Lecture Notes in Computer Science 1667

Edited by G. Goos, J. Hartmanis and J. van Leeuwen

Springer

Berlin
Heidelberg
New York
Barcelona
Hong Kong
London
Milan
Paris
Singapore
Tokyo

Jan Hlavička   Erik Maehle
András Pataricza (Eds.)

Dependable Computing – EDDC-3

Third European Dependable Computing Conference
Prague, Czech Republic, September 15-17, 1999
Proceedings

 Springer

Series Editors

Gerhard Goos, Karlsruhe University, Germany
Juris Hartmanis, Cornell University, NY, USA
Jan van Leeuwen, Utrecht University, The Netherlands

Volume Editors

Jan Hlavička
Czech Technical University in Prague
Department of Computer Science and Engineering
Karlovo nam 13, CZ-12135 Prague 2, Czech Republic
E-mail: hlavicka@cslab.felk.cvut.cz

Erik Maehle
Medizinische Universität zu Lübeck, Institut für Technische Informatik
Ratzeburger Allee 160, 23538 Lübeck, Germany
E-mail: maehle@iti.mu-luebeck.de

András Pataricza
Technical University of Budapest
Department of Measurement and Information Systems
Pázmány P. sétány 1/d, H-1521 Budapest, Hungary
E-mail: pataric@mit.bme.hu

Cataloging-in-Publication data applied for

Die Deutsche Bibliothek - CIP-Einheitsaufnahme

Dependable computing : proceedings / EDCC-3, Third European Dependable Computing
Conference, Prague, Czech Republic, September 15 - 17, 1999. Jan Hlavicka ...
(ed.). - Berlin ; Heidelberg ; New York ; Barcelona ; Hong Kong ; London ;
Milan ; Paris ; Singapore ; Tokyo : Springer, 1999
(Lecture notes in computer science ; Vol. 1667)
ISBN 3-540-66483-1

CR Subject Classification (1998): B.1.3, B.2.3, B.3.4, B.4.5, C.3-4, D.2.4,
D.2.8, D.4.5, E.4, J.7

ISSN 0302-9743
ISBN 3-540-66483-1 Springer-Verlag Berlin Heidelberg New York

Typesetting: Camera-ready by author
SPIN: 10705369   06/3142 – 5 4 3 2 1 0   Printed on acid-free paper

The idea of creating the European Dependable Computing Conference (EDCC) was born at the moment when the Iron Curtain fell. A group of enthusiasts, who were previously involved in research and teaching in the field of fault-tolerant computing in different European countries, agreed that there is no longer any point in keeping previously independent activities apart and created a steering committee which took the responsibility for preparing the EDCC calendar and appointing the chairs for the individual conferences. There is no single European or global professional organization that took over the responsibility for this conference, but there are three national interest groups that sent delegates to the steering committee and support its activities, especially by promoting the conference materials. As can be seen from these materials, they are the SEE Working Group "Dependable Computing" (which is a successor organization of AFCET) in France, the GI/ITG/GMA Technical Committee on Dependability and Fault Tolerance in Germany, and the AICA Working Group "Dependability of Computer Systems" in Italy. In addition, committees of several global professional organizations, such as IEEE and IFIP, support this conference.

Prague has been selected as a conference venue for several reasons. It is an easily accessible location that may attract many visitors by its beauty and that has a tradition in organizing international events of this kind (one of the last FTSD conferences took place here). However, there is one other fact, which may not be known by the general public, that makes Prague a special place for organizing a conference on dependable computing. It was here in 1957 that the first fault-tolerant computer in the world was set into operation. It was a relay computer SAPO that had three ALUs working in the TMR mode. The machine was designed by Professor Antonin Svoboda at the Institute of Mathematical Machines, which he founded and managed for some time. Thus this conference can be seen as a way in which the Czech Technical University pays tribute to this great man of science.

Preparing an international conference is always a question of teamwork and I was lucky to have the opportunity to work with an excellent team. Availability of modern means of communication, especially the Internet, made it relatively easy to form such a team across several borders and to coordinate its activities during the last two years. It is impossible to name all those who contributed to the success of the EDCC-3. Let me mention at least some of them.

The main load of responsibility naturally lay on the shoulders of the conference chairs. Each of them, being responsible for his or her sector, invested much effort and did an excellent job. In addition to three face-to-face meetings they exchanged thousands of e-mails, phone calls, and written messages while fine-tuning the final image of the conference. At this point it should be mentioned that each of the program co-chairs established a team within his own workplace and received very important support from his host institution. These institutions, namely, the Medical University of Lübeck in Germany and the Technical University of Budapest in Hungary, deserve our sincere thanks, because without their generous support the conference would hardly be what it is now.

The Czech Technical University, as the main organizer of this year's conference, offered us the services of its CTU Congress Agency. In cooperation with the finance and local arrangements chair, this agency arranged the conference venue, accommodations, and social program, and handled registration. Its staff worked very efficiently and helped to keep the conference budget within reasonable limits.

The list of those who contributed to the success of the conference would be incomplete without our sponsors. Six local companies responded to our call and helped us to create a fund from which we could finance the participation of students and active participants from countries having restricted access to freely convertible currency.

Finally, I can conclude that it was a pleasure to work with people who are so dedicated to their jobs and so dependable (no pun intended!) in their activities. I can only wish that the conference participants enjoy both the technical and social program of the conference as much as we enjoyed preparing it.

Prague, June 1999

Jan Hlavička
EDCC-3 General Chair

The Third European Dependable Computing Conference can already rely on the traditions defined by the previous two conferences in this series. EDCC-1 was held in Berlin, on 4-6 October, 1994; and EDCC-2 in Taormina, on 2-4 October, 1996.

Originating from two former conference series – the "International Conference on Fault-Tolerant Computing Systems" and the "International Conference on Fault-Tolerant Systems and Diagnostics," EDCC was one of the pioneers in the unification of scientific life in the two parts of Europe after the political barriers had vanished.

The main focus of the conference reflects the changes in the rapidly growing and ever more extensive field of computer applications. In addition to the traditional topics in dependable computing, such as testing, general hardware and software reliability, safety and security, the rapid development of the infrastructural background of research and of practical applications triggered a shift in the main topics during the last decade.

The growing importance of the field of dependability both in technology and in everyday life is prominently indicated by the fact that the European Community defined, in its 1999 Workprogramme of the 5th Framework Programme on Information Society Technologies, an autonomous Cross-Programme Action under the title "Dependability in services and technologies."

This action defines the main objective of forthcoming European research: "To develop technologies, methods and tools that will meet the emerging generic dependability requirements in the information society, stemming both from the ubiquity and volume of embedded and networked systems and services as well as from the global and complex nature of large-scale information and communication infrastructures, from citizens (especially with respect to enhancing privacy), administrations and business in terms of technologies (hardware and software), tools, systems, applications and services. The work must reflect the wide scalability and heterogeneity of requirements and operating environments. There will be an emphasis on risk and incident management tools as well as on privacy enhancing technologies. The scope includes self-monitoring, self-healing infrastructures and services."

We hope that our conference will contribute to these goals. Fortunately, the conference received a large number of submissions. All papers were sent to four reviewers, two program committee (PC) or steering committee members and two external experts. No paper was processed with less than three reviews returned to the PC.

The PC held a two-day meeting in Budapest, as the final phase of decision making, after receiving the reviews. The basic principle adopted by the PC was to "discuss until consensus is reached." According to this principle, whenever a remarkable difference was detected between the reviews, a new PC member was assigned to consider the paper and all previous reviews. If there was a difference of opinion between the PC members familiar with the candidate's paper, a new PC member was assigned to lead a consensus discussion among them. Any PC member with a conflict of interest was excluded from the discussion of the corresponding paper. Finally, after four rounds of discussion, the

PC selected 26 papers (3 of them for the industrial track) out of the 71 submissions from 25 countries.

In order to facilitate fast feedback from the international scientific community, the organizers decided to follow the successful pattern of other conferences, such as that of IEEE FTCS, and introduced the Fast Abstract Session for the presentation of results from work in progress. Twenty submissions were selected by the program co-chairs for presentation in this form.

In addition to our regular scientific program, a Dinner Speech is delivered by Prof. Dr. Winfried Görke from the University of Karlsruhe, Germany. Prof. Görke is a very well-known European pioneer in the fields of testing and fault-tolerant computing. He played an important and outstanding role in establishing connections between researchers in Western and Eastern Europe in the difficult times of the Iron Curtain and is one of the founders of the German Special Interest Group of Fault-Tolerant Computing. In his speech in the historic environment of the Bethlehem's Chapel in Prague he talks about the history of fault-tolerant computing in Europe.

The Conference was organized by

- SEE Working Group "Dependable Computing," France
- GI/ITG/GMA TC on Dependability and Fault Tolerance, Germany
- AICA Working Group "Dependability of Computer Systems," Italy

under the auspices of the Council of European Professional Informatics Societies (CEPIS), and in cooperation with

- Czech Technical University in Prague
- IFIP Working Group 10.4 "Dependable Computing and Fault-Tolerance"
- IEEE TC on Fault-Tolerant Computing
- EWICS Technical Committee on Safety, Reliability and Security (TC7).

The organizers gratefully acknowledge the help of all reviewers, the staff at the Medical University of Lübeck, the Czech Technical University in Prague and the Technical University of Budapest. The organizers express their thanks to Ram Chillarege at IBM for supporting the review process by making available to them the electronic reviewing system originally prepared for FTCS-28.

A few days before our PC meeting the sad news reached us that Dr. Flaviu Cristian from UC San Diego, USA, had passed away on Tuesday, April 27, after a long and courageous battle with cancer. Being a leading expert in the field of distributed fault-tolerant systems we had also asked him to review some papers, which he, however, could not complete because of his illness. Flaviu Cristian was born in Romania in 1951, and moved to France in 1971 to study computer science. He received his Ph. D. from the University of Grenoble, France in 1979, where he carried out research in operating systems and programming methodology. He went on to the University of Newcastle upon Tyne, UK and worked in the area of specification, design, and verification of fault-tolerant software. In 1982 he joined IBM Almaden Research Center. While at IBM, he received the Corporate Award, IBM's highest technical award, for his work on the Advanced Automation System for air traffic control. Subsequently he joined UC San

Diego as professor in the Department of Computer Science and Engineering in 1991. He was elected a Fellow of the Institute for Electrical and Electronic Engineers in 1998 for his contributions to the theory and practice of dependable systems. Flaviu Cristian's work on the design and analysis of fault-tolerant distributed systems was fundamental, and he was widely regarded as one of the technical leaders in his field. The impact of his work was felt both in the theory and in the practice of fault-tolerance.

We express our gratitude to Springer Verlag for publishing the proceedings of the conference. This year two important changes were made for additional distribution of information:

- Springer will offer, in addition to the print version, an electronic form of the proceedings.
- Similarly, the final text of the fast abstracts will be made available via the web at the URL: http://www.inf.mit.bme.hu/edcc3/ .

July 1999

András Pataricza,
Erik Maehle
EDCC-3 Program Co-Chairs

Organizing Committee

General Chair

Jan Hlavička
Czech Technical University
Prague, Czech Republic

Program Co-Chairs

Erik Maehle
Medical University of Lübeck
Germany

András Pataricza
Technical University of Budapest
Hungary

Finance and Local Arrangements Chair

Publicity Chair

Hana Kubátová
Czech Technical University
Prague, Czech Republic

Karl-Erwin Grosspietsch
German National Research Center
for Information Technology (GMD)
St. Augustin, Germany

International Liaison Chairs

North America:
Dimiter Avresky
Boston University
USA

Asia:
Takashi Nanya
University of Tokyo
Japan

EDCC Steering Committee

Algirdas Avizienis, USA
Mario Dal Cin, Germany
Jan Hlavička, Czech Republic
Andrzej Hławiczka, Poland
Hermann Kopetz, Austria
Jean-Claude Laprie, France

Brian Randell, UK
Ernst Schmitter, Germany
Luca Simoncini, Italy
Pascale Thévenod-Fosse, France
Jan Torin, Sweden
Raimund Ubar, Estonia

Program Committee

External Referees

Anceaume, E.
Avresky, D.
Bartha, T.
Belli, F.
Boichat, R.
Chessa, S.
Crouzet, Y.
Csertán, Gy.
Deconinck, G.
DiGiandomenico, F.
Dilger, E.
Draber, S.
Elnozahy, E.N.
Ezhilchelvan, P.
Fabre, J.C.
Fantechi, A.
Fetzer, C.
Geisselhardt, W.
Gil, P.
Gnesi, S.
Görke, W.
Gössel, M.
Grandoni, F.
Grosspietsch, K.-E.
Hazelhurst, S.
Ibach, P.
Kaaniche, M.
Kaiser, J.

Kalbarczyk, Z.
Kanoun, K.
Karl, H.
Kermarrec, A.M.
Kopetz, H.
Korousic-Seljak, B.
Krasniewski, A.
Kropf, T.
Landrault, C.
Latella, D.
Ma, Y.
Madeira, H.
Masum, A.
Mock, M.
Mostefaoui, A.
Mura, I.
Nicolaïdis, M.
Noyes, D.
Obelöer, W.
Pedone, F.
Peng, Z.
Petri, A. Jr.
Petri, S.
Piestrak, S.
Polze, A.
Puaut, I.
Puschner, P.
Racek, S.

Raik, J.
Raynal, M.
Rodrígues, L.
Romanovski, A.
Rufino, J.
Santi, P.
Schlichting, R.
Schneeweiss, W.
Selényi, E.
Silc, J.
Silva, L.M.
Simon, Gy.
Skavhaug, A.
Sobe, P.
Stalhane, T.
Sziray, J.
Tangelder, R.
Tarnay, K.
Telek, M.
Urbán, P.
Vergos, H.
Vernadat, F.
Vierhaus, T.
Voges, U.
von Henke, F.
Waeselynck, H.
Werner, M.
Yarmolik, V.N.

Table of Contents

Keynote Speech

Reliable and Secure Operation of Smart Cards 3
  H.H. Henn, IBM Germany, Böblingen, Germany

Session 1: Dependability Modelling
  Chair: Jean-Claude Laprie, LAAS-CNRS, Toulouse, France

Dependability Modelling and Sensitivity Analysis of Scheduled Maintenance
Systems 7
  A. Bondavalli, I. Mura (CNUCE/CNR, Pisa, Italy), K.S. Trivedi (Duke University, Durham, USA)

Evaluation of Video Communication over Packet Switching Networks 24
  K. Heidtmann (University of Hamburg, Germany)

Dependability Evaluation of a Distributed Shared Memory Multiprocessor System 42
  M. Rabah, K. Kanoun (LAAS-CNRS, Toulouse, France)

Session 2a: Panel
  Moderator: Fevzi Belli, University of Paderborn, Germany

Software Reliability Engineering – Risk Management for the New Millenium.... 63
  F. Belli (University of Paderborn, Germany)

Session 2b: Fast Abstracts
  Chair: Dimiter Avresky, Boston University, USA

List of Fast Abstracts 67

Session 3: Protocols
  Chair: István Majzik, Technical University of Budapest, Hungary

Muteness Failure Detectors: Specification and Implementation 71
  A. Doudou (EPFL, Lausanne, Switzerland), B. Garbinato (United Bank of Switzerland, Zürich, Switzerland), R. Guerraoui, A. Schiper (EPFL, Lausanne, Switzerland)

A Fault Tolerant Clock Synchronization Algorithm for Systems with Low-Precision
Oscillators 88
  H. Lonn (Chalmers University of Technology, Gothenburg, Sweden)

Avoiding Malicious Byzantine Faults by a New Signature Generation Technique . 106
  K. Echtle (University of Essen, Germany)

An Experimental Evaluation of Coordinated Checkpointing in a Parallel Machine 124
L.M. Silva, J.G. Silva (Universidade de Coimbra, Portugal)

Session 4: Fault Injection 1
Chair: Janusz Sosnowski, Warsaw University of Technology, Poland

MAFALDA: Microkernel Assessment by Fault Injection and Design Aid 143
M. Rodríguez, F. Salles, J.-C. Fabre, J. Arlat (LAAS-CNRS, Toulouse, France)

Assessing Error Detection Coverage by Simulated Fault Injection 161
C. Constantinescu (Intel Corporation, Hillsboro, USA)

Considering Workload Input Variations in Error Coverage Estimation 171
P. Folkesson, J. Karlsson (Chalmers University of Technology, Göteborg, Sweden)

Session 5: Fault Injection 2
Chair: David Powell, LAAS-CNRS, Toulouse, France

Fault Injection into VHDL Models: Experimental Validation of a Fault-Tolerant
Microcomputer System 191
D. Gil (Universidad Politécnica de Valencia, Spain), R. Martínez (Universitat de València, Spain), J.V. Busquets, J.C. Baraza, P.J. Gil (Universidad Politécnica de Valencia, Spain)

Can Software Implemented Fault-Injection be Used on Real-Time Systems? 209
J.C. Cunha (Instituto Superior de Engenharia de Coimbra, Portugal), M.Z. Rela, J.G. Silva (Universidade de Coimbra, Portugal)

Session 6: Safety
Chair: Bernd Eschermann, ABB Power Automation AG, Baden, Switzerland

Integrated Safety in Flexible Manufacturing Systems 229
R. Apfeld (Berufsgenossenschaftliches Institut für Arbeitssicherheit, St. Augustin, Germany), M. Umbreit (Fachausschuß Eisen und Metall II, Mainz, Germany)

A Method for Implementing a Safety Control System Based on Its Separation
into Safety-Related and Non-Safety-Related Parts 239
T. Shirai, M. Sakai, K. Futsuhara (Nippon Signal Co., Japan), M. Mukaidono (Meiji University, Japan)

Session 7: Hardware Testing
Chair: Raimund Ubar, Tallin Technical University, Estonia

Design of Totally Self-Checking Code-Disjoint Synchronous Sequential Circuits . 251
J.W. Greblicki, S.J. Piestrak (Wrocław University of Technology, Poland)

Path Delay Fault Testing of a Class of Circuit-Switched Multistage Interconnection
Networks 267

M. Bellos (University of Patras, Greece), D. Nikolos, H.T. Vergos (University
of Patras, and Computer Technology Institute, Patras, Greece)

Diagnostic Model and Diagnosis Algorithm of a SIMD Computer 283

S. Chessa (CNR, Pisa, and University of Trento, Italy), B. Sallay, P. Maestrini
(CNR, Pisa, Italy)

Session 8: Built-In Self-Test

Chair: Bernd Straube, Fraunhofer Gesellschaft, Institute for Integrated Circuits,
Germany

Pseudorandom, Weighted Random and Pseudoexhaustive Test Patterns Generated
in Universal Cellular Automata 303

O. Novák (Technical University Liberec, Czech Republic)

A New LFSR with D and T Flip-Flops as an Effective Test Pattern Generator for
VLSI Circuits 321

T. Garbolino, A. Hławiczka (Silesian Technical University of Gliwice, Poland)

Transparent Word-Oriented Memory BIST Based on Symmetric March Algorithms 339

V.N. Yarmolik (Belorussian State University, Minsk, Belarus, and Bialystok
University of Technology, Poland), I.V. Bykov (Belorussian State University,
Minsk, Belarus), S. Hellebrand, H.-J. Wunderlich (University of Stuttgart,
Germany)

Session 9: Networks and Distributed Systems

Chair: Gilles Muller, INRIA/IRISA, Rennes, France

Achieving Fault-Tolerant Ordered Broadcasts in CAN 351

J. Kaiser, M.A. Livani (University of Ulm, Germany)

Directional Gossip: Gossip in a Wide Area Network 364

M.-J. Lin (University of Texas at Austin, USA), K. Marzullo (University of
California, San Diego, USA)

Efficient Reliable Real-Time Group Communication for Wireless Local Area
Networks 380

M. Mock (GMD, St. Augustin, Germany), E. Nett (University of Magdeburg,
Germany), S. Schemmer (GMD, St. Augustin, Germany)

Session 10: Software Testing and Self-Checking

Chair: Luca Simoncini, CNUCE/CNR, Pisa, Italy

A Case Study in Statistical Testing of Reusable Concurrent Objects 401

H. Waeselynck, P. Thévenod-Fosse (LAAS-CNRS, Toulouse, France)

Fault-Detection by Result-Checking for the Eigenproblem 419
  P. Prata (Universidade da Beira Interior, Covilhã, Portugal),
  J.G. Silva (Universidade de Coimbra, Portugal)

Concurrent Detection of Processor Control Errors by Hybrid Signature Monitoring 437
  Y.-Y. Chen (Chung-Hua University, Hsin-Chu, Taiwan)

Author Index 455

Keynote Speech

Reliable and Secure Operation of Smart Cards

Horst H. Henn, Chief Architect for Smart Cards, IBM Germany, Böblingen, Germany

Reliable and Secure Operation of Smart Cards

Horst H. Henn

Smart Card Solution Development, Dept. 3289
IBM Germany, Böblingen,
Schönaicher Str. 220
D-71032 Böblingen, Germany
hhenn@de.ibm.com

Smart cards are a key system component in distributed web based applications. Smart cards perform highly critical operations like electronic payment, digital signature and key management. Secure and dependable operation must be assured in normal and manipulated environment. Typical failure modes and attacks as well as protection schemes are described for smart card hardware and software. Certification methodology of smart card systems for state of the art systems like GELDKARTE and MONEO as well as requirements for ITSEC=6 security level are evaluated.

Session 1

Dependability Modelling

Chair: Jean-Claude Laprie, LAAS-CNRS, Toulouse, France

Dependability Modelling and Sensitivity Analysis of Scheduled Maintenance Systems

Andrea Bondavalli[1], Ivan Mura[1], and Kishor S. Trivedi[2]

[1] CNUCE/CNR, Via Santa Maria 36,
I-56126 Pisa, Italy
{a.bondavalli, ivan.mura}@cnuce.cnr.it
[2] CACC, Dept. of ECE, Duke University, Box 90291
NC 27708 Durham, USA
kst@ee.duke.edu

Abstract. In this paper we present a new modelling approach for dependability evaluation and sensitivity analysis of Scheduled Maintenance Systems, based on a Deterministic and Stochastic Petri Net approach. The DSPN approach offers significant advantages in terms of easiness and clearness of modelling with respect to the existing Markov chain based tools, drastically limiting the amount of user-assistance needed to define the model. At the same time, these improved modelling capabilities do not result in additional computational costs. Indeed, the evaluation of the DSPN model of SMS is supported by an efficient and fully automatable analytical solution technique for the time-dependent marking occupation probabilities. Moreover, the existence of such explicit analytical solution allows to obtain the sensitivity functions of the dependability measures with respect to the variation of the parameter values. These sensitivity functions can be conveniently employed to analytically evaluate the effects that parameter variations have on the measures of interest.

1 Systems with Multiple Phases and Multiple Missions

With the increasing complexity and automation encountered in systems of the nuclear, aerospace, transportation, electronic, and many other industrial fields, the deployment of processing systems in charge of performing a multiplicity of different control and computational activities is becoming common practice. Very often, the system and its external environment can be altered during the operation, in a way that the behaviour during a time interval can be completely different from that within other periods.

The operational scenario devised for the Scheduled Maintenance System (SMS) problem is a typical one in the context of the on-board aeroplane control systems. SMS are to be used during their life-time for multiple missions. The system is run for a finite number of missions, and then it has to pass a maintenance check. Such maintenance can be more or less extensive and accurate. Typically, it is the case that after a prefixed number of missions the system is completely checked, so that all its components are as good as new ones after that. Moreover, other kinds of maintenance actions are usually performed between two major checks. For instance, some highly critical components could be checked and possibly repaired after each mission, and some others could be replaced after some missions even if they are still working. Anyway, these partial checks are not able to guarantee the absence of faulty components in the system, and thus the dependability figures of the SMS inside a mission are affected by the past history of the SMS inside the previous missions. Within each mission, an SMS behaves as a phased mission system (PMS), that is it is has to carry out various operational phases, each of them possibly having specific dependability requirements and particular failure criteria. Specifically, the typical phases of an aeroplane mission include a take off, ascent, cruise, descent, approach and landing phases. Once again, since the same architectural components are to be used by the system, the behaviour of the SMS during a particular phase is affected by its past evolution while inside other phases of the same mission.

It is quite intuitive that an SMS can be reduced to a PMS, by simply disregarding the multiple missions, and considering all the phases to be executed as being part of a long mission. In this way, all the methods that have been proposed for the dependability analysis of PMS, also apply to SMS. Because of their deployment in critical applications, the dependability modelling and analysis of PMS has been considered a task of primary relevance, and many different approaches have appeared in the literature [4, 8, 13, 15, 17-19]. However, the modelling of complex systems always poses formidable problems, and PMS do not represent an exception to the rule. Moreover, the phased behaviour adds a further degree of complexity to the analysis of these systems. Modelling a PMS can be a complex task even inside one single phase; when a multiplicity of phases and the dependencies among them are to be taken into account, additional difficulties are encountered. The sole methodology specifically designed for the dependability modelling and evaluation of the SMS has been proposed by Somani *et al.*, who implemented it within the EHARP tool [18] (an extension of the HARP tool). Some further extensions of EHARP for the SMS problem were introduced by Twigg *et al.* in [20]. The EHARP tool is based on a separate Markov chain modelling of the SMS inside the various phases, an approach that is able to effectively master the complexity and the computational cost of the analysis. However, as carefully explained in [15], this separate Markov based modelling approach requires a relevant amount of user-assistance to correctly model the dependencies among successive phases.

In this work, we show how the general methodology based on the Deterministic and Stochastic Petri Nets (DSPN) proposed in [15] for the modelling and evaluation of PMS can be applied to the specific case of the SMS problem. Thanks to the expressiveness of the DSPN, the modelling of systems showing a phased behaviour becomes quite intuitive and simple. The specific features of SMS are easily accommodated within our general modelling scheme, and the resulting model is defined in a very compact way, with a dramatic reduction in the number of the interactions with the user and the consequent reduction in possible errors. Indeed, the treatment of the dependencies among phases is moved from the low level of the Markov chains to the more abstract and easier to handle level of the DSPN. The evaluation procedure of the DSPN model of an SMS is supported by the existence of an efficient analytical solution method for the transient probabilities of the underlying marking process.

Moreover, we offer in this paper another relevant contribution to the study of systems with multiple phases, either PMS or SMS. The existence of analytical expressions for the time-dependent marking occupation probabilities of the DSPN models of this class of systems allows us to explicitly derive the sensitivity functions of the dependability measures of interest, that is the analytical form of the derivatives of the measures with respect to the variations of a set of parameters. The steady-state sensitivity analysis of DSPN has been presented in [6], whereas the time-dependent sensitivity analysis of DSPN models is a task that has not been attacked yet, to the best of our knowledge. Such a transient sensitivity analysis can fruitfully complement the means available for the study of PMS and SMS, providing guidelines for the system optimisation, and in some cases avoiding or limiting the need of performing long batches of evaluations for a number of different values of the parameters [9].

The rest of this paper is organised as follows. Section 2 describes the most peculiar characteristics of SMS, and presents a simple case study that we will consider as a convenient application example throughout the paper. In Section 3 we introduce our DSPN approach and detail it by completely carrying out the modelling of the SMS taken as example. Then, the analytical solution of the DSPN models of SMS is briefly addressed in Section 4. In that same section, we also discuss on the opportunity and advantages offered by the sensitivity analyses to gain deeper insights into models and systems, and present the general guidelines for the derivation of the sensitivity functions for the measures of interest. Section 5 presents the results of a numerical evaluation conducted on the example of SMS, aiming at demonstrating the advantages of performing sensitivity analyses. Finally, Section 6 presents some concluding remarks.

2　The SMS Problem

Consider a SMS that executes m missions, each mission being characterised by a specific number of phases of given durations. We denote with n_i the number of phases mission i is divided in, $i = 1, 2, ..., m$. Moreover, denote with $P_{i,j}$ the j-th phase to be performed during mission i, $j = 1, 2, ..., n_i$, $i = 1, 2, ..., m$. As long as we are interested in an exact analytical solution, phase duration is restrained to be deterministic. In fact, only approximate solution techniques have been proposed in the literature for the case of random phase durations. This assumption can be more or less restrictive, depending on the very nature of the events that lead to phase changes. Anyway, we assume that phase $P_{i,j}$ has a constant duration $\tau_{i,j}$, $j = 1, 2, ..., n_i$, $i = 1, 2, ..., m$.

After completing the m missions, the SMS is subject to a complete maintenance check. Obviously, the study of system dependability can be limited to the period between two complete checks of the system, because after the check, the system is reset to its initial condition. Moreover, between these major checks, the system may be subject to less exhaustive and less expensive maintenance actions, which however affect the dependability figures of the system. Therefore, a proper modelling of the maintenance actions plays a relevant role for an accurate dependability evaluation. All the maintenance actions are considered instantaneous, because they are performed when the system is non operative. Therefore, they are also referred to as discrete repairs. The picture in Figure 1 shows an example of a possible maintenance schedule during the SMS life-time.

The proper scheduling of maintenance actions is a non trivial problem. From a dependability viewpoint, the best possible option is to completely check the SMS at end of each mission. However, the cost of such simplistic solution is unacceptable because of the consequent under utilisation of the system. On the other hand, increasing the number of missions between two complete checks worsens the dependability figures of the SMS, with the risk of incurring in a catastrophic failure. The proper balance between system utilisation and dependability of operation can be formulated as an optimisation problem, for which dependability modelling provides a useful solution tool.

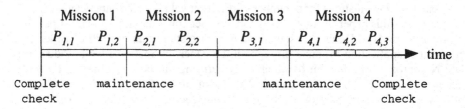

Fig. 1. Life-cycle of a SMS

To better explain our DSPN approach through an application case, we consider a simple example of SMS, inspired by the one that has been studied in [20]. Consider a system equipped with two components. Component A is a primary unit providing some functionality to the system, and component B acts as a backup unit for component A. The system is equipped with a switching logic, so that when A fails, the control of operation is immediately passed to B.

The system executes cyclically two different types of mission. Mission *1* encompasses a single phase $P_{1,1}$ of fixed duration $\tau_{1,1}$, whereas mission *2* is a two phased mission, whose phases $P_{2,1}$ and $P_{2,2}$ have duration $\tau_{2,1}$ and $\tau_{2,2}$, respectively. The time to failure of component A is exponentially distributed, with parameter $\lambda_{1,A}$ during the missions of type *1*, and parameters $\lambda_{2,A}$ during the type *2*, respectively, whereas the time to failure of component B is constantly λ_B. The switching part is assumed to be fault-free. The system is assumed to be functional as long as either A or B are working.

The following scheduled maintenance actions are undertaken during system lifetime:
- The system is subject to a complete and exhaustive maintenance check each one hundred missions.
- Primary unit A is replaced at the end of each mission, if failed. After the replacement, A takes again the role of primary unit.
- Backup unit B is subject to a partial check at the end of each α pairs of missions.

So, after one hundred missions all the components are checked, and the system is restored to the initial condition. The Reliability of the system must be studied over the time interval between the beginning of the first mission and the end of the hundredth one. System failure is defined as the failure of A and B, and can be a catastrophic event that leads to a relevant economic loss. The occurrence probability of a system failure during the one hundred missions is denoted by F, and can be computed as $1-R$, where R is the Reliability of the system at the end of the one hundred missions.

Moreover, from a point of view of the system optimisation, we intend to determine whether it is economically convenient to increase the number α of checks, or to increase the coverage c of the intermediate checks. Increasing the number of checks on the backup unit B has the effect of reducing the occurrence probability F. However, the check is a long operation, which requires the system to be not operative for a long period. For a global optimisation of the maintenance actions, the cost of such under utilisation of the system must be weighted with the potential cost paid in case of system failure. Suppose a cost Φ is paid in case F occurs during the one hundred missions, and a cost φ is paid (say in terms of time) to perform the partial check of B each α pairs of missions. The cost φ of the check and the overage c that it provides obviously depend from each other: the higher the target coverage, the more expensive the check required. We use the mathematical notation $\varphi = \varphi(c)$ to denote such dependency. Then, to optimise the SMS with respect of the schedule of the maintenance, one should minimise the following overall expected cost function:

$$Cost = \Phi \cdot Prob[F] + \varphi(c) \cdot \left\lfloor \frac{50}{\alpha} \right\rfloor = \Phi \cdot (1 - R) + \varphi(c) \cdot \left\lfloor \frac{50}{\alpha} \right\rfloor \qquad (1)$$

We now briefly present the EHARP approach to the modelling and evaluation of SMS, by discussing its application to the example sketched above. EHARP is a tool especially designed for the Reliability analysis of SMS. The failure-repair model of the SMS is built as a continuous-time Markov chain, which may be different for each phase and each mission of the SMS. In the case of our example, there are two different Markov models, because the failure characteristics of the two SMS components differ during the missions of type 1 and 2.

The various Markov models are of course dependent from each other, in that the same components are to be used within various phases and missions. For instance, in our example if the primary A fails during the first phase of a type 2 mission, this will affect the operation in the successive second phase, and thus the memory of the past evolution is to be kept from one phase to the other. Similarly, if the backup component B fails and it is not repaired by a maintenance check at the end of the mission, then such a latent failure will affect the dependability of the subsequent missions. To model these dependencies, a set of phase-to-phase mapping functions must be specified. Starting from the final state occupation probability vector of a phase, these functions assign the initial state occupation probabilities over the states of the Markov chain of the next phase. Similarly, a set of mission-to-mission mapping functions need to be specified, to map the state occupation probabilities at the end of a mission to the start of the next one. In the EHARP environment, these functions are restricted to be linear functions, so that they can be represented as matrices.

It is worthwhile observing that the specification of the mapping matrices requires a considerable amount of user interaction. Though not conceptually complicated, the manual specification of these matrices may become a long and tedious job, and more importantly it certainly becomes an error-prone task for large Markov models.

A non trivial point the author of [20] also consider, is the specification of the maintenance actions. The definition language of the EHARP tool allows the introduction of maintenance directives such as the following one:

Repair X at interval n if B = True

whose meaning is to declare that component X is to be repaired at the end of the n-th mission, provided that predicate B holds of the state of the system at that time. All the repair directives have to be manually translated into mapping matrices, and are included in the same mapping matrices used to represent the dependence among successive phases and successive missions. Indeed, the instantaneous repair caused by maintenance actions is easily incorporated into the structural changes the SMS usually experiences as a result of the phase-dependent characteristics.

However, this treatment of the maintenance actions further increases the amount of user-assistance needed to define the models. As the authors of [20] themselves affirm:

> [...] manual specification of the state to state mapping is tedious except for very small systems. Much energy has been devoted to compact specification methods for state dependent failure mechanisms, but the authors do not know a compact specification method for discrete repairs.

As we shall see in the following, the DSPN approach to the modelling of SMS overcomes this limitations of the methods in the literature, completely avoiding the need of any user-assistance in the treatment of the phase dependencies and in the specification of the maintenance actions.

3 The SMS Problem Viewed as a PMS

The methodology we apply in this section to the modelling of our example of SMS is directly derived from the one we devised for PMS in [15]. The additional specific features of SMS are immediately included in our general modelling scheme, and exploited to achieve a compact representation of the multiple missions performed during the life-cycle. We show the potentialities of the DSPN approach and highlight the advantages it offers with respect to the classical modelling with Markov chains.

The modelling of the SMS is based on a single DSPN modelling approach, though the model is logically split in the following three parts:
- the Mission Net submodel (MN), which represents the consecutive execution of the various missions between two complete checks of the SMS.
- the Phase Net submodel (PhN), which models the alternation of phases during the execution of the various missions;
- the System Net submodel (SN), which represents the failure-repair model of the system components inside the various phases;

It is worth noting that the different submodels logically reflect the inherent hierarchy of the problem, that is the one existing among life-cycle, missions, and phases of a SMS. Each of the submodels may be dependent from the other ones. So, the evolution of the SN submodel is made dependent from the marking of the PhN and MN to model the mission and phase particularities of the failure/repair characteristics of the system. Similarly, the PhN evolution may be governed by the status of the MN submodel, and vice versa.

These dependencies are conveniently modelled through the use of marking-dependent guards on transitions, timed transition priorities, halting conditions, reward rates, etc. These expressive modelling features are already available under the Stochastic Reward Nets and Stochastic Activity Networks modelling paradigms and their associated automated tools SPNP [7] and UltraSAN [16], and are being more and more included in other automated tools for the evaluation of system dependability, such as DSPNexpress [11, 12], PANDA [1], and SURF-2 [2].

We now apply our modelling methodology to the example of PMS defined in the last section. The topmost level submodel MN shown in Figure 2 includes a single token circulating in it, four places M_1, M_2, W_1, and W_2, and four immediate transitions end_1, end_2, $start_1$, and $start_2$. A token in place M_i models the execution of a type i mission, and the firing of a transition end_i represents its completion, $i = 1, 2$. Place W_i and transition $start_i$, $i = 1, 2$, are employed to model the synchronisation between the MN and the PhN submodels at the end of each mission. The place *Count* has been included to provide a compact representation of the SMS, by exploiting its cyclic behaviour. The number of tokens in place *Count* keeps track of the number of missions performed by the SMS. The MN model is not limited to have a particular structure. A simple chain linking all the possible missions can be used if the SMS does not exhibits any regular pattern in the execution of the missions. More compact structures as the one shown in Figure 2 can be defined if some missions are periodically performed.

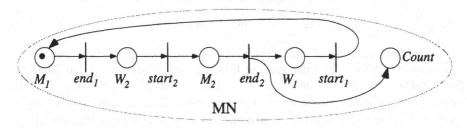

Fig. 2. Topmost MN submodel of a SMS

Since a mission starts only after the preceding one has completed, the definition of the MN model is to be completed by a set of enabling conditions, also called guards, that control the firing of the immediate transition end_i and $start_i$, $i = 1, 2$. These enabling conditions are defined in terms of the marking of the PhN submodel shown in Figure 3, and are listed in Table 1. Notice that these marking dependent guards are not intended to substitute the classic enabling rules of Petri net model transitions, rather they represent additional constraints that must be fulfilled for a transition to be eligible for firing.

Table 1. MN marking dependent enabling conditions

Transition	Enabling condition
end_1, end_2	$m(Stop) = 1$
$start_1$, $start_2$	$m(P_1) = 1$

The PhN submodel concisely represents in a single net the two possible types of mission executed by the SMS. To explain the evolution of the PhN model, suppose first that the SMS solely executes mission of type 2, which consist of two consecutive phases. The two deterministic transitions t_1^{Det} and t_2^{Det} model the time needed for the SMS to perform the two phases of a type 2 mission. A single token circulates in the PhN. A token in place P_1 enables transition t_1^{Det}, modelling the execution of the first phase of the mission. Similarly, a token in the place P_2, enables transition t_2^{Det}, modelling the execution of the second phase. To represent on this same model the execution of the single phased type *1* missions, too, we introduce the immediate transition h_1, which directly moves the token to the place *Stop*. Thus, a single phase mission is modelled by skipping the deterministic transition t_2^{Det}.

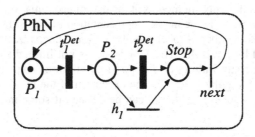

Fig. 3. PhN submodel of a SMS

This dynamic selection of the path to be followed is modelled by the enabling conditions shown in Table 2, which rule the firing of the PhN transitions depending on the marking of the MN submodel. As soon as it reaches place *Stop*, the token is moved back to place P_1 by the instantaneous transition *next*, which models the beginning of the next mission. It is worthwhile observing that this compact modelling of the set of possible missions becomes particularly convenient when several missions are repeated between the complete maintenance checks.

Table 2. PhN marking dependent parameters

Transition	Firing time	Enabling condition
t_1^{Det}	$\tau_{1,1}$, if $m(M_1) = 1$ $\tau_{2,1}$, if $m(M_2) = 1$	TRUE
t_2^{Det}	$\tau_{2,2}$	$m(M_2) = 1$
h_1	instantaneous	$m(M_1) = 1$
next	instantaneous	$m(W_1) + m(W_2) = 1$

Following the same approach as in the case of the PhN, we define a single SN submodel that actually specialises into different models, depending on the marking of the SMS. The SN submodel for our example of SMS is shown in Figure 4.

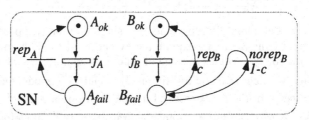

Fig. 4. System Net submodel

A token in place A_{ok} or A_{fail} models the fact that component A is correctly working or failed, respectively, and similarly for component B. The failure process of components A and B is modelled by the exponential transition f_A and $f_B = \lambda_B$, respectively. Since the failure intensity is different depending on the type of mission, the firing time of f_A is dependent on the marking of the MN submodel, as specified in Table 3.

Table 3. Marking dependent firing rates of the SN submodel

Transition	Firing rate
f_A	$\lambda_{1,A}$ if $m(M_1) = 1$, $\lambda_{2,A}$ if $m(M_2) = 1$

The discrete repairs that take place as a consequence of the maintenance actions are modelled by introducing the immediate transitions rep_A, rep_B, and $norep_B$. These immediate transitions are enabled at the end of those missions for which a maintenance action has been scheduled. To ensure a proper sequence of firing of the immediate transitions in the model, the discrete repair transition are assigned a priority higher than that of transition *next* in the PhN submodel. The two conflicting transitions rep_B and $norep_B$ fire with probability c and $1-c$, modelling the coverage of the intermediate maintenance check on component B. To properly model the execution of the scheduled maintenance action, the enabling conditions shown in Table 4 are added to the immediate transitions rep_A, rep_B, and $norep_B$.

Table 4. SN marking dependent enabling conditions

Transition	Enabling condition
rep_A	$m(Stop) = 1$
rep_B	$m(Stop) = 1$ & $m(Count) = \alpha \cdot i$, $i = 1, 2, ..., \lfloor 50/\alpha \rfloor$
$norep_B$	$m(Stop) = 1$ & $m(Count) = \alpha \cdot i$, $i = 1, 2, ..., \lfloor 50/\alpha \rfloor$

Similarly, we can model maintenance directives requiring the repair of components between two phases of a mission, or whatever change of configuration that takes place at the end of a phase. Moreover, as we have detailed in [15], this same mechanism of conditioning the evolution of a part of the model through a set of marking dependent parameters can be used to model more general scenarios of multi phased missions. In particular, by conditioning the MN and PhN submodels to the marking of the SN one it is possible to represent more dynamic and flexible SMS, where the next phase or mission to be performed can be chosen depending on the state of the system.

It is important to spend a few words in pointing out the advantages of the DSPN modelling of SMS. First of all, the high-level approach turns out in a overall SMS model that is concise, easy to understand and to modify. Moreover, the whole modelling procedure limits the possibility of introducing errors inside the models. Various structural properties of the separate Petri net submodels can be checked to increase the confidence that can be put in the modelling itself. Further, the links among the various submodels are expressed through predicates of the marking, in a clear and unambiguous way. The tedious process of manual description of the mapping and the translation of maintenance directives into matrices, which is necessary with the EHARP approach, is completely eliminated. Indeed, the mapping between successive phases and missions and the maintenance actions are completely specified at the level of the DSPN modelling. The mapping at the level of the underlying Markov chains is automatically obtained from the analysis of the reachability graph of the DSPN model, thus dramatically reducing the amount of user-assistance needed to define the SMS models. Finally, as we shall see in the following, these modelling capabilities are also sustained by a very efficient analytical solution technique.

4   Analytical Solution and Sensitivity Snalysis

As it has been proved in [5], a DSPN model can be analytically solved in terms of the time-dependent marking occupation probabilities by applying the results of the MRGP theory, provided that at most one deterministic transition is enabled in each of the possible markings of the net. This condition is obviously satisfied for the DSPN model of a SMS, because the only deterministic transitions of the model are those in the PhN, and they get enabled sequentially, one at the time. Moreover, due to the special structure of the system, the computationally efficient method proposed in [15] applies for the solution of the models. In the following, we briefly recall that method, for deriving first the exact analytical expression for the transient marking occupation probabilities, and second the sensitivity of the dependability measures with respect to the parameter variations.

4.1   Reliability at Mission Completion Time

To avoid a cumbersome notation, during this solution step we flatten the multiple mission structure of the SMS, reducing it to a PMS structure. Thus, we renumber the phases along the various missions, so that we consider a single long mission, during which all the $N = \sum_{i=1}^{m} n_i$ phases of the SMS are sequentially executed. Let τ_i denote the time the SMS spends in phase i of the mission, and Q_i denote the transition rate matrix that describes the evolution of the SN submodel while the SMS executes phase i, $i = 1, 2, ..., N$. During the execution of a phase i, the evolution of the marking process underlying the DSPN model follows that of a simple continuous-time Markov chain, and is thus described by the exponential of the matrix Q_i.

According to the results presented in [15], the vector $\pi(t)$ of the time-dependent marking occupation probabilities of the DSPN model can be explicitly computed for any time $t \geq 0$. From vector $\pi(t)$ all the dependability measures of interest can be obtained. For instance, we can obtain the Reliability R of the SMS at the end of the last phase N, which is given by the following expression:

$$R = \pi_0 \cdot \left(\prod_{h=1}^{N} e^{Q_h \tau_h} \Delta_h \right) \cdot \beta \tag{2}$$

where π_0 is the vector of initial probability assignment, Δ_h is the branching-probability matrices which account for the branching probabilities as the deterministic transition i fires $i = 1, 2, ..., N$, and β is a vector that selects the successful states at the end of the hundredth mission. It is worthwhile observing that evaluating the preceding formula to obtain the transient state probability matrix only requires us to derive matrices $e^{Q_h \tau_h}$, and Δ_h, $h = 1, 2, ..., N$. All the required matrices can be derived from the analysis of the DSPN reachability graph. The solution of the single DSPN model is reduced to the cheaper problem of deriving the transient probability matrices of a set of homogeneous, time-continuous Markov chains whose state spaces are proper subsets of the whole state space of the marking process.

4.2   Sensitivity Analysis

The existence of an analytic expression for the marking dependent occupation probabilities allows to evaluate the derivatives of the dependability measures of interest with respect to the variations of some parameters, the so-called sensitivity functions [9]. These functions can be conveniently employed to perform an analytical study of the effects that the parameter variations have on the dependability. Indeed, the absolute value of the derivative indicates the magnitude of the variations of the measure for a small perturbations of the parameter, and its sign reveals whether an increase of the parameter value causes a corresponding increase or instead a decrease of the measure.

Obviously, whenever the dependence of the measure of interest from the parameters only involves simple functions that can be computed at a limited computational cost, the sensitivity analysis can be conveniently conducted through multiple evaluations, to plot the dependability measures for the whole range of parameter values. However, when more parameters can be varied simultaneously, this approach tends to become expensive in terms of the number of evaluations. In this scenario, the study of the sensitivity functions represents a suitable strategy to point out which parameters of the system most significantly impact on the measures of interest. Indeed, by comparing the partial derivatives with respect to the varying parameters it is possible to identify those to which the measures are sensitive the most.

Conversely, when the dependability measure object of the evaluation is a complex function, performing multiple evaluations can easily become an expensive task. For instance, consider the formula for the SMS Reliability given by Equation (2), and suppose we want to estimate the effect that varying the failure rate λ_A has on the measure. Then, since the parameter λ_A appears inside the transition rate matrices Q_i, for each value of λ_A we need to evaluate a set of matrix exponentials. In this case, the sensitivity function of the Reliability with respect to parameter λ_A can fruitfully complement the means available for the study of a SMS, in some cases avoiding or limiting the need of performing long batches of evaluations for a number of different values of the parameters.

We now obtain the sensitivity function of the Reliability R given by Equation (2), with respect to an independent parameter θ, that is we consider $R = R(\theta)$. The analytical derivation of this derivative is just an example of the sensitivity studies that can be performed once the analytical expression for the dependability measures are available. The initial probability vector, the duration of phases, the firing rates of exponential transitions, as well as the probability mass functions ruling the firing of immediate transitions may be dependent on parameter θ. Let us denote with $\rho(\theta)$ the sensitivity function, defined as the derivative of $R(\theta)$ with respect to θ:

$$\rho(\theta) = \frac{\partial}{\partial \theta} R(\theta) = (\frac{\partial}{\partial \theta} \pi_0) \prod_{h=1}^{N} e^{Q_h \tau_h} \Delta_h \cdot \beta + m_0 \cdot \frac{\partial}{\partial \theta} \left(\prod_{h=1}^{N} e^{Q_h \tau_h} \Delta_h \right) \cdot \beta \quad (3)$$

The derivative of the product that appears in the last term of Equation (3) is obtained as follows:

$$\frac{\partial}{\partial \theta} \prod_{h=1}^{N} e^{Q_h \tau_h} \Delta_h = \sum_{k=1}^{N} \left[\left(\prod_{h=1}^{k-1} e^{Q_h \tau_h} \Delta_h \right) \frac{\partial}{\partial \theta} e^{Q_k \tau_k} \Delta_k \left(\prod_{h=k+1}^{N} e^{Q_h \tau_h} \Delta_h \right) \right] \quad (4)$$

Last, the derivative of $e^{Q_k \tau_k} \Delta_k$ can be obtained as follows:

$$\frac{\partial}{\partial \theta} e^{Q_k \tau_k} \Delta_k = \frac{\partial}{\partial \theta} \left(e^{Q_k \tau_k} \right) \Delta_k + e^{Q_k \tau_k} \frac{\partial}{\partial \theta} \Delta_k \quad (5)$$

By combining the intermediate results given by Equation (3), (4), and (5), we obtain the most general formula for the sensitivity function $s(\theta)$, for it takes into account the dependence from θ of any other parameter of the DSPN model. It is worthwhile observing that, with respect to the evaluation of the Reliability R, the estimation of the sensitivity function only requires an additional small computation effort. Indeed, mostly the same matrices are required, according to Equations (2) and (3), (4), and (5). The only non trivial computation is that of the derivative of the matrix exponential, for which efficient algorithms have been defined [3, 10, 14]. Thus, once the value of the Reliability $R(\theta)$ has been derived, its derivative $\rho(\theta)$ can be evaluated too with a limited additional effort for a given value of θ. The pointwise derivatives of the measure can be employed to increase the accuracy of the approximations of the measure over continuous intervals, through an interpolation approximation. Thus, the number of points at which the measure is plotted can be drastically reduced still achieving a good level of accuracy.

5 Numerical Evaluation

In this section we present the results of a numerical evaluation of the dependability figures for the example of SMS we modelled above. In a first evaluation session we estimate R, the Reliability of the SMS at the mission completion time, with varying the values of some parameters, and complement the analysis by exploiting the information provided by the sensitivity functions. Then, mainly dealing with the sensitivity functions, we study in detail the cost function defined by Equation (1), to provide some hints for possible system optimisation.

The general analytical expression for Reliability R, given by Equation (2), can be rewritten according to the particular structure of our example of SMS. Since the firing rates of transitions f_A and f_B have different values depending on the type of mission, there are two distinct transition rate matrices, which we denote with Q_1 and Q_2. Similarly, there are two types of maintenance checks, that is the one performed at the end of each mission, which solely involves component A, and that performed each α pairs of missions, which affects both A and B. These two types of check are translated into two distinct branching probability matrices, denoted by Δ_1 and Δ_2, respectively. As an instance, the following equation shows the formula of R for $\alpha = 2$:

$$R = \pi_0 \cdot (X \cdot Y \cdot X \cdot Z)^{25} \cdot \beta \tag{6}$$

where $X = e^{Q_1 \tau_{1,1}} \Delta_1$, $Y = e^{Q_2(\tau_{2,1}+\tau_{2,2})} \Delta_1$, and $Z = e^{Q_2(\tau_{2,1}+\tau_{2,2})} \Delta_2$. For this same value of $\alpha = 2$, we also show the sensitivity function of R with respect to the failure rate of the backup unit λ_B, denoted by $\rho(\lambda_B)$. According to the equations derived in the previous section, the sensitivity function $\rho(\lambda_B)$ takes the following form:

$$\rho(\lambda_B) = \pi_0 \cdot \left[\sum_{h=1}^{25} (X \cdot Y \cdot X \cdot Z)^{h-1} \cdot \left(\frac{\partial}{\partial \lambda_B}(X \cdot Y \cdot X \cdot Z) \right) \cdot (X \cdot Y \cdot X \cdot Z)^{25-h} \right] \cdot \beta \tag{7}$$

The derivative of matrix $XYXZ$ is obtained according to Equation (5). It is worthwhile observing that the matrix powers computed during the evaluation of the Reliability for a given value of λ_B according to Equation (6) can be conveniently reused when evaluating the sensitivity function $\rho(\lambda_B)$ in Equation (7), thus reducing the required computational cost.

We assume that at the beginning of operation both component A and B are perfectly working, and therefore the initial probability vector π_0 is the one that assigns probability 1 to the marking in which both A and B are correctly working. Vector β selects those marking that represents a proper system state, that is all the markings except the one in which both A and B have failed. The fixed value parameters, that is the phase duration and the failure process of the primary unit A are given in Table 5. Hour (h) is the unit in which all time-related measures are expressed.

Table 5. Fixed value parameters of the SMS model

Duration of the phases	Failure rates of components
$\tau_{1,1} = 15h$, $\tau_{2,1} = 5h$, $\tau_{2,2} = 10h$	$\lambda_{1,A} = 0.001/h$, $\lambda_{2,A} = 0.002/h$

The parameters related to the backup unit B, that is its failure intensity during the various missions, the coverage and the frequency of the check, are variable within the ranges specified by Table 6.

Table 6. Parameter values for component B

Failure rate	Check coverage	Frequency of the check
$\lambda_B \in [10^{-1}\lambda_{1,A}, 10\lambda_{1,A}]$	$c \in [0.6, 0.99]$	$\alpha = 1, 2, 5$

We first evaluate the Reliability R of the SMS with varying the failure rate of the backup unit λ_B within the considered range of values, for the various possible values of the period length α between two intermediate maintenance checks, and a fixed value of the coverage $c = 0.95$. The curves shown in Figure 5 help in clarifying the effect that the choice of a particular frequency has on the Reliability of the system.

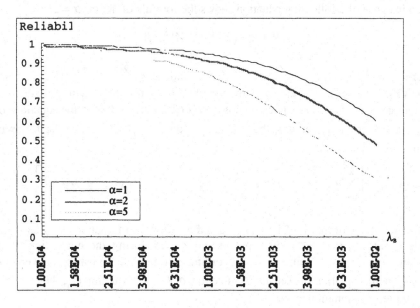

Fig. 5. Reliability of the SMS for different settings of parameters

From the results shown in Figure 5, it is possible to identify a range of values of the failure rate λ_B, specifically the values on the left side of the plots, for which changing the period α does not impact significantly on the final measure, whereas relevant changes in the SMS Reliability results can be observed for higher values of λ_B. As it would be expected, if reliable components are employed, the frequency of the check does not necessarily need to be particularly high to achieve satisfactory results.

We now approximate the results obtained for the Reliability of the SMS by using the interpolation technique and compare the quality of the approximate results with respect to the amount of information that is needed to compute them. Letting $\alpha = 2$, we interpolate the Reliability by considering an increasing number of interpolation points (the so-called interpolation nodes) to obtain more and more accurate approximation of the original Reliability figures. We consider four different approximate Reliability curves, obtained by interpolating the function and its derivative in two, three, four, and five nodes. The relative error introduced by the various interpolations over the whole interval of values considered for λ_B is shown in Figure 6. As it can be observed from the comparison in Figure 6, with five interpolation nodes we obtain a very tight approximation of the original curve, which was evaluated at one hundred points to produce the corresponding curve shown in Figure 5.

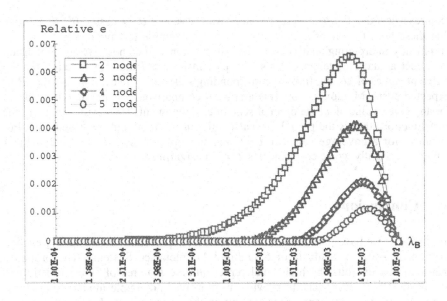

Fig. 6. Accuracy of Reliability approximation

We now conduct a different set of numerical evaluations to study the cost function defined by Equation (1) with varying the coverage c of the check on the backup unit B, for a fixed value $\lambda_B = \lambda_{I,A}$ of component B failure rate.

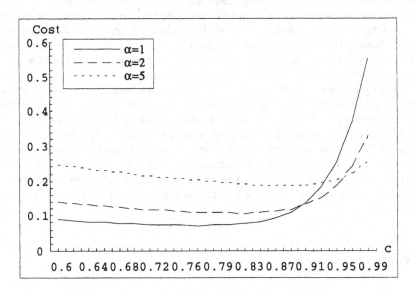

Fig. 7. Expected cost as a function of the intermediate check coverage

We assume the cost Φ of the system failure as being unitary, and proportionally define the cost function $\varphi(c) = k_I \cdot e^{k_2 c}$ in a way that a check providing coverage 0.6

requires a cost of $10^{-6}\Phi$, whereas a check with coverage 0.99 costs $10^{-2}\Phi$. Notice that these specific values are only chosen as an example to have the possibility of graphically interpreting the trends of the cost function, and do not have any pretension to reflect actual maintenance costs. We plot in Figure 7 the cost function for the different values of α, and find the corresponding values of c that minimise the SMS expected costs. Moreover, from this graphical comparison, it is possible to identify, for any given value of c, the optimal schedule of the maintenance with respect to the cost function, that is the period α that results in the minimum expected cost. For instance, for a coverage value of $c = 0.95$, the optimal period is $\alpha = 2$, $\alpha = 5$ provides a slightly worse cost, whereas $\alpha = 1$ is significantly more expensive.

6 Conclusions

In this paper we have introduced a new modelling approach for dependability evaluation and sensitivity analysis of Scheduled Maintenance Systems. The proposed methodology exploits the high level representative features of Deterministic and Stochastic Petri net models, to provide an intuitive and simple modelling strategy. Compared to the other approaches existing in the literature, which are mainly based on Markov chain modelling tools, the DSPN approach offers significant advantages, drastically limiting the amount of user-assistance needed to define the model of a SMS. Moreover, the DSPN model of a SMS can be analytically solved in terms of the time-dependent marking occupation probabilities for the purposes of dependability evaluation. The solution technique is very efficient in terms of computational cost, requires only standard numerical algorithms, and can be easily automated.

Furthermore, owing to the existence of the explicit analytical solution for the transient marking occupation probabilities, we have obtained the sensitivity functions of the dependability measures with respect to the variation of the parameter values. These sensitivity functions can be conveniently employed to analytically evaluate the effects that parameter variations have on the measures of interest.

To better show the advantages of our approach, we have applied our modelling methodology to an example of SMS that has been inspired by a case study encountered in the literature. We have completely carried out the modelling, derived the sensitivity function of the Reliability, and performed a set of numerical evaluations with the aim of finding the most appropriate schedule of maintenance for the example of SMS. By exploiting the additional information provided by the sensitivity functions, we have obtained very accurate approximations of the dependability measures through an interpolation approach, achieving a significant reduction of the evaluation computational costs.

References

1. S. Allmaier and S. Dalibor, "PANDA - Petri net analysis and design assistant," in Proc. Performance TOOLS'97, Saint Malo, France, 1997.
2. C. Beounes, M. Aguera, J. Arlat, C. Bourdeau, J.-E. Doucet, K. Kanoun, J.-C. Laprie, S. Metge, J. Moreira de Souza, D. Powell and P. Spiesser, "SURF-2: a program for dependability evaluation of complex hardware and software systems," in Proc. IEEE

FTCS'23, Fault-Tolerant Computing Symposium, Toulouse, France, 1993, pp. 668-673.

3. J. T. Blake, A. Reibman and K. S. Trivedi, "Sensitivity analysis of reliability and performability measures for multiprocessor systems," Duke University, Durham NC, USA 1987.

4. A. Bondavalli, I. Mura and M. Nelli, "Analytical Modelling and Evaluation of Phased-Mission Systems for Space Applications," in Proc. IEEE High Assurance System Engineering Workshop (HASE'97), Bethesda Maryland, USA, 1997, pp. 85 - 91.

5. H. Choi, V.G. Kulkarni and K.S. Trivedi, "Transient analysis of deterministic and stochastic Petri nets.," in Proc. 14th International Conference on Application and Theory of Petri Nets, Chicago Illinois, USA, 1993, pp. 166-185.

6. H. Choi, V. Mainkar and K. S. Trivedi, "Sensitivity analysis of deterministic and stochastic petri nets," in Proc. MASCOTS'93, 1993, pp. 271-276.

7. G. Ciardo, J. Muppala and K.S. Trivedi, "SPNP: stochastic petri net package.," in Proc. International Conference on Petri Nets and Performance Models, Kyoto, Japan, 1989.

8. J. B. Dugan, "Automated Analysis of Phased-Mission Reliability," IEEE Transaction on Reliability, Vol. 40, pp. 45-52, 1991.

9. P. M. Frank, "Introduction to System Sensitivity Theory," New York, Academic Press, 1978.

10. P. Heidelberger and A. Goyal, "Sensitivity analysis of continuous time Markov chains using uniformization," in Proc. 2-nd International Workshop on Applied Mathematics and Performance/Reliability models of Computer/Communication systems, Rome, Italy, 1987.

11. C. Lindemann, "Performance modeling using DSPNexpress," in Proc. Tool Descriptions of PNPM'97, Saint-Malo, France, 1997.

12. C. Lindemann, "Performance modeling using deterministic and stochastic petri nets," John Wiley & Sons, 1998.

13. J.F. Meyer, D.G. Furchgott and L.T. Wu, "Performability Evaluation of the SIFT Computer," in Proc. IEEE FTCS'79 Fault-Tolerant Computing Symposium, June20-22, Madison, Wisconsin, USA, 1979, pp. 43-50.

14. J. K. Muppala and K. S. Trivedi, "GSPN models: sensitivity analysis and applications," in Proc. 28-th ACM Southeast Region Conference, 1990.

15. I. Mura, A. Bondavalli, X. Zang and K. S. Trivedi, "Dependability Modeling and Evaluation of Phased Mission Systems: a DSPN Approach," in Proc. DCCA-99, San Jose, CA, USA, 1999.

16. W. H. Sanders, W. D. Obal II, M. A. Qureshi and F. K. Widjanarko, "The *UltraSAN* modeling environment," Performance Evaluation, Vol. 21, pp. 1995.

17. M. Smotherman and K. Zemoudeh, "A Non-Homogeneous Markov Model for Phased-Mission Reliability Analysis," IEEE Transactions on Reliability, Vol. 38, pp. 585-590, 1989.

18. A. K. Somani, J. A. Ritcey and S. H. L. Au, "Computationally-Efficent Phased-Mission Reliability Analysis for Systems with Variable Configurations," IEEE Transactions on Reliability, Vol. 41, pp. 504-511, 1992.

19. A. K. Somani and K. S. Trivedi, "Phased-Mission Systems Using Boolean Algebraic Methods," Performance Evaluation Review, Vol. pp. 98-107, 1994.

20. D. W. Twigg, A. V. Ramesh, U. R. Sandadi, A. Ananda and T. Sharma, "Reliability computation of systems that operate in multiple phases and multiple missions," Boeing Commercial Airplane Group

Evaluation of Video Communication over Packet Switching Networks

PD Dr. Klaus Heidtmann
Telecommunication and Computer Networks Division,
Department of Computer Science, University of Hamburg
Vogt-Kölln-Str. 30, D-22527 Hamburg, Germany
Email: heidtmann@informatik.uni-hamburg.de

Abstract. Real-time video communication as a component of distributed multimedia systems for new evolving applications like video telefony and video-conferencing is strongly dependent on the quality of service provided by its communication support. Dependability attributes of the undelying communication system playing a predominant role with regard to the quality achievable from applications and users point of view. Especially video compression reduces data rates by removing the original redundancy of video sequences but creates dependencies between data of different images enabling extensive error propagation. So real-time video communication becomes extremely sensitive to faulty transmitted, lost or too late arriving data. This dependability inherent for instance in most packet switching networks results in low video quality.

In this paper we study video communication via best-effort networks, which present the actual communication infrastructure. First we illustrate the effect of transmission deficiencies on the visual quality of the received video. Then an analytical model of dependability is developed, which reflects the transmission of MPEG and H.261 coded video streams. We apply our model to compute appropriate or even optimal parameters for video encoders. Forward error control using error correcting codes provides the communication process with fault tolerance, which may improve the quality of video transmission by systematic redundancy. So we extend our model to determine the required level of redundancy. Finally we discuss further mechanisms of fault tolerance to achieve high video quality even in case of modest or even low quality of service delivered by communication systems.

Keywords: multimedia system, real-time video communication, visual quality, dependability evaluation, best-effort network, quality of service, forward error control

1 Introduction

Currently new emerging services, particularly distributed multimedia applications, e.g. video telefony and video-conferencing, are of great importance in industry, academic research and standardization. Large scale deployment of such applications will impose very high constrains on the overall system components, such as networks and end-systems. The requirements range from high data rates, due to the voluminous nature of video data, to severe temporal constraints, due to the continuous nature and real-time requirements of audio and video communication.

A multimedia system is characterized by the computer-controlled integrated generation, manipulation, representation, storage and communication (!) of independent digital information. This information is often coded in continuous (time dependent) media (e.g., audio, video). Uncompressed video data requires considerable amount of capacity which is often not available, even with todays technology. In case of multimedia communication for instance a very high bandwidth, reserved exclusively for a single point-to-point communication, is necessary for the transfer of uncompressed video data over digital networks. A simple calculation shows that the transmission of uncompressed video streams in a multimedia system requires a network providing megabit data rates for each application. Such a network is expensive and in many cases not available at all. Therefore most multimedia systems handle digital video and audio data streams in compressed form. Some techniques and related implementations already exist, while the development of more refined techniques and implementations is continuing. The most important video compression techniques today are MPEG, H.261, H.263 and we focus on these well established and standardized techniques [Efs 98].

The use of appropriate compression techniques considerably reduces the data transfer rates in many cases without much loss in quality. But applied to video transmission it must be handled with great care because it augments error propagation. Video compression techniques reduce data rates by interframe coding, where many or nearly all frames refer to others. These dependencies imply that a faulty, lost or too late received reference frame prevents the decompression of any frame that refers to it although these dependent frames may not be directly affected by an error. As a consequence compressed data are very sensitive to faults, losses and too long transmission delays. Furthermore in distributed applications with real-time requirements, such as real-time audio and video communication, reliability of the underlying network is also prevailing because timing restrictions usually do not allow for retransmissions in case of transmission errors or losses. Since multimedia data is seldom send directly as raw data, that is without any form of compression, special care has to be taken to guard the transmission against the typical hazards of data communication like bit errors, delays or losses.

Because networks consist of limited resources, traffic loads can exceed the supply of data transmission capacity available at a certain time and location. Consequently the network or some parts of it may become overloaded or congested. So even if the total capacity might be sufficient to handle a given total demand on network resources, differences in the distribution of the demands can form intermediate or local bottlenecks appearing as either longer delays or losses. Although the internetworking technology tries to do its best to deliver transmitted data timely and correctly, due to the inability to predict traffic correctly and because there is no access control to manage limited resources, a certain quality of the network's service cannot be guaranteed. Thus one speaks of a best-effort network. Well-known examples are the global Internet, Ethernet and mobil networks [BNC 99].

As with other classes of distributed applications distributed multimedia systems are strongly dependent on the quality of the underlying communication system or communication network offering its services with a level of Quality-of-Service (QoS). This dependency centers on the continuity of service delivered by the communication system, on the overall performance level achieved and especially on the real-time requirements of continuous media e.g. in real-time audio and video communication. Besides performance characteristics the reliability properties of a communication system are playing a predominant role with regard to its quality of service [Hei 97]. So multimedia applications like real-time audio- and video communication with their usually strict requirements for throughput and bounded delays do not perform very favorably when run over a best-effort network. Because of data losses or high delays the service offered by an application can deteriorate: a video might freeze, or worse, show artifacts because of losses, video thus degrades to still image display. Audio streams became unintelligible when portions of the data stream are missing.

To support the solution of these problems this paper presents a reliability and performance study of real-time video communication. The derived model reflects the transmission of coded video streams and is still analytically tractable. So it can be applied to evaluate the quality of computing and communication systems for this class of applications. To show this the paper comprises some case studies applying the introduced model. However, our results can also be used to obtain high QoS for end-users by an appropriate parameterization of the video encoder and the forward error control (FEC). This parameterization comprises a careful tuning of video coding parameters to the actual state of the network and to the transmission capacity required dynamically by the application.

In section 2 we will shortly describe the features of real-time video communication, which determine the quality of the received video. This includes the principal assumptions concerning video communication as viewed throughout this paper and the methods of video compression and encoding as far as they are relevant in our context. Some examples for the degradation of visual quality caused by video transmission are given in section 3. Section 4 comprises the analytical model, which allows us to quantitatively evaluate the quality of video transmitted over packet switching networks. In the case studies of section 5 we make use of the advantages inherent in our analytical model: namely, the excellent usability for comprehensive parameter studies. The case studies provide valuable hints for good or optimal parameterization of video encoders and for a model based network management to support high quality of video communication in real-time. In section 6 we sketch a desirable extension of the model as it has been developed to investigate the potential of forward error control in achieving high quality of video communication. Finally we mention additional methods to improve the reliability and quality of video communication like information dispersal, where the video stream is split and transmitted over different network paths, and reservation of network resources to guarantee the provided quality of network service.

2 Coding and Transmission of Video Data

Let us now describe the way video communication is assumed to take place throughout this paper and as it is reflected by our model and the case studies. Think of video telefony as a simple example application. A sending end-system takes a video sequence while another receiving end-system has to display it at the same time. In video telefony an end-system takes pictures of a speakers face and these pictures are simultaneously displayed on the monitor of the receiving end-system for the listener.

Of course, transmission deficiencies have some negative impact on the quality of the stream redisplayed by the receiver. We assume that the network will lose, corrupt and delay data units during their transmission. In case of corrupted data being delivered we suppose that, as a consequence of real-time communication requirements, retransmission of data will not be acceptable. If transmission delays exceed the required delay bounds of real-time video communication, data arrive too late to be timely displayed within the video sequence. So they are useless for the receiver. Therefore, from the receiver point of view the effect of data corruption or excessive delay is the same as a complete loss. Losses can be caused by several reasons: Load may exceed the buffering or processing capacity of network routers or end-systems. If one particular router or the receiving host receives more packets than it can process or store in its buffers it has to discard the data packets. Traffic may also exceed the capacity of physical networks. In this situation collisions can occur and sent data becomes garbled. Sometimes access to the media is restricted so that the capacity cannot be surpassed. Depending on the type used (e.g. copper, optical, fiber, microwave) specific transmission technologies exhibit a loss rate caused by material and environment. Factors like electric influence, light, temperature or air pressure can effect the frequency of errors on a line or a wireless transmission medium. Any component whose participation is mandatory for a specific connection like routers or other hosts may cause a failure, if it breaks down.

A moving picture is simply a succession of still pictures. Accordingly, one can achieve a degree of compression by independently compressing each still picture in the sequence that makes up the moving picture. A pictures encoded as an independent still image is called I-frame (intraframe). Because it is encoded independent of other frames in the so-called intraframe mode, it can be displayed independently of the content of other frames. This approach of intraframe coding fails to exploit the considerable redundancy present in all video sequences. Even in a moving picture with a lot of action, the differences between adjacent still pictures are generally small compared to the amount of information in a single still picture. This suggests that an encoding of the differences between adjacent still pictures is a fruitful approach to compression. Typically, many of the pixels will change little or not at all from one frame to the next, or the change simply involves the movement of a pattern of pixels from one location on a frame to a nearby location on the next frame. These redundancies are exploited in an interframe mode.

For interframe mode, similar blocks of pixels common to two or more successive frames are replaced by a pointer that references one of the blocks. This so-called motion vector gives the displacement of the block in the current frame with reference to its match in the anchor frame. Typically, the motion vector for a block is obtained by minimizing a cost function that measures the difference between a block and each predictor candidate. The search range could encompass only small displacements or could range up to the entire frame size. The reference pictures must be transmitted and received before an interframe can be decoded and displayed. If a frame is encoded as an interframe based on the most recent preceding I- or P-frame, which ever is closest, it is called P-frame (predictive frame).

The relative frequency of these types of frames within a video stream is a considerable parameter and must satisfy several trade-offs. At least the first picture of a video stream must be an intraframe. More interframes means more computation and a stronger dependence among different frames. As we know from other fields of fault tolerant computing such dependencies decrease reliability by error propagation. A single fault may not only destroy the current frame but also the frames that depend on the current one. Other important aspects for the picture sequence structure in an implementation are time constraints, buffer size or the desired compression and quality trade-off. The standard H.261 defines two types of frames, i.e. I- and P-frames, while e.g. MPEG defines additional optional frame types [EfS 98].

Each frames is subdivided into macroblocks each representing 16x16 pixel. The format CIF (Common Interface Format) provides 396 macroblocks (288x352 pixel) per frame while QCIF (Quarter CIF) reduces to 99 macroblocks per frame. A macroblock can be encoded in intraframe or interframe mode and is then called I- or P-macroblock. An I-macroblock is encoded independent of other macroblocks and can be displayed independently of the context of other macroblocks. P-macroblocks are predicted taking into account the content of an I- or P-macroblock of the preceding frame and thus depend on the presence and correctness of this reference macroblock. Frames that contain at least one P-macroblock are called P-frames, while I-frames comprise only I-macroblocks.

Video encoding leads to data streams with either constant or variable bit rate. A constant bit rate implies constant data volumes for any frame resulting in varying picture quality. A constant picture quality over time is achieved by varying the data volume of frames, i.e. a variable bit rate. In the following we prefer a constant picture quality resulting in a variable bit rate to be transmitted over a packet switching network. Measurements of bit rates etc. are given for instance in [HKZ 99, Bai 99].

The subsequent investigation considers the following situation: A video coder in the sending end-system compresses and encodes a video stream in real-time. This data stream is given to the communication system, which fragments the data into packets, transmits the single data packets over the network to the receiving end-system and reassembles the received data packets to a data stream, which is passed to the video decoder of the receiver site. After decoding in the receiving end-system the video data is displayed here. So based on the arriving data stream the video decoder in the receiving end-system reconstructs the sent video in real-time as good as possible to display it. Applications with this scenario are for instance video telephony and video-conferencing.

3   Deterioration of the Visual Quality

The following investigation evaluates video communication from the end-users point of view at the receiving end-system in so far as the received and displayed video differs from the video stream right before transmission. Notice that we do not compare the displayed video with the original pictures sequence before compression, but with the already compressed and thereafter sent video data. (s. Fig. 3.1).

The loss of information as a consequence of lossy compression used by video systems is not a subject of our evaluation. Only the deterioration of the video quality as an effect of the transmission is considered. This deterioration is visible on the monitor of the receiving end-system and is also indirectly affected by the encoding and compression, especially with regard to error propagation.

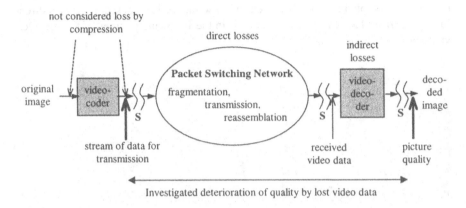

Fig. 3.1. Schematic view of video communication (S: interface of investigation)

Frames with faulty, lost or too late received data are called direct losses. They prevent the video decoder in the receiving site from decoding other frames which refer to directly lost frames. So we call frames with a lost reference frame indirect losses. Hence, direct losses occur in the network during transmission, while indirect losses appear in the decoder during decoding (s. Fig. 3.1 and Fig. 3.2).

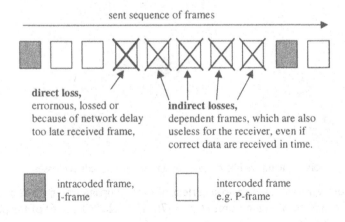

Fig. 3.2. Example of direct and indirect losses of frames

Fig. 3.3 compares an original picture of a video sequence with its received version to observe the degradation caused by a direct or indirect loss. The video sequence is coded with H.261, resolution QCIF, quantization factor 1and picture rate 30 frames/s. The received and degraded picture is shown on the left side. During transmission three macroblocks (no. 12 – no. 14) of the second group of blocks were lost, which represent the beginning of the middle line. So the following macroblocks of this group of blocks move up three positions within this group, while the following group of blocks for the upper part of the picture remains unaffected. Hence, in the received picture the middle line and its successor line are moved to the left, so that the face of the newscaster is cut in disarranged slices. This degradation of the first picture in the received video sequence is a consequence of a direct loss. The sliced face can also be observed in the following pictures of the received video as an example of indirect losses.

Fig. 3.3. Sent vs received video frame with 3 directly lost macroblocks during transmission

Now we compare the corresponding pictures (no. 26) of two received video sequences. The left picture of Fig. 3.4 belongs to the video, which was transmitted perfectly, while the right blurry frame indicates the loss of 15 previous P-frames (no. 2 – no. 16) in the received video sequence. This illustrates the degradation of the visual quality of a so-called indirectly lost frame.

Fig. 3.4. Perfectly received picture vs blurry frame as an example of indirect losses

Finally we demonstrate the disastrous effect of error propagation in form of indirect losses. Fig. 3.5 shows some frames (no. 1, 76, 151, 226, 301, 376) of the perfectly received example video.

Fig. 3.5. Frames of a perfectly received video

For the video sequence shown in Fig. 3.6 the data stream generated by the video encoder was fragmented into data packets of size 512 Byte. 1% of the data packets were discarded as direct loss during transmission. This is a relatively small amount of lost information, for instance an audio stream with a loss of 1% is as perceptible as a perfect one. But in case of video coding a lot of frames may refer to the few lost ones. As a consequence many dependent P-frames can not be correctly decoded forcing degradation of visual quality as a form of error propagation.

Fig. 3.6. Frames of a video sequence with 1% directly and much more indirectly lost data

4 Dependability Model for Video Communication

While compression algorithms manipulate video data in a controlled way and intentionally without much loss in video quality, the above discussed losses occur unintentionally and may result in low video quality. In the following we evaluate the video quality by means of the expected number of losses and by the probability of losing a frame. The basic quantity of our evaluation is the probability ε_c for the direct loss of a data packet in the network and the number of data packets for I- and P-frames c_i resp. c_p.

Based on these quantities we want to compute the probability that a randomly chosen frame is lost. This probability is a characteristic quantity for the quality of the received video and for the quality of service delivered by the communication system. It can be computed for our situation using a probabilistic dependability model. This contribution is restricted to an analytical evaluation of this model. Its simulative evaluation allowing for less restrictive assumptions is an ongoing work. Notice e.g. that the loss of several sequential packets (burst) is not as bad as statistically independent losses of single packets under the assumption that the mean loss probability is identical in both situations. So our following results are pessimistic as they represent a lower bound on the actual quality.

We assume that packet or fragment losses in the network or in an end-system are mutually independent for the subset of data transferred via the considered point-to-point connection. This independence assumption concerning packet or fragment losses is a rather approximate one in a large number of networks. However, keep in mind that this assumption refers only to losses of packets transmitted via one point-to-point connection and not for all data units transported by the communication network or switched by one switching node. This makes our independence assumption much more acceptable than supposing independent losses for bit error etc. The losses we assume include losses in the end-systems, e.g. buffer overflow.

A frame is viewed as useless if at least one of its data packets is lost. In this case the video decoder may substitute the corresponding section of an old picture for the missed data. But the spectator will regard this old part as an impairment, especially if this old section does not fit very well into the actual picture because it is faded in another environment. To avoid this problem of unsuitable sections the decoder can present the entire old picture until a complete, fault-free and actual set of data packets to represent a new frame is received. But transitions from a former picture to a new one without intermediate frames as missing links may appear as jerks.

With the probability ε_c for the direct loss of a data packet in a packet switching network we also know the probability $1-\varepsilon_c$ that a data packet is received correctly and timely. If a frame consists of c_i resp. c_p data packets and the losses of single data packets are statistically independent, then the probability for the direct loss of an I- resp. P-frame is given by

$$\varepsilon_i = 1 - (1-\varepsilon_c)^{c_i} \quad \text{resp.} \quad \varepsilon_p = 1 - (1-\varepsilon_c)^{c_p}$$

Now we consider the loss probability of frames between two consecutive I-frames with distance n. This implies that there are $n_p = n-1$ P-frames between two consecutive I-frames. In the special case n_p=0 there is no P-frame between two consecutive I-frames. To derive the probability of losing an arbitrary frame we begin with those events that cause the most indirect losses and we define the following disjoint events:

1. The loss of an I-frame implies the severest consequential damages, i.e. the indirect loss of all n_p P-frames until the next I-frame. So this event causes the total loss of n frames (one I-frame and n_p P-frames), and therefore the following number of lost frames is expected

$$n_{\varepsilon,i}(n) = n\,\varepsilon_i\,.$$

2. The other disjoint events are defined by the fact that the j-th P-frame is lost as the first. In other words: the previous I-frame and the j-1 P-frames between this I-frame and the lost P-frame were received correctly and the j-th P-frame is lost. In this case all n_p-j P-frames between the lost P-frame and the following I-frame are lost indirectly. This results in the loss of n_p+1-j P-frames and in the following expected number of lost frames $(1-\varepsilon_i)\,(1-\varepsilon_p)^{j-1}\,(n_p+1-j)\,\varepsilon_p$ for j=1 to n_p. With subscripts j=0 to n_p-1 this looks like

$$(1-\varepsilon_i)\,(1-\varepsilon_p)^j\,(n_p\text{-}j)\,\varepsilon_p$$

The sum of the probabilities for the last defined disjoint events yields the expected number of lost P-frames between two consecutive I-frames with n_p intermediate P-frames:

$$n_{\varepsilon,p}(n) = (1-\varepsilon_i)\,\varepsilon_p \sum_{j=0}^{n_p-1} (1-\varepsilon_p)^j\,(n_p\text{-}j) = \frac{1-\varepsilon_i}{\varepsilon_p}((1-\varepsilon_p)^n + n\varepsilon_p - 1)$$

The expected total loss of frames with respect to a group of frames with length n, i.e. an I-frame and its n_p subsequent P-frames until the next I-frame, is the sum of the probabilities for I- and P-frames derived above in 1. and 2. Dividing this sum by the total number n of frames in the group yields the probability $\varepsilon_f(n)$ that an arbitrary frame of such a group of length n is lost (frame loss probability)

$$\varepsilon_f(n) = \frac{n_{\varepsilon,i}(n) + n_{\varepsilon,p}(n)}{n} = \varepsilon_i + \frac{1-\varepsilon_i}{n\varepsilon_p}((1-\varepsilon_p)^n + n\varepsilon_p - 1) = 1 - \frac{1-\varepsilon_i}{n\varepsilon_p}(1-(1-\varepsilon_p)^n)$$

Now we consider the widely used MPEG and H.261 standards for video compression.

The MPEG algorithm assumes up to three types of frames by means of compression: I-, P- and B-frames. These frames are organized in so-called groups of pictures (GOP) with length n, what we called group of frames in our model. Every GOP starts with an I-frame (intraframe), which is encoded independent of other frames and thus can be displayed independently of the content of other frames, which is important to limit effects of error propagation within the total video stream. The other n-1 frames in a GOP are optional interframes and can be divided into two classes: P- and B-frames. MPEG has a forward prediction mode for P-frames where a reference frame in the past is used to predict areas of the current P-frame. Because of intermediate B-frames the reference frame is not necessarily the preceding frame, but the last I- or P-frame some time in the past. So P-frames (predictive frames) are predicted taking into account the content of the last I- or P-frame and thus are dependent on the presence and correctness of those frames. The B-frames (interpolated frames) are bi-directionally interpolated based on the content of the two neighbouring I- resp. P-frames, which precede and follow immediately the set of successive B-frames, where the interpolated B-frame belongs to. B-frames use interpolation for even better compression. The GOP structure, which is defined by the appearance and order of B- and P-frames between two I-frames, is not predefined in the standard but is one of the optimization possibilities for the encoder. Typical coding patterns are: IPPP (each I-frame is followed by three P-frames, no B-frames) or IBBPBB. Further details on the MPEG standard can be found for instance in [ISO 93, Tan 96, EfS 98]. Our model can be directly applied to MPEG encoded video streams as long as only I- and P-frames are used. For additional B-frames the above model can be extended straight forward.

A major difference between MPEG and H.261 is the way they take care of motion information between consecutive frames: Whereas MPEG specifies a coding pattern for GOPs, H.261 attempts to predict the current picture from only the previous one, i.e., there is no bi-directional interpolation. This is due to the strict timing requirements of online applications like video telefony and video-conferencing. So the H.261 standard defines just two types of frames: I- and P-frames. Our generic model above can be applied to H.261 video streams in two ways: on frame level or on macroblock level. On frame level I- and P-frames of the model are identical to those of H.261. On macroblock level the I- and P-macroblocks of the video stream take the place of I- and P-frames in our model. The group of frames from one I-frame to the next with distance n is replaced by a so-called group of macroblocks [HeW 99].

5 Case Studies

Our various case studies are meant to illustrate the areas of applicability of the analytical model presented in the foregoing part of this paper. We selected two studies, which quantitatively evaluate and compare the video quality of different variants of video encoding and investigate the implications of varying network dependability. The results can for instance be used to adequately parameterize the video encoder.

First we study the influence of the length of the group of frames n on the frame loss probability $\varepsilon_f(n)$ for different packet loss probabilities ε_c. Experiments, where H.261 video sequences were transmitted over the Internet, showed packet losses of about 10% between INRIA in France and the University College London (UCL) in Great Britain as well as packet losses of about 20% between INRIA and the Lawrence Berkeley Laboratory (LBL) in California [BoT 98]. Another measurement of packet loss and delay in the Internet is given in [ASW 98, Sie 98]. In mobile communication packet loss probabilities of 0.01 were observed [MRP 97].

Fig. 5.1 illustrates how the number of interframes n_p represented by the length $n=n_p+1$ of a group of frames increases the probability $\varepsilon_f(n)$ of losing an arbitrary frame. The data of any frame is divided into 99 or 396 data packets ($c_i=c_p=99$ resp. $c_i=c_p=396$). Each packet is directly lost during transmission with probability ε_c regardless of its length. The proposed Internet standard [TuH96] for instance provides this number of packets to transmit H.261 encoded video streams over the Internet. The probability for a lost frame is high because each frame is fragmented into 99 or 396 data packets. Notice the logarithmic scaling of the frame loss probability to see its immense increase when more interframe coding. For instance the frame loss probability is increases by the factor of 2 from no interframe coding ($n=1$) to two interframes ($n=3$) and by the factor of 3 if four interframes are used ($n=5$). This is observed for all packet loss probabilities and should be considered when compression is used. Fig. 5.1 shows the trade-off between video compression efficiency (many interframes) and quality of the received video (high frame loss probability). The frame loss probability in case of 99 data packets is much better than the other. So because of smaller frame loss probability a lower resolution leading to only 99 data packets may result in higher video quality at the receiver than a higher resolution video with 396 data packets implying more lost frames.

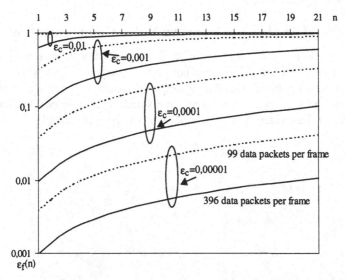

Fig. 5.1. Frame loss probability $\varepsilon_f(n)$ vs group of picture length n (compression efficiency)

Fig. 5.2 shows the influence of the packet loss probability ε_c on the frame loss probability $\varepsilon_f(n)$. Frames are fragmented into 99 data packets each and $n_p=n-1$ interframes are inserted between two consecutive I-frames. We see that small groups of pictures imply an acceptable frame loss probability when packet loss probability is limited by 0,005. Whereas frame loss probability is high for large groups of frames even for small packet loss probabilities. So an acceptable quality of the received video sequence quantified by the frame loss probability $\varepsilon_f(n)$ can only be guaranteed for small groups of frames and low packet loss probability. Further case studies are given in [HeW 99].

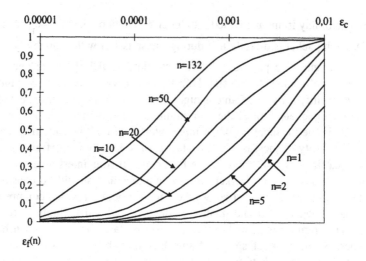

Fig. 5.2. Influence of packet loss probability ε_c on the frame loss probability $\varepsilon_f(n)$ for several group of picture lengths n

6 Proposed Methods to Improve Video Communication

As we have seen video communication with its usually strict requirements for throughput and bounded delays does not perform very favorably when run over a best-effort network. Because of data losses or high delays the service offered by an application can deteriorate. But there some simple fault-tolerance mechanisms to ensure more robust video communication. We now give an example.

Fig. 6.1. Robust coding with absolute (right) instead of relative (left) macroblock addresses

The videocoder and -decoder we used identifies a macroblock of a frame by a relative address. Assume that two macroblocks MB1 and MB2 are coded followed by a macroblock MB3, which image has not changed since the previous frame and therefore is not coded by the videocoder. When the next macroblock MB4 is coded it has the relative address 2, because it is the second macroblock after the latest co-ded macroblock MB2. But if MB2 is lost during transmission the decoder uses the relative address of macroblock MB4 and refers it to the macroblock, which was co-ded before MB2, i.e. MB1. So MB4 will be presented as the second macroblock after MB1 and will be not be shown correctly at its original position 4 but misplaced at position 3 the original position of MB3. Something like this happened for the left picture of Fig. 6.1 (s. also Fig 3.3). We substituted the relative macroblock addresses of the H.261 videocodec by absolute addresses to reduce the impact of losses. The result is shown at the right side of Fig 6.1, where the degradation of video quality is restricted to a wrong colored rectangle at an unessential position, where original data was lost. The pictures of Fig. 6.1 illustrate the improvement of visual quality achieved in a very simple way by substituting absolute for relative macroblock addresses.

After we have investigated the peculiarities of timing and loss sensitive applications over best-effort networks we now briefly discuss forward error control to improve the quality of video communication.

A well-known principle dating from the still rather early days of data communication is to eliminate redundancy which accidentally exist in the user data to be transmitted via a communication network and to replace this original, less useful redundancy by some much more useful redundancy specifically oriented to support forward error control. One could observe this principle e.g. in text transmission, where the considerable redundancy of natural language texts was eliminated by coding algorithms such as Shannon-Fano code and replaced by redundancy being able to recover particularly well from the type of errors to be expected for the underlying transmission channel (e.g. CRC-based checksums [Tan 96]). This situation in text transmission is similar to todays video communication, where a lot of redundancy (in space and time) exists in the video sequences to be transmitted. Video compression considerably reduces the redundancy, thereby significantly reducing the throughput required to transmit the compressed video stream. And, as in data communication, researchers and developers of video communication systems are becoming increasingly aware that video streams after their compression should be transmitted together with some intelligently determined redundancy so that the receiver would be able to correct as many as possible of the transmission errors occurred, i.e. to achieve some error control without retransmitting the data (cf. Forward error control, FEC). For recent approaches to achieve forward error control in video communication, cf. e.g. [ABE 96].

A question which arises if one first eliminates redundancy as for instance inherent in a video stream and thereafter adds redundancy into the stream again, is what kind of efficiency gain would have to be expected as a consequence of the fact that the newly added redundancy is carefully chosen as opposed to the original accidental redundancy. Note, that compression can be used to reduce the amount of user data to be transmitted; the throughput gained by this compression may then be used to transmit additional redundancy (e.g. for some FEC).

In order to compare between the coding variants with and without forward error control we extend our analytical model. We will consider an algorithm without any prioritization of data units transmitted. However, our model reflects the PET coding algorithm as developed at International Computer Science Institute (ICSI) at Berkeley, which allows one to choose priorities in a very flexible way for the different types of data units transmitted. For special investigations on PET and MPEG with constant bit rate see [Wol 97a,b]. Other approaches are reported in [BoT 98, CaB 97, Car 97, LMS 97, PRC 98, RiV 98, Riz 97, RoS 97].

We study the influence of forward error control on the probabilities of losing I- and P-frames (ε_i resp. ε_p) which were derived in the third section. The number of data packets c_i for one I-frame without redundant coding increases by r_i to c_i+r_i as a consequence of using a redundant error correcting code, e.g. PET [ABE 96]. To decode the I-frame after transmission only any c_i data packets out of c_i+r_i are necessary and must be correctly received. So we can combine all disjoint events that exactly j data packets for j=0 to r_i out of all c_i+r_i send data packets are lost. This combined event occurs if a subset of at least c_i data packets is received correctly. The probabilities of the disjoint event sum up to the probability $\varepsilon_i(\varepsilon_c,c_i,r_i)$ of the combined event. The notion of the brackets indicate that this probability is a function of the packet loss probability ε_c of the network, the number c_i of data packets for an I-frame and the number r_i of redundant data packets.

$$\varepsilon_i(\varepsilon_c,c_i,r_i) \; = \; 1 - \sum_{j=0}^{r_i} \binom{c_i+r_i}{j} \varepsilon_c^{\,j}\, (1-\varepsilon_c)^{\,c_i+r_i-j}.$$

The corresponding sum with c_p and redundancy r_p instead of c_i and r_i can be given for the probability $\varepsilon_p(\varepsilon_c,c_p,r_p)$ of losing a P-frame with the same redundant coding.

Obviously, the new formula includes the irredundant coding used in section 4 as a special case for $r_i=0$ resp. $r_p=0$. Now we can assign the above derived expressions $\varepsilon_i(\varepsilon_c,c_i,r_i)$ and $\varepsilon_p(\varepsilon_c,c_p,r_p)$ for ε_i and ε_p to the formula of section 4 and compute the frame loss probability when using the proposed kind of forward error control. This new variant of the formula for the frame loss probability can be applied to quantify the improvement of video quality achieved by the forward error control and to evaluate this improvement with regard to the overhead of redundant coding with r_i resp. r_p redundant data packets.

After we have investigated the peculiarities of timing and loss sensitive applications over best-effort networks and the benefit of forward error control, we will briefly explain some other recommendations to improve the quality of video communication.

First we propose the method of information dispersal to exploit different network routes. The data stream produced by a multimedia application on one side of an end-to-end connection is to be split into multiple substreams. These streams are send over different physical paths of the network. The multimedia application on the other end receives data packets from these multiple links and uses them to reconstruct the original stream. So one hopes to achieve three different goals.

If the different network routes are mutually independent, meaning that the network performance on one does not directly influence performance on the other ones, chances are that the bad effect of already existing bottlenecks will only impact part of our data transmissions. By splitting the traffic we reduce the data load put on a single network link and its routers. Although the total data load remains the same, we disperse our data requirements evenly out over distributed resources thus reducing likelihood that a bottleneck is caused by our data packets. By using additional forward error control the communication becomes partly loss-resilient. If losses do not exceed the amount of redundancy spend for the protection we can endure a certain number of losses or excessive delays. So if we spend enough redundancy even the loss of an entire substream send over a specific route can be tolerated by the combination of forward error control and information dispersal. In addition, by splitting the data stream and having parts following different routes through the network, it becomes more difficult to eavesdrop on the data since only parts of it will pass through most routers on the way. This is, of course, a welcome side-effect. In order to evaluate the feasibility of information dispersal we designed and implemented an audio communication which was used as a test bed for experiments directly applying controlled data dispersal onto different access points (providers) of the global Internet. The results can be found in [Sie 98, ASW 98].

Until now we accept the best-effort character of networks and try to improve the quality of video communication by additional mechanisms being implemented in the end-systems [CTC 96, JaE 97]. The network itself remains the same. Another more rigorous approach establishes networks with guarantied quality of service by reserving network resources. A solution proposed to deal with limited resources are the so-called service categories in ATM networks [Sta 98] and the reservation protocols like RSVP or ST-2 [WoS 97], which implement mechanisms to allow sending or receiving hosts to request resources on routers that are part of the static data transmission path. But all these reservation techniques my even be available tomorrow. We developed a prototype of a client-server based reservation protocol for Fast-Ethernet. A server process controls the network resources. It receives the transmission requests of the client stations and allocates some bandwith for them with respect to the actual state of the network.

7 Summary and Outlook

In this paper we quantitatively evaluated the quality of video communication from the users point of view. Therefore we introduced an analytical model of dependability reflecting transmission of video streams, which images were compressed according to video coding standards such as MPEG and H.261. This model considers aspects of performance, reliability and availability to determine the quality of the video presented by the receiving computer depending on properties of besteffort networks, which present the actual communication infrastructure. Several simplifying assumptions were required to obtain a model, which is still analytically tractable and which thus gives us interesting insights in the dependability of video communication. We applied our model for instance to compute appropriate or even optimal parameters for video encoders and extended it to determine the required level of redundancy for forward error control. These results can serve as a decisive factor for network management, especially for controlling network traffic and quality of network service. Case studies demonstrated the trade-off between the efficiency of video encoding, the fault-tolerance of the communication process and the quality of the received video. So we showed that even with an analytical model interesting insight can be gained into the quality of video communication as achieved by different video encoding schemes and by additional methods of fault tolerant communication. We conclude that standard video coding algorithms and the proposed mechanisms to achieve or increase fault tolerance offer the potential for high video quality even in case of using communication systems with modest or even low quality of delivered service.

This contribution assumes video communication using compression algorithms with two types of frames, namely I- and P-frames. It can simply be extended to video communication with more types of frames. But it is clear in advance that the use of for instance B-frames will force stronger and a greater number of dependencies between video frame with more problematic consequences. This type of frames may be included in video sequences coded according to MPEG or H.263 and must be handled with great care. The last mentioned standard was designed for smaller bit rates than 64 kb/s [ITU 98]. A fragmentation of H.263 data packets for transmission via the Internet is proposed in [Zhu 97]. Probably, H.263 will also be used by many applications with higher data rates and thus replace its predecessor H.261, which can be viewed as a special parameterization of H.263. The new standard provides more efficient compression and improved error recovery, which predestinate it for instance to mobil video communication. For these reasons we are interested to modify our model for H.263 to include so-called PB-frames, which are combinations of one P- and one B-frame.

Currently we are working at an extended analytical model of a birth and death process where the states represent some levels of performance resulting in different probabilities ε_c for losing data packets. Another project deals with simulation models and simulative evaluation of real-time audio and video communication. Evidently, our presented analytical model in particular does not reflect situations where losses or transmission errors occur in bursts or correlate. Simulation models will allow us to cover such situations and other special realistic refinements. Measurements of the load produced by distributed multimedia applications and of the resulting network traffic for communication will be used to calibrate and tune our models. Furthermore, we are going to construct a general load generator and network simulator to perform a lot of experiments which are not feasible in a real network environment.

References

[ABE 96]   Albanese, A., Blömer J., Edmonds J., Luby M., Sudan M., Priority Encoding Transmission, IEEE Trans. Information Theory 42, 6, Nov. 1996

[ASW 98]   Siemsglüss S., Albanese A., Wolfinger B., Information Dispersal to Improve Quality-of-Service on the Internet, Proc. SPIE Intern. Symp. on Voice, Video, and Data Communications, Vol. 3529, Boston/Mass., Nov. 1998

[Bai 99]   Bai G., Load Measurement and Modeling for Distributed Multimedia Applications in High-Speed Networks, Dissertation, FB Informatik University Hamburg, Uni Press Bd. 107, Lit Verlag, Hamburg, 1999

[BNC 99]   Bull D., Canagarajah N., Nix A. (ed.), Mobile Multimedia Communications, Academic Press, London, 1999

[BoT 98]   Bolot J., Turletti T., Experience with Rate Control Mechanisms for Packet Video in the Internet, ACM SIGCOMM Computer Communication Review, 28, 1, Jan. 1998

[CaB 97]   Carle G., Biersack E., Survey of Error Recovery Techniques for IP-based Audio-Visual Multicast Applications, IEEE Network Magazine 11, 6, 1997

[Car 97]   Carle, G., Error Control for Real-Time Audio-Visual Services, Seminar High Performance Networks for Multimedia Applications, Dagstuhl, 1997

[CTC 96]   Chen, Z., Tan S.M., Campbell R.H., Li Y.: Real Time Video and Audio in the World Wide Web, World Wide Web Journal, vol. 1, 1996

[EfS 98]   Effelsberg W., Steinmetz R., Video Compression Techniques, dpunkt-verlag, Heidelberg, 1998

[GBL 98]   Gibson J., Berger T., Lookabaugh et al., Digital Compression for Multimedia, Morgan Kaufmann Publ., 1998

[HBD 98]   Hafid A., Bochmann G., Dssouli R., Distributed Multimedia Applications and QoS: A Review, Electronic J. on Networks and Distrib. Processing 2, 6, 1998

[Hei 97]   Heidtmann K., Zuverlässigkeitsbewertung technischer Systeme, Teubner, Stuttgart, 1997

[HeW 99]   Heidtmann K., Wolfinger B., Analytische Leistungsbewertung von Videokommunikation gemäß H.261 über verlustbehaftete Paketvermittlungsnetze, 10. ITG/GI-Fachtagung über Messung, Modellierung und Bewertung von Rechen- und Kommunikationssystemen MMB '99, Trier, 1999

[HKZ 99]   Heidtmann K., Kohlhaas C., Zaddach M., Messung der Netzlast und Bewertung der Bildqualität bei Videokommunikation über Paketvermittlungsnetze, 15. GI/ITG-Fachtagung über Architektur von Rechensystemen ARCS'99, Jena, 1999

[ISO 93]   International Standard ISO/IEC 11172: Information technology – Coding of moving pictures and associated audio for digital storage media up to about 1.5 Mbit/s, Part 2: Video, 1993

[ITU 93]   Video codec for audivisual services at px64 kbits, ITU-T Recommendation H.261, 1993

[ITU 98]   Video coding for low bit rate communication, ITU-T Recommendation H.263, 1998

[JaE 97]   Jacobs, S., Eleftheriadis A., Adaptive video applications for non-QoS networks, Proc. 5th Intern. Workshop of Quality of Service IWQoS'97, New York, 1997.

[LMS 97]   Luby, M., Mitzenmacher M., Shokrollahi A. et al., Practical Loss-Resilient Codes, Proc. 29th ACM Symp. on Theory of Computing, 1997

[Lu 96]   Lu G., Communication and Computing for Distributed Multimedia Systems, Artech House, 1996

[MRP 97]   Messier A., Robinson J., Pahlavan K., Performance Monitoring of a Wireless Campus Area Network, LCN'97, 1997

[PRC 98]   Podolsky M., Romer C., McCanne S., Simulation of FEC-Based Error Control for Packet Audio on the Internet., Proc. INFOCOM'98, San Francisco, March 1998

[RiV 98]   Rizzo L., Vicisano L., RMDP: an FEC-based Reliable Multicast protocol for wireless environments, ACM Mobile Computing and Communications Review 2, 2, April 1998

[Riz 97]   Rizzo L., Effective erasure codes for reliable computer communication protocols, ACM Computer Communication Review 27, 2, April 1997

[RoS 97]   Rosenberg, J., Schulzrinne H., An A/V Profile Extension for Generic Forward Error Correction in RTP, Internet-Draft draft-ietf-avt-fec, Internet Engineering Task Force, 1997

[Sie 98]   Siemsglüss S., Information Dispersal to Improve Quality-of-Service on the Internet, diploma thesis, Depart. Computer Science, Univ. Hamburg, 1998

[Sta 98]   Stallings W., High Speed Networks, Prentice-Hall, 1998

[Tan 96]   Tanenbaum A.S., Computer Networks, 3rd ed., Prentice Hall, 1996

[TuH 96]   Turletti T., Huitema C., RTP Payload Format for H.261 Video Stream, Prop. Internet Stand., RFC 2032, Oct. 1996

[Wol 97a]   Wolfinger B., On the Potential of FEC Algorithms in Building Fault-tolerant Distributed Applications to Support High QoS Video Communications, ACM Symp. Principles of Distributed Computing PODC'97, Santa Barbara, 1997

[Wol 97b]   Wolfinger B., Efficiency Video Encoding without and with FEC: Analytical Models for QoS Evaluations, 1st World Congress on System Simulation, Singapore, 1997

[WoS 97]   Wolf, L.C., Steinmetz R., Concepts for Resource Reservation in Advance, J. Multimedia Tools and Applications, State of the Art in Multimedia Computing 4, 3, May 1997.

[Zhu 97]   Zhu C., RTP Payload Format for H.263 Video Streams, Proposed Internet Standard, RFC 2190, Sept. 1997

Dependability Evaluation of a Distributed Shared Memory Multiprocessor System

Mourad Rabah and Karama Kanoun

LAAS-CNRS — 7 Avenue du Colonel Roche
31077 Toulouse Cedex 4 — France
{rabah, kanoun}@laas.fr

Abstract. This paper deals with the dependability evaluation of a Multipurpose, Multiprocessor System (MMS) under investigation by a system manufacturer. MMS is symmetric with a DSM and a CC-NUMA. As the system is scalable, we consider two architectures: a reference one composed of four nodes and an extended one with an additional spare node. A set of dependability and performability measures is evaluated for these architectures with two categories of application users, accepting different service degradation levels. Modeling is based on GSPN to which reward rates are added to evaluate performability measures. The originality of our approach is the clear separation between the architectural and the service concerns. The results allow us to quantify the influence of the main parameters and to compare the dependability of the systems under consideration. They can thus be used for supporting the manufacturer design choices as well as the potential user configuration choices.

1. Introduction

Nowadays, computer systems are becoming more and more complex. They are composed of hardware and software components interacting together to ensure the required service. Even though specific applications may need the design of specific systems to achieve the required functions, economic reasons lead to use basic support systems (computers, operating systems, middleware) available on the market. This situation gave rise to a category of systems that can be referred to as multipurpose systems that are — to some extent — application-independent basic systems. Many system providers have developed generic systems that can be used in several application domains. Such systems can be either complete support systems (such as: LOGISIRE, developed by ABG, Germany [1], the TRICON system developed by TRICONEX, USA [2], Alpsa-8000-P320 developed by CEGELEC, France [3]), or generic components that can be integrated into complete systems (such as the Votrics system for hardware fault tolerance developed by ALCATEL Austria [4]). Even though most of the time, basic support systems are composed of Commercial Off-The-Shelf components (COTS), careful design, development and validation are needed to provide dependable and high-performance support systems. The evaluation of performability measures constitutes a powerful means for assessing the dependability and performance of such systems. The Multipurpose, Multiprocessor

System, MMS considered in this paper, under investigation by a system manufacturer is scalable and most of its components are COTS. It uses a Distributed Shared Memory (DSM) and a Cache-Coherent Non-Uniform Memory Access. A recent tutorial on "Distributed Shared Memory Concepts and Systems" [5] showed that 1) building of commercial systems that follow the DSM paradigms is still in its infancy despite the amount of research work performed in the domain and 2) most of the existing multiprocessor systems based on DSM are research prototypes. Hence the importance of the commercialization of such systems.

A reference MMS architecture is defined. It is composed of four nodes. It can be used for various applications requiring different performance and/or dependability levels. Based on this reference architecture, a whole family can be defined for applications necessitating either higher performance or higher dependability levels or both. Our aim is to provide a framework for the dependability evaluation of the reference architecture with different application needs and more generally to define a framework (for the system manufacturer) for modeling efficiently new systems of the same family based on this reference architecture.

In this paper, we define a set of dependability and performability measures that are evaluated for the reference architecture and an extended one (using a spare node) with two examples of application users requiring different service degradation levels. The results allow the quantification of the influence of the main parameters on the defined measures and the comparison of the considered systems.

The paper is organized as follows. Section 2 presents the systems under consideration. Section 3 defines the performability measures. Section 4 describes the modeling approach and illustrates it through an example, while Section 5 presents some results. Section 6 concludes the paper.

2. Presentation of the Systems under Consideration

We first present the reference architecture with its associated failure modes. Two types of users are then defined together with their associated service levels and maintenance policies. Finally an extended architecture is defined.

2.1 The Reference Architecture

The reference architecture is composed of 16 processors grouped into 4 identical nodes as shown in Figure 1. The nodes are connected through an interconnection network composed of two redundant rings. Each ring is connected to each node via a controller. To ensure high availability, all nodes are connected to a centralized diagnostic equipment (Deq) that is redundant. Its role is to log and analyze all error events in the system, initiate system reboots and control them. The DEq does not contribute to service accomplishment; however the system cannot reboot without it.

MMS has two external disks. Each disk is a dual access RAID (Redundant Array of Independent Disks). The RAID's disks can be stopped, changed and synchronized without stopping the RAID system (on-line maintenance). Each RAID is shared by two nodes. If a node, or its interconnection controller, fails, the RAID can be used by the other nodes. The failure of both RAIDs makes external storage unavailable.

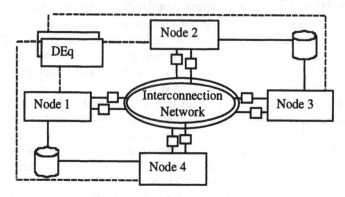

Fig. 1. MMS reference architecture

As indicated in Figure 2, each node has:

- a set of four independent processors; each processor has a two-level private cache where data from other node memories can be replicated or migrated;
- a local bus;
- a set of dedicated controllers such as interruption and reboot controllers;
- a local Random Access Memory, RAM (composed of four banks) and its controller; a node is available as long as a memory bank is available and it can use any other node memory bank as the RAMs of the four nodes constitute the distributed shared memory of MMS;
- a Remote Cache Controller (RCC), interconnecting the node to the rings via two controllers;
- a set of Peripheral Component Interconnect (PCI) buses, with slots for connecting external devices (through Ethernet, FDDI connections, etc.), connected to the local bus by a bridge;
- an internal disk, connected through an interface to the PCI bus;
- miscellaneous devices, such as power supply units and fans.

In addition to the redundant diagnostic equipment, DEq, and to the redundancy of several components (interconnection network, power supply, system disk, swap and external disks), MMS includes other facilities to reduce system downtime following error detection, among which:

- a node is held available as long as at least one processor, one memory bank, one power supply unit, all fans, the local bus and PCI buses with their connectors and controllers are available;
- the memories feature single error correction and double error detection codes;
- the architecture can be automatically reconfigured: the load of a failed processor can be partitioned among the other processors and the load of a whole node can be partitioned among the other nodes (the node is isolated).
- the components of an isolated node are not accessible by the other nodes;

- the internal disks can be hot plugged;
- a software failure of a processor leads to system reboot;
- the automatic system (re)configuration can be performed when the system is in operation or during reboot (if a failure is identified by the on-line tests);
- the reboot can be complete with all on-line tests or fast with a reduced test set;
- self-detected errors of the Operating System (OS) lead to system automatic reboot, while non-self-detected errors of the OS require a manual reboot;
- while detected errors of a component necessitating system reboot lead to a proper reboot, non-detected errors lead a brutal reboot (without saving properly the main parameters for example).

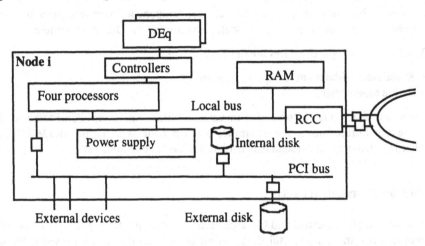

Fig. 2. Main components of a node

It is intended that some failures (whose nature is to be determined by the system manufacturer according to some criteria) will lead to system reconfiguration without reboot or with fast reboot. However, we assume in this paper that any component failure necessitating system reconfiguration forces a complete reboot. This assumption can be easily modified for those failures needing system reconfiguration without reboot or with a fast reboot.

2.2 Architectural Failure Modes

Given the large number of components (processors, memory banks, disks, buses, interconnections, controllers, interfaces, etc.) and the specific influence of their failure on system state and performance, a multitude of failure modes can be defined, related to the nature of the failed components. Generally, they are identified by a Preliminary Risk (or Hazard) Analysis: the consequences of all component failures are analyzed, individually and in combination. Usually states with equivalent consequences are grouped into the same failure mode.

For the purpose of the study, from the Preliminary Risk Analysis, seven architectural failure modes have been defined, including five levels of performance degradation. The table giving the detailed correspondence between elementary component failures and the architecture failure modes spreads in more than four pages for the reference MMS. The identified failure modes are:

- B: loss of one or more components among the redundant components; the processing capacity of the architecture is not impaired. B is referred to as the benign failure mode.
- D0: loss of one processor or one memory bank or connections to external devices or loss of the diagnostic equipment, DEq.
- DD: loss of the two external disks.
- Di: loss of i nodes[1] i = {1, 2, 3}.
- C: loss of the four nodes, or loss of a critical component: interconnection network, all power supply units, and non-self-detected errors of the Operating System.

In addition, two specific states are defined:

- OK: the state without any component failure.
- Reb: the reboot state.

Note that states with components in various failure modes are considered in the most severe failure mode. For example, when a node is in failure mode D1 and another is in D0 or B, the system is considered in the failure mode D1.

2.3 Service Degradation Levels

The above MMS properties and the architecture failure modes are user-independent. However, even though graceful degradation of the architecture is provided by the supporting architecture, this possibility can be exploited differently by the users for different application requirements. For instance, some applications will accept a degraded service provided by three, two or even only one node, while others will only accept the loss of some processors, without loosing a whole node. Indeed, the architectural failure modes lead to service degradation levels that are strongly related to the user's specific application needs.

It is worth noting that B and C have the same meaning for all applications: in B the entire service is performed (*ES*) while in C there is no service (*NS*). Between B and C, several service degradation levels can be defined according to user's needs and to the architecture failure modes.

To illustrate the mapping between architectural failure modes and service degradation levels, we consider two examples of users, denoted X and Y.

- **User X:** The service is considered as entire in states OK and B. X accepts a degraded service as long as at least three nodes are available without a critical component failure: NS correspond to D2, D3 and C. Between ES and NS, we have defined two significant service degradation levels: minor and major degradation

---

[1] Let us recall that a node is available as long as at least one processor, one memory block out of four, one power supply unit, all fans, the local bus and PCI buses with their connectors or controllers are available.

levels (respectively referred to as mD and MD). The mapping between the architectural failure modes and the service degradation levels is given in Table 1.

- **User Y** needs the entire capacity of the system and does not accept any service degradation. The entire service is delivered in OK, B and DD. NS gathers all other failure modes.

The states belonging to the same service degradation level are grouped into a class state. These classes are denoted respectively: ES-S, mD-S, MD-S and NS-S.

Table 1. Mapping between architectural failure modes and service degradation levels

Service levels	Entire service (ES)	Minor degradation (mD)	Major degradation (MD)	No Service (NS)	Reboot
X	OK, B	D0, DD	D1	D2, D3, C	Reb
Y	OK, B, DD	—	—	D0, D1, D2, D3, C	Reb

User X corresponds most likely to a potential user of MMS as he takes advantage of the architecture reconfigurations offered by the manufacturer. User Y has been only defined to allow comparison between the two types of users without considering complex situations. Note that state group DD is in ES for Y while it is in mD for X.

2.4 Maintenance

Although maintenance management is user-dependent, the system supplier usually proposes a maintenance contract. In order not to suspend system activities after each failure and call for a paying maintenance, two maintenance policies are defined:

- **Immediate maintenance**: for NS-S (as defined by the user's needs). However some time is needed for maintenance arrival. Immediate maintenance is thus performed in two steps: maintenance arrival (during this time, the system is unavailable) and repair.
- **Delayed maintenance**: for the other states with service degradation: the system continues to be used until a period of time in which its activities can be stopped for repair. Different delays may be allocated to the different service levels. Delayed maintenance is also performed in two steps: a maintenance delay during which a degraded service is delivered and repair.

The repair is followed by a system reboot.

2.5 Extended Architecture

To illustrate the approach, we also consider an extended architecture that features a fifth node used as a spare. The four basic nodes are used in the same manner as in the reference architecture. In case of failure of a first node, the latter is replaced by the spare node. We have thus four systems: the reference architecture (composed of 4 nodes) combined with users X and Y, and the extended architecture (5 nodes), also with users X and Y. For the four systems above, we assume immediate maintenance for NS-S and delayed maintenance for the other states. For the sake of conciseness, these systems will be respectively referred to as X4, Y4, X5 and Y5.

The failure modes and service degradation levels defined for the reference architecture apply to the extended architecture as well, since the spare does not contribute to service accomplishment in the absence of a failure.

3. Dependability and Performability Measures

Dependability measures are user-dependent: they are defined according to the service degradation levels. For user Y, we have considered a conventional availability measure: the system is available in ES-S states and unavailable in NS-S.

While this measure still holds for X, three additional *dependability levels* are defined corresponding to the three service levels:

- LE(t): dependability level associated with the entire service, ES, at time t.
- Lm(t): dependability level associated with the minor service degradation level.
- LM(t): dependability level associated with the major service degradation level.

Let e(t) denote the system state at time t. According to the partitions defined in Section 2.3, we have:

- $LE(t) = Prob \{ e(t) \in ES\text{-}S \}$
- $Lm(t) = Prob \{ e(t) \in mD\text{-}S \}$
- $LM(t) = Prob \{ e(t) \in MD\text{-}S \}$

For X, the classical availability and unavailability are respectively defined by:
$A(t) = Prob \{ e(t) \in \{ES\text{-}S, mD\text{-}S, MD\text{-}S\} \} = LE(t) + Lm(t) + LM(t)$
$UA(t) = Prob \{ e(t) \in \{NS\text{-}S, Reb\} \} = 1 - A(t)$

An additional measure of interest for X and Y is the system unavailability due to system reboot:
$UA_{Reb}(t) = Prob \{ e(t) \in Reb \}$.

The steady state measures are respectively denoted: LE, Lm, LM, A, UA and UA_{Reb}. LE and A will be expressed in terms of probability. Lm, LM, UA and UA_{Reb} will be expressed as the sojourn times per year in the considered service level.

As the system continues operation even in the presence of component failures, with performance degradation, *performability* measures are of prime interest as indicated in [6], [7], [8] and [9]. Performability measures the performance of the system in presence of failures. We assume here that all states in a given service degradation class have the same reward rate. Let r_Z denote the reward rate of the class state z: r_Z is the performance index in the class state Z (these indexes are estimated by the user according to his application). The expected reward rate, W(t), at time t is defined by:
$E[W(t)] = r_{ES\text{-}S} LE(t) + r_{mD\text{-}S} Lm(t) + r_{MD\text{-}S} LM(t) + r_{UA} UA(t)$.

The expected reward rate at steady state is:
$E[W] = r_{ES\text{-}S} LE + r_{mD\text{-}S} Lm + r_{MD\text{-}S} LM + r_{UA} UA$.

The above equation shows that the dependability measures are special cases of the expected reward rate with specific performance indexes (equal to zero or one).

In the rest of the paper, we will evaluate the steady unavailability, UA, the steady unavailability due to system reboot, UA_{Reb}, the dependability levels LE, Lm and LM and the expected reward rate at steady state, E[W]. When necessary, other measures such as the Mean Down Time, MDT (due to NS-S), or the Mean Time To Failure, MTTF, will be evaluated to put emphasis on specific behaviors.

4. Dependability Modeling

As the system is modular, with COTS components on which various specific applications can be run, our modeling approach has the same properties. It is modular, it uses generic sub-models and it is based on the separation of architectural concerns (including all basic hardware and software components) from those related to the user's application (i. e., service concerns). Modularity is useful for mastering complexity. The elaboration of generic sub-models is useful for modeling efficiently similar architectures thanks to the reuse of sub-models. The separation of concerns property allows reuse of the part of the model related to the system architecture, when the basic architecture is to be used with different service requirements.

Model construction is based on Generalized Stochastic Petri Nets (GSPN). The GSPN is then transformed into a Stochastic Reward net [10] by assigning reward rates to tangible markings (i. e., the states of the Markov chain associated with the GSPN). The Markov Reward model [11] associated with the Stochastic Reward net is then processed to obtain dependability and performance measures.

The GSPN of the components and their structural interactions are established in a first step. Any structured modeling approach can be used. However, to support the mapping between the service degradation levels and the architectural failure modes, specific places corresponding to the various failure modes are created and put into a layer, identified as the failure mode layer. The latter constitutes the interface between the architectural and the service parts of the model. Once the needs of a user are identified, the mapping between the service degradation levels and the failure modes can easily be achieved. The maintenance is managed according to the user policy in the service model. The interactions between the different parts of the model are depicted in Figure 3[2].

The architectural model is the same for users X and Y, whereas the service model is different. It can be argued that the model is over-dimensioned for Y as we have considered several failure modes that will be grouped into the same service degradation level. However, as we have built only a small part of the model that is specific to Y, there is no loss of time. The gain is even more substantial for the system manufacturer who will be able to provide to potential system buyers quantified dependability and performability measures, based on the same model (requiring only small adaptations for specific situations).

---

[2] Note that functional interactions between the components may appear; they will be taken into account in a specific part of the service model.

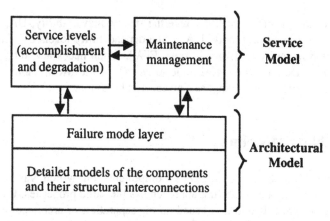

Fig. 3. Interactions between the different parts of the model

4.1 System Model

In the architectural model, a block model is associated to each component, including controllers, power supply units, fans, buses, diagnostic equipment, etc. When identical components have the same behavior with respect to the evaluated measures, they are modeled by one block. This is for example the case of the four processors and the four memory banks within a node. Considering the model of the reference architecture, given the number of different components, the architectural model is composed of 40 blocks (among which 19 are different). The GSPN of the reference system has 183 places and 376 transitions for X4 (182 places and 351 transitions for Y4). The GSPN for the extended system has 215 places and 580 transitions for X5 (213 places and 643 transitions for Y5). We have first derived the Markov chain for X4 and Y4 with two successive failures before system unavailability (i. e., truncation of order 2) and the Markov chain corresponding to a truncation of order 3. The error related to the dependability measures is less than 1%. We have thus considered models with a truncation of order 2 to process models with less number of states and hence reduce the execution time for sensitivity analyses where several executions are needed.

To illustrate the approach, we present the GSPN related to the processors within a node. Our objective is to show how the architectural model communicates with service model through the failure mode layer.

4.2 The Processor Model

The four processors of a node are modeled by the GSPN of Figure 4. The upper part of the figure gives a simplified view of the service model (corresponding to X4): places in the left side represent the four service levels and places in the right side represent the maintenance states: P_{main}: call for delayed maintenance, P_{Reb}: reboot state and P_M: the repairman presence place. The lower part of the figure gives the architectural model with the failure mode layer.

Not all transitions are shown, for the sake of clarity. In particular, in the architectural model, the enabling conditions Ci associated with the transitions are indicated at the bottom of the figure.

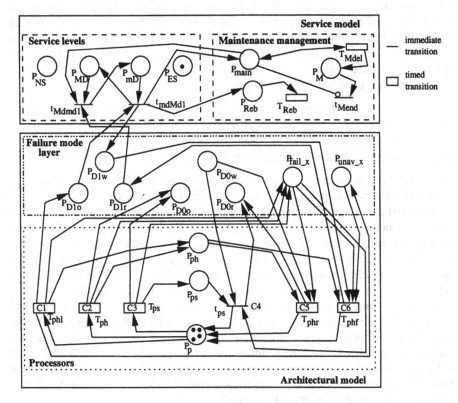

Transition	Rate	Definition
T_{ph}	$M(P_p)*\lambda_{ph}$	Processor's hardware failure; $M(P_p)$: marking of P_p; λ_{ph}: failure rate.
T_{ps}	$M(P_p)*\lambda_{ps}$	Software failure of a processor.
T_{phl}	λ_{ph}	Hardware failure of the last processor.
t_{ps}	-	The processor becomes available after software failure and reboot.
T_{phr}	μ_{ph}	Processor repair after a hardware failure without node isolation.
T_{phf}	μ_{ph}	Repair of one processor, reintegration of the node
T_{Mdel}	σ_{Mdel}	Delayed maintenance rate.
T_{Reb}	σ_{Reb}	Reboot rate.
t_{Mend}	-	End of maintenance intervention (no more failures).
t_{mdMd1}	-	Change of service degradation level after the last processor failure.
t_{Mdmd1}	-	Change of service degradation level after a repair from MD-S.

C1: $M(P_{ph}) = 3$ and $M(P_{NS}) = M(P_{unav\_x}) = 0$ C3: $M(P_{NS}) = M(P_{unav\_x}) = 0$ C5: $M(P_M) = 1$
C2: $M(P_{ph}) > 3$ and $M(P_{NS}) = M(P_{unav\_x}) = 0$ C4: $M(P_{Reb}) = 1$ C6: $M(P_M) = 1$

Fig. 4. GSPN of the four processors of a node

In the architectural model, P_p gives the number of operational processors of node x (its initial marking is 4). After a software failure of a processor (transition T_{ps}), the system is rebooted through t_{ps}. A hardware failure of a processor (transition T_{ph}) leads to a minor service degradation level. However the failure of the last processor (transition T_{ph1}) leads to a major service degradation level. P_{ps} represents the number of processors with a software failure waiting for reboot and P_{ph} those with a hardware failure waiting for repair. The failure mode layer gathers all the architecture's failure information. Figure 4 shows only information used or updated by the processor model. Each failure mode Z has 3 places:

1. P_{Zo}: occurrence of a failure bringing the system into failure mode Z that has to be taken into account in the service model;
2. P_{Zw}: waiting for repair;
3. P_{Zr}: end of repair; the service degradation level has to be accordingly updated.

Also the interface contains places summarizing the state of each node x: P_{fail_x} (number of failures in x) and P_{unav_x} (when it is marked, node x is unavailable).

The model is explained through an example. Let us assume that the last available processor in node x fails. The firing of T_{ph1} removes a token from P_p and puts a token in the following places: 1) P_{ph} (there is an additional processor failure in node x), 2) P_{fail_x} (there is an additional failure in node x), 3) P_{unav_x} (node x becomes unavailable) and 4) P_{D1o} (D1 failure mode). The failure is thus recorded in the failure mode layer to update the service model. Assuming that the system was in mD, the token from P_{D1o} enables t_{mdMd1} whose firing changes the current service level from mD to MD and puts a token in P_{D1w} meaning that the failure has been recorded and is waiting for repair. Also it puts a token in P_{main} for an additional call for maintenance. The presence of a token in P_{main} enables T_{Mdel}, corresponding to the delayed maintenance call. The firing of T_{Mdel} means that a repairman has arrived and the repair is performed. After the repair of a processor of node x, the token is moved from P_{D1w} to P_{D1r} and the service level returns to mD consuming a token from P_{D1r}.

4.3 Model Parameters

The nominal values of the model parameters (failure rates, repair time, maintenance delay and arrival times) have been either provided by the system manufacturer or assigned according to our experience. Sensitivity analyses have been performed to evaluate their relative influence on dependability and performability measures. Unless specified, the results of the next section have been obtained using the nominal values.

5. Results

Based on the models of the reference architecture and the extended architecture, as well as on the nominal parameter values, the dependability measures presented in Section 3 have been evaluated for users X and Y and several sensitivity analyses have been carried out. We have selected a subset of results to show the influence of some parameters. We give the results related to user X, then to Y, before summarizing.

5.1 User X

Influence of the Maintenance Time. The immediate maintenance time is equal to the sum of the maintenance arrival time and the repair time (Cf. 2.4). The nominal value of each time is 2 hours and it is assumed that all components have the same repair time. In order to analyze the influence of the maintenance time on dependability, we carry out a sensitivity analysis with respect to the repair time.

Table 2 shows that the sojourn time in mD-S, Lm, is not sensitive to the repair time, while the sojourn time in MD-S, LM, and the unavailability are affected. To a large extent, the unavailability of the system is due to the reboot time as shown by the last column. The difference between the last two columns gives the unavailability due to NS-S. Reducing the repair time by one hour reduces the sojourn time in NS-S by 21 min per year (from 35 min to 14 min). Using the nominal values of the parameters, the mean time to failure (MTTF) is 42033 hours (4.8 years) and the mean downtime (MDT) due to NS-S is 2 h 43. The sojourn time in NS-S is 34 min per year (= 2 h 43 min / 4.8 years); which is in accordance with the 35 min obtained from Table 2.

Table 2. X4 dependability measures in h/year (and probability) according to the repair time

Repair time	LE (probability)	Lm	LM	UA	UA_{Reb}
2 h	0.98913	47h40	46h13	1h20	0h45
1 h	0.98926	47h42	45h23	0h58	0h44

Influence of the Reboot Time. The nominal reboot time is 20 min. Table 2 suggests that on average there are two system reboots per year. Table 3 confirms this result for different values of the reboot time. As mentioned in Section 2.1, it is assumed that all system reconfigurations force a reboot. In addition, the re-insertion of the off-line repaired component(s) necessitates a system reboot. The results of Tables 2 and 3 argue in favor of performing a reconfiguration without a reboot whenever possible or with fast reboot (lasting less time).

Also Table 3 shows that the 35 min of unavailability due to NS-S are independent from the reboot time (it is given by the difference between UA_{Reb} and UA).

Table 3. X4 dependability measures according to the reboot time

Reboot time	LE (probability)	Lm	LM	UA	UA_{Reb}
10 min	0.98916	47h41	46h18	0h57	0h23
20 min	0.98913	47h40	46h13	1h20	0h45
30 min	0.98910	47h41	46h09	1h41	1h07

Influence of the Maintenance Delay. Immediate maintenance is performed only when the system is in NS-S. When the system is in a degraded service state, maintenance is delayed. The average nominal maintenance delay is one week for both minor and major service degradation states. Table 4 shows that if the maintenance delay is two weeks for mD-S, the time spent in mD-S, Lm, is almost multiplied by two. On the other hand, when the delay is reduced to two days for MD-S, the time spent in MD-S, LM, is significantly reduced. In both cases, unavailability is not affected.

Table 4. X4 dependability measures according to maintenance delay in mD-S and MD-S

Delay in mD-S / MD-S	LE (probability)	Lm	LM	UA
1 week / 1 week	0.98913	47h40	46h13	1h20
2 weeks / 1 week	0.98378	94h33	46h15	1h19
1 week / 2 days	0.99274	47h51	14h25	1h19

Another possibility could be to perform the delayed maintenance in a more regular manner: i. e., to make periodic maintenance even without any error reported. However, periodic maintenance could be more expensive than on-request maintenance if the time between two maintenance interventions (i. e., its period) is too short (to improve system availability). A tradeoff has to be made: the periodicity can be optimized through the evaluation of the number of visits to the delayed maintenance states. The models we have developed can be modified to model periodic maintenance: this modification affects only the maintenance part of the model and its interactions with the failure mode layer.

Influence of the Hardware Failure Rate (λ_{ph}). The nominal hardware failure rate of a processor is 10^{-6}/h. Table 5 shows the sensitivity of system dependability to this failure rate. If this rate is one order of magnitude lower, the unavailability is reduced by 8 min per year, whereas if the failure rate is one order of magnitude higher, it is increased by 1 h 09 min per year. The most influenced level corresponds to the minor service degradation level. This is due to the presence of 16 processors in the system whose first three successive failures lead to minor service degradation.

Table 5. X4 dependability measures according to λ_{ph}

λ_{ph}	LE (probability)	Lm	LM	UA
1.0E-07	0.99145	28h02	45h40	1h12
1.0E-06	0.98913	47h40	46h13	1h20
1.0E-05	0.96602	245h20	49h52	2h29

Influence of the Remote Cache Controller (RCC) Failure Rate. The nominal failure rate of an RCC is 10^{-7}/h. Table 6 shows that system dependability is affected by the value of this failure rate. Indeed, a failure rate of 10^{-5}/h increases the system unavailability by 14 min per year and doubles the sojourn time in LM (corresponding to the major service degradation level, MD-S). The most influenced level is LM; this is due to the presence of 4 RCCs whose failures lead to MD-S.

Table 6. X4 dependability measures according to λ_{RCC}

λ_{RCC}	LE (probability)	Lm	LM	UA
1.0E-07	0.98913	47h40	46h13	1h20
1.0E-06	0.98855	47h42	51h13	1h21
1.0E-05	0.98282	47h47	101h10	1h34

Influence of the Spare Node. Table 7 gives the dependability measure for the extended architecture, system X5. These results are to be compared with those of Table 2. It can be seen that the system unavailability is unaffected but the time spent in MD-S, LM, is considerably reduced. The "Spare use" column indicates the time during which the spare is used. For the nominal values, this time is 46 h 25 per year: it is distributed among mD-S and ES-S. Note that the major service degradation level, LM, corresponds here to the loss of 2 nodes before maintenance achievement. A sojourn time in MD-S of 14 min per year shows that the double failure is unlikely.

Table 7. X5 dependability measures

Arrival / repair times	LE (probability)	Lm	LM	UA	UA$_{Reb}$	Spare use
2 h / 2 h	0.99426	48h46	0h14	1h19	0h45	46h25
1 h / 2 h (or 2 h / 1h)	0.99433	48h28	0h14	0h58	0h44	45h35

Expected Reward Rate. Let us assume that the performance index of a given state class represents the percentage of system processing capacity in this class (an index of 0.6 for example, means that the processing capacity is 60 %). We have thus $r_{ES-S} = 1$ and $r_{UA} = 0$. In this context, Table 8 gives the expected reward rate at steady state with various values of the performance indexes r_{mD} and r_{MD}. Obviously, X5 has higher expected reward rate than X4. Note that X5 is less sensitive to the performance index associated to MD-S because of the reduced sojourn time in MD-S. The last line gives the system availability.

Table 8. Expected reward rate at steady state, E[W]

Performance indexes	E[W] for X4	E[W] for X5
$r_{mD} = 0.8$; $r_{MD} = 0.6$	0.996650	0.998726
$r_{mD} = 0.8$; $r_{MD} = 0.7$	0.997178	0.998728
$r_{mD} = 0.9$; $r_{MD} = 0.7$	0.997722	0.999285
$r_{mD} = 0.9$; $r_{MD} = 0.8$	0.998250	0.999288
$r_{mD} = 1$; $r_{MD} = 1$ (A)	A = 0.999849	A = 0.999850

5.2 User Y

For Y, the service is either entire or nil. The availability results according to the repair time are summarized in Table 9. Reducing the repair time improves the availability of the system. This is not surprising since most of the failures lead to immediate maintenance. Note that, as opposed to what was observed for X4, system unavailability is mainly due to NS-S (difference between the last two columns): 3 h 25 min compared to 24 min of unavailability due to system reboot.

Table 9. Y4 availability according to the repair time

Repair time	A (probability)	UA	UA$_{Reb}$
2 h	0.99957	3h49	0h24
1 h	0.99970	2h37	0h24

Considering the nominal values, the MTTF is 7175 h and the MDT due to NS-S is 3 h 09 min. This means that immediate maintenance is called on average a little bit more than once a year and the reboot time of 24 min corresponds to system reboot after maintenance: the system does not exercise reboots in ES-S as all failures are tolerated without system reconfiguration. Recall that for X4, the immediate maintenance is called on average once every 4.8 years, but the system is rebooted on average twice a year. The maintenance delay rate does not influence the availability of the system: the maintenance is delayed only for benign failures that do not affect service delivery. Sensitivity analyses with respect to hardware processor and to the RCC failures are similar to those obtained for X4.

Influence of the Spare Node. The presence of a spare node directly impacts the availability of the system since the first node failure can be tolerated. Table 10 shows that unavailability is divided by 3 for Y5 compared to Y4 (Table 7). Moreover, it can be seen that the unavailability is of the same order of magnitude as for X4 (these values are 1h20 and 58 min from Table 2). Considering the nominal values of the parameters, the time during which the spare is used is 93h 08 min. This time is almost equal to the sum of Lm and LM of Table 2, line 1, that is 93 h 53 min. The difference (45 min) corresponds to the time spent in states without an external disk (failure mode DD defined in Section 2; also Cf. Table 1).

Table 10. Y5 dependability

Repair time	A (probability)	UA	UA$_{Reb}$	Spare use
2 h	0.99986	1h15	0h41	93h08
1 h	0.99990	0h55	0h40	92h17

5.3 Tradeoff Dependability - Performance

Columns 3 and 4 of Table 11 report, from the previous tables, the expected reward rate and availability of the four systems for the nominal values of the parameters (for Y, the expected reward rate is equal to availability). It shows that the reference architecture provides better availability for user X and better performance for Y: there is thus a tradeoff between system performance and availability. On the other hand, the extended architecture provides better availability and better performance for Y. However, the difference between X and Y availability is not significant. This result is sensitive to the coverage factor c (the probability of successful switching from the failing node to the spare one), as shown in columns 5 and 6 that give the same measures for a lower coverage factor (respectively 0.95 and 0.85).

Table 11. Comparison of the reference and extended architectures

Measure	User	4 nodes	5 nodes (c=1)	5 nodes (c=0.95)	5 nodes (c=0.85)
Expected reward rate	X	0.99825	0.99929	0.99924	0.99913
	Y	0.99957	0.99986	0.99984	0.99981
Availability	X	0.99985	0.99985	0.99985	0.99985
	Y	0.99957	0.99986	0.99984	0.99981

5.4 Summary of Results

The main results presented in this paper can be summarized as follows:
For user X:

- system unavailability is mainly due to the reboot time;
- the no service states are reached on average once each 4.8 years but the system is rebooted twice a year;
- the maintenance delay affects only the sojourn time in states with minor and major service degradation; while the repair time affects system unavailability;
- the addition of a spare does not affect system unavailability but reduces the sojourn time in states with major service degradation.

For user Y:

- system unavailability is mainly due to the maintenance time;
- the no service states are reached on average once a year and the system is rebooted once a year (following system maintenance);
- the addition of a spare considerably reduces system unavailability.

The results revealed the existence of a tradeoff between system availability and system performance. Sensitivity analyses showed the influence of the failures rates of the processors and the remote cache controllers on system dependability. For example selecting a processor with a failure rate one order of magnitude higher to the nominal value assumed by the manufacturer will increase the system unavailability by 50 %.

6. Conclusions

This paper was devoted to the dependability evaluation of a multipurpose, multiprocessor system, MMS, under investigation by a system manufacturer. We have presented a reference architecture and an extended architecture and compared their dependability measures considering two examples of users with different service requirements. Modeling is based on GSPNs to which reward rates are added to evaluate performability. The modeling approach is modular, as many of other published approaches (see e. g., [8], [12], [13] and 14]). The originality of our approach is the separation between the architectural and the service concerns. This separation of concerns is very important in particular as we are considering a system manufacturer perspective, in which the user's needs are explicitly accounted for. In a typical user's perspective, as the user is interested in comparing possible architectural solutions for the same service purposes, there is no need to consider explicitly service concerns and usually emphasis is put on architectural concerns. Note that, even though several publications have been devoted to multiprocessors systems (see e. g., [15] and [16]), none of them addressed explicitly the manufacturer and the user concerns at the same time. Moreover none considered in detail the system architecture with all components.

The results presented for MMS can be classed into two categories: those supporting the manufacturer choices and those that will support the potential user choices. Of course, these results are not independent and have to be used together. Proper design choices by the manufacturer will — hopefully — be of great benefits for the user.

From the manufacturer perspective, the results are mainly related to:

- the selection of the processors and of the remote cache controllers, RCC, according to the impact of their failure rates on dependability measures (and their cost most probably);
- the decision concerning the reboot policy: reboot after system reconfiguration or not, reboot with or without on-line tests;
- the provision of a spare node. With respect to this point, a tradeoff should be made between the dependability improvement and the additional difficulty for developing the underlying mechanisms for the insertion of the spare into the system.

From the user perspective, the results concern:

- the selection of the maintenance policy: delayed or immediate maintenance, tradeoff between the maintenance guaranteed time and the cost of the maintenance contract (to agree on with the system provider);
- the selection between the reference architecture and the extended one, and more generally between all available solutions.

Another important point of interest concerns the exploitation by the user of the various degradation possibilities offered by the architecture. According to the service expected by the application, the user has to make choices concerning service degradation levels he can accept and the tradeoff between performance and availability. This choice may affect the architecture of the applicative software.

The work is under progress. More specifically, additional performability measures are under investigation, particularly to study some specific points such as the dependability improvement induced by distributed, shared memories. Also, other extended architectures are under consideration. As the architectural model is modular, and the component models are generic, their modeling is based on extensive reuse of the GSPN developed for the reference and the extended architectures considered in this paper.

References

1. T. Kloppenburg, "LOGISIRE — A Safe Computer System for Process-Automation", *Proc. 3rd Intern. GI/IGT/GMA Conf.*, Bremerhaven, Germany, Springer-Verlag, 1987.
2. Triconex, TRICON Technical Product Guide, Version 9 Systems, Irvine, Triconnex Corporation, , 1996.
3. J. Poueyo and J.P. Dalzon, "Mastering Safety of Opel and Distributed Systems in Compliance with IEC 61508", *Proc. IFAC 2nd Symp. on Information Control Manufacturing (INCOM'98)*, Nancy-Metz, France, pp. 511-516, 1998.
4. G. Wirthumer, "Votrics — Fault Tolerance Realized in Software", *Proc. 8th IFAC Int. Conference on Computer Safety, Reliability and Security (SAFECOMP'89)*, Vienna, Austria, pp. 135-140, 1989.
5. J. Protic, M. Tomasevic and V. Milutinovic, Eds. *Distributed Shared Memory — Concepts and Systems*, IEEE Computer Society, 1998.
6. J.F. Meyer, "On Evaluating the Performability of Degradable Computing Systems", *Proc. 8th IEEE Int. Symp. Fault-Tolerant Computing (FTCS-8)*, Toulouse, France, pp. 43-52, 1978.
7. J. Arlat and J.-C. Laprie, "Performance-Related Dependability Evaluation of Supercomputer Systems", *Proc. Proc. 13th Int. Symp. on Fault-Tolerant Computing (FTCS-13)*, Milano, Italy, IEEE Computer Society Press, pp. 276-283, 1983.
8. J.F. Meyer and W.H. Sanders, "Specification and Construction of Performability Models", *Proc. Int. Workshop on Performability Modeling of Computer and Communication Systems*, Mont Saint Michel, France, pp. 1-32, 1993.
9. L.A. Tomek, V. Mainkar, R.M. Geist and K.S. Trivedi, "Reliability Modeling of Life-Critical, Real-Time Systems", *Proceeding of the IEEE, Special Issue on Real-Time Systems*, 82 (1) , pp. 108-121, 1994.
10. G. Ciardo, J. Muppala and K.S. Trivedi, "SPNP: Stochastic Petri Net Package", *Proc. 3rd Int. Workshop on Petri Nets and Performance Models*, Los Alamitos, CA, USA, pp. 142-151, 1989.
11. R.A. Howard, *Dynamic Probabilistic Systems*, New York, J. Wiley and Sons, 1971.
12. K. Kanoun, M. Borrel, T. Moreteveille and A. Peytavin, "Availability of CAUTRA, a subset of the French Air Traffic Control System", *IEEE Transactions on Computers*, Vol. 48, No. 5, pp. 528-535, 1999.
13. M. Nelli, A. Bondavalli and L. Simoncini, "Dependability Modeling and Analysis of Complex Control Systems: An Application to Railway Interlocking", *Proc. 2nd European Dependable Computing Conf.*, Taormina, Italy, Springer-Verlag, 1996.
14. N. Fota, M. Kâaniche and K. Kanoun, "Dependability Evaluation of an Air Traffic Control System", *Proc. 3rd IEEE Int. Computer Performance & Dependability Symposium (IPDS)*, Durham, NC, pp. 206-215, 1998. To appear in *Performance Evaluation*, Elsevier-Science, North-Holland, 1999.
15. A. Marsan, G. Balbo and G. Conte, "A Class of Generalized Stochastic Petri Nets for the Performance Analysis of Multiprocessor Systems", *ACM Transactions on Computers*, 2 (2), pp. 93-122, 1984.
16. J.K. Muppala, A. Sathaye, R. Howe, C and K.S. Trivedi, "Dependability Modeling of a Heterogeneous VAX-cluster System Using Stochastic Reward Nets", *Hardware and Software Fault Tolerance in Parallel Computing Systems*, Ed. D.R. Avresky, pp. 33-59, 1992.

Session 2a

Panel
Software Reliability Engineering
Risk Management for the New Millenium

Moderator: Fevzi Belli, University of Paderborn, Germany

Invited Panelists:

Ram Chillarege, IBM Thomas J. Watson Research Center, USA
Bojan Cukic, West Virginia University, USA
Raghu Singh, Federal Aviation Administration, USA
Harald Stieber, Fachhochschule Nürnberg, Germany
Mladen Vouk, North Carolina State University, USA

Software Reliability Engineering
Risk Management for the New Millenium

Fevzi Belli

University of Paderborn,
Department of Electrical and Electronics Engineering
Warburger Str. 100, D-33098 Paderborn, Germany
Fevzi.Belli@sigma.uni-paderborn.de
http://adt.uni-paderborn.de/

Software Reliability Engineering (SRE) refers to those software production processes that design reliable performance and functionality into information & knowledge processing systems. In short, SRE seeks to build such systems that do what we want. The question is whether a general risk management (which we want, including the aspects of safety, security, etc.) can be achieved by the approaches used in SRE. If not, why not? If so, how?

In detail, the panel will address aspects of SRE like:

– software failure models
– reliability growth models
– testing methods for reliability assessment
– operational profiles as a means for software validation
– process evaluation, e.g. models like the Capability Maturity Model
– test and verification methods for off-the-shelf components
– tools for experimental investigation of software reliability
– the wide spectrum of SRE applications, ranging from information systems to knowledge-based expert systems, etc.

Session 2b

Fast Abstracts

Chair: Dimiter Avresky, Boston University, USA

List of Fast Abstracts

The Fast Abstracts are presented at the conference in short talks, and also in a poster session. They are published in a separate volume, and also on the World Wide Web.

http://www.inf.mit.bme.hu/edcc3/

Using Wyner-Ash Codes to Improve UDP/IP Transmission
M. Arai, A. Yamaguchi, K. Iwasaki (Tokyo Metropolitan University, Japan)

Fault Tolerance Software Library for Support of Real-Time Embedded Systems
S. Bogomolov, A. Bondarenko, A. Fyodorov (LGTCM Soft Lab, Saint-Petersburg, Russia)

Defect Oriented TGP for Combined I_{DDQ}-Voltage Testing of Combinational Circuits
E. Gramatová, J. Bečková, J. Gašpar (Slovak Academy of Sciences, Bratislava, Slovakia)

An Approach for the Reliability Optimization of N-Version Software under Resource and Cost/Timing Constraints
I.V. Kovalev (Technical University of Krasnoyarsk, Russia),
K.-E. Grosspietsch (GMD, St. Augustin, Germany)

Detection of Race Occurrence in Distributed Applications
H. Krawczyk, B. Krysztop, J. Proficz (Technical University of Gdańsk, Poland)

Evaluating System Dependability in a Co-Design Framework
M. Lajolo (Politecnico di Torino, Italy),
L. Lavagno (Università di Udine, Italy),
M. Rebaudengo, M. Sonza Reorda, M. Violante (Politecnico di Torino, Italy)

Backward Error Recovery in the APEmille Parallel Computer
P. Maestrini (Consiglio Nazionale delle Ricerche, Pisa, Italy),
T. Bartha (Hungarian Academy of Sciences, Budapest, Hungary)

Formal Verification of Fault Tolerance Techniques in UML
I. Majzik, J. Jávorszky (Technical University of Budapest, Hungary)

Reaching Byzantine Agreement under the Non-Cooperative Byzantine Failure Mode Assumption
A. Masum (University of Essen, Germany)

Measure an e-site's QoS with Multi-Workload
F. Nan, H.X. Wei, X.Y. Chen (IBM China Research Lab, Beijing, P. R. China)

τ-Calculus, a Multilevel Specification Methodology
J.-L. Paillet (LIM-CMI, Marseille, France)

A Fault-Tolerant Approach for Mobile Agents
S. Petri, C. Grewe (Medical University of Lübeck, Germany)

Designing the Reconfiguration Strategies of Fault Tolerant Servers
B. Polgar (Technical University of Budapest, Hungary)

Recovery Strategies for Distributed Multimedia Applications
L. Romano, G. Capuozzo (University of Naples, Italy),
A. Mazzeo, N. Mazzocca (2nd University of Naples, Italy)

Error Detection Based on the Self Similar Behavior of Network Traffic
W. Schleifer (CERN, Geneva, Switzerland)

Efficient Probabilistic Diagnosis for Large Systems
E. Selényi (Technical University of Budapest, Hungary),
T. Bartha (Hungarian Academy of Sciences, Budapest, Hungary)

A Systematic Approach to Software Safety
R. Singh (Federal Aviation Administration, Washington, DC, USA)

Fault-Tolerant Web Services on a Computing Cluster
P. Sobe (Medical University of Lübeck, Germany)

Evaluating FPU Tests with Fault Inserter
J. Sosnowski, T. Bech (Warsaw University of Technology, Poland)

Dependability Model of an Authentication System
V. Vais, S. Racek (University of West Bohemia, Plzen, Czech Republic),
J. Hlavička (Czech Technical University, Prague, Czech Republic)

Session 3

Protocols

Chair: István Majzik, Technical University of Budapest, Hungary

Muteness Failure Detectors: Specification and Implementation*

Assia Doudou[1], Benoit Garbinato[2], Rachid Guerraoui[1]**, and André Schiper[1]

[1] École Polytechnique Fédérale, Lausanne (Switzerland)
{Doudou, Guerraoui, Schiper}@epfl.ch
[2] United Bank of Switzerland, Zürich (Switzerland)
Garbinato@ubs.com

Abstract. This paper extends the failures detector approach from crash-stop failures to muteness failures. Muteness failures are malicious failures in which a process stops sending algorithm messages, but might continue to send other messages, e.g., "I-am-alive" messages. The paper presents both the specification of a muteness failure detector, denoted by $\Diamond M_A$, and an implementation of $\Diamond M_A$ in a partial synchrony model (there are bounds on message latency and clock skew, but these bounds are unknown and hold only after some point that is itself unknown). We show that, modulo a simple modification, a consensus algorithm that has been designed in a crash-stop model with $\Diamond S$, can be reused in the presence of muteness failures simply by replacing $\Diamond M_A$ with $\Diamond S$.

1 Introduction

A fundamental characteristic of distributed systems is the notion of partial failures: part of a system might have failed while the rest might be correct. Coping with partial failures usually requires to get some (even approximative) knowledge about which processes have failed and which have not.

1.1 Background: Crash Detectors

Traditionally, failure detection mechanisms were usually mixed up with the distributed protocols using them. Relatively recently, Chandra and Toueg suggested an approach where failure detection is encapsulated within a so-called *failure detector* and decoupled from the rest of the distributed protocol [3]. Roughly speaking, a failure detector is a distributed oracle that provides hints about partial failures in the system; a process p typically consults its failure detector module to know whether a given process q has crashed or not. Formally, a failure detector is described according to axiomatic *completeness* and *accuracy* properties. Completeness expresses the ability of a failure detector to eventually detect

---

* Research supported by OFES under contract number 95.0830, as part of the ESPRIT BROADCAST-WG (number 22455).
** Rachid Guerraoui is currently a Faculty Hire at HP Labs, Palo Alto (CA).

failures, while accuracy expresses its ability to eventually avoid false suspicions (i.e., falsely suspecting correct processes). By decoupling failure detection from other algorithmic issues, Chandra and Toueg provided an abstraction that avoids focusing on operational features of a given model, such as the asynchrony of the transmission and the relative speeds of processes. Features related to failure detection are encapsulated within a separate module: the failure detector becomes a powerful abstraction that simplifies the task of designing distributed algorithms[1] and proving their correctness. For example, Chandra and Toueg have described an algorithm that solves the consensus problem in an asynchronous system augmented with an *eventually strong* failure detector, denoted by $\Diamond S$. The axiomatic properties of $\Diamond S$ encapsulate the amount of synchrony needed to solve the consensus problem in the presence of crash failures and hence to circumvent the well-known *FLP* impossibility result.[2] Other agreement algorithms, e.g., [15], have later been designed on top of the same failure detector $\Diamond S$. Although $\Diamond S$ cannot be implemented in a purely asynchronous system (this would contradict the FLP impossibility result), when assuming practical systems however, e.g., those that provide some kind of partial synchrony, implementations of such a failure detector do exist [3]. A failure detector acts as a modular black-box of which implementation can change with no impact on the algorithm using it, as long as that implementation ensures the adequate completeness and accuracy properties.

1.2 Motivation: From Crash to Muteness Failures

The motivation of our work is to explore the applicability of the *failure detector* approach to a broader context, where failures are not only crash failures but might have a more malicious nature. In a crash-stop model, it is usually assumed that either a process correctly executes the algorithm that has been assigned to it, or the process crashes and completely stops its execution. Some authors have discussed the applicability of the failure detector approach in system models where processes can crash and recover, and communication links are not always reliable [1,14,13,4]. In each of those models however, the notion of failure (and thus of an incorrect process) is completely independent from the algorithms run by processes in the system. This is no more the case with a Byzantine failure model, i.e., with malicious failures.

A process is said to commit a Byzantine failure when it deviates from the specification of its algorithm [11]: the process might not have necessarily stopped its execution, but might send messages that have nothing to do with those it is supposed to send in the context of its algorithm. Malicious failures are thus intimately related to a given algorithm. To illustrate this point, consider a process q

---

[1] Hereafter, we sometimes refer to distributed algorithms as protocols.

[2] *Consensus* is a fundamental problem that consists, for a set of processes, in deciding on the same final value among a set of initial values. The FLP impossibility result states that no algorithm can solve consensus in an asynchronous distributed system if one process can fail by crashing [7].

that is part of a set Ω of processes trying to agree on some value. Suppose now that q executes agreement protocol $\mathcal{A}$, which is proven to be correct, whereas all other processes in Ω execute a different agreement protocol $\mathcal{A}$', also proven to be correct. With respect to processes executing $\mathcal{A}$', q is viewed as a Byzantine process, that is a *faulty* process, although it executes correct algorithm $\mathcal{A}$. So, the fact that the notion of failure is relative to a given algorithm in a Byzantine model has an important consequence: it is impossible to achieve a complete separation of the failure detector from the algorithm using it. A consequence is an intrinsic circular dependency: if algorithm $\mathcal{A}$ relies on some failure detector $\mathcal{D}$, the latter must in turn be specified and thus implemented in terms of $\mathcal{A}$ (at least partially).

Our paper can be seen as a first step towards understanding how this circular dependency can be explicitly taken into account, when *specifying* and *implementing* failure detectors in a Byzantine model. On the other side, it is well-know that the consensus problem is at the heart of many other agreement problems. So, having a solution to the consensus yields to solution to other agreement problems like atomic broadcast [3], atomic commitment [9] and membership [8]. Therefore, by allowing to solve consensus, the failure detector allows indirectly to solve other agreement problems that are fundamental in the context of fault-tolerance. Thus, the ultimate motivation behind extending the paradigm of failure detectors to Byzantine model, is to give a correct abstraction in this model, which allows to solve other agreement problems like atomic broadcast.

Muteness Failure Detectors To simplify our discussion, rather than considering all possible Byzantine behaviours, we introduce a weaker malicious failure model that we call the *muteness* failure model. Intuitively, a process p is said to be *mute* with respect to algorithm $\mathcal{A}$ if p stops sending $\mathcal{A}$'s messages to one or more processes. Crash failures are particular cases of mute failures, which are themselves particular cases of Byzantine failures. Interestingly, distinguishing mute failures from other Byzantine failures allows us to clearly separate liveness issues from safety issues: muteness failures are those preventing the progress in consensus algorithms and should be captured at the failure detector level, whereas other kinds of Byzantine failures can be handled at the algorithmic level [12, 5].

We restrict our work to a class of distributed algorithms, which we call *regular round-based algorithms*. Roughly speaking, this class includes all algorithms that have a regular and round-based communication pattern. Most consensus algorithms that make use of unreliable failure detectors belong to that class, including the centralised algorithm of [3] and the decentralised algorithm of [15]. By analogy with crash failure detectors, we define muteness failure detector $\Diamond M_{\mathcal{A}}$ as one that tries to capture muteness failures with respect to a given algorithm $\mathcal{A}$. We show that our specification of $\Diamond M_{\mathcal{A}}$ does indeed make sense in the context of regular round-based algorithms, and we then describe an implementation of $\Diamond M_{\mathcal{A}}$ in a partial synchrony model where there exist bounds on message latency and clock skew, but these bounds are unknown and hold only after some unknown point in time.

1.3 Contribution: Preserving the Modularity of Failure Detectors

The key contribution of our work is to show that, even though a muteness failure detector is inherently related to a given algorithm, we can still partly preserve the modularity of the failure detector approach. This result is conveyed along four dimensions.

1. From the specification point of view, we define the muteness failure detector $\Diamond M_{\mathcal{A}}$ in terms of axiomatic properties. By doing so, we provide an abstraction that helps proving the correctness of consensus algorithms in a Byzantine model.
2. From the algorithmic point of view, the dependency between the failure detector and the algorithm using it can be reduced to a simple well-defined interaction. Modulo this interaction, we can reuse the decentralised consensus algorithm of [15] (initially designed for the crash-stop model) as it is, in a model with mute processes, by merely replacing the failure detector $\Diamond \mathcal{S}$ with $\Diamond M_{\mathcal{A}}$.
3. From the implementation point of view, we isolate the dependency between some algorithm $\mathcal{A}$ and the implementation of its corresponding $\Diamond M_{\mathcal{A}}$ in some function $\Delta_{\mathcal{A}}(r)$; the latter is used to increment the timeout at the beginning of each round r. Roughly speaking, the correctness of $\Diamond M_{\mathcal{A}}$'s implementation does not only rely on partial synchrony assumptions made on the system, but also on time assumptions made on algorithm $\mathcal{A}$. Intuitively, those assumptions state a set of necessary conditions for finding a function $\Delta_{\mathcal{A}}$ that makes our implementation of $\Diamond M_{\mathcal{A}}$ satisfy adequate completeness and accuracy properties.
4. From the practical point of view, defining an adequate abstraction of failure detectors in Byzantine model to solving the consensus problem can be viewed as a cornerstone to solving other agreement problems like atomic broadcast, which is powerful primitive to build fault tolerant applications.

1.4 Roadmap

Section 2 presents our model and formally introduces the notion of muteness failures. Section 3 defines the properties of the muteness failure detector $\Diamond M_{\mathcal{A}}$ and specifies the class of algorithms that we consider. Section 4 presents our implementation of $\Diamond M_{\mathcal{A}}$. We then prove the correctness of our implementation in a partial synchrony model, provided some timing assumptions on algorithms using $\Diamond M_{\mathcal{A}}$. Section 5 shows how a consensus algorithm designed in a crash-stop model, namely the decentralised protocol of [15], can be reused in the context of muteness failures. Finally, Section 6 describes the research results that relate to ours, and Section 7 closes the paper with some concluding remarks and open questions.

2 The Model

This section introduces our model, basically made of processes participating in a distributed algorithm, via the execution of a local automata. We also formally define the muteness failure model that we consider, and discuss how it relates to other failure models.

2.1 Algorithm & Automata

We consider an *asynchronous* distributed system, i.e, there is no upper bound on the time required for a computation or a communication. The system is composed of a finite set $\Omega = \{p_1, ..., p_N\}$ of N processes, fully interconnected through a set of reliable communication channels. Hereafter, we assume the existence of a real-time global clock outside the system: this clock measures time in discrete numbered ticks, which range T is the set of natural numbers $\mathbb{N}$. We define distributed algorithm $\mathcal{A}$ as a set of deterministic automata $\mathcal{A}_p$ run by processes in the system. We sometimes refer to $\mathcal{A}_p$ as an *algorithm* rather than an automata but it should be clear that we mean the local automata run by some correct process p.

2.2 A Restricted Byzantine Model

Byzantine failures can be split into *undetectable* and *detectable* failures [10]. Undetectable failures are those that cannot be detected from received messages, e.g., a Byzantine process that cheats on its initial value when participating to some agreement protocol. Faced with the impossibility to detect such failure, a process that commits only undetectable failures is considered as correct by the other correct processes. Among detectable failures, we have (1) *commission* failures (with respect to some algorithm), i.e., messages that do not respect the semantics of the algorithm and (2) *omission* failures (with respect to some algorithm), i.e., expected algorithm messages that never arrive. According to this classification, muteness can be seen as a permanent omission failure, i.e., a mute process is a process that stop sending any algorithm messages to one or more correct processes.

Muteness Failures. Each algorithm $\mathcal{A}$ generates a set of messages that have some specific syntax. We say that a message m is an $\mathcal{A}$ message if the syntax of m corresponds to the syntax of the messages that could be generated by $\mathcal{A}$. Note that a message m sent by a Byzantine process that carries a semantical fault but has a correct syntax is considered as an $\mathcal{A}$ message.

Based on this definition, we define a *mute* process as follows. A process q is *mute* with respect to some algorithm $\mathcal{A}$ and some process p if q prematurely stops sending $\mathcal{A}$ messages to p. We say that process q fails by *quitting algorithm $\mathcal{A}$ with respect to some process p*. A muteness failure pattern F is a function from $\Omega \times T$ to 2^{Ω}, where $F(p, t)$ is the set of processes that quit algorithm $\mathcal{A}$ with respect to p

by time t. By definition, we have $F(p,t) \subseteq F(p,t+1)$. We also define $quit_p(F) = \bigcup_{t \in T} F(p,t)$ and $correct(F) = \Omega - \bigcup_{p \in \Omega} quit_p(F)$. We say that q is *mute to* p if $q \in quit_p(F)$, and if $q \in correct(F)$, we say q is *correct*.

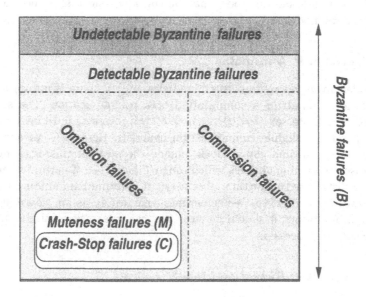

Fig. 1. A Classification of Byzantine Failures

Muteness failures constitute a subset of Byzantine behaviours and a superset of crash-stop failures. Figure 1 conveys this idea, with B denoting the set of all possible Byzantine failures, M the set of muteness failures, and C the set of crash-stop failures. A crashed process is a mute process with respect to all other processes. Note that $M \not\subseteq C$ because a mute process might stop sending messages without crashing.

A Minimum Number of Correct Processes. Let f be the upper bound on the number of faulty processes tolerated in the system. The FLP impossibility shows that in an asynchronous model no agreement problem can be solved if $f > 0$. However, different tacks were proposed in the literature to circumvent this impossibility like extending the asynchronous model with failure detectors, postulating some probabilistic behaviour about the system message, etc. However, all the proposed algorithms assume a minimum number of correct processes, refered hereafter as $N - f$. In the crash-stop model, the value of f is less than $N/2$ and in the Byzantine model this value is less than $N/3$. [3]

---

[3] For the detailed proof of this result see the work done by Bracha and Toueg in [2].

3 Muteness Failure Detector

This section formally presents the $\Diamond M_A$ muteness failure detector and the class of algorithms that can use that detector.

3.1 The $\Diamond M_A$ Muteness Failure Detector

A muteness failure detector is a distributed oracle aimed at detecting mute processes. Since the notion of muteness failure is related to some algorithm A, the notion of muteness detector is also related to A. Formally, the $\Diamond M_A$ muteness failure detector is expressed in terms of the following two properties:

Eventual Mute Completeness. There is a time after which every process that is mute to a correct process p, with respect to A, is suspected by p forever.

Eventual Weak Accuracy. There is a time after which a correct process p is no more suspected to be mute, with respect to A, by any other correct process.

3.2 Regular Round-Based Algorithms

There are algorithms for which the use of $\Diamond M_A$ makes no sense. More precisely, for such algorithms, it is impossible to implement $\Diamond M_A$, even in a completely synchronous model. Intuitively, these algorithms are those for which a mute process cannot be distinguished from a correct process, even in a completely synchronous system, i.e., algorithms where muteness can be a correct behaviour. Therefore, we define here a class of algorithms, named C_A, for which the use of $\Diamond M_A$ does indeed make sense. We characterise this class by specifying the set of attributes that should be featured by any algorithm $A \in C_A$. We qualify such algorithms as *regular round-based*.

Attribute (a). Each correct process p owns a variable $round_p$ that takes its range $\mathcal{R}$ to be the set of natural numbers $\mathbb{N}$. As soon as $round_p = n$, we say that *process p reaches round n*. Then, until $round_p = n+1$ process p is said to be *in round n*.

Attribute (b). In each round, there is at most one process q from which all correct processes are waiting for one or more messages. We say that q is <u>the</u> *critical process of round n* and its explicitly awaited messages are said to be *critical messages*.

Attribute (c). With at least $N - f$ correct processes participating in algorithm A, each process p is critical every k rounds, $k \in \mathbb{N}$ and if in addition p is correct then it sends a message to all in that round.

Intuitively, Attribute (a) states that A proceeds in rounds, while Attribute (b) defines the notion of critical process and restricts the number of such processes to one in each round. Finally, Attributes (c) expresses, in terms of rounds, that a correct process is critical an infinite number of times, and that it should therefore not be mute. Interestingly, many agreement protocols that we know of feature these three attributes. In particular, both the centralised consensus algorithm of [3] and the decentralised consensus algorithm of [15] are instances of class C_A. They trivially feature Attributes (a), (b) and (c), since they proceed in asynchronous rounds and rely on the rotating coordinator paradigm; in particular, we have $k = N$ for their instance of Attribute (c).

4 An Implementation for $\Diamond M_A$

In the crash-stop failure model, the implementation of some failure detector $\mathcal{D}$ can be made independent of the messages sent by the algorithm using $\mathcal{D}$. For example, this is the case of the timeout-based implementation of $\Diamond \mathcal{P}$ sketched in [3], which sends periodically its own "p-is-alive" messages: such messages are completely separate from those generated by the consensus algorithm (or by whatever algorithm using the failure detector).[4] This independence is made possible because a crashed process stops sending any kind of messages, no matter whether they are generated by the algorithm or by the local failure detector module. In some sense, we can say that, in a crash-stop model, incorrect processes have a coherent behaviour with respect to the messages they send: if they stop sending messages related to the failure detector, they also stop sending messages related to the algorithm.

In the muteness failure model, on the contrary, incorrect processes can stop sending algorithm messages without crashing. In other words, they can play by the rule as far as messages "p-is-alive" are concerned, and at the same time they can stop sending any other messages. So, the periodic reception of messages from the failure detector module of some process p is no longer a guarantee that an algorithm message will eventually arrive from p. Consequently, an implementation of $\Diamond M_A$ based on independent messages cannot help to capture mute processes.

4.1 An Algorithm $\mathcal{I}_D$ for Implementing $\Diamond M_A$

Algorithm 1 gives an implementation $\mathcal{I}_D$ of the muteness failure detector $\Diamond M_A$. It relies on a timeout mechanism and is composed of three concurrent tasks. Variable Δ_p holds the current timeout and is initialised with some arbitrary value $init_\Delta > 0$ that is the same for all correct processes. In addition, $\mathcal{I}_D$ maintains a set $output_p$ of currently suspected processes and a set $critical_p$ containing the processes that p is allowed to add to its $output_p$ set. These two sets are initially empty. A newly suspected process is added to $output_p$ by Task 1 as follows: if p does not receive a "q-is-not-mute" message for Δ_p ticks from some process q that is in $critical_p$, q is suspected to be mute and inserted in the $output_p$ set.

---

[4] Note that this implementation is correct only if we assume that failure detector messages and algorithm messages do not prevent each other from reaching their destination.

Algorithm 1 Implementation $\mathcal{I}_{\mathcal{D}}$ of Muteness Failure Detector $\Diamond M_{\mathcal{A}}$

1: {*Every process p executes the following :*}

2: $\Delta_p \leftarrow init_\Delta$; $output_p \leftarrow \emptyset$; $critical_p \leftarrow \emptyset$; {*Initialisation*}

3: **for all** $q \in critical_p$ **do** {*Task 1*}
4:   **if** $(q \notin output_p) \wedge (p$ did not receive "q-is-not-mute" during Δ_p ticks) **then**
5:     $output_p \leftarrow output_p \cup q$

6: **when** receive "q-is-not-mute" from $\mathcal{A}_p$ {*Task 2*}
7:   **if** $(q \in output_p)$ **then**
8:     $output_p \leftarrow output_p - q$

9: **when** receive $new\_critical_p$ from $\mathcal{A}_p$ {*Task 3*}
10:   $critical_p \leftarrow new\_critical_p$
11:   $\Delta_p \leftarrow g_{\mathcal{A}}(\Delta_p)$

Interactions between $\mathcal{A}_p$ and $\Diamond M_{\mathcal{A}}$. Figure 2 sketches how algorithm $\mathcal{A}_p$ executed by a correct process p and $\Diamond M_{\mathcal{A}}$ interact: besides queries to $\Diamond M_{\mathcal{A}}$ (arrow 1), our implementation $\mathcal{I}_{\mathcal{D}}$ handles two more interactions with $\mathcal{A}_p$. Tasks 2 and 3 are responsible for that. Each time p receives a message from some process q (arrow 2), algorithm $\mathcal{A}_p$ delivers "q-is-not-mute" to $\mathcal{I}_{\mathcal{D}}$ (arrow 3). As a consequence, Task 2 removes process q from $output_p$ in case q was suspected. At the beginning of each round, $\mathcal{A}_p$ delivers a $new\_critical_p$ set to $\mathcal{I}_{\mathcal{D}}$ (arrow 4) containing the *critical processes* of the new round. Task 3 updates $critical_p$ accordingly to the set $new\_critical_p$. In addition, Task 3 also computes a new value for timeout Δ_p by applying some function $g_{\mathcal{A}}$ on the current value of Δ_p. Since the timeout is updated in each new round, there exists a corresponding function $\Delta_{\mathcal{A}} : \mathcal{R} \rightarrow \mathcal{T}$ that maps each round n onto its associated timeout $\Delta_{\mathcal{A}}(n)$. For instance, if function $g_{\mathcal{A}}$ doubles the current timeout Δ_p, then $\Delta_{\mathcal{A}}(n) = 2^{n-1} init_\Delta$.

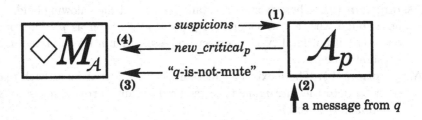

Fig. 2. Interactions between $\mathcal{A}_p$ and $\Diamond M_{\mathcal{A}}$

4.2 Assumptions for Proving the Correctness of Algorithm $\mathcal{I}_D$

Our algorithm $\mathcal{I}_D$ does not approximate the bound on communication delays, as does the implementation of $\Diamond\mathcal{P}$ in [3], but rather the maximum delay between two consecutive $\mathcal{A}$'s messages sent by some correct process. Therefore, proving the correctness of this implementation, even when assuming a partial synchrony model, is not a straightforward task. Indeed, the delay between two consecutive $\mathcal{A}$'s messages does not depend only on transmission delay, but also depends on the communication pattern of algorithm $\mathcal{A}$.

In order to prove the correctness of implementation $\mathcal{I}_D$, we then rely on (1) partial synchrony assumptions, and (2) time assumptions on algorithm $\mathcal{A}$ and on the timeout function of $\mathcal{I}_D$, i.e., on function $\Delta_\mathcal{A}$. In addition, we assume that there are permanently $N - f$ correct processes participating in distributed algorithm $\mathcal{A}$.[5]

Partial Synchrony Assumptions. The *partial synchrony* model assumed here is slightly weaker than those discussed in [6], a reference paper by Dwork et al. on consensus in partial synchrony. In the model they consider, the bound δ on communication delays and the bound ϕ on processes' relative speeds do exist but they are either unknown, *or* known but they hold only after some *Global Stabilisation time*(hereafter GST) that is itself unknown. In the following, we assume a system where δ and ϕ are both unknown *and* hold only after some unknown GST. Such a weaker partially synchronous system is also the one assumed by Chandra and Toueg for their implementability proof of $\Diamond\mathcal{P}$ [3]. From now on, we consider the system only after GST, i.e., we assume only values of the global clock that are greater or equal than GST.

Time Assumptions on $\mathcal{A}$ and $\mathcal{I}_D$. In order to state those assumptions, we need a few definitions. We say that some round n is *reached* as soon as at least one correct process p reaches n; once a round is reached, it remains so forever. For some round n we say that n is *completed* if all correct processes have received all the critical messages of round n.

Assumption (a). There exists a constant β such that the following holds. Let n be a round with a correct critical process p. As soon as p is in round n together with at least $N - f$ correct processes, then n is completed in some constant time β.

Assumption (b). There exists a function $h : \mathcal{R} \to \mathcal{T}$ that maps each reached round n onto the *maximum time* required by any correct process in some round $m < n$ to reach n.

Assumption (c). There exists a function $\Delta_\mathcal{A}$ such that the following holds. There exists a round n' such that $\forall n \geq n'$ where n is a reached round, we have:

---

[5] We will come back to this additional assumption in Section 4.4, where we discuss what happens if it does not hold forever.

$$\Delta_A (n) > h(n) \;\wedge\; \Delta_A (n+1) - h(n+1) > \Delta_A (n) - h(n).$$

Intuitively, this means that after round n', the timeout $\Delta_A (n)$ associated with any reached round $n \geq n'$ is larger and grows faster than $h(n)$.

Corollary 41 *From Assumption (a) to (c), we can easily infer that:*

$$\exists n' \in \mathcal{R}, \forall n \geq n', \; \Delta_A (n) > h(n) + \beta.$$

4.3 Correctness Proof of Algorithm $\mathcal{I}_D$

We now prove that, when used by any regular round-based algorithm, $\mathcal{I}_D$ satisfies the Eventual Mute Completeness and the Eventual Weak Accuracy properties, under the assumptions of Section 4.2. This is formally expressed by Theorem 42.

Theorem 42 *When used by an algorithm A of class C_A, $\mathcal{I}_D$ ensures the properties of $\Diamond M_A$ in the partial synchrony model, under Assumptions (a) to (c).*

PROOF: We first prove the Mute Completeness property, which is needed to prove the Eventual Weak Accuracy property.

Eventual Mute Completeness. By Attribute (c) of any algorithm $A \in C_A$, we infer that each process is critical in an infinite number of rounds. Therefore, each process q is eventually added the set of $critical_p$ of a correct process p. If q is mute to process p, that means q stops sending messages to p forever. Thus the algorithm A_p of process p stops receiving messages from q and algorithm $\mathcal{I}_D$ stops receiving "q-is-not mute" messages (Task 2). Therefore, there is a time t after which process p timeouts on q and inserts it in its $output_p$ set (Task 1). Since q stops sending messages to p forever, process q is never removed from $output_p$ and q is suspected forever to be mute by p. Hence, there is a time after which the Eventually Mute Completeness holds forever.

Eventual Weak Accuracy. From the Eventual Mute Completeness a correct process is never blocked forever by a mute process. Therefore, any correct process executes an infinite sequence of rounds. Let p and q be two correct processes. We know that q can only be added to $output_p$ in rounds r where q is the critical process of r. From Corollary 41, we have $\exists n' \in \mathcal{R}, \forall n \geq n', \Delta_A (n) > h(n) + \beta$. Let n be any such round where q is the critical process, and assume that p just reached n, i.e., p is at the beginning of round n. There are two possible cases:

Case 1. Process $q \notin output_p$ at the beginning of round n, i.e, when p starts round n it does not suspect q. Since $\Delta_A (n) > h(n) + \beta$, the timeout Δ_p is larger than the maximum time required by any correct process (includes q) to reach round n, plus the time needed by round n to be completed. As consequence, process p receives the expected critical messages from q without suspecting q. Thus, q is not added to $output_p$. Furthermore, thanks to Corollary 41, we infer that q will not be added to $output_p$ in n, nor in any future round where q will be critical.

Case 2. Process $q \in output_p$ at the beginning of round n, i.e, when p starts round n process q is already suspected by p. Therefore, q was suspected by p in some round $r < n$, where q was r's critical process. Since each correct process executes an infinite sequence of rounds, from the assumption that there are always $N - f$ participating correct processes and from Attribute (c), we know that process q eventually reaches round r as well as at least $N - f$ correct processes and hence sends a message to all in that round. So, there is a round $r' \geq n$, where p eventually receives q's messages and consequently removes q from $output_p$. Since for round r' we also have $\Delta_A (r') > h(r') + \beta$ and $q \notin output_p$, we fall back on Case 1.

Therefore, there exists a round $max(r', n)$ after which process q is never suspected to be mute by any correct process p. Thus, there is a time after which the Eventual Weak Accuracy holds forever. □

4.4 The Problem of Ensuring $\Diamond M_A$ Properties Forever

It is worth noting that several distributed algorithms do not ensure the participation of $N - f$ correct processes *forever*. With such an algorithm A, we say that correct process p *terminates* when A_p yields its last result and p stops participating in A. This is in particular the case for both the centralised and decentralised agreement algorithms described in [3] and [15] respectively. The problem is that, with less than $N - f$ correct processes, we cannot guarantee anymore that a correct process executes an infinite sequence of rounds and sends regular messages to all. As a consequence, $\mathcal{I}_D$ cannot ensure Eventual Weak Accuracy *forever*.

Often, however, such algorithms also guarantee that once a correct process terminates, all correct processes are then able to eventually terminate without using $\Diamond M_A$ anymore.[6] In other words, such algorithms only need $\mathcal{I}_D$ to ensure $\Diamond M_A$ properties *as long as no correct process terminates*. Again, this is the case of both aforementioned agreement algorithms.

5 Putting $\Diamond M_A$ to Work

This section gives an example of a distributed agreement algorithm that can be combined with $\Diamond M_A$, namely the decentralised consensus algorithm of [15]; this algorithm is also known as *Early Consensus*, hereafter *EC*. We already known that EC is a regular round-based algorithm (Section 3.2). We now show that EC satisfies, in the partial synchrony model defined earlier, Assumptions (a) to (c) (state in Section 4.2). We start by recalling the basic insight of the EC algorithm, and then we proceed with the proofs.

---

[6] Chandra & Toueg's point out that failure detector properties need only to hold *"long enough for the algorithm to achieve its goal"* [3, page 228].

5.1 Background: Overview of Early Consensus

The detailed EC algorithm can be found in [15], hereafter we outline the basic idea. EC is based on the rotating coordinator paradigm and proceeds in asynchronous rounds, each one being divided into two phases. In Phase 1 of every round r, algorithm EC tries to decide on the estimate of the coordinator p_c of round r. The coordinator p_c starts by broadcasting its current $estimate_c$. When a process receives $estimate_c$, it reissues (broadcasts) this value to all. Once process has received $estimate_c$ from $N - f$ processes, it broadcasts a $decision$ message containing $estimate_c$ and decides on it. Phase 1 is illustrated in Figure 3.

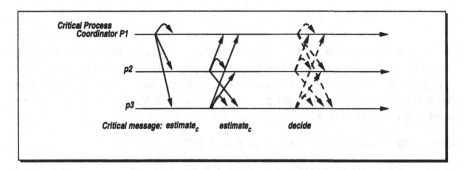

Fig. 3. Phase 1 of Early Consensus

If p_c is suspected by at least $N - f$ processes, Phase 2 ensures that if any process decides on $estimate_c$ in round r, then all correct processes that start round $r + 1$ set their current estimate to $estimate_c$. This is ensured as follows. When a process suspects coordinator p_c, it broadcasts a $suspicion$ message. Once a process has received at least $N - f$ $suspicion$ messages, it broadcasts its current $estimate$ in a so-called $GoPhase2$ message. Once a process has received $N - f$ $GoPhase2$ messages, it checks if one of the received estimates is the estimate of p_c.[7] If an estimate sent by p_c is found the process adopts it and moves to round $r + 1$. Phase 2 is illustrated in Figure 4.

5.2 Usability Proof of $\Diamond M_{\mathcal{A}}$ by Algorithm EC

In this section we show that the EC algorithm satisfies the time assumptions stated in Section 4.2.

Lemma 51 *Assumption (a) holds with $\mathcal{A} = EC$.*

---

[7] An estimate is composed of two fields: (1) the value of the estimate and (2) the identifier of the process who proposed this estimate.

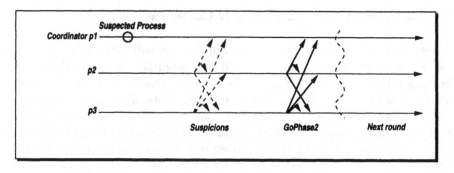

Fig. 4. Phase 2 of Early Consensus

PROOF: Let n be a round with a correct critical process p, and assume that p is is in round n together with at least $N - f$ correct processes. Since we are after GST, process p sends its current estimate in bounded time $\leq \phi$. The estimate is then received by all other correct processes in bounded time $\leq \delta + \phi$. Therefore, round n is completed in a constant time $\beta = \phi + \delta$. □

Lemma 52 *Assumption (b) holds with $\mathcal{A} = EC$.*

PROOF: This proof shows the existence of function h which, as already said, computes the maximum time required by any correct process in some round $m < n$ to reach n. Let p_i be a correct process in the most advanced round, let say n. Let p_j be a correct process in the less advanced round, let say m. In EC, each correct process sends a *GoPhase2* message to all before proceeding to the next round. Therefore, process p_i already sent message $(p_i, m, 2, -)$ to all, when it was in round m.

Since we are after GST, message $(p_i, m, 2, -)$ is received by each correct process in a bounded time $\leq \delta$. Each correct process delivers this message and relays it to all the other processes in bounded time $\leq (N+1)\phi$. So, any correct process, in particular process p_j which is in round m, collects $N - f$ GoPhase2 messages and proceeds to the next round in bounded time $\leq (2\delta + (N + 1)\phi)$. Therefore, process p_j reaches round n in bounded time $\leq (n - m)(2\delta + (N + 1)\phi)$. Since the worse case is $m = 1$, we can roughly bound the time needed by process p_j to reach round n by $(n - 1)(2\delta + (N + 1)\phi)$. We have thus proved the existence of a linear function $h(n) = (n - 1)(2\delta + (N + 1)\phi)$ for algorithm EC. □

Lemma 53 *Assumption (c) holds with $\mathcal{A} = EC$.*

PROOF: Immediate from Lemma 52, if we define exponential function $\Delta_{\mathcal{A}}(n) = 2^{n-1}init_\Delta$. □

Theorem 54 *If $\mathcal{A} = EC$ and $\Delta_{\mathcal{A}}(n) = 2^{n-1}init_\Delta$, $\mathcal{I}_{\mathcal{D}}$ ensures the properties of $\Diamond M_{\mathcal{A}}$ in the partial synchrony model.*

PROOF: Immediate from Lemmas 51 to 53, and from Theorem 42 □

6 Related Work

Beside our work, we know of two research efforts that aim at extending the notion of failure detectors to Byzantine models and solving consensus using such detectors. Malkhi and Reiter considered a system model where all messages are exchanged using a causal-order reliable broadcast primitive [12]. They defined the notion of *quiet process* that is close to our notion of *mute process*. They also introduced a failure detector, noted $\Diamond S$ (bz), and they expressed its properties in terms of *Strong Completeness* and *Eventual Weak Accuracy*. The aim of $\Diamond S$ (bz) is to track processes that prevent the progress of the algorithm using it. The failure detector $\Diamond S$ (bz) is shown to be strong enough to solve consensus.

In [10], Kihlstrom et al. define two classes of failure detectors: (1) the eventual Weak Byzantine failure detector $\Diamond W$ (Byz), and (2) the eventual Strong Byzantine failure detector $\Diamond S$ (Byz). Both detectors are shown to be strong enough to solve consensus. Contrary to the specification proposed by Malkhi and Reiter, and contrary to the one we propose, these classes of failure detectors capture all the *detectable* Byzantine failures. Consequently among the set of failures captured by $\Diamond W$ (Byz) or $\Diamond S$ (Byz) there are failures that prevent the progress of the algorithm, i.e., muteness failures (in point-to-point communication network) or quietness failures (in causal-order reliable broadcast communication network).

Neither [12] nor [10] address the fundamental circularity problem (i.e., the dependency between the algorithm and the Byzantine fault detector), which we believe is a fundamental issue when applying the failure detector approach in the context of Byzantine failures. This is probably because none of those papers discuss the correctness of Byzantine fault detector implementations. In [12], the authors did not address the implementability issues, while authors of [10] present a non-proved implementation that roughly aims to insert timeout mechanism in the branch of the algorithm where there are expected messages: but this is far from proving that this implementation provides the expected properties of the failure detector. By focusing on mute detectors and restricting our work to regular round-based algorithms, we could address the circularity problem and describe a correct implementation of mute detectors in a partial synchrony model.

7 Concluding Remarks

The motivation of this paper was to extend failures detectors for crash-stop failures to malicious failures. The extension was however not straightforward because, in a malicious environment, the notion of fault is intimately related to a given algorithm. It is thus impossible to specify a Byzantine fault detector that is independent from the algorithm using it (unlike in a crash-stop model). Furthermore, given the necessity of a two-ways interaction between the fault detector and the algorithm, one might end up with a fault detector that is impossible to implement, even in a completely synchronous model. This paper can be viewed as a first step towards better understanding these issues in a Byzantine environment. The paper focuses on muteness failures. Muteness failures are malicious failures in which a process stops sending algorithm messages, but might continue to send other messages. The paper presents both a definition of a mute detector $\Diamond M_A$ and a protocol for implementing $\Diamond M_A$ in a partial synchrony model. The mute detector $\Diamond M_A$ is strong enough to solve consensus in an asynchronous distributed system with mute failures. Although the implementation of $\Diamond M_A$ and the algorithm using it must cooperate, which is actually inherent in the problem, we have confined that interaction inside a specific module. Furthermore, we have shown that, modulo that interaction, one can reuse a consensus algorithm designed in a crash stop model.

Open Questions We restricted our work to the class of *regular round-based* distributed algorithms. Although many algorithms belong to that class, it would be interesting to see whether one could extend this class and still be able to provide a sensible implementation of $\Diamond M_A$ in a partial synchrony model. In fact, some of the attributes of that class could indeed be relaxed. For instance, we required (*) *the permanent participation of a majority of correct processes in the algorithm.* This assumption is not really needed as long as, once a correct process terminates, all correct processes are able to eventually terminate without using $\Diamond M_A$ anymore. In other words, $\Diamond M_A$ properties are actually only needed *as long as no correct process terminates.* We can thus replace (*) by (**) *there is at least a majority of correct processes participating in the algorithm, as long as no correct process terminates.* It would be interesting to find out whether other attributes can be relaxed and whether the time assumptions that we require to implement $\Diamond M_A$ are just *sufficient* or *necessary.*

References

1. M. Aguilera, W. Chen, and S. Toueg. Failure detection and consensus in the crash-recovery model. In *12th International Symposium on Distributed Computing.* Springer Verlag, LNCS 1499, September 1998.
2. G. Bracha and S. Toueg. Asynchronous consensus and broadcast protocols. *Journal of the Association for Computing Machinery,* 32(4):824–840, October 1985.
3. T. D. Chandra and S. Toueg. Unreliable failure detectors for reliable distributed systems. *Journal of the ACM,* 43(2):225–267, March 1996.
4. Danny Dolev, Roy Friedman, Idit Keidar, and Dahlia Malkhi. Failure detectors in omission failure environments. In *Proceedings of the Sixteenth Annual ACM Symposium on Principles of Distributed Computing,* page 286, Santa Barbara, California, August 1997.
5. A. Doudou and S. Schiper. Muteness detectors for consensus with byzantine processes (brief announcement). In *Proceedings of the 17th Annual ACM Symposium on Principles of Distributed Computing (PODC'98),* Puerto Vallarta, Mexico, June 1998. ACM. An extended version of this brief annoucement is available as a Technical Report, TR 97/230, EPFL, Detp d'Informatique, October 1997, under the title "Muteness Failure Detector for Consensus with Byzantine Processes".
6. C. Dwork, N. Lynch, and L. Stockmeyer. Consensus in the presence of partial synchrony. *Journal of the ACM,* 35(2):288–323, apr 1988.

7. M. Fischer, N. Lynch, and M. Paterson. Impossibility of Distributed Consensus with One Faulty Process. *Journal of the ACM*, 32:374–382, April 1985.

8. R. Guerraoui and A. Schiper. Consensus service: a modular approach for building agreement protocols in distributed systems. In *IEEE 26th Int Symp on Fault-Tolerant Computing (FTCS-26)*, pages 168–177, June 1996.

9. Rachid Guerraoui. Revisiting the relationship between non-blocking atomic commitment and consensus. In Jean-Michel Hélary and Michel Raynal, editors, *Distributed Algorithms, 9th International Workshop, WDAG '95*, volume 972 of *Lecture Notes in Computer Science*, pages 87–100, Le Mont-Saint-Michel, France, 13–15 September 1995. Springer.

10. Kim Potter Kihlstrom, Louise E. Moser, and P. M. Melliar-Smith. Solving consensus in a Byzantine environment using an unreliable fault detector. In *Proceedings of the International Conference on Principles of Distributed Systems (OPODIS)*, pages 61–75, December 1997.

11. L. Lamport, R. Shostak, and M. Pease. The Byzantine Generals Problem. *ACM Transactions on Programming Languages and Systems*, 4(3):382–401, July 1982.

12. D. Malkhi and M. Reiter. Unreliable Intrusion Detection in Distributed Computations. In *Proc. 10th Computer Security Foundations Workshop (CSFW97)*, pages 116–124, June 1997.

13. O.Babaoğlu, R.Davoli, and A.Montresor. Failure Detectors, Group Membership and View-Synchronous Communication in Partitionable Asynchronous Systems. Technical Report UBLCS-95-18, Department of Computer Science University of Bologna, November 1995.

14. R. Oliveira, R. Guerraoui, and A. Schiper. Consensus in the crash-recover model. Technical Report 97/239, École Polytechnique Fédérale de Lausanne, Switzerland, August 1997.

15. A. Schiper. Early consensus in an asynchronous system with a weak failure detector. *Distributed Computing*, 10(3):149–157, April 1997.

A Fault Tolerant Clock Synchronization Algorithm for Systems with Low-Precision Oscillators

Henrik Lonn

Department of Computer Engineering
Chalmers University of Technology
412 96 Gothenburg
hlonn@ce.chalmers.se

Abstract. In this paper we present a new fault tolerant clock synchronization algorithm, the Fault Tolerant Daisy Chain algorithm. It is intended for internal clock synchronization of systems using a broadcast bus with Time Division Multiple Access (TDMA) communication, or other systems where clock readings are broadcast at regular intervals. The algorithm allows synchronization after each clock reading and is therefore tolerant to oscillators with large drift rates. Clock hardware is simplified since it is not necessary to store the collected clock readings until the next synchronization, nor is it necessary to schedule synchronization events. Theoretical bounds on clock skew are derived assuming non-Byzantine and Byzantine faults and compared with three different convergence synchronization algorithms. A simulated fault injection study is also presented, where the proposed algorithm was found to tolerate transient faults better than the theoretically best among the convergence algorithms, particularly at high drift rates.

1. Introduction

Most distributed systems require an agreed timebase. The timebase is represented by a number of clocks, one in each node, that are synchronized at regular intervals. Synchronized clocks are used in distributed control systems to avoid timing variations that would otherwise result in poor control performance [1]. In safety-critical systems, synchronized clocks are necessary for many fault tolerance mechanisms.

Numerous clock synchronization methods for distributed systems have been presented. In this paper we will concentrate on clock synchronization in safety-critical systems using a broadcast bus. We specifically consider cost-sensitive application areas such as the automotive industry, and therefore require a clock synchronization algorithm that tolerates low-precision oscillators, i.e. large clock drift.

Because synchronized clocks are so important for correct system operation, fault tolerant algorithms are necessary. Many of the previously proposed fault tolerant clock synchronization algorithms operate on a set of clock readings collected from the other

† This work was supported by grant form the Volvo Research Foundation

clocks in the system. When all clocks have collected clock readings from all other clocks, the synchronization algorithm is applied and all clocks are corrected. Assuming that only one node at a time can transmit its clock reading on the bus, clocks can only be adjusted every n^{th} transmission. In the mean time, each node must store the collected clock readings, and the clocks will drift apart due to the slightly differing rates of their oscillators.

In this paper we present the fault tolerant Daisy Chain clock synchronization algorithm. With this method, clocks are synchronized after each message transmission or clock reading. It is thus not necessary to keep track of the instant when the adjustment should be calculated and applied, and no clock readings need to be stored. The original Daisy Chain algorithm was described in [2]. Below, we modify the algorithm to tolerate faults and derive the theoretical bounds on clock skew. Depending on parameter settings, both Byzantine and non-Byzantine faults are tolerated.

The rest of the paper is organized as follows: In Section 2 we explain how clock readings can be distributed in a system with broadcast bus. In Section 3 the fault model of such system is discussed. Section 4 describes different existing clock synchronization algorithms and in Section 5 the new fault tolerant Daisy Chain algorithm is presented. A theoretical comparison is made in Section 6 while Section 0 contains a simulation study. The paper is closed with a Summary and Conclusions Section. In appendix, a sketch of the proof of the Daisy Chain algorithm is given.

2. Obtaining clock readings

When communication consists of broadcast messages on a bus, the arrival time of a frame can be used as an accurate measure of the sender's time. Because sending times of messages are scheduled before run-time and known by all nodes, it is not necessary to broadcast explicit clock values over the network. The difference between actual and expected arrival time at the receiving node is a measure of the current time-skew between the two clocks. This approach means that it is possible to transmit clock readings with every message without any communication overhead. The use of *á priori* known times for system events for clock synchronization was first presented in [3].

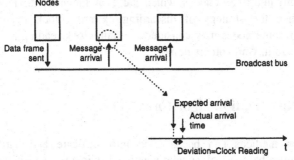

Fig 1. Using difference between actual and expected message arrival time as clock readings

3. Fault model

With the clock distribution method described above, clock faults will occur as messages arriving at the wrong time. The cause of this may be both transient and permanent faults, but we assume that many of the permanent faults can be detected and masked. For example, a "deaf" node will stop sending messages and will not subsequently affect the correct nodes. In a distributed system, the most difficult failures to tolerate are Byzantine failures. A Byzantine failure is such that the same information is interpreted differently by its receivers [4], which makes it difficult to tolerate.

Transient failures are most likely caused by electromagnetic interference. We assume that electromagnetic interference can cause messages to

- Be corrupted
- Arrive too early
- Arrive too late

Message corruption occurs when a disturbance forces a transmitted "0" to be interpreted as a "1" and *vice versa*. A corruption of frame contents can be detected with a very high probability if a checksum is used. However, if a disturbance affects the first bit of a message, the fault may not be detected. There are two cases:

- If the disturbance occurs just before the message arrival and drives the bus to the same value as the first bit, a too early message arrival is recorded.
- If the disturbance drives the opposite value until just after the message arrival, a too late arrival is recorded

In none of these cases the fault is detected using the checksum, but has to be tolerated by the clock synchronization algorithm..

In most cases failures will be non-Byzantine and thus affect all nodes, although the propagation delay will cause the perceived time of the failure to differ slightly. However, disturbances with low energy may be effective in some nodes, but not in others. One reason is that nodes are physically separated and therefore experience different field strengths. Other reasons include component variations, problems with terminations, capacitive and inductive couplings to ground and adjacent cables.

Byzantine faults also occur if the clock source of a sending node is too slow or fast. Since the receiving nodes also have varying clock rates, the timing fault will be perceived differently in different nodes, which causes an inconsistent view of the fault. For example, when the strategy of discarding extreme clock readings is used (explained below), some nodes may consider a certain clock reading to be above the threshold and discard it, while others do not.

4. Clock synchronization algorithms

Synchronization methods can be grouped into software and hardware based approaches. Hardware based clock synchronization requires that clocks are connected via a dedicated network for clock signals and is therefore not relevant here. Software synchronization algorithms use clock readings exchanged e.g. via broadcast messages. Software algorithms can be divided into consistency and convergence methods. With the consistency methods all clocks agree on the set of clock readings with an agreement protocol. The agreement protocol can be the same as the ones used for general agreement problems, such as the ones proposed in [4]. Once the protocol has finished and all clocks have the same vector of clock values, the new clock value could be the mean or midpoint of these.

The convergence methods are such that faults are tolerated without the overhead associated with consistency methods. Faults are neutralized by the way the new clock value is calculated based on the collected clock readings. For any algorithm to tolerate m arbitrary, or Byzantine faults, a total of n>3*m clocks are required [4]. Below we will review three convergence clock synchronization methods.

In the Fault Tolerant Average method (FTA) [5], the new clock value is the average of all n clocks except the m fastest and m slowest clocks. Maximum skew is:

$$\delta_{max} = (\varepsilon + 2\rho R)\frac{n-2m}{n-3m} \tag{1}$$

ε is the reading error of a remote clock, R is the re-synchronization interval and ρ the maximum drift rate between any two clocks.

Since clock readings are collected during the n timeslots preceding a synchronization, the values are up to n timeslots old when used in the clock adjustment function. At this time, the clock reading may deviate with up to $2\rho \cdot Tn$ from the real value, where T is the duration of a timeslot. In the worst case, the age of the clock readings used in the fault tolerant average calculation are between 2m and n timeslots. The total error in the adjustment function due to age is bounded by

$$\frac{\sum_{i=2m+1}^{n} i \cdot T \cdot 2\rho}{(n-2m)} = (n+2m+1)\rho T \tag{2}$$

The effect of this error is identical to the clock reading error ε and (1) therefore becomes

$$\delta_{max} = (\varepsilon + (n+2m+1)\rho T + 2\rho R)\frac{n-2m}{n-3m} \tag{3}$$

The Interactive Convergence Algorithm (CNV) is described in [6]. Clocks are adjusted to the average of all clock readings, replacing with zero those with a skew exceeding δ_{max}. Maximum skew is:

$$\delta_{max} = \frac{2n\varepsilon + 2\rho S(n-2m) + 2\rho nR}{n-3m} \tag{4}$$

Where S is the interval during which clock values are exchanged. S<=R since all clocks have to be read between synchronizations.

In the Midpoint Algorithm (MP) [7], clocks are adjusted to the mean of the fastest and slowest clocks, excluding the m fastest and m slowest clocks. Worst case skew is

$$\delta_{max}=4\varepsilon+4\rho R \tag{5}$$

Just like with algorithm FTA, the clock reading term must be modified to account for the age of the clock values. Only two clock readings are used, but these may be n and n-1 timeslots old in the worst case. (5) is thus modified to

$$\delta_{max}=4(\varepsilon+(n+n-1)\cdot 2\rho T/2) +4\rho R=4\varepsilon+(8n-4)\cdot\rho T +4\rho R \tag{6}$$

5. Daisy-Chain synchronization

With the previously described clock synchronization algorithms, clock readings are collected from all other clocks before an adjustment value is calculated and applied. If adjustments were performed more often, a clock's value would change compared to the reading given to the other clocks, and their adjustments would be based on invalid clock vectors. With Daisy-Chain synchronization, all nodes synchronize their clocks to the node that is currently sending in a Daisy-Chain fashion. To limit the effect of faulty clocks, no adjustment is made if the clock reading deviates more than a threshold value, D.

Since clock adjustments are made after each message, clock drift cannot increase skew as much as if the time between synchronizations were longer. Also, the complexity of the clock synchronization hardware can be reduced since it does not have to decide whether to synchronize or not after each message, and because a set of clock values does not have to be stored for the synchronization.

5.1 Algorithm description

Each time a message is received, each node calculates the clock deviation between the local clock and the senders' clock. A receiving node j calculates the clock deviation $\delta_{i,j}$ between itself and the sending node i. As indicated above, the deviation between the expected arrival time and the actual time is used, and a correction is made for the propagation delay of the message. If the resulting clock deviation is larger than the threshold value D, it is replaced by 0. To avoid that correct clock readings are discarded, D must be larger than the sum of maximal clock skew and clock reading error, i. e. $D\geq\delta_{max}+\varepsilon$.

The local clock of j is then adjusted by adding $\dfrac{\delta_{i,j}}{r}$ to the current clock value, where the parameter r depends on the system size and the number of faults to tolerate. The adjustment term can be both negative and positive, depending on which node is faster.

Since clocks are only adjusted with a fraction of the clock deviation, the impact of a faulty clock on the rest of the system is limited. On the other hand, several adjustments with correct clock readings are required to reduce the clock skew after a synchronization with faulty clock readings.

If we let r=n, the algorithm is the same as CNV, except that clock readings are not collected from all nodes prior to synchronization.

The derivation of the skew bounds for the Daisy Chain Algorithm can be found in Appendix. Below, we present the requirements and attainable performance when non-Byzantine and Byzantine faults, respectively, exist.

Theorem 1. If at most f synchronizations involving non-Byzantine faults occur among any n consecutive synchronizations, where 2f<n, the Daisy Chain algorithm can maintain a clock skew of δ_{max} where

$$\delta_{max} = \rho R \left(2r + \frac{4f}{1 - f/r - \left(1 - \frac{1}{r}\right)^{n-f}} \right) + \varepsilon \left(2 + \frac{3f/r}{1 - f/r - \left(1 - \frac{1}{r}\right)^{n-f}} \right) \tag{7}$$

The parameter r must be chosen so that the denominator in (7) is >0, i.e.

$$1 - f/r - \left(1 - \frac{1}{r}\right)^{n-f} > 0 \tag{8}$$

The inequality holds if

$$r > \frac{f(f+1)}{2} \tag{9}$$

Theorem 1b. If at most m synchronizations involving Byzantine faults occur among any n consecutive synchronizations, where 3m<n, the Daisy Chain algorithm can maintain a clock skew of δ_{max} where

$$\delta_{max} = \rho R \left(2r + \frac{6m}{1 - 2m/r - \left(1 - \frac{1}{r}\right)^{n-m}} \right) + \varepsilon \left(2 + \frac{6m/r}{1 - 2m/r - \left(1 - \frac{1}{r}\right)^{n-m}} \right) \tag{10}$$

The parameter r must be chosen so that the denominator in (10) is >0, i.e.

$$1 - 2m/r - \left(1 - \frac{1}{r}\right)^{n-2m} > 0 \tag{11}$$

This holds if

$$r > m(2m+1) \tag{12}$$

When we compare performance, the Daisy Chain algorithm is called DC_B when Byzantine faults are taken into account and DC otherwise.

6. Comparison

Maximum skew depends on two critical system parameters, namely the clock reading error, ε and the clock drift, ρ. The contribution to the total clock skew from each of these parameters is therefore interesting to study. We compare $\delta_{max}(\rho,\varepsilon)$ with $\varepsilon=0$ to investigate the skew contribution from clock drift and set $\rho=0$ to study the skew contribution from clock reading error.

We assume that a broadcast bus is used, and nodes send messages according to a schedule that is defined before run-time. In such system the reading error, ε, can be very small since all nodes receive the same physical message and differences in propagation delay can be compensated for. It will be the precision of the clock reading, i.e. the granularity of the clock, that decides ε.

Clock drift depends on the type of oscillators that is used. Low-accuracy oscillators are cheaper and we therefore want the clock synchronization to be particularly tolerant to large ρ.

The FTA, CNV and MP algorithms only allow clock synchronization to be done after every n^{th} clock reading, i.e. when clock readings from all clocks have been collected. Compared to the Daisy Chain algorithm their resynchronization interval is thus n times longer.

Below we show the contribution to δ_{max} from ρ for each of the algorithms. In the expression for δ_{max} (Equations (1)-(10)) we have first let $\varepsilon=0$ and divided by ρ. Further down δ_{max} is divided by ε while $\rho=0$.

R is substituted with nT for algorithms FTA, CNV and MP, where T is the resynchronization interval for Daisy Chain synchronization. The S parameter used for the CNV algorithm equals (n-1)T, since this would be the period during which clock readings are collected if clock readings are broadcast in turn.

Table 1. Contribution to clock precision, δ_{max}, from clock drift, ρ ($\varepsilon=0$)

FTA:	$\dfrac{\delta_{max}}{\rho} = \left((n+2m+1)T + 2R\right)\dfrac{n-2m}{n-3m} = \dfrac{n-2m}{n-3m}(3n+2m+1)T$	(13)
CNV:	$\dfrac{\delta_{max}}{\rho} = \dfrac{2S(n-2m)+2nR}{n-3m} = \dfrac{2T(n-1)(n-2m)+2n^2T}{n-3m}$	(14)
MP:	$\dfrac{\delta_{max}}{\rho} = (8n-4)T + 4R = (12n-4)T$	(15)
DC:	$\dfrac{\delta_{max}}{\rho} = T\left(2r + \dfrac{4f}{1-\dfrac{f}{r}-\left(1-\dfrac{1}{r}\right)^{n-1}}\right)$	(16)
DC$_B$	$\dfrac{\delta_{max}}{\rho} = T\left(2r + \dfrac{6m}{1-2m/r-\left(1-\dfrac{1}{r}\right)^{n-m}}\right)$	(17)

Table 2. Contribution to clock skew, δ_{max}, from clock reading error, ε ($\rho = 0$)

FTA:	$$\frac{\delta_{max}}{\varepsilon} = \frac{n-2m}{n-3m}$$	(18)
CNV:	$$\frac{\delta_{max}}{\varepsilon} = \frac{2n}{n-3m}$$	(19)
MP:	$$\frac{\delta_{max}}{\varepsilon} = 4$$	(20)
DC:	$$\frac{\delta_{max}}{\varepsilon} = 2 + \frac{3f/r}{1-\frac{f}{r}-\left(1-\frac{1}{r}\right)^{n-f}}$$	(21)
DC$_B$:	$$\frac{\delta_{max}}{\varepsilon} = 2 + \frac{6m/r}{1-\frac{2m}{r}-\left(1-\frac{1}{r}\right)^{n-m}}$$	(22)

For the DC algorithm, we also have to choose a value for the parameter r. In Table 3, the optimal values for r when $\varepsilon=0$ are listed for different system sizes and number of faults. These values are the solution to the equation $\frac{\partial}{\partial r}\delta_{max} = 0$ with $\varepsilon=0$, and thus minimize (16). A disadvantage is that these values are non-integers, and unique for each system size. However, rounding r to the nearest integer does not affect performance significantly. For f=1 we can use r=2, and for f=2 and m=1 we use r=4 for most system sizes. The advantage is that this division is a simple right-shift of the binary value.

To minimize the contribution from ε, r should be as large as possible, as δ_{max} decrease monotonically with r. However, since we focus on low-precision oscillators, an r that minimizes the sensitivity to clock drift should be chosen.

Table 3. Optimal value of parameter r with respect to skew contribution from ρ

Nodes, n	Optimal r, non-Byzantine faults			Optimal r, Byzantine faults		
	f=1	f=2	f=3	m=1	m=2	m=3
4	1.97	-	-	5.07	-	-
5	2.09	5,15	-	4.25	-	-
6	2.17	4,36	-	4.06	-	-
7	2.24	4,20	10,51	4.02	17.72	-
8	2.29	4,18	7.74	4.03	11.93	-
9	2.32	4,21	6.94	4.06	10.11	-
10	2.35	4,26	6.61	4.09	9.27	38.39
15	2.41	4.51	6.45	4.27	8.27	14.30
20	2.41	4.67	6.65	4.37	8.27	12.73

Table 4. Key to symbols used in tables and diagrams

CNV	The interactive convergence algorithm
MP	The Midpoint algorithm
FTA	The fault tolerant average algorithm
DC	The Daisy Chain algorithm
DC_B	The Daisy Chain algorithm, a Byzantine fault model assumed
D	Threshold size. Clock readings deviating more than D are discarded
r	Division parameter used in the Daisy Chain algorithm
n	System size
m	number of Byzantine faults
f	number of non-Byzantine faults
ε	Clock reading error
ρ	Clock drift
δ_{max}	Maximum clock skew
T	Time between clock readings

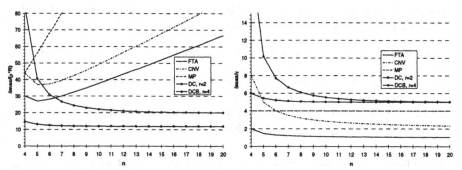

Fig. 2. Skew contribution from clock drift for different system sizes ($\varepsilon=0$, m=f=1). **Fig. 3.** Skew contribution from clock reading error for different system sizes ($\rho=0$, m=f=1).

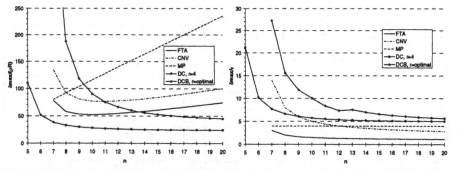

Fig. 4. Skew contribution from clock drift for different system sizes ($\varepsilon=0$, m=f=2). **Fig. 5.** Skew contribution from clock reading error for different system sizes ($\rho=0$, m=f=2).

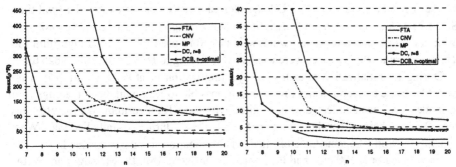

Fig. 6. Skew contribution from clock drift for different system sizes (ε=0, m=f=3).

Fig. 7. Skew contribution from clock reading error for different system sizes (ρ=0, m=f=3).

Above, expressions (13)- (22) are plotted for system sizes between 4 and 20 nodes. The diagrams show the skew contribution from ρ (left) and ε (right). With two or more Byzantine faults, the optimal value for r varies too much with system size to be kept constant. The parameter is then taken from Table 3 and rounded to the nearest integer for DC with Byzantine faults. The same r is used both in the $\delta_{max}/(\rho T)$ and δ_{max}/ε diagrams.

Regarding skew contribution from ρ, the averaging methods loose performance with system size as their resynchronization interval increase. The Daisy Chain algorithm on the other hand performs better with increased size since the resynchronization interval is constant while the impact of the faults decreases.

7. Simulation study

The comparison in Section 6 only refers to the worst case scenario with a given number of faults. In reality, we do not know how many faults that occur in a certain interval and when they occur. In this section we use probabilistic fault injection in an eight node system to evaluate the performance of the Daisy Chain method and compare it with the (theoretically) best of the averaging methods, FTA. We study both average skew and the fraction of time the system is in synchrony.

7.1 System description

The simulated system consists of a group of nodes executing a simple TDMA communication protocol. The nodes send messages of equal length in consecutive order. Each node is considered synchronized for as long as correct messages are received from at least half of the ensemble. When all nodes have lost synchronization, the nodes are re-initialized using the ID resynchronization algorithm [8].

The exclusion of extreme clock values, i.e. those deviating more than D from the local value, is implemented using a *reception window*. A node only receives messages whose first bit arrives within a 2·D long interval centered on the expected arrival time. Since TDMA communication is used, it is not meaningful to try to receive messages at arbitrary times, and a reception window is therefore used for the FTA algorithm too. Three different window sizes were used corresponding to D=0.25, 0.5 and 0.625 μs.

During re-initialization after loss of synchronization or at system startup it is not possible to use a reception window, nor is it possible to wait until clock readings from all nodes have been collected as is required with the FTA algorithm. We therefore use the Daisy Chain algorithm with r=1 and D=∞ during re-initialization. When synchronization is regained, the original synchronization scheme is resumed.

Each timeslot is 100 bits, and the simulated bitrate is 1Mbit/s. Messages are 98 bits long and we assume that it contains a checksum with 100% coverage, i. e. all faults are detected.

Nodes have a fixed, clock rate that lies between 1-ρ and 1+ρ, where ρ is 10^{-4} and 10^{-5} respectively. A propagation delay between each station of 1 m was used. With most realistic propagation delays and transmission speeds, each node must know the delay from each node and compensate for it. This compensation will not be exact, however, so the small delays used in our simulation correspond to the residual differences and contribute to the reading error.

The system model was simulated in Bones Designer, a tool for asynchronous simulation. The system was implemented using hierarchical block diagrams, see Fig. 8. A more detailed description of the simulation can be found in [9].

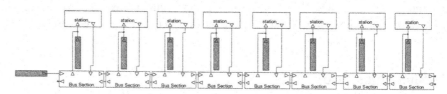

Fig. 8. Top level block diagram of the simulated system

7.2 Simulation Fault model

In the simulation, only transient faults on the bus are modeled. We do not include clocks with the wrong rate or nodes sending messages at arbitrary times. The reason is that we assume that nodes are fail silent and therefore detect their own failures.

We assume that transient faults appear as i) disturbances that affect the bus and ii) disturbances that affect message reception in the individual nodes. Type ii) faults are injected independently at each node.

The simplified view of the simulation model in Fig. 8 shows the type i) fault injector as a horizontal and the type ii) injectors as vertical dark boxes.

Disturbances of both types have a duration that is uniformly distributed between 0 and 1 timeslot length. The time between disturbances is exponentially distributed with mean values 10, 50 and 100 timeslot lengths for type i) and 10 times longer for each of the injectors of type ii). If the error intensity is higher than this, most systems cannot operate anyway and the quality of synchronization is of less interest.

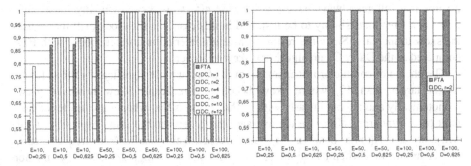

Fig. 9. Fraction of time the system is synchronized. Clock drift is $\rho=10^{-4}$ (left) and $\rho=10^{-5}$ (right)

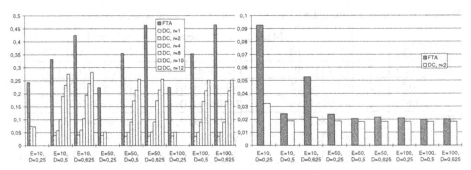

Fig. 10. Average skew [μs]. Clock drift is $\rho=10^{-4}$ (left) and $\rho=10^{-5}$ (right)

7.3 Results

The system was executed for a time corresponding to 10^5 timeslots. The simulation was iterated 10 times for each parameter setting. Ten different random seeds were used which resulted in ten independent tuples of each observed variable. The tuples consist of one value for each parameter setting. Two quantities were measured, the fraction of time the system was synchronized and the average skew. The former quantity is obtained by measuring the total time that 5 or more nodes were synchronized. Skew was measured as the time difference between the fastest and slowest clock. Skew measurements were only taken when the system was synchronized.

Three different values of D were simulated. The smallest, D=0.25, resulted in poor performance while there was no significant difference between D=0.5 and D=0.625. The reason for this is that clock skew frequently exceed the small D and therefore many clock readings were discarded.

The average time the system is synchronized (denoted uptime) is generally higher with the Daisy Chain Algorithm. The difference is large at high drift rate and high error intensity, while it is not statistically significant at lower drift rate and error intensity.

The average skew is higher with the FTA algorithm than for most parameter selections of the Daisy Chain Algorithm. This is because the theoretical formulas assume that failures always have a worst case effect on skew. In reality most faults cause clock readings simply to be lost, and in this case it is the clock drift that causes the skew to increase. Since the resynchronization interval is n times longer with FTA compared to the Daisy Chain algorithm, skew is higher.

The choice of parameter r does not seem to affect uptime significantly for as long it is not larger than 12, where skew becomes significant. Skew however grows monotonically and almost linearly with r. The reason is that when there are less than 1 fault per n synchronizations on the average, the 2r term in the skew expression (A.4) will dominate. Another observation is that average skew benefits from frequent losses of synchronization when r is high. This is because with a high r, the synchronization used during the reinitialization phase is better at reducing skew.

Table 5. Simulation results, uptime [%]. Clock drift, $\rho=10^{-5}$, 95% confidence interval.

			Mean time between faults [Timeslots]		
Alg.	D	r	10	50	100
DC	0.25	2	81.73±0.89	99.861±0.041	99.861±0.041
	0.5	2	89.97±0.22	99.969±0.01	99.969±0.01
	0.625	2	89.97±0.35	99.967±0.011	99.967±0.011
FTA	0.25		77.78±0.96	99.944±0.033	99.944±0.033
	0.5		89.82±0.32	99.963±0.013	99.963±0.013
	0.625		89.73±0.28	99.9643±0.0098	99.9643±0.0098

Table 6. Simulation results, uptime [%]. Clock drift, $\rho=10^{-4}$, 95% confidence interval.

			Mean time between faults [Timeslots]		
Alg.	D	r	10	50	100
DC	0.25	1	63.4±1.3	99.28±0.19	99.77±0.13
		2	79.0±1.1	99.749±0.052	99.948±0.018
	0.5	1	89.94±0.34	99.84±0.034	99.9696±0.0099
		2	89.84±0.3	99.823±0.033	99.9666±0.0093
		4	90.04±0.23	99.835±0.037	99.968±0.015
		8	90.11±0.26	99.844±0.027	99.9708±0.01
		10	90.00±0.23	99.835±0.039	99.9651±0.0089
		12	89.99±0.24	99.825±0.036	99.969±0.011
		30	77.4±1.3	94.7±1.2	95.7±1.1
	0.625	1	89.95±0.23	99.872±0.032	99.965±0.012
		2	89.86±0.4	99.829±0.043	99.968±0.011
		4	89.81±0.25	99.829±0.037	99.964±0.018
		8	90.1±0.19	99.845±0.029	99.9703±0.0098
		10	89.78±0.26	99.828±0.036	99.963±0.012
		12	89.96±0.34	99.825±0.048	99.968±0.014
		30	82.93±0.90	97.94±0.91	98.49±0.91
FTA	0.25		58.3±1.1	98.16±0.11	98.766±0.03
	0.5		87.14±0.20	99.059±0.047	99.336±0.016
	0.625		87.47±0.33	99.021±0.044	99.207±0.014

Table 7. Simulation results, clock skew [ns]. Clock drift, $\rho=10^{-5}$, 95% confidence interval

Alg.	D	r	Mean time between faults [Timeslots]		
			10	50	100
DC	0.25	2	32.37±0.52	18.362±0.015	18.362±0.015
	0.5	2	18.83±0.11	18.2325±0.0037	18.2325±0.0037
	0.625	2	21.63±0.13	18.2465±0.0063	18.2465±0.0063
FTA	0.25		92.7±4	21.09±0.54	21.09±0.54
	0.5		24.46±0.21	19.963±0.023	19.963±0.023
	0.625		52.8±1.5	20.25±0.13	20.25±0.13

Table 8. Simulation results, skew [ns]. Clock drift, $\rho=10^{-4}$, 95% confidence interval.

Alg.	D	r	Mean time between faults [Timeslots]		
			10	50	100
DC	0.25	1	73.8±1.7	38.22±0.73	36.52±0.68
		2	72.65±0.63	51.962±0.068	50.93±0.033
	0.5	1	39.73±0.12	35.903±0.024	35.418±0.013
		2	57.55±0.11	51.555±0.033	50.774±0.023
		4	100.78±0.12	90.533±0.042	89.075±0.035
		8	189.79±0.48	172.887±0.093	170.175±0.07
		10	233.02±0.46	214.14±0.11	210.825±0.082
		12	275.77±0.63	255.35±0.14	251.476±0.096
		30	500.3±1.2	596.39±0.94	608.9±1.6
	0.625	1	41.28±0.21	35.921±0.024	35.409±0.018
		2	59.92±0.22	51.6±0.034	50.76±0.023
		4	104.177±0.084	90.604±0.05	89.075±0.036
		8	194.8±0.3	173.028±0.091	170.182±0.071
		10	239.07±0.36	214.29±0.1	210.844±0.089
		12	282.84±0.37	255.57±0.14	251.51±0.098
		30	614.3±1.3	733.5±1.9	753.64±0.95
FTA	0.25		243.15±1	222.98±0.37	223.94±0.17
	0.5		332.24±0.9	354.9±0.5	352.81±0.51
	0.625		425±1.2	463.8±0.52	464.56±0.38

8. Summary and conclusions

In this paper we have described the fault tolerant Daisy Chain clock synchronization algorithm. The algorithm is intended for systems using a broadcast bus with a TDMA communication protocol. Its strength is that clocks are re-synchronized after each message transmission. A large clock drift will therefore be less critical than with traditional algorithms, where clock adjustment can only be performed every n[th] message in an n node system.

However, the effect of faults is potentially greater. With the Daisy Chain method only one value is available at a synchronization, and it is used unless it deviates more than the threshold value, D. With the averaging methods, faulty or extreme clock readings are completely removed from the calculation of the adjustment value. In small systems with many faults, the averaging methods therefore can guarantee a higher clock precision than the Daisy Chain method. For the same reason, the clock rate will be more constant with the averaging methods. However, the difference is small, since the allowed adjustments should be smaller than the required clock granularity.

Of the convergence synchronization methods, the Fault Tolerant Average algorithm has the best theoretical performance, and it was therefore compared to the Daisy Chain algorithm in a simulation study. The simulations showed that the Daisy Chain algorithm managed to keep the simulated 8-node system synchronized a larger proportion of time compared to the FTA algorithm. The reason is that the theoretical performance assumes that each fault behaves in a worst case manner. The probability for this is small, and in reality the contribution to skew from faults is unnecessarily pessimistic. In most cases, the transient fault causes the message to be corrupted and the clock reading is lost. In this case it is the time between clock adjustments that is most important for the clock skew.

The simulation results are of course affected by the communication protocol model used. With a more "clean" analysis modeling only the clocks and the exchange of clock values we could remove this dependency. However, the algorithm is intended for an environment similar to the simulated system and we believe it is in such context the algorithms should be evaluated.

References

1   B. Wittenmark, Nilsson, J, Törngren, M, "Timing problems in real-time control systems," presented at 1995 American Control Conference, Seattle, Washington, 1995.
2   H. Lonn and R. Snedsbol, "Synchronisation in safety-critical distributed control Systems," presented at IEEE International Conference on Algorithms and Architectures for Parallel Processing, ICA^{3}PP, Brisbane, Australia, 1995.
3   O. Babaglou and R. Drummond, "(Almost) No Cost Clock Synchronization," presented at 17th Fault-Tolerant Computing Symposium , FTCS-17, Pittsburgh, PA, USA, 1987.
4   L. Lamport, R. Shostac, and M. Pease, "The Byzantine Generals Problem," *ACM Transacctions on Programming Languages and Systems*, vol. 4, pp. 382-401, 1982.
5   H. Kopetz and W. Ochsenreiter, "Clock Synchronization in Distributed Real Time Svstems," *IEEE Trans. Computers.*, vol. 36, pp. 933-940, 1987.
6   L. Lamport and P. M. Melliar-Smith, "Synchronizing Clocks in the Presence of Faults," *Journal of the ACM*, vol. 32, pp. 52-78, 1985.
7   J. Lyndelius and N. Lynch, "A New Fault Tolerant Algorithm for Clock Synchronisation," *Information and Computation*, vol. 77, pp. 1-36, 1988.
8   H. Lonn, "Initial Synchronization of TDMA Communication in Distributed Real-Time Systems," In: 19th IEEE International Conference on Distributed Computing Systems (ICDCS'99), Austin, Texas, USA, 1999.
9   H. Lonn, "A Simulation Model of the DACAPO protocol," Department of Computer Engineering, Chalmers University, Gothenburg, Technical Report 99-1, 1999.
10 H. Lonn, "The Fault Tolerant Daisy Chain Clock Synchronization Algorithm," Department of Computer Engineering, Chalmers University, Gothenburg, Technical Report 99-2, 1999.

Appendix. Proof of correctness

Because the full proof of the algorithm requires more than ten pages, we only sketch the derivation of the skew bounds and refer the reader to [10] for the complete proof.

Non-Byzantine fault hypothesis, Theorem 1

One Successful synchronization. First, consider what happens when a clock ensemble is synchronized once with the Daisy Chain algorithm. If the synchronization is successful, clock skew is changed from $\delta^{(i)}$ to $\delta^{(i+1)}$ where

$$\delta^{(i+1)} \le (\delta^{(i)} + 2\rho R)(1 - \frac{1}{r}) + \frac{2\varepsilon}{r} \qquad (A.1)$$

$\delta^{(i)}$ is the clock skew immediately after synchronization i. By the time of the next synchronization, R time units later, skew has increased by $2\rho R$. At this time, all clocks receive a clock reading. Denote the clock value of the fastest and slowest clocks c_p and c_q respectively and that of the clock sending the clock reading c_s. Clock skew at the time of the synchronization is

$c_p - c_q = \delta^{(i)} + 2\rho R$

After the synchronization clock p has adjusted its time to $c_p' = c_p + (c_s - c_p \pm \varepsilon)/r$ and clock q to $c_q' = c_q + (c_s - c_q \pm \varepsilon)/r$, where ε is the clock reading error.

Skew after the adjustment is

$$c_p' - c_q' = c_p + (c_s - c_p \pm \varepsilon)/r - c_q + (c_s - c_q \pm \varepsilon)/r \le c_p - c_q - (c_p - c_q - 2\varepsilon)/r = (\delta^{(i)} + 2\rho R)(1 - \frac{1}{r}) + \frac{2\varepsilon}{r}$$

One Synchronization with faulty clock readings. If non-Byzantine faults occur during the synchronization, one or more of the clocks will not get the correct clock value. Since clock deviations up to D can be used for adjustments, in the worst case some nodes make a clock adjustment of $\pm D/r$, while others find the clock reading to be (just) above the threshold value and discard it. Clock skew increase from $\delta^{(i)} + 2\rho R$ just before the synchronization to

$$\delta^{(i+1)} \le \delta^{(i)} + 2\rho R + \frac{D}{r} \qquad (A.2)$$

Scenario with n consecutive synchronizations. Consider a scenario where at most f faults can occur during any n consecutive synchronizations. After such scenario, clock skew changes from $\delta^{(i)}$ to $\delta^{(i+n)}$ due to a faulty clock or clock reading where

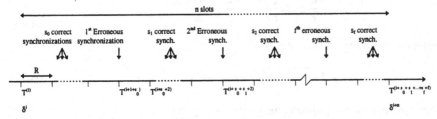

Fig. 11. Scenario with f faults during n timeslots

$$\delta^{(i+n)} = \left(\delta^{(i)} + 2\rho R\right)\left(1-\frac{1}{r}\right)^{n-f} + \left(\frac{D}{r}+2\rho R\right)\sum_{j=1}^{f}\left(1-\frac{1}{r}\right)^{\sum_{i=j}^{f} s_i} + \left(2\varepsilon+2\rho Rr\right)\left(1-\left(1-\frac{1}{r}\right)^{n-f}\right) - 2\rho R \qquad \text{(A.3)}$$

This can be seen if we consecutively apply (A.1) for the s_j correct synchronizations and (A.2) for the faulty synchronizations. (A.3) is maximized if $s_1,..s_f$ is 0 and therefore s_0 is n-f. The bound on $\delta^{(i+n)}$ is

$$\delta^{(i+n)} \le \left(\delta^{(i)} + 2\rho R\right)\left(1-\frac{1}{r}\right)^{n-f} + \left(\frac{D}{r}+2\rho R\right)\cdot f + \left(2\varepsilon+2\rho Rr\right)\left(1-\left(1-\frac{1}{r}\right)^{n-f}\right) - 2\rho R$$

Since all faulty synchronizations are found at the end of the n timeslot scenario (s_0=n-f), skew is maximum after the nth synchronization.

We find the smallest worst case skew, δ_{max}, that the algorithm can maintain by letting $\delta^{(i)}$+2ρR= δ_{max}, and require that $\delta^{(i+n)}$+2ρR $\le \delta_{max}$. The addition of 2ρR accounts for clock drift after the clock synchronization.

$$\delta^{(i+n)} \le \left(\delta_{max}+2\rho R\right)\left(1-\frac{1}{r}\right)^{n-f} + \left(\frac{D}{r}+2\rho R\right)\cdot f + \left(2\varepsilon+2\rho Rr\right)\left(1-\left(1-\frac{1}{r}\right)^{n-f}\right) - 2\rho R + 2\rho R \le \delta_{max} \Rightarrow$$

$$\delta_{max} \ge \rho R\left(2r + \frac{2f}{1-\left(1-\frac{1}{r}\right)^{n-f}}\right) + D\left(\frac{f/r}{1-\left(1-\frac{1}{r}\right)^{n-f}}\right) + 2\varepsilon \qquad \text{(A.4)}$$

We see that δ_{max} increases with D, and we therefore make it as small as possible. In order for all correct clock readings to be accepted,

D$\ge \delta_{max}$+ε

If we let D=δ_{max}+ε and solve for δ_{max} we get

$$\delta_{max} = \rho R\left(2r + \frac{4f}{1-f/r-\left(1-\frac{1}{r}\right)^{n-f}}\right) + \varepsilon\left(2 + \frac{3f/r}{1-f/r-\left(1-\frac{1}{r}\right)^{n-f}}\right) \qquad \text{(A.5)}$$

The denominators in (A.5) must be >0, i. e.

$$1-f/r-\left(1-\frac{1}{r}\right)^{n-f} > 0 \Rightarrow \left(1-\frac{1}{r}\right)^{n-f} < 1-f/r$$

Using Taylor expansion gives the inequality

$$1-\frac{a}{r} < \left(1-\frac{1}{r}\right)^{a} < 1-\frac{a}{r}+\frac{a(a-1)}{2r^2} \qquad \text{(A.6)}$$

Using the lower bound in (A.6) gives:

$$1-\frac{n-f}{r} < 1-f/r \Rightarrow n > 2f \qquad \text{(A.7)}$$

The upper bound in (A.6) combined with (A.7) gives

$$\left(1-\frac{1}{r}\right)^{n-f} \le \left(1-\frac{1}{r}\right)^{2f+1-f} = \left(1-\frac{1}{r}\right)^{f+1} < 1 - \frac{f+1}{r} + \frac{f(f+1)}{2r^2} < 1-f/r \Rightarrow r > \frac{f(f+1)}{2}$$

and we have shown the statements of Theorem 1.

Byzantine fault hypothesis, Theorem 1b

One Synchronization with faulty clock readings. If we assume Byzantine faults are present, clock skew changes from $\delta^{(i-k)}$ to $\delta^{(i)}$ due to a faulty clock or clock reading where

$$\delta^{(i)} \le \delta^{(i-1)} + 2\rho R + \frac{2D}{r} \tag{A.2b}$$

This is because in the worst case, the same clock reading is interpreted as +D in the fastest node and -D in the slowest node. Skew therefore increase by 2D/r apart from the increase due to clock drift.

If we replace the D in (A.2) by 2D and do the same analysis as for the non-Byzantine case, we arrive at the following bound on δ_{max}:

$$\delta_{max} = \rho R \left(2r + \frac{6m}{1 - 2m/r - \left(1-\frac{1}{r}\right)^{n-m}} \right) + \varepsilon \left(2 + \frac{6m/r}{1 - 2m/r - \left(1-\frac{1}{r}\right)^{n-m}} \right) \tag{A.8}$$

The denominators in (A.8) must be >0, i. e.

$$1 - 2m/r - \left(1-\frac{1}{r}\right)^{n-m} > 0 \Rightarrow \left(1-\frac{1}{r}\right)^{n-m} < 1 - 2m/r \tag{A.9}$$

If we combine the lower bound of the Taylor expansions in (A.6) with (A.9) we get the requirement:

$$1 - \frac{n-m}{r} < 1 - 2m/r \Rightarrow n > 3m \tag{A.10}$$

Combining (A.10) with (A.9) and the upper bound in (A.6) means that a sufficient (but not required) criterion is that

$$\left(1-\frac{1}{r}\right)^{n-m} < \left(1-\frac{1}{r}\right)^{3m+1-m} = \left(1-\frac{1}{r}\right)^{2m+1} < 1 - \frac{2m+1}{r} + \frac{2m(2m+1)}{2r^2} < 1 - 2m/r \Rightarrow r > m(2m+1) \tag{A.11}$$

Avoiding Malicious Byzantine Faults by a New Signature Generation Technique

Klaus Echtle

University of Essen, Fb 6 / Informatik, D-45117 Essen
http://www.cs.uni-essen.de/echtle
echtle@informatik.uni-essen.de

Abstract. Agreement problems like interactive consistency, reliable broadcast, group membership, etc. require a high protocol overhead when they must be solved under general (and thus hard) fault assumptions. Known signature methods contribute to more efficient solutions by protecting forwarded information from being altered undetectably. This paper presents a new signature generation technique, which prevents the occurrence of malicious Byzantine faults in the sender with very high probability. Hence, it is not necessary to exchange multicast messages among the receivers for an equality check. This advantage opens an extended design space of agreement protocols with fewer messages, fewer timeouts and thus lower execution times. The new unique signature generation algorithm (called *UniSig*) is based on alternately stepwise generation of coded sequence numbers and digital signatures. Different messages cannot obtain the same valid signature, because the steps to increment the coded sequence number are included in UniSig. Deviations from the program execution path are very likely to lead to detectably corrupted signatures. Hence, for each sequence number a valid signature can be generated only once.
Keywords. Malicious Byzantine Faults, Agreement Protocols, Digital Signatures for Fault Tolerance.

1   Introduction

Byzantine faults have been considered in the literature for a long time [22, 26]. Originally the term Byzantine was used to characterize two-face behaviour of a node towards a set of other nodes. Later it was used more generally to express arbitrary behaviour of faulty nodes [21]. There are two types of Byzantine faults when messages are multicast:

- *Partial distribution fault*: A faulty multicast sender may distribute a message to a subset of the receivers only.
- *Malicious Byzantine fault*: A faulty multicast sender may send different message contents to different receivers, where the messages cannot be identified as wrong by the receivers: The deviating copies have the same sequence number and appear consistent with respect to message format, code, check word, etc., see figure 1. Remark: If a message is not consistent, it is obviously wrong. This trivial case is <u>not</u> called a malicious Byzantine fault.

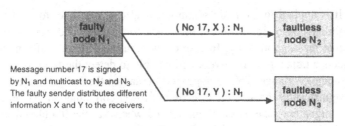

Fig. 1 Malicious Byzantine fault

Signature techniques cannot prevent partial distribution faults. However, they are a countermeasure against malicious Byzantine faults [19]. Therefore, we focus on this particular fault type here. We do not distinguish whether its cause lies in the sending node itself or in communication ressources it uses.

Do malicious Byzantine faults occur at all ? This question has sometimes been asked, because the assumption of these faults leads to costly protocols in terms of message number and execution time. Roughly speaking, the correct answer is: "Yes and no!" Extensive series of experiments have been conducted, where not even a single malicious Byzantine has been observed [18]. In these experiments single bus communication protected by check words is used. Due to the physical and the code-based support malicious Byzantine faults are extremely rare, as can be expected. However, in different communication scenarios an increased probability of such faults is realistic. If a multicast message leaves the sender through different (point-to-point or bus) links, the processor replicates the message. Then, it must be taken into account that the copies can be different. Even if the processor signs the message only once before replication (this should generally be preferred) there is the possibility of wrong distribution, because the processor has access to any message previously generated and stored somewhere in the memory. A faulty processor might mix up and/or alter these messages in an unpredictable way.

It is interesting to note, that even the assumption of partial distribution faults only may lead to a behaviour that cannot be distinguished from malicious Byzantine faults: In a system of, say, four nodes $N_1, ..., N_4$ a faulty multicast sender N_1 sends message X to nodes N_2 and N_3 only (see figure 2). Afterwards it sends a different message Y (with the same sequence number 17) to N_4 only. This appears as a malicious Byzantine fault to the receivers.

This paper introduces a particular signature algorithm which makes the occurrence of malicious Byzantine faults extremely unlikely, regardless of the communication

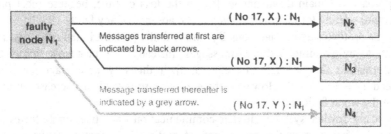

Fig. 2 Malicious Byzantine behaviour caused by partial distribution faults

structure. It is applied to the node sending a multicast message, forcing it with very high probability not to sign different messages consistently and pretend to the receivers the same message idendity. In case of distributing different information under a single sequence number the receivers will be able to detect the fault locally – without further message exchange. This new property enlarges the design space of agreement protocols significantly towards the direction of lower communication overhead.

The new signature scheme is recommended whenever the likelihood of malicious Byzantine faults (or quasi-malicious Byzantine faults according to figure 2) requires an appropriate countermeasure. This might not be the case in many direct bus structures. However, the scheme exhibits advantages in many communication systems (direct or non-direct point-to-point networks and others) where a sender reaches different receivers via different outgoing links.

After a brief survey of protocol techniques dealing with such faults in section 2 the exact fault model is defined in section 3. Then, the new signature scheme is presented with respect to the basic idea (section 4), concrete signature functions (section 5), their implementation (section 6) and a (re-) configuration scheme (section 7). Usage of the signature technique in agreement protocols is demonstrated in section 8. Finally, section 9 draws conclusions and discusses further research.

2 Known Countermeasures against Byzantine Faults

Msany types of the agreement problem such as provision of a consistency vector [14], atomic broadcast [4], distributed diagnosis [2, 6] and others have been successfully solved under the fault hypothesis of malicious Byzantine faults. All known solutions are based on a few fundamental protocol elements:

- Receivers exchange the information they have obtained [24]. This widely used approach guarantees to reveal the distribution of deviating message copies. As its main disadvantage it adds drastically to the message complexity. The number of messages highly depends on whether signatures are used or not.
- Receivers wait until the maximum transfer delay along the longest possible forwarding sequence among faulty nodes has elapsed [24]. If a validated deviating message copy is received up to this point in time, a malicious Byzantine fault is detected and the message discarded. Otherwise the message is delivered locally. Remark: If signatures are used, validation is performed on each received message. Without signatures, it is based on an appropriate majority decision. In this approach the main disadvantage lies in the loss of time, because most protocols require waiting for the timeout even in the absence of any fault.
- Some protocols avoid malicious Byzantine faults (at least in the main cases of execution) by avoiding multicast messages. Instead, these protocols simply forward information along a chain of nodes [5, 8]. In this way the average message overhead is kept very low. However, the execution time tends to increase, in particular for the worst fault case.
- In many smaller systems simpler communication links like single buses are preferred. They reduce the occurrence of malicious Byzantine faults by physical

methods and structures, as well as by coding techniques [23, 25]. This approach is very efficient. However, it causes performance problems in larger systems. More-over, if high dependability demands require redundant buses, the problem of malicious Byzantine faults returns and must be defeated by additional means.

The mentioned limitations cannot be overcome generally. Various formal proofs have shown that the limitations are hard [15]. Therefore, one has sometimes moved from the original agreement problems to similar problems, which require less overhead and are still appropriate for particular practical problems – approximate agreement [7] instead of exact agreement, for example.

A straight-forward approach to avoid the occurrence of Byzantine faults is simply the central generation of a unique signature in the multicast sender. This method works well up to a certain degree of dependability. Highest requirements, however, cannot be satisfied this way, because the sender usually stores a lot of messages inter-nally and can mix them up in an unpredictable way. This possibility decreases depen-dability and, moreover, makes dependability predictions difficult when complex soft-ware is applied. It may be necessary to validate many parts of the operating and com-munication system.

The new signature scheme presented in the next section can be seen as an exten-sion of the latter approach, where only code properties of signature generation and usual addressing properties of the hardware count. The proposed approach can be widely recommended, because it only costs execution of very few instructions and provides a clear dependability improvement.

3 System Model and Fault Model

We consider a distributed system consisting of n nodes $N_1, \dots, N_n$. The nodes are interconnected by any type of communication system, whether redundant or not. A collection of processes runs on the nodes. The processes interact by the exchange of messages.

Messages are transmitted in a context known by the communicating processes. The contexts of interest here are logical multicast channels used for the execution a fault-tolerant agreement protocols. Forming and management of contexts by membership protocols etc. is beyond the scope of this paper. The v communication contexts estab-lished dynamically during the lifetime of a system are denoted by $C_1, \dots, C_v$. Each context maintains its own variable to express its current sequence number.

The system is required to tolerate faults in up to F nodes. The fault tolerance method is not dealt with here. A particular method may restrict F with respect to n. The signature scheme does not impose restrictions on the number F of faulty nodes.

A faulty node may exhibit any wrong behaviour, including any local corruption and generation of any message at any time to be sent via any outgoing link – except breaking the signatures. Wrong messages must not be signed correctly. This is the usual assumption for signatured protocols, in principle. However, it has a modified meaning here, because the assumption is made for the internal process of signature generation within a node, not only for the sent information. In other words, we presuppose that an algorithm is unable to generate an undetectably wrong signature, even when executed on a faulty node. We do not make this restriction for just any algorithm. Instead, we design a very special algorithm (see next section) where the probability of undesired signing of wrong message copies is extremely low. Absolute guarantees can never be given for signatured protocols, of course.

In practice, our assumption means that we have to tolerate random changes of the state information, as are typically caused by technical faults, not by intentional attacks! A faulty processor may corrupt data, keep copies of data, mix up addresses, may arbitrarily branch to any subroutine, etc. However, we must presuppose that it does not create a signature-breaking algorithm just by chance when being faulty. This property requires a careful design of the signature generation algorithm (consisting of few instructions only), where the local key has to be protected by a special code. It is unlikely to be broken, because both the data and the algorithms necessary for breaking do not exist within the respective node. Traditional signatures are based on the same principle of keeping some information secret.

4 New Signature Scheme

The idea of the signature scheme preventing malicious Byzantine faults can be explained by the following (non-realistic) scenario: Each node N_i which must multicast a message at first interacts with some helper nodes N_{i1}, N_{i2} etc. arranged in a so-called cosign cycle (see figure 3). The message is sequentially co-signed by each node of the cycle. If different message contents with the same sequence number are submitted to the cycle each faultless node in the cycle refuses to cosign. Provided that the fault number F does not exceed the number of nodes in the cycle, this primitive approach prevents malicious Byzantine faults for any message idendity, which means: for any sequence number in a given communication context.

Obviously, this seems to be the most costly solution and is not practicable. A better approach uses only a single helper node in the cycle, a so-called cosign-partner N_{i1} (see figure 4). This scheme performs the same service provided that the partners do not collaborate [11, 13] if faulty: N_{i1} may omit to cosign, but not cosign a wrongly submitted message.

If we think further about cosign partners, it can be concluded that N_{i1} can be simplified. It need not provide the full functionality of a node. Its function of deciding

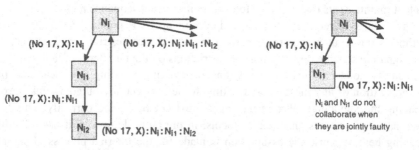

Fig. 3 Cosign cycle   **Fig. 4** Cosign partner

on a sequence number and cosigning if necessary can be performed by a very simple device. The new idea is to implement N_{i1} efficiently just by a piece of software within N_i, and prevent collaboration by a special signature scheme. It must ensure that for each *sequence number* s at most one signature can be generated. The signature generation algorithm is called Unique Signature Algorithm, *UniSig* for short.

Usual signature functions are not appropriate for this purpose. A faulty node N_i might compose a message from any sequence number s and information X, sign and send it. Then it uses s again by attaching it to a different information Y, signing and sending the message. Thus a malicious Byzantine fault has occurred with the non-identical messages (s, X):N_i and (s, Y):N_i. Receivers which obtain only one of these messages cannot detect the fault.

This problem is avoided by UniSig, which is based on the following principles:

- A multicast sender N_i protects the sequence number s for a context C_j by a *check word* c. There is a function ω which maps s to c. However, node N_i does not know this function. This prevents N_i from generating an appropriate check word for an illegal sequence number.

- Node N_i only knows the functions to "increment" s and c consistently. For the sequence number s the function is simply $\alpha(s) = s + 1$. For the check word the function $\beta(c)$ is more complicated, depending on ω. Function β is completely independent from the explicit sequence number s.

- In node N_i a boolean check function $\gamma(s, c)$ is implemented to test whether $\omega(s) = c$. In case of detected inconsistency, both s and c are destroyed. A faulty node should be unable to "conclude" ω from β or γ and apply ω to any number in order to obtain a consistent c for a wrong sequence number.

- Furthermore, node N_i knows a signature function $\sigma(s, c, m)$ which generates a signature for sequence number s, the corresponding check word c, and the message contents m.

- Functions β and σ are not directly implemented in node N_i. They are executed alternately in steps $\beta'(c)$, $\sigma'(s, c, m)$, $\beta''(c)$, $\sigma''(s, c, m, t)$, etc. (see figure 5). This guarantees that signature generation depends on the stepwise progress made in incrementing the check word c. Hence, valid signatures cannot be generated without incrementing c. Once a signature generation has been started the old pair (s, c) is no longer available.

- Finally, all nodes own a Boolean function $\tau(s^*, m^*, t^*)$ to check the correctness of a signature t^* they receive in a message with sequence number s^* and contents m^*.

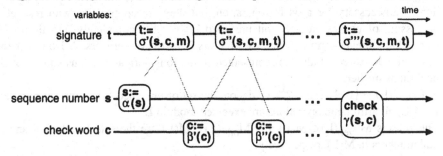

Fig. 5 Signature generation scheme

Remark 1: Functions β, γ, σ and τ depend on the node N_i and on the context C_j they are used in. However, instead of writing $\beta_{ij}(c)$, $\gamma_{ij}(c)$, $\sigma_{ij}(c)$ and $\tau_{ij}(s, m, t)$ we use the simplified notations $\beta(c)$, $\gamma(c)$, $\sigma(c)$ and $\tau(s, m, t)$, because we focus on a single sender node and a single context to explain the signature scheme. Concrete functions are provided in section 5.

Remark 2: An asterisk is used to distinguish message elements before (without *) and after the transfer (with *). In the absence of communication faults $s* = s$, $t* = t$ and $m* = m$ hold.

5 UniSig Signature Generation Functions

The main challenge of designing UniSig is the definition of appropriate functions ω, α, β, γ, σ and τ. They must follow the principles specified in section 4, and, moreover, enable very efficient implementations. Whenever a message has to be sent UniSig is executed. It should not add significantly to the time consumption of the communication software. Consequently, only up to some tens of instructions are acceptable for UniSig. There is no need for high computational overhead, because the signatures need not be crytographically strong. Intelligent attacks are not assumed. The signatures need only reveal technical faults, which cause more or less random effects.

Appropriate functions are based on combined multiplication and addition schemes. All calculations are done in modulo arithmetics, because the inverse functions are much more complex compared to arithmetics in an infinite space. Attention must be payed to the inverse functions, because they support breaking of the signatures. It was decided not to calculate modulo a prime number for efficiency reasons. Arithmetics modulo 2^L for a sufficiently high integer L is more appropriate because the modulo operation means simply an *and*-operation with a mask word.

The functions defined next are all based on L = 60. This means they work in unsigned 60 bit integer arithmetic. The keys, parameters, and the final signature are also 60 bit. This could appear as unnecessarily long. However, memory capacity and communication speed are not that critical nowadays. 60 bits do not cause noticable overhead. On the other side, 60 bits provide a very good protection against arbitrary "guesses" of keys or signatures. Probabilities in the range of 2^{-60} are negligible. A number format of 60 bits is best supported by processors which allow for long integers of 64 bits, as most commonly used processors do (sometimes several instructions are necessary for a 64 bit operation, but they are cooperative with respect to processing of carries etc.). 60 bit unsigned integer fits completely into the 64 bit signed long integer format, which uses 63 bits for positive numbers. A 1-bit overflow of 60 bit additions can also be represented in the long format and thus simplifies the operations further.

Let $M(L) = \{0, 1, 2, \ldots, 2^L-1\}$ denote the set of unsigned L-bits integer numbers. In M(L) all arithmetic operations are executed modulo L.

The subsets $M_{even}(L) \subset M(L)$ and $M_{odd}(L) \subset M(L)$ are the sets of all even and all odd numbers in M(L), respectively.

The decision for unsigned 60 bit instead of signed 64 bit integers is also a primitive yet effective contribution to the resilience of the signature. It can be assumed that inverse functions are not likely to be implemented in particularly 60 bits, if at all existing in any part of the software. Nevertheless, we do not build the resiliency of the signature on this observation. We just take it as an extra improvement beyond the other resilience properties. There is a further extra: Multiplicative inverses are not guaranteed to exist when calculations are executed modulo 2^L, because 2^L is not a prime for $L > 1$. Consequently, the well-known Euklid's algorithm to find the multi-plicative inverse does not work. Instead, a more complex algorithm is necessary to find either the inverse or its non-existence for an unsigned 60 bit number. This algo-rithm is more than just an extension of Euklid's algorithm and thus unlikely to exist somewhere in a node.

The functions are based on the following data:

- For efficiency reasons the signature function is not applied directly to the whole information m of a message. Instead a usual check word $\chi(m)$ is formed first. Then, signature generation is applied to $\chi(m)$. The function $\chi(m)$ can be a known hash function like CRC, preferably a 60 bit CRC or at least a 32 bit CRC.
- Signature generation uses the following parameters the respective node keeps <u>secret</u>:

  a   *signature generation key* chosen from $M_{odd}(60)$,

  p   parameter from $M_{odd}(60)$,

  q   parameter from $M_{even}(60)$,

  r   chosen such that $(p + q) \cdot r = 1$ in $M(60)$.

  The sum $p + q$ is odd. Consequently the multiplicative inverse r exists in $M(60)$. The numbers a, p and q should be sequences of 60 bits, which appear arbitrarily chosen. They need not be prime.

- Check functions use the following <u>public</u> parameters:

  b   *signature check key* chosen from $M_{odd}(60)$. Note that b is independent from a !

  d   chosen such that $d = (p + q) \cdot a \cdot b$ in $M(60)$.

  The reason behind this formula will become clear when the respective functions σ and τ are explained.

For all of the functions α, β, γ, σ and τ we must carefully distinguish the specification from the implementation. The first is a mathematical formula to define the function. The latter is the way to describe how a function value is calculated. The implemen-

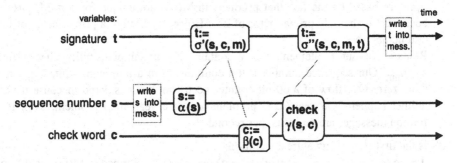

Fig. 6 Functions used in UniSig

tation may deviate from the specification formula in order to ensure a good protection against signature breaking fault effects. As will be explained later an implementation should never generate the values of the three expressions $p+q$, $(p+q) \cdot a$, and $\chi(m) \cdot (p+q)$.

Now we define the functions to execute alternately the steps of sequence number incrementation and signature generation. In principle any number of steps can be taken. However, it turned out, that even very small numbers of steps are sufficient. We take only one for β (hence $\beta = \beta'$) and two for σ (see figure 6). s is written to the message before, t after signature generation. Function

ω maps a sequence number to a check word: $c := \omega(s) := (p + q) \cdot a \cdot s$,   formed in $M(60)$. Note that the definition of the sequence number's check word uses the signature generation key a. Function ω is not implemented. It just expresses the pre- and post-conditions of a consistent increment of both s and c.

α increments the sequence number: $s_{new} := \alpha(s) := s + 1$,   formed in $M(60)$. The implementation calculates accordingly: **s := s + 1**.

β increments the check word of the sequence number:
$c_{new} := \beta(c) := (p + q) \cdot (c \cdot r + a)$,   formed in $M(60)$. The implementation avoids $p + q$ as an intermediate result by calculating the following two assignments sequentially: **c := c · r + a;   c := c · q + p · c**.
The implemented function β satisfies the specified function β because it delivers
$(c \cdot r + a) \cdot q + p \cdot (c \cdot r + a) \; = \; (p + q) \cdot (c \cdot r + a)$.
β satisfies the postcondition that (s_{new}, c_{new}) are consistent provided that the pre-condition of consistent (s, c) is satisfied. The proof is based on the consistency definition ω: Consistency of (s, c) means $c = (p + q) \cdot a \cdot s$. We can substitute c in the formula expressing the function value
$\beta(c) \; = \; (p + q) \cdot ((p + q) \cdot a \cdot s \cdot r + a) \; = \; (p + q) \cdot (1 \cdot a \cdot s + a) \; = \; (p + q) \cdot a \cdot (s + 1)$.
Hence, the postcondition holds. Remark: The equation above uses $(p + q) \cdot r = 1$.

γ checks whether s and c are consistent: $\gamma(s, c) := (c = (p + q) \cdot a \cdot s)$,   formed in $M(60)$. The function value is boolean. The implementation avoids critical inter-mediate results by calculating   **c · b = s · d**.   This boolean value satisfies the specification of γ, because from $d = (p + q) \cdot a \cdot b$ we conclude
$c \cdot b = s \cdot d \; \Leftrightarrow \; c \cdot b = s \cdot (p + q) \cdot a \cdot b \; \Leftrightarrow \; c = (p + q) \cdot a \cdot s \; \Leftrightarrow \; \gamma(s, c)$.
The above implications from right to left are obvious, the implications from left to right are based on the fact that products in $M(60)$ are unique for $b \in M_{odd}(60)$, because 2 is the only prime factor of 2^{60}. However, 2 is not a prime factor of the odd number b.
Remark: In our implementation γ contains additional plausibility checks like $s \geq s_{min}$. Our sequence number starts counting from a minimum value s_{min}, not from zero. Overflow of a 60-bit counter needs not be considered, because it will neither happen as a year 2000 problem nor as a year 3000 problem, even if a million messages are multicast per second.

σ' is the first step of signature generation:
    $t := \sigma'(s, c, m) \; = \; 2^{60} - \chi(m) \cdot (p + q) \cdot a \cdot (s - 1) \cdot s$,   formed in $M(60)$, is the so-

called *pre-signature*. It is implemented by $\mathtt{t := -x \cdot c \cdot s}$, where x is the variable containing the previously calculated hash function $\chi(m)$ of the message (CRC for example). The result of the unary minus is interpreted unsignedly in M(60). The equivalence between specification and implementation is obvious, when we recall that σ' is executed between incrementing the sequence number s and incrementing the check word c. At this point in time c is still consistent to the old sequence number, which is $s - 1$ with respect to the new value in variable s. Hence, $c = (p + q) \cdot a \cdot (s - 1)$.

σ'' is the second step of signature generation:

$t_{new} := \sigma'(s, c, m, t) = \chi(m) \cdot (p + q) \cdot a \cdot s$, formed in M(60). If we omit parameter t, we obtain the global signature specification: $\sigma(s, c, m) = \chi(m) \cdot (p + q) \cdot a \cdot s$. In the specification of σ'' parameter t is only written to indicate that its implementation accesses the pre-signature t. The implementation of σ'' calculates $\mathtt{t := t + x \cdot c \cdot s}$. Again, x is the variable containing the previously calculated $\chi(m)$. The verification of the implementation must take into account that, after calculation of the pre-signature, β has been applied to increment check word c. Then, $c = (p + q) \cdot a \cdot s$ holds. Consequently, the implementation of σ'' provides in M(60):

$$t + x \cdot c \cdot s = 2^{60} - \chi(m) \cdot (p + q) \cdot a \cdot (s - 1) \cdot s + \chi(m) \cdot (p + q) \cdot a \cdot s \cdot s =$$
$$0 + \chi(m) \cdot (p + q) \cdot a \cdot (-s \cdot s + s + s \cdot s) = \chi(m) \cdot (p + q) \cdot a \cdot s = \sigma(s, c, m).$$

τ is the boolean signature check function:

$\tau(s^*, m^*, t^*) := ((s^* + 1) \cdot \chi(m^*) \cdot d = t^* \cdot b)$. The implementation calculates accordingly $\mathtt{(s^* + 1) \cdot \chi(m^*) \cdot d = t^* \cdot b}$ in M(60).

In contrast to the other functions mentioned above, τ is not executed in node N_i which generates the signature. Instead, each receiver of a multicast message applies it to the message it receives. The received message consists of sequence number s^*, contents m^* and signature t^*. Note that the sequence number has been written to the message by the sender before incrementing it. Hence $s^* + 1$ corresponds to the new sequence number s in the sender. Function τ delivers true for a correctly signed message, because from the three substitutions

$d = (p + q) \cdot a \cdot b$, $t^* = \chi(m^*) \cdot (p + q) \cdot a \cdot s$, and $s^* + 1 = s$ in the signature check equality $(s^* + 1) \cdot \chi(m^*) \cdot d = t^* \cdot b$, we obtain the generally true statement $s \cdot \chi(m^*) \cdot (p + q) \cdot a \cdot b = \chi(m^*) \cdot (p + q) \cdot a \cdot s \cdot b$.

Usually a receiver applies further tests besides τ. Its communication software checks whether s^* is the successor of the sequence number received immediately before. It also checks whether $\chi(m^*)$ and m^* are consistent.

The mathematical relationships between the functions are clear from the definitions and proofs above. Now, the design decisions behind these functions, taken to make them resilient to malicious Byzantine faults, are outlined.

The values delivered by the implementations should never pass check τ, if the sequence number of a message has been used for a different message before. We cannot prevent a sender node N_i from reusing an old sequence number, because it can be obtained by just decrementing a newer sequence number or by reading it from a sent message it still keeps in a buffer. However, we prevent generation of a signature

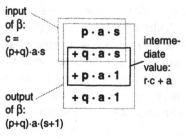

input
of β:
c =
(p+q)·a·s

p · a · s

+ q · a · s

+ p · a · 1

+ q · a · 1

interme-
diate
value:
r·c + a

output
of β:
(p+q)·a·(s+1)

c

b · (p + q) · a · s

d

Fig. 7 Implementation of β   **Fig. 8** Implementation of γ

consistent to a wrong sequence number. Undetectably wrong signatures are made very unlikely by requiring several arithmetic operations for their generation.

According to functions ω and σ, the check word and the signature are multiples of the sequence number. However, the respective factors are not used directly. They are composed of two factors $(p+q)$ and a, one of which is subdivided further into two terms p and q of a sum. This enables mathematical operations to generate check word $c = (p + q) \cdot a \cdot (s + 1)$ for a successor sequence number $s + 1$, and signature $s = \chi(m) \cdot (p + q) \cdot a \cdot s$ without generating parts of the product explicitly. As was mentioned earlier in this section we avoid generating the values of expressions like $p + q$, $(p + q) \cdot a$ or $\chi(m) \cdot (p + q)$. Multiplication of these values by a wrong sequence number s or by $\chi(m)$ of a wrong message m would cause dangerous results: undetectably wrong check words or signatures !

The implementations find ways to avoid dangerous values. β starts with a check word $c = (p + q) \cdot a \cdot s$ and must generate $c_{new} = (p + q) \cdot a \cdot (s + 1)$ thereof. Instead of simply adding $(p + q) \cdot a$, the implementation of β first removes $(p + q)$ by multiplication with its inverse r. Then, separate multiplications with p and q, respectively, and a final addition provide the result, as is depicted in figure 7.

The check γ does not factorize the check word or multiply the sequence number with a dangerous factor. Instead both s and c are multiplied with further factors which must lead to the same product on both sides of the equality formula $b \cdot c = d \cdot s$ (see figure 8).

σ' calculates a pre-signature, which containes a term $-\chi(m) \cdot (p + q) \cdot a \cdot s \cdot s$ of a sum, whereas σ" calculates an expression containing a term $X(m) \cdot (p + q) \cdot a \cdot s \cdot s$ of a sum. The terms ensure that the two parts are not dangerous multiples of either $\chi(m)$ or s. The final addition removes the terms.

In the execution sequence α, σ', β, γ, σ", any deviation from correct intermediate results is very unlikely to be "repaired" by succeeding operations, even when fault-affected. In the whole chain operations do neither repeat nor compensate previous operations, nor are their results independent from any previous result.

6   Implementation and Evaluation

The implementation of functions α, σ', β, γ, σ'' is rather simple. The complete program is shown below in an assembler-like style. Each line stands for a macro providing a single 60 bit arithmetic operation each. A 60 bit addition macro typically consists of two instructions, a long addition as well as an and-operation with a 60 bit mask. If a processor supports unsigned arithmetics in its instruction set, a 60 bit multiplication is implemented accordingly. Otherwise, four 32 bit multiplications and appropriate additions of carries are necessary.

The program has to be executed in a sender node whenever it multicasts a message. Therefore, low execution time counts. The program typically executes much faster than the rest of the communication software, because it is rather short and free of loops. If we assume two instructions for an arithmetic macro and a single instruction for transfers and comparisons, then only 31 instructions have to be executed per run.

The more additional checks we include in γ the more additional instructions are required. Additional checks contribute to a further increase in detection coverage. One can think of range checks of the sequence number or of testing the non-corrupted presence of program code and constant data, using signatures over the respective memory contents (checking it requires a loop).

We implemented all functions defined in section 5 in assembly language for a spe-

```
UniSig Data:
a, b, d, p, q, r  -- parameters of UniSig.
R1, R2            -- register variables for temporary intermediate
results.
s, c              -- sequence number s and its check word c.
x                 -- check character of message m.
t                 -- signature to be formed for message m.

UniSig Program:
          transfer s  → m[...]  -- copy old sequence number
                               -- into message.

alpha:    add   s, 1  → s       -- increment sequence number.

sigma':   mult  x, c  → R1      -- calculate pre-signature - x · c · s
          mult  rR, s → R1
          negative R1 → t

beta:     mult  c, R  → c       -- new check word c := c · r + a
          add   c, a  → c
          mult  p, c  → R1      --                    c := c · q + p · c
          mult  c, q  → c
          add   c, R1 → c

gamma:    mult  c, b  → R1      -- check consistency of s and c:
          mult  s, d  → R2
          exit if R1 • R2       -- exit if c · b • s · d.
          .........             -- further checks.

sigma'':  mult  x, c  → R1      -- calc. final signature t + x · c · s
          mult  R1, s → R1      --     (here, t is the pre-signature)
          add   t, R1 → m[...]  -- write signature into message.
          transfer 0  → t       -- destroy signature variable.
```

cial simulated processor, where we could vary the word length L. The following parameters have been used finally: a = 933778034205795679, b = 2172103073000046589, d = 548239610506104991, p = 146778819810877069, q = 197140581391336328, r = 664930812394331453, L = 60. Many other sets of parameters have also been generated by a special algorithm for that purpose.

The simulator allows for fault injection into registers both temporarily and permanently, similar to [17, 20]. The first means flipping a bit after exactly one randomly chosen instruction. The latter means setting a sepcified bit to a constant value of either zero or one after each instruction. This is a simple standard fault injection technique.

After a run under fault injection, we test whether a malicious Byzantine fault has occurred. This undesired event happens if a message is generated with both,

- a wrong sequence number s or a wrong message contents m,
- and a signature t consistent to s and m.

Wrong s and t are obtained from executing the program above under fault injection. Wrong m are obtained from copying up to sixteen words to a message under fault injection (the longer a message is the less critical it is).

Here, fault injection is not appropriate to quantify the portion of undetectable malicious Byzantine faults. The probability of an undetectable malicious Byzantine fault should be that low that not even a single one is observed during millions of runs. However, if we would have observed such fault we revealed a weakness in our scheme, or at least in its implementation. In other words, fault injection serves more for testing than for quantification. Testing must not be neglected, because formal analysis cannot quantify the resilience of the scheme. Recall that we assumed faults in the processor when generating the signature, not only faults during message transfer along the communication system. This is a severe difference. Faults during the transfer are much simpler to deal with mathematically because faultless transfer is characterized by an idendity function mapping sent data to received data. Computation, however, means complicated mapping of values even in the absence of faults. The extremely large space for possible changes in the presence of faults normally induces strong restrictions to the potential of mathematical analysis. Roughly speaking, it is either not accurate or not tractable. Consequently, we need tests.

Permanent faults of types stuck-at-0 and stuck-at-1 have been injected to each bit of the 14 variables a, b, d, p, q, r, R1, R2, s, c, x, t, m1 or PC. Variable m1 is the (randomly chosen) first 32 bit word of the message contents m. PC is the 32 bit program counter. Its faults cause control flow errors. A total of $2 \cdot (12 \cdot 60 + 2 \cdot 32) = 1568$ experimental runs with permanent faults have been executed. Furthermore, temporary faults have been injected to 4000 runs. Temporary faults are flips of a randomly chosen bit in one of the variables a, b, d, p, q, r, R1, R2, s, c, x, t, m1 or PC after a randomly chosen instruction. As was expected, an undetectable malicious Byzantine fault did not occur in any of the runs under fault injection.

7 Configuration and Reconfiguration of Signature Generators

The principles from section 4 guarantee with high probability that a faulty processor can only generate a unique signature for any sequence number. However, further countermeasures are necessary to prevent replication and misuse of UniSig. Most operating systems allow for dynamic process duplication with respect to both program and data. Hence, a faulty node may generate replicates of UniSig and generate two or more signatures for a sequence number. Additional principles on UniSig realization are necessary:

- UniSig can run in any part of the memory, but uses absolute addresses only.
- After the local operating system of node N_i has allocated memory for UniSig, the UniSig program is formed by other nodes, transferred to N_i and loaded to memory. It is essential that other nodes check, whether node N_i does not own more than one UniSig per communication context C_j.

These principles lead to the following protocol, which is only required for the establishment of a new context, not during normal operation (see figure 9): N_i multicasts the address range where it wants to execute UniSig for a new context. A sufficient number of nodes different from N_i check whether there have not been previous requests for UniSig-allocation for the context. The distributed management of contexts does not mean high overhead since nodes must know anyway the communication contexts they are involved in. If the checks are passed, all the nodes generate UniSig with absolute addressing for the respective address range in N_i. Then, they execute an agreement protocol to tolerate wrong decisions of faulty nodes. Finally, the UniSig programs are transferred to N_i, which applies majority voting on the incoming UniSigs and loads a majority UniSig to the particular address range.

After a fault in N_i has been detected, the respective context is destroyed in all nodes using it. An efficient way of context recovery does not exist. Instead a new context with a new sequence number is established by the (re-) configuration protocol.

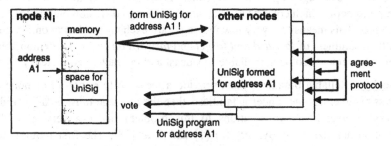

Fig. 9 (Re-) Configuration protocol

8 Exploitation in the Design of Agreement Protocols

Avoiding malicious Byzanine faults by the new signature technique enables the design of new agreement protocols with less overhead. Protocol design is simplified as follows: Once a receiver has obtained a multicast message and validated its signature, it can "conclude" that a deviating replica (same context, same sequence number, consistent signature) does not exists anywhere in the system. Other receivers of the respective message receive either an identical copy or no copy at all. Equality of the copies received at different locations needs not be checked. Hence, extra messages are not necessary for that purpose.

This effect of the UniSig signature scheme enables two novel protocol elements, which can be used as building blocks of a complete agreement protocol:

- Protocol element: *Forward and forget*. After a message has been multicast by sender N_i, each receiver N_j forwards the message to all respective other receivers. In this way a faultless receiver makes sure that all other receivers have obtained the message as well. Node N_j needs not wait until it obtains the message from other receivers, because decisions on equality of copies are superfluous. Hence, after forwarding the received message, N_j can immediately deliver it locally and forget it globally. Message copies received later on must be identified as outdated (sequence number déjà vu) and ignored. Node N_j needs not wait for messages forwarded from other nodes to itself. Consequently, there is no need for a timeout! The main advantage of *forward and forget* is the potential to construct entirely timeout-free special types of agreement protocols. Timeouts always cause a high delay because they are determined with respect to the worst-case execution time (or message delay), which typically exceeds the normal durations by orders of magnitude. Protocols can become much faster when being free of timeouts.

- Protocol element: *Forward on request*. The sender simply diffuses the multicast message to all receivers. In the absence of faults not any further message is required. This solution presupposes that receivers know the point in time when to expect a multicast message. Then, each faultless receiver can send a *request message* to ask the sender and/or other receivers for the message after its timeout has expired. Depending on the chosen compromise between time consumption and message overhead, different nodes can be asked either sequentially or in parallel. The main advantage of *forward on request* is the possibility to construct an agreement protocol, which consists of pure simple message diffusion only in the absence of faults. This means that very few messages are exchanged (during only 1 phase).

Now, the usefulness of *forward and forget* and *forward on request* is demonstrated by two new agreement protocols: reliable broadcast and interactive consistency.

Protocol 1: Reliable broadcast must provide a message to either all or none of the faultless receivers. If the sender is faultless, then the message must be delivered to all faultless receivers. Known solutions to this problem under a very general fault assumption are *streets of Byzantinum* [1] and *Veto* [13]. The first requires always timeouts because it is strictly phase-oriented. The latter is timeout-free in the faultless case, but requires timeouts in the presence of faults. Now, we add the new *forward and forget* solution without any timeout.

In this protocol the sender N_i applies UniSig and distributes the message to all receivers N_{j1}, N_{j2}, etc. (see figure 10). Each receiver first checks whether the sequence number, the signature, and the other contents in the received message are consistent, whether the sequence number fits to the respective context, and whether the sequence number appears for the first time. If all these examinations are passed,

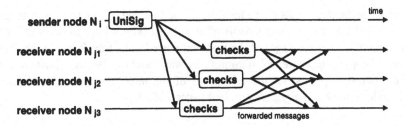

Fig. 10 Reliable broadcast protocol according to the *forward and forget* principle

the message is locally delivered and immediately forwarded to all other receivers. Cosigning the forwarded messages is not necessary.

After (faulty or faultless) sender node N_i has reached at least one faultless receiver, forwarding of the unique message (deviating replicas cannot exist due to UniSig) guarantees that all faultless receivers will obtain the message. This is sufficient for reliable broadcast.

Protocol 2: Interactive consistency must provide identical copies of a so-called consistency vector [22] to all faultless nodes. If a sender is faultless, then its sent value must appear in the respective element of the consistency vector. Well-known solutions to this problem are *pruned oral messagse* POM [16], *signed messages* SM [24], and many others. Now we modify SM by making the message transfer in the second phase optional according to *forward on request*. In the following we only consider the part of the protocol which processes the value of a single sender node.

In this protocol the sender N_i applies UniSig to a message containing N_i's value. Then the message is distributed to all receivers (see figure 11). Each receiver N_j applies the same checks as in the reliable broadcast protocol explained before (see figure 10). If the checks are not passed or the message does not arrive until timeout, then N_j sends a request message to the other receivers. On receipt of the request these receivers cosign and forward their replica of the message to N_j (provided they have received a replica of the message at all). Then, the known scheme of SM is applied: In the next phase N_j only accepts messages with at least two signatures. In the phase thereafter three signatures are required, etc.

The new variant of SM requires an extra phase for the request messages. However, in the faultless case (which hopefully happens in far more than 99% of the protocol executions) most of the messages are saved. If SM is executed among n nodes in the absence of faults, messages are only exchanged in the first two phases. Processing of

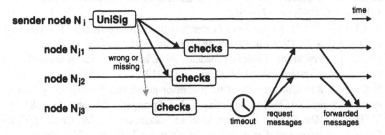

Fig. 11 Interactive consistency protocol according to the *forward on request* principle

a single sender's value costs n –1 messages in the first and $(n-1) \cdot (n-2)$ messages in the second. The new variant with *forward on request* skips all messages of the second phase. Only the n – 1 messages of the first phase need to be transferred in the absence of faults. This is the theoretical minimum as was shown in [9]. An illustration with concrete numbers points out the advantage of the new protocol variant: For, say, n = 10 nodes only 9 messages are required instead of 81.

9 Conclusion

UniSig executes alternately the steps for generating both a coded sequence number and a signature. The steps apply special functions, which are very likely to deliver a non-consistent signature to a multiply used sequence number. This enables the receiver to detect locally the corruption of the message. Malicious Byzantine faults cannot occur among consistently signed messages. Hence, UniSig is an effective countermeasure against malicious Byzantine faults. It is also very efficient, since only few instructions have to be executed – much less than many parts of conventional communication software.

UniSig has been tested by a usual fault injector. Not any malicious Byzantine fault occurred. We expect that UniSig makes these faults that extremely rare that it is hopeless to wait for such fault in reasonable time. This consideration triggered the development of a new fault injection technique, which is subject to current research. It primarily aims at generation of non-covered faults rather than realistic faults. This goal has already been applied successfully to the communication level [3, 10, 12]. Now it is applied to the processor level, where faults are generated in a completely different way (modification of state information instead of sending particular messages).

A further branch of current research is the design of further agreement protocols using the *forward and forget* and *forward on request* principles.

References

1 Ö. Babaoglu, R. Drummond: Streets of Byzantium: network architectures for fast reliable broadcast; IEEE Trans. on Software Eng., vol. SE-11, no. 6, 1985, pp. 546 – 554.

2 Y. Chen, W. Bücken, K. Echtle: Efficient algorithms for system diagnosis with both processor and comparator faults; IEEE Transactions on Parallel and Distributed Systems, vol. 4, no. 4, 1993, pp. 371 – 381.

3 Y. Chen, K. Echtle: Evaluation of deterministic fault injection for fault-tolerant protocol testing; FTCS-21, Digest of Papers, IEEE Press, 1991, pp. 418 – 425.

4 F. Cristian: Synchronous atomic broadcast for redundant broadcast channels; The Journal of Real-Time Systems, vol. 2, 1990, pp. 195 – 212.

5 F. Cristian: Reaching agreement on processor-group membership in synchronous distributed systems; Distributed Computing, vol. 4, Springer, 1991, pp. 175 – 187.

6 M. Dal Cin: On distributed system-level self-diagnosis; 4th Int. Conf. on Fault-Tolerant Computing, Informatik-Fachberichte 214, Springer, 1989, pp. 186 – 196.

7 D. Dolev, N. Lynch, S. Pinter, E. Stark, W. Weihl: Reaching approximate agreement in the presence of faults; 3rd Symp. on Reliability in Distributed Software and Database Systems, Conf. Proc., IEEE Press, 1983, pp. 145 – 154.

8 K. Echtle: Fault masking and sequence agreement by a voting protocol with low message number; 6th Symp. Reliability in Distributed Software and Database Systems, Conf. Proc., IEEE Press, 1987, pp. 149 – 160.

9 K. Echtle: Distance agreement protocols; FTCS-19, Digest of Papers, IEEE Press, 1989, pp. 191 – 198.

10 K. Echtle, M. Leu: The EFA fault injector for fault-tolerant distributed system testing; Fault-Tolerant Parallel and Distributed Syst., Conf. Proc., IEEE Press, 1992, pp. 28 – 35.

11 K. Echtle, M. Leu: Fault-detecting network membership protocols for unknown topologies; 4th Int. Working Conf. on Dependable Computing for Critical Applications DCCA-4, Conf. Proc., Springer, 1994, pp. 69 – 90.

12 K. Echtle, M. Leu: Test of fault-tolerant distributed systems by fault injection; Fault-Tolerant Parallel and Distributed Systems, IEEE Press, 1995, pp. 244 – 251.

13 K. Echtle, A. Masum: A multiple bus broadcast protocol resilient to non-cooperative Byzantine faults; FTCS-26, Digest of Papers, IEEE Press, 1996, pp. 158 – 167.

14 P. Ezhilchelvan: Early stopping algorithms for distributed agreement under fail-stop, omission, and timing fault types; 6th symp. Reliability in Distributed Software and Database Systems, Conf. Proc., IEEE Press, 1987, pp. 201 – 212.

15 M. Fischer, N. Lynch, M. Paterson: Impossibility of distributed consensus with one faulty process; Journal of the ACM, vol. 32, no. 2, 1985, pp. 374 – 382.

16 F. DiGiandomenica, M. L. Guidotti, F. Grandoni, L. Simoncini: A gracefully degradable algorithm for byzantine agreement; 6th Symp. Reliability in Distributed Software and Database Systems, Conf. Proc., IEEE Press, 1987, pp. 188 – 200.

17 E. Jenn, J. Arlat, M. Rimén, J. Ohlsson, J. Karlsson: Fault injection into VHDL models: the MEFISTO tool; FTCS-24, Digest of Papers, 1994, pp. 66 – 75.

18 H. Kopetz, G. Grünsteidl, J. Reisinger: Fault-tolerant membership service in a synchronous distributed real-time system; Dependable Computing for Critical Applications, Dependable Comp. and Fault-Tolerant Systems, vol. 4, Springer, 1991, pp. 411 – 429.

19 M. Leu: Relative signatures for fault tolerance and their implementation; 1st European Dependable Computing Conf. EDCC-1, LNCS 852, Springer, 1994, pp. 563 – 580.

20 T. Lovric: Processor fault simulation with ProFI; European Simulation Symposium ESS 95, Conf. Proc., 1995, pp. 353 – 357.

21 D. Powell: Failure mode assumptions and assumption coverage; FTCS-22, Digest of Papers, 1992, pp. 386 – 395.

22 M. Pease, R. Shostak, L. Lamport: Reaching agreement in the presence of faults; Journal of the ACM, vol. 27, no. 2, 1980, pp. 228 – 234.

23 J. Rufino, P. Verissimo, G. Arroz, C. Almeida, L. Rodrigues: Fault-tolerant broadcasts in CAN; FTCS-28, Digest of Papers, 1998, pp. 150 – 159.

24 H. R. Strong, D. Dolev: Byzantine agreement; Compcon 83, Conf. Proc., IEEE Press, 1983, pp. 77 – 81.

25 C. Temple: Avoiding the babbling-idiot failure in a time-triggered communication system; FTCS-28, Digest of Papers, 1998, pp. 218 – 227.

26 J. Turek, D. Shasha: The many faces of consensus in distributed systems; Computer, IEEE Press, June 1992, pp. 8 – 17.

An Experimental Evaluation of Coordinated Checkpointing in a Parallel Machine

Luis Moura Silva   João Gabriel Silva

Departamento Engenharia Informática
Universidade de Coimbra, Polo II
3030 – Coimbra, Portugal
luis@dei.uc.pt

Abstract. Coordinated checkpointing represents a very effective solution to assure the continuity of distributed and parallel applications in the occurrence of failures. In previous studies it has been proved that this approach achieved better results than independent checkpointing and message logging. However, we need to know more about the real overhead of coordinated checkpointing and get sustained insights about the best way to implement this technique of fault-tolerance. This paper presents an experimental evaluation of coordinated checkpointing in a parallel machine. It describes some optimization techniques and presents some performance results.

1. Introduction

Checkpointing and rollback-recovery is a very effective technique for recovering the application from partial or total system failures. There are several papers in the literature about checkpointing algorithms for distributed and parallel systems. A comprehensive survey is presented in [1]. Basically, the checkpointing algorithms can be divided in two main classes: independent and coordinated checkpointing.

In the former class of algorithms the application processes are allowed to establish checkpoints in an independent way and no synchronization is enforced between their checkpoint operations. When there is a failure the system will search in stable storage and will try to find some set of local checkpoints that taken together correspond to a consistent state of the application. This requires each process to keep several checkpoints in stable storage and there is no certainty that a global consistent state can be built. Consequently, this approach presents two main drawbacks: (i) the possibility of occurring the *domino-effect* [2] during the rollback operation; (ii) and the storage overhead that is required to maintain several checkpoints in stable storage.

In the second approach -coordinated checkpointing- a global checkpoint is taken periodically and the processes have to synchronize between themselves to assure that their set of local checkpoints corresponds to a consistent state of the application [3]. In coordinated checkpointing the recovery phase is simple and quite predictable since all the processes roll back to their last committed checkpoints. This approach avoids the *domino-effect* and presents a lower memory overhead in stable storage. Some overhead is introduced during the checkpoint operation due to the synchronization of processes and some people argue that independent checkpointing is better than coordinated checkpointing because of the overhead that is caused by this synchronization. However, we have implemented both schemes and performed an experimental study in a commercial parallel machine [4]. The results were truly the opposite: coordinated checkpointing presents better results and independent checkpointing is almost difficult to use in practice due to the huge memory overhead that is imposed to the stable storage system.

Taking this fact into account we decided to analize in some more detail what actually are the main sources of performance overhead in the different phases of a coordinated checkpointing algorithm. At the same time we try to provide some optimization techniques that do not depend from the underlying hardware and can be easily ported to any distributed or parallel systems.

In this paper, we present the results of an experimental study that was conducted in a commercial parallel machine. We have done an implementation of coordinated checkpointing in four different versions: using a blocking algorithm, a non-blocking one, using main-memory checkpointing and checkpoint staggering. We present the performance penalty that is introduced by each version.

The rest of the paper is organized as follows: section 2 presents an overview about the coordinated checkpointing algorithm. Section 3 presents the performance results and includes a comparison between the different versions. Section 4 describes some of the related work and, finally, section 5 concludes the paper.

2. Coordinated Checkpointing

In [5] we have presented an algorithm to implement a coordinated global checkpoint for distributed applications. To some extend that algorithm has some similarities with another one that was presented in the same conference [6]. For lack of space we only present a brief overview of our algorithm.

Every site should take a local checkpoint and the algorithm assures that the set of local checkpoints must result in a consistent recovery line, to which processes can roll back in case of failure. This means that processes must coordinate their checkpoints.

The distributed system is composed by a number (N) of sites $DS = \{S_1, S_2, ..., S_N\}$ that only communicate through asynchronous messages. There is one site that is called the *coordinator* that is responsible for periodically initiating a global checkpoint. For the sake of clarity it is assumed that every site (S_i) runs an application process (P_i). The nth checkpoint of process P_i is called by $chkp_i(n)$. A global checkpoint includes all the local checkpoints together with the state of the communication channels. A message that is sent from P_i to P_k is called by m_{ik}.

To avoid the *domino-effect* the algorithm must assure that the set of checkpoints belonging to the same recovery line forms a consistent global state. According to that algorithm, a global checkpoint -GC(n)- forms a consistent global state if it observes the three following rules:

- **Rule 1**: For every message m_{ij} sent from P_i to P_j and consumed before $chkp_j(n)$, then the sending of that message must have happened before $chkp_i(n)$;

- **Rule 2**: For every message m_{ij} sent before $chkp_i(n)$ and consumed after $chkp_j(n)$, then that message must be saved to be replayed if the processes have to roll back to that recovery line;

- **Rule 3**: Processes can take another checkpoint (n+1) only if the previous global checkpoint is already complete.

This last rule means that a global checkpoint contains only one local checkpoint for each process, and each of those checkpoints is identified by the same ordinal number.

2.1 The Global Checkpoint Algorithm

In our algorithm the checkpoint event is triggered periodically by a local timer mechanism at the *coordinator* site. The associated Recovery Manager takes a checkpoint of the application process running on that site and sends a message - chkp_req(n) - to the other sites in the network. Checkpoints are assigned with ordinal numbers from a monotonically increasing number (CN), which is incremented every time a global checkpoint is created. That message - chkp_req(n) - contains the new value of the Checkpoint Number. That number (CN) is piggybacked in each outgoing application message. When each of the remaining sites receives the - chkp_req(n)   - message it takes a *tentative* checkpoint of its application processes and sends an acknowledge message to the coordinator site - chkp_ack(n).

The application processes are only suspended during the time of taking a checkpoint of its state. Then, they proceed normally while the checkpointing protocol is still running. When the *coordinator* site receives the acknowledgements of all the other sites it transforms the *tentative* checkpoints into *permanent* checkpoints, by broadcasting a message - chkp_commit(n) - to the network. This means that every process needs to keep two checkpoints in stable storage, to prevent a situation of failure while the current checkpoint is being taken. Without losing generality, let us assume that each site S_i only runs one application process P_i. Now let us see how the algorithm avoids the so-called *orphan* messages and identifies the *missing* messages, in order to be saved.

Orphan messages may happen since we assume that the communication channels can be non-FIFO and the asynchronism of the network may violate the causal order between messages. *Missing* messages are simply in transit during the checkpointing algorithm. Let us take a look to Figure 1.

Message m_1 was sent by process P_2 before taking checkpoint (n) and it is consumed by P_1 after its correspondent checkpoint. This is an example of a *missing* message, and it is easily identified since the message carries with it the CN of the sender process. In that case $m_1.CN = (n-1)$ while $P_1.CN = (n)$. In order to be replayed in case of rollback, that message is logged in stable storage by the receiver process in a place called the *Msg_Log*. Before committing the global checkpoint the *coordinator* has to be sure that all the *missing* messages have been logged in stable storage. It requires the execution of a separated protocol to collect all the *missing* messages. For lack of space we refer the interested reader to [4] for more details about the algorithm that has been used to collect the *missing* messages.

The other message, m_2, is an example of a message that violates rule R1 of Definition 1. It is an *orphan* message since it was sent by a process after taking its checkpoint ($P_2.CN = n$) and it arrives at site S_3 before taking the nth checkpoint ($P_3.CN = (n-1)$). Since message m_2 has a CN higher than the CN of the receiver site, it means that the checkpointing algorithm is already running; process P_2 has been taking its checkpoint (n) but the message `chkp_req(n)` destined to site S_3 did not arrive yet. So, the way to avoid that *orphan* message is to take a checkpoint at site S_3 before consuming it. Later, when the proper message - `chkp_req(n)` - arrives at S_3 it will be discarded since the nth checkpoint was already taken and the message became redundant. The CN counter forbids the occurrence of *orphan* messages and facilitates the task of detecting *missing* messages. Upon rollback, those messages that were saved in the *Msg_Log* are introduced on the message queue of the application process.

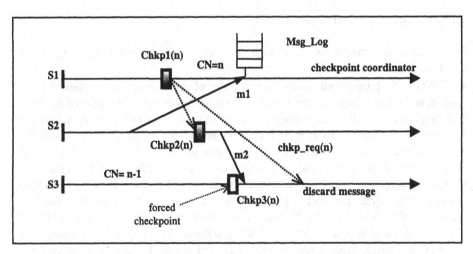

Fig. 1. Avoiding orphan messages and identifying missing messages.

The algorithm is non-blocking, in the sense that after a process takes its local checkpoint it proceeds with its computation without waiting for the others. All the synchronization is done in background in order to reduce the performance degradation. It was also proved in [5] that the global checkpoint achieved by this algorithm corresponds to a consistent system state, thereby it is *domino-effect* free.

3. An Experimental Study

In this section, we present the results of an experimental study that was conducted in a commercial parallel machine. The whole algorithm of coordinated checkpointing that was presented in the previous sub-sections was implemented in a run-time library (CHK-LIB) that we have developed for the Parix operating system[1] [7]. That library provides reliable and FIFO communication and the programming interface resembles the functionality of MPI.

The testbed machine was a Parsytec Xplorer, with 8 transputers (T805). In that machine, each processor has 4 Mbytes of main-memory, and all of them have direct access to the host file system. In our particular case, the host machine was a SunSparc2. Stable storage was implemented on the disk of the host machine. The I/O bandwidth between the parallel machine and the Sun Workstation is only 1Mb/sec. We should keep in mind that, for this particular platform, the central I/O system is a potential point of bottleneck. Besides, we have conducted our study in small machine. Therefore, we could not take any immediate conclusions about the scalability of the algorithms.

3.1 The Application Benchmarks

To evaluate the checkpointing scheme we have used the following application benchmarks:

- **ISING**: This program simulates the behaviour of Spin-glasses. Each particle has a spin, and it can change its spin from time to time depending on the state of its direct 4 neighbours and the temperature of the system. Above a critical temperature the system is in complete disarray. Below this temperature the system has the tendency to establish clusters of particles with the same spin. Each element of the grid is represented by an integer, and we executed this application for several grid sizes.

- **SOR**: successive overrelaxation is an iterative method to solve Laplace's equation on a regular grid. The grid is partitioned into regions, each containing a band of rows of the global grid. Each region is assigned to a process. The update of the points in the grid is done by a Red/Black scheme. This requires two phases per iteration: one for black points and other for red points. During each iteration the slave processes have to exchange the boundaries of their data blocks with two other neighbours, and at the end of the iteration all the processes perform a global synchronization and evaluate a global test of convergence. Each element of the grid is represented in double precision, and we executed this application for several grid sizes.

- **ASP**: solves the All-pairs Shortest Paths problem i.e. it finds the length of the shortest path from any node i to any other node j in a given graph with N nodes by using Floyd's algorithm. The distances between the nodes of the graph are represented in a matrix and each process computes part of the matrix. It is an

---

[1] Parix is a product of Parsytec Computer GmbH.

iterative algorithm. In each iteration there is one of the process which has the pivot row. It broadcasts its value to all the other slaves. We executed the problem with two graphs of 512 and 1024 nodes.

- **NBODY**: this program simulates the evolution of a system of bodies under the influence of gravitational forces. Every body is modeled as a point mass that exerts forces on all other bodies in the system and the algorithm calculates the forces in a three-dimensional dimension. This computation is the kernel of particle simulation codes to simulate the gravitational forces between galaxies. We ran this application for 4000 particles.
- **GAUSS**: solves a system of linear equations using the method of Gauss-elimination. The algorithm uses partial pivoting and distributes the columns of the input matrix among the processes in an interleaved way to avoid imbalance problems. In every iteration, one of the processes finds the pivot element and sends the pivot column to all the other processes. We used two systems of 512 and 1024 equations.
- **TSP**: solves the travelling salesman problem for a dense map of 16 cities, using a branch and bound algorithm. The jobs were divided by the possible combinations of the first three cities.
- **NQUEENS**: counts the number of solutions to the N-queens problem. The problem is distributed by several jobs assigning to each job a possible placement of the first two queens. We used this algorithm with 13 queens.

These applications have different patterns of communication and different models of computation. For instance, TSP and NQUEENS follow the Master/Worker model and hardly communicate. The other applications follow the SPMD model and involve more inter-process communication, although with different levels of task granularity.

3.2 Versions of Coordinated Checkpointing

In order to evaluate the importance of the implementation aspects we decided to implement the coordinated checkpointing algorithm presented in section 2 using four different techniques. These techniques can be used in any other implementation since they do not make use of any particular feature of the underlying system. The versions we have considered are described as follows:

- **Coord_NB**: this scheme uses a non-blocking checkpointing protocol. While the state of a process is being saved to stable storage the process remains blocked. It resumes at the end of that operation. It does not need to wait for the rest of the protocol that will be executed in the background.
- **Coord_B**: this scheme uses a blocking checkpointing protocol. This means that all the application is frozen while the global checkpoint is being taken. The execution of the application processes is only resumed when the global checkpoint is committed in stable storage.
- **Coord_NBM**: this scheme uses a non-blocking checkpointing protocol. The checkpoint of each process is firstly saved to a local snapshot area in main memory.

When this memory copy operation is over the application process is allowed to resume with its computation. There is a checkpointer thread that will be responsible for writing the checkpoint data into the stable storage and for the rest of the protocol. These operations are done in a concurrent way.

- **Coord_NBMS**: this scheme is an extension of the previous scheme (Coord_NBM). The only difference is that it uses a checkpointing staggering technique in order to reduce the contention in the access to the stable storage, that is implemented in a central disk of the host machine. The processors are organized in a virtual ring and execute a token-based protocol: a process that has the token is allowed to write the checkpoint to stable storage. When that operation is finished it sends the token to the next one that will write its checkpoint. The operation continues until the last processor writes its checkpoint. At this point, the checkpoint coordinator can initiate the commit phase. With this token-based protocol, only one processor has access to stable storage at a time, thus reducing the potential bottleneck of using a global disk.

Some other possible optimization techniques could have been included like incremental and copy-on-write checkpointing. However, these techniques were not possible to implement in Transputer-based machines. Besides, these techniques are not entirely portable to across different systems.

3.3 Performance Results

In the first part of our experiments we have only considered the first version the protocol: Coord_NB. The other versions will be considered in the second part of this section.

- **Part I: Performance of Coord_NB**

In our parallel machine, processors are numbered from 0 to 7. Processor 0 of that machine works as the checkpointing coordinator. Among other tasks it is the one responsible for triggering periodically the checkpoint operation. Each processor has a checkpointer thread that will be responsible for the checkpointing protocol. Stable storage was implemented on the disk file system of the host machine, and every processor writes its checkpoint into a different checkpoint file. Each checkpoint is first saved into a temporary file. When the global checkpoint is committed all the temporary checkpoint files are renamed to permanent, where each file has the CN number as suffix. This is necessary to assure the integrity of at least one checkpoint file in the occurrence of a system failure during the execution of the checkpointing protocol.

Table 1 presents the overhead per checkpoint and the checkpoint duration for all the benchmarks. These values correspond to a single global checkpoint of the application. In this first implementation of coordinated checkpointing (Coord_NB) every process is blocked while its checkpoint is being saved to stable storage. As soon as this operation is finished, the process resumes its computation. The checkpointing protocol is performed in a non-blocking way and the application processes are only blocked during the checkpoint saving operation.

Table 1. Overhead per Checkpoint and Checkpoint Duration (`Coord_NB`).

Applications	Size of Global Checkpoint (Kb)	Checkpoint Duration (sec)	Overhead per Checkpoint (sec)
ISING 2048	19463	39.75	35.34
SOR 1280	15994	36.15	36.06
GAUSS 1024	11806	22.36	22.36
ASP 1024	7230	14.82	14.00
NBODY 4000	3540	11.91	4.39
TSP 16	2884	45.69	0.97
NQUEENS 13	2845	22.65	0.79

We can see in Table 1 that for the first four applications (ISING, SOR, GAUSS, ASP) the checkpoint duration is quite close to the overhead per checkpoint. For these four applications the degree of concurrency due to the non-blocking nature of the checkpointing protocol is not that significant as we might expect. We can then conclude that for those loosely synchronous applications the checkpoint saving clearly dominates the total performance overhead. In this case, the non-blocking nature of the protocol is not a major benefit. For the last three applications (NBODY, TSP, NQUEENS) the checkpoint duration is much higher than the overhead per checkpoint. The reason is simple: in our system the application processes can only be checkpointed when they execute some library call (i.e. when they send or receive a message). These three applications are more computation-intensive and by this reason they take more time to perform a global checkpoint involving every process of the application. The overhead per global checkpoint is directly related to the size of the global checkpoint. For the ISING and SOR application it is around 36 seconds, while for the TSP and NQUEENS application it is less than 1 second.

In Figure 2 we present the variation of the checkpoint duration and the overhead per checkpoint for the ISING application when we consider different increasing sizes of the problem. Two things can be observed: first, there is an almost linear increase of the overhead per checkpoint. This is directly related with the increase in the overall size of the checkpoint. Secondly, the checkpoint duration is only visibly different for the bigger sizes of the problem. For the lower sizes, the duration and the overhead are almost equal. By this Figure, we can conclude that the most important source of overhead is the operation of checkpoint saving to stable storage and not the checkpointing protocol.

In Table 2 we present the maximum number of *missing* and *orphan* messages that were observed in our experiments.

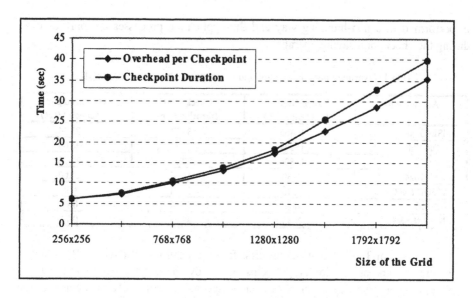

Fig. 2. Overhead per Checkpoint and Checkpoint Duration (ISING).

Table 2. Number of Missing and Orphan Messages.

Applications	Max. Number of Missings	Max. Size of Msg_Log (bytes)	Max. Number of Orphans
ISING 256	4	1152	0
ISING 512	1	544	0
ISING 768	1	800	0
ISING 1024	1	1056	1
ISING 1280	1	1312	1
ISING 1536	1	1568	0
ISING 1792	0	0	0
ISING 2048	0	0	0
SOR 256	1	2080	0
SOR 512	1	4128	0
SOR 768	1	6176	0
SOR 1024	1	8224	0
SOR 1280	1	10272	0
GAUSS 512	0	0	0
GAUSS 1024	1	8232	0
ASP 512	7	14560	0
ASP 1024	0	0	0
NBODY 4000	0	0	0
TSP 16	0	0	0
NQUEENS 13	0	0	0

The occurrence of *orphan* messages was actually very uncommon. Only for two of the cases (ISING 1024 and ISING 1280) we found the occurrence of one *orphan* message. The occurrence of *missing* messages was more common. For most of the applications, the average number of *missing* messages per checkpoint was around 1. For the applications with a higher computation to communication ratio the number of *missing* messages was 0. Only in two cases we have observed the occurrence of more than one *missing* message: ISING(256) with 4 and ASP(512) with 7 *missing* messages.

In the third column we present the maximum size of the message log in bytes. It is quite clear that when there is the occurrence of *missing* messages the stable storage overhead to store those messages is absolutely insignificant.

- **Part II: Performance of all the Versions**

In the second part of our experiments we decided to compare the performance of all the versions that were implemented. The comparison is presented in Table 3, where the overhead is presented in seconds.

Table 3. Overhead per Checkpoint (`Coord_NB`, `Coord_B`, `Coord_NBM`, `Coord_NBMS`).

Applications	Coord_NB	Coord_B	Coord_NBM	Coord_NBMS
ISING 256	6.10	6.62	2.54	0.63
ISING 512	7.36	7.88	2.35	0.81
ISING 768	9.98	10.45	2.90	0.78
ISING 1024	13.22	13.76	1.85	0.13
ISING 1280	17.30	17.80	2.89	0.25
ISING 1536	22.76	23.53	-----	-----
ISING 1792	28.69	29.15	-----	-----
ISING 2048	35.34	35.95	-----	-----
SOR 256	6.91	7.47	3.50	1.09
SOR 512	10.39	10.97	5.15	2.42
SOR 768	16.45	16.74	7.04	4.70
SOR 1024	24.84	25.55	-----	-----
SOR 1280	36.06	36.36	-----	-----
GAUSS 512	10.47	10.57	5.42	1.14
GAUSS 1024	22.05	22.36	10.47	1.91
ASP 512	7.80	7.96	3.24	0.91
ASP 1024	14.00	14.92	4.15	1.51
NBODY 4000	4.39	6.36	0.98	0.27
TSP 16	0.97	30.10	0.23	0.24
NQUEENS 13	0.79	5.42	0.14	0.13

The two last schemes (`Coord_NBM` and `Coord_NBMS`) use a main-memory checkpointing scheme. This means they would require some additional memory in every local processor. For this reason, they could not be used in some of the benchmarks with a large application state.

In Table 3 we can see that the scheme with the blocking checkpointing protocol (`Coord_B`) performs always worse than the first scheme, that used a non-blocking protocol (Coord_NB). The difference was mostly significant for the TSP and NQUEENS applications.

The major difference happened when we used the main-memory checkpointing technique. With this optimization most of the checkpoint activity is performed in the background. This technique resulted in a significant reduction in the overhead per checkpoint. If we compare the overhead of Coord_NB with the overhead of Coord_NBM we can see reductions in the order of 50% to 85%. The scheme that used a checkpoint staggering technique (Coord_NBMS) was able to reduce the overhead per checkpoint even further: there were reductions from 71% to 99%.

These results allow us to conclude that the use of those two optimization techniques - *main-memory checkpointing* and *checkpoint staggering* - is very effective in the reduction of the performance overhead. The only drawback of main-memory checkpointing is the additional storage memory that is required in every processor and this may restrict its use with applications that have a large application state.

The picture becomes more visible in Figure 3, where we present the overhead per checkpoint when using those four schemes in the ISING applications. For a grid size bigger than 1280x1280 there was no available memory in each node to use those two schemes that rely in the main-memory checkpointing technique. Nevertheless, up to that problem size we can see that there is no visible increase in the overhead of Coord_NBM and Coord_NBMS, while for the other two schemes there was an almost linear increase. Coord_NB and Coord_B present a similar performance because they do not use main-memory checkpointing.

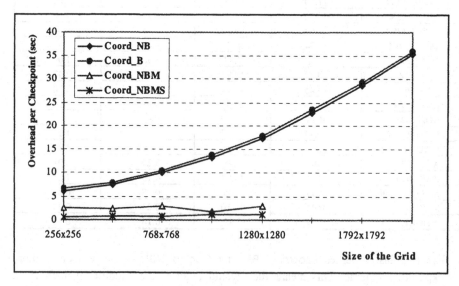

Fig. 3. Overhead per Checkpoint ISING: Coord_NB, Coord_B, Coord_NBM, Coord_NBMS.

Figure 3 corroborates the claim that the main source of overhead is not the protocol synchronization, but rather the checkpoint saving in stable storage. Interestingly, we can achieve a higher reduction in the performance overhead if we try to optimize the operation of checkpoint saving rather than the nature of the checkpointing protocol.

Reducing the checkpoint size, performing the checkpoint concurrently with the computation or reducing the contention in the access to stable storage are three possible techniques that can be used effectively to reduce the overhead of checkpointing.

In our case it was not possible to reduce the checkpoint size, since it was not possible to implement incremental checkpointing. However, this technique would not pay off in those applications that make use of most of the address space. The two other techniques were implemented and proved to be successful.

Figure 4 presents the time each processor takes to write its checkpoint to stable storage, when using the GAUSS(1024) application and those four versions of coordinated checkpointing.

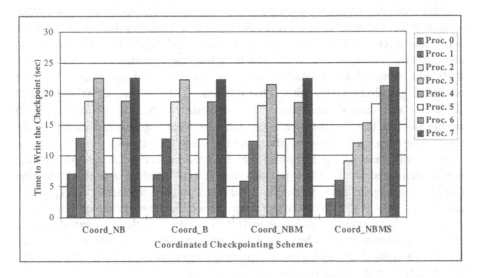

Fig. 4. Time to finish the checkpoint of every processor (GAUSS 1024).

It can be seen that processor 0 is always one of the first ones to finish its checkpoint. This processor 0 is the one connected to the host machine, where there is the stable storage system. Processors 3 and 7 are usually the last ones to complete their checkpoints. This was expected since these two processors are the most far away from processor 0. The processors in the machine are organized in a two-dimensional grid.

An interesting result is related with the Coord_NBMS scheme, where we can clearly observe the effects of the token-based protocol. The virtual ring was organized in the increasing order of the processor's numbers and this fact explains the shape of those columns. Coord_NBMS is the scheme that presents the higher checkpoint duration, although it is the scheme that incurs in the lower checkpoint overhead. The difference in the checkpoint duration to the other schemes was around 2 seconds for that particular application. This result was somehow expected: when we force some ordering in the checkpoint saving this will delay the commit of the global checkpoint. Anyway, that metric of checkpoint duration is irrelevant for fault-tolerance purposes.

We have also implemented that checkpoint staggering technique with the first two schemes, Coord_NB and Coord_B. However, there was no visible reduction in the overhead, and in some of the cases it was even worse. Thereby, we concluded that checkpoint staggering was only effective when used with main-memory checkpointing.

4. Related Work

Some other interesting experimental studies were presented in the literature For instance in [6] was presented another study that was conducted in a system of 16 diskless Sun 3/60 workstations, connected by a 10Mbits Ethernet, running a special version of the V-Kernel. With a checkpoint interval of 2 minutes the overall overhead was in the order of 1% to 5.8%. Some optimization techniques, like incremental and copy-on-write checkpointing, were used to reduce the performance overhead. That study has shown that the synchronization of the individual processes to form a consistent global checkpoint added little overhead. The overhead of writing data to stable storage clearly dominates. That implementation was performed by a modification of the V-kernel, while our schemes were implemented on top of the operating system, without any modification to the underlying system.

In [8] was presented the performance of a consistent checkpointing algorithm that was implemented on the Mach micro-kernel. It was based on a 2-phase blocking scheme. Some optimization techniques were included like incremental checkpointing and the use of a RAM-based stable storage device. For one of the benchmarks the average overhead ranged from 3% up to 16%. The upper checkpoint interval was 4.5 minutes. Another application benchmark presented an overhead of 14% and 23%. That scheme made use of special hardware support to implement the stable storage and was only able to tolerate single processor failures.

In [9] there were presented some checkpointing methods for shared-memory multiprocessors. Their results showed that non-blocking copy-on-write checkpointing reduces considerably the overhead in the execution time. Four schemes were implemented: sequential checkpointing, simple and concurrent main-memory checkpointing, and copy-on-write checkpointing. The scheme that takes less time to complete a checkpoint is the sequential technique, but it is also the scheme that presents the higher overhead. Main-memory and copy-and-write checkpointing were very effective in order to overlap the checkpoint writing with the execution of the target program. They increase the checkpoint time, but reduce considerably the total overhead. All those experiments were taken on a 4-processor shared-memory machine, where 3 of the processors were used by the application itself, and the remaining one by the checkpointer. This fact would give a positive contribution to the final results. Nevertheless, they did not address the problem of consistent checkpointing in message-passing distributed-memory systems.

A checkpointing tool for the Intel iPSC/860 multicomputer was presented in [10]. It implements three consistent checkpointing algorithms: (i) *Chandy-Lamport*; (ii) *Synch-and-stop*; (iii) and *Network-Sweeping*. The second algorithm freezes the whole system before taking a global checkpoint, while the third scheme is a variation of the Chandy-Lamport algorithm that tries to minimize the number of marker messages by exploiting the routing characteristics of the multicomputer. Two optimizations were also included: main-memory checkpointing and compression. Some performance results were taken with six application benchmarks and the same interesting conclusion was also achieved: the checkpointing algorithm is not the relevant factor for the checkpoint time and overhead. The dominant factor is, indeed, the time to write the checkpoint data to stable storage.

In [11] was presented a simulation study that compares the behavior of three checkpointing protocols. This study presents some interesting results since it was able to evaluate the relevance of several factors in the performance of checkpointing, like the network topology, the size of the system and the communication pattern of application. It was concluded that the checkpoint size is always the dominating factor.

The idea of staggered checkpointing has been previously presented in [12]. However, no experimental results have been presented in that paper.

In [13] was presented another experimental study that was conducted in a parallel machine. That paper presents some discussions about the effect of memory and I/O bandwidth in a checkpointing algorithm that is mainly directly oriented for DSM systems.

Finally, in [14] was presented another experimental study but that paper was more focused on a direct comparison between coordinated checkpointing and message logging.

5. Conclusions

This paper presented some experimental results about the implementation of coordinated checkpointing in a commercial parallel machine. The results that were presented are mostly oriented to this particular architecture and cannot be directly generalized to any other system or platform. In our case, the stable storage was implemented in the central disk of the host machine that has a low I/O bandwidth and represents a single point of failure. Another study that uses parallel I/O to improve the bandwidth of stable storage was presented in [15]. Nevertheless, this study presents some important insights about the use of checkpointing parallel machines with a central I/O system.

In the paper we have presented an effective algorithm that includes a protocol for saving the in-transit messages at the time of a global checkpoint. This algorithm has been implemented in four different versions and their behavior has been analized. The most important observation from our experimental study is that the cost of checkpointing is dominated by the writing of the local checkpoints to stable storage.

The overhead of synchronizing the checkpoints is negligible and presents a minor contribution to the overall performance cost.

This allow us to conclude that if we want to achieve a significant reduction in the performance overhead we should try to optimize the operation of checkpoint saving. Three possible solutions can be then be used: (i) reducing the checkpoint size; (ii) performing the checkpoint concurrently with the computation; (iii) or reducing the contention in the access to stable storage.

In our particular case, the use of optimization techniques like main-memory checkpointing and checkpoint staggering were able to reduce considerably the performance overhead of our coordinated algorithm. Whenever possible the system should try to perform the checkpoint concurrently with the computation, and use an ordering technique to reduce the congestion in stable storage, specially when it is implemented in a shared global disk. More details about this study and related issues can be obtained in [4].

Acknowledgments

This work was partially supported by the Portuguese *Ministério da Ciência e Tecnologia*, the European Union through the R&D Unit 326/94 (CISUC) and the project PRAXIS XXI 2/2.1/TIT/1625/95 (PARQUANTUM).

References

1. E.N.Elnozahy, D.B.Johnson, Y.M.Wang. "A Survey of Rollback-Recovery Protocols in Message Passing Systems", Technical Report CMU-CS-96-181, School of Computer Science, Carnegie Mellon University, October 1996
2. B.Randell. "System Structure for Software Fault-Tolerance", IEEE Trans. on Software Engineering, Vol. SE-1 (2), pp. 226-232, June 1975
3. K.M.Chandy, L.Lamport. "Distributed Snapshots: Determining Global States of Distributed Systems", ACM Transactions on Computer Systems, Vol. 3, No. 1, pp. 63-75, February 1985
4. L.M.Silva, "Checkpointing Mechanisms for Scientific Parallel Applications", PhD Thesis presented at the Univ. of Coimbra, Portugal, January 1997, ISBN 972-97189-0-3
5. L.M.Silva, J.G.Silva. "Global Checkpointing for Distributed Programs", Proc. 11th Symposium on Reliable Distributed Programs, Houston USA, pp. 155-162, October 1992
6. E.N.Elnozahy, D.B.Johnson, W.Zwaenepoel. "The Performance of Consistent Checkpointing", Proc. 11th Symposium on Reliable Distributed Systems, pp. 39-47, 1992
7. "Parix 1.2: Software Documentation", Parsytec Computer GmbH, March 1993
8. G.Muller, M.Banatre, N.Peyrouze, B.Rochat. "Lessons from FTM: An Experiment in the Design and Implementation of a Low Cost Fault-Tolerant System", IEEE Transactions on Reliability, pp. 332-340, June 1996
9. K.Li, J.F.Naughton, J.S.Plank. "Real-Time Concurrent Checkpoint for Parallel Programs", Proc. 2nd ACM Sigplan Symposium in Principles and Practice of Parallel Programming, pp. 79-88, March 1990

10. J.S.Plank, K.Li. "ickp - A Consistent Checkpointer for Multicomputers", IEEE Parallel and Distributed Technology, vol. 2 (2), pp. 62-67, Summer 1994

11. B.Bieker, E.Maehle. "Overhead of Coordinated Checkpointing Protocols for Message Passing Parallel Systems", Workshop on Fault-Tolerant Parallel and Distributed Systems, IPPS'99, San-Juan, Puerto-Rico, April 1999

12. N.Vaidya. "On Staggered Checkpointing", Proc. 8th IEEE Symposium on Parallel and Distributed Processing, SPDS, October 1996

13. G.Cabillic, G.Muller, I.Puaut. "The Performance of Consistent Checkpointing in Distributed Shared Memory Systems", Proceedings 14th Symposium on Reliable Distributed Systems, SRDS-14, September 1995

14. N.Neves, K.Fuchs. "RENEW: A Tool for Fast and Efficient Implementation of Checkpoint Protocols", Proc. 28th Int. Symposium on Fault-Tolerant Computing, FTCS-28, pp. 58-67, Munich, June 1998

15. L.M.Silva, J.G.Silva, S.Chapple, L.Clarke, "Portable Checkpointing and Recovery", Proc. 4th Int. Symp. on High-Performance Distributed Computing, HPDC-4, Pentagon City, USA, pp.188-195, August 1995

Session 4

Fault Injection 1

Chair: Janusz Sosnowski, Warsaw University of Technology, Poland

MAFALDA: Microkernel Assessment by Fault Injection and Design Aid

Manuel Rodríguez, Frédéric Salles, Jean-Charles Fabre and Jean Arlat

LAAS-CNRS, 7 Avenue du Colonel Roche, 31007 Toulouse cedex 4 - France
E-mail: {rodriguez, salles, fabre, arlat}@laas.fr

Abstract. MAFALDA is a generic experimental environment that is intended to support, for several microkernel candidates, both objectives of characterization of the failure modes in the presence of injected faults (internal or external) and of the incorporation of wrappers to improve these failure modes. After a short classification of current microkernel architectures and of their interactions between the application layer and the microkernel functional components, the paper presents the main features of MAFALDA with a focus on the fault injection and wrapping modules. The implementation of these modules is then described distinguishing the two main modes of interactions identified (library-based or trap-based). Some experimental results are presented that show the usefulness of the tool. The paper concludes by a summary of the main characteristics of MAFALDA and a brief discussion of our future work.

1. Introduction

Mainly motivated by economic reasons, the use of COTS (Commercial-Off-The-Shelf) components for the development of computer systems encompassing critical applications as well, is becoming ubiquitous. However, such components are seldom developed to meet such demanding dependability requirements and moreover systems integrators have usually little information and guarantee on their design and validation processes, as well as on their failure modes. Accordingly, qualifying, integrating and combining COTS components raise major concerns and challenges to system integrators.

Several recent related studies have been carried out that address the important issue of objectively characterizing and improving the behavior of COTS software components (e.g., see [1, 2]). Due to their impact on the behavior of the overall system, much attention has been paid to COTS operating systems (OSs). In particular, FINE [3] and BALLISTA [4] addressed respectively the Unix OS and several POSIX-compliant OSs. MAFALDA environment (Microkernel Assessment by Fault Injection and Design Aid) focuses on the emerging microkernel technology.

Microkernel technology is very appealing today in the design and implementation of either general purpose OSs or specific ones targeted at a given application domain. This technology provides basic components, on which or from which, OS services can be easily implemented. These components are often not specific to a given system and can be obtained off-the-shelf since today many vendors provide microkernels. On this basis, it is up to the system designer integrating such COTS components to develop dedicated upper layer software. This is the current practice in OS development including for systems with stringent dependability requirements such as embedded systems aiming at critical applications (e.g., railway, space, avionics, etc.).

The design issues involved when considering to incorporate a microkernel for developing a given system depends of course on several considerations: the functional components offered, the flexibility to customize the microkernel, the performance of the interaction between the application processes and the microkernel, the various addressing modes and related protection mechanisms, etc. Still, the decision to use COTS microkernels in critical systems raises additional concerns related to dependability issues. Accordingly, the assessment of the behavior of these components in the presence of faults is of high interest since upper software layers have to deal with the failure modes of the selected microkernel.

Three main failure modes can be identified whatever the perturbation affecting the microkernel (either an erroneous kernel call or an internal fault):

- *Detected error*: the perturbation is successfully identified and reported by the microkernel system calls or at least an exception is raised to the application layer.
- *Crash*: the microkernel freezes and at least a warm restart (or even a hardware restart) is necessary.
- *Propagated error*: the microkernel propagates erroneous data that can corrupt the application layer, and thus the failure or the hang of the application.

Of course, the impact of these outcomes on the application layers may depend on the specification of the system and of the level of redundancy implemented at these layers. When no service interruption can be afforded, then all three outcomes may well lead to a failure of the system. However, whenever error processing can be carried out at the upper layers, it is likely that the ability to detect errors is of great help. Moreover, for what concerns undetected errors, although this is context dependent, it is likely that a propagated error will have a more severe impact than a system crash. Accordingly, in the sequel, we will consider that an *application failure* occurs when an error is propagated to the application layer.

Clearly, the ability to get insights on their failure modes is a major data entry, not only for supporting the decision whether to select a given microkernel, but also for guiding the subsequent design decisions, including the incorporation of additional protection mechanisms.

Accordingly, the aim of the MAFALDA is twofold:

1. The first aim is to provide objective quantitative data regarding the failure modes of a candidate microkernel. Using fault injection at various levels, MAFALDA enables to establish a better understanding of the microkernel behavior in the presence of faults. MAFALDA supports: i) *robustness assessment*, by analyzing the microkernel response to invalid calls that could result from faults affecting the application processes, and ii) *fault containment assessment*, by analyzing the consequences of internal faults affecting both the data and code segments of the microkernel. The results provided by MAFALDA comply with the failure classification considered earlier, but also include further useful insights (e.g., by means of detailed observation traces).

2. The second aim is to provide means to improve the failure modes depicted by the analysis of the faulty behavior. Such an improvement relates to the addition *of encapsulation mechanisms* in order to enhance the error detection capabilities of the microkernel, so as to reduce the proportion of application failures and system crashes. This encapsulation is based on the notion of *wrappers* monitoring the management of the microkernel system calls. Because the services provided by most microkernel basic components often exhibit simple specifications (e.g., synchronization, communication, etc.), it is possible to devise simple models (*predicates*) describing their expected behaviors. This allows for the development of wrappers, that not only can filter the invocation patterns, but also can dynamically check for the adequacy of the operation of a specific component.

These two objectives i.e., assessment of failure modes and definition of wrappers, were respectively introduced and covered in two previous papers [5] and [6]. This paper concentrates on the design and implementation of MAFALDA, the tool that supports the two above objectives, for several types of microkernel candidates. The consistent implementation of the injection and containment mechanisms into a single environment procures a rather unique feature to MAFALDA.

The contribution of MAFALDA to the design of systems based on COTS microkernels has two main facets:

- it may help microkernel *integrators* in the selection of a candidate microkernel according to the observed behavior in the presence of faults and also it provides means to improve its behavior thanks to the notion of wrappers that can be tailored according to upper layers requirements.
- it may also benefit microkernel *providers* by supporting objective data to better design and implemented their product. This is of course of high interest when the delivered microkernel itself has been customized (notion of microkernel instance) to fit customer's requirements.

The organization of the paper is as follows. Section 2 describes the various architectures of microkernel-based systems and proposes a classification of microkernels from several viewpoints, i) supported functional components and ii) application/microkernel interactions (mainly, *library-based* or *trap-based*). This classification supports the detailed presentation of the main features of MAFALDA in Section 3. Section 4 deals with implementation issues; in particular, it describes how MAFALDA supports fault injection and containment for the microkernels corresponding to each of the two modes of application/microkernel interactions identified in Section 2. To illustrate the usefulness of the tool, some experimental results are presented in Section 5. Finally, Section 6 concludes the paper by summarizing the main interests of MAFALDA for the design and the implementation of microkernel-based systems with dependability requirements, and by addressing our future plans.

2. Microkernel-Based Systems

Microkernel technology aims at providing very basic OS functions to system designers: synchronization mechanisms (semaphores), multi-threaded process management including scheduling facilities, memory management, communication mechanisms, interrupt handling. On top of it, different types of OS services can be developed as upper software layers (in fact middleware) with different objectives and usage. The middleware is always composed of several processes complementing the microkernel basic components that are running on top of the microkernel.

The set of components within the microkernel may vary a lot depending on the microkernel candidate. Some are real runtime kernels (e.g. Chorus [7, 8], VxWorks [9]) on which applications or system services can readily be executed, while others implement only very few basic mechanisms upon which system services have to be developed to obtain an actual runtime layer (e.g., QNX [10]). This makes the definition of a microkernel somewhat fuzzy. Indeed, what is called a microkernel varies a lot. However, for us, and as it is usually admitted, a microkernel is composed of a minimal number of components (see Table 1) that make it a real autonomous runtime kernel. As shown on the table, Chorus and VxWorks are fully compliant with this definition. The microkernel components themselves can be selected off-the-shelf or customized according to the targeted application domain. A microkernel instance is thus a compound of off-the-shelf and designed on purpose components.

Table 1. Microkernels functional components

Functional component	Chorus	VxWorks	QNX
Tasks management	X	X	external service
Scheduling	X	X	X
Synchronization	X	X	X
Communication	X	X	
Memory management	X	X	external service
Interrupt handling	X	X	X

One very important issue when considering our objective, is the way application/middleware interact with the microkernel. Two cases are distinguished:

1. The microkernel software is provided as a set of *library functions* and combined at compile or load-time to the application/middleware software. In this case, the resulting stand-alone software executes in a single address space, normally in supervisor mode. Accordingly, no protection mechanism based on the available memory management unit (MMU) is provided, i.e., all internal data structure can be accessed without any control. This is the case of today's version of VxWorks.
2. The microkernel software is running in supervisor mode within a separate address space. The application/middleware software is normally running in user mode, each individual microkernel process being in a separate address space. The interaction between the application processes and the microkernel software, i.e., the microkernel system calls, is often implemented by a *trap mechanism*. This is the case of Chorus ClassiX.

The distinction between microkernels implemented only as a library of basic services or implemented as a true kernel whose internal functions can only be accessed through a trap mechanism is a significant difference in many respects. This distinction is summarized in Figure 1. However, the distinction is not that clear since, in the later case, system calls are also provided to upper layers as libraries. In this case, part of the system call is executed in the user address space and the trap mechanisms invoke internal functions in supervisor space. The invocation of internal functions is accompanied by a change of the addressing/running mode. Clearly this approach has an impact on the performance of the system calls (context switch *vs.* simple jump).

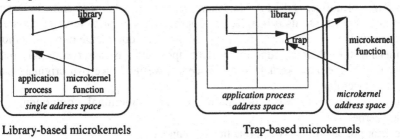

Library-based microkernels   Trap-based microkernels

Fig. 1. Library *vs.* Trap-based microkernels

The above distinction has many impacts as far as dependability is concerned. From a design viewpoint, clearly the library-based interaction does not ensure that a deviant application process will not corrupt other application processes and even the microkernel internal functions shared between all application processes. Because of the clear distinction between kernel space and application address spaces, the trap-based interaction provides enhanced error confinement. Trap-based microkernels also offers a single entry point into the microkernel address space that can be used for many aims regarding the assessment and the encapsulation of the microkernel functions.

3. Guidelines and Architecture

After a short exposition of the objectives that have led to the design of MAFALDA, we present the main assumptions considered for selecting the fault model to be supported by the tool. The modules that compose the architecture of MAFALDA are then described. Finally, the main steps of conducting a fault injection campaign with MAFALDA are identified. Finally, some examples of experimental results that can be obtained are given.

3.1 Design objectives

Our first objective is the characterization of the behavioral profile of a given COTS microkernel instance in the presence of faults. This analysis concerns both the evaluation of i) the robustness of its interface towards external faults, and ii) the intrinsic coverage of its internal error detection mechanisms. The first point is related to the aptitude of the microkernel to cope with an external stress. This property characterizes the capacity of the microkernel to detect an error propagating from the application level of the system, through its interface. The second point is related to the assessment of its own internal error detection and fault tolerance.

The corresponding fault models result from the analysis of the possible origin of a fault whose activation is prone to lead directly, or by propagation of the resulting error, to an erroneous behavior of the microkernel. Two forms of fault injection must thus be considered: i) the corruption of the input parameters during the invocation of a microkernel primitive, and ii) the injection of faults into the code and data segments of the microkernel. On its principle, this approach is similar to most of classic fault injection tools. Nevertheless, we propose here to complement this method by considering the abstract functional decomposition characterizing the internal architecture of the microkernel. In consequence, we introduce two original forms of analysis, concerning:

1. the robustness and error detection for each functional component of the microkernel,
2. the error propagation between functional components.

This consideration leads to the notion of a modular workload, tailored to the internal functional architecture of the candidate microkernel. Such a workload, composed of a set of independent application processes, is suitable for the activation of the primitives exported by each single functional component (see Figure 2).

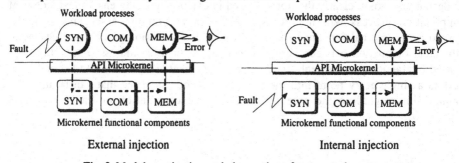

Fig. 2. Modular activation and observation of propagated errors

As illustrated on this figure the analysis of the behavior and data produced by the workload processes provide specific insights for the corresponding microkernel components. This scheme facilitates the observation of the error propagation between components. Indeed, the functional failure of a distinct component from the one targeted by the injection will be interpreted as the consequence of the propagation of an internal error within the microkernel.

Another major objective is to elaborate on the behavioral assessment for providing guidance and support to contain the effect of both external and internal faults that may affect the behavior of the target microkernel. Preventing faults from impacting the upper layers can only be achieved by external mechanisms. This claim leads to the notion of *wrapper*. The wrapping concept supported by MAFALDA mainly elaborates on executable assertions (e.g., see [11, 12]). Regarding to efficiency concerns, the accuracy of fault containment wrappers depends on the ability to identify a semantic error in the service delivered by the microkernel. This can be achieved by modeling the expected behavior of its functional components in the absence of faults. Because microkernel component specifications are easy to understand, their modeling allows for the easy definition of predicates. Once embedded into wrappers, taking the form of executable assertions, these predicates can be dynamically verified and any violation can thus be interpreted as a faulty behavior of the corresponding component.

3.2 Fault assumptions and fault/error model

Two forms of injection can be associated to each of the fault models identified:

- The evaluation of the robustness of the interface of the target microkernel corresponds to the analysis of the propagation of an error from the application level to the executive level. This approach consists in a corruption on a randomly selected byte, among the byte chain that constitutes the set of parameters passed to the microkernel during the invocation of one of its primitive. Only calls from the workload process corresponding to the selected functional component tested are susceptible to be corrupted, while the other calls remain unchanged.

- The second form of injection has for objective to simulate the occurrence of a physical fault (consecutive to the failure of the physical support of the system) or a software fault (design or development) into the microkernel. Here again, the injection process consists in a corruption on a randomly selected byte within the address space of the targeted functional module, in its text segment, as well as in its data segment.

For both forms of injection, the applied binary operation consists in performing one or several bit flips on the designated byte. This model is in accordance with most of the software fault injection tools.

The question of the representativity of this model of software error simulation, compared to the pathology induced by the occurrence of real faults, is crucial. Several Software Implemented Fault Injection studies (SWIFI) were dedicated to the analysis of the relationship between faults injected by software and physical faults. The tool EMAX [13] has been developed to extract a realistic fault model from the observation of failures due to the occurrence of physical faults in a microprocessor. This study showed a large proportion of control flow errors affecting the address and data buses, whose symptoms correspond from an informational point of view, to the inversion of one or several bits. The work presented in [14] showed that errors observed when injecting transient faults at the gate level in a simulation model of a processor can always be simulated by software at the informational level. The work described in [15] associates the occurrence of physical faults and errors at the functional level in a functional model of a processor. This study concluded that almost 99% of the bit-flip faults could be emulated by software. Finally in [16] the SWIFI technique is compared to two different fault injection techniques (ion radiation and physical injection at the pins level). This analysis showed that a simple bit flip model allows generating errors similar to errors observed by physical injection. All these studies tend thus to support the pertinence of the SWIFI technique based on bit(s) corruption at the target system informational level.

3.3 Architecture overview

Figure 3 illustrates the general architecture and the different modules of MAFALDA, as well as their respective interactions. On the target machine, we can identify: (1) the workload processes (Wpi) in charge of the activation of the microkernel functional components, (2) the injection module responsible for the implementation of the fault injection process, and (3) the wrapping module supporting the executable assertions. A host machine is running the controller module dedicated to the general coordination of the whole experiment. It is noteworthy that as suggested by this figure, in order to speed up experiments, up to 10 target systems can be used in parallel.

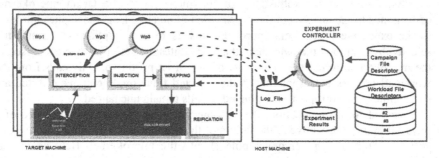

Fig. 3. MAFALDA architecture

The *injection* module is responsible for injecting faults, according to the model previously introduced. Depending on the type of fault specified in the *campaign file descriptor*, the injection target is either the microkernel code and data segments, or the input system call parameters.

The *wrapping* module constitutes a generic support for the implementation of various error detection and fault containment wrappers, as executables assertions upon the microkernel.

Clearly both *injection* and *wrapping* modules require a high level of *controllability*. This requirement is obvious as far as the parameter fault injection is concerned. In this case, the invocation of microkernel services plays the role of injection trigger, and such an event must be systematically intercepted. Concerning the *wrapping* module the controllability must be extended to all events susceptible to induce the update or the verification of an executable assertion, i.e. microkernel service invocations, returns from invocation, and even calls to some internal functions. The implementation of this property is a charge of the *interception* module, responsible for the behavioral reflection.

Besides controllability, the implementation of the wrappers may require access to specific microkernel data structures identified in the definition of the assertions. Here comes the notion of reification which aims at providing a satisfying level of the *observability* to implement the wrappers. The fulfillment of this property is the responsibility of the *reification* module.

On the host machine, for each injection campaign is associated a unique *campaign file descriptor* that entirely defines the parameters required by MAFALDA for proceeding to an experiment cycle: the type of faults to be injected, the functional component target of the injection, and a reference to a workload file descriptor.

The *workload file descriptor* contains the specification of the workload process. The *controller* interprets this file and extracts all the necessary information to install the workload processes on the target machine.

During an experiment, the *log file* collects the raw outcomes produced by the modules located on the target machine:
1. the reports of injection returned by the injector (injection time, location, fault type),
2. the events notified by the observation mechanisms (first time of fault activation, fault masking, detection of an error),
3. the detection status notified by the wrappers (assertion violation, error propagation),
4. the output produced during the execution of the workload processes, including normal (results of computation) and abnormal (notification of an application failure) data.

At the end of an experiment cycle, the controller analyzes the collected outcomes stored in the log file, to conclude on the experiment result. This information as well as a short synthesis of the most significant campaign attributes (e.g., error latencies, error messages) are archived in the *experiment result file*.

3.4 Fault injection campaign and measures

Figure 4 summarizes the main steps of a fault injection campaign. First, the set of workload processes is executed in the absence of an injected fault, so as to collect a trace of their behavior as well as the results produced under normal operation.

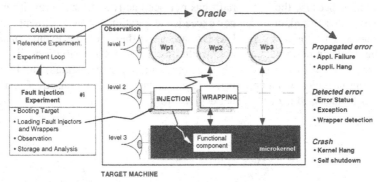

Fig. 4. Scheduling of a fault injection campaign

In addition to output data, this trace includes internal values and processes scheduling. These data constitute the *Oracle* used *a posteriori* to diagnose the propagation of an error to the application level. After this initial step, the *controller* executes the experiments sequentially. For each of them, the target machine is rebooted, avoiding thus any perturbation due to the potential presence of a residual fault from the previous experiment. Then the workload processes (W*pi*) responsible for the activation of the microkernel components are executed simultaneously. Depending on the type of injection, a single fault in randomly injected affecting either the targeted functional component through its

- interface: corruption of an incoming parameter from the corresponding workload process, or
- internal state: corruption of a code or data segment location.

The last step consists in the observation of the target system behavior. The various outcomes and traces produced are collected for the duration of the experiment.

The different failure modes of the candidate microkernel are grouped according to three distinct observation levels.

- The highest level (application level) concerns the observation of the symptoms of a propagated error: application failure due to an erroneous behavior or incorrect results, or hang of a workload process. Diagnosing such situations is carried out by an *a posteriori* analysis of the collected outcomes. The data produced by each workload process are compared to the initial *Oracle*, then application hang and application failure correspond respectively to an incomplete or erroneous data.
- The second level of observation (interface level) corresponds to the notification of a detected error. When issued from the internal detection mechanisms of the microkernel, the notification takes typically the form of an error status or an exception, whereas wrapper mechanisms return specific extended error status.
- The last level of observation (kernel level) concerns microkernel crashes, i.e., microkernel hang or self shutdown. A shut down decision is consecutive to the detection of a critical faulty state (e.g., internal data inconsistency, hardware failure) for which no recovery procedure can be undertaken. At this level, a microkernel hang diagnosis is established by testing the microkernel activity at the end of the experiment.

Finally, MAFALDA considers the case where no failure or error report is observed, either because the initial fault has not been activated, or the resulting error has been covered, masked, or its latency exceeds the duration of an experiment.

The measures provided by MAFALDA are a synthesis of the events observed during the fault injection campaign, including i) errors distribution, ii) errors propagation, iii) notifications distribution (exceptions, errors status), and iv) the corresponding latencies when appropriate (e.g., for the exceptions raised). Clearly the set of events synthesized is microkernel dependent.

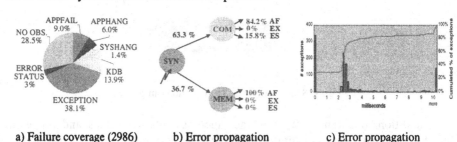

a) Failure coverage (2986)   b) Error propagation   c) Error propagation

Fig. 5. Sample of campaign results synthesis

To illustrate the types of results produced, Figure 5 shows a sample of results obtained when applying MAFALDA to the synchronization component of the Chorus/ClassiX microkernel. A more comprehensive analysis of the results obtained can be found in [5].

Figure 5-a shows the distribution of errors reported. Besides the propagation of errors that had no observable consequences (28.%), the figure indicates that from roughly 3000 experiments, more than 50% of them were successfully detected by internal errors mechanisms of the microkernel (error status, exception, kdb), while about 7.4% of the errors led to a fail silent behavior of the microkernel (system hang, application hang). An application failure occurred in 9% of the cases, in which applications delivered an incorrect service as a consequence of a non-detected propagated error.

Figure 5-b analyzes the propagation of errors between the functional components. In this case, we observe that most of the errors propagate to the communication module, which reveals that the communication module is more dependent on synchronization than the memory module.

As an example of timing measurements, Figure 5-c gives the latency distribution of the exceptions raised. In particular, the curves reveal that 30% of the exceptions are raised immediately, while 50% are distributed in an interval from 2.4 to 4 milliseconds.

4. Implementation Issues

This section provides insights on how fault injection and wrapping techniques are implemented by MAFALDA.

4.1 Microkernel fault injection

Fault injection into the microkernel address space takes advantage of the debugging hardware features existing in most of the modern microprocessors so as to inject faults by software and monitor the activation of the faults, in the same manner as Xception [17]. Figure 6 shows an overview of the microkernel fault injection technique using MAFALDA.

As shown in Figure 6-a, MAFALDA defines both temporal and spatial fault injection triggers, at the expiration of which a handler is activated responsible for injecting either a permanent or a transient fault. Such a fault can be aimed at either code or data segments.

As an example, Figure 6-b describes how MAFALDA carries out the injection of a transient fault into the code segment of the microkernel. When the temporal trigger expires and the target assembly instruction is reached by the processor program counter, an exception handler is activated. The handler signals the activation of the fault, and corrupts the assembly instruction applying a bit-flip mask to it. In order to simulate a transient fault, trace mode is then set up, and execution is allowed to resume. Now, the faulty instruction executes. If no failure occurs, the handler takes over the CPU again, resets the trace mode, recovers the faulted bits, and finally resumes execution.

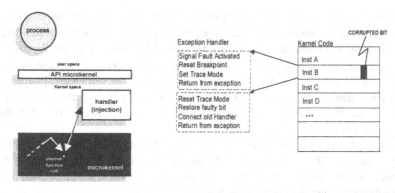

a) Overview   b) Transient fault into microkernel code segment

Fig. 6. Microkernel fault injection

4.2 Parameter fault injection

Techniques concerning parameter fault injection are different whether library-based microkernels or trap-based microkernels are considered, as shown in Figure 7.

Library-based microkernels do not have a common kernel call entry point and, in addition, sometimes they embody part of primitive service code into system libraries. When an application process performs a system call, it first executes such library routines at the same privilege level than the process, and then a jump-like assembly instruction drives the execution flow into the kernel. In order to perform fault injection into system call input parameters, MAFALDA provides a fault injection library which runs on top of the system libraries, as shown in Figure 7-a.

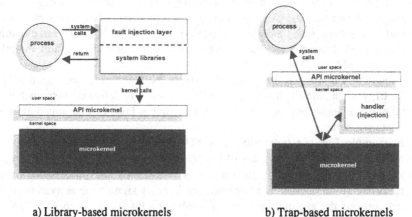

a) Library-based microkernels   b) Trap-based microkernels

Fig. 7. Parameter fault injection

The fault injection library works as follows: when a system call containing the target parameters is executed by a process, the fault injection layer intercepts it, randomly selects one input parameter of the system call, then applies a bit-flip mask to it, and finally lets the original call proceed into the system libraries.

Trap-based microkernels are characterized by the fact that they all have a single kernel call entry point to the microkernel. Fault injection is carried out by intercepting target system calls before they enter the microkernel, as shown in Figure 7-b.

The simplest and more efficient way to transparently put it into practice consists in *trapping* such a single kernel call entry point. For such a purpose, MAFALDA utilizes the debugging hardware features of the microprocessor to program a hardware breakpoint, so an exception is automatically raised by the underlying hardware whenever the kernel call entry point of the microkernel is reached in the processor program counter register. The handler attached to this exception is responsible for corrupting the input parameters. Once parameters have been injected, the handler lets the system call continue into the kernel. The advantages of this approach are that i) binary processes can be run as workload, and ii) workloads with specific activation profiles (i.e., matching a particular application domain) can be readily used.

4.3 Fault containment wrappers

Implementation issues for fault containment wrappers are also different for library-based microkernels or trap-based microkernels (Figure 8). In general, several approaches can be identified for wrapping: i) insert the fault containment wrapper into the kernel, ii) use a middleware process as a wrapper, or iii) embody the wrapper into libraries. In some cases, the primitive service is optimized partially into libraries, and thus the system call is not delivered to the kernel unless it is absolutely necessary that the kernel manage the call. With approaches i) and ii), only the primitive service part located into the microkernel is wrapped. Unlike i) and ii), embodying the wrapper into libraries accounts for primitive service optimizations.

Concerning *library-based microkernels*, MAFALDA's fault containment wrappers must cater for the part of the primitive service implemented into libraries. MAFALDA thus defines wrappers as an additional layer to the system libraries. Whenever a system call is made by a process, it first enters the *library-based wrapper*, where the call is filtered appropriately. Then, the call is allowed to resume into the system libraries. Finally the wrapper is activated again when the call returns, making it possible to perform further checks. The checks carried out encompass both input parameters (call to the kernel), and the system state resulting after the execution of the system call (return from the kernel). The latter requires that wrappers can access internal structures within the microkernel [18]. To solve this problem, an additional module, called side API, is attached to the microkernel, which acts as the reification module shown in Figure 3. This module can exhibit such microkernel internal data to upper layers of the system, and consequently, wrapping can be efficiently implemented. In order to give a general view of issues concerning wrapping with library-based microkernels, the above outlined concept of library-based wrapper is shown in Figure 8-a.

Wrappers for *trap-based microkernels* rely on a *metakernel protocol* to prevent errors from propagating. The metakernel protocol is defined on the basis of two important concepts, [6]: *behavioral reflection* and *reification*. Behavioral reflection correspond to the ability of intercepting every system call and reflecting a behavioral modification on the kernel. The implementation of this concept allows user system calls and internal function calls within the microkernel to be intercepted.

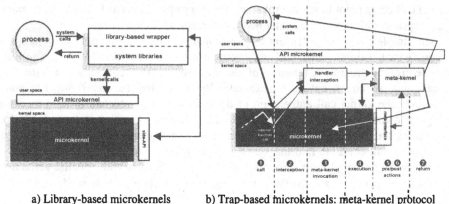

a) Library-based microkernels   b) Trap-based microkernels: meta-kernel protocol

Fig. 8. Fault containment wrappers

Behavioral reflection is put into practice by programming the internal hardware debugger. Reification allows internal structures within the microkernel to be exhibited to upper layers of the system. Reification, therefore, permits the internal state of the microkernel to be both observed and controlled. It corresponds to the module *reification* shown in Figure 3, being implemented as a module added to the microkernel which defines the so-called *metainterface*. Figure 8-b illustrates the metakernel protocol of MAFALDA. Every system call or internal function call is trapped by a handler, which passes control to the metakernel. The latter carries out checks during the *pre-actions* and *post-actions*, taking advantage of the metainterface to access the information needed. The actual execution of the primitive or method takes place between such pre- and post-actions, but it can be skipped or eventually replaced by another primitive or method. Finally, execution is resumed by returning to either the user application or the microkernel, whether it was a user system call or a microkernel internal function call, respectively.

4.4 Contribution of fault injection and wrappers

We show here how fault injection and wrapping interact when either library or trap-based techniques are considered.

The location of the wrappers is important, and has to respect the following rules:

- All system calls must be intercepted by the wrapper, and preferably after the data were corrupted by fault injection.
- The wrapper must filter system calls before they reach the system libraries.
- The wrapper must filter the return of every system call.

Accordingly, wrappers for library-based microkernels and fault injectors are respectively located as shown in Figure 9. Concerning trap-based microkernels, the metakernel protocol of Figure 8-b defines the overall behavior of MAFALDA, since it comprises not only wrapping, but also both parameter fault injection and microkernel fault injection. Indeed, the pre-actions performed by the metakernel can easily include parameter injection, regardless of the meta-interface. On the other hand, a microkernel internal function call can be accessed and corrupted on the same bases of microkernel fault injection, namely: pre-actions support bit-flip injection, while post-actions provide for fault removal.

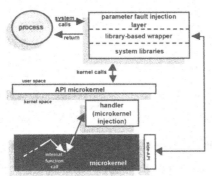

Fig. 9. Library-based microkernels: Fault Injection & Wrapping

5. Examples of Results

In this section we provide some results obtained with MAFALDA in assessing and enhancing an instance of the Chorus/ClassiX r3.1 microkernel running on a Pentium machine (target machine), and monitoring experiments from a Sun station with Solaris 2.5.1 (host machine).

Even though the Chorus/ClassiX is a trap-based microkernel, some primitive services are optimized into libraries. As a consequence, MAFALDA could successfully apply trap-based techniques as well as library-based techniques to such microkernel. The evaluation of the Chorus/ClassiX microkernel by fault injection is reported in [5], while the microkernel enhancement by wrappers is reported in [6].

For sake of brevity, we focus our analysis on the fault coverage increase provided by the use of wrappers with MAFALDA. Two wrappers have been designed: a *synchronization wrapper*, catering for library-based wrapping techniques, and a *scheduling wrapper*, which follows the metakernel protocol principle. The efficiency of these wrappers is analyzed in Figure 10.

Figure 10-a shows the efficiency of the synchronization wrapper. It reveals that when microkernel fault injection was performed into the standard (i.e., not wrapped) synchronization module, about 9% of the injected errors led to an application failure. However, when the synchronization module is encapsulated with the wrapper, the same fault injection campaign led to a decrease on the rate of application failures to 2.2%. In the case of parameter fault injection, the 87% of application failures observed without wrapping the microkernel, are totally covered by the wrapper. The efficiency of the scheduling wrapper is shown in Figure 10-b. The wrapper enhanced the rate of the application failures, which was reduced to 2.3%. It is worth noting that the wrapper also had a positive impact on the percentage of application hangs and system hangs, which reduced to 3.9% and 1.1%, respectively. MAFALDA allowed these remaining failures to be examined in detail off-line. They clearly were out of the error domain of the scheduling model developed by the proposed wrapper. Thus, MAFALDA offers suitable means to set new grounds for the development of improved wrappers.

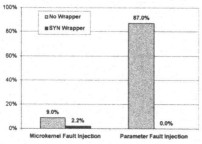
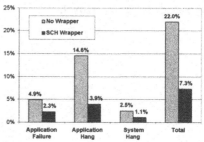

a) SYN: Application failure distribution   b) SCH: Wrapping for microkernel fault

Fig. 10. Wrapper efficiency

6. Summary and Conclusion

The Assessment of a COTS Microkernel by Fault Injection with MAFALDA is certainly one of the main interest for the design of a target system. The results obtained clearly enable the system designer to decide on which microkernel candidate his application needs fit. It is worth noting however that COTS microkernels are not always used in a standard configuration, but that a specific instance of the microkernel is developed on purpose. This is mostly the case for safety critical systems in which some components must be replaced according to application domain standards (e.g. scheduling policy as in ARINC 653 for avionics systems [19]). MAFALDA is thus a very useful tool to qualify a given microkernel instance.

The faults considered in MAFALDA include software faults affecting the application/middleware software (parameter fault injection) and physical faults that could affect also the core functions of the microkernel (microkernel fault injection). The interpretation of the results obtained varies from one system to another. This is the first dimension of MAFALDA regarding Design Aid. For safety critical system, the main aim is to handle the error information returned and place the application in a safe state. For more generic system dependable architecture, replication strategies may be implemented to also handle crashes. In this case, only physical faults can be considered and the main assumption is that the runtime layer (including software and hardware) is fail silent. MAFALDA provides more features to these aims by means of wrappers. The later are used to improve both the returned error information and the fail silent assumption, preventing as far as possible application failures. Indeed, the encapsulation framework provided by MAFALDA is a second dimension of the Design Aid features of the tool. Dedicated wrappers can be implemented according to the application needs and for a given microkernel instance. Their efficiency depends very much on the abstraction level where the modeling of the internal components has been done. It is up to the system designer to decide on this abstraction level and define accordingly the metainterface for the implementation of the wrappers. The metainterface defines the expected observability and controllability required by the wrappers. This notion enables a standard configuration (binary version) to be used when the microkernel provides the implementation of the required metainterface. Requesting such implementation from the microkernel provider is the price to pay for improving the system designer confidence in a given microkernel.

From the microkernel provider viewpoint, MAFALDA has also some interesting features. Indeed, understanding better the various application failure scenarios has a direct impact on the design and the implementation of the microkernel. This observation is also important for the microkernel crashes that are expected to be minimal. This is of course mandatory in most applications, even for non-critical ones.

From our experiments we can already draw some preliminary lessons. Microkernel that take advantage of handling separate address spaces often make use of trap mechanisms for the implementation of the microkernel system call. This features provides a single point of access to the microkernel functions and thus can be easily intercepted for implementing additional controls.

The failure modes of the microkernel in the presence of faults not only rely on the implementation of the correct microkernel functions (including on-line error detection mechanisms) but also design choices regarding the microkernel components. Being aware of these design choices is mandatory for the development of upper layers. Clearly, one of the benefits of MAFALDA is to make clear such design decisions. The selection of the appropriate microkernel finally relies on its functionalities and other properties, such as easy customization. However the later is not of prime importance as far as dependability is concerned; the observed failure modes and the capacity to improve this behavior by means of wrappers is decisive. This will be illustrated in the next future by a comparative campaign of various well known microkernels (such as Chorus, VxWorks, QNX, etc) using MAFALDA. Dealing with real-time aspects is another fundamental features in dependable systems in general and safety critical ones in particular. Clearly MAFALDA must be improved to handled more explicitly these aspects. This is one of our current activity.

Acknowledgments: This work was partially supported by ESPRIT Project 20072, Design for Validation (DeVa). Manuel Rodríguez is currently supported by Thomson-CSF (SRTI SYSTEM) in the framework of the Laboratory for Dependability Engineering (LIS). LIS is a Cooperative Laboratory between Aerospatiale Matra Airbus, Électricité de France, Matra Marconi Space France, Technicatome, Thomson-CSF and LAAS-CNRS.

References

[1] P. Koopman, J. Sung, C. Dingman, D. Siewiorek and T. Marz, "Comparing Operating Systems using Robustness Benchmarks", in *Proc. 16th IEEE Symp. on Reliable Distributed Systems,* Durham, NC, USA, 1997, pp. 72-79.

[2] J. Voas, "Certifying Off-The-Shelf Software Components", *Computer,* vol. 31, pp. 53-59, June 1998.

[3] W. Kao, R. K. Iyer and D. Tang, "FINE: A Fault Injection and Monitoring Environment for Tracing the UNIX System Behavior under Faults", *IEEE Transactions on Software Engineering*, vol. 19, pp. 1105-1118, 1993.

[4] P. Koopman and J. DeVale, "Comparing the Robustness of POSIX Operating Systems", in *29th IEEE Int. Symp. on Fault-Tolerant Computing*, Madison, WI, USA, 1999, pp. 30-37.

[5] J.-C. Fabre, F. Salles, M. Rodríguez and J. Arlat, "Assessment of COTS Microkernels by Fault Injection", in *Proc. 7th Dependable Computing for Critical Applications*, San Jose, CA, USA, 1999, pp. 19-38.

[6] F. Salles, M. Rodríguez, J.-C. Fabre and J. Arlat, "MetaKernel anf Fault Containment Wrappers", in *29th IEEE Int. Symp. on Fault-Tolerant Computing*, Madison, WI, USA, 1999, pp. 22-29.

[7] Chorus, "Chorus/ClassiX r3 - Technical Overview", no. Technical Report CS/TR-96-119.8, Chorus systems, 1996.

[8] Chorus, "Chorus/ClassiX r3.1b for ix86 - Product Description", no. Technical Report CS/TR-96-221.1, Chorus systems, 1996.

[9] VxWorks, "VxWorks Realtime Kernel", WindRiver Systems, (see http://www.wrs.com/products/html/vxwks52.html), 1998.

[10] D. Hildebrand, "An Architectural overview of QNX", in *1st Work. on Micro-Kernels and Other Kernel Architectures*, Seattle, WA, USA, 1992, pp. 113-126.

[11] A. Mahmood, D. M. Andrews and E. J. McCluskey, "Executable Assertions and Flight Software", in *Proc. 6th Digital Avionics Systems Conf.*, Baltimore, Maryland, USA, 1984, pp. 346-351.

[12] C. Rabéjac, J.-P. Blanquart and J.-P. Queille, "Executable Assertions and Timed Traces for On-Line Software Error Detection", in *Proc. 26th Int. Symp. on Fault-Tolerant Computing*, Sendai, Japan, 1996, pp. 138-147.

[13] G. A. Kanawati, N. A. Kanawati and J. A. Abraham, "EMAX: An automatic Extractor of High-Level Error Models", in *Computing Aerospace Conff.*, San Diego, CA, USA, 1993, pp. 1297-1306.

[14] E. Czeck, "Estimates of the Abilities of Software-Implemented Fault Injection to Represent Gate-Level Faults", in *Int. Work. on Fault and Error Injection for Dependability Validation of Computer Systems*, Gothemburg, Sweden, 1993.

[15] M. Rimén, I. Ohlsson and J. Torin, "On Microprocessor Error Behavior Modeling", in *24th Int. Symp. on Fault Tolerant Computing*, Austin, Texas, USA, 1994, pp. 76-85.

[16] E. Fuchs, "Validating the Fail-Silent Assumption of the MARS Architecture", in *proc. 6th Dependable Computing for Critical Applications*, Garmisch-Partenkirchen, Germany, 1998, pp. 225-247.

[17] J. Carreira, H. Madeira and J. G. Silva, "Xception: A Technique for the Experimental Evaluation of Dependability in Modern Computers", *IEEE Transactions on Software Engineering*, vol. 24, pp. 125-136, February 1998.

[18] F. Salles, J. Arlat and J. C. Fabre, "Can We Rely on COTS Microkernels for Building Fault-Tolerant Systems?", in *Proc. 6th Future Trends of Distributing Computing Systems*, Tunis, Tunisia, 1997, pp. 189-194.

[19] ARINC-653, "Avionics Application Software Standard Interface (ARINC 653)", ARINC Working Group, (see http://www.arinc.com/home.html).

Industrial Track Paper

Assessing Error Detection Coverage by Simulated Fault Injection

Cristian Constantinescu

Intel Corporation, Server Architecture Lab, CO3-202,
5200 NE Elam Young Parkway, Hillsboro, OR 97124-6497, USA
cristian.constantinescu@intel.com

Abstract. Server dependability is of increasing importance as more critical applications rely on the client-server computing model. As a consequence, complex fault/error handling mechanisms are becoming common features of today servers. This paper presents a new simulated fault injection method, which allows the assessment of the effectiveness of error detection mechanisms without using expensive test circuits. Fault injection was performed in two stages. First, physical fault injection was performed on a prototype server. Transient faults were injected in randomly selected signals. Traces of the signals sensitive to transients were captured. A complex protocol checker was devised for increasing error detection. The new detection circuitry was simulated in the second stage of the experiment. Signal traces, injected with transient faults, were used as inputs of the simulation. The error detection coverage and latency were derived. Fault injection also showed that coverage probability was a function of fault duration.

1 Introduction

High dependability has become a major concern to server manufacturers and information technology professionals as client-server computing model has been gaining more acceptance in the mission critical enterprise arena. As a consequence, enhanced fault/error handling mechanisms are embedded into the latest generations of high end servers. Typically, the fault/error handling process consists of error detection, isolation and diagnosis of the faulty field replaceable unit, reintegration of the unit if the fault/error is transient, replacement by a spare if a permanent or intermittent fault is detected and spares are available, and graceful degradation if no spares are available. High error detection coverage (i. e. conditional probability that an error is detected, given that an error occurs) is paramount for properly handling errors.

Fault/error injection is commonly used for assessing the effectiveness of fault tolerance mechanisms and deriving coverage probabilities. Numerous physical, software and simulated methodologies have been developed in order to perform fault injection experiments. Physical and software fault injection are performed on the target system. The most commonly used approaches for performing physical fault injection are: injection at the IC pin level [1, 5, 18, 20], electromagnetic interference

[18] and heavy-ion radiation [17, 18]. Software tools, such as FIAT [24], EFA [8], DOCTOR [12], FERRARI [16], Xception [3], and results of software fault injection experiments [2, 4, 25] were presented in literature. Simulation models were frequently used as an alternative to physical and software fault injection. ADEPT [10], DEPEND [11] and MEFISTO [15] are among the most well known fault injection simulation tools. Scan Chain Implemented Fault Injection (SCIFI) and VHDL simulated fault injection were used in [9]. Combined implementations, based on hardware, software and simulated fault injection were employed in [1, 23, 28]. A survey of fault injection tools and techniques was provided in [13].

A new simulated fault injection method is presented in this paper. Our approach is based on a temporal language, PROTO [29], and allows the determination of the effectiveness of error detection mechanisms without costly silicon implementations of the detection circuitry. The fault injection experiment described herein consisted of two stages. First, transient faults were physically injected in a two-way Pentium® Pro processor based prototype server, according to the methodology presented in [5]. Traces of the signals sensitive to transient faults were captured and error detection coverage was derived. Complex circuitry, employing an algorithm for checking protocol violations, was devised in order to improve error detection. In the second stage of the experiment the new detection mechanism was simulated and faults were injected in traces of the signals which exhibited high sensitivity to transients. This approach allowed us to evaluate the efficacy of the protocol checker, derive the error detection coverage probability and determine the detection latency.

The paper is organized as follows. Simulated fault injection is described in Section 2. Section 3 presents the fault injection experiments. Signal sensitivity to transient faults is assessed. Error detection coverage and detection latency are derived. Section 4 concludes the paper.

2 Simulated Fault Injection

A new simulated fault injection approach was developed for assessing the efficacy of error detection mechanisms. The PROTO language was used to describe the detection circuitry. PROTO is a temporal language which models the behavior of complex devices as a series of timed expressions. It is primarily based on temporal flow (sequential events with triggering and completion points) and temporal finite state machine (repetitive events and finite state machine) constructs. PROTO couples the Intel Hardware Description Language (iHDL) design model with the validation environment, allowing functional validation of the design without using costly test circuits. Commonly, a PROTO simulation consists of the following steps:
- Temporal behavior of the device is specified in the PROTO language
- Specification is compiled into a simulation model
- Simulation model is executed

The PROTO model can be executed in two modes: stand-alone and lock-up. In the first mode traces from a real machine are captured in trace files. The simulation runs independently, using the trace files as inputs. Alternatively, an iHDL based Register Transfer Level (RTL) model can be used, if traces from the real system are not available. In the second mode the PROTO simulation is executed in lock-step with the

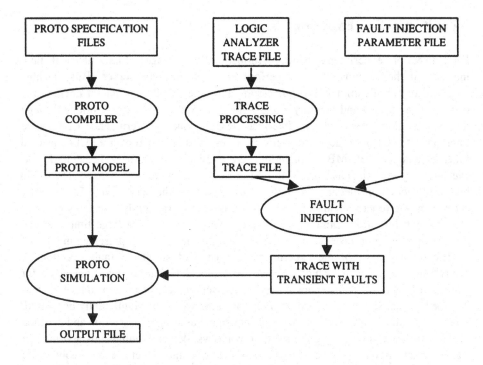

Fig. 1. Block diagram of the simulated fault injection

RTL model. The RTL model provides the input for the simulator through an Application Program Interface (API) opened pipe. Both approaches store the results in output files. The first execution mode, using traces captured from a real machine, was employed in our experiments.

Simulated fault injection followed the procedure depicted in Fig. 1. The main steps of the experiment were:

- Create and compile the PROTO specification files of the detection circuitry. The PROTO model was obtained in this way.

- Process the traces of the signals which were sensitive to transient faults. A PROTO compatible trace file was the result of this step.

- Create the fault injection parameter file. This file provided the following information: names of the injected signals; starting point of the fault injection; duration of the fault(s); fault type. Two types of faults were injected: type "1", when the signal was pulled to one, and type "0" when the signal was forced to zero.

- Inject the faults described by the parameter fife into the trace file. An AWK program was developed for performing the fault injection. This step of the experiment created trace files which contained transient faults.

- Run the PROTO simulation, in stand-alone mode, using the fault injected traces as inputs. Simulation results were stored in an output file.

- Analyze the output file. Derive error detection coverage probability and detection latency. The fault injection approach described above was used for assessing the effectiveness of the protocol violation checker.

3 Fault Injection Experiments

Fault injection experiments were performed in two stages. First, physical fault injection at the IC pin level was performed on a prototype server. This machine consisted of two Pentium® Pro processors, connected to the peripheral devices and memory over an I/O and memory bridge. The disks were linked to the bridge through the Small Computer System Interface (SCSI) and a Peripheral Component Interconnect (PCI) interface card. Network access was provided over a PCI connected Ethernet adapter. 256 MB of memory were available. A Linpack benchmark was executed on the machine under the Microsoft NT operating system. The main fault/error detection mechanisms initially employed by the server were ECC, parity and watch-dog timers. Transient faults were injected in randomly selected signals, at random time instances. Duration of the faults was varied over a large time interval. Signal sensitivity to transients was derived using the methodology presented in [5].

The second stage of the experiments consisted of simulated fault injection. A sophisticated mechanism, which checked for protocol violations, was considered for augmenting error detection capabilities of the server. The detection algorithm was designed so that signal sensitivity to transient faults would be significantly decreased. The main features of the checker were: detect signal assertion/deassertion and duration of the active state outside predefined time windows, detect simultaneous assertion of signals which should never be active at the same time, and detect a wrong sequence of operations. In order to evaluate the effectiveness of the protocol checker we injected faults similar to those used in the first phase (i. e. same number of transients, identical durations), in all signals which exhibited high sensitivity to transients.

This section gives the results of both physical and simulated fault injection experiments and discusses the impact of checking for protocol violations on error detection coverage. Over 2000 transient faults were injected in each phase of the experiment. We decided to inject only transients because these faults were the most frequently experienced by modern computers [14, 19, 26]. For the sake of brevity only three examples are presented here.

3.1 Analysis of Signal Sensitivity to Transient Faults

Results of the physical fault injection in signal A are given in Fig. 2.1. Duration of the faults (type "1") was varied from 25 ns to 120 μ s. Although 90% of the 25 ns faults induced no errors, the remaining 10% led to undetected errors. The percentage of undetected errors increased to 27% and 77%, for 50 ns and 100 ns transients, respectively. 6% of the errors were detected in the case of 100 ns faults. None of the errors induced by 200 ns faults were detected. The percentage of detected errors increased from 3% to 90% as fault duration was varied from 2 μ s to 120 μ s. Faults shorter than 25 ns, injected in signal A, induced no errors and all errors induced by faults longer than 120 μ s were detected.

Simulated fault injection showed that checking for protocol violations significantly improved detection of the errors induced by transients (Fig. 2.2). 23% and 60% of the errors induced by 100 ns and 200 ns faults, respectively, were detected. All errors

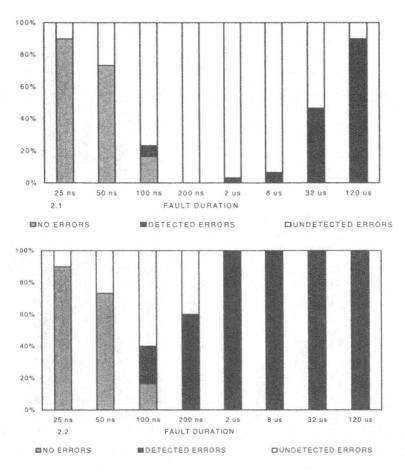

Fig. 2. Sensitivity of signal A to transient faults (type "1"faults).
2.1 - initial, 2.2 - improved detection

generated by $2\,\mu$ s – $120\,\mu$ s faults were detected. Short transients (25 ns – 50 ns) continued to induce undetected errors. The average detection latency was 350 ns.

Multi-point faults induced a larger number of undetected errors. It also has to be stressed that undetected errors were induced even it the case of very short transients, i. e. 10 ns. Fig. 3.1 shows the results of the physical fault injection in signals A (type "1" faults) and B (type "0" faults). The percentage of undetected errors increased from 30% in the case of 10 ns transients to 100% for $2\,\mu$ s faults. Only 3% of the errors induced by 25 ns, 50 ns and 100 ns faults were detected. The percentage of detected errors increased from 20% to 90% as fault duration was varied from $8\,\mu$ s to $120\,\mu$ s.

Checking for protocol violations provided better error detection, as it is showed in Fig. 3.2. The percentage of detected errors increased from 23%, in the case of 25 ns faults, to 100% for $2\,\mu$ s transients and longer. None of the errors induced by 10 ns faults were detected. The average detection latency was 240 ns.

Fig. 4.1 gives the results of physical fault injection simultaneously performed in

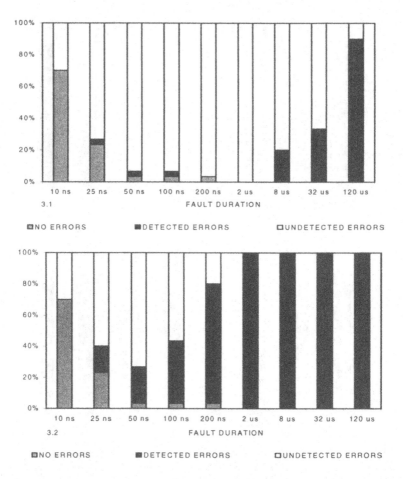

Fig. 3. Sensitivity of signals A and B to transient faults (A type "1" faults, B type "0" faults)
3.1 - initial, 3.2 - improved detection

three signals: A (type "1" faults), B and C (type "0" faults). Comparing with the previous cases three-point transient faults led to more undetected errors. Only 6%, 30% and 83% of the errors induced by the 200ns, 32 μ s and 120 μ s faults were detected, respectively. No errors were detected in the case of 2 μ s and 8 μ s faults.

As Fig. 4.2 shows, checking for protocol violations significantly improved error detection. The percentage of detected errors ranged from 33% for 25 ns faults to 100% in the case of 2 μ s – 120 μ s faults. Yet, none of the errors induced by short transients (10 ns) were detected. In the case of three-point faults the average detection latency increased to 1.18 μ s.

3.2 Derivation of Error Detection Coverage Probability

Statistical inference methods are commonly employed for estimating the coverage probability. Sampling in partitioned and nonpartitioned spaces, stratified and two-stage

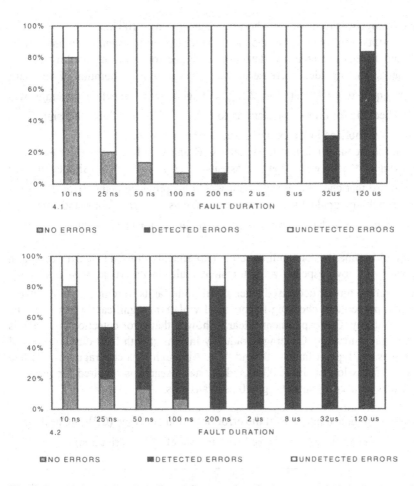

Fig. 4. Sensitivity of signals A, B and C to transient faults (A type "1" faults, B and C type "0" faults) 4.1 - initial, 4.2 - improved detection

sampling were the main techniques used in [21, 22]. Multi-stage, stratified and combined sampling techniques were employed for deriving confidence intervals of the coverage probability in multi-dimensional spaces of events [6, 7].

In this work we were particularly interested in deriving independent coverage probabilities and their confidence intervals for each duration of the injected transient faults. Because of schedule requirements the sample size used in our experiments was limited to 30. Confidence intervals were derived with the aid of Student t distribution, when estimated values of the coverage were in $0.1 \leq c \leq 0.9$ range. χ^2 distribution was used for $c < 0.1$ and $c > 0.9$ [27].

Table 1 shows the 90% confidence intervals of the error detection coverage probability. Signal A detection was characterized by a very low coverage for errors induced by transient faults in the 25 ns - 8 μ s range. Coverage improved for 32 μ s and longer faults. Simulated fault injection showed that checking for protocol violations significantly improved the coverage in the 200 ns – 120 μ s range. Yet, low detection coverage was observed for short transients (25 ns – 100 ns).

Similar results were obtained in the case of multi-point transient faults injected in signals A and B: unacceptable low detection coverage for errors induced by 10 ns - 8 μ s transients, and a gradual increase of the coverage with the duration of the faults which were equal to or longer than 32 μ s. Higher error detection coverage was attained by checking for protocol violations for 100 ns – 120 μ s faults. No significant improvement was noticed in the case of 10 ns – 50 ns transients.

Faults simultaneously injected in signals A, B and C led to lower error detection coverage even in the case of long transients (8 μ s – 32 μ s). Simulated fault injection showed that checking for protocol violations provided better error detection. Coverage probability gradually increased from 25 ns to 2 μ s faults and remained steady for longer faults. No improvement was observed for errors induced by 10 ns faults.

Single and multi-point physical fault injection experiments showed that error detection coverage was very low, especially for transient faults in the 10 ns – 8 μ s range. Detection coverage further decreased when multi-point faults were injected. Simulated fault injection proved that checking for protocol violations significantly increased the coverage probability. Our experiments clearly showed that error detection coverage is a function of fault duration. Coverage gradually increased with fault duration, for all injected signals and type of faults ("0" and "1"). Although high coverage was attained in the case of faults longer than 200 ns, additional research is required for properly detecting errors induced by short (e. g., 10 ns) transients.

Table 1. 90% confidence intervals of the error detection coverage (CPV – Checking for Protocol Violations is used; * derived with the aid of χ^2 distribution)

Signal Name	Fault Duration								
	10 ns	25 ns	50 ns	100 ns	200 ns	2 μ s	8 μ s	32 μ s	120 μ s
A	-	*.0, .077	*0.0, .077	*.0, .177	*.0, .077	*.0, .13	*.0, .177	.309, .624	.805, .995
A CPV	-	*.0, .077	*0.0, .077	.155, .445	.674, .926	.923, 1.*	.923, 1.*	.923, 1.*	.923, 1.*
A&B	*.0, .077	*.0, .13	*0.0, .13	*.0, .13	*.0, .077	*.0, .077	.074, .326	.185, .482	.805, .995
A&B CPV	*.0, .077	.074, .326	.1, .367	.245, .555	.676, .926	.923, 1.*	.923, 1.*	.923, 1.*	.923, 1.*
A,B&C	*.0, .077	*.0, .077	*0.0, .077	*0.0, .077	*0.0, .177	*0.0, .077	*0.0, .077	.155, .445	.716, .951
A,B&C CPV	*.0, .077	.245, .555	.445, .755	.481, .785	.674, .926	.923, 1.*	.923, 1.*	.923, 1.*	.923, 1.*

4 Conclusions

High error detection coverage have become paramount for achieving today's dependability requirements of enterprise class servers. A new simulated fault injection method has been developed in order to evaluate the effectiveness of error detection mechanisms. First, faults were physically injected into a prototype server in order to asses signal sensitivity to transient faults. A complex protocol checking mechanism was devised for improving error detection. In the second stage of the experiment a simulation model of the new detection circuitry was developed. Traces captured from the physical system were injected with transient faults and used as inputs of the simulation. This approach was successfully used to derive the error detection coverage and detection latency of the protocol checker, without using expensive test circuits.

Physical fault injection experiments showed that several signals were sensitive to transient faults and the error detection coverage was unacceptably low. It was noticed that multi-point faults induced a larger number of undetected errors, comparing with single-point faults. Also, in the case of multi-point faults, shorter transients (i. e. 10 ns versus 25 ns) were capable of inducing undetected errors. Additional fault injection experiments are ongoing to find out whether this behavior is implementation specific.

Simulated fault injection proved that checking for protocol violations improved error detection, providing significantly higher coverage probabilities. It was also observed that detection coverage was a function of fault duration: the longer the transient fault, the higher the coverage. Although the simulated protocol checker detected most of the errors induced by faults in the 200 ns – 120 μ s range, further research has to be carried out for improving detection of shorter transients. In general, it has to be stressed that injecting only permanent faults would lead to overly optimistic estimates of the coverage probability.

Acknowledgement

The author wishes to thank Steve Almquist for development of the simulation model, and Jean Arlat and the anonymous reviewers for their valuable comments.

References

1. Arlat, J. et al: Fault Injection for Dependability Validation: a Methodology and Some Applications. IEEE Trans. Software Engineering, 2 (1990) 166-182
2. Barton, J., Czeck, E., Segall, Z., Siewiorek, D.: Fault Injection Experiments using FIAT. IEEE Trans. Computers, 4 (1990) 575-582
3. Carreira, J., Madeira, H., Silva, J. G.: Xception: A technique for the experimental evaluation of dependability in modern computers. IEEE Trans. Soft. Engineering, 2 (1998) 125-136
4. Chillarege, R., Bowen, N.: Understanding Large Systems Failures-A fault Injection Experiment., Proc. 19th FTCS Symposium (1989) 356-363
5. Constantinescu, C.: Validation of the fault/error handling mechanisms of the Teraflops supercomputer. Proc. 28th FTCS Symposium (1998) 382-389

6. Constantinescu, C.: Estimation of coverage probabilities for dependability validation of fault-tolerant computing systems. Proc. 9th Annual Conf. Computer Assurance, Gaithersburg (1994) 101-106

7. Constantinescu, C.: Using Multi-stage & Stratified Sampling for Inferring Fault Coverage Probabilities. IEEE Trans. Reliability, 4 (1995) 632-639

8. Echtle, K., Leu, M.: The EFA Fault Injector for Fault Tolerant Distributed System Testing. Proc. Fault Tolerant Parallel and Distributed Systems Workshop, (1992) 28-35

9. Folkesson, P., Svensson, S., Karlsson, J.: A comparison of simulated based and scan chain implemented fault injection. Proc. 28th FTCS Symposium (1998) 284-293

10. Ghosh, A., Johnson, B.: System-Level Modeling in the ADEPT Environment of a Distributed Computer System for Real-Time Applications. Proc. IEEE International Computer Performance and Dependability Symposium (1995) 194-203

11. Goswami, K., Iyer, R.K., Young, L.: DEPEND: A Simulation Based Environment for System Level Dependability Analysis. IEEE Trans. Computers, 1 (1997) 60-74

12. Han, S., Shin, K., Rosenberg, H.: DOCTOR: An Integrated Software Fault Injection Environment for Distributed Real-Time Systems. Proc. IEEE International Computer Performance and Dependability Symposium. (1995) 204-213

13. Hsueh, M.C., Tsai, T. K., Iyer, R. K.: Fault injection techniques and tools. IEEE Computer, 4 (1997) 75-82

14. Iyer, R. K.: Experimental Evaluation. Special Issue 25th FTCS Symp. (1995) 115-132

15. Jenn, E. et al.: Fault Injection into VHDL Models: The MEFISTO tool. Proc. 24th FTCS Symposium (1994) 66-75

16. Kanawati, G., Kanawati, N., Abraham, J.: FERRARI: A Tool for the Validation of System Dependability Properties. Proc. 22nd FTCS Symposium (1992) 336-344

17. Karlsson, J. et al.: Using Heavy-ion Radiation to Validate Fault Handling Mechanisms. IEEE Micro, 1 (1994) 8-32

18. Karlsson, J. et al.: Application of Three Physical Fault Injection Techniques to the Experimental Assessment of the MARS Architecture. Proc. 5th DCCA Conference (1995) 150-161

19. Lala, P. K.: Fault Tolerant and Fault Testable Hardware Design. Prentice Hall Int., New York (1985)

20. Madeira, H., Rela, M., Moreira, F., Silva, J. G.: A General Purpose Pin-level Fault Injector. Proc. 1st European Dependable Computing Conference, (1994) 199-216

21. Powel, D., Martins, E., Arlat, J., Crouzet, Y.: Estimators for fault tolerance coverage evaluation. IEEE Trans. Computers, 2 (19 95) 261-274

22. Powel, D., Cukier, M., Arlat, J.: On stratified sampling for high coverage estimators. Proc. 2nd European Dependable Computing Conference (1996) 37-54

23. Scott, D. T., Ries, G., Hsueh, M., Iyer, R. K.: Dependability Analysis of a High-Speed Network Using Software-implemented Fault Injected and Simulated Fault Injection. IEEE Trans. Computers, 1 (1998) 108-119

24. Segal, Z., Lin, T.: FIAT: Fault Injection Based Automated Testing Environment. Proc. 18th FTCS Symposium (1988) 102-107

25. Silva, J. G. et al: Experimental Assessment of Parallel Systems. Proc. 26th FTCS Symposium (1996) 415-424

26. Siewiorek, D. P., Swarz, R. S.: The Theory and Practice of Reliable Design. Digital Press, Digital Equipment Corp., Bedford, Massachusetts (1984)

27. Trivedi, K. S.: Probability and Statistics with Reliability, Queuing, and Computer Science Applications. Prentice-Hall (1982)

28. Walter, C. J.: Evaluation and Design of an Ultra reliable Distributed Architecture for Fault Tolerance. IEEE Trans. Reliability, 4 (1990) 492-499

29. PROTO Language. Design Technology Documentation PROT03, Intel Corp (1995)

Considering Workload Input Variations in Error Coverage Estimation

Peter Folkesson and Johan Karlsson

Laboratory for Dependable Computing, Department of Computer Engineering,
Chalmers University of Technology, S-412 96 Göteborg, Sweden
{peterf, johan}@ce.chalmers.se

Abstract. The effects of variations in the workload input when estimating error detection coverage using fault injection are investigated. Results from scan-chain implemented fault injection experiments using the FIMBUL tool on the Thor microprocessor show that the estimated error non-coverage may vary by more than five percentage units for different workload input sequences. A methodology for predicting error coverage for a particular input sequence based on results from fault injection experiments with another input sequence is presented. The methodology is based on the fact that workload input variations alter the usage of sensitive data and cause different parts of the workload code to be executed different number of times. By using the results from fault injection experiments with a chosen input sequence, the error coverage factors for the different parts of the code and the data are calculated. The error coverage for a particular input sequence is then predicted by means of a weighted sum of these coverage factors. The weight factors are obtained by analysing the execution profile and data usage of the input sequence. Experimental results show that the methodology can identify input sequences with high, medium or low coverage although the accuracy of the predicted values is limited. The results show that the coverage of errors in the data cache is preferably predicted using data usage based prediction while the error coverage for the rest of the CPU is predicted more favourably using execution profile based prediction.

1 Introduction

Since fault-tolerant computer systems are often used for protecting large investments and even lives, validating such systems before they are being put to use is imperative. Experimental validation methods such as fault injection have become particularly attractive for estimating the dependability of computer systems [8]. As fault-tolerant systems typically contain several mechanisms for detecting and handling errors in order to avoid system failures, it is of particular interest to measure the efficiency of these mechanisms, i.e., to measure the error detection coverage.

It is well known that the workload program has significant impact on the dependability measures obtained from fault injection experiments [4], [6]. Thus, the program must be carefully chosen when evaluating fault-tolerant systems. The ideal is to use the real program that will be used during actual operation of the system.

The results of fault injection experiments may also be affected by the workload input sequence [3]. Fault injection experiments conducted on a Motorola MVME162 board executing a parser evaluating algebraic expressions clearly show the impact of the input domain on estimated dependability measures [2]. Thus, both the program and the input sequence to the program must be considered when validating fault-tolerant systems.

We have used the FIMBUL tool [5] to investigate the effects of workload input variations on fault injection results. We show, for three different programs, that variations in input domain significantly affects the estimated error coverage. A solution to the problem of accurately estimating error coverage when the input domain varies could be to perform fault injection experiments for many input sequences. However, conducting fault injection experiments for a large number of input sequences is very time consuming. To speed up the validation process, a methodology for predicting the error coverage for a particular input sequence based on fault injection results obtained for another input sequence is presented.

The remainder of the paper is organized as follows. The experimental set-up used for investigating the effects of workload input variations on fault injection results is described in Sect. 2. In Sect. 3, results obtained from fault injection experiments clearly demonstrate that the input sequence affects the estimated error coverage. The methodology for predicting error coverage is presented in Sect. 4 and applied on three different workloads in Sect. 5. Finally, the conclusions of this study are given in Sect. 6 together with a discussion about the advantages/disadvantages of the methodology and the need for further research.

2 Experimental set-up

The target system for the fault injection experiments was the Thor microprocessor, a 32 bit stack oriented RISC processor developed and sold by Saab Ericsson Space AB [10]. The Thor processor is primarily intended for embedded systems in space applications and includes several advanced error detection mechanisms to support fault tolerance. Access to the internal logic of the CPU is provided via internal and boundary scan chains using a Test Access Port (TAP).

The FIMBUL (Fault Injection and Monitoring Using Built-in Logic) tool was used to conduct the fault injection experiments on Thor. FIMBUL is able to inject faults into the internal logic of Thor via scan-chain implemented fault injection (SCIFI). This technique can be more than 100 times faster than e.g. simulation based fault injection, and yet produce very similar results [5].

This section gives a short overview of Thor and FIMBUL, and a description of how they were configured during the experiments.

2.1 The Thor processor

The Thor processor uses a stack oriented instruction set architecture which gives compact machine code due to frequent use of an implicit operand addressing mode. A stack based architecture also provides a high locality of data references resulting in high hit rates of the data cache and fast context switching since only the stack pointer needs to be updated.

A block diagram of the Thor chip is given in Fig. 1. A four stage instruction pipeline is found in the middle of the figure. The pipeline consists of an *Instruction Fetch* stage (*IF*), an *Address Generation* stage (*AG*), an *Operand Fetch* stage (*OF*) incorporating a 32 word (128 byte) direct mapped write-back data cache, and an *EXecute* stage (*EX*). An instruction enters the pipeline in the IF stage and is then passed from one stage to the next each system clock cycle except when a pipeline stall occurs, e.g., when the EX stage is performing a multicycle operation or waits for a write operation to slow memory.

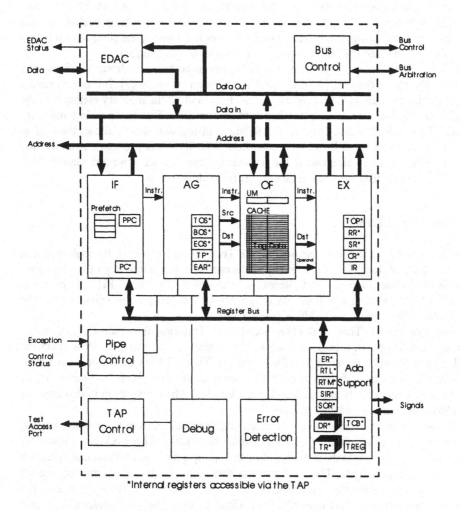

*Internal registers accessible via the TAP

Fig. 1. Block diagram of the Thor processor

On-chip support for real-time processing specifically for the Ada language is available on Thor and is handled by the *Ada support* block. This includes task scheduling and dispatch, communication between tasks, time handling, accurate delays and fast interrupt handling.

The support for fault tolerance includes several internal error detection mechanisms. The error detection mechanisms are controlled and supervised by the *Error Detection* block and consist of *control flow checking, run-time checks, memory data checks* and *master/slave comparator operation.* In this study, we consider estimation of the error detection coverage of the run-time checks and control flow checking mechanism. The run-time checks include those which are commonly found in other microprocessors (division by zero checks etc.), as well as Thor specific checks such as index array bound checks. The control flow checking mechanism uses a signature monitoring scheme that checks the control flow of the program execution during run-time (see [9] for a general description of this technique).

The *TAP control* and *Debug* blocks implements the test and debug facilities. The TAP conforms to the IEEE 1149.1 standard for boundary scan [7]. It provides access to 101 chip-pin signals via a boundary scan-chain, and all the memory elements in the cache and 18 internal registers (marked with an asterisk in Fig. 1) via an internal scan-chain. The TAP also gives access to a debug scan-register, which allows the user to set breakpoints. When a breakpoint condition is fulfilled, the processor halts and the values of the memory elements in the scan-chains can be read or written via the TAP. This feature provides very powerful support for fault injection.

2.2 The FIMBUL tool

The test and debug facilities included in the Thor processor is used for fault injection by the FIMBUL tool. Transient bit-flip faults can be injected into any of the locations accessible by the boundary and internal scan-chains of the Thor CPU. The points in time for fault injection are chosen by programming the debug scan-register to halt the processor when a particular address is accessed.

The tool uses a Thor evaluation board [11], featuring the Thor CPU, memory circuits and I/O ports, installed on a Sun UNIX workstation using an SBus interface. All communication between FIMBUL and the Thor CPU is performed via UNIX device drivers. The software needed to communicate with Thor in order to inject faults and collect data is executed on the workstation. The workstation is also used for workload generation and data analysis.

There are three phases involved in conducting fault injection campaigns using FIMBUL: the *set-up, fault injection* and *analysis phases.* The workload chosen for fault injection experiments is analysed in the set-up phase to produce configuration data for the experiments. The configuration data contains all the information needed to perform fault injection experiments, e.g. when and where to inject faults, the number of faults to inject and which workload to use. The configuration data also determines the operation mode for the FIMBUL fault injection module. There are four operation modes: *normal, normal reference, detail* and *detail reference.* In normal mode, the CPU state, i.e. the contents of the Thor scan-chains, is logged when a fault injection experiment terminates. In detail mode, the CPU state is logged after each instruction executed since fault injection allowing the error propagation to be analysed in detail. No fault injection is performed in the corresponding reference modes to obtain data from fault free executions.

The configuration data is read and interpreted by FIMBUL in the fault injection phase. After initializing the Thor evaluation board, the workload is downloaded and FIMBUL starts operating in reference mode. Then, the first fault injection experiment is performed according to the information given in the configuration data. Fault injection is made by programming the debug-scan register to halt the processor when an address given in the configuration data is accessed. The contents of the boundary and internal scan-chains of Thor are then read and the bits stated in the configuration data are inverted and written back to the CPU. The workload execution is then resumed (the CPU state is now logged after each instruction executed since fault injection if FIMBUL operates in detail mode). Workload execution continues until a time-out value has been reached, an error has been detected or the program finishes its execution, whichever comes first. Then, the CPU state is logged and the Thor evaluation board is reinitialized and another fault injection experiment begins.

The data logged in the fault injection phase is analysed in the analysis phase to obtain dependability measures about the target system. The dependability measures obtained include the percentage of detected, latent and overwritten errors as well as the percentage of faults leading to incorrect results, i.e. the error non-coverage.

2.3 Experiments conducted

FIMBUL executed on a 50 MHz Sun Sparc Classic workstation equipped with a Thor evaluation board. The evaluation board used 512 KB RAM and was clocked with 12.5 MHz. The workstation used its own 2 GB disk space for storing results and managing the experiments. FIMBUL operated in normal mode since most of the experiments were focused on measuring error non-coverage. Using this set-up, FIMBUL injected approximately one fault every two seconds. The detail reference mode was sometimes used for further investigation, e.g. studying the impact of input domain variations on workload execution.

The faults injected were single bit-flips in the internal state elements (latches and flip flops). Single bit-flip faults were selected to model the effects of Single Event Upsets, which are common in the space environment. The FIMBUL tool is capable of injecting faults into 2250 of the 3971 internal state elements of Thor (see Fig. 1). The data cache of Thor contains 1824 of the injectable state elements while 426 injectable state elements are located in the other parts of Thor, hereafter called *register part* or *registers*. The injected faults were selected randomly by sampling the fault space using a uniform sampling distribution. We define the fault space as the Cartesian product $F = L \times T$, where L is the set of all fault locations (state elements) and T the set of all time points when faults can be injected.

Three different workloads written in the Ada language were considered. One is an implementation of the Quicksort algorithm. It uses recursion to sort an array containing seven data elements of the Ada predefined type *float*. The size of this workload is 756 bytes and it utilizes 27 of the 80 instructions of the Thor CPU. The execution time is close to a few thousand clock cycles depending on the initial sort order of the elements. The second workload is an implementation of the non-recursive Shellsort algorithm. Again, a seven element array of the Ada predefined type float is sorted. The size of the workload is 600 bytes and it utilizes 29 of the 80 instructions of Thor. Execution time is a bit lower than for the Quicksort workload, but again varies depending on the initial sort order of the elements. The third workload implements an algorithm solving the Towers of Hanoi puzzle. The size is 1724 bytes and it utilizes 27 different instructions. Execution time varies around five thousand clock cycles depending on the input sequence used.

Seven elements were sorted by the sort workloads in the experiments. Twenty-five initial permutations of these seven elements were chosen among all the 5040 possible permutations as input sequences for the workloads. These are alphabetically denoted A-Y, where the sort order varies from A="the seven elements are already sorted" to Y="the elements are sorted backwards". Seven different input sequences were used for the Towers of Hanoi workload, see Sect. 5.3.

3 Results for the Quicksort workload

The results for the Quicksort workload, obtained when injecting 4000 faults for each of the input sequences A-Y, are given in Fig. 2. The observed error non-coverage is shown for each input sequence. Major differences can be observed. Only 7.80% non-covered errors were obtained for input sequence N while 13.67% non-covered errors were obtained for input sequence Y with the corresponding 95% confidence intervals for the two sequences of ±0.94% and ±1.10% respectively. Thus, error non-coverage was estimated with a difference of more than five percentage units. These results clearly demonstrate that the input sequence affects the error detection coverage.

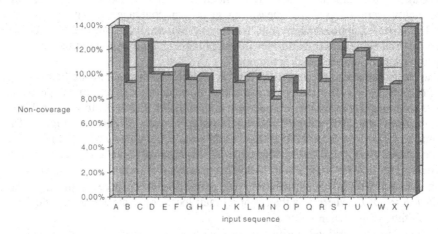

Fig. 2. Error non-coverage for Quicksort using different input sequences.

4 A methodology for predicting error coverage

The goal of a fault injection experiment is usually to provide a single error coverage factor which can be used in an analytical model for calculating the reliability, availability or safety of the target system. Such a single measure of error detection coverage, c, can be obtained as a weighted sum of the coverage factors obtained for different input sequences:

$$c = \sum_{i=1}^{n} c_i \cdot w_i \tag{1}$$

where c_i is the coverage estimated for input sequence i and w_i is the weight factor for input sequence i. Clearly w_i is the probability of occurrence for input sequence i during real operation.

There are several practical problems in estimating the coverage factor this way. First, the probability distribution of the input sequences must be established, which could be a difficult task for many applications. Second, the number of input sequences could be extremely large and it would therefore be impossible to perform fault injection experiments to estimate the coverage factor for each input sequence.

A practical solution to these problems would be to use a manageable number of input sequences which, for example, are selected based on educated guesses about the input sequence distribution. Even if the number of input sequences is reduced to, say, between 10 and 100, it is quite time consuming to conduct fault injection experiments to estimate the error coverage (or non-coverage) for every input sequence. To speed up this process, we propose a methodology for predicting the error coverage for a particular input sequence based on the results from fault injection experiments with another *base-* or *reference-*, input sequence. Thus, the goal of our research is to find efficient ways to estimate the c_i values in (1). Estimation of the weight factors, w_i, is another problem which is not addressed in this paper.

Two different techniques for predicting the error coverage are proposed. One is based on the fact that workload input variations cause different parts of the workload code to be executed different number of times. The other takes into account that the input variations alter the usage of data.

4.1 Execution profile based prediction

One reason for the observed coverage variations is that the *execution profile* of a program varies for different input sequences. A program can be divided into basic blocks [1], and each basic block is executed a different number of times depending on the input sequence. An example of how the workload execution profile may vary for two different input sequences is given in Fig. 3.

Let $P_{nce,i}$ denote the probability that a fault results in a non-covered error, given that the fault is activated during execution of basic block i. It is reasonable to assume that the probabilities $P_{nce,a}$ and $P_{nce,b}$ for two basic blocks a and b varies, but that the probability $P_{nce,i}$ is constant for each basic block i for all input sequences since the activity of the system during execution of the basic block is the same regardless of input sequence used, i.e. the same instructions are always executed.

Assume that $P_{nce,C} > P_{nce,n}$ for all blocks $n \in \{A, B, D, E\}$ in Fig. 3. The non-coverage is then higher for a system that processes input X than input Y (assuming faults activated with equal probability for all points in time during the execution of the workload) since the proportion of the time spent executing block C is $14*8/(7*1+3*0+14*8+9*8+3*1)*100\%=58\%$ for input X and only $14*3/(7*1+3*1+14*3+9*3+3*1)*100\%=53\%$ for input Y.

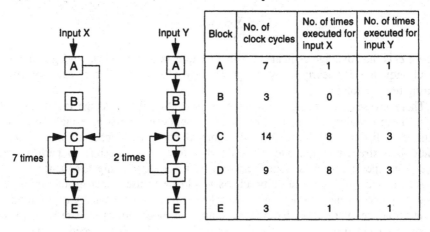

Block	No. of clock cycles	No. of times executed for input X	No. of times executed for input Y
A	7	1	1
B	3	0	1
C	14	8	3
D	9	8	3
E	3	1	1

Fig. 3. Workload execution profile varies for different input data.

The execution profile based prediction technique calculates the predicted non-coverage $\bar{c}_{ep}$ for a particular input sequence p using the following equation:

$$\bar{c}_{ep} = \sum_{i=1}^{n} P_{nce,i} \cdot w_{ep,i} \tag{2}$$

where the basic blocks of the workload are numbered 1 to n. $P_{nce,i}$ is estimated using fault injection experiments for the base input sequence as

$$P_{nce,i} = \frac{n_{nce,i}}{n_{e,i}} \tag{3}$$

where $n_{nce,i}$ is the observed number of faults activated when block i is executing resulting in non-covered errors, and $n_{e,i}$ is the total number of faults activated during execution of block i.

$w_{ep,i}$ is the weight factor for block i, i.e. the proportion of faults activated during execution of block i for input sequence p out of the total number of faults activated for input sequence p. If all faults are assumed to be activated with an equal probability for all points in time, the weight factor can be estimated as the proportion of the whole execution time spent executing block i, for input sequence p. Assume that block i executes for k_i clock cycles that the workload executes for l_p clock cycles for input sequence p. $w_{ep,i}$ is then calculated as $w_{ep,i} = \dfrac{ki}{lp} \cdot x_{p,i}$ where $x_{p,i}$ is the number of executions of block i for input sequence p.

4.2 Data usage based prediction

Another reason for variations in error detection coverage is that different input sequences lead to different usage of data. (We here use the term data in a generic sense covering all types of data used by a program, including the program counter, hardware and user stack pointers, pointers used by the application program, application data, etc.) Error detection coverage clearly varies for different classes of data items. For example, errors in application data are less likely to affect control flow or memory access behaviour, than errors affecting application pointers or the program counter. Thus, when error detection relies on control flow checking and memory access checking, the error detection coverage is lower for errors that affect application data compared to errors that affect application pointers or the program counter. The amount of application data used by a program varies for different input sequences, which leads to variations in error detection coverage.

Based on these observations, a technique for predicting error coverage, or non-coverage, for a particular input sequence can be proposed. The different types of data items used by a program are divided into n classes, such that the error detection coverage is similar for the data items in a given class. As an approximation, we assume that the error detection coverage is the same for all data items in each class. Clearly, the classification must be made such that this approximation is valid.

The data usage based prediction technique calculates the predicted non-coverage $\bar{c}_{dp}$ for a particular input sequence p using the following equation:

$$\bar{c}_{dp} = \sum_{i=1}^{n} P_{ncd,i} \cdot w_{dp,i} \tag{4}$$

where the data classes are numbered 1 to n. $P_{ncd,i}$ is the probability that a fault in a data item in class i leads to a non-covered error, estimated using the fault injection experiments for the base input sequence as

$$\hat{P}_{ncd,i} = \frac{n_{ncd,i}}{n_{d,i}} \tag{5}$$

where $n_{ncd,i}$ is the observed number of faults injected in data items in class i resulting in non-covered errors, and $n_{d,i}$ is the total number of faults injected into data items in class i. The technique relies on the assumption that $P_{ncd,i}$ is approximately constant for different input sequences.

$w_{dp,i}$ is the weight factor for data class i for input sequence p. The weight factor is calculated as the percentage of the fault space $F = L \times T$ (see Sect. 2.3) containing data in class i during the execution using input sequence p. The weight factor is obtained by investigating the state space of the microprocessor during a single fault free run of the application program using input sequence p.

5 Applying the methodology

5.1 Predictions for the Quicksort workload

The FIMBUL tool is not always able to identify the basic block executing when a non-covered error is activated. We therefore assume, as an approximation, that this block is the same as the one executing when the fault is injected. This is a reasonable approximation for the register part since most of the faults injected in the register part resulting in non-covered errors have short activation latencies. However, the approximation is inadequate for the data cache since the fault injected cache lines are often used during execution of basic blocks other than the one executing when the fault is injected. Data usage based prediction is better suited for predicting the effects of faults injected into the data cache. To demonstrate how the two prediction techniques work for different parts of the processor, the results are presented separately for the register part and the data cache.

Table 1 shows the execution profiles of the Quicksort workload for the input sequences used in this study. Several differences can be observed between the profiles, e.g. block C93 is executed between one and nine times depending on the input sequence and block CF6 is not executed at all for input sequence A and up to five times using other input sequences.

For each basic block, the right-most column of Table 1 gives the estimated probability that a fault injected into the register part results in a non-covered error, given that the fault is activated during execution of the basic block. The predictions are based on 1500 faults injected into the register part during execution of each basic block for input sequence M. (The Quicksort workload contains 21 basic blocks, therefore a total of 31500 faults were injected). The last two rows of Table 1 show the error non-coverage predicted using equation (2) vs. the observed error non-coverage when injecting 4000 faults into the Thor register part for each input combination.

The results show that the execution profile based prediction technique correctly predicts that input sequences F, J, T and Y should have the highest error non-coverage and A the lowest. However, the predicted non-coverage is sometimes much higher than the observed non-coverage, e.g. for sequences A, D and P. One reason for the discrepancies between the predicted and observed non-coverage may be the low number of non-covered errors observed leading to a low confidence in the results. The 95% confidence intervals for the observed non-coverage values are around ±0.2%. Another reason may be that the assumption that the block executing when a fault is activated is the same as the one executing when the fault is injected, sometimes is inaccurate.

The results of execution profile based prediction on the register part is also shown in the left diagram in Fig. 4. The right diagram in Fig. 4 shows the results of data usage based prediction on the register part. Again, input sequence M was chosen as the base input sequence. The data used by the workload was divided into six classes. One class consists of the elements to be sorted, another of pointers to the elements to be sorted, three classes contains a particular value of the status register and the sixth class contains all other data.

Table 1. Execution profiles for different input sequences to the Quicksort workload. Thor registers fault injected.

Block start-address	No. of instr. (k_i)	No. of executions per input sequence ($x_{p,i}$)																								$P_{nce, i}$ input M
		A	B	C	D	E	F	G	H	I	J	K	L	M	N	O	P	Q	R	S	T	U	V	W	X	Y	
C46	8	3	7	5	6	6	7	7	5	6	7	7	5	6	7	6	7	7	8	6	8	7	7	7	7	6	1.19%
C4F	3	3	7	5	6	6	8	7	5	6	7	8	5	6	7	6	7	7	8	6	8	7	7	7	7	6	2.01%
C52	26	3	6	4	5	5	5	6	5	5	4	6	4	5	6	5	6	5	6	5	6	4	5	6	6	3	0.07%
C6D	12	8	12	11	14	12	9	10	13	12	9	11	8	14	15	11	14	15	9	10	10	8	8	11	14	8	0.40%
C7B	9	5	4	5	7	5	1	2	6	4	2	3	2	5	6	4	6	5	1	3	1	2	1	3	4	2	0.07%
C87	12	8	13	10	11	11	14	14	11	15	8	13	15	16	16	12	14	14	14	12	15	9	12	14	15	8	0.47%
C93	9	5	5	4	4	4	6	6	4	7	1	5	9	7	7	5	6	4	6	5	6	2	5	6	5	2	0.00%
C9D	5	3	8	6	7	7	8	8	7	8	7	8	6	9	9	7	8	10	8	7	9	7	7	8	10	6	0.27%
CA3	21	3	7	5	6	6	7	7	5	6	7	7	5	6	7	6	7	7	8	6	8	7	7	7	7	6	2.04%
CBA	27	3	7	5	6	6	7	7	5	6	7	7	5	6	7	6	7	7	8	6	8	7	7	7	7	6	1.39%
CD8	8	3	7	5	6	6	7	7	5	6	7	7	5	6	7	6	7	7	8	6	8	7	7	7	7	6	0.07%
CE1	5	3	7	5	6	6	7	7	5	6	7	7	5	6	7	6	7	7	8	6	8	7	7	7	7	6	0.40%
CE7	8	3	6	5	5	6	7	7	5	6	7	7	5	6	7	6	6	6	8	6	7	7	7	6	7	6	0.00%
CF0	5	3	8	6	7	7	8	8	7	8	7	8	6	9	9	7	8	10	8	7	9	7	7	8	10	6	0.00%
CF6	4	0	2	2	2	2	3	2	2	3	3	2	2	4	3	2	2	5	2	2	3	3	2	2	4	3	0.07%
CFC	5	3	6	4	5	5	5	6	5	5	4	6	4	5	6	5	6	5	6	5	6	4	5	6	6	3	0.98%
D02	5	1	2	2	3	2	2	2	3	1	2	3	1	2	3	2	3	3	2	2	2	1	1	3	2	1	0.00%
D09	5	3	6	4	5	5	5	6	5	5	4	6	4	5	6	5	6	5	6	5	6	4	5	6	6	3	0.60%
D0F	5	1	3	1	1	2	2	3	1	3	1	2	2	2	2	2	2	1	3	2	3	2	3	2	3	1	0.00%
D16	4	3	6	4	5	5	5	6	5	5	4	6	4	5	6	5	6	5	6	5	6	4	5	6	6	3	0.00%
D24	13	1	1	1	1	1	1	1	1	1	1	1	1	1	1	1	1	1	1	1	1	1	1	1	1	1	0.20%
Predicted non-coverage		0.60%	0.69%	0.66%	0.66%	0.68%	0.72%	0.69%	0.65%	0.78%	0.70%	0.65%	0.63%	0.68%	0.65%	0.68%	0.67%	0.68%	0.73%	0.68%	0.78%	0.74%	0.69%	0.66%	0.78%		
Observed non-coverage		0.28%	0.61%	0.52%	0.49%	0.54%	0.70%	0.59%	0.58%	0.52%	0.68%	0.66%	0.51%	0.59%	0.64%	0.62%	0.47%	0.61%	0.60%	0.64%	0.74%	0.66%	0.64%	0.63%	0.68%	0.71%	

The results in Fig. 4 show that the data usage based prediction method fails to predict whether the error non-coverage is high or low for a particular input sequence, while the execution based prediction technique correctly identifies the input sequences with the highest, or lowest, error non-coverage (although the predicted value is sometimes too high, probably due to the reasons discussed above).

The results using data usage based prediction on the data cache are shown in Table 2. An analysis of the Quicksort workload shows that the data most sensitive to fault injection in the data cache are the elements to be sorted. Two data classes were therefore used for the data usage based prediction technique. One class contains the elements to be sorted while the other class contains all other data. Table 2 gives the weight factors for these two classes for each input sequence. The right-most column gives the estimated probability that a fault injected into a cache line containing the data in the class will lead to a non-covered error. The estimations are based on examination of 351 fault injected cache lines leading to non-covered errors (out of a total of 3019 injections) for input sequence M.

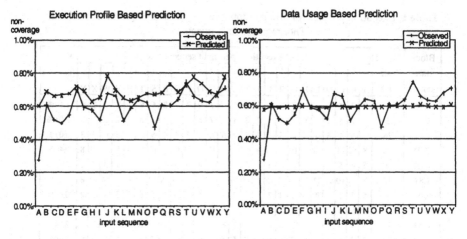

Fig. 4. Predicted vs. observed non-coverage for Quicksort. Thor registers fault injected.

Table 2 also gives the error non-coverage, predicted using equation (4), as well as the observed values estimated using 3000 faults injected into the data cache for each input sequence. A comparison shows that the predicted values are generally lower than the observed values, but that the relative differences between the predicted values correspond well to the relative differences between the observed values. This shows that the technique is capable of pointing out the input sequences with the highest (or lowest) error non-coverages.

Table 2. Weight factors and non-coverage for different input sequences to Quicksort. Thor data cache fault injected.

Critical data class	Weight factors for the data classes for each input sequence ($w_{dp,i}$) (%)																									$\hat{P}_{ncd,i}$
	A	B	C	D	E	F	G	H	I	J	K	L	M	N	O	P	Q	R	S	T	U	V	W	X	Y	input M
Elements to sort	24.72	20.20	23.81	20.81	21.49	22.00	20.93	21.06	21.25	24.95	21.06	20.68	20.78	20.93	21.37	20.34	22.73	21.28	22.99	22.41	23.75	22.28	21.10	20.47	26.37	43.05%
Other data	75.28	79.80	76.19	79.19	78.51	78.00	79.07	78.94	78.75	75.05	78.94	79.32	79.22	79.07	78.63	79.66	77.27	78.72	77.01	77.59	76.25	77.72	78.90	79.53	73.63	3.39%

Predicted non-cov. (%)	13.19	11.40	12.83	11.64	11.91	12.11	11.69	11.74	11.82	13.28	11.74	11.59	11.63	11.69	11.86	11.46	12.40	11.83	12.50	12.27	12.81	12.22	11.75	11.51	13.85
Observed non-cov. (%)	16.87	11.39	15.84	12.05	12.12	12.91	11.52	11.99	10.35	16.45	11.47	11.75	11.63	9.60	11.85	10.24	13.78	11.21	15.32	13.70	14.43	13.40	10.73	11.06	16.79

In addition, we have also used execution profile based prediction on the data cache. In this case, 1000 faults were injected for each basic block. (A total of 21000 faults were injected).

A comparison of the results obtained when using execution profile based and data usage based prediction on the data cache is shown in Fig. 5 (input sequence *M* was used as the base sequence for both prediction techniques). The diagrams show the observed vs. predicted error non-coverage for the different input sequences *A-Y* for each prediction technique. The observed values are estimated using 3000 faults injected for each input sequence.

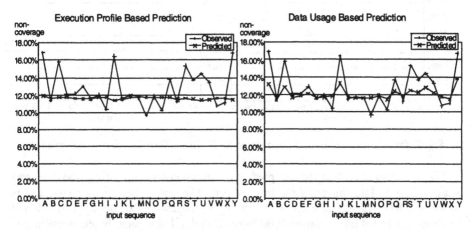

Fig. 5. Predicted vs. observed non-coverage for Quicksort. Thor data cache fault injected.

The results show that the data usage based prediction technique succeeds in identifying the input sequences with the highest non-coverage (*A, C, J, S, U* and *Y*) while the execution profile based prediction technique is clearly inadequate.

5.2 Predictions for the Shellsort workload

To verify the validity of the observations made in Sect. 5.1, a second workload was investigated. Fig. 6 shows the observed vs. predicted error non-coverage for various input sequences using the Shellsort workload when fault injecting the data cache. The observed error non-coverage is based on 2000 injected faults for each input sequence. Also in these experiments, the input sequence *M* was used as the base sequence for both prediction methods. The left diagram shows the results for execution profile based prediction based on a total of 4000 faults injected during execution of the whole workload. The right diagram shows the results for data usage based prediction based on examination of 744 injected faults leading to non-covered errors.

In contrast to the results for the Quicksort workload, the observed non-coverage varies much less for the different input sequences. Both prediction methods correctly point out input sequence *A* as having the lowest non-coverage but do not find any input sequence with an exceptionally high non-coverage.

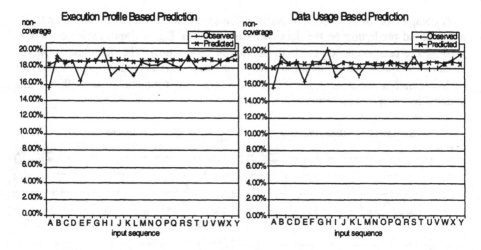

Fig. 6. Predicted vs. observed non-coverage for Shellsort. Thor data cache fault injected.

Fig. 7 shows the observed vs. predicted error non-coverage using the Shellsort workload when fault injecting the register part. The observed error non-coverage is based on 4000 faults injected for each input sequence. Execution profile based prediction is based on a total of 4000 injected faults. Data usage based prediction is based on examination of 435 injected faults leading to non-covered errors.

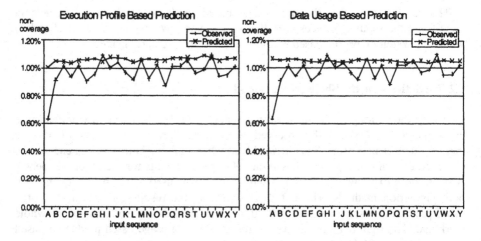

Fig. 7. Predicted vs. observed non-coverage for Shellsort. Thor registers fault injected.

The observed non-coverage differences are much smaller, just as for the data cache, and neither method finds any input sequence with an exceptionally high non-coverage. Only the execution profile based prediction method correctly identifies input sequence *A* as having the lowest error non-coverage.

5.3 Predictions for the Towers of Hanoi workload

The methodology described in Sect. 4 was applied on a third workload. The workload chosen is an implementation of an algorithm solving the Towers of Hanoi puzzle, see Fig. 8.

Fig. 8. Towers of Hanoi puzzle.

The purpose is to move the three discs of one tower stick to another by dropping the discs on any of the three available tower sticks. A larger disc may never be placed on top of a smaller one. The implementation uses a 3x3 floating point matrix containing non-zero values, representing the discs, and zero values, representing no disc. The locations of these values in the matrix determine the current configuration of the three towers. The algorithm recursively solves the problem of moving the discs to the right-most tower stick.

Seven different tower configurations (*A-G*) were used as the initial input sequences for the algorithm, see Fig. 9. Input sequence *A* was chosen as the base sequence.

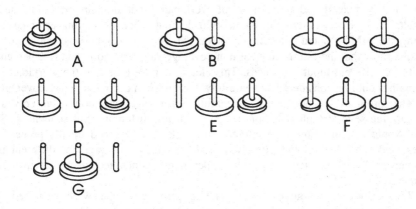

Fig. 9. Input sequences for Towers of Hanoi.

Fault injection results show that almost all of the non-covered errors were activated when fault injecting the cache. The faults injected into the register part are therefore neglected in these experiments and only the data usage based prediction technique was used. The critical data was found to be the zeros and floating point values representing the discs. 50 out of 167 non-covered errors were due to faults injected into zeros while 100 were due to faults injected into disc values out of a total of 10000 faults injected into the cache.

The error non-coverage predicted using equation (4) is given for each of the input sequences *A-G* in Table 3. The predicted error non-coverage is highest for input sequences *E* and *F*. The last row of Table 3 shows the error non-coverage estimated using around 7500 faults injected into all available fault locations for each of the input sequences. The results show that the observed error non-coverage is indeed highest for input sequences E and F (2.55% vs. 2.71%).

Table 3. Predicted non-coverage for Towers of Hanoi. Only data cache considered.

	Input sequence						
	A	B	C	D	E	F	G
Zero value data usage	0.10668	0.09737	0.10985	0.11450	0.17536	0.13475	0.10909
Disc data (non-zero value) usage	0.05083	0.05524	0.05638	0.05395	0.05346	0.06404	0.06381
Other data usage	0.84249	0.84739	0.83377	0.83155	0.77118	0.80121	0.82710
Zero data non-coverage	0.047	-	-	-	-	-	-
Disc data non-coverage	0.197	-	-	-	-	-	-
Other data non-coverage	0.0020	-	-	-	-	-	-
Predicted non-coverage (data cache only)	1.67%	1.71%	1.79%	1.77%	2.03%	2.05%	1.93%
Observed non-coverage (whole CPU)	1.87%	1.38%	1.84%	1.67%	2.55%	2.71%	1.79%

6 Conclusion

This paper investigated the impact of workload input domain on fault injection results. The effects of varying the workload input when estimating error coverage using the FIMBUL fault injection tool on the Thor processor was examined. The results show that the estimated error non-coverage can vary more than five percentage units for different input sequences. This clearly demonstrate that the workload input domain should be considered and carefully chosen when estimating error coverage.

The problem of accurately estimating error coverage could be solved by performing several fault injection campaigns using different input sequences. Since this would be very time consuming, a methodology to speed up the process was presented. The methodology involves predicting error coverage for different input sequences based on fault injection experiments conducted using another input sequence.

Two different techniques for predicting error coverage were proposed. One technique uses the fact that workload input variations cause different parts of the workload code, i.e. basic blocks, to be executed. The other technique takes into account that workload input variations alter the usage of data. Prediction is made by calculating coverage factors for each basic block or sensitive data based on fault injection results for a single input sequence. The error coverage for a particular input sequence is then predicted by means of a weighted sum of these coverage factors. The weight factors are obtained by analysing either the execution profile or the data usage profile of the input sequence using a single fault free run of the program.

Another way of estimating error coverage could be to carry out fault injection campaigns where the input sequence is selected randomly for each injected fault. The selection should be made according to the input sequence distribution. However, many of the advantages associated with the prediction methodology would be lost. Identifying the basic blocks and data most sensitive to faults can be useful when trying to improve the error coverage of the target system. The prediction based methodology can also be useful for identifying the input sequences with the lowest (worst case) error coverage. Also, there is no need to perform any new fault injection experiments if the input sequence distribution for the target system is altered.

Results show that error coverage for the register part of Thor, i.e. all parts of the CPU except the cache, is predicted more favourably using execution profile based prediction, while error coverage for the data cache is predicted more favourably using data usage based prediction. Since it is not always possible to identify the basic block which activates a non-covered error using FIMBUL, this block is assumed to be the same as the one executing when the fault is injected. This approximation requires the data usage based prediction technique to be used on the data cache since faults injected into the data cache have longer activation latencies than faults injected into the register part.

The results also show that although data usage based prediction fails to predict the actual error coverage, it can be useful for finding the input sequences with the most extreme error coverages, particularly when the error coverage differences are prominent. These input sequences could then be used in fault injection campaigns to estimate the real coverage values.

More research is needed to refine the methodology. In this paper, the input sequence used as the base input sequence was selected arbitrarily. It may be more favourable to select it according to certain criteria, e.g. an input sequence that causes all of the basic blocks of the workload code to be executed and as many critical data items to be used as possible. Perhaps several input sequences should be used as base input sequences for certain workload programs.

A method for identifying the critical data items for the data usage based prediction technique needs to be developed. The data belonging to various data classes were easily identifiable for the workloads used in this study since the same values were always used (albeit in a different sort order) for each input sequence, often enabling identification by simply studying the values. For other workloads the corresponding sensitive variables would sometimes have to be identified, e.g. by tracing the values and locations of the variables during execution of the workload.

Simulation based fault injection would probably allow the error coverage of the whole CPU to be predicted using execution profile based prediction only, since the higher observability available in the simulations should enable identification of the basic blocks activating the non-covered errors. This would completely eliminate the need for the data usage based prediction technique as well as the approximations made about which block that activates a non-covered error. The accuracy of the predicted values should thereby improve.

Although the methodology managed to identify input sequences with high, medium or low non-coverage for the workloads used in this study, more research is needed to determine whether the methodology is applicable to other workloads and other systems. The workloads used in this study had low complexity and performed similar floating point array manipulations but nevertheless provided a good starting point for our research. Larger programs can easily be investigated with FIMBUL since the SCIFI technique is very fast. Such programs typically consist of a number of subprograms, e.g. subroutines for sorting etc., and error coverage for each of these subroutines could probably be used to estimate the total error coverage.

In addition to these issues, the possibility to expand the methodology for estimating not only overall error coverage, but the coverage of specific error detection mechanisms as well, should also be investigated.

Acknowledgements

We wish to thank Magnus Legnehed, Stefan Asserhäll, Torbjörn Hult, and Roland Pettersson of Saab Ericsson Space AB as well as Prof. Jan Torin for their support of this research.

References

1. A. Aho, R.Sethi, and J. Ullman, "Compilers: Principles, Techniques and Tools", Reading, MA: Addison Wesley, 1985.
2. A. Amendola, L. Impagliazzo, P. Marmo, and F. Poli, "Experimental Evaluation of Computer-Based Railway Control Systems", in *Proc. 27th Int. Symp. on Fault-Tolerant Computing (FTCS-27)*, pp. 380-384, (Seattle, WA, USA) June 1997.
3. C. Constantinescu, "Using multi-stage and stratified sampling for inferring fault-coverage probabilities", *IEEE Transactions on Reliability*, 44 (4), pp. 632-639, 1995.
4. E. Czeck, and D. Siewiorek, "Observations on the Effects of Fault Manifestation as a Function of Workload", *IEEE Transactions on Computers*, 41 (5), pp. 559-566, May 1992.
5. P. Folkesson, S. Svensson, and J. Karlsson, "A Comparison of Simulation Based and Scan Chain Implemented Fault Injection", in *Proc. 28th Int. Symp. on Fault-Tolerant Computing (FTCS-28)*, pp. 284-293, (Munich, Germany) June 1998.
6. U. Gunneflo, J. Karlsson, and J. Torin, "Evaluation of Error Detection Schemes Using Fault Injection by Heavy-ion Radiation", in *Proc. 19th Int. Symp. Fault-Tolerant Computing (FTCS-19)*, pp. 340-347, 1989.
7. Test Technology Technical Committee of the IEEE Computer Society, *IEEE standard test access port and boundary-scan architecture*, USA 1990.
8. R. K. Iyer, "Experimental Evaluation", in *Special Issue of Proc. 25th Int. Symp. on Fault-Tolerant Computing (FTCS-25)*, Pasadena, CA, USA, 1995.
9. Mahmood A., et al, "Concurrent Error Detection Using Watchdog Processors - A Survey", *Transactions on Computers*, vol. 37, No. 2, February 1988, pp. 160-174.
10. Saab Ericsson Space AB, *Microprocessor Thor, Product Information*, September 1993.
11. Saab Ericsson Space AB, *Workstation Board Specification*, Doc. no. TOR/TNOT/0015/SE, February 1993.

Session 5

Fault Injection 2

Chair: David Powell, LAAS-CNRS, Toulouse, France

Fault Injection into VHDL Models: Experimental Validation of a Fault Tolerant Microcomputer System

D. Gil[1], R. Martínez[2], J. V. Busquets[1], J. C. Baraza[1], P. J. Gil[1]

[1] Grupo de Sistemas Tolerantes a Fallos (GSTF)
Departamento de Informática de Sistemas, y Computadores (DISCA)
Universidad Politécnica de Valencia, Spain
{dgil, jcbaraza, vbusque, pgil}@disca.upv.es
[2] Instituto de Robótica, Universitat de València, Polígono la Coma s/n,
E-46980, Paterna, Valencia, Spain
Rafael.Martinez@uv.es

Abstract. This work presents a campaign of fault injection to validate the dependability of a fault tolerant microcomputer system. The system is duplex with cold stand-by sparing, parity detection and a watchdog timer. The faults have been injected on a chip-level VHDL model, using an injection tool designed with this purpose. We have carried out a set of injection experiments (with 3000 injections each), injecting transient and permanent faults of types stuck-at, open-line and indetermination on both the signals and variables of the system, running a workload. We have analysed the pathology of the propagated errors, measured their latency, and calculated both detection and recovery coverage. We have also studied the influence with the fault duration and fault distribution. For instance, system detection coverage (including non-effective faults) is 98% and the system recovery coverage is 95% for short transient faults (0.1 clock cycles).

1. Introduction

The fault injection is a technique of Fault Tolerant Systems (FTSs) validation which is being increasingly consolidated and applied in a wide range of fields, and several automatic tools have been designed [1]. The fault injection technique is defined in the following way [2]:

Fault injection is the validation technique of the Dependability of Fault Tolerant Systems which consists in the accomplishment of controlled experiments where the observation of the system's behaviour in presence of faults is induced explicitly by the voluntary introduction (injection) of faults to the system.

The fault injection in the hardware of a system can be implemented within three main techniques:

1. *Physical fault injection*: It is accomplished at physical level, disturbing the hardware with parameters of the environment (heavy ions radiation, electromagnetic interference, etc.) or modifying the value of the pins of the integrated circuits.

2. *Software Implemented Fault injection (SWIFI)*: The objective of this technique, also called Fault Emulation, consists of reproducing at information level the errors that would have been produced upon occurring faults in the hardware. It is based on different practical types of injection, such as the modification of the memory data, or the mutation of the application software or the lowest service layers (at operating system level, for example*)*.

3. *Simulated fault injection*: In this technique, the system under test is simulated in other computer system. The faults are induced altering the logical values during the simulation.

This work is framed in the simulated fault injection, and concretely in the simulation of models based on the VHDL hardware description language. We have chosen this technique due fundamentally to:

- The growing interest of the simulated injection techniques [3], [4], [5], [6], [7], [8] as a complement of the physical fault injection [9], [10], [11], [12], [13] (these have been traditionally more numerous and developed) and Fault Emulation (SWIFI) [14], [15], [16], [17], [18] experiments. The greatest advantage of this method over the previous ones is the Observability and Controllability of all the modelled components. The simulation can be accomplished in different abstraction levels. Another positive aspect of this technique is the possibility of carrying out the validation of the system during the design phase, before having the final product.

- The good perspectives of modelling systems and faults with VHDL, that has been consolidated as a powerful standard to analyse and design computer systems [19].

This work follows the one carried out in the paper [20], where the study of the error syndrome of a simple microcomputer was presented, errors were classified and latencies were measured. To do that, we performed an injection campaign by means of a fault injection tool deployed for such a purpose [21].

In present work, we intend to perform the validation of a fault tolerant system. The VHDL model of the microcomputer used in the previous paper has been enhanced and we have added mechanisms for the detection and recovery of errors. Using our own fault injection tool, we have performed an injection campaign on the system and we have calculated the coverage and latencies on the detection and recovery of the produced errors.

In section 2, we present the main elements of the fault injection tool. In section 3 we describe the computer system, based on a simple 16 bit-microprocessor. In section 4, we describe the fault models used in the injection. In section 5 we set the conditions and parameters of the injection experiments: type of fault, place where to inject, injection instant, duration of the fault, place where the errors should be detected, etc. In section 6 we present the obtained results, basically concerning the coverage factors and the propagation latencies. Finally, in section 7 we explain some general conclusions and possible future lines of continuation of the work.

2. The fault injection tool

We have developed an injection tool for automatic fault injection in VHDL models at gate-level, register-level and chip-level.

The injection tool is composed by a series of elements designed around a commercial VHDL simulator. A more comprehensive description of the tool and the aspects currently in progress can be seen in [21]. The main components of the tool are:

Configuration file. Fault injection experiments are defined in a file using the following parameters:

1. Experiment name.
2. Total number of injected faults.
3. Fault injection time instant.
4. Fault duration (transient faults).
5. Places (signals/variables) where faults are injected.
6. Fault value.
7. Output file: result.

Macro generator. This is a program that writes a file with calls to the *macros* that perform the injection. The parameters of the *macros* are defined in the configuration file so that they can vary from one experiment to another. The *macros* have been written by the command-language of the simulator.

Simulator. It has been used the commercial VHDL simulator V-System/Windows by Model Technology [22] for IBM-PC (or compatible). It is a simple and easy to use event-driven simulator. When activated by the user, the simulator executes the file with macros and generates the output text file *.lst* for every injection. The *.lst* file contains the trace of the whole simulation.

Data analyser. This program analyses the output file *.lst* for each injection, and compares it to the reference fault-free output file to provide the following information: type of the injected fault, type of error, latencies (propagation, detection, recovery) and coverage (detection, recovery) estimators. The results of the comparison are stored in the file *result*.

VHDL component library. It is a set of VHDL models used to build or modify models of Fault-Tolerant Systems, to be able to validate them. It has the VHDL models at gate, register or chip level.

System. It is a VHDL model to be studied/validated. The proposed tool deals with models at gate, register or chip level.

VHDL injector library. This library comprises injector models in VHDL that can be added to the system model. These models allow the injection of new faults to make available a large set of fault types. They can be applied to signals, in structural architectures of the model (stuck-at, open line, indetermination, short, bridging, delay or bit-flip faults). They can also be applied at algorithmic level in behavioural architectures of the model, changing the syntactical structures of the VHDL code [23]. They are called respectively *saboteurs* and *mutants* in [7]. The automatic control of *saboteurs* and *mutants* are currently under development.

In short, the tool is easy to use and versatile, and it is appropriate to perform injection experiments in medium complexity systems.

3. Computer system

We have built the VHDL model of a fault-tolerant microcomputer. Fig. 1 shows the block diagram of the system. The system is duplex with cold stand-by sparing, parity detection and watchdog timer.

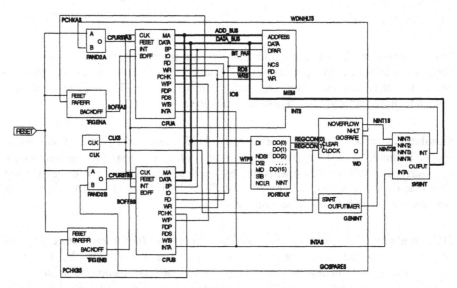

Fig. 1. Block diagram of the computer system.

The structural architecture of the model is composed by the following components:

- Main Central Processing Unit (CPUA) and spare CPU (CPUB).
- RAM memory (MEM).
- Output parallel port (PORTOUT).
- Interrupt controller.
- Clock generator.
- Watchdog timer.
- Pulse generator (GENINT).

- Two back-off cycle generators (TRGENA, TRGENB).
- Two AND gates (PAND2A, PAND2B).

Each component is modelled by a behavioural architecture with usually one or more concurrent processes. Both main and spare processors are an enhanced version of the MARK2 processor [24]. Now, both Data and Address busses are wider (16 bits and 12 bits respectively). We have also added new registers, instructions and addressing modes. This way, the processor is more versatile and both stack and interrupts are improved. In addition, several control signals have been added for parity control (PCHK) and generation of the back-off cycle (BOFF). Parity is added to the data that is checked for every memory read. In case of error, the signal PCHK is asserted. The parity bit is generated in the write cycles.

The description of this system is around 1500 lines of VHDL code. The code is divided into 10 entities, 11 architectures and 1 packages, excluding the STD and IEEE libraries of service. In addition, 416 bytes are used to store the machine code executed by the CPU.

As mentioned before, several fault-tolerance mechanisms have been added to increase the dependability of the system. The error detection mechanisms include the parity check and program control flow check by watchdog timer.

If the processor detects a parity error, the back-off generator asserts such a signal for a fixed time (that may be configured). The processor waits for such a time in case the cause of the error finishes. Once this time expires, the processor re-executes the last instruction. In case the parity error persists, the back-off signal is generated for a permanent time.

We have used a periodic interrupt (NINT2) to cope with the program flow errors. Each time the interrupt is received, the response routine resets the watchdog timer to avoid its overflow. Subsequently, the component GENINT is activated to produce a new interrupt. These actions are done through the output parallel port.

An error of program control flow during the interrupt routine will produce an overflow of the Watchdog timer. This situation will activate the processor interrupt signal (NINT1) in order to recover the system from a checkpoint previously stored in stable memory.

There is a second memory bank with a backup copy of the recovery point and a variable that indicates the active bank. This way, the data integrity is ensured at any time.

In case of two successive overflows of the Watchdog timer, the NHLT signal will be asserted to stop permanently the main CPU and start the spare processor. The spare processor recovers the recovery checkpoint from the stable memory to continue with the main processor tasks.

4. Fault models

For the injection experiments, we aim at using a variety of faults that would represent the most usual physical faults. Although the most used model is *stuck-at* (0, 1), as VLSI ICs integration density rises, it becomes more necessary to introduce new and more complex models. In this way, it is proved that in CMOS technology, only the 64% of defects can be modelled as *stuck-at* faults [23].

In our work we have considered two new models in addition to the classical *stuck-at* model: *indetermination* and *open-line* (high-impedance). This models represent real faults that occur in IC's as will be seen later.

Moreover, the used injection technique allows an easy implementation of these four fault models by the use of special simulator commands to modify the value of signals and variables of the VHDL model (section 5 describes this technique in detail). In fact, the way to inject faults is to assign to the signal or variable the modified value ('0': stuck-at 0, '1': stuck at 1, 'Z': open-line or 'X': high impedance) at injection time. Other fault models, as *short* and *bringing*, forces to modify the VHDL model with *saboteurs* components.

The injected values belong to the multivalued type *std-logic*, declared in the IEEE STD-logic-1164 package. This type has a resolution function to manage the value of output signals connected in parallel. All the VHDL model bit-like or register-like variables and signals are declared of type *std-logic*.

Next, we describe in short the physical mechanisms implied in the *indetermination* and *open-line* fault models, to justify their inclusion.

The *indetermination* model allows to represent transient physical faults of different types: transient in power supply, cross-talk, electromagnetic interferences (light, radio, etc.), temperature variation, α radiation and cosmic radiation (the last ones are very important in space applications.)

These physical faults can vary directly the values of voltage and current of the logical levels of the circuit nodes. They also can generate e^--h^+ pairs, which are swept by the electric field of the depletion zones of the PN unions in the transistors. This produces a current of e^--h^+ pairs which may produce the variation of the logical levels, and therefore their indetermination.

Fig. 2, summarises some causes and mechanisms of this type of faults.

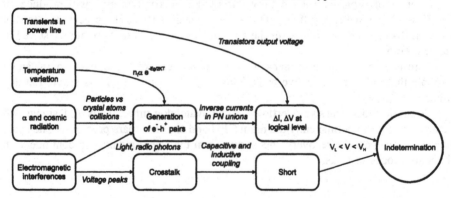

Fig. 2. Some causes and mechanisms of the indetermination transient faults.

On the other hand, *open-line* represents permanent physical faults that produce a high impedance state in the transistor oxide, metal or semiconductor layers, and also in its connections. Some examples of this type of faults are [25]:

- Manufacturing faults, which affect to masks, and consequently, to the layout.
- Electro-migration in the metals.
- Thin-oxide breakdown.
- Electric stress.

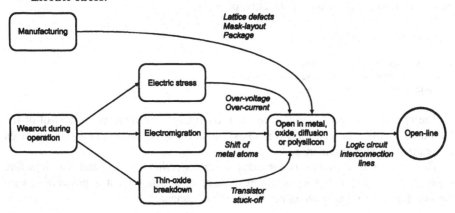

Fig. 3. Some causes and mechanisms of the open-line permanent faults.

Fig. 3, represents some causes and mechanisms of this type of faults.

Notice that some of the causes of the open-line faults may also cause permanent indeterminate faults.

5. Fault injection experiments

The used injection technique and the parameters of the injection campaign are summarised below.

5.1 Injection technique

This injection technique is based on special simulator commands. These commands allow changing values to signals and variables without changing the VHDL model. The components and architectures of the model are not changed at all. The injector concatenates several commands in macros. The macros are executed from the simulator environment. Next, we indicate the sequence of pseudo-commands used in the manipulation of signals and variables [7]:

Manipulation of signals

1. **Simulate_Until** *[injection instant]*
2. **Modify_Signal** *[signal name] [fault value]*
3. **Simulate_For** *[injection duration]*
4 **Restore_Signal** *[signal name]*
5. **Simulate_For** *[observation time]*

The sequence of pseudo-commands is thought to inject transient faults, which are the most common and difficult to detect [26]. To inject permanent faults, the sequence is the same, but omitting steps 3 and 4. To inject intermittent faults, the sequence consists of repeating steps 1 to 5, with random separation intervals. The elements between brackets constitute the injection parameters.

Manipulation of variables

1. **Simulate_Until** *<injection instant >*
2. **Assign_Variable** *<variable name> <fault value>*
3. **Simulate_For** *<observation time>*

The operation is similar to the injection on signals, but there is no control of the fault duration. For this reason it is not possible to inject permanent faults on variables using the simulator commands.

The command sequence is included in an *injection macro*, and the injection parameters are passed as parameters of the macro. In this way, it is possible to vary the injection conditions without modifying the command code.

5.2 Parameters of the injection campaign

The following list describes the fault injection experiment conditions of the injection campaign of this work.

1. **Number of faults**: n = 3000 single faults in every injection campaign. This guarantees the statistical validity of the results.

2. **Workload:** The workload is a simple program that obtains the arithmetic series of n integer numbers.

$$series = \sum_{k=1}^{n} k \ . \tag{1}$$

3. **Fault types:** The injected faults are transient/permanent, stuck-at 0, stuck-at 1, open-line, or indetermination and they may affect the signals and the variables in the model.

4. **Place where the fault is injected:** The faults are systematically injected on any atomic signal (sets of signals, like buses, are divided into their bits) and variable of *the* model, in both the external structural architecture and the behavioural architectures of the components. Faults are not injected in the spare CPU, since it is off while the system is working properly.

5. **Values of the faults:** The values of faults are produced according a Uniform distribution along the available range of signals and variables.

6. **Time instant when the fault is injected:** The time instant of injection is distributed according to different types of probability distribution functions

(Uniform, Exponential, Weibull, Gaussian), typical of the transient faults [27], in the range:

$$[0, t_{workload}] .$$

where $t_{workload}$= workload simulation duration without faults.

7. **Simulation duration:** The simulation duration includes the execution time of the workload and the recovery time with the spare CPU ($t_{Simul} = t_{Workload} + t_{Spare}$). In our case, we have chosen a value of 500μS.

8. **Fault duration:** The experiments has selectively chosen the following values: 100, 1000, 10000, 250000 and 500000 ns, equivalent to 0.1, 1.0, 10.0, 100.0, 250.0, and 500.0 clock cycles respectively (the processor cycle is 1000 ns.) In some experiments, the duration is randomly generated in the range [0.1T-10.0T], where T is the CPU clock cycle. It is been intended to inject "short" faults, with a duration equal to a fraction of the clock cycle (the most common faults, as described in [28]), as well as "long" faults, which will ensure in excess the propagation of the errors to the detection signals.

9. **Analysis results:** For every injection experiment, two files are compared: the simulation result with and without fault. The estimated coverages and latencies of the detection and recovery mechanisms are automatically recorded. The Fault-tolerance mechanisms predicate graph [2] is shown in Fig. 4. The diagram shows the fault pathology, what means the process that follows the faults since they are injected until the detection and recovery by the fault-tolerant system.

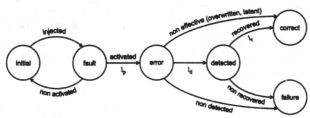

Fig. 4. Fault-tolerance mechanisms predicate graph.

The following parameters are obtained from the sample data:
- The percentage of activated faults. A fault is called activated when it produces a change on a signal or variable. The percentage is calculated based on the total number of injected faults, n.
- Error detection coverage. We have distinguished two types of coverage estimators:
  * Coverage of the detection mechanisms

$$C_{d(mechanisms)} = \frac{N_{Detected}}{N_{Activated}} . \quad (2)$$

* Global system coverage

$$C_{d(system)} = \frac{N_{Detected} + N_{Non-effective}}{N_{Activated}} \, .$$

(3)

The faults that do not affect the running application are called non-effective faults. A non-effective fault is usually produced when the faulty information is overwritten by the normal execution, or because the faulty data remains dormant in an unused part of the system. In the latter case, the fault may eventually become effective. The non-effectiveness of faults is related to intrinsic characteristics of the system. We define a more global coverage called System Coverage.

• Recovery coverage. Divided also in two types of coverage estimators:
  * Coverage of the recovery mechanisms

$$C_{(mechanisms)} = \frac{N_{Detected\_recovered}}{N_{Activated}} \, .$$

(4)

* Global system coverage

$$C_{r(system)} = \frac{N_{Detected\_recovered} + N_{Non-effective}}{N_{Activated}} \, .$$

(5)

• Propagation, detection and recovery latencies:
  * Lp = tp – tinj, where tp is the time instant the fault is visible at the signals of the external structural architecture. Tinj is the injection time instant.
  * Ld = td – tp, where td is the time instant the error is detected by detection mechanisms.
  * Lr = tr – td, where tr is the time instant the recovery mechanisms finish the recovery process.

6. Results

The experiments have been carried out on a PC-compatible with *Pentium* processor at 200Mhz.

Every set of 3000 injections has been divided in two sets with 1500 each, due to lack of disk space and to keep reasoble the simulation time. Some aspects about the time necessary to perform the experiments are:

– The execution of the workload with faults, 1500 fault injections last for around 4 hours.
– For the analysis of the simulations, 1500 simulaciones last for around 2 hours.

These times depend on the workload complexity and the machine power.

The results have been grouped, depending on the particular aspect of the fault tolerant system validation which is intended to remark, into the following headings:

1. Influence of the fault duration.
2. Influence of the type of probability distribution of the injection instant.

6.1 Influence of the fault duration

The parameters of the injection campaign are, summarised:

- number of injections per experiment, n = 3000.
- place = *Random* (all the atomic signals and variables of the model).
- value = *Random* ('0', '1', 'Z', 'X').
- instant = *Uniform* $(0, t_{workload})$.
- duration = 0.1 T, 1.0 T, 10.0 T, 100.0 T, 250.0T, 500.0 T

Fig. 5 shows the percentage of activated errors related to the fault duration.

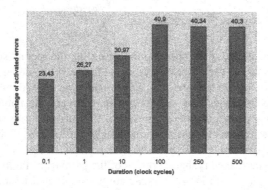

Fig. 5. Percentage of activated errors related to the fault duration.

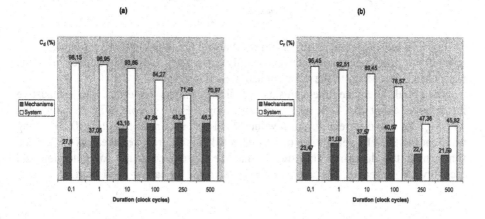

Fig. 6. Coverages related to the fault duration. (a) Detection coverage. (b) Recovery coverage.

As it can be seen, there is a nearly logarithmic growth in the interval [0.1T-10.0T], which corresponds with transient faults of short duration. For 100.0T the slope is steeper, and from that point, the percentage is stabilised at 40%. The last segment corresponds with transient faults of longer duration and permanent faults, where the spare CPU is activated.

Fig. 6 presents both detection and recovery coverages related to the fault duration, indicating the type of coverage as defined earlier. The figure shows that Cd (mechanisms) grows with fault duration, and it holds constant from 100.0T and above in approximately 48%. However, Cd (global system) follows the opposite behaviour. In the interval [0.1T- 10.0T] the values are quite high (between 93% and 98%). For 100.0T the coverage is around 84% and from 250.0T and above it is stabilised around 70%. As expected, the global system is affected mostly by longer faults, even though the percentage of detected faults also grows with fault duration. This tendency is explained as follows: there is a important decrease of the percentage of non-effective errors while increases the percentage of non-detected error that produces system failure. From (2) and (3) the expression for Cd (system) is:

$$C_{d(system)} = C_{d(mechanisms)} + \frac{N_{Non-effective}}{N_{Activated}} . \tag{6}$$

the first term increases as the duration increases, but the second strongly decreases as the duration increases. The global effect is that the detection coverage decreases.

The recovery coverage follows the same behaviour as Cd until 100.0T, with slightly smaller percentages. This means that the recovery mechanisms are working well, and almost any detected error is recovered. Cr(system) varies between 79% and 95%, while Cr(mechanisms) varies approximately between 23% and 41%. But Cr decreases notably between 250.0T y 500.0T, to reach 47% for $C_{r(system)}$ and 22% for Cr(mechanisms). The reason is that a portion of the permanent faults affects the spare system performance (even though the faults are not originated in such a CPU) and it precludes the system recovery. From (4) and (5) the expression for Cr(system) is:

$$C_{r(system)} = C_{r(mechanisms)} + \frac{N_{Non-efective}}{N_{Activated}} . \tag{7}$$

Fig. 7 shows the latencies lp, ld and lr related to the fault duration. As can be seen, lp < ld << lr. The checkpoint recovery greatly contributes to the total latency. There is not a clear dependency to the duration inside each interval.

The Fault-tolerance mechanisms predicate graphs give us an exhaustive information about the fault and error pathology. For example, Fig. 8 shows the coverage for two different duration values: 0.1T (short transient faults), 100.0T (long transient faults). The percentage of non-detected and non-recovered errors grows as a function of the duration. This means that the system coverage for detection and recovery has decreased. We can also see the latencies for each type of fault.

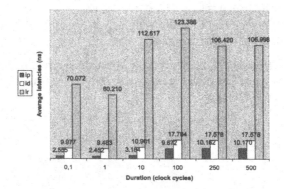

Fig. 7. Average latencies (propagation, detection and recovery) related to fault duration.

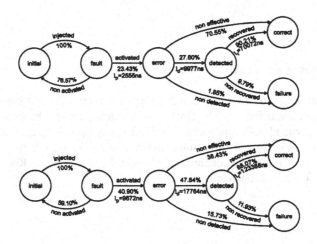

Fig. 8. FTM predicate graphs for different fault durations. (a) 0.1T. (b) 100.0T.

6.2   Influence of the fault distribution

The following figures show the same results as the previous ones but as a function of the statistical distribution of the time instant the fault is injected.

The parameters of the injection campaign are, summarised below:

- number of injections per experiment, n = 3000.
- place = *Random* (all the atomic signals and variables of the model).
- value = *Random* ('0', '1', 'Z', 'X').
- instant = with different statistical distributions:
    * *Uniform* $(0, t_{workload})$.
    * Exponential, $\alpha = 0.005$
    * Weibull, $\alpha = 0.001$, $\beta = 3.0$

> * Gaussian, $\mu = t_{workload}/2$, $\sigma = t_{workload}/8$

- duration = *Random* (0.1T, 10.T), with increments of 0.1T. We are focused on the effect of the short transient faults.

As it can be seen in Fig. 9, the percentage of activated errors is slightly influenced by the distribution type. The values lay between 28.13% for Uniform distribution and 29.57% for Weibull distribution.

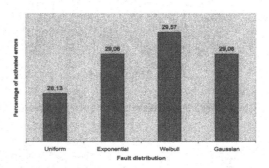

Fig. 9. Percentage of activated errors related to the fault distribution.

Fig. 10 presents coverage for detection and recovery. The differences between distributions are small for Cd. The Uniform distribution makes the largest difference among others (around 95% compared to 97% in the system coverage). Regarding Cr, there is a larger variation of the results. Uniform and Gaussian distributions present larger values for Cr than Exponential and Weibull ones (around 30% compared to 20% on the coverage of mechanisms).

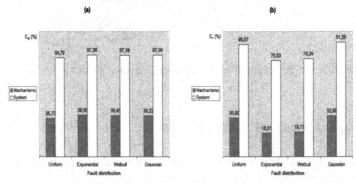

Fig. 10. Coverages related to the fault distribution. (a) Detection cov. (b) Recovery coverage.

Regarding latencies, Fig. 11 corroborates the differences previously shown in Fig. 7 : lp < ld << lr. In addition, there are important differences among the distributions, summarised as:

- lp, ld (Exponential, Weibull) > lp, ld (Uniform, Gaussian)
- lr (Exponential, Weibull) < lr (Uniform, Gaussian)

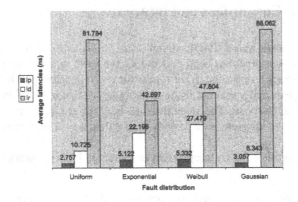

Fig. 11. Average latencies (propagation, detection and recovery) related to fault distribution.

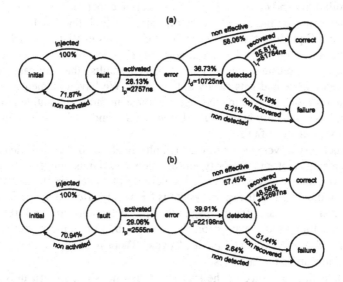

Fig. 12. Fault-tolerance mechanisms predicate graphs for two types of fault distribution. (a) Uniform. (b) Exponential.

Fig. 12 shows the fault-tolerance mechanisms predicate graphs for two important cases: Uniform and Exponential distribution. The values for the coverage and latency are the ones discussed before. The percentage of activated errors and detection coverage is similar. The most important difference is the increase of the percentage of non-recovered errors for the Exponential distribution (around 51% compared to 14% of the Uniform distribution). This fact produces a decrease on the recovery coverage. The recovery latency for the Exponential distribution is much lower than that of Uniform distribution (42697 ns compared to 81784 ns).

7. Summary. Conclusions and future work

An injection campaign into a VHDL model of an 16-bit fault tolerant microcomputer system running a workload has been performed. We have injected transient faults (in groups of 3000 in each experiment), of types stuck-at, open-line and indetermination, on the model signals and variables, using the simulator commands of an injection tool designed with that purpose. The objective has been to study the pathology of the propagated errors, to measure their latency, and calculate the detection and recovery coverages.

The most important conclusions that can be extracted from the work and the results are:

- We have proven the good performance of the used injection technique (automatic alteration of variables and signals of the model by the use of special simulator commands). Worth to mention the easy implementation, and the high controllability and observability of the injection experiments.

- We have showed the usefulness of the injection tool, that has been designed to work on PC platforms and inject faults at chip-level in VHDL models.

- The detection recovery has an almost logarithmic growth related to the fault duration for transient faults. For permanent faults, the coverage tends to a maximum value and gets steady at this value. We have obtained values among 28% and 48%. The system coverage for transient faults (including non-effective faults) has reach very high values (between 93% and 98%), while it decreases to 70% for permanent faults.

- The recovery coverage for transient faults is close to the fault detection one. This means that the majority of the detected faults are finally recovered. However, the recovery coverage for permanent faults greatly decreases (until 22%), indicating that the spare system is frequently affected by the fault.

- The average values for propagation (lp), detection (ld) and recovery (lr) latencies follows the expression: $lp < ls \ll lr$. For transient faults, $lp \approx 2.7$ Tcycle, $ld \approx 10$ Tcycle and $lr \approx 81$ Tcycle. There is not a clear influence of the fault duration on the latencies.

- The detection coverage of the transient faults does not significantly varies for different distributions of the fault instant. However, the type of distributions has influenced the recovery coverage and latencies. In both cases, the Exponential and Weibull distributions have a similar behaviour between them, and different than Uniform and Gaussian. Nevertheless, to analyse the dependency with the fault distribution, it is important to notice the influence of the workload, because it determines the sensibility of fault in a given instant.

Summarising, the system detects and recovers transient faults well enough (with values for Cd and Cr above 90%). Regarding latencies, the worst case is the lr, due to the checkpoint recovery of the control flow transient faults. Regarding the permanent faults, the detection recovery is high (Cd >= 70%) but the recovery coverage notably decreases (around 45%). The performance of the cold-start spare is affected by permanent faults (even though the faults are not originated in such a CPU).

The information presented here can be used to improve the design of detection and recovery mechanisms to optimise the values of coverage and latency.

It is intended to complete this work in a short term in the following aspects:

- Verifying the dependence on the workload (the dependence of faults on the workload is an important factor [26]) and on the type of model. In the latter sense, it seems convenient to test the tool with more structural models.
- Verify in detail the contribution of each detection and recovery mechanisms on the coverages and latencies.
- Testing new injection techniques that can modify the VHDL code, starting from the idea of *saboteurs* (at structural level) and *mutants* (at behavioural level) [7].
- Improve the detection mechanisms that may be present inside the CPU, and validate them by fault injection.

8. References

1. J. Clark., D. Pradhan, "Fault Injection. A method for validating computer-system dependability", *IEEE. Computer*, June 1995.
2. J. Arlat, A. Costes, Y. Crouzet, J. Laprie, D. Powel. "Fault Injection and Dependability Evaluation of Fault-Tolerant Systems". *IEEE Transactions on Computers*, Vol 42, n°. 8, pp. 913-923. August 1993.
3. K. Goswami, K. Iyer, "DEPEND: A simulation-based environment for system level dependability analysis", *Tech. Rep. CRHC-92-11*, Center for Reliable and High Performance Computing, University of Illinois (USA) 1991.
4. G. Choi, K. Iyer, "FOCUS: An experimental environment for fault sensitivity analysis", *IEEE Transactions on Computers*, Vol. 41, pp. 1515-1526, Dec. 1992.
5. P. Folkesson, S. Svensson, J. Karlsson. "A Comparison of simulation-based and scan chain implemented fault injection". *28th International Symposium on Fault Tolerant Computing (FTCS-28)*, pp. 284-293. Munich, Germany. June 1998.
6. J. Clark, D. Pradhan, "REACT: Reliable Architecture Characterization Tool", *Tech. Rep. TR-92-CSE-22*, Univ. of Massachusetts, June 1992.
7. Jenn E., Arlat J., Rimen M., Ohlsson J., Karlsson J. "Fault Injection into VHDL Models: The MEFISTO Tool", *FTCS-24*, IEEE, 1994, pp. 66-75.
8. T. Delong, B. Johnson, Profeta III, "A fault Injection Technique for VHDL Behavioral-Level models", *IEEE Design and Test of Computers*, Vol 13, n° 4, Winter 1996.
9. J. Arlat, M. Aguera, L. Amat, Y. Crouzet, J. C. Fabré, J. C. Laprie, E. Martins, D. Powell, "Fault injection for dependability validation: a methodology and some applications", *IEEE Transactions on Software Engineering*, Vol.16, pp.166-182, Febrero 1990.
10. U. Gunneflo, "Physical fault injection for Validation of Dependable Computing Systems and a Fault-Tolerant Computer design for Safety-critical missions", PhD thesis, Chalmers Univ. Of Technology, Göteborg (Sweden), 1990.
11. P. Gil, "Sistema Tolerante a Fallos con Procesador de Guardia: Validación mediante Inyección Física de Fallos", D. Ph. Thesis, Departamento de Ingeniería de Sistemas, Computadores y Automática, Univ. Politécnica de Valencia, September 1992.
12. J. Karlsson, P. Folkesson, J. Arlat, Y. Crouzet, G. Leber. "Integration and Comparison of Three Physical Fault Injection Techniques". *Predictably Dependable Computer Systems*. Chapter V: Fault Injection, pp. 309-329. Springer Verlag, 1995.
13. R. J. Martínez, P. J. Gil, C. Martín, C. Pérez, J.J. Serrano . "Experimental Validation of High-Speed Fault-Tolerant Systems Using Physical Fault Injection", *in Seventh*

Dependable Computing for Critical Applications, DCCA'7. IEEE Computer Society Press. Pending of publication. pp. 233-249, 1999.

14. Z. Segall, et al. "FIAT: Fault-Injection Based Automated Testing Environment", *Proc. 18th Symp. on Fault-Tolerant Computing Systems (FTCS-18)*, Tokyo (Japan), IEEE CS Press, pp. 102-107, June 1988.

15. G. A. Kanawati, N. A. Kanwati, J. A. Abraham: "FERRARI: A Tool for the Validation of System Dependability Properties", *Proceedings 22th Symp. on Fault-Tolerant Computing Systems (FTCS-22)*, Boston, Massachusetts (U.S.A.), pp. 336-344, July, 1992.

16. W. Kao, R. K. Iyer, D. Tang, "FINE: A Fault Injection and Monitor Environment for Tracing the UNIX System Behavior under Faults", *IEEE Transactions on Software Engineering*, Vol. 19, No. 11, pp. 1105-1118, Nov. 1993.

17. S. Han, H. A. Rosenberg, K. G. Shin, "DOCTOR: An IntegrateD SOftware Fault InjeCTiOn EnviRonment", *Technical report, Univ. of Michigan*, December 1993.

18. J. C. Fabre, F. Sallés, M. Rodriguez, J. Arlat. "Assesment of COTS microkernel by fault injection". *Proceedings Seventh IFIP International Working Conference on Dependable Computing for Critical Applications (DCCA-7)*, pp. 19-38. San José, EEUU. Enero 1999.

19. IEEE Standard VHDL Language Reference Manual, IEEE Std 1076-1993.

20. D. Gil, J. C. Baraza, J. V. Busquets and P. Gil. "Fault Injection into VHDL Models: Analysis of the Error Syndrome of a Microcomputer System". *Proc. Of the 24th Euromicro Conference*. Västeras, Sweden, 1998.

21. D. Gil, J.V. Busquets, J.C. Baraza and P. Gil. "A Fault Injection Tool for VHDL Models". *Fastabs of the 28th Fault Tolerant Computing Symposium (FTCS-28)*. Munich, Germany. 1998.

22. Model Technology, "V-System/Windows User's Manual. Version 4", 1994.

23. Armstrong J.R., Lam F.-S., Ward P.C. "Test generation and Fault Simulation for Behavioral Models". *In Performance and Fault Modeling with VHDL*. (J.M.Schoen ed.), pp.240-303, Englewood Cliffs, Prentice-Hall, 1992.

24. J. R. Armstrong, "Chip-Level Modeling with VHDL", Prentice Hall, 1989.

25. E. A. Amerasekera, F. N. Najm. "Failure Mechanisms in Semiconductor Devices". John Wiley & Sons. 1997.

26. R. Iyer and D. Rosseti. "A measurement-based model for workload dependence of CPU errors". *IEEE Trans. Comput.* vol. C-35. pp. 511-519. June 1986.

27. D. P. Siewiorek, "Reliable Computer Systems. Design and Evaluation", *Digital Press*, 1994.

28. H. Cha, E. M. Rudnick, G. S. Choi, J. H. Patel, R. K. Iyer, "A fast and accurate gate-level transient fault simulation environment". *Proceedings 23rd Symp. on Fault-Tolerant Computing Systems (FTCS-23)*, Toulouse (France), pp. 310-319, June, 1993.

Can Software Implemented Fault-Injection be Used on Real-Time Systems?[‡]

João Carlos Cunha[1], Mário Zenha Rela[2], João Gabriel Silva[2]

[1] Departamento de Engenharia Informática e de Sistemas
Instituto Superior de Engenharia de Coimbra
Quinta da Nora, 3030 Coimbra – Portugal
jcunha@isec.pt
[2]Departamento de Engenharia Informática
Universidade de Coimbra, Pólo II
3030 Coimbra – Portugal
{mzrela,jgabriel}@dei.uc.pt

Abstract. Software Implemented Fault Injection (SWIFI) is a well-established technique for fault injection, but with a significant drawback for Real-Time Systems: intrusiveness, also known as "probe effect". In fact, for most fault models, additional code has to be run on the same processor that executes the application. The danger lies in some deadlines being missed as a consequence of that overhead.

This paper identifies the sources of intrusiveness, and discusses the procedures to measure it. The question of what level of intrusiveness can be considered acceptable is also addressed.

A Pentium version of an existing SWIFI tool (Xception), developed with no real-time considerations in mind, was tested on a system composed by off-the-shelf (COTS) components (a standard PC with a Pentium processor and a commercial real-time multitasking kernel). Data collected using this platform shows that the intrusiveness can be quite significant.

A technique called "Routine Specialization" is proposed to lower that overhead. Results obtained from a "real-time-oriented" injector (RT-Xception) taken from the same system, show a very significant improvement. A comparison with data from other authors shows that with this change SWIFI becomes a viable technique for a wide range of real-time applications.

[‡] This work was partially supported by the portuguese Ministério da Ciência e Tecnologia and the European Union through the R&D Unit 326/94 (CISUC) and the project PBIC/C/TIT/2450/95 (SAFIRA II)

1 Introduction

Fault injection is a widely used technique for Dependability evaluation and validation. Software Implemented Fault Injection (SWIFI), also known as fault emulation, is being used in a growing number of situations [1, 2, 3, 4, 5, 6, 8, 10, 11, 12, 13, 15, 18, 19, 21, 24, 25] due to its intrinsic flexibility and portability among different platforms, if compared with hardware-based approaches.

Basically, one can distinguish two types of SWIFI, according to the moment when the faults are injected: off-line and runtime [9]. Off-line fault-injection consists on the modification of the program's image (code or data) before it is loaded into the target system and executed. No additional interference is required while the workload executes. When the instructions/data are reached during the execution, the error becomes active. This technique presents a minimum intrusiveness, but at the cost of a very limited fault model. In fact, transient faults are impossible to emulate on processor functional units or buses. The only exception is the case of faults injected in the program's data image, that become active the first time that memory location is accessed. Permanent faults are also limited to memory faults in the code segment (and thus can only emulate some types of processor faults, such as an instruction decode error). Faults are only triggered when the corrupted memory is accessed and thus no time-based trigger exists.

An early approach to SWIFI, FIAT [21], used a similar approach, corrupting a task memory image using compiler and loader information. Other SWFI tools that used this technique had low time intrusiveness. DOCTOR [8], used in the distributed real-time system HARTS, uses the modification of the application executable image by changing some instructions generated by the compiler. In the real-time system MARS error detection mechanisms were evaluated using a similar approach [6], by injecting faults on the application's code and data prior to the execution. Minimum intrusiveness elects off-line fault injection as the preferred approach for real-time systems.

On the other hand, runtime fault-injection has the ability to inject a wider fault model. The fault-injection process consists on the execution of corruption code, concurrently to the target workload, that emulates the effects of the intended fault. This approach permits a whole spectrum of fault types and locations, since the injection code can emulate the effects of any processor, memory or bus error, given that the fault is able to manifest itself in components accessible by software. The moment this corruption is performed may be triggered by any external event (as a timeout or any target process-generated interrupt), by exceptions/traps (as instruction fetch or data access), or by inserting the injection instructions in the normal execution path of the target program. However, the execution of extra code leads inevitably to a time overhead. This overhead can be reduced if the injection code is fully prepared in an off-line phase but, unlike the off-line injection, the corruption is performed in runtime. This means that the precise location of the fault is already known (only instruction fetch or code insertion triggers are allowed). The fault-injection tools used on MARS, as well as the DOCTOR tool, use this runtime fault-injection and off-line injection setup approach for injecting errors by mutilating messages exchanged between processes.

Other tools are very time-consuming, because they don't have any temporal restrictions. FINE [12] uses a software monitor to trace instruction flow and to corrupt instructions in specific addresses, and the FERRARI tool [11], uses the UNIX *ptrace* function to corrupt the process memory image in run-time by inserting software traps at specified instruction addresses. Another approach is followed by the ProFI tool [15] that executes the target system in trace-mode in order to invoke the fault injection routine before each instruction. An extensive fault model is then possible to simulate.

Furthermore, the capability to have a time-based trigger is extremely important to obtain meaningful statistical results that reflect random hardware faults. DEFINE[13], Ftape [24] and Xception [1], do support this trigger mode. Having a time-based trigger means that the injector has no idea about the instruction where the fault is to be injected. This implies, for several fault models (e.g. injection on the ALU or system buses), that the current instruction needs to be decoded on-line. On CISC machines this is a particularly hard task. Obviously, none of these tools was built targeting real-time systems.

These facts elect runtime fault-injection as the most complete fault-injection technique, along with the capability to provide a time trigger. However, this technique has a major drawback, which is the extra time overhead needed to execute the corruption code. This intrusiveness is particularly undesirable whenever real-time systems need to be evaluated: beyond corrupting the state of the target component, the fault-injection instructions may alter the behavior of the workload, thus some deadlines may be missed. This problem is known as "probe effect" [7].

The correct operation of a real-time system depends on the capability of the system to comply with time constraints. The fault-injection mechanism must not affect the timing of the target system, in a way that it may not comply with those timing conditions. As far as we know, the verification of these conditions has never been evaluated by other SWIFI with a wide error model, in order to determine their applicability to real-time systems. This is in the subject of this paper.

In section 2 we present measured values for the intrusiveness associated to Software Implemented Fault Injection, using a Pentium version of the Xception fault injector [1]. In section 3 we identify the sources of that intrusiveness and discuss the techniques that can be used to reduce it. These ideas are then applied to a new SWIFI tool, RT-Xception, which uses the same extensive fault model as Xception, but has a totally new approach to the fault-injection core design and implementation. RT-Xception is described in section 4 along with the supported fault model. The RT-Xception intrusiveness is then measured and its applicability to real-time environments evaluated. Those results are presented in section 5. The last section contains the concluding remarks and ideas for future work.

2 Intrusiveness and Real Time Fault Injection

In order to be able to use Software Implemented Fault-Injection in Real-Time Systems we need to guarantee that the time interference due to the fault-injection process is both predictable and negligible.

The first requirement is central in Real-Time Systems, where predictability is the key issue, rather than low response time or high throughput, to guarantee that deadlines are fulfilled. The second requirement is needed if we do not want SWIFI to significantly restrict the range of real-time applications where it can be used. These two requirements essentially mean that the disturbance caused by SWIFI must have an upper bound, and that this bound should be as low as possible. We considered that the experimental way was the most viable approach to find whether SWIFI fulfilled those two requirements.

We had two requirements for the platform to use on our experiments - it had to be COTS to have a clear practical significance, and we should be able to compare the results obtained with data published by other researchers. The data we needed had to enable us to define approximately what is the time behavior expected from a platform for real-time systems.

We found what we were looking for in [23]. In this paper, the real-time capabilities of Windows CE 2.0 are evaluated and compared against QNX's Neutrino 1.0. The measurements were carried out with an Intel Pentium MMX processor at 200Mhz on a standard PCI ATX motherboard, with the cache enabled. We naturally decided to use exactly the same hardware configuration. The sole difference resides on the real-time multitasking kernel used - because of source code availability and because it has a certain level of memory protection between processes (a surprisingly rare capability in real-time multitasking kernels, in spite of the effectiveness of memory protection as an error detection method), we chose SMX$^\circledcirc$ (Simple Multitasking Executive), a commercial real-time kernel from Micro Digital Inc, USA, working in 16-bit protected mode [20].

Our first step was to verify that our platform was indeed comparable to those used in [23]. The main temporal figure of merit used in [23] is the kernel response-time to an asynchronous external event, namely the latency for interrupt handling at thread level. By measuring the time that elapses between an interrupt and the beginning of the associated task execution (interrupt handling latency) we can evaluate the time the kernel takes to respond to an external stimulus. The results are presented in Table 1, and clearly show that our platform is quite similar to the other two. The measure for the SMX kernel corresponds to the time to activate a Link Service Routine after an interrupt occurs. These values present a very small standard deviation: just 0.14 µs.

Table 1. Interrupt handling latencies (values in microseconds)

	SMX 3.2	Windows CE 2.0	QNX Neutrino 1.0
average	3.1	9.5	1.9
maximum	3.9	13.4	3.6

We have then tested an existing version of a SWIFI tool developed in our group, Xception [1], under the described test platform. This tool was built with no real-time considerations in mind, so time resolution was a performance factor, not a requirement.

Since the only measures that we wanted to take were related to time intrusiveness, for all the measurements described in this paper we always executed the injector with a null injection mask. This means that it performed all the normal tasks of an injection, except that in the end it did not modify any bit in the target system because none was specified in the injection mask.

We observed that the delay introduced by Xception at the moment where the fault was injected was about 240 μs, with small variations for different types of faults injected, which makes it easy to calculate a tight upper bound and thus guarantees predictability. But this delay is two orders of magnitude greater than the measured interrupt handling latency of approximately 3 μs (Table 1). This overhead is clearly far from negligible. While this figure does not prevent such fault injector from being used in real-time applications, it significantly restricts the scope of applications where it can be used to only those that are quite "slow real-time".

This overhead can be explained by the computations that have to be performed by the fault injector. Xception supports a very powerful fault model (it injects various types of transient faults and provides both temporal and spatial triggers), which requires in many cases that several instructions be analyzed in order to affect the desired register/operand according to the specified fault-type. Having in mind that the target system is a Pentium-based machine, instruction decode is a specially hard work.

As stated in the introduction, some existing fault-injection tools seek to overcome this probe-effect by using a pre-runtime approach, and thus by restricting the fault model. Besides, temporal triggers are not supported, in spite of their importance for statistically significant dependability evaluation.

We wanted to keep the full fault model. In the following section we will analyze in detail the reasons for the measured overhead, and propose an approach to lower it.

3 The Complexity of SWIFI

Disturbing a system in a precise and controlled way is a very delicate and complex process; it is the opposite of doing it in an uncontrolled way. An analogy can be drawn with a human being: anyone can hurt someone else with a knife; a surgeon, however, has to be very knowledgeable and precise to manipulate a specific point in a patient's body. In the same way, to use fault-injection for evaluation/validation purposes, the disturbance affecting the computer system must agree with a fault model, and this requires a lot of information and computation. Since extra code executes in the target system, it may disturb the workload and even interfere with its outcome. SWIFI tools must then be extremely careful in order to reduce the impact on the target system to the intended corruption only.

Xception is based on the idea that no software based monitoring of the target program progress is needed to select the injection instant, as this would represent an unacceptable overhead. Instead standard hardware resources like breakpoint registers and timers are used to trigger the injection. These resources are commonly available in modern processors. There is thus essentially no time overhead associated with the selection of the moment where the fault should be injected, since breakpoint registers and timers can be set up before the application starts.

The overhead results from two other phases: the injection phase, where an error that emulates the occurrence of the intended fault is introduced in the system, and the data collection phase, where a description of the system state at the moment of injection is stored somewhere for later analysis.

3.1 Fault Injection

Let us examine the injection phase first. To understand the time overhead involved, we must have a precise idea of the fault/error model supported by the tool, particularly those aspects that contribute to the higher overhead.

1. **Transient faults** occur much more frequently than permanent faults [17]. To inject them, we cannot use zero overhead off-line techniques like making static changes in the code or initial data image of a program (although it may be possible, if we only want to inject memory faults that occur the first time the memory location is accessed). We have to let the program execute, interrupt it at the right moment and inject the fault.

2. **Permanent faults** are not considered in our fault-injector. While some permanent faults, as memory faults on program's code segment, are very easy to emulate (the memory cells must only be corrupted once) others are more difficult or even extremely painful to emulate. For example, to emulate a data memory fault, the fault-injector should be triggered every time that memory location is written, in order to corrupt it again. To emulate a permanent register fault the work is even harder, regardless the approach followed to do it: a) every instruction to execute should be decoded to find out if the register is being used, in order to corrupt it; b) before every instruction, the register is corrupted; c) corruption code is added off-line before every instruction that reads the register. For most fault models, the

injection of permanent faults presents a prohibitive overhead. Since the vast majority of hardware faults are transients, we decided to inject only these.

3. **Precise fault location.** To be as close as possible to the faults that do occur in real systems, the errors injected should emulate a number of fault locations as large as possible. Along with the memory and internal data and address buses, the hardware building blocks of the target processor should be considered, such as Processor Registers, Integer Unit, Memory Management Unit and the Floating-Point Unit. This means that the error to be injected depends on the instruction that is being executed at the injection moment. For instance, to inject a fault in the Integer Unit, the result of an integer instruction can be tampered with, but to inject in the Floating-Point Unit a floating point instruction must be executing for us to interfere with it's results. The point here is that we must know which is the instruction that is going to be executed when the fault injection is triggered.

4. **Time based trigger.** The support for temporal triggering (specified as the time from the startup of the application until the moment when a fault should be injected) is essential when evaluating a system's dependability. Injecting faults with a uniform distribution during the application's execution time is one of the best ways to model randomly occurring hardware faults. The problem is that, when an injection moment is specified, there is no way of knowing *a priori* which instruction is going to be in execution when that moment comes. Since we have just seen that the injection procedure depends on that instruction, we will have to decode it in run-time, which is a significant source of overhead, mainly for processors with complex instruction sets like the Intel x86 architecture.

When the user specifies a spatial trigger e.g. the occurrence of a particular code address, the injector can look at the code before the application is started to see which instruction is in that address, so that the decoding will not have to be performed at run time. But this optimization is not always possible for all spatial triggers. For instance, if the occurrence of a particular data address is specified, the injector will still have to decode the instruction at runtime since many different instructions can access that address.

External-event triggering, which is invoked by activating an interrupt line, giving the possibility to synchronize a fault injection with the controlled system, also requires run-time decoding of instructions.

5. **Fault type.** The type of fault to inject can be stuck-to-zero, stuck-to-one, bridging faults and bit-flip, thus allowing a broad range of faults to be emulated. The fault type parameter also identifies the number and position of the bits that are to be affected. This is normally implemented by the use of a mask that is ANDed, ORed, or XORed with the data to be affected, and is responsible for only a small part of the overhead.

An additional fault-type relevant for real-time systems is a *time delay*. Injecting such fault involves just occupying the processor for the specified time delay. This can be used, for example, to force a task to miss a deadline. The overhead here is not a problem, since a delay is exactly what the user intends.

A point to clarify here is what happens if the instruction that is being executed when the injection moment occurs is not appropriate for the specified fault model, e.g. if it is an integer instruction when we wanted to emulate a fault in the floating-point unit. We might consider that this corresponds to the situation where a fault occurs in a functional unit that is not being used - a non-effective transient fault (i.e. it never became an error [14]). But modern processors are pipelined, which means that even if the instruction that is being issued at the moment is not of the particular type we are looking for, there may be another one of that type in the pipeline, that would be affected by a fault in the target functional unit. We should thus look for the relevant instruction type in an instruction "window", or sequence, that roughly corresponds to the pipeline depth, or at least to those phases that can be affected by a fault in the relevant execution unit. This means that if the first instruction is not adequate for the kind of fault we want to inject, we single-step the program for some more instructions looking for a suitable one.

Besides, if we would give up whenever the first instruction encountered was not of the correct type, we would have a very low fault-activation rate, leading to very lengthy fault-injection campaigns.

In our case, we settled for a three-instruction window. This raises even further the probe effect, as most of the sources of overhead already described are multiplied by three, plus the overhead of the single step process itself.

3.2 Data Collection

Regarding the data collection phase, its overhead results from the time it takes to gather the data related to the fault injection process, such as the task that was executing when the fault was injected, register contents, etc. followed by the storage of that data in a safe place (e.g. some sort of stable memory). This data is used as a "marker" for the point where a fault was effectively injected (note that we cannot predict exactly where a temporal trigger will be activated).

The collection of data may require that the program be stopped again at the instruction that immediately follows the injection, so that the saved information includes the major consequences of an injection (e.g. the new program counter value, or what has been read after a memory access was corrupted). This is a situation that requires an additional single-step, consuming even more time.

It should be clear now that the process of injecting a fault is far from trivial, leading to the overheads reported in section 2.

4 Using SWIFI on Real-Time Systems

In the previous section we have identified the main sources of unwanted intrusiveness of software fault-injection in real-time systems: the fault-injection action itself and the acquisition of data in the neighborhood of the injection point.

4.1 Specialized Routines

To lower the time overhead we devised a new approach, that we call *specialized routines*. It has some points in common with program specialization, where a special compiler tries to use all knowledge available before program execution to reduce the generality of the code and thus make it more efficient [16]. In our case, we essentially substitute the exception handler used in Xception, which is capable of handling all fault types, triggers and locations, with a set of routines tuned to a particular fault type and location. For instance, if we want to inject a fault in the integer unit we do not have to fully decode the instruction, but only to determine whether it is an integer instruction and in which register/memory cell will it's result be stored. This is a partial decode that can use decoding tables for speed.

Unlike Muller's approach [16], our program specialization is fully manual. This way, we can achieve the best performance gains and have full control over the final code. Since this portion of the code is relatively small, code specialization is easily done.

This approach moves off-line most of the data analysis, thus making the injection routine extremely fast. It is also predictable, since we can bound the number of executed instructions: the code has no infinite loops and we limit the maximum the number of decoded instructions. We can expect that even if several machine instructions have to be checked to find an instruction that fulfills the fault-model criteria, this does not lead to a meaningful overhead.

The drawback of specialized code is the requirement for larger code and data segment sizes that have to be devoted to the fault injection routines. However, since real-time is the concern, this is a price we are ready to pay. But a bigger problem may arise from this larger code: a real error may alter the program flow into the fault-injection code. This problem can be minimized if the address space of the injection code is somehow separated from the target system (e.g. in different memory segments).

An additional performance gain can be achieved by programming the exception routines in assembly language. It also provides determinism (there is greater control from the programmer as opposed e.g. to C++). Since this is an architecture dependent part on any fault injector, the use of assembly language is a reasonable option.

4.2 RT-Xception: A Software Fault-Injector with Real-Time Constraints

We have thus developed a new SWIFI tool, RT-Xception, for the Pentium processor, using the *specialized routines* technique just described.

Similarly to Xception, in RT-Xception several kinds of events can trigger the injection of a fault: a specific instruction being fetched, a certain address being used for a load or for a store, or a predefined time elapsed from the start of the program. Additionally, RT-Xception supports fault-injection triggering by external events.

The fault locations supported by RT-Xception are: Integer Unit, FPU, Registers, MMU, Address Bus, Data Bus and Memory.

RT-Xception is basically composed by two modules: the Experiment Management Environment (EME) and the Injection Run Controller (IRC). The former runs in a host computer while the later is embedded into the target system.

This ensures that the only steps in the fault injection experiment that shall be executed concurrently in the target system are the fault injection itself and data collection: all experiment generation and control, and result analysis are done off-line.

Host System (Experiment Management Environment)

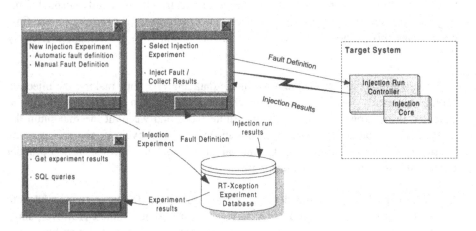

Fig. 1. Architecture of RT-Xception

The Experiment Management Environment (EME) is a set of Windows-based applications with Graphical User Interfaces providing an easy way to define and execute fault injection experiments, and to collect and analyze the results. All the experiment definitions and results are stored in a standard database file.

Each fault-injection experiment is composed by a sequence of fault-injections, executed one at a time.

The Injection-Run Controller (IRC) is a module embedded in the target system that receives the fault description from the Fault Injector's EME through a TCP/IP connection. It starts the fault triggering and prepares the Injection Core that will corrupt the target system. This Injection-Run Controller is thus dependent of the target system's architecture, both operating system and processor, but the conceptual model of the injector is very similar among different architectures.

The IRC is also responsible for collecting data during the process of injecting faults, in order to have information about the system's state and fault effect. This data consists on the processor context (register values) and operating system context. After the injection of each fault, the Target System is resetted and, on restart, data is sent to the Experiment Management Environment, before the next fault injection.

In order to have the least possible overhead, the collected data is stored in a local dedicated stable memory and, only after the experiment terminates, it is sent to the EME. This stable memory is based on a standard flash-ram memory, with an IDE interface. Since this memory is much slower than conventional RAM, the collected information is temporarily kept on main memory and only after terminating the fault injection (the Injection Core exception routine), a low-priority task is invoked to copy the data to flash-ram. The only drawback is that if the system crashes or hangs before the data is copied into stable-storage this data is lost.

As we have discussed in the previous section, we have written the RT-Xception's core code using a new approach: routine specialization. Thus, instead of generic routines, we used one specialized routine for every fault injection case. The number of 'if' or 'case' control structures was reduced to a minimum, and decoding is done only to the extent needed by the intended fault type, using basically table lookup.

According to this approach, when the IRC receives the description of the fault to inject, it simply selects the specific injection routine and performs all required initializations. When the fault trigger interrupts the processor, this specialized routine is called to execute the intended corruption and associated data collection.

Let us see some examples.

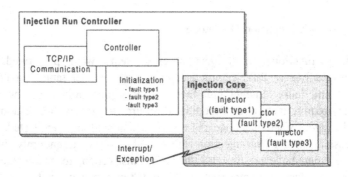

Fig. 2. Architecture of the Injection Run Controller

To inject faults in registers, the Injection Core performs the following steps: it collects and stores the system context (with time information), corrupts the target register on the stack, stores the new system context, and restores it with the corrupted value. For this type of fault no instruction decoding is needed at all. During the initialization phase (prior to the application execution), the fault information was analyzed and the target register identified.

Faults in memory are injected in a similar way since no instruction decode is needed. A memory segment descriptor is previously setup (the SMX kernel works with segmented memory). When the trigger interrupts the processor the injection routine saves the system context, corrupts the selected memory location according to the fault mask and type, and restores the system context.

Faults in the Integer Unit are possibly the hardest to inject. In this fault type the injection routine must decode the instruction, decide if it is an Integer Unit (IU) instruction, what is the target operand (memory or register), prepare the injection, execute the instruction, and then corrupt the target. If the decoded instruction is not an IU instruction, it places the processor in single-step mode until a valid instruction is found, or until a maximum number of decoded instructions is met. We considered that if, after the fault trigger, no three consecutive instructions use the IU, this fault is considered one that never became active: it simply "vanishes". This prevents randomly large time overheads due to the fault injection process if an applicable instruction takes too long to find. For the other functional units a similar approach is used.

In the following section we present the experimental results obtained after injecting faults with RT-Xception. The figures for Xception are also presented so that their intrusiveness can be compared.

5 Experimental Results

5.1 Measuring RT-Xception Overhead

Several fully functional fault-injection experiments were performed, using a representative subset of RT-Xception's fault models: register faults, memory faults, and integer unit faults. Integer unit faults differ significantly from the other two because they require instruction decoding. Both time trigger (with a random timeout) and spatial trigger (based on a code address, chosen at random) were tested.

In the case of Integer Unit injection with spatial trigger on a randomly chosen code address, we could have pre-decoded the target instruction, to enable the use of a simpler, and thus faster, injector routine. We didn't do it because not all of the spatial triggers have that possibility (e.g. the spatial triggers associated to data addresses), and in this way the measure is representative of the more complex cases.

Since the only measures that we intended to take were related to time intrusiveness, no fault was injected. This was possible without changing anything in the injector, just by specifying a null injection mask (the mask that specifies which bits in the target word should be affected), so that no bits were changed.

The average and maximum overheads measured for these cases are presented in Table 2.

Table 2. RT-Xception average/maximum overhead (values in µs)

Fault locations	Time trigger with data collection	time trigger without data collection	spatial trigger with data collection	spatial trigger without data collection
Registers	8.5 / 8.7	4.2 / 4.3	5.5 / 5.6	1.2 / 1.3
Memory	9.3 / 9.9	4.7 / 5.8	6.2 / 6.8	1.6 / 2.1
Integer Unit	19 / 20	12.2 / 14	16.3 / 16.9	9.1 / 10.8

The main point here is that the overhead for RT-Xception is close to two orders of magnitude lower than the overhead of Xception which, as stated in section 2, was around 240 µs (see also Table 3). It is also clear that these figures are of the same order of magnitude as the interrupt handling latencies presented in section 2 for the Windows CE 2.0, QNX's Neutrino 1.0 and SMX 3.2.

We believe that these figures represent a negligible overhead, and thus prove that, through routine specialization, SWIFI becomes a feasible approach for almost all real-time applications, without any compromise in the range of fault models offered.

Looking closer, we can see that the overhead of RT-Xception is different for each target functional unit, as expected, since the fault injection is performed by different routines. Integer unit faults are the slowest because of the need to decode the instructions up to 3 times.

This variable delay among different fault models didn't happen when the original Xception was used because the injection steps were almost the same, regardless of fault location, type or trigger.

To evaluate the impact of fault-injection on the system's behavior, the system context is collected before and after the fault is injected. This obviously leads to an extra overhead and, as we can observe from the collected figures, this overhead can be very expressive. However, quite often no data collection at the fault injector level is needed because the consequences of the fault are analyzed at the application level, thus lowering significantly the fault-injector intrusiveness.

The difference between the overhead of the time and spatial based triggers should also be explained, as we have said before that by using hardware resources like breakpoint registers and timers triggering consumes no processor time. The problem is that we used the same timer that is used by the multitasking kernel to preempt tasks. To share the timer without disturbing the kernel some additional reprogramming of the timer is needed, which consumes around 3 μs per injection. We are considering the use of a different timer that exists in the local APIC (Advanced Programmable Interrupt Controller) of the most recent versions of the Pentium processor, that should bring the overhead for time based trigger to exactly the same values of spatial-based trigger. The problem is that this would prevent RT-Xception from running in the older versions of the processor.

The overheads presented are also very stable and thus predictable, because the injector routines have been written in assembly and have no variable loops and few 'if' statements, allowing us to easily count the maximum number of executed instructions.

A legitimate question is whether the low overheads presented by RT-Xception are due to the routine specialization technique or just to the use of assembly language. To find that out we implemented in C++ the routines we used for our previous tests for the spatial trigger case. As can be seen in Table 3, the big difference happens when going from Xception to RT-Xception in C++ (Xception is also written in C++). The case is that RT-Xception (both C++ and assembly versions) use the routine specialization technique, while Xception has a general object-oriented approach.

Table 3. Differences caused by routine specialization and the implementation language, compared to Xception, using a spatial trigger (average times in μs)

Fault locations	Xception (C++)	RT-Xception (C++)	RT-Xception (asm)
Registers	225	11.5	5.5
Memory	240	12.5	6.2
Integer Unit	260	29	16.3

Finally it should be noted that assembly language has been used because of its adequacy to the very low level manipulations performed by the injector routines, and not just for speed.

The size of code and data occupied by RT-Xception, was not a major concern. However, large injector code or data sizes can be quite intrusive, if the propagation of an injected fault reaches these memory areas. Since our system has segmented memory, we have hosted the fault-injector on its own code and data segments. The processor's memory management unit guarantees memory protection between segments, and so this problem is practically eliminated, being present only in some shared memory areas (such as the stack segment).

Nevertheless, we have measured the memory occupation by RT-Xception, as presented in Table 4. The fault-injection core occupies only 10 Kbytes of code, for the full fault model. The IRC (Injection-Run Controller) module has a large code memory overhead, comprising communication routines, message decoding, stable memory management, etc. Furthermore, it is written in C++, since its operation during the fault-injection is null. This size could be reduced, but it will have a marginal impact on the system, due to the use of segmented memory. On the other hand, the injection core data segment has a larger size than the IRC, due to the decoding tables.

Table 4. Memory overhead

Memory areas	IRC	Injection core	Total
Code segment	21 Kb	10 Kb	31 Kb
Data segment	5 Kb	13 Kb	18 Kb

The C++ version of RT-Xception presents a larger code size: the injection core has 14 Kbytes (summing up to a total of 35 Kbytes). Data size is equal, since the decoding tables are the same.

A comparison to Xception is also mandatory. Xception's code segment has 59 Kbytes and data segment has 7 Kbytes. The much larger code segment is mainly due to the complex decoding mechanism and, since no detailed decoding tables are used (only some general tables), its data size is much smaller.

5.2 An Example Application

We took yet another approach to assert the applicability of RT-Xception for real-time tasks.

We considered the common structure of real-time applications, which are usually composed by repeated INPUT, COMPUTE, OUTPUT cycles as they interact with the external world. If we measure the program execution time on every iteration, i.e. the elapsed time since a time trigger and the output of the result, we can observe different values on different cycle iterations. This is mainly due to the existence of alternate paths in the code and fluctuations in synchronization time and scheduling moments in multiprocess programs. This random oscillation of the application output's time fits usually inside an interval, which we call a "execution jitter".

The designer of a real-time system has to take into account this jitter, that is hard to calculate beforehand in systems that are not statically scheduled, by including a safety margin well beyond this variation when calculating the systems ability to fulfill the application deadlines.

Thus, while it is impossible to state a general rule, it seems reasonable to accept that if the overhead imposed by a SWIFI tool fits inside this execution jitter, that tool should be usable to inject faults in such system. This is a very simple way to verify if a fault-injection tool is suitable for a particular real-time system.

In order to get an idea of how big this jitter can be, we took some measures with a real-time application adapted from a commercial gas-fired ceramic furnace controller. A PID (Proportional/Integral/Derivative) algorithm is used to control the temperature set-point. This application is composed of two main periodic tasks. One task ("PID") reads the most recent temperature input from the furnace, compares it against the current set-point and evaluates the new aperture value for the gas valve. The other task ("MoveServo") reads the current position of the gas valve, receives the desired aperture from the first task and commands the opening or closing of the valve by means of a servomotor. The first task is invoked every 880 milliseconds, while the second task is called every 220 milliseconds. This means that every fourth time the MoveServo task is called after the PID task. A more detailed description of this application may be found in [22].

We measured the elapsed time between the stimulus and the output of results by the application tasks. (Table 5 and Fig. 3).

Table 5. Test application output latency (values in μs)

	PID	MoveServo	MoveServo (after PID)
Max	1826	1910	3638
Min	1719	1705	3562
Average	1754	1744	3562
Standard Deviation	40	41,5	40

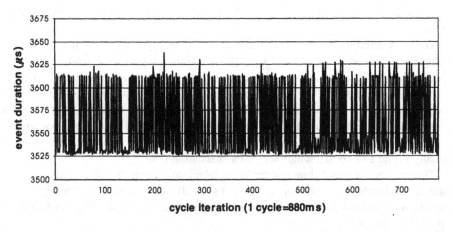

Fig. 3. Application output latency for the case where both tasks executed (PID followed by MoveServo)

As can be seen from Fig. 3, the application's execution jitter (about 80 μs) is much higher than the overhead caused by RT-Xception (below 17 μs), which ensures with great probability that it can be used for this application since it's intrusiveness will be almost undetectable.

Obviously, the above results do not guarantee that RT-Xception is universally applicable in real-time applications. We just think that it makes a strong case for its applicability to a wide range of real-time systems.

6 Conclusions and Current Work

In this paper we investigated whether software implemented fault-injection (SWIFI) could be used in real-time systems. We have proposed two practical rules to measure the intrusiveness of any SWIFI tool on any real-time system, with any workload: first, the injector's overhead must be of the same order of magnitude of the real-time kernel's interrupt latency; second, the injector's overhead must be clearly inside the workload's output jitter, due to different execution times from cycle to cycle.

We took a general SWIFI tool, measured the overhead it imposes on the target application and found it to be significant. Having identified the main sources of intrusiveness, we developed a new SWIFI tool (RT-Xception) that supports the same extensive fault model while limiting the overhead imposed on the application.

The key for these results relies on a new approach for the fault injector implementation: routine specialization. Having one specialized routine for each fault case reduces drastically the complexity of the injection core and the injection time penalty. Thus SWIFI intrusiveness becomes both predictable and negligible for almost all real-time applications, having been measured to lie in the range of 1 μs to 20 μs (on a Pentium MMX at 200MHz).

The experimental method may not be sufficiently formal for some applications. Although we can state that the overhead of our fault-injection technique is predictable, since the number of executed instructions and the number of cache rows used are bounded, we are currently working on analytical means to calculate the worst case execution time for RT-Xception.

Since RT-Xception is now quite stable, we expect to use it to evaluate a distributed real-time fault-tolerant system based on dynamic redundancy, presently being readied in our laboratory.

References

1. Carreira, J., Madeira, H., Silva, J.G.: Xception: A Technique for the Experimental Evaluation of Dependability in Modern Computers. IEEE Trans. on Software Engineering, February (1998) 125-135
2. Chillarege, R., Bowen, N. S.: Understanding Large System Failures: A Fault Injection Experiment. FTCS-19, Chicago-IL (1989)
3. Choi, G., Iyer, R. K.: FOCUS: An experimental Environment for Fault Sensitivity Analysis. IEEE Trans. on Computers, vol. 41 (1992) 1515-1526
4. Czeck, E. : Estimates of the Abilities of Software-Implemented Fault-Injection to Represent Gate-Level Faults: IEEE Int'l Workshop on Fault and Error Injection for Dependability Validation of Computer Systems, Gothenburg-Sweden (1993)
5. Echtle, K., Leu, M.: The EFA Fault Injector for Fault-Tolerant Distributed System Testing. Workshop on Fault-Tolerant Parallel and Distributed Systems (1992)

6. Fuchs, E.: An Evaluation of the Error Detection Mechanisms in MARS using Software-Implemented Fault Injection. EDCC-2, Taormina-Italy (1996)

7. Gait, J.: Probe Effect. IEEE Trans. on Parallel and Distributed Systems (1992)

8. Han, S., Rosenberg, H. A., Shin, K. G.: DOCTOR: an Integrated Software Fault Injection Environment. IEEE Int'l Workshop on Integrating Error Models with Fault Injection, Annapolis-Maryland-USA (1994)

9. Hsueh, M.-C., Tsai, T. K., Iyer, R. K.: Fault Injection Techniques and Tools. IEEE Computer, April (1994) 75-82

10. Jenn, E., Arlat, J., Rimén, M., Ohlsson, J., Karlsson, J.: Fault Injection into VHDL Models: The MEFISTO Tool. FTCS-24, Austin-Texas-USA (1994)

11. Kanawati, G.A., Kanawati, N.A., Abraham, J. A.: FERRARI: A Flexible Software-Based Fault and Error Injection System. IEEE Trans. on Computers, vol. 44 (1995) 248-260

12. Kao, W., Iyer, R. K., Tang, D.: FINE: A fault Injection and Monitoring Environment for Tracing the UNIX System Behavior under Faults. IEEE Trans. on Software Engineering, vol. 19 (1993) 1105-1118

13. Kao, W., Iyer, R. K., Tang, D.: DEFINE: A Distributed Fault Injection and Monitoring Environment. Workshop on Fault-Tolerant Parallel and Distributed Systems (1994)

14. Laprie, J.C.: Dependability: Basic Concepts and Terminology. Springer-Verlag (1991)

15. Lovric, T.: Processor Fault Simulation with ProFI. European Simulation Symposium (1995) 353-357

16. Muller, G., Marlet, R., Volanski, E. N., Consel, C., PU, C., Goel, A.: Fast, Optimized SUN RPC Using Automatic Program Specialization. 18th International Conference on Distributed Computing Systems, Amsterdam-The Netherlands, May (1998)

17. Powell, D, Veríssimo, P. Bonn, G., Waeselynck, F., Seaton., D.: The Delta-4 Approach to Dependability in Open Distributed Computing Systems. FTCS-18, Tokyo (1988)

18. Rimen, M., Ohlsson, J., Torin, J.: On Microprocessor Error Behaviour Modelling. FTCS-24, Austin-Texas (1994)

19. Rosenberg, H.A., Shin, K.G.: Software Fault Injection and its Application in Distributed Systems. FTCS-23, Toulouse (1993)

20. SMX® Simple Multitasking Executive, http://www.smxinfo.com

21. Segall, Z., Vrsalovic, D., Siewiorek, D., Yaskin, D., Kownacki, J., Barton, J., Dancey, R., Robinson, A., Lin, T: FIAT: Fault Injection Based Automated Testing Environment. FTCS-18, Tokyo (1988)

22. Silva, J.G., Prata, P., Rela, M., Madeira, H.: Practical Issues in the Use of ABFT and a New Failure Model. FTCS-28, Munich-Germany (1998)

23. Timmerman, M.: Is Windows CE 2.0 a real threat to the RTOS World?. Real-Time Magazine, vol. 98-3 (1998)

24. Tsai, T.K., Iyer, R.K., Jewitt, D.: An Approach towards Benchmarking of Fault-Tolerant Commercial Systems. FTCS-26, Sendai-Japan (1996)

25. Young, L.T.: A Hybrid Monitor Assisted Fault Injection Environment, DCCA-3, Sicily-Italy (1993)

Session 6

Safety

Chair: Bernd Eschermann, ABB Power Automation AG, Baden, Switzerland

Industrial Track Paper
Integrated Safety in Flexible Manufacturing Systems

Dipl.-Ing. Ralf Apfeld

Fachbereich Maschinenschutz/Steuerungstechnik, Berufsgenossenschaftliches Institut für Arbeitssicherheit, 53754 Sankt Augustin, Germany

Dr.-Ing. M. Umbreit

Fachausschuß Eisen und Metall II, Prüf- und Zertifizierungsstelle im BG-Prüfzert 55130 Mainz, Germany

R.Apfeld@hvbg.de
Smbg.umbreit@t-online.de

Abstract. In the case of machine tools, turning machines, milling machines and machining centres the machine user is part of the production process. To give the worker more possibilities to intervene in the production process it is desirable to work close to the motions of the machine axis. Intelligent computer based systems are able to introduce new safety technologies into the machines. A close connection between motion control and safety monitoring can realize protection corridors in space and velocity. Therefore new technologies, e. g. movement monitoring, are necessary to avoid hazardous situations. Many manufactures of power drive systems established a new technology for fault tolerant movement controls. In comparison to former monitoring systems the reaction time can be decreased by more than one order of magnitude. The authors present the application and the way of validation and testing of such complex systems.

1 Introduction

Today just-in-time-manufacturing requires highly flexible machinery working in a complex network, which is realized by software driven manufacturing cells. While some standards still do not allow software driven systems for specific safety functions, things have recognizably changed for safety devices during the last five years. Light curtains, laser scanners and safety PLCs (Programmable Logic Controller) are increasingly used for area guarding, safe muting or processing of the emergency stop. The safety functions of reduced velocity, protection against unintended movements or muting of fences are realized using redundant PLC architectures. Software-driven highly complex systems are becoming more and more state-of-the-art in the machinery sector. To ensure that the electronic based solution is in accordance with the machinery directive, nearly all manufacturers want to have their products certified. The BG-Institute for Occupational Safety (German: Berufsgenossenschaftliches Institut für Arbeitssicherheit BIA) has been certifying such systems for more than 15 years.

The benefits of modern technology on a machining centre and the certification procedure used by the BIA will be illustrated.

2 Safety functions for machining centres

2.1 Machining centers: concept and scope

Machining centres are for example used for cutting cold metal work material. They are numerically controlled and capable of carrying out two or more machining processes (e.g. milling, drilling, turning). The tools will be changed automatically from a magazine or similar storage unit in accordance with the machining programme [2]. Machining centres are operated in different modes [3]:

- automatic cycle (mode 1) for automatic production with closed guards
- setting (mode 2) to programme the system with opened guards
- optional mode (mode 3) for manual intervention under restricted operating conditions with programme execution in real-time for test purposes with open guards.

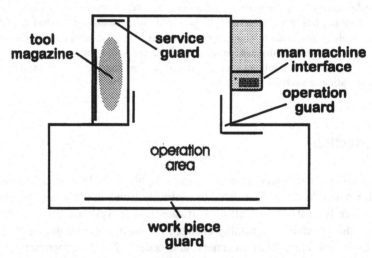

Figure 1: Ground plan of a machine tool, safety areas

A ground plan of a machine tool (Figure 1) shows two safety areas: tool magazine and operational area. Several times a day the user has to enter the operational area, while the tool magazine is only important for the initial set-up or in the case of maintenance.

The speed monitoring of dangerous machine movements is done with external equipment. Dangerous areas are separated with safety guards, but this may lead to lower productivity of the machine, which can be shown by the example of an important German manufacturer of turning machines: A turning machine works with 60 tools on a revolver tool device, which is driven by a high dynamic AC-drive. The tool exchange is made manually. In the case of a fault the revolver accelerates very fast (within some 10 ms) to 1500 RPM (Rotations per Minute). To change all tools the user has to open the safety guard, install a new tool, close the guard and rotate the revolver to the next tool-position and so on, 60 times for all tools! This procedure results in a high inacceptance of safety requirements: the user will try to manipulate the guard-locking device for the sake of better ergonomic working conditions, but with the risk of losing his hands in the case of a fault in the control system.

Very often the user's claim is to work close to the machine motions to observe for example the process for a highly expensive work piece. In totally manually controlled machines (e. g. small milling machines) such observations are possible because all movements are directly controlled by the user. If the automatic motion is controlled in a safe way, the same can be done in a processor controlled machine. All dangerous areas in space and also in velocity space can be observed by an integrated monitoring device. In a highly flexible way the machine can be adapted to the work of the user and not vice versa. The safety functions realized by the integrated monitoring software are listed in Table 1.

Table 1. Safety-related functions of power drive systems in machinery

Safety-related stopping process	Fastest stopping process of the Power Drive (PD) monitored by the NC.
Safety-related standstill	No unexpected movements are possible.
Safety-related operational stop	The motor is under position control of the PD. The monitoring of unexpected movements is active in PD and NC. Fastest reaction in case of unexpected restart.
Safety-related reduced speed	PD and NC ensure that the speed does not exceed certain risk dependent limits.
Safety-related limited increment	PD and NC ensure that a certain defined relative distance is not violated by one of the axes.
Safety-related limited absolute position	PD and NC ensure that a certain defined absolute position is not violated by one of the axes.

2.2 Hazards in machining centres

Machining centres present a wide range of hazards, not least because of their wide application as rotating tool and "stationary" workpiece machine tools. Protection against contact with moving cutting tools, especially when being rapidly rotated in the spindle, or in the case of fast moving work pieces is of great importance. Other hazards can be caused by the fast movement of a tool inserted into the spindle by a tool robot during automated tool exchange. When power-operated mechanisms are provided for workpiece transfer, they can also create hazardous situations during loading/unloading and workpiece alignment or clamping [2].

2.3 Risk estimation

[3] lists 19 groups of hazards and gives a detailed description of 30 individual hazardous situations, the operating modes with associated activities and the hazardous zones related to each hazard.

A safety measure is provided by [4], which defines 5 categories. The category to be fulfilled by the control system depends on the risks at the machining center. In most cases category 3 is appropriate, meaning "a single fault does not lead to the loss of the safety function".

2.4 External safety equipment

In general safety measures are external safety devices and equipment, e.g. contactors, position switches, cams, monitoring devices. If a safety critical state is detected those devices control a switching action in the power circuits of the machine. This can lead to interactions which can reduce the availability of the machine. Examples are charge and discharge of the intermediate circuit, damage to the power transistors and contactors in case of switching inductive load, loss of position reference and others.

Regarding personal safety in the case of external safety equipment other aspects shall also be considered. A very important factor is the human reaction time. When applying external enabling devices (enables a motion while pressed) the decisive action is to recognize the danger early and to avoid an injury by releasing the enabling button.

Investigations at Fachausschuß Eisen und Metall II in Mainz showed, that even if the person who has to press the enabling device is very concentrated on the sudden dangerous event, a reaction time of 400 ms is possible. A DC-servo motor controlled machine axis moves several ten centimetres in this time. Considering the more probable case that the person is concentrated on the process but not on a possible danger, the reaction time is more than one second and the axis would move one meter and more.

Automatically controlled external monitoring devices for reduced speed and standstill can improve this situation. However, the signal path from the output contacts to the power circuits of the machine is generally carried out by more than one contactor and time delays cannot be avoided.

2.5 New architectures to integrate safety functionality

The risk analysis requires category 3 for all of the safety-related parts, which provide the safety functions of Table 1. According to EN 954-1 [4] "Safety-related parts of control systems according to category 3 shall be designed so that a single fault in any of these parts shall not lead to the loss of the safety function. Whenever reasonably practicable the single fault shall be detected at or before the next demand upon the safety function". The requirement of fault tolerance in the case of a single fault will be achieved by the following structure.

Figure 2 shows a typical architecture of a machine tool control system. In these systems at least 2 microcontrollers are implemented for functional reasons. The Numerical Control (NC) is responsible e. g. for complex interpolations in space, while the digital Power Drives (PDs) have to control the motions of the axes. This results in a natural diverse redundant system with the exception of the process interfaces. To achieve a totally redundant control system the only hardware changes are commonly extensions to the input and output interfaces for sensors (e. g. rotational sensors, guard switches, control switches) and actuators (e. g. guard interlocking, relays and final switching devices). All safety-related functions can be implemented within these two channels by software. The redundancy meets the requirement that no single fault leads to a malfunction.

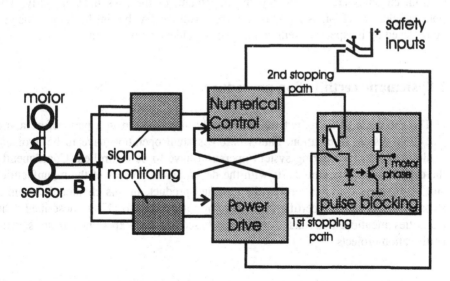

Figure 2: Architecture of a fault-tolerant Numerical Control System

Nevertheless, this architecture does not meet the requirement of fault detection. This is for example covered by an additional implementation of cross monitoring and so called forced dynamisation: PD and NC calculate the safety-related values independently and test input and output paths. All these parameters are monitored in both channels and compared with the values of the other path. To achieve a good diagnostic coverage the cross monitoring is not only restricted to compare output signals but also to compare a lot of intermediate calculation results inside the controllers (e.g. position values, speed values, input and output values, safety-related machine parameters).

To detect faults in the signal processing of static inputs by cross monitoring, the signal has to change within the so-called fault recognition time. For example the input signal of the emergency stop changes only on demand. If these redundant input signals change at every standstill of the machine for a short time, PD and NC could monitor correct execution and lock any further action in the case of differences. This mechanism is called "forced dynamisation". The time interval between the test procedures can be monitored by PD and NC.

The main important motion sensors are the rotational sensors of each axis. Normally all electronic parts of the safety-related control system have to be redundant. However, it is possible to reduce the number of rotational sensors to only one, if the output signal of this device is highly dynamic. Therefore the fault detection has to be made in a highly dynamical way by the two channels.

Figure 2 also shows an example of safe pulse blocking. The main features are the two stopping paths:

- stopping of the impulses generated by PD to control the motor
- switch-off of the opto-couplers, which transmit the pulses to the end stage of the PD.

Both channels are able to stop the movement of the axes independently. The opto-coupler switch-off is currently realized with a relay, but in the future this can be replaced by inexpensive semiconductors to achieve a faster fault reaction.

3 Systematic certification procedure

The life cycle of a product can be roughly distinguished in a part before and a part after system installation. Faults before system operation have to be avoided. Faults which happen during system operation have to be controlled. Consequently the certification procedure starts with the development process of the manufacturer and also covers modifications of the certified product. In this chapter the main 8 steps of the systematic certification procedure according to [1] are described. The quantities mentioned in this chapter are based on the experience from several certification projects.

3.1 Review of the specification

Special emphasis is put on the validation of the specification. Beside others the following points have to be investigated:
- Does the requirement specification deal in a correct, clear, unequivocal and consistent way with every safety-relevant function, external/internal interfaces, the reaction in the case of power failure and restart, internal self tests and reactions etc.?
- Are the documentation rules adequate for the application?
- Is the specification of a form that it can be understood by developers and programmers?
- Is there an adequate process to control changes in the specification?
- Are development tools used by the manufacturer?

All recognised problems will be discussed in several review sessions and lead to changes in the specification.

3.2 Design review and test case specification

Besides the validation of the specification, project organisation (formal mechanisms in the manufacturer's organisation), documentation (design documents and manuals, reviews with machine manufacturers as users of the NC and PD) and functional tests (test of all safety-related machine functions with different combinations) are subjects of the approval. Several reviews of the design documents normally lead to test cases for systematic testing and changes in the design.

3.3 Statical analysis

In several recursive steps NC and PD soft- and hardware are analysed by the safety experts. The safety-related software of NC and PD has a typical extent of about 1000 - 2000 instructions each. Since category 3 is needed for these applications, a static analysis is sufficient. This is done according to the software rules [5] and partly with the help of an analyser tool, which generates a metrics table (Table 2) including the number of statements, the cyclomatic number (number of independent paths) and others [6,7].

Table 2. Metrics Table

AXIS	LOW	HIGH	VALUE
Number of statements	1	50	23
Directly called components	0	7	2
Cyclomatic number	1	10	7
Number of unconditional jumps	0	0	0

Number of entry nodes	1	1	1
Number of exit nodes	1	1	1
Number of exits of cond struct	0	4	0
Number of nested levels	0	4	4
Comments frequency	0.20	1	0.70
Average size of statements	2	10	6.30
Vocabulary frequency	1	4	2.69

In addition to this more statistical analysis, the control graph in Figure 3 shows the structure of the function. All structure elements, like "if then else", "case", "while", "branch", "goto" etc. are represented. Any violation of the rules of structured programming technique can be found in such a graph and has to be corrected as far as possible. Every weak point of the software has to be investigated in greater detail and should finally be improved.

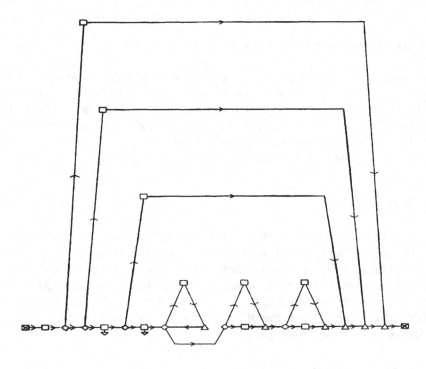

Figure 3: Control - Graph

3.4 Walk-throughs

The analyses are accompanied by several walk-through sessions of the software. The correct and complete realisation of the requirement specifications, the software rules and the software codex of the manufacturer will be checked during the walk-throughs. In most cases, parts of the source code and documentation have to be improved. Very often, the programmer recognizes faults by himself while explaining the software. It is therefore very important that the programmer attends the walk-through meetings without the presence of his manager.

3.5 Systematic tests

During the reviews of the specification, the design documentation, the static analysis and the walk-throughs several test cases are generated, which will be prepared by the manufacturer. All test cases are executed and documented in the presence of BIA-experts during several sessions.

For all monitoring functions special tests are realized to validate their presence, the correct function and completeness. All tests are carried out manually and partly automatically at a real simulation station to guarantee that the conditions are close to the practice. More than 100 test cases will be constructed during the careful analysis of the design documents to prove the system reaction under real-time conditions. For every test case, the system reaction will be monitored and documented.

The execution of the test cases may reveal serious faults. In one project, some I/O-information in a redundant architecture could be blocked by a high priority interrupt of the NC channel so that the machine started up with full acceleration. The fault was corrected using additional software algorithms in both channels.

3.6 EMI and environmental testing

The robustness of the safety-related system towards expected operating strain and external influences is checked by means of EMC-tests, mechanical shock and vibration tests, temperature and humidity tests, several electrical and climatic tests.

3.7 Site-acceptance tests

The installation manual, which describes in detail the installation, is also an important item in the type test approval. A complete machine test is required after installation of the safety-related system. Typically a more than 100-page-document describes the operating conditions using the software driven safety functions (see Table 1). During a site acceptance test the safety experts check the usefulness of the installation manual with the support of the machine manufacturer. Necessary changes have to be implemented after the first meetings together with the machine manufacturer.

In most cases, the point of view of the machine manufacturer differs from that one of the control manufacturer. Therefore it is very often necessary to change the instruction manual. For this reason, the BIA requires also review sessions in the presence of a machine manufacturer.

3.8 Modification phase

Due to user requests, there is normally a need to change NC- and PD-software several times. All modifications are documented according to BIA´s requirements.

The old and new version numbers have to be clearly documented. The affected programmes will be listed and a description of the modification has to be made. The origin of the modification request has to be documented. In several enclosures the listings of the modified code are supplied together with the code walk-throughs after the modification. Each modification has to be signed by the software engineer and certified after testing by the BIA.

4 Conclusions

This paper shows that machinery safety can be achieved using the application-specific C-standards and the requirements of EN 954-1 [4]. It could be demonstrated that the use of the German prestandard DIN V VDE 0801 [1] is necessary for the certification of computerized safety-related systems. In future the international standard IEC 1508 [8] will be used instead of the German prestandard.

The described procedure will also be applied to less complex systems like adjustable speed drives for material transfer, sawing and grinding units etc. These units usually include one processor and can be enhanced for safety purposes.

5 Acknowledgement

Some parts of this paper are based on the work of Dietmar Reinert and Michael Schaefer, both BIA, Germany.

References

1. DIN V VDE 0801: Grundsätze für Rechner in Systemen mit Sicherheitsaufgaben, mit Anhang A1. Beuth-Verlag, Berlin 1990 und 1994.
2. CEN/TC 143/WG 4 N155: Machine tools - Safety. Working Document. Brussels 1997.
3. prEN 12417 Werkzeugmaschinen, Sicherheit Bearbeitungszentren, 1996
4. EN 954-1: Safety of machinery. Part 1: General principles for design. Brussels 1997.
5. M. Schaefer, A. Gnedina, T. Börner, K.-H. Büllesbach, W.Grigulewitsch, G. Reuß, D. Reinert: Programmierregeln für die Erstellung von Software für Steuerungen mit Sicherheitsaufgaben, Wirtschaftsverl. NW, Dortmund/Berlin 1998, ISBN 3-89701-212-X
6. McCabe, T. J.: A complexity measure. IEEE Transactions on Software Engineering 2: 308-320 (1976). 228, 363
7. Dumke, Reiner: Softwareentwicklung nach Maß, Vieweg 1992
8. DIN VDE 0801 (IEC 1508): Entwurf: Funktionale Sicherheit. Sicherheitssysteme, Teile 1-7. Beuth-Verlag, Berlin 1996.

A Method for Implementing a Safety Control System Based on Its Separation into Safety-Related and Non-Safety-Related Parts

Toshihito SHIRAI[1], Masayoshi SAKAI[1], Koichi FUTSUHARA[1] and Masao MUKAIDONO[2]

[1] Nippon Signal Co., Ltd.
1-13-8, Kamikizaki, Urawa-shi, Saitama-ken, 338-8588, Japan

[2] Meiji University
1-1-1, Higashimita, Tama-ku, Kawasaki-shi, Kanagawa-ken, 214-8571, Japan

Abstract. International safety standards recommend that control systems should be separated into safety-related and non-safety-related parts. The control circuit is required to have such an interlock function that the control output of the safety-related part gives permission to the control output of the non-safety-related part. This paper describes the methods of separating and combining the safety-related and non-safety related parts in Chapter 2. In Chapter 3, a configuration example of the control circuit for producing a control output is presented. The control circuit is constructed by two fail-safe techniques, or dynamic fail-safe signal processing and voltage-above-supply-voltage processing. The proposed control circuit has such a fail-safe characteristic that it produces no output when the frequent check of its functioning detects a failure in any of its elements. An interlock device constructed by using the two fail-safe processing techniques and containing high-output semiconductor switching elements is shown.

1 Introduction

The control systems of machinery and the like contain both safety-related functions and non-safety-related functions in many cases. International safety standards presently proposed and discussed for control systems recommend the method of handling control systems by separating them into safety-related and non-safety-related parts [1], [2]. If a control system is treated as divided into safety-related and non-safety-related parts, components such as solenoid valves that issue a control output to machine control elements must combine output signals from these two groups of parts to generate the control output. The control output generating component is required to have such an interlock function that the control output of a safety-related part gives permission to the control output of a non-safety-related part. The international safety standards rank safety according to failure behavior and failure detection capability, and specify the minimum requirement that the safety function must not be lost due to a failure [1], [2].

This paper describes the separation of a control system into safety-related and non-safety-related parts, and proposes a single-channel control circuit that performs an AND operation on the control output of the safety-related part and the control output of the non-safety-related part, and has an interlock function. It also describes the method of connecting the safety-related part with the non-safety-related part. A single-channel control circuit is constructed by the dynamic fail-safe signal processing method, so that it produces a control output (safety information) only when it checks to see that it is normal. It has such a fail-safe characteristic that it frequently check the functions of its input, logic operation and output sections (based on continuous monitoring [3]) and produces no output when a failure is detected in any one of its elements.

2 Separation and Combination of Safety-Related and Non-Safety-Related Parts in Control System

Figure 1 shows the method of separating a control system into a safety-related part and a non-safety-related part. When safety and danger are defined for the control object of the control system, the function of assuring the safety of the control object (safety-related function) is included in the safety-related part. For example, the function of preventing collision between an operator and a machine's movable part is included in the safety-related part. In Fig. 1, the emergency stop button and the safety confirmation sensor comprise the safety-related part. A function not directly related to safety (non-safety-related function), such as productivity or operability, is included in the non-safety-related part. In Fig. 1, the non-safety-related part is a sequencer, for example.

In Fig. 1, the AND gate A is a control circuit with such an interlock function that the control output of the safety-related part issues permission to the control output of the non-safety-related part. In other words, the control circuit is represented by the AND gate A. The control circuit has start and restart interlock functions as specified in the draft international standard IEC 61496-1 (1997), for example. Provided with these functions, it performs an AND operation on the binary output signal Lb of the safety-related part and the binary output signal La of the non-safety-related part. The binary output signal Lb normally indicates safety and is thus termed a safety-related signal. The binary output signal La is a operation command, for example. $Lb = 1$ indicates a safe state, and $Lb = 0$ indicates a hazardous state. $La = 1$ indicates a operation command, and $La = 0$ indicates the absence of a operation command. Only when $Lb = 1$ or only when safety is assured, the control output $Lc = 1$ is produced by $La = 1$ to start a machine, for example. Actually, the control circuit is equipped with a high-output switching element that directly drives a solenoid valve, for example. The control circuit needs such a fail-safe characteristic that when a

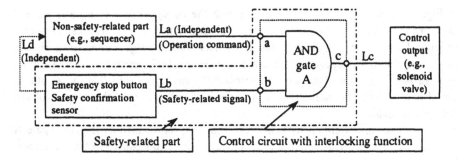

Fig. 1. Separation and combination of safety-related and non-safety-related parts.

failure occurs in one of its elements, it does not incorrectly produce the control output $Lc = 1$, so that it is included in the safety-related part. The control circuit represented by the AND gate A is required to have such a characteristic that if it is faulty, it produces no output when the input is available only at either of the input terminals a and b. It is also required not to allow such a situation that a failure in the non-safety-related part causes the safety-related part to produce a hazardous output. That is, it is required to assure independency of the interface between the output signal La of the non-safety-related part and the input terminal a of the AND gate from any failure that may occur in the safety-related and non-safety-related parts. This independency is also required when a signal from the safety-related part is utilized in the non-safety-related part. A special level converter circuit that uses an ac signal is utilized to construct the interface. This paper assumes that the control object is in the safe sate when no control output is produced.

3 Configuration of Control Circuit with Interlock Function

Concrete methods for constructing fail-safe control circuits are presented in none of the draft international safety standards. The control circuit discussed in this paper achieves the above-mentioned fail-safe characteristic of a single-channel system and the independency of signal transmission by signal processing with ac signals (dynamic fail-safe signal processing [4], [5]) and signal processing with a voltage above the supply voltage (voltage-above-supply-voltage processing [4]).

In dynamic fail-safe signal processing, safety is indicated by ac signals transmitted by ac operations, including the on/off switching of circuit elements, and danger is indicated by dc signals of voltage not exceeding the supply voltage. Assume that the circuit is constructed so that it does not self-oscillate when it fails. In other words, when the circuit fails, it does not transmit ac signals and does not incorrectly indicate safety. The circuit is considered to be in the normal operating state when it outputs an ac signal and in the faulty state when it does not output an ac signal. The functioning of the circuit is performed and at the same time, checked by using the ac signal. The check is made approximately at the period of the ac signal. For example, in Fig. 1, Lc = 1 indicates the state in which the ac signal is present, and Lc = 0 indicates the state in which the ac signal is absent. When the circuit fails, its output becomes Lc = 0, stopping the machine. In dynamic fail-safe signal processing, signals of voltage above the supply voltage can be processed. In the control circuit of Fig. 1, such an AND operation function (fail-safe AND gate [5]) is used that the ac output signal is produced only when two input signals of voltage above the supply voltage are both available.

The control circuit with interlock function, represented by the AND gate A in Fig. 1, is discussed in detail below. The control circuit consists of an interface, logic operation circuit, and output circuit.

3.1 Interface

The interface is required to have the essential function of transmitting the two input signals La and Lb. It also is required to have such a fail-safe characteristic that it does not incorrectly indicate safety when the input signal Lb indicates the hazardous state (requirement 1) and to assure the independency of signal transmission so that an input signal is not directly transmitted as output (requirement 2).

Figure 2 schematically illustrates the method of interfacing the non-safety-related part output signal La and the safety-related part output signal Lb, both being input to the control circuit. To meet the requirement 2) described above, the input signals are isolated by photocouplers from the output signals. The dc input signals La and Lb are supplied to the PT3-PD1 and PT4-PD2 photocouplers, respectively. The phototransmitters PT1 and PT2 connected to the signal generator SG1 are supplied with ac signals. The photodetectors PD1 and PD2 turn on and off in synchronism with the ac signals. When La = 1 is taken as high level, the switching of the photodetector PD1 causes the ac signal to flow to the phototransmitter PT3, switches the photodetector PD3, and inputs the ac signal to the rectifier circuit Rec1. The rectifier circuit Rec1 converts the ac input signal into a dc signal of voltage above the supply

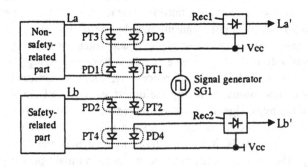

Fig. 2. Schematic configuration of interface.

voltage Vcc and equivalent to La' = 1. When La = 0 is taken as no-voltage level, the ac signal is not input to the rectifier circuit Rec1, and a dc signal of the same voltage as the supply voltage Vcc and equivalent to La' = 0 is output from the rectifier circuit Rec1. This achieves signal transmission based on the above-mentioned voltage-above-supply-voltage processing method. Lb is similarly transmitted. This circuit meets the requirement 1) described above. When a photocoupler fails, for example, the ac signal is not input to the corresponding rectifier circuit, and the output of the rectifier circuit goes logic 0.

3.2 Output Circuit

Figure 3 schematically illustrates the configuration of the output circuit. The on-failure detection circuit continuously monitors the high-output semiconductor switching element Tr to see that a hazardous short-circuit failure is not caused during the output current turn-off period (off-period) and output current turn-on period (on-period). That is, the high-output semiconductor switching element Tr is constantly checked for its off-performance. As soon as a short-circuit failure occurs, the output current is cut off by the separate switching element ra.

Figure 3(b) shows the method of monitoring the semiconductor switching element Tr for a short-circuit failure. During the off-period, the check signal generator SG2 switches the photodetector PD6. If the semiconductor switching element Tr is turned off, the switching current flows to the phototransmitter PT5, so that the photodetector PD5 is switched and Lp' is converted to an ac signal. As the monitor output p, the rectifier circuit Rec3 produces an dc signal of voltage above the supply voltage Vcc and equivalent to logic 1, which reports the normal state. If a short-circuit failure is caused in the semiconductor switching element Tr, Lp assumes the level of the supply voltage Vcc. No current flows to the phototransmitter PT5, Lp' becomes a dc signal, and the monitor output p becomes a dc signal of the same level as the supply voltage Vcc and equivalent to logic 0, thereby reporting the failure. During the

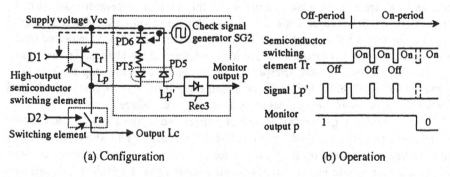

(a) Configuration (b) Operation

Fig. 3. Method of monitoring high-output semiconductor switching element.

on-period, the short-circuit failure of the semiconductor switching element Tr is not known until it is actually turned off. The semiconductor switching element Tr is instantaneously turned off by the check signal generator SG2. The photodetector PD6 is clamped on. Since the semiconductor switching element Tr is instantaneously turned off periodically, Lp' becomes an ac signal when the semiconductor switching element Tr can turn off. As the monitor output p, the rectifier circuit Rec3 produces a dc signal of voltage above the supply voltage Vcc and equivalent to logic 1, reporting the normal state. When the semiconductor switching element Tr develops a short-circuit failure, as described above, the monitor output p becomes a dc signal of the same level as the supply voltage Vcc, reporting the failure. The higher the frequency of checking the off-performance, the faster the short-circuit failure can be detected. This frequent switching action can be successfully performed by a semiconductor switch, but is difficult to accomplish with an electric circuit using contacts because of reliability.

3.3 Logic Operation Circuit

Figure 4 shows an configuration example of the logic operation circuit of the control circuit represented by the AND gate A in Fig. 1. In Fig. 4, AND1 to AND5 are AND operation circuits. The safety-related signal Lb' transmitted by the interface and the monitor output p based on the off-performance check (off-condition check) of the semiconductor switching element Tr are input to AND1, where they are ANDed. The self-hold circuit 1 produces the output signal Sa2 = 1 when Sa1 = 1 is input as its hold signal and a start command is input as its trigger signal. As long as the hold signal Sa1 = 1 is available, the self-hold circuit 1 continues to produce the output signal Sa2 = 1, irrespective of its trigger signal. Sa2 = 1 indicates the permission to start the machine. The permission to start the machine is given by the start command only when safety is assured and when a short-circuit failure is not caused in the semiconductor switching element Tr. The signals Sa2 and La' are input to AND3. The signals D1 and D2 are produced on the condition that both the signals Sa2 and La' are at least logic 1. Only when the machine is permitted to start, the signals D1 and D1 each go logic 1 or 0 (switching element on or off) according to whether the signal La' is logic 1 or 0 (e.g., start or stop). If danger is indicated or if a short-circuit failure is caused in the semiconductor switching element Tr, the signals D1 and D2 go logic 0 (off), irrespective of the signal La', and stop the supply of power to the machine. Each time the switching element ra turns on, it is back-checked by the self-hold circuit 2 to see that it has no short-circuit failure.

The start and restart interlocks specified in the international safety standards are accomplished by the self-hold circuit 1. The above-mentioned international safety standard IEC61496-1, for example, states that the automatic start of the machine should be prevented when the input signal Lb indicates danger and then safety or when the power to the circuit is restored. When the signal Lb indicates danger or when the circuit power is lost, the self-hold condition is cleared, the signals D1 and D2 both go logic 0, and the semiconductor switching element Tr and the

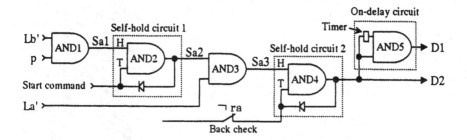

Fig. 4. Schematic configuration of logic operation circuit.

switching element ra cut off the load current. When Sa1 = 1 is then input, the self-hold circuit 1 does not output logic 1 until the start command is input. Unless the start command is input again or the intention to start the machine is indicated again, the signals D1 and D2 maintain the logic 0 level, and the two switches keep the load current off.

The on-delay circuit causes the semiconductor switching element Tr to turn on later than the switching element ra that is connected in series with the semiconductor switching element Tr. The switching element ra does not directly turn on and off the load current, but the semiconductor switching element Tr directly turns on and off the load current. The switching element ra and the semiconductor switching element Tr can be compared to a machine main switch and a machine start switch, respectively. The two elements also have a diversity along the time axis. Normally, the machine is started as the main switch and start switch are sequentially turned on and is stopped as the start switch and main switch are sequentially turned off. The semiconductor switching element Tr and the switching element ra are driven in this way.

3.4 Fail-Safe Interlock Device

Figure 5 shows the approximate configuration and appearance of the interlock device implemented based on the above-mentioned dynamic fail-safe signal processing and voltage-above-supply-voltage processing methods. The interlock device consists of logic and output sections. The logic section includes an AND circuit (fail-safe AND gate), two fail-safe self-hold circuits, and a fail-safe on-delay circuit (such a timer circuit that its time delay is not shortened when it fails). These circuits are connected based on voltage-above-supply-voltage processing, and the logic operating parts of the respective circuits are constructed based on dynamic fail-safe signal processing [5]. The output of the interlock device can directly drive an electromagnetic switch, solenoid valve, or a lock-type door switch solenoid, for example. The interlock device includes some portions of the above-mentioned output circuit and logic operation circuit. The control circuit with interlock function shown in

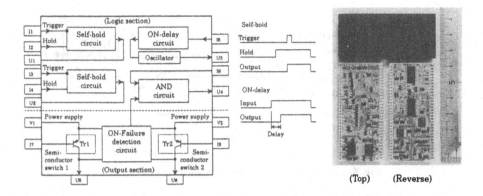

Fig. 5. Configuration and appearance of interlock device (hybrid IC 24 V, 0.6 A, ×2 outputs).

Fig. 1 can be accomplished in a fail-safe manner by constructing interfaces and the like as its external circuit.

4 Conclusions

When a control system is divided into a safety-related part and a non-safety-related part, the method of combining the safety-related part and the non-safety-related part has been presented, and the safety requirements of the control circuit that processes signals from the safety-related part and the non-safety-related part and produces a control output have been described. The control circuit integrated as a high-output device by using the dynamic fail-safe signal processing and voltage-above-supply-voltage processing techniques has been concretely shown.

The control system constructed by separating it into the safety-related part and the non-safety-related part can prove its safety in a relatively straightforward manner. This type of control system is also advantageous in that there are relatively few constraints as to the modification of the control function by the user for a purpose not related safety, or productivity improvement, for example. A safety-related control circuit must have such a characteristic that it assures safety even when it fails. This requirement is defined in the international safety standards proposed by Europe and the revised robot safety standard in the United States, and is becoming the world's common safety requirement.

References

1. ISO/IEC DIS 13849-1, Safety of machinery: Safety-related parts of control systems (1997).
2. Draft IEC 1508, Functional safety: Safety-related systems (1995).

3. PrEN 50100-1, Safety of machinery: Electro-sensitive protective devices (1994).
4. K. Futsuhara, N. Sugimoto and M. Mukaidono: A Method of Constructing Safety Device with Consideration of Noise-Induced Errors, Proc. of 2nd Int. Conf. on Human Aspects of Advanced Manufacturing and Hybrid Automation, pp. 921-928 (Aug. 1990).
5. M. Kato, M. Sakai, K. Jinkawa, K. Futsuhara and M. Mukaidono: LSI Implementation and Safety Verification of Window Comparator Used in Fail-Safe Multiple-Valued Logic Operations, IEICE Trans. Electron., Vol. E76-C, No. 3, pp. 419-427 (Mar. 1993).

Session 7

Hardware Testing

Chair: Raimund Ubar, Tallin Technical University, Estonia

Design of Totally Self-Checking Code-Disjoint Synchronous Sequential Circuits

Jerzy W. Greblicki and Stanisław J. Piestrak

Wrocław University of Technology, Institute of Engineering Cybernetics
50–370 Wrocław, Poland
{jwg,sjp}@residue.ict.pwr.wroc.pl

Abstract. Several design methods of self-checking synchronous sequential circuits (SMs) have been proposed in the literature. In this paper, we present a new approach to designing totally self-checking (TSC) code-disjoint (CD) SMs protected against errors using unordered codes. It is assumed that D flip-flops are used as the memory elements and that the circuit should be TSC for all single stuck-at faults (except for the faults on the clock lines), and CD for all input unidirectional errors. The initial 2-level AND-OR equations (with all products shared) are checked for self-testing by verifying some algebraic conditions. All stuck-at-1 faults which cannot be detected during normal functioning are identified. Then, the circuit is modified to the AND-AND-OR circuit with generally higher fault coverage. The resulting circuit is minimized using the well known SIS CAD tools. The whole design process has been automated by using the newly developed software tools that accept the BLIF representation of a SM and are compatible with the SIS tools. Many benchmark SMs can now be implemented as TSC with 100% fault coverage.

1 Introduction

Self-checking (SC) digital circuits, are a class of highly reliable circuits that allow for concurrent error detection during normal functioning. Their main applications include those wherein errors caused by internal faults should be detected as soon as possible, at best immediately at the first occurrence.

For SC sequential circuits (SM's), the main problem is to check whether a sequence of outputs is incident to a given sequence of inputs. Since a fault may affect the state transition function as well as the output function, this generally requires the correctness of both. One notable common restriction in all known SC synchronous SM's is that faults on the clock lines do not occur. Several design methods for SC SM's that have been proposed in [1]–[16] can be divided into three groups.

The first group of methods generalizes the built-in parity circuit approach for combinational circuits (CC's) to a SM M specified by the logic circuit, see e.g. [1]. For a given fault set F, a faulty M is simulated for every f in F to find all changes of outputs. On this basis, a table of faulty functions is constructed that contains all incorrect output combinations produced after occurrence of any internal fault. Then, a flow table of a checking SM M_k is constructed on the basis of the flow table of a M and a table of faulty functions. Unfortunately, this design seems to be prohibitively time-consuming for any larger M.

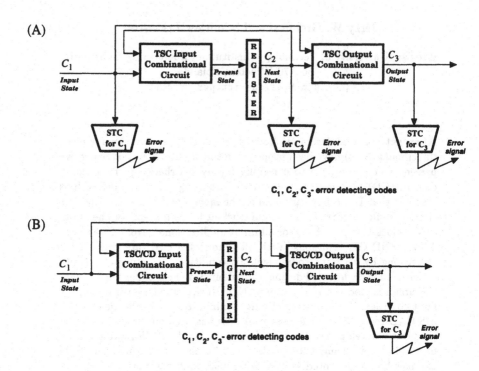

Fig. 1. Self-checking sequential circuit (Mealy type): (A) Model 1; (B) Model 2.

The second group of methods commences with a SM given by a flow table and considers using either parity or m/n codes for internal and output state assignment, so that the resulting circuit is totally self-checking (TSC) [2]–[12]. These designs rely on using self-testing checkers (STC's) that continuously monitor whether the input, internal, and/or output state represents a codeword and eventually produce the error signal at the occurrence of the first error (Fig. 1(A)). Essentially, the main problem is to guarantee that combinational input (excitation) and output circuits are TSC and that the checkers are ST even for incomplete encodings. The ultimate goal is the minimum hardware implementation of all extra circuits, so that an alternative scheme (functionally equivalent) from Fig. 1(B) is also worth of consideration. It offers the potential of hardware savings — no STCs are needed to check inputs and internal states — at the cost of increasing the complexity of the input and output CCs however. Unfortunately, meeting the requirements for TSC and code-disjoint (CD) by both CCs has been a rather difficult problem, and no successful attempts have been reported in the literature yet. TSC SM's using m/n and Berger encodings of internal and output states, using D flip-flops as memory elements, were proposed in [5]–[12].

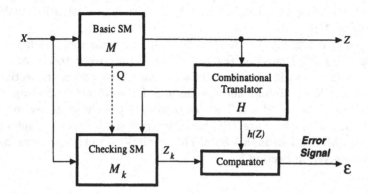

Fig. 2. Block diagram of a SC SM built on the basis of algebraic model.

Finally, the most general are the algebraic approaches considered in [13]–[16] wherein SC is achieved from the specification rather than the logic design level. This group of methods relies on checking the algebraic relations between output signals of the basic SM M and a checking SM M_k, where M_k evaluates the correctness of functioning of M by analyzing input and output sequences of M. The general scheme of a SC SM that uses a checking SM M_k which is homomorphic to a basic SM M is shown in Fig. 2. The circuit H transforms the outputs produced by M so that they can be compared against outputs produced by M_k. H is a combinational circuit whose structure depends on the chosen criterium of checking. The comparator checks whether the state transitions in M and M_k are incident, by observing whether the condition $Z_k = h(Z)$ is satisfied in each cycle. Any mismatching between them indicates error in either M or M_k. The design goal is to find a reduced SM M_k and a circuit H which ensure detection of internal faults of a specified class in the system from Fig. 2. An attempt is made to have $|Q_k| \ll |Q|$, so that most extra hardware expenses would go into H. Unfortunately, none of the referenced works achieved this goal.

These methods have the following limitations:

1. Inputs are not protected against errors; the 2-rail check part for inputs is generated from the primary inputs by the bank of inverters.
2. The problem whether a subset of codewords actually used is sufficient to guarantee that all STCs used are ST for internal faults.
3. No analysis of the fault and error coverage in a SM itself has been done. Hence, neither the efficiency of a code and the resulting realization of a SC SM nor any indication what class of faults is particularly troublesome is provided.

4. Overall, it is impossible to derive any conclusions whether a TSC realization of a particular SM is feasible at all, and if not — why.

Here, we will present a new approach to designing TSC/CD SMs protected against errors using unordered codes. We will limit our attention to Model 1 circuit of Fig. 1(A).

This paper is organized as follows. Section 2 presents some background material regarding TSC circuits, the properties of unordered codes, and surveys easily-testable realizations of the STCs for unordered codes. In Section 3 the properties of TSC IF circuits and the methods for verification and improvement of the ST property are given. The design results presented in Section 4 show that designing SMs which are TSC for all internal single stuck-at faults is feasible for many MCNC benchmark SMs. The conclusions and suggestions for future research are given in Section 5.

2 Preliminaries

2.1 Self-Checking Circuits

The concept of a TSC combinational circuit (CC) H with encoded inputs and outputs was introduced in [23] and [32]. It was extended to include SMs in [3], [7], and [14]. Let F be the set of likely faults f in a circuit considered.

Definition 1 *A SM is called* self-testing *(ST) with respect to F if for every fault f from F it produces a noncode space output for at least one code space input.*

Definition 2 *A SM is called* fault-secure *(FS) with respect to F if for every fault f from F and for every code space input it produces either a correct output or a noncode space output (i.e. a detectable error).*

Definition 3 *A SM is called* totally self-checking *(TSC) with respect to F if it is both ST and FS with respect to F.*

Definition 4 *A circuit H is called* code-disjoint *(CD), if it maps the input code space to the output code space and the input non-code space to the output noncode space.*

Definition 5 *A circuit H is called a* self-testing *checker (STC) if it is both ST and CD.*

Here F includes all single stuck-at-z (s/z), $z = \{0, 1\}$ faults.

2.2 Unordered Codes

A number of unordered codes have been proposed in the literature, see [17]–[22]. Their most important properties are that they detect all unidirectional errors and are naturally suited to implement inverter-free (IF) circuits [19]. Amongst unordered codes, we are particularly interested in the following codes.

1. A K-pair 2-rail code is a systematic code which uses K check bits ($c_{K-1}, \ldots,$ c_1, c_0) which are the bit-by-bit complements of the $I = K$ information bits ($x_{I-1}, \ldots, x_1, x_0$), i.e. for any $0 \leq i \leq K-1$ we have $c_i = \overline{x_i}$. The 2-rail codes have been the most frequently used in SC circuits, due to their advantages: simple design of circuitry and generally easy hardware implementation. Their disadvantage is very high 100% redundancy.

2. An *m-out-of-n code* (*m/n code, constant-weight code*) is one in which all valid codewords have exactly m 1s and $n - m$ 0s. Its capacity equals to $|C_{m/n}| = \binom{n}{m}$, where $C_{m/n}$ denotes all m/n codewords. The $\lfloor n/2 \rfloor/n$ code is the optimal unordered code [18], in the sense that there is no other unordered code of codeword length n which has more codewords than the $\lfloor n/2 \rfloor/n$ code. The disadvantage of m/n codes is that they are nonsystematic, which does not cause any problems if used to encode internal states of the SMs. Notice however that a K-pair 2-rail code is nothing else but a special case of an incomplete $K/2K$ code with only 2^K out of $\binom{2K}{K}$ all codewords used. (*Note:* A code is *incomplete* if some of its codewords are not used.)

The TSC SMs considered here use the 2-rail and $1/n$ codes only, so we will briefly survey the most efficient available realizations of the STCs for these codes, for completeness. Since 2-rail codes are generally incomplete, we are particularly interested in easily-testable STCs. A more detailed survey of the STCs for other unordered and unidirectional error detecting codes can be found e.g. in [24] and [25].

Several implementations of the STCs for complete 2-rail codes have been described in [23], [26]. The first design of the STCs for incomplete 2-rail codes was considered by Marouf and Friedman [27], but the most general results (so far) were given later by Khakbaz [28], and Özgüner [29]. First, Khakbaz [28] showed that if a K-pair 2-rail code has four distinct codewords then, under some conditions, a tree-like STC for this code can be built with 2-pair 2-rail modules. Then, Özgüner [29] showed that an STC having a non-tree structure can be built for many incomplete 2-rail codes for which the method from [28] fails. One common requirement in all the above design procedures is that any incomplete 2-rail code for which an STC is constructed has the property that any input line is 0 (or 1) for at least two input codewords. More generally, since 1968 — when the self-checking circuits were introduced, there has been a consensus that no combinational checker ST for any single s/z fault can be constructed for *any* error-detecting code (EDC) which has some input lines which are 0 (or 1) for only one input codeword. Indeed, no STC for any such a code (except for the $1/n$ codes with $n \geq 4$) has ever been reported in the open literature yet. One, a very frequently occurring class of such an incomplete K-pair 2-rail code is one which contains exactly $2^K + 1$ consecutive codewords corresponding to the decimals 0, 1, 2, ..., 2^K. In this code, the most significant bit (MSB) of an information (check) part of a codeword is 1 (0) for exactly one codeword corresponding to 2^K, i.e. for (10...0 01...1). Recently, we have solved this open problem in [30]. For instance, such a code appears on the 2-rail encoded outputs of the MCNC benchmark SMs 'dk16' and 'dk17' ($K = 3$).

Several STC's for $1/n$ codes have been proposed [31]–[33]. The least complex known STCs for the $1/n$ codes are the following: the $1/4$, $1/7$, $1/8$, $1/11$, and $1/12$ codes — [31]; the $1/5$ and $1/6$ codes — [32], all other $1/n$ codes ($n \leq 9$) — [33].

3   Design of Self-Checking Inverter-Free Circuits

Basically, three properties of TSC/CD SMs should be considered: ST, FS, and CD, but only the ST property will be presented here, due to the following. It was shown in [3] that any IF CC using m/n codes on its inputs and outputs is FS; this can be easily generalized to include any other unordered code as well. As for CD, we have attempted to design TSC/CD SM benchmarks, according to Model 2 of Fig. 1(B), but we have failed: we were unable to design a single benchmark SM considered here with perfect fault and error coverage. Hence, the approaches presented here will apply to Model 1 of Fig. 1(A), wherein the CD property is assured by the STCs placed on all interfaces of a SM. As a result, the only our concern in this section is whether the input and output IF CCs can be fully exercised by codewords actually used.

3.1   Unordered Codes and Inverter-Free Circuits

Let X and Y be two binary n-tuples. We say that X covers Y (written $Y \leq X$) if and only if X has 1's everywhere Y has 1's. If neither $Y \leq X$ nor $X \leq Y$, then we say X and Y are unordered (written $X \not\subseteq Y$). In later discussions the relation $<$ will be used whenever $Y \leq X$ and $Y \neq X$. A set of binary n-tuples C is called *unordered code* if for every $X, Y \in C$, $X \neq Y$ implies $X \not\subseteq Y$. A code C is able to detect all unidirectional errors if and only if it is unordered [19]. The IF functions of a circuit $\mathbf{H}$ with unordered input code space C_{IN} can be derived as follows.

Definition 6 *We say that a word X_i of an unordered code C_{IN} corresponds to an implicant m_i, written $X_i \leftrightarrow m_i$, if m_i is a product of uncomplemented variables x_k which correspond to 1's in X_i. Any such a product will be called a complete unordered product.*

For instance, for the $X = (001101)$ we have $X \leftrightarrow x_3 x_4 x_6$, since X has 1's on the bits x_3, x_4, and x_6. The functions z_j of a circuit $\mathbf{H}$ can be expressed as

$$z_j = \sum_{m_i \in M_j} m_i, \quad j = \{1, 2, \ldots, s\}, \tag{1}$$

where: $\sum$ denotes logic OR and M_j is the set of all implicants m_i which correspond to the inputs $X_i \in C_{IN}$ for which z_j is 1.

A CC that implements (1) and uses only complete unordered products is *nonconcurrent*. i.e. for any $X_i \in C_{IN}$ exactly one product is 1 (this property could be useful while designing TSC/CD SMs of Fig. 1(B)). Smith [19] proved that an IF circuit **H** with unordered input and output code spaces is FS for any single s/z fault and that if **H** is ST for single s/z faults and CD for single input errors, it preserves ST and CD for multiple unidirectional errors and s/z faults. Henceforth, only the ST and CD properties shall be considered explicitly w.r.t. single input errors and faults.

3.2 Formal Conditions for Self-Testing

An algebraic approach — starting with the sum-of-products logic functions (1) — hence applicable to minimal-level (as well as their multi-level) implementations was presented in [2], [3], [6], [8], [9], [37]–[39]. The TSC/CD bit-sliced 2-level AND-OR CC's using complete m/n codes, designed to realize SC synchronous and asynchronous SM's, were proposed in [6], [8], [9]. A more general approach that allow to design TSC/CD CC's using m/n codes and shared logic was given in [37] and extended to an ST or/and CD NOT-AND-OR CC using any input EDC in [38]. If a basic circuit is not ST for some faults, a modification method of introducing one (AND) or two (AND-OR) extra gate levels was also suggested. The usefulness of this approach was demonstrated on the new STC's for all arithmetic codes with check base $A = 3$. Finally, the formal conditions of designing TSC/CD PLA's using any input unordered code (directly applicable to an ordinary 2-level AND-OR circuit as well) were presented in [39]. Here, however, we shall concentrate on IF circuits only.

Let **H** be an n-input s-output CC that translates an unordered closed code C_{IN} into an unordered code C_{OUT} according to the functions (1) using complete products. Let $m_i(x^*)$ denote the set of bits that occur in m_i. For given $m_i = x_{i_1} x_{i_2} \ldots x_{i_a}$ and $m_j = x_{j_1} x_{j_2} \ldots x_{j_b}$, the relation $m_i \subseteq m_j$ holds *iff* $(\forall x_{i_r} \in m_i(x^*))(\exists x_{j_p} \in m_j(x^*) \mid x_{i_r} = x_{j_p})$ [3]. E.g. for $m_i = x_4 x_5$, $m_j = x_2 x_4 x_5 x_6$, and $m_k = x_3 x_5$ we have $m_i \subseteq m_j$ and $m_i \not\subseteq m_k$. A *divider* m_j *of an implicant with respect to* x_k $m_j(x_k)$ is obtained by assigning $x_k = 1$ in m_j [2], [3].

Note: Assuming that the initial functions (1) do not contain identical AND gates feeding the same outputs (the circuit **H** is irredundant), only $s/1$ faults on the inputs of AND gates need to be considered. It is justified as follows. All other $s/1$ faults other than the $s/1$ faults on the inputs of AND gates are detected by the latter tests as well. Any $s/0$ fault of the AND gate that realizes m_j is detected by the codeword $X_j \leftrightarrow m_j$. The same X_j detects the $s/0$ fault on the output of the OR gate fed by m_j.

Let M be the set of all implicants m_j which correspond to all codewords $X_j \in C_{IN}$ and $z^*(m_j)$ denote a set of functions z_i containing an implicant m_j (i.e. such that $z_i(X_j) = 1$).

Theorem 1 *The circuit* **H** *that implements (1) using shared AND gates is ST for any single $s/1$ fault, if*

$$(\forall m_j \in M)\,(\forall x_k \in m_j(x^*))\,(\exists m_l \mid z^*(m_j) \neq z^*(m_l) \text{ and } m_j(x_k) \subseteq m_l).$$

$$(2)$$

Theorem 1 serves as a formal algebraic tool to verify that a given 2-level AND-OR circuit $\mathbf{H}$ realized using complete products is ST w.r.t. s/1 faults. If Theorem 1 does not hold for some x_k in m_j, it indicates that this circuit is not ST for the $x_k/1$ fault on the input of m_j.

3.3 Elimination of s/1 Faults Untested by Input Codewords

Some s/1 faults on the input lines of an AND gate $m_j = \underbrace{(x_{j_1} \ldots x_{j_a})}_{p_u} x_{j_{a+1}} \ldots x_{j_b}$,

which are untested by input codewords, can be made testable by attempting to implement m_j in two levels, provided that the AND gate of the first level — p_u — is shared with another AND gate $m_i = \underbrace{(x_{j_1} \ldots x_{j_a})}_{p_u} x_{i_{a+1}} \ldots x_{i_b}$ in which

all s/1 faults untested in p_u of m_j are fully tested. For instance, consider two sample functions with one untested s/1 fault (marked by an arrow)

$$z_1 = \cdots + x_1 x_2 \overset{\downarrow}{x_3} + \cdots$$
$$z_2 = \cdots + x_2 x_3 x_4 + \cdots$$

Notice that sharing the AND gate that generates the product $p_u = x_2 x_3$ to implement these two products as $x_1(x_2 x_3)$ and $(x_2 x_3) x_4$, allows us to eliminate the untested fault $x_3/1$ in the AND gate $m_j = x_1 x_2 x_3$. By using this concept, Theorem 1 can now be generalized as follows.

We introduce the following notions. Let $p_u \subseteq m_j$. p_u is called a *proper subimplicant* of m_j iff p_u contains at least two variables and $p_u \neq m_j$ (p_u can be realized using one AND gate that could be shared). Let $m_j = (x_{j_1} \cdot \ldots \cdot x_{j_a}) \cdot p_1 \cdot \ldots \cdot p_r$. The *set of proper subimplicants* of m_j will be denoted by $m_j(p^*) = \{p_1, p_2, \ldots, p_r\}$. The *set of all subimplicants* used in the circuit $\mathbf{H}$ will be denoted by P: it corresponds to all shared AND gates that form the first level. Let $p_u \subseteq m_j$. A *divider* $m_j(p_u)$ of an implicant m_j w.r.t. a proper implicant p_u is an expression obtained by assigning $p_u = 1$ in m_j.

Theorem 2 *Consider an IF CC $\mathbf{H}$ that implements (1) with inputs from an unordered code C_{IN} and outputs from an unordered code C_{OUT} with some AND gates implemented in two levels and shared.*
The 3-level AND-AND-OR realization of the circuit $\mathbf{H}$ is ST for any single s/1 fault, if all three following conditions hold ($\forall m_j \in M$) :

1) $(\forall x_k \in m_j(x^*)) (\exists m_l \mid z^*(m_j) \neq z^*(m_l)$ and $m_j(x_k) \subseteq m_l)$. \hfill (3)

2) $(\forall p_u \in m_j(p^*)) (\exists m_l \mid z^*(m_j) \neq z^*(m_l)$ and $m_j(p_u) \subseteq m_l)$. \hfill (4)

3) $(\forall p_u \in P) (\forall x_k \in p_u(x^*)) (\exists m_j, m_l \in M, m_j \neq m_l \mid p_u \in m_j(p^*)$
   and $p_u \in m_l(p^*)$ and $z^*(m_j) \neq z^*(m_l))$ \hfill (5)

The conditions (3)–(5) respectively guarantee that the circuit **H** is ST for all s/1 faults: (i) on the primary input lines x_k that feed directly the AND gates of the 2nd level; (ii) on the input lines p_u of the AND gates of the 2nd level; and (iii) on the primary input lines x_k that feed the AND gates of the 1st level (which are shared). All these three cases can be observed on the logic scheme presented later in Fig. 3. If all three conditions (3)–(5) of Theorem 2 hold, the circuit is not only ST but it also preserves complete products, which could be advantageous for CD. If none of the two above approaches work, one can use the method of improving testability of untested s/1 faults given by Diaz [3]. It relies on removing some literals corresponding to untested s/1 faults in the 2-level AND-OR functions. Here, unlike in [3], the use of shared AND gates could be assumed, whenever possible. However, the limitation of the Diaz's approach is that the resulting ST circuit may not be FS or CD anymore; hence, a designer must pay special attention to that problem.

3.4 Design Example

Design a TSC excitation circuit for the SM specified by Table 1(A), using D flip-flops as memory elements. It is assumed that the three input states $\{I_1, I_2, I_3\}$ are encoded using the 1/3 code (for which an STC can be built) rather than using an incomplete 2-pair 2-rail code composed e.g. of three codewords $\{(00\ 11), (01\ 10), (10\ 01)\}$ (for which an STC is not known). Five internal states are encoded using an incomplete 2/4 code (Table 1(B)).

Table 1. Synchronous sequential machine (A) Transition table; (B) Encoding.

(A)

S^I	I_1	I_2	I_3
A	E	C	A
B	C	E	A
C	D	B	A
D	B	D	C
E	B	C	E

(B)

$(y_4 y_5 y_6 y_7)$	$(x_1 x_2 x_3)$		
	100	010	001
(1100)	(1010)	(0101)	(1100)
(0110)	(0101)	(1010)	(1100)
(0101)	(1001)	(0110)	(1100)
(1001)	(0110)	(1001)	(0101)
(1010)	(0110)	(0101)	(1010)

The next state functions $\{y_4', y_5', y_6', y_7'\}$ for the encoding given in Table 1(B) will be conveniently expressed by writing k for x_k ($k = 1, 2, 3$) and y_k ($k = 4, 5, 6, 7$):

$$y_4' = 145 + 157 + 247 + 256 + 3\,\overset{\downarrow}{4}\,5 + 346 + 35\,\overset{\downarrow}{6} + 35\,\overset{\downarrow}{7}$$

$$y_5' = 146 + 147 + 156 + 245 + 246 + 257 + 3\,\overset{\downarrow}{4}\,5 + 347 + 35\,\overset{\downarrow}{6} + 35\,\overset{\downarrow}{7}$$

$$y_6' = 145 + 146 + 147 + 256 + 257 + 346$$

$$y_7' = 156 + 157 + 245 + 246 + 247 + 347$$

Verification of the ST property of the above circuit according to Theorem 1 reveals that three s/1 faults in three shared AND gates — 345, 356, and 357 — are untested during normal functioning; each untested s/1 line is marked with an arrow.

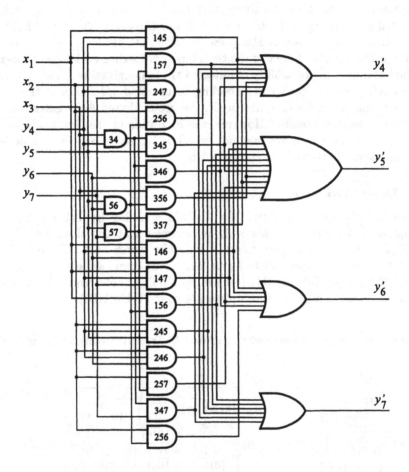

Fig. 3. Logic scheme of the excitation circuit.

Now suppose that all three AND gates containing undetected faults are realized in two levels and are shared with some other products. For instance, the products 345 (with untested input line 4) and e.g. 346 (fully tested) can be realized in two levels using shared AND gate $p_1 = 34$. A similar modification applies to 356 and 256 (sharing $p_2 = 56$) as well as to 357 and 257 (sharing $p_3 = 57$). As a result, the following AND-AND-OR equations are received, wherein all three first-level shared AND gates are marked by parentheses:

$$y_4' = 145 + 157 + 247 + 2(56) + (34)5 + (34)6 + 3(56) + 3(57)$$

$$y_5' = 146 + 147 + 156 + 245 + 246 + 2(57) + (34)5 + 347 + 3(56) + 3(57)$$
$$y_6' = 145 + 146 + 147 + 2(56) + 2(57) + (34)6$$
$$y_7' = 156 + 157 + 245 + 246 + 247 + 347$$

Verification of the ST property of thus modified circuit according to Theorem 2 reveals that all s/1 faults can be tested during normal functioning now. The logic scheme of the above circuit is shown in Fig. 3.

4 Results

We have prepared a software CAD package that allows for a fully automatic design, verification, and modification (if undetected faults are found) of TSC SMs. Its present version allows the synthesis according to two proposed design approaches:

1. The 2-level AND-OR circuit with shared AND gates and
2. The 3-level AND-AND-OR circuit with shared AND gates on either level.

The TSC SMs are designed under the following assumptions:

1. Inputs are encoded using a 2-rail code.
2. Internal states are encoded using an $1/n$ code.
3. Outputs are encoded using a 2-rail code.
4. Any TSC SM is realized according to the scheme of Fig. 1(A).
   Note: We have failed to obtain a realization of Fig. 1(B) which would be TSC/CD for both the excitation and output circuits. Since all benchmark SMs considered are Mealy-type (see Table 2), hence obtaining a TSC/CD realization for only one of them does not make much sense, as we are anyway forced to use an STC to protect the remaining non-CD circuit. Such a task would certainly be easier for any Moore-type SM.
5. Only if a 2-level AND-OR circuit, despite using shared AND gates, still contained some undetected s/1 faults, we attempted to find (automatically) a 3-level AND-AND-OR TSC realization, also with shared AND gates whenever possible (see Table 3).
6. Either version containing the lowest possible number of undetected faults was implemented using multi-level IF circuits obtained by using SIS. Obviously, all first-level shared AND gates of the 3-level AND-AND-OR realization — which were introduced to improve ST — were preserved (see the last two columns of Table 3). (*Note:* The complexity of the STCs was not taken into account.)

The efficiency of using these two techniques — aimed at improving the ST of a SM — was tested on a subset of the MCNC benchmark SMs whose basic characteristics are included in Table 2. The actual design results of their TSC versions can be evaluated according to the data given in Table 3. (*Note:* The excitation and output circuits use shared gates.)

Table 2. Characteristics of some benchmark SMs

Circuit	#states	#inputs	#outputs	#products
dk14	7	3	5	56
dk15	4	3	5	32
dk16	27	2	3	108
dk17	8	2	3	32
dk512	15	1	3	30
donfile	24	2	1	96
ex2	19	2	2	72
ex3	10	2	2	36
ex5	9	2	2	32
ex7	10	2	2	36
lion	4	2	1	11
lion9	9	2	1	25
mc	4	3	5	10
modulo12	12	1	1	24
bbara	10	4	2	160

From Table 3 it is seen that sharing AND gates in the 2-level AND-OR realization (Theorem 1) is sufficient for four circuits only: 'dk14', 'dk512', 'donfile', and 'modulo12'. However, an automatic introduction of shared AND gates forming the first level of the 3-level AND-AND-OR realization (Theorem 2) eliminated all undetected s/1 faults in all but two circuits: 'mc' and 'bbara'. It also allowed us to eliminate only a few undetected s/1 faults in the latter two circuits. The major problem with these circuits is that the output states have highly irregular patterns of various weights which result in highly incomplete encodings. These, in turn, as it can be seen from Table 3, gave us a rather limited chance to improve testability by sharing some extra AND gates. Our analysis of the type of undetected s/1 faults in 'mc' and 'bbara' suggests that achieving the 100% faults coverage is feasible, provided that some further extensions of the approach presented here could be found or some other m/n codes ($m > 1$) codes are used to encode internal states.

Overall, we have shown that many circuits can be made TSC for all faults in both the SM and all STCs used as well. This observation remains in a sharp contrast with the previous results e.g. from [11] and [12], wherein: (1) no analysis of faults detectable during normal functioning by a limited set of codewords actually used was done; and (2) the testability of the embedded STCs was ignored. The detailed analysis of some benchmark SMs considered in [11] and [12] has convinced us that most of these designs cannot be made ST for 100% of single s/z faults by any ad hoc design. Another important open problem found while designing SC SMs (solved by us elsewhere) [30], was the need for an STC for incomplete K-pair 2-rail codes composed of the first $2^{K-1}+1$ codewords, $K \geq 3$. Such a code occurs on inputs and outputs of many benchmark SMs considered in [11] and [12] and, since no STC for such a code was available until now, this is

Table 3. Characteristics of TSC/CD realizations of some benchmark SMs

Circuit	Number of undet. faults		Number of literals	
	AND-OR	AND-AND-OR	Non-minimized	Minimized by SIS
dk14	–	–	1344	1194
dk15	4	–	824	643
dk16	2	–	1316	1086
dk17	2	–	404	251
dk512	–	–	240	178
donfile	–	–	576	576
ex2	20	–	808	419
ex3	14	–	436	212
ex5	10	–	368	158
ex7	16	–	452	202
lion	12	–	162	51
lion9	18	–	258	92
mc	64	56	880	309
modulo12	–	–	96	60
bbara	432	406	2608	1956

one of our arguments that these circuits could not have been made ST for 100% of faults.

5 Conclusions

The new approach to designing totally self-checking (TSC) code-disjoint (CD) synchronous sequential machines (SMs) has been presented. It was assumed that the inputs and outputs of the TSC/CD SMs are encoded using 2-rail codes, the internal states are encoded using 1-out-of-n codes, and D flip-flops are used as the memory elements. The ultimate goal of the design was to obtain the realization of the SM which is TSC for all single stuck-at faults (except for the faults on the clock lines) and CD for all input unidirectional errors.

First, the initial functions in the form of 2-level AND-OR equations of the combinational excitation and output circuits are generated. Assuming that all products are shared, the circuits are checked for ST and fault-secureness, by verifying some algebraic conditions. All s/1 faults which cannot be detected during normal functioning (i.e. by applying only those codewords which are actually used) are identified. Next, a modification procedure is used that looks for products which can be partitioned into such subproducts, which, if shared, could be better testable and hence would result in a ST AND-AND-OR circuit. Finally, the modified circuits are minimized using well known SIS CAD tools, which guarantee that no new undetected faults are introduced.

Most part of the whole design process has been automated by the newly developed software tools. These tools use the BLIF (Berkeley Logic Interchange

Format) representation of a SM as the input and generate the representation of a TSC/CD version of a SM which is compatible with the SIS minimization tools. The analysis of various benchmark SMs showed that a TSC SM with 100% fault coverage can be built for many more circuits for which all previous methods have failed. For those SMs for which some undetected faults still remain, their number can be significantly reduced.

The future work will be aimed at extending the approach presented here and further attempts to design TSC SMs which are TSC for 100%, in particular those for which we failed till now. We will extend our CAD tools to include other unordered encodings on the inputs (Berger code) and outputs of a SM (concatenated unordered codes) which would ensure the existence of an STC which is ST for 100% even by an incomplete subset of codewords used. We will look for other more powerful techniques that would allow for an automatic improvement of the testability of an initial circuit containing undetected faults. Also, we will still attempt to show the feasibility of designing a TSC/CD Mealy-type SM (Fig. 1(B)), which would potentially lead to less complex circuits, as they do not need STCs to monitor inputs and internal states.

Acknowledgements

This research was supported by the grant No. 8 T11C 005 13 from Komitet Badań Naukowych, Poland.

References

1. E. S. Sogomonyan and E. V. Slabakov, *Self-Checking Devices and Fault-Tolerant Systems*, Radio i Svyaz, Moscow, 1989 (in Russian).
2. M. Diaz, "Design of totally self-checking and fail-safe sequential machines," in *Dig. Pap. 4th Int. FTC Symp.*, Urbana, IL, 1974, pp. 3–19 – 3–24.
3. M. Diaz *et al.*, "Unified design of self-checking and fail-safe combinational circuits and sequential machines," *IEEE Trans. Comput.*, vol. C-28, pp. 276–281, March 1979.
4. F. Özgüner, "Design of totally self-checking asynchronous and synchronous sequential machines," in *Dig. Pap. 7th Int. FTC Symp.*, June 1977, pp. 124–129.
5. V. I. Maznev, "Synthesis of totally self-checking sequential circuits," *Autom. Remote Control*, vol. 38, pp. 913–920, No. 6, 1977.
6. V. V. Sapozhnikov, Vl. V. Sapozhnikov, and V. G. Trokhov, "Design of self-checking sequential networks," *Avtom. Vychisl. Tekh.*, vol. 11, pp. 6–11, No. 3, 1977.
7. R. David and P. Thevenod-Fosse, "Design of totally self-checking asynchronous modular circuits," *J. Des. Autom. Fault-Tolerant Comput.*, vol. 4, pp. 271–287, Oct. 1978.
8. V. V. Sapozhnikov and Vl. V. Sapozhnikov, "Synthesis of totally self-checking asynchronous automata," *Autom. Remote Control*, vol. 40, pp. 124–133, No. 1, 1979.
9. V. V. Sapozhnikov and Vl. V. Sapozhnikov, *Discrete Automata with Error Detection*, Energoatomizdat, Leningrad, SU, 1984 (in Russian).
10. T. Nanya and T. Kawamura, "A note on strongly fault secure sequential circuits," *IEEE Trans. Comput.*, vol. C-36, pp. 1121–1123, Sept. 1987.

11. N. K. Jha and S.-J. Wang, "Design and synthesis of self-checking VLSI circuits," *IEEE Trans. Comp.-Aided Des.*, vol. 12, pp. 878–887, June 1993.

12. C.-S. Lai and C.-L. Wey, "*SOLiT*: an automated system for synthesising reliable sequential circuits with multilevel logic implementation," *IEE Proc.-Comput. Digit. Tech.*, vol. 142, pp. 49–54, Jan. 1995.

13. V. V. Danilov *et al.*, "An algebraic model for the hardware monitoring of automata," *Autom. Remote Control*, vol. 36, pp. 984–981, No. 6, 1975.

14. J. Viaud and R. David, "Sequentially self-checking circuits," in *Dig. Pap. 10th Int. FTC Symp.*, Kyoto, Japan, Oct. 1980, pp. 263–268.

15. N. S. Shcherbakov and B. P. Podkopaev, *Structural Theory of Hardware Checking of Digital Devices*, Mashinostroenie, Moscow, 1982 (in Russian).

16. R. A. Parekhji, G. Venkatesh, and S. D. Sherlekar, "Concurrent error detection using monitoring machines," *IEEE Design and Test of Computers*, vol. 12, No. 3, pp. 24–32, Fall 1995.

17. J. M. Berger, "A note on error detection codes for asymmetric binary channels," *Inform. Contr.*, vol. 4, pp. 68–73, Mar. 1961.

18. C. V. Freiman, "Optimal error detection codes for completely asymmetric binary channels," *Inform. Contr.*, vol. 5, pp. 64–71, Mar. 1962.

19. J. E. Smith, "The design of totally self-checking check circuits for a class of unordered codes," *J. Des. Autom. Fault-Tolerant Comput.*, vol. 2, pp. 321–342, Oct. 1977.

20. G. P. Mak, J. A. Abraham, and E. S. Davidson, "The design of PLAs with concurrent error detection," in *Dig. Pap. 12th Int. FTC Symp.*, Santa Monica, CA, June 1982, pp. 303–310.

21. J. E. Smith, "On separable unordered codes," *IEEE Trans. Comput.*, vol. C-33, pp. 741–743, Aug. 1984.

22. S. J. Piestrak, "Design of TSC code-disjoint inverter-free PLA's for separable unordered codes," in *Proc. ICCD'94, Int. Conf. on Computer Design: VLSI in Computers & Processors*, Cambridge, MA, Oct. 10–12, 1994, pp. 128–131.

23. W. C. Carter and P. R. Schneider, "Design of dynamically checked computers," in *Proc. IFIP Conf.*, Edinburgh, Scotland, Aug. 1968, pp. 878–883.

24. S. J. Piestrak, *Design of Self-Testing Checkers for Unidirectional Error Detecting Codes*, Scientific Papers of Inst. of Techn. Cybern. of Techn. Univ. of Wrocław, No. 92, Ser.: Monographs No. 24, Oficyna Wyd. Polit. Wrocł., Wrocław 1995, 112 pp.

25. S. J. Piestrak, "Design of encoders and self-testing checkers for some systematic unidirectional error detecting codes," *J. of Microelectronic Systems Integration*, Sp. Issue on Defect and Fault Tolerance in VLSI Systems, vol. 5, pp. 247–260, No. 4, 1997.

26. J. F. Wakerly, *Error Detecting Codes, Self-Checking Circuits and Applications*, North-Holland, New York, 1978.

27. M. A. Marouf and A. D. Friedman, "Design of self-checking checkers for Berger codes," in *Dig. Pap. 8th Int. FTC Symp.*, Toulouse, France, June 1978, pp. 179–184.

28. J. Khakbaz and E. J. McCluskey, "Self-testing embedded parity checkers," *IEEE Trans. Comput.*, vol. C-33, pp. 753–756, Aug. 1984.

29. F. Özgüner, "Design of totally self-checking embedded two-rail code checkers," *Electr. Lett.*, vol. 27, pp. 382–384, 14th Feb. 1991.

30. S. J. Piestrak, "Design method of combinational self-testing checkers for a class of incomplete 2-rail codes," submitted to *IEEE Trans. Comput.*

31. V. Rabara, "Design of self-checking checker for 1-out-of-n code ($n > 3$)," in *Proc. 4th Int. Conf. on Fault-Tolerant Syst. Diagnostics*, Brno, Czechoslovakia, Sept. 28–30, 1981, pp. 234–240; also appears as: V. V. Sapozhnikov and V. Rabara, "Universal

synthesis algorithm for $1/n$ testers," *Probl. Inf. Transm.*, vol. 18, pp. 209–218, No. 3, 1982.

32. D. A. Anderson and G. Metze, "Design of totally self-checking check circuits for m-out-of-n codes," *IEEE Trans. Comput.*, vol. C-22, pp. 263–269, Mar. 1973.

33. S. J. Piestrak, "Design method of self-testing checkers for 1-out-of-n codes," in *Proc. 6th Int. Conf. on Fault-Tolerant Syst. Diagnostics*, Brno, Czechoslovakia, Sept. 1983, pp. 57–63.

34. S. J. Piestrak, "Design method of totally self-checking checkers for m-out-of-n codes," in *Dig. Pap. 13th Int. FTC Symp.*, June 28–30, 1983, Milan, Italy, pp. 162–168.

35. S. J. Piestrak, "The minimal test set for sorting networks and the use of sorting networks in self-testing checkers for unordered codes," in *Dig. Pap. 20th Int. FTC Symp.*, Newcastle upon Tyne, UK, June 1990, pp. 457–464.

36. S. J. Piestrak, "General design procedure of self-testing checkers for all m-out-of-n codes with $m \geq 3$ using parallel counters," in *Proc. 4th IEEE Int. On-Line Testing Workshop*, July 7–9, 1998, Capri, Italy, pp. 182–186.

37. S. J. Piestrak, "PLA implementation of totally self-checking circuits using m-out-of-n codes," in *Proc. ICCD'85*, Port Chester, N.Y., Oct. 1–3, 1985, pp. 777–781.

38. S. J. Piestrak, "Design of high-speed and cost-effective self-testing checkers for low-cost arithmetic codes," *IEEE Trans. Comput.*, vol. C-39, pp. 360–374, March 1990.

39. S. J. Piestrak, "General design principles of self-testing code-disjoint PLA's," *Proc. ATS'93 — 2nd Asian Test Symp.*, Beijing, China, Nov. 18–19, 1993, pp. 287–292.

Path Delay Fault Testing of a Class of Circuit-Switched Multistage Interconnection Networks

M. Bellos[1], D. Nikolos[1,2] & H. T. Vergos[1,2]

[1]Dept. of Computer Engineering and Informatics, University of Patras, 26 500, Rio, Greece
tarka@ceid.upatras.gr, {nikolosd, vergos}@cti.gr
[2]Computer Technology Institute, 3, Kolokotroni Str., 262 61 Patras, Greece

Abstract. In this paper we consider path delay fault testing of a class of isomorphic Multistage Interconnection Networks (MINs) with centralized control using as representative the nxn Omega network. We show that the number of paths is $3n^2-2n$ and we give a method for testing those applying only $2(3n-2)$ pairs of test vectors. We also show that this is the least number of test vector pairs that are required for testing all paths of the MIN. We also give a path selection method such that: a) the number of selected paths, that is, the number of paths that must be tested, is a small percentage of all paths and the propagation delay along every other path can be calculated from the propagation delays along the selected paths, b) all the selected paths are tested by using $2(3\log_2 n+1)$ test vector pairs. Both methods derive strong delay–verification test sets.

1 Introduction

Multistage Interconnection Networks (MINs) represent a compromise between the single bus and the crossbar switch interconnections from the point of view of implementation complexity, cost, connectivity and bandwidth. A MIN consists of alternating stages of links and switches. Many kinds of MINs have been proposed and built for use in massively parallel computers [1, 2].

The testing of MINs has been widely considered with respect to the state stuck-at fault model, the link fault model and the switch fault model [for example 3, 4]. However, physical defects in integrated circuits can degrade circuit performance without altering their logic functionality. Apart from this, increasing performance requirements of the contemporary VLSI circuits makes it difficult to design them with large timing margins. Thus imprecise delay modeling and the statistical variations of the parameters during the manufacturing process may result in circuits with greater delays than the expected ones. The change in the timing behavior of the circuit is modeled by two popular fault models. One is the gate delay fault model where delays violating specifications are assumed to be due to a single gate delay [5, 6]. The other is the path delay fault model where a path is declared faulty if it fails to propagate a transition from the path input to the path output within a specified time interval [7]. The latter model is deemed to be more general since it captures the cumulative effect of small delay variations in gates along a path as well as the faults caused by a single gate.

A physical path of a circuit is an alternating sequence of gates and lines leading from a primary input to a primary output of the circuit. In delay fault test generation we associate two logical paths with each physical path. A logical path is a pair (T, p) with $T = \overline{x} \rightarrow x, x \in B = \{0, 1\}$, being a transition at the input of p. In the case of delay fault testing the test set consists of pairs of vectors. The cardinality of the test set, that is, the number of pairs of vectors depends on the number of the paths that must be tested and the percentage of the paths that can be tested in parallel. Throughout the paper the term test session is used to denote the application of a test vector pair. The number of physical paths in a contemporary circuit is prohibitively large in order for all the paths to be tested for path delay faults. To this end to reduce the paths that must be tested for path delay faults various path selection methods have been proposed (for example [8–11]) although none of them has proven to be satisfactory for the general case.

In this paper we address the problem of testing for path delay faults a class of isomorphic circuit-switched MINs with centralized control, using as representative the Omega network [12]. We consider that the network has been implemented as a set of b/M M-bit slices [13], where b is the size of the bus of each source and destination of the network, $1 \leq M \leq b$ and each slice has been implemented as a VLSI chip. For M=b the network has been implemented on a single chip (probably on a single wafer). The test sets that we derive are strong delay–verification test sets, therefore, their application ensures that if the circuit under test (CUT) functions correctly at a speed it will also operate correctly at every lower speed. In section 2 we present the terminology that will be used in this paper. In section 3 we present the main features of the Omega network and we show that the number of physical paths is $O(n^2)$. In section 4 exploiting the inherent parallelism of the Omega network we show that it can be tested for path delay faults in $O(n)$ test sessions. We also show that the derived test set is a strong delay-verification test set. In section 5 we present a new path selection method such that: a) the paths, which are selected for testing constitute a small percentage of the total number of paths; the delay along the rest paths can be calculated from the propagation delays along the selected paths, b) the propagation delays along n of the selected paths are measured in parallel during each test session. According to this method the required number of test sessions is $O(\log_2 n)$. The application of this method cuts down the test effort as well as the test application time significantly. We also show that the derived test set is a strong delay–verification test set. The conclusions are given in section 6.

2 Preliminaries

A two pattern test $T = <V_1, V_2>$ is said to be a robust delay test for a path P, for a rising or falling transition at the output of the path, if and only if, when P is faulty and test T is applied, the circuit output is different from the expected state at sampling time, independent of the delays along gate inputs not on P [14]. A robust test may actually propagate transitions to an output through more than one path to that output in the circuit; such a test is called Multiple-Path Propagating Robust Test (MPP-RT) [15]. A robust test that propagates the fault effect through only a single path to an output in the circuit will be called a Single-Path Propagating Robust Test (SPP-RT) for that output. For example consider the circuit in Figure 1 [15]. The test $< V_1, V_2>$, with $V_1=(a=1, b=0, c=1, d=1)$ and $V_2=(a=0, b=0, c=0, d=1)$ for a falling transition at the output y is a MPP-RT, which sensitizes and propagates fault effects robustly along both the paths a-3-y and c-3-y to the output y. The test $<V_1, V_2>$ with $V_1= (a=0, b=0, c=1, d=1)$ and $V_2 = (a=0, b=0, c=0, d=1)$ for a falling transition at the output y is a SPP-RT, which sensitizes and propagates the fault effect robustly only along the single path c-3-y. We define a robust test as Multiple SPP-RT (M-SPP-RT) if it propagates the effect of one or more faults along distinct paths or along paths starting from the same primary input and ending at distinct outputs without internal reconvergent fanouts. For example in Figure 4.a the test $< V_1, V_2>$, with $V_1= (X_{0i}=0, X_{1i}=0, c=0)$ and $V_2= (X_{0i}=1, X_{1i}=1, c=0)$, is a M-SPP-RT that propagates the effect of delay faults along the distinct paths X_{0i}-3-7-Y_{0i} and X_{1i}-5-8-Y_{1i}. Also the test $<V_1, V_2>$ with$V_1= (X_{0i}=0, X_{1i}=1, c=0)$ and $V_2= (X_{0i}=0, X_{1i}=1, c=1)$), is a M-SPP-RT that propagates the effect of delay faults along the paths c-4-7- Y_{0i} and c-2-5-8-Y_{1i}. We have to note that in the circuit of Figure 1 the test $< V_1, V_2>$, with $V_1=(a=0, b=0, c=0, d=1)$ and $V_2=(a=1, b=0, c=0, d=1)$ is not a M-SPP-RT because the paths a-2-5-x and a-3-5-x reconverge.

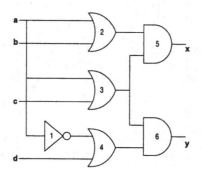

Fig. 1.

A robust test is said to be a Hazard-Free Robust Test (HFRT) if no hazards can occur on the tested path during the application of the test, regardless of the gate delay values. Therefore, a M-SPP-HFRT $< V_1, V_2>$ has to provide steady, glitchless, sensitizing values at all the off-path inputs along more than one paths, when the primary inputs changed from V_1, to V_2.

Robust tests may not exist for all path delay faults in an arbitrary circuit. Some nonrobust tests can be shown to be valid if certain other faults have been tested robustly [16]. Such tests are called Validatable Nonrobust (VNR) tests. The term RV tests is used to denote tests that are robust or validatable nonrobust. A circuit is RV - testable if there is a robust or a VNR test for any single path delay fault. It has been shown in [17] that the fact that a circuit functions correctly at a clock speed does not imply that it will also function correctly at a lower clock speed. A set of path delay tests is called a strong delay–verification test set if the correct response of the CUT at a speed implies correct operation at any lower speed [17]. A circuit which has a strong delay-verification test set is called a delay-verifiable circuit [17].

3 Omega Networks

We consider nxn Omega MINs, where $n=2^k$. An Omega MIN is constructed from $N=\log_2 n$ stages of switches, where each of the stages has n/2 2x2 switches. The switch stages are labeled from 1 to N. There are also the stages 0 and N+1 which are formed from the source and destination nodes respectively. The interconnection pattern between adjacent stages is the perfect shuffle permutation [18]. This holds for all pairs of stages except N and N+1. Figure 2 shows an 8x8 Omega MIN.

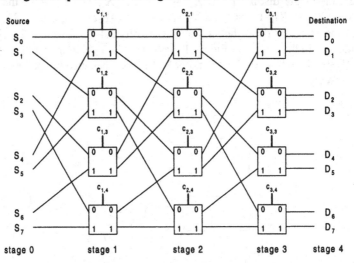

Fig. 2. 8x8 Omega Network

An inherent property of the Omega MIN is that distinct paths of the MIN may have common links and switches. Thus, a conflict appears when any two sources are trying to set any switch of the network in complementary states.

Each switch S, as shown in Figure 3.a has a pair of input data buses X_0, X_1, a pair of output data buses Y_0, Y_1 and a control signal c. All four buses are identical in size and unidirectional. The two states of the switch S are determined by the control line c as follows: the *direct* state shown in Figure 3.b, where the values of X_0, X_1 are propagated to Y_0, Y_1 respectively, and a *cross* state shown in Figure 3.c, where the values of X_0, X_1 are propagated to Y_1, Y_0 respectively. The upper input and output are labeled with 0 while the lower are labeled with 1. Each switch is constructed from 2M 2->1 multiplexers, where M is the size of the buses. Each pair of multiplexers, see Figure 3.*d*, accepts two lines of X_0, X_1 buses, the control signal c and drives the corresponding lines of buses Y_0, Y_1.

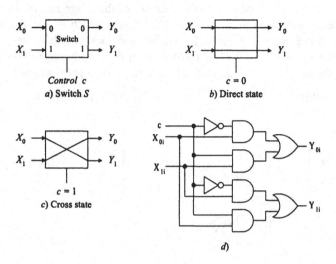

Fig. 3.

Without loss of generality we consider that each link between sources and switches, between switches, as well as switches and destinations is a single virtual line, that may actually represent either one physical line or a physical bus. For testing purposes any value of the virtual line is always applied to every line of the physical bus that it may represent. Paths along the MIN are formed by concatenation of subpaths along links and subpaths through switches of the MIN as well as by subpaths sourcing from the control signals. We will hereafter present the analysis based on virtual lines (or simply lines). The analysis will be valid for all M lines of the bus. We note that to every virtual path or line correspond two logical virtual paths.

In an nxn Omega MIN we distinguish the paths in two sets: those not including subpaths sourcing from a control input and those which do. Since the connections of sources to destinations change dynamically during system operation, delays that stem from the control signals are also significant. Let P be the set consisting of all virtual paths starting from any source and ending at any destination. Since there are n sources and there is only one path from one of them to all the destinations, the number of all possible virtual paths is n^2. That is the cardinality of P, denoted $|P|$, is

$$|P| = n^2.$$

Let L be the set consisting of all paths starting from the control input of a switch and ending at any destination. Figures 4.*a* and 4.*b* present the subpaths from the control input of a switch through two of its 2M multiplexers for $X_{0i}=0$ and $X_{1i}=1$ and for $X_{0i}=1$ and $X_{1i}=0$. Since the transition, during delay testing, propagates from the control input through 2M multiplexers and along the lines of the bus, in this case we refer also to virtual paths. For computing the number of the virtual paths starting from a control input we observe that at every stage the control input of a switch can be seen as the root of two full binary trees having the destinations as leaves. Each such tree has a depth of N-i+1, where i is the number of the stage and $i \in \{1, 2, ..., N\}$. The latter means that every such tree has 2^{N-i+1} leaves which is also the number of virtual paths. Since each stage has n/2 switches and each switch is the root of two trees, there are $2*(n/2)*2^{N-i+1}$ virtual paths starting from each stage's control inputs. Thus the cardinality of L is equal to the sum of the virtual paths starting from every control input, which is: $$|L| = \sum_{i=1}^{N} 2\frac{n}{2}2^{N-i+1} = 2\frac{n}{2}2(2^{N}-1) = 2n(n-1)$$

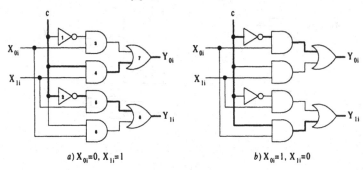

a) $X_{0i}=0, X_{1i}=1$ b) $X_{0i}=1, X_{1i}=0$

Fig. 4.

Therefore the total number of virtual paths is equal to: $|P| + |L| = 3n^2 - 2n$ and the number of all logical virtual paths is: $|LV| = 2(3n^2 - 2n)$

The number of physical lines is equal to $M(3n^2 - 2n)$, however the propagation delays along the M lines of the bus are measured in parallel.

Although the number of the virtual paths of an nxn Omega network is $O(n^2)$ we will show in the next section that due to the inherent parallelism of the network the propagation delay along various paths can be measured in parallel.

4 Method One: Parallel Testing

It is well known that in an Omega network when the control inputs get a set of values each source is connected to a different destination. Throughout this section we consider that all control inputs of stage i, for i=1, 2, ..., N, of the Omega network take the same value c_i. Then changing the value of the control inputs of a stage i the switches of this stage from the direct state go to the cross state or from the cross state go to the direct state, and all paths from sources to destinations are changed. Then taking into account that in the Omega network only one path exists from a specific source to a specific destination we conclude that for the two sets of values of $c_1c_2...c_N$ and of $c_1'c_2'...c_N'$, with $c_1c_2...c_N \neq c_1'c_2'...c_N'$, a common path from the source to destination in both configurations of the network does not exist. Therefore, applying to $c_1c_2...c_N$ all possible values, that is 2^N different values, we ensure that each source has been connected to each destination. A feature of the Omega network is that every source can be connected to every destination. Thus taking into account that we have n destinations we conclude that at least n value combinations of the control signals are necessary so that each source to be connected to each destination. From the above discussion we conclude that 2^N is the least number of configurations that ensures that all possible paths from sources to destinations have been established. For each configuration, that is a value of $c_1c_2...c_N$, we can measure the delays along n virtual paths, hence $2*2^N$ test sessions are required in order to measure the delays along all logical virtual paths from sources to destinations. Let T_p denote the number of test sessions required to measure the delays along all paths from sources to destinations. Then :

$$T_p = 2*2^N = 2n \qquad (1)$$

As we have already observed at every stage i a control input can be seen as a root of two full binary trees having the destinations as leaves. We have also shown that every such tree has 2^{N-i+1} virtual paths from the root to the leaves. For any combination of values of $c_{i+1}c_{i+2}...c_N$ two paths starting from the control input of each switch of the stage i are established, that is we have $2*n/2$ virtual paths, along which the delay can be measured in parallel. Then taking into account that to each switch of the stage i correspond two trees each one with 2^{N-i+1} virtual paths we conclude that $2 * 2 * 2^{N-i+1} / 2$ test sessions are required for measuring the propagation delay along the logical virtual paths starting from a control input of stage i. Taking into account that i=1, 2, ..., N we get that the total number of test sessions T_L for measuring the propagation delays along the virtual paths starting from control inputs is :

$$T_L = 2 * \sum_{i=1}^{N} 2^{N-i+1} = 4(2^N-1) = 4(n-1) \qquad (2)$$

From relations (1) and (2) we get: $T_p + T_L = 2(3n-2)$.

Therefore, while the number of virtual paths of a nxn Omega network is $O(n^2)$ we have shown that the number of the required test sessions is $O(n)$. In a circuit with n outputs the maximum number of paths that can be tested in parallel is equal to n. Then taking into account that the number of all logical virtual paths of the nxn Omega network is equal to $2(3n^2-2n)$ and the fact that $2(3n-2)$ test sessions are required we conclude that this is the optimal number of test sessions required to test all possible paths.

From the above discussion it is evident that all paths of an Omega MIN are sensitizable. Furthermore it is evident that the derived test set consists of M-SPP-HFRT test vector pairs, that test all paths of the MIN. Since the M-SPP-HFRT tests are a subset of the RV-tests and we test all paths of the MIN, from Theorem 1 in [17] we conclude that the proposed test set is a strong delay-verification test set. This implies that the correct function of the circuit at the tested speed ensures correct operation at any lower speed.

5 Method Two: Path Selection Based Method

It has been shown in [8] that by measuring the delays along a suitable very small set Δ of physical paths, the propagation delay along any other path can be calculated. However, this method can not exploit the inherent parallelism of Omega or their isomorphic networks. The method proposed in this section exploiting the parallelism of the Omega networks derives a basis with cardinality n times smaller than that derived by the method of [8]. For simplifying the analysis, we examine the sets P, L separately.

5.1 Set P

As a first step, we represent the MIN as a graph where each switch, source and destination is represented by a node of the graph and each link by a line. We observe that the graph is a collection of full binary trees with root nodes connected by links at stages m and m+1 with m$\in$ {1, 2, ..., N-1}. When N is even we choose m=N/2 and the binary trees on the left as well as on the right are of depth m, while when N is odd we choose m = $\lfloor N/2 \rfloor$, where $\lfloor x \rfloor$ denotes the integer part of x, and the binary trees on the left are of depth m, while the ones on the right are of depth m+1. The left trees have as leaves the sources and the right the destinations. We define m' to be the depth of the right tree and it is equal either to m if N even, or to m+1 if N is odd.

Figure 5 presents one pair of the above trees along with their interconnection. We denote a pair of such trees as a t-structure. All t-structures are similar. In every nxn Omega network there are exactly n different t-structures since there are n different links between the stages where the connection of a pair of trees takes place. These t-structures do not have any virtual paths in common because the connection between any two tree pairs that form a t-structure is distinct. The latter property does not eliminate the possibility of having common subpaths.

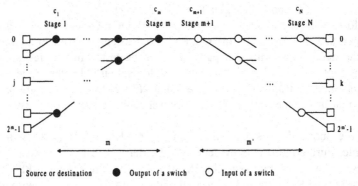

Fig. 5.

Lemma 1. The n t-structures represent all virtual paths of set P.

Proof. a) N is even, that is N=2m. Then the two trees of a t-structure have the same number m of levels and therefore have 2^m leaves each. The number of virtual paths, denoted V, of each t-structure is: $V = 2^m 2^m = 2^{2m} = 2^N = n$ ($N=\log_2 n$)

b) N is odd, that is N=2m+1. Then the left tree of a t-structure has m levels and the right tree has m+1. Thus, they have 2^m and 2^{m+1} leaves respectively. The number of virtual paths of a t-structure is: $V = 2^m 2^{m+1} = 2^{2m+1} = 2^N = n$ ($N=\log_2 n$)

In both cases we have n t-structures and any two of them represent distinct virtual paths, therefore, the number of virtual paths in each case is n^2. ■

Any two virtual paths of a t-structure cannot be tested in parallel for delay faults since every possible pair of virtual paths requires at least one of the switches at stages m and m+1 to be in contradictory states. For example, in Figure 2, the paths from S_0 to D_0 and S_4 to D_2 belong to the same t-structure and the propagation delays along them cannot be measured in parallel because the switches at the stages m=1 and m+1=2 cannot be in the direct and cross state simultaneously. On the contrary, virtual paths belonging to different t-structures can be tested in parallel for path delay faults, provided that two or more virtual paths do not force common switches in contradictory states. If no conflict arises, n virtual paths one from each t-structure can be tested in parallel by a single test session.

We define Q as the set of the following paths of a t-structure:

- All paths from one source to all destinations. The number of these paths is equal to the number of leaves of the right tree. We denote this set as Q_A.
- All paths from all sources except the one assumed in a) to a single destination. The number of these paths is equal to the number of leaves of the left tree minus 1. We denote this set as Q_B.

Theorem 1. If the propagation delays along all paths of set Q of a t-structure are known, the propagation delay along any path of a t-structure can be calculated.

Proof. Without loss of generality suppose that Q contains all paths from the source with address 0 to all $2^{m'}$ destinations and the paths from sources with addresses 1 to 2^m-1 to the destination with address p, where $0 \leq p \leq 2^{m'}-1$. Let j->k be a path from source with address j, $0 < j \leq 2^m-1$ to the destination with address k with $0 \leq k \leq 2^{m'}-1$ and k≠p. Then the propagation delay along the path j->k can be calculated as :

$$d(j\text{->}k) = d(j\text{->}p) + d(0\text{->}k) - d(0\text{->}p) \qquad ■$$

We will show in the sequel that there is no need to measure the propagation delays along all virtual paths belonging to the set Q for every t-structure. The n t-structures of the network can be split in two parts: the left will contain the left trees and the right the right trees. All left trees have the same depth, as well as all right trees have the same depth. We will present an algorithm that manipulates the control signal values of the switches, such that n virtual paths, each belonging to a distinct t-structure, can be tested in parallel. The algorithm takes advantage of the fact that two t-structures can have common switches that form subtrees either on the right or the left part, as shown in Figure 6. This can be used in minimizing both the number of virtual paths that need to be tested and the number of test sessions required. The algorithm first manipulates the switches of the right part and next those of the left part. Each stage's control signals are set by a bit of an N-bit binary number. Control signals of stage i, $i \in \{1, 2, ..., N\}$ are controlled by bit c_i. Hence the m leftmost bits represent the control signals' values for the left part of the MIN while the rest for the right part.

Let p_1 and p_2 be two sources in two different t-structures TS_1 and TS_2, as shown in Figure 6. The two t-structures have common switches that form a subtree of l levels. Suppose that the delays along all virtual paths starting from p_1 and ending at the destinations in set S_1 and those along all virtual paths starting from p_2 and ending at the destinations of set S_2 are known. Then measuring the delay along a virtual path starting from p_1 and ending at a destination of S_2 and a path starting from p_2 and ending at a destination of S_1 we can calculate the delays along all virtual paths starting from p_1 or p_2 and ending at any destination in sets S_1 and S_2. For example, suppose that we want to calculate the propagation delay along path p_1->j, where j is a destination in S_2. If we know the propagation delay along p_1->k, k is in S_2, then the propagation delay of p_1->j can be calculated from the propagation delays of p_1->k, p_2->j and p_2->k as : $d(p_1$ ->j) = d(p_2->j) + d(p_1->k) - d(p_2->k)$.

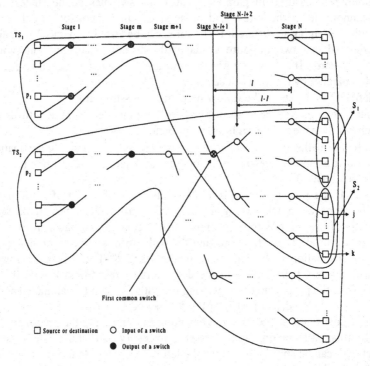

Fig. 6.

The following algorithm establishes all virtual paths along which the propagation delay must be measured.

Algorithm 1

Consider that all control inputs of stage i, for i = 1, 2, ..., N take the same value of c_i. Then one control bit is required for describing the state of the switches of every stage. Hence for the N stages we need N bits, $c_1, c_2, ..., c_N$. Set $m = \lfloor N/2 \rfloor$ and $m' = \lceil N/2 \rceil$, where $\lceil x \rceil$ denotes the least integer greater than or equal to x.

Step 1. Set $c_1 ... c_m\ c_{m+1} .. c_N = 0 ... 00$.

`Step 2.` Apply two test sessions, one for transition 0->1 and the other for 1->0.

`Step 3.` Set $c_m c_{m+1} .. c_N = 0 ... 01$.

`Step 4.` Apply two test sessions, one for transition 0->1 and the other for 1->0.

`Step 5.` Shift left $c_m c_{m+1} .. c_N$ (consider that the rightmost bit is filled with a zero).

`Step 6.` If $c_m \neq 1$ then go to step 4.

`Step 7.` Set $c_1 c_2 ... c_m c_{m+1} = 100 ... 0$

`Step 8.` Apply two test sessions, one for transition 0->1 and the other for 1->0.

`Step 9.` Shift right $c_1 c_2 ... c_m c_{m+1}$ (consider that the leftmost bit is filled with a zero).

`Step 10.` If $c_{m+1} \neq 1$ then go to step 8 else end.

From the above algorithm we conclude that $2(m' + m + 1) = 2N + 2$ test sessions are required.

Theorem 2. The propagation delays along any path of set P that has not been measured during the application of the algorithm can be calculated from the measured propagation delays.

Proof. By steps 1, 2, 3, 4 the propagation delays along 2n virtual paths for n trees of the form of Figure 7.a have been measured. Thus for each tree we know the propagation delays along virtual paths from the same source to two destinations, since switches on the left side of the MIN remain unchanged. These n trees are of depth 1. After the first iteration of steps 5, 6, 4 switches at stage N-1 are considered and the propagation delays along n more virtual paths have been measured. These n virtual paths are distinct compared to the previous virtual paths established since the proposed algorithm manipulates a different stage of switches at each iteration. Thus any of the n virtual paths established from a source end at a distinct destination.

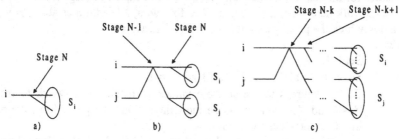

Fig. 7.

Suppose that from source i the virtual path ends at a destination of S_j. Then the virtual path starting from j ends at a destination of S_i since the switch that is manipulated is common for both virtual paths. From the above, we can calculate the propagation delays along all virtual paths starting from i or j and ending at a destination of $S_i \cup S_j$. The latter means that two trees of depth 1, with their right subtrees connected by a switch at stage N-1, can be combined to form two trees of depth 2 from the same sources, as shown in Figure 7.b. This is possible for every pair of such trees and thus after each iteration we have n trees available.

After k-1 iterations of steps 5, 6, 4 the propagation delays along the virtual paths of n trees of depth k have been measured or calculated. Suppose that we consider two such trees i, j that have a common switch at stage N-k. At the next iteration of steps 5, 6, 4 this switch is set to the cross state. Now a virtual path is established from i to a destination of S_j and another one from j to a destination of S_i. In the same manner we can calculate the propagation delays along all virtual paths from i or j to $S_i \cup S_j$ thus forming two trees of depth k+1 that start from i and j, as shown in Figure 7.c.

After m' iterations the propagation delays along all virtual paths of n m'-depth trees are known which means that we know all the propagation delays along all virtual paths of each of the n Q_A sets.

In the same manner, steps 7-10 of Algorithm 1 provide the information for calculating the propagation delays along all virtual paths of n m-depth trees that each ends at a specific destination. Hence we know the propagation delays along all virtual paths in the Q_B sets. Thus we can calculate the propagation delays along all virtual paths of all the Q_A and Q_B sets and from Theorem 1 we can calculate the propagation delays along all virtual paths of set P. ∎

5.2 Set L

For path delay fault testing of paths starting from the control input of a switch, the inputs X_0 and X_1 of the switch must be set to complementary values.

Figures 4.*a* and 4.*b* present the subpaths from the control input of a switch through two of its 2M multiplexers for $X_{0i}=0$ and $X_{1i}=1$ and for $X_{0i}=1$ and $X_{1i}=0$ respectively. Therefore for path delay fault testing of the paths starting from the control input of a switch at least two sessions are required, one with $X_{0i}=0$ and $X_{1i}=1$ and one with $X_{0i}=1$ and $X_{1i}=0$.

Consider for the rest of this section that all control inputs of stage i, for i=1, 2, ..., N of the network take the same value c_i. The following Algorithm establishes virtual paths along which the propagation delays must be measured.

Algorithm 2.

Step 1. Set i=1.

Step 2. Set $c_j=0$ for all j∈ {1, 2, ..., N} with j ≠ i.

Step 3. Set the sources to the suitable values such that each switch to receive $X_0=0$ and $X_1=1$ and measure the delays along the paths from the n/2 c_i inputs to the n destinations.

Step 4. Set each source to its complement and measure the delays along the paths from the n/2 c_i inputs to the n destinations.

Step 5. If i<N then set i=i+1 and go to step 2 else end.

We note that in each one of the steps 3 and 4 two measurements are required, one for the transition 0->1 and one for transition 1->0. Therefore Algorithm 2 applies $4N = 4\log_2 n$ test sessions.

After the application of Algorithm 2 we have measured the propagation delays along all paths starting from a control input $c_{i,j}$ of the switch j of stage i that pass through the output $Y_0(i,j)$ or $Y_1(i,j)$ of the switch and ends at a destination D_k with $c_{i+1,j_i} = c_{i+2,j_2} = ... = c_{N,j_{N-i-1}} = 0$, where $j_1, j_2, ..., j_{N-i-1} \in \{1, 2, ..., n/2\}$.

For example, we can see from Figure 2 that such a path is the path from $c_{1,1}->D_0$, which is established when we have $S_0 = 0$ and $S_4 = 1$ (for $S_0 = 1$ and $S_4 = 0$ we have another path from $c_{1,1}\text{->}D_0$) and $c_{2,1} = c_{3,1} = 0$. The propagation delays along the path $c_{1,1}\text{->}D_3$, which is established when we have $S_0 = 0$, $S_4 = 1$ and $c_{2,1} = c_{3,1} = 1$, has not been measured. However, the propagation delay along $c_{1,1}\text{->}D_3$ can be calculated from the propagation delays along paths $c_{1,1}\text{->}D_0$ (was measured), $S_0\text{->}D_0$ and $S_0\text{->}D_3$ as : $d(c_{1,1}\text{->}D_3) = d(S_0\text{->}D_3) + d(c_{1,1}\text{->}D_0) - d(S_0\text{->}D_0)$

We note that the paths $S_0\text{->}D_0$ and $S_0\text{->}D_3$ belong to P, hence the propagation delays along them are already known.

Theorem 3. The propagation delays along any virtual path of set L that has not been measured during the application of Algorithm 2 can be calculated from the measured propagation delays, during the application of Algorithm 2, and the propagation delays along paths of set P.

Proof. Let $c_{i,j}$ denote the control input of switch j of stage i, then $j \in \{1, 2, ..., n/2\}$. Consider a path that starts from a control input $c_{i,j}$, passes through Y_z, with $z = 0$ or $z = 1$ that ends at D_w such that at least one of c_{i+1,j_1}, c_{i+2,j_2}, ..., $c_{N,j_{N-i-1}}$ is equal to 1.

The propagation delay along the path $c_{i,j}$ -> Y_z -> D_w has not been measured. Consider the following paths:

The path $c_{i,j}$ -> Y_z -> $D_{w'}$, with $w' \neq w$, such that $c_{i+1,j_1} = c_{i+2,j_2} = ... = c_{N,j_{N-i-1}} = 0$.

The propagation delay along this path has been measured during the application of Algorithm 2.

The paths $S_x\text{->}Y_z\text{->}D_w$ and $S_x\text{->}Y_z\text{->}D_{w'}$ (these belong to P, hence the propagation delays along them are already known). Then :

$$d(c_{i,j} \text{ -> } Y_z \text{ -> } D_w) = d(S_x\text{->}Y_z\text{->}D_w) + d(c_{i,j} \text{ -> } Y_z \text{ -> } D_{w'}) - d(S_x\text{->}Y_z\text{->}D_{w'}) \quad \blacksquare$$

From Theorems 2 and 3 we conclude that with $2(3\log_2 n + 1)$ test sessions we have obtained all the needed information in order to calculate the propagation delays along all paths in sets P and L.

The first method can also be used to derive the maximum speed of the CUT and ensures that the circuit will function correctly for lower speeds. We have shown that the second method can alternatively be used to derive the maximum speed of the CUT. Since the application of the first method ensures that the circuit functions correctly for lower speeds and the maximum speed can alternatively be derived following the second method, we conclude that, when either the first or the second method is used, it is ensured that the CUT will function correctly for all speeds lower than the maximum. Therefore, the test set derived following the second method is also a strong delay-verification test set.

6 Conclusions

We have presented two methods for path delay fault testing of the nxn circuit switched Omega MIN with centralized control. Following the first and the second method respectively $2(3n - 2)$ and $2(3\log_2 n + 1)$ test sessions are required, while the total number of logical paths is equal to $2(3n^2 - 2n)$. The application of the first method requires only verification that the outputs have the correct value one clock period after the application of the second test vector of each test vector pair. The application of the second method requires the measurement of the propagation delays along the selected paths, therefore the application of this method requires a more aggressive tester. However, for large values of n the number of test vector pairs required by the second method is significantly smaller than that required by the first method hence the second method is preferable. We present comparison results in Table 1.

Both methods give strong delay-verification test sets, therefore their application ensures that if the CUT functions correctly at a speed it will operate also correctly at all lower speeds.

Table 1. Comparison results.

MIN	Number of logical virtual paths T	Number of test sessions		Reduction		
		method one T_1	method two T_2	$\frac{T - T_1}{T}100\%$	$\frac{T - T_2}{T}100\%$	$\frac{T_1 - T_2}{T_1}100\%$
16x16	1472	92	26	93.75	98.23	71.74
32x32	6016	188	32	96.88	99.45	82.98
64x64	24320	380	38	98.44	99.85	90.00
128x128	97792	764	44	99.19	≈100	94.24
256x256	392192	1532	50	99.6	≈100	96.74
512x512	1570816	3068	56	99.8	≈100	98.17
1024x1024	6287360	6140	62	99.9	≈100	98.99

Table 2. Test vectors and established paths for 8x8 Omega network.

$S_0S_1S_2S_3S_4S_5S_6S_7$	$c_1c_2c_3$	Virtual paths
P T T T T T T T T*	0 0 0	S_0-D_0, S_1-D_1, S_2-D_2, S_3-D_3, S_4-D_4, S_5-D_5, S_6-D_6, S_7-D_7
T T T T T T T T	0 0 1	S_0-D_1, S_1-D_0, S_2-D_3, S_3-D_2, S_4-D_5, S_5-D_4, S_6-D_7, S_7-D_6
T T T T T T T T	0 1 0	S_0-D_2, S_1-D_3, S_2-D_0, S_3-D_1, S_4-D_6, S_5-D_7, S_6-D_4, S_7-D_5
T T T T T T T T	1 0 0	S_0-D_4, S_1-D_5, S_2-D_6, S_3-D_7, S_4-D_0, S_5-D_1, S_6-D_2, S_7-D_3
L 0 1 0 1 0 1 0 1	0 0 T	$c_{3,1}$-D_0, $c_{3,1}$-D_1, $c_{3,2}$-D_2, $c_{3,2}$-D_3, $c_{3,3}$-D_4, $c_{3,3}$-D_5, $c_{3,4}$-D_6, $c_{3,4}$-D_7
1 0 1 0 1 0 1 0	0 0 T	$c_{3,1}$-D_0, $c_{3,1}$-D_1, $c_{3,2}$-D_2, $c_{3,2}$-D_3, $c_{3,3}$-D_4, $c_{3,3}$-D_5, $c_{3,4}$-D_6, $c_{3,4}$-D_7
0 0 1 1 0 0 1 1	0 T 0	$c_{2,1}$-D_0, $c_{2,1}$-D_2, $c_{2,2}$-D_4, $c_{2,2}$-D_6, $c_{2,3}$-D_1, $c_{2,3}$-D_3, $c_{2,4}$-D_5, $c_{2,4}$-D_7
1 1 0 0 1 1 0 0	0 T 0	$c_{2,1}$-D_0, $c_{2,1}$-D_2, $c_{2,2}$-D_4, $c_{2,2}$-D_6, $c_{2,3}$-D_1, $c_{2,3}$-D_3, $c_{2,4}$-D_5, $c_{2,4}$-D_7
0 0 0 0 1 1 1 1	T 0 0	$c_{1,1}$-D_0, $c_{1,1}$-D_4, $c_{1,2}$-D_1, $c_{1,2}$-D_5, $c_{1,3}$-D_2, $c_{1,3}$-D_6, $c_{1,4}$-D_3, $c_{1,4}$-D_7
1 1 1 1 0 0 0 0	T 0 0	$c_{1,1}$-D_0, $c_{1,1}$-D_4, $c_{1,2}$-D_1, $c_{1,2}$-D_5, $c_{1,3}$-D_2, $c_{1,3}$-D_6, $c_{1,4}$-D_3, $c_{1,4}$-D_7

*T denotes a 0->1 and a 1->0 transition.

Although the analysis has been made using the nxn circuit-switched Omega network with centralized control, it is valid for all isomorphic to the Omega networks [12], that can be obtained by suitably permuting switching elements and associated links of the Omega network. As an example in Tables 2 and 3 we give the test vector pairs, derived from Method two for the 8x8 Omega and Generalized Cube (Figure 8) networks respectively. The virtual paths that are tested in any case can be different, hence the paths along which the propagation delays must be calculated from the measured delays are also different.

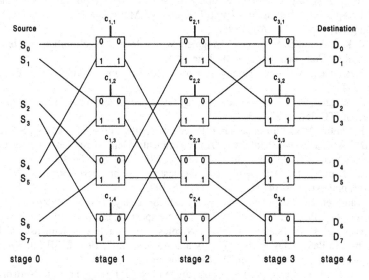

Fig. 8. 8x8 Generalized Cube Network

Table 3. Test vectors and established paths for 8x8 Generalized Cube network.

	$S_0S_1S_2S_3S_4S_5S_6S_7$	$c_1c_2c_3$	Virtual paths
P	T T T T T T T T	0 0 0	S_0-D_0, S_1-D_1, S_2-D_2, S_3-D_3, S_4-D_4, S_5-D_5, S_6-D_6, S_7-D_7
	T T T T T T T T	0 0 1	S_0-D_1, S_1-D_0, S_2-D_3, S_3-D_2, S_4-D_5, S_5-D_4, S_6-D_7, S_7-D_6
	T T T T T T T T	0 1 0	S_0-D_2, S_1-D_3, S_2-D_0, S_3-D_1, S_4-D_6, S_5-D_7, S_6-D_4, S_7-D_5
	T T T T T T T T	1 0 0	S_0-D_4, S_1-D_5, S_2-D_6, S_3-D_7, S_4-D_0, S_5-D_1, S_6-D_2, S_7-D_3
L	0 1 0 1 0 1 0 1	0 0 T	$c_{3,1}$-D_0, $c_{3,1}$-D_1, $c_{3,2}$-D_2, $c_{3,2}$-D_3, $c_{3,3}$-D_4, $c_{3,3}$-D_5, $c_{3,4}$-D_6, $c_{3,4}$-D_7
	1 0 1 0 1 0 1 0	0 0 T	$c_{3,1}$-D_0, $c_{3,1}$-D_1, $c_{3,2}$-D_2, $c_{3,2}$-D_3, $c_{3,3}$-D_4, $c_{3,3}$-D_5, $c_{3,4}$-D_6, $c_{3,4}$-D_7
	0 0 1 1 0 0 1 1	0 T 0	$c_{2,1}$-D_0, $c_{2,1}$-D_2, $c_{2,2}$-D_1, $c_{2,2}$-D_3, $c_{2,3}$-D_4, $c_{2,3}$-D_6, $c_{2,4}$-D_5, $c_{2,4}$-D_7
	1 1 0 0 1 1 0 0	0 T 0	$c_{2,1}$-D_0, $c_{2,1}$-D_2, $c_{2,2}$-D_1, $c_{2,2}$-D_3, $c_{2,3}$-D_4, $c_{2,3}$-D_6, $c_{2,4}$-D_5, $c_{2,4}$-D_7
	0 0 0 0 1 1 1 1	T 0 0	$c_{1,1}$-D_0, $c_{1,1}$-D_4, $c_{1,2}$-D_1, $c_{1,2}$-D_5, $c_{1,3}$-D_2, $c_{1,3}$-D_6, $c_{1,4}$-D_3, $c_{1,4}$-D_7
	1 1 1 1 0 0 0 0	T 0 0	$c_{1,1}$-D_0, $c_{1,1}$-D_4, $c_{1,2}$-D_1, $c_{1,2}$-D_5, $c_{1,3}$-D_2, $c_{1,3}$-D_6, $c_{1,4}$-D_3, $c_{1,4}$-D_7

The application of the proposed methods to a wider class of MINs (for example Delta and Banyan MINs) as well as their extension for path delay fault diagnosis are under investigation.

References

1. H. J. Siegel, *Interconnection Networks for Large-Scale Parallel Processing*, 2nd ed., New York: McGraw-Hill, 1990.
2. T. Feng, "A survey of Interconnection Networks", Computer, pp. 12–27, December 1981.
3. D. P. Agrawal, "Testing and Fault Tolerance of Multistage Interconnection Networks", Computer, pp. 41 – 53, April 1982.
4. V. P. Kumar and S. M. Reddy, "Augmented shuffle-exchange multistage interconnection networks", Computer, pp. 30 – 40, June 1987.
5. Z. Brasilai and B. Rosen, "Comparison of ac self-testing procedures", Proc. of ITC-83, pp. 560-571.
6. K. D. Wagner, "The error latency of delay faults in combinational and sequential circuits", Proc. of ITC-85, pp. 334 - 341.
7. G. L. Smith, "Model for delay faults based upon paths", Proc. of ITC-85, pp. 342 - 349.
8. J. D. Lesser and J. J. Shedletsky, "An Experimental Delay Test Generator for LSI Logic", IEEE Trans. on Computers, vol. C-29 (3), pp. 235 – 248, March 1980.
9. W. K. Lam, et al., "Delay fault coverage, test set size and performance trade-offs", IEEE Trans. on CAD, vol. 14 (1), pp. 32 - 44, Jan. 1995.
10. S. Tani, et al., "Efficient Path Selection for Delay Testing Based on Partial Path Evaluation", Proc. of 16th IEEE VLSI Test Symposium, pp. 188 - 193, 1998.
11. T. Haniotakis, Y. Tsiatouhas and D. Nikolos, "C-Testable One-Dimensional ILAs with Respect to Path Delay Faults : Theory and Applications", 1998 IEEE Int. Symposium on Defect and Fault Tolerance in VLSI Systems, pp. 155 - 163.
12. C. Wu and T. Feng, "On a Class of Multistage Interconnection Networks", IEEE Transactions on Computers, vol. C-29 (8), pp. 694 – 702, August 1980.
13. M. A. Franklin, D.F. Wann and W.J. Thomas, "Pin Limitations and partitioning of VLSI Interconnection Networks", IEEE Trans. on Computers, vol. C-31, pp. 1109 – 1116, November 1982.
14. C. J. Lin and S. M. Reddy, "On Delay Fault Testing in Logic Circuits", IEEE Trans. on CAD, pp. 694 – 703, September 1987.
15. K. Pramanick and S. M. Reddy, "On the Design of Path Delay Fault Testable Combinational Circuits", Proc. of Fault Tolerant Computing, pp. 374 – 381, 1990.
16. J. Lin, S. M. Reddy and S. Patil, "An Automatic Test Pattern Generator for the Detection of Path Delay Faults", Proc. of Int'l Conf. on CAD, pp. 284 – 287, 1987.
17. W. Ke and P. R. Menon, "Synthesis of Delay – Verifiable Combinational Circuits", IEEE Trans. on Computers, pp. 213 – 222, Feb. 1995.
18. H. S. Stone, "Parallel Processing with the perfect shuffle", IEEE Trans. on Computers, vol.C-20, pp. 153 - 161, 1971.

Diagnostic Model and Diagnosis Algorithm of a SIMD Computer

Stefano Chessa[1,2], Balázs Sallay[1], and Piero Maestrini[1]

[1] Istituto di Elaborazione dell'Informazione del CNR, Pisa, Italy
[2] Dipartimento di Matematica, University of Trento, Italy

Abstract. Self-diagnosis of systems comprising large numbers of processors has been studied extensively in the literature. The APEmille SIMD machine, a project of the National Institute of Nuclear Physics (INFN) of Italy, was offered as a test bed for a self-diagnosis strategy based on a comparison model.

Because of the general machine architecture and some design constraints, the standard assumptions of the existing diagnosis models are not completely fulfilled by the diagnosis support built in APEmille. This circumstance led to the development of a specific diagnostic model derived from the PMC and comparison models. The new model introduces the concept of direction-related and direction-independent faults.

The consistency of this model with the APEmille architecture is discussed, and possible fault scenarios which are particularly critical for the correctness of the diagnosis are examined. It is shown that the limited hardware redundancy, extended with simple functional tests, is sufficient for obtaining valid diagnosis with the presented model.

1 Introduction

Fault-tolerance is a stringent requirement for systems which perform critical tasks that must be completed without errors. In most cases, this does not apply to general purpose computers as the reliability of present day machines is satisfactory. However, massive parallel systems are a notable exception. If we consider a parallel machine composed of thousands of processors, each having a *Mean Time Between Failures* (MTBF) of 10 years, the MTBF of the entire machine could be as small as a few days. Since massively parallel systems are used to perform huge computations that may require several days or weeks, fault-tolerance becomes a vital requirement. In such an environment, techniques involving hardware or data replication are too expensive, and those based on system-level diagnosis appear to be good alternatives.

System-level diagnosis was introduced by Preparata, Metze, and Chien [1]. They proposed a model (hereafter referred as the *PMC model*) of systems composed of several units, capable of testing each other along system interconnections. The test of unit v, performed by unit u, proceeds as follows:

– u sends a test input sequence to v;

- v performs a test program using the input sequence and sends the results to u;
- u compares the results provided by v with the expected results and produces the test outcome. The test outcome is binary: 0 if the test passes and 1 if it fails.

Observe that a test requires a bi-directional connection between u and v.

Assuming permanent faults, each unit can be either faulty or fault-free. The tests performed by fault-free units are always reliable, while the tests performed by faulty units are unreliable. This test invalidation rule is summarized in Table 1. A different invalidation rule, known as the *BGM model*, assumes that tests of faulty units are also reliable even if executed by faulty units [2].

Table 1. The PMC invalidation rule

tester unit	tested unit	outcome
fault-free	fault-free	0
fault-free	faulty	1
faulty	fault-free	any
faulty	faulty	any

Comparison models are another derivation of the PMC model, suitable for the case where the units comprising the system are identical. Here, the outputs of the units can be compared by comparators, and the diagnosis algorithm derives the system diagnosis from the comparison results [3]. Comparison-based diagnosis has been studied extensively also in view of application to wafer-scale testing [4, 5], and it has been shown that it can tolerate faults affecting comparators [6].

In the PMC model, as well as in its derivations, the set of the test outcomes, called the *syndrome* of the system, is collected by a reliable external diagnoser (*centralized diagnosis*) which executes a diagnosis algorithm aimed at identifying the faulty units. An extensive survey on system-level diagnosis can be found in [7].

In this paper we discuss the application of the system-level diagnosis approach to the APEmille massively parallel machine [8,9], which is the latest member of the APE family, now next to the assembly and test stage before the final release. The APE family has been developed mainly to solve some theoretical physics problems which require massive computations like the *Lattice Gauge Theory* [10]. This problem, requiring massive floating-point computations that can be easily parallelized, has led to the development of dedicated parallel processors. The APE family has been one of the most significant developments in this area.

The complexity of the computations involved in such problems may easily require several days or weeks even in such a high-performance environment, thus we may expect that multiple faults occur during a single job execution. For this reason, APEmille was chosen as an ideal test bed for the application of self-diagnosis strategy. A preliminary proposal to this purpose had already appeared in [11]. It was foreseen that self-diagnosis could be implemented in *diagnosis sessions* preceding or interrupting job execution. Diagnosis sessions involve mutual tests of processors in order to provide a syndrome to be collected by the host computer, which, in turn, executes the diagnosis algorithm. After the faulty components are identified and replaced, the current job is resumed using a suitable recovery strategy. Following this proposal, the APEmille processors were designed to incorporate both customary fault detecting and correcting features based on data encoding, which had already been exploited in the previous members of the APE family, and additional hardware supports aimed at executing the tests needed by the self-diagnosis algorithm.

This paper reviews such hardware supports and some relevant hardware features of the forthcoming machine. Based on the actual design, it revises the diagnostic model and the diagnosis algorithm of the preliminary proposal, matching the abstract model with the real machine implementation.

2 Diagnosis of Regular Systems

In general, a diagnosis algorithm partitions the set $\mathcal{N}$ of the system component units into three sets: $\mathcal{K}, \mathcal{F}, \mathcal{U}$ of units identified by the algorithm as fault-free, faulty, and suspect, respectively. If $\mathcal{N}_f$ is the actual fault set, the diagnosis is said to be *correct* if $\mathcal{F} \subseteq \mathcal{N}_f$ and $\mathcal{K} \subseteq \mathcal{N} - \mathcal{N}_f$, and it is said to be complete if $\mathcal{U} = \emptyset$ (i.e. $\mathcal{K} \cup \mathcal{F} = \mathcal{N}$).

The *diagnosability* of a system is defined as the maximum number of faults for which a correct and complete diagnosis is always obtainable regardless of which components are affected by these faults. The classical theory of system-level diagnosis states that the diagnosability is upper-bounded by the minimum indegree of the units in the system [1]. However, in most practical cases, the interconnection structure of the system only allows each unit to be tested by a small number of neighbors. This is the case of regular or quasi-regular structures, where diagnosability is a small constant, although the number of units may become very large. In order to overcome this limitation, several recent papers [12–14] use a probabilistic approach to ensure a diagnosis which is correct with high probability, although possibly incomplete.

In [15,16] we proposed a different approach to achieve deterministic diagnosis correctness of two-dimensional toroidal grids. This approach can be easily extended to other regular interconnected systems like three-dimensional grids, hypercubes and so on. The diagnosis algorithm proceeds through three steps:

- In the first step (*Local Diagnosis*), it performs a preliminary classification of units exploiting tests between adjacent units.
  Initially, it builds set $\mathcal{F}$ of faulty units. If unit u tests an adjacent unit v as faulty but v tests u as fault-free, then v is faulty and it is put in set $\mathcal{F}$ by the diagnosis algorithm. Note that $\mathcal{F}$ may be empty at the end of this step.

Then the algorithm locates distinct pairs of units which are not yet classified and test each other as faulty. Such units are labelled as *dual* and put in set $\mathcal{D}$. With the construction of set $\mathcal{D}$ we trade a faulty unit for an unknown one, as one of them is surely faulty; this way, some faults are separated and more reliable assumptions can be made about the number of faults in the remaining part. All the other units are classified as Z and are put in set $\mathcal{Z}$. Adjacent Z-units test each other with 0 and must be in the same state (either faulty or fault-free).

– In the second step (*Fault-Free Core Identification*), adjacent Z-units are combined into Z-aggregates. A Z-aggregate contains units which are in the same state (all faulty or all fault-free), and is separated from the other Z-aggregates by faulty and dual units. The Fault-Free Core *FFC* is defined as the union of Z-aggregates of maximum cardinality.

– The last step (*Augmentation*) exploits the tests executed by the units in the FFC to recursively expand the FFC by attaching dual units and other Z-aggragates. It also identifies other faulty units.

The diagnosis algorithm is correct if the FFC is non-empty and actually fault-free. Given a syndrome σ, the minimum number of faults which might cause an incorrect diagnosis is given by $T_\sigma = \#\mathcal{F} + \frac{1}{2}\#\mathcal{D} + \alpha$, where $\#$ denotes the cardinality of a set and α is the maximum cardinality of the Z-aggregates. T_σ is asserted by the algorithm itself, and it can be compared with the expected number of faults to decide if the diagnosis is acceptable.

Exploiting certain topological properties of two-dimensional toroidal grids, it is proven that, for any syndrome, a lower bound to T_σ is given by the syndrome-independent bound $T(n) \in \Theta(n^{\frac{2}{3}})$, where n is the number of units in the system [16].

This algorith can be easily adapted to perform comparison-based diagnosis. In this case, it would use the following assumptions:

1. If the output sequences of two units, performing the same job on the same data set, are identical (i.e. they are compared with 0), they are both faulty or they are both fault-free. We will call such units 0-connected units.
2. If the output sequences of two units disagree, at least one of the units is faulty. We will call such units 1-connected units.

To obtain a correct diagnosis, it is generally enough to ensure that Assumption 1 is true. With Assumption 1 it is possible to *aggregate* a block of 0-connected units, since all units in the block must be in the same state. The use of Assumption 2 usually increases the completeness of the diagnosis through the Augmentation step. Note that the identification of faulty units in the Local Diagnosis is no longer possible, therefore set $\mathcal{F}$ will be always empty at the end of this step.

3 APEmille Architecture

APEmille is a *SIMD* machine in the teraflop range. It consists of up to 4096 processing elements which execute the same task synchronously. Each processing element (*Jmille*) consists of a processor unit incorporating a large register file and its private memory. Jmille performs floating-point arithmetic operations in single and double precision, as well as logical operations. Instructions are either register-to-register operations or memory accesses.

The instruction flow to Jmilles is provided by an instruction processor, called *Tmille*. Tmille controls the sequence of instructions and it is also able to perform integer operations to manipulate its control variables. Jmille processors communicate through communication units, called *Cmille*, which implement a logical scheme where the Jmilles are interconnected in a three-dimensional torus. Each Jmille is identified by a triple (x, y, z) of integers corresponding to its position, and it is connected to six neighbors. Two routing styles are implemented by the Cmille units: *rigid* and *broadcast*.

- **Rigid** : Each Jmille (x, y, z) sends data to a destination $(x + \Delta x, y + \Delta y, z + \Delta z)$, where the offset vector $(\Delta x, \Delta y, \Delta z)$ is the same for all Jmilles.
- **Broadcast** : A single Jmille is the source and all the other Jmilles are the destinations. A broadcast can also be two-dimensional: in this case the grid is partitioned into planes, each plane having a different source. Similarly, a single-dimensional broadcast is also possible.

The physical architecture of APEmille differs from its logical architecture in several points. The main difference is that the APEmille is actually a three-dimensional toroidal grid of clusters, where each cluster is composed of eight Jmille, one Tmille, and one Cmille processors (Figure 1). The Tmille and Cmille provide instruction decoding and routing capabilities for the entire cluster. Every cluster is arranged on a single board. All Tmille processors are synchronized and distribute the same instruction sequence to the respective boards. This means that all Jmille processors in the machine are also synchronized and execute the same instruction sequence. Tmille processors also implement the communication between APEmille and the host computer.

Cmille units (and, consequently, boards) are connected as a three-dimensional torus, each Cmille being connected to six adjacent Cmilles by bi-directional buses along three directions (namely X^+, X^-, Y^+, Y^-, Z^+, and Z^-). The data sent along these buses are encoded with a single error correcting, double error detecting code (*EDAC*) [17].

Boards can be *wrapped* by setting an appropriate Cmille register. A wrapped board is logically disconnected from the other boards and behaves as if it were a small 2-ary three-dimensional hypercube.

Consider the following example of rigid communication. Let us assume an offset $(1, 0, 0)$ and consider in particular Jmilles $(0, 0, 0)$ and $(1, 0, 0)$, belonging to the same board. The communication proceeds as follows: Each Jmille sends the packet to the Cmille in its board. The packet sent by Jmille $(0, 0, 0)$ must be delivered to $(1, 0, 0)$ in the same board, so Cmille can start immediately the delivery. However, the packet sent by the Jmille $(1, 0, 0)$ must be sent to $(2, 0, 0)$, which belong to a different board. Therefore the packet sent by $(1, 0, 0)$ requires a remote communication with the adjacent Cmille along bus X^+, which is slower

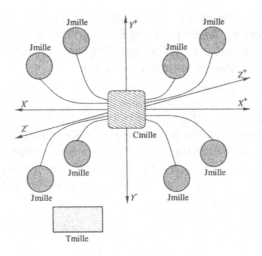

Fig. 1. APEmille cluster

than a local communication. This apparent contradiction with the SIMD model is solved by allowing the Cmille network to signal to Tmilles that the instruction flow must be stopped, until all the communications have been completed. The fetching of instructions is resumed when all packets have reached their destinations.

Another important difference between the physical and the logical architecture is that Cmille is actually partitioned into four slices. The slices are identical and perform the same task on different data sections. Every packet sent by a Jmille is partitioned into four distinct sections, and each slice implements the routing for one packet section.

The inter-board buses (X^+, X^-, Y^+, Y^-, Z^+, and Z^-) are also partitioned and each partition is managed by a slice.

APEmille can operate in three different modes. The *system mode* allows the host computer to access all the memories of APEmille to set up a new task or to read out the results at the end of a task. Once the program and the data have been written and the Cmille and Tmille registers have been set to initial values, the machine is set in *run mode* to execute the program. The third mode (*equal mode*) is used to perform self-test.

4   APEmille Diagnosis Support

The tests aimed at the self-diagnosis of APEmille are controlled by a test program which runs chiefly in equal mode and compares the data of adjacent Jmilles in a board (*intra-board test*) or that of two selected Jmilles (*witness Jmilles*) of adjacent boards (*inter-board test*). Before and after comparisons, the program runs in system mode in order to load Tmille processors with the test program and Jmille memories with identical data, and to read out results from the comparator registers, respectively. Since comparisons involve data transmitted along the buses, the inter-board tests consist of two phases. In the positive phase board (a, b, c) compares its own witness Jmille data with those of boards $(a - 1, b, c)$, $(a, b - 1, c)$, and $(a, b, c - 1)$, while in the negative phase they are confronted to the witness Jmille data of boards $(a + 1, b, c)$, $(a, b + 1, c)$, and $(a, b, c + 1)$. We allow that the program occasionally performs some dedicated tests on some critical hardware parts which affect the validity of the comparison results. The number of such 'non-comparison' tests should be minimized, since we do not aim at executing a thorough functional test at this level and environment.

After the test program is executed, the diagnosis algorithm transforms the set of individual comparator outputs and dedicated test results into an abstract, binary comparison outcome, and identifies the fault-free and faulty boards by considering these outcomes. It also reveals the confidence level of the diagnosis (the syndrome-dependent threshold T_σ) in terms of a minimal number of faults which would invalidate the diagnosis, if they were actually present in the system.

Self-diagnosis is a complement to a thorough functional test. This latter performs the board test in the conventional sense. It propagates precalculated test patterns for gate-level faults from the board input to the tested part, as well as the obtained output values of the tested part to the board output. The self-diagnosis operates at a higher level, and does not specify a gate-level fault model. Instead, it is based on assumptions about the possible comparison outcomes between boards which may contain faults.

Since some parts of the board are not activated at all in equal mode, we cannot expect the diagnostic algorithm to detect all faults in the system. Such faults are, for instance, those in the run-mode communication mode controller in the Cmille processor. Instead, we aim at the correct diagnosis of those general parts of the boards that have an effect on the comparison results. These parts include the Jmille processing units and the Tmille instruction decoding and sequencing units.

There are several kinds of hardware supports to deal with faults and errors occurring in the Tmille, Cmille, and Jmille subsystems. The main supports are embedded into the *Equal* module of Cmille. Since Cmille is four-sliced, the Equal module is replicated in every slice.

Some of the supports are aimed mainly at performing error detection and/or correction and are active in run mode, whereas other supports have been introduced for the purpose of self-diagnosis.

Error detection mechanisms: These mechanisms are active in run mode. When they detect a fault they raise an exception which stops the machine to allow the execution of a diagnosis session. They can be divided into two classes: Data encoding and Tmille fault-detection.

– Data encoding: As anticipated in Section 3, data stored in the memories and data sent along the buses connecting two boards or two units in the same board are encoded with an EDAC. Single errors are corrected, while double errors originate an exception.

The encoding is applied to individual data sections, to be managed by Cmille slices. Single errors are counted in a register, and Cmille raises an exception when this number reaches a certain threshold.

- Tmille fault-detection: When a Tmille fetches a new instruction from the program memory, it extracts a single bit signature from the memory EDAC, and sends it to every slice of the Cmille residing in the same board. Each slice delivers its copy of the signature to three slices in adjacent boards along either the positive or negative buses (e.g. X^+, Y^+, Z^+), and receives three signatures from the adjacent boards (in the above example, coming from the buses X^-, Y^-, Z^-).

Every slice performs comparisons between the signatures received from adjacent boards and the one generated in the board. The comparisons are performed by self-checking comparators [18]. In case of disagreement, the Cmille raises an exception which, if unmasked, stops the machine.

Observe that it is possible to mask all these exceptions and proceed with the computation. This is useful during the test sessions: the accumulated disagreements constitute a syndrome, which can be combined with the syndrome provided by the diagnosis mechanisms and decoded by a diagnosis algorithm.

Diagnosis mechanisms: These mechanisms are active only when APEmille is set to equal mode. This mode is used only for test purpose and enables comparisons between Jmilles. In the diagnosis session the Jmille processors are loaded with the same data and the same test program. If no faults occur, all the Jmilles read and write synchronously the same data, from, or into the respective memories. The equal mode provides two main features: the *Local Equal* and the *Remote Equal*. The Local Equal executes comparisons between Jmilles in the same board, and it is used to perform a preliminary diagnosis of the board. The Remote Equal performs comparisons between two witness Jmilles of adjacent boards, and the results of these comparisons provide a syndrome for the diagnosis algorithm.

Note that the exchange of data between Jmilles is disabled in both Local and Remote Equal in order to prevent fault propagation.

- Local Equal: In this mode every board is wrapped, the communications are disabled, and the Jmilles in each board are logically connected in a ring. When a Jmille reads data from its memory, it sends the data to the Cmille. Each Cmille slice receives a data section from each Jmille in the board, and compares data coming from Jmilles which are adjacent in the logical ring. For every memory read operation, every Cmille slice performs eight comparisons in parallel by means of self-checking comparators, and the comparison outcomes produced in the sequence are ORed in the slice register file. The individual slices of any Cmille compare different data sections provided by the same pair of adjacent Jmilles, which, however, can interchange data sections between slices by executing suitable shift operations. This technique can be used to ensure that, in different times, all the slices perform comparisons of the same data, and a single faulty slice cannot mask partial Jmille faults.

– Remote Equal: The Remote Equal performs comparisons between two witness Jmilles of adjacent boards. When the witness Jmille reads data from the local memory, it forwards the data to Cmille, which delivers them to three Cmilles in adjacent boards along either the positive or negative buses (the positive or negative buses can be selected dynamically by the test program), and receives from the opposite directions the data from the witness Jmilles of the adjacent boards. The received data are compared with the data provided by the witness Jmille in the board. The comparisons are executed by self-checking comparators and ORed in sequence in Cmille registers. Since Cmille is sliced, the comparators and the registers are replicated.

5 Diagnostic Model of APEmille

The self-diagnosis begins with an *intra-board diagnosis* phase which relies on the Local Equal tests. In this case, individual boards may declare themselves as faulty by comparing the data of the Jmilles constituting the board. One should not expect that a faulty board necessarily declares itself faulty, because a fault external to the Jmilles may mask Jmille faults or make the Jmilles behave equally. For example, a fault in the instruction decoding function of Tmille may cause the Jmilles to execute the same wrong instruction sequence during this phase. However, we expect that the intra-board diagnosis detects disagreements between Jmille units if the remainder of the board is fault-free.

A board failing the intra-board phase is immediately identified as faulty, and it will be treated accordingly by the algorithm presented in Section 2. If not fault-free, a board passing this phase can be faulty in the following ways:

– the Jmille units are affected by the same fault;
– there is a fault in the remainder of the board which masks Jmille faults;
– Jmilles are all fault-free, but a fault in the remainder of the board makes them behave the same wrong way.

The subsequent phases of the diagnosis algorithm exploit the results of the Remote Equal tests to decide whether the boards passing the intra-board phase are indeed fault-free. The following of this section deals with the invalidation model used in these phases of the self-diagnosis and with a diagnosis algorithm, derived from the original algorithm described in Section 2, which complies with this model.

The present implementation of APEmille prevents comparators, built in the Cmille slices, from observing a small part of the functionalities of the containing and the adjacent boards. This is somewhat different from the standard assumption of comparison models [3]. If faults occur in the unobservable parts, Assumption 1 of Section 2 may be violated, and this may lead to the aggregation of fault-free and faulty boards, thus causing a wrong diagnosis.

We examine what parts of the boards are outside the range of the comparators. In this analysis, we disregard occurring in path from the comparator outputs to the host reading the syndrome. Such faults are dangerous, but can be dealt with by introducing a suitable readout test, to be described later.

It should be observed that in the APEmille boards the hardware parts involved in a comparison depend on the direction of the comparison. A considerable part of the Cmille hardware are implemented in three copies, belonging to the X, Y, and Z directions, respectively. Thus, a number of faults affect comparison results in only one direction. In case a fault-free board does not detect a fault affecting a different direction in the adjacent board, like in the cases of Figure 2, the algorithm of Section 2 may base the diagnosis on false assumptions. In the example, the Y-directional part of board B is faulty (because of a comparator fault, for instance), thus the B-C comparison result is unreliable. However, if the remainder in board B is good, the entirely fault-free board A will assume that B is fault-free and handle its connections as they were its owns. Consequently, a comparison model-based algorithm may incorrectly conclude that boards A and C are in different states (case a), or in the same state (case b).

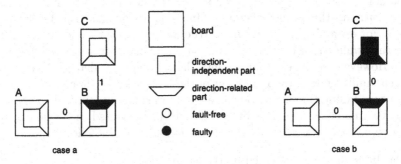

Fig. 2. Violation of Assumption 1

Unless a large number of non-diagnostic (i.e. not comparison-based) tests are devoted to faults affecting direction-related parts, it is practically impossible to avoid the risk that Assumption 1 be violated. Therefore we use a diagnosis model which is based on invalidation rules different from those of the standard comparison model. For this, we model the APEmille board as the union of four functions: a direction-independent core (basically, Tmille and the witness Jmille processors, and some Cmille parts), and direction-related parts, one for all the three directions. Similarly, we define direction-related and direction-independent faults, affecting these parts. We call a board strongly fault-free (SFF) if its direction-independent part and all its direction-related parts are fault-free. We call a board fault-free with respect to a δ direction (FF_δ, $\delta \in \{X, Y, Z\}$) if the direction-independent part and at least the direction-related part corresponding to δ are fault-free. Note that the model does not distinguish between the hardware parts dealing with the δ^+ and δ^- buses; they together constitute the δ direction-related part.

Given the previous definition, we use the following criterion as the basis for aggregation:

If the adjacent boards A and B are compared with a 0 result in a δ direction, then either

- *both A and B are FF_δ, or*
- *the direction-independent parts in both A and B are faulty.*

In other words, with at least one fault-free direction-independent part we will detect a direction-related fault affecting the direction of the actual comparison. Table 2 enlists possible states of two adjacent boards together with the outcomes allowed by the assumption. It should be observed that the invalidation rules of Table 2 are somewhat weaker than the original assumptions of the comparison model, because they allow that a fault-free board be connected with 0 to another board that is partly faulty. However, with respect to the δ direction it resembles the stronger BGM model [2], since in lines 2-5 they prescribe a 1 outcome even if both boards are faulty but at least one direction-independent part is fault-free. Section 6 discusses why this model is consistent with the actual hardware of APEmille.

Table 2. Assumed invalidation rule

	direction-independent part		δ direction-related part		allowed outcome
	of board A	of board B	of board A	of board B	in direction δ
1	fault-free	fault-free	fault-free	fault-free	0
2	fault-free	faulty	any	any	1
3	fault-free	fault-free	faulty	any	1
4	fault-free	fault-free	any	faulty	1
5	faulty	fault-free	any	any	1
6	faulty	faulty	any	any	0 or 1

Under the rules of Table 2, a board A that is 0-connected with 3 other boards along 3 distinct directions can be declared as strongly fault-free and the 3 adjacent boards as fault-free with respect to the direction of the test, otherwise all the 4 boards would be faulty (Figure 3). We will call such conditionally fault-free boards strongly zero (SZ) and weakly zero (WZ_δ) boards, respectively.

Consequently, a 0-connected block of SZ boards are all in the same state, either all fault-free or all faulty. The satisfactory condition for their fault-freeness is that the number of faults in that part does not exceed the number of SZ boards plus the number of WZ boards which are situated on the boundary of this block. Figure 4 shows such a block, for the sake of simplicity in two dimensions.

The property of Table 2 implicitly contains the assumption that a board that is influenced by a δ direction-related fault either outputs the same test responses

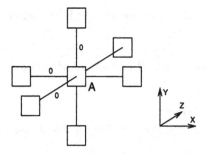

Fig. 3. Strongly zero board A

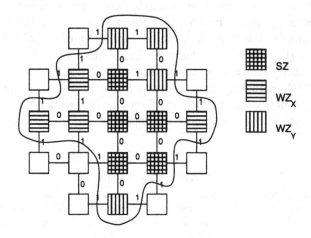

Fig. 4. Boards in identical state

to the δ^+ and δ^- buses during the positive and negative phases of the diagnostic test, or that its different responses, being a fault affecting the δ direction, are detected by a FF_δ neighbor. This would not be necessarily true, either, but a short dedicated test, as described in Section 6, will circumvent this problem.

Considering this feature, after the identification of the Fault-Free Core (FFC) of SFF and FF_δ boards the diagnosis algorithm can go further by extending the FFC: if a board A within the FFC is FF_δ and is 0-connected to the FFC in the direction δ, then the 1-comparison on the other side of A is reliable. According to this, we can identify board B in Figure 5/b and 5/c as faulty, but we cannot do this in Figure 5/a. Moreover, we can sometimes estimate to what extent board B is faulty: in case c the direction-independent part of board B is faulty, otherwise it could not produce a 0 result on the opposite side in the δ direction; however, in case b it is possible that only the δ direction-related part of board B is faulty, the general parts being fault-free.

It should be observed that extension rules slightly differ when we consider cable faults between boards in the model. In this case, a 1 result between boards A and B of Figure 5/c does not imply necessarily that the direction-independent

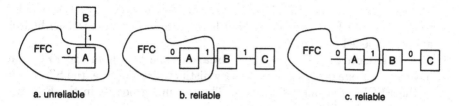

Fig. 5. Reliable and unreliable 1-connections

parts of boards B and C would be faulty, but the cable between A and B can be faulty as well. By replacing the suspicious cable and repeating the self-diagnosis we can obtain more informative results. In addition, it is possible that the diagnosis ends with one or more pairs of adjacent strongly fault-free boards, still comparing each other with outcome 1. In this case, unless all boards in the FFC are actually faulty (which however can be excluded if the number of faults in the system is below T_σ), this means that the link connecting the two boards must be faulty.

5.1 Diagnosis Algorithm for APEmille

After the test program for the intra-board and inter-board tests are executed, the syndrome is downloaded to the host computer which generates the abstract inter-board comparison result, as explained in Section 6. With respect to the algorithm described in Section 2, we add a preliminary phase of intra-board diagnosis, and we modify the Fault-Free Core Identification and the Augmentation steps according to the proposed model. The diagnosis algorithm proceeds as follows:

1. **Intra-board Diagnosis.** The boards passing the intra-board diagnosis are labelled as Z (zero), whereas failing boards are labelled as F (faulty).
2. **Local Diagnosis.** Adjacent 1-connected Z-boards are classified in distinct pairs and are labelled as D (dual) in the same way as described in Section 2.
3. **Fault-Free Core Identification.** 0-connected Z-boards are combined into Z-aggregates. Z-boards having no 0-connected Z neighbors become Z-aggregates of cardinality 1. The Fault-Free Core (*FFC*) is defined as the union of Z-aggregates of maximum cardinality. The FFC is non-empty and contains only fault-free direction-independent parts if the number of faults does not exceed a syndrome-dependent bound T_σ [16]. The boards in the FFC are labelled as FF.
4. **Augmentation.** First, the FFC is extended recursively by appending D-boards and other Z-aggregates which are 0-connected to at least one FF board. Then the set of faulty boards is extended. If a board in the FFC has a 0-connection on one side but 1 on the opposite side of the same direction, the neighbor connected with 1 is faulty (see Figure 5) and is labelled as F. Here we assume that suspicious cables have already been replaced. If the faulty board is 0-connected with another board at the opposite side of the given direction, the direction-independent part of it is faulty, and is labelled

as FDI. Last, the set of faulty units are further extended in a way similar to the recursive FFC expansion: boards that are 0-connected to FDI boards are also labelled as FDI.

5. **Classification of** SFF **and** FF_δ **boards.** The boards in the FFC that have at least one 0-connection in every distinct direction (i.e. the SZ boards of the FFC) are strongly fault-free. The remaining boards in the FFC are not necessarily SFF.

6. **Final conclusions.** SFF boards are fault-free, F and FDI boards are faulty. Boards labelled FF are known to be fault-free in the direction-independent part, and possibly faulty in some direction-related part. If there are boards labelled D or Z, the diagnosis is incomplete and these boards are suspects.

6 Compliance of the Model with the APEmille Hardware

In this section we explain why it is reasonable to apply the diagnostic model, described in the previous section, in the actual environment of APEmille diagnosis.

6.1 Test Outcome Generation of the Result Set

The abstract comparison result assumed by the model is a binary outcome, actually constructed by combining information obtained from 8 slice comparators (4 for each board) and from other diagnosis-related checks. The outcome is derived as follows:

- If any one of the built-in error detection mechanisms signals an on-line error, the abstract outcome related to one direction or to all directions will be 1, depending whether the problem affects only one direction or the direction-independent part of the board. For example, a mismatch in any copy of a comparator register bit is direction-related, whereas an error detected by the Tmille memory EDAC is a general error.
- If any one of the dedicated tests fail, the connection checked by the test will convey a 1 abstract result. These tests are explained in the next section.
- If any one of the eight comparator registers contains 1, the abstract result will be 1.

6.2 Consistency with the Hardware Design

In order to comply with the diagnostic assumptions described in Section 5, the diagnostic test should satisfy the following requirements:

I. If two adjacent boards are connected with 0, then both boards are fault-free with respect to the direction of the connection, or both contain faulty direction-independent parts.

II. A faulty board should produce the same test responses during the positive and negative phases of the test. This could be regarded as a special case of the first requirement, but we treat this problem with special attention.

The way these requirements are satisfied is rather a practical issue than an algorithm-related one. We still discuss possible problems here in some detail to justify our assumptions by enlisting the situations that may violate them. We explain briefly how they are prevented by the replicated design of Cmille or detected by additional functional tests. A large part of possible faults are automatically covered by the redundant 4-sliced design of the Cmille unit, under the reasonably safe assumption that at least one of the 8 Cmille slices in any two compared boards works correctly. The Jmille test program shifts Jmille data systematically, so that possibly faulty fragments can reach every slice. Among the fault scenarios, however, there are some that either affect non-replicated parts of the board or violate the rules of Table 2 even if they affect only one slice.

The following problems affect Assumption I:

- *The 1 comparison result is properly generated in the comparison register, but a fault in the Cmille slice or the Tmille processor prevents reading them out.* We assign a test to this problem which loads data into the witness Jmilles so that every adjacent board have different data, in a way similar to a 3D-chessboard. Performing operations in equal mode should set the comparator registers, thus, after reading out the register contents, we can check if they can be set and read out.

- *Disagreements between Jmille outputs can be masked by faults in the data paths of the Cmille equal module.* Consider two Cmille slices of two adjacent boards, as illustrated in Figure 6. Faults affecting part a are indistinguishable from Jmille faults, therefore they will not invalidate the diagnosis. On the other hand, identical faults either at locations b and d or at b and c' may produce a 0 result when a fault-free and a faulty direction-independent part or two fault-free such parts are confronted, which result should be 1 even if there are direction-related faults. These faults are especially dangerous because they have a local effect on only one Cmille slice. However, we can extend the above described functional test to cover this type of faults with suitable test patterns that depend on the used fault model. A Jmille may fail to provide the required test patterns, but in this case another, fault-free Cmille slice will signal the difference. This test extension increases somewhat the required number of read-out operations, but it still remains a small constant.

- *The comparators or comparator registers are faulty.* The APEmille architecture provides a 3-fold protection against these faults: the redundancy of the four-slice Cmille implementation, the self-checking and redundant design of the comparators and comparator registers, and the described dedicated test, which is an exhaustive test for the comparators as well.

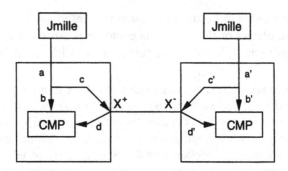

Fig. 6. Cmille data path problems

Furthermore, we must ensure that a faulty board produces the same outputs during the positive and negative phases of the test in a given direction. This could be violated due to direction decoding faults or bus driver stuck-at faults: if such a fault affects one or more bits, then the board sometimes sends data to the wrong direction or does not send any data when it should. For example, if in Figure 7 everything is fault-free except that board B is unable to send data to the negative direction on a given bit, the positive phase of the diagnostic test will conclude with 0s in all the comparator registers, because the fault is not activated. In the negative phase, however, board A will detect that board B is faulty but the B-C comparison remains 0, so the diagnostic algorithm may run into contradictions. To avoid this problem, we extend the dedicated test with a phase when the transmitting capabilities of the boards are tested: we send a certain codeword and its bitwise complement to the positive direction, and we check in the next board if they arrive. Next, we repeat this test in the negative directions.

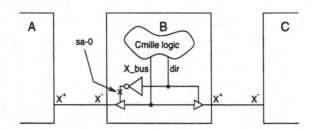

Fig. 7. Problems with direction control

7 Conclusion and Further Work

The present paper has described a self-diagnosis approach in a practical environment where the abstraction level of the existing diagnostic model is not adequate.

A more detailed comparison-based diagnostic model has been presented which takes into account the circumstance that comparison results do not necessarily depend on the state of the entire board. It has been described how the actual implementation complies with the abstract model, and a short dedicated test session has been given to cover certain fault scenarios which could otherwise violate the new model.

The relation between the abstract model and the physical implementation has now been analyzed by considering a number of possible situations that could endanger the applicability of the model. The research is continuing with the goal of validating the preceding analysis by means of VHDL simulation, using fault injection based on a gate-level fault model. The field application to APEmille is planned for the near future.

References

1. Preparata, F., P, Metze, G., and Chien, R., T., "On the Connection Assignment Problem of Diagnosable Systems". IEEE Transactions on Computers, Vol. EC-16, No. 12, pp. 848-854, December 1967.

2. Barsi, F., Grandoni, F., and Maestrini, P., "A Theory of Diagnosability of Digital Systems". IEEE Transactions on Computers, Vol. C-25, No. 6, pp. 585-593, June 1976.

3. Malek, M., "A Comparison Connection Assignment for Diagnosis of Multiprocessor Systems", Proceedings of the 10th Symposium on Computer Architecture, pp. 31-35, May 1980.

4. Rangarajan, S., Fussel, D., and Malek, M., "Built-in Testing of Integrated Circuit Wafers, IEEE Transactions on Computers, Vol. 39, No. 2, pp. 195-205, February 1990.

5. Chessa, S., and Maestrini, M., "Self-Test of integrated Circuit Wafers", Proceedings of European Test Workshop, Sete, France, June 1996, pp.54-58.

6. Sallay, B., Maestrini, P., and Santi, P., "A Comparison-Based Diagnosis Algorithm Tolerating Comparator Faults", to appear in IEE Proceedings on Computers and Digital Techniques.

7. Barborak, M., Malek, M., and Dahbura, A., T., "The Consensus Problem in Fault-Tolerant Computing", ACM Computing Surveys, Vol. 25, No. 2, pp. 171-220, June 1993.

8. Tripiccione, R., "Ape100 and beyond", International Journal on Modern Physics, sec.C vol.4, 1993, pp.13-23.

9. Bartoloni, A., Battista, C., Cabasino, S., Cosimi, M., D'Agostini, U., Marzano, F., Panizzi, E., Paolucci, P.S., Rapuano, F., Rinaldi, W., Sarno, R., Todesco, G.M., Torelli, M., Vicini, P., Cabibbo, N., Fucci, A. and Tripiccione, R., "APEmille: a Parallel Processor in the Teraflops Range", INFN report, March 1995.

10. Shigemitsu, J., "Lattice Gauge Theory: A Status Report", Proceedings of the XXVII International Conference on High Energy Physics (edited by P. J. Bussey and I. G. Knowles). Institute of Physics Publishing, 1995, pp. 135- 156.

11. Aglietti, F., Centurioni, E, Chessa, S., D'Auria, I., Franzinelli, F, Maestrini, P., Michelotti, A., Pagliai, I., and Tripiccione, R., "Self-Diagnosis of APEmille", Proceedings of EDCC-2 Conference on Dependable Computing, Gliwice, Poland, May 1996, pp. 73-84.

12. Somani, A., K. and Agarwal, V., K., "Distributed Diagnosis Algorithm for Regular Interconnected Systems", IEEE Transactions on Parallel and Distributed Systems, Vol. 41, No. 7, pp. 899-906, July 1992.

13. LaForge, L., E., Huang, K., and Agarwal, V., K., "Almost Sure Diagnosis of Almost Every Good Element", IEEE Transactions on Computers, Vol. 43, No. 3, pp. 295-305, March 1994.

14. Huang, K., Agarwal, V.K., LaForge, L., and Thulasiraman, K., "A Diagnosis Algorithm for Constant Degree Structures and Its Application to VLSI Circuit Testing", IEEE Transactions on Parallel and Distributed Systems, Vol. 44 No. 4, pp. 363-372, April 1995.

15. Maestrini, P. and Santi, P., "Self-Diagnosis of Processor Arrays Using a Comparison Model", Proceedings of the 14th SRDS-Symposium on Reliable and Distributed Systems, Bad Neuenahr, Germany, September 1995, pp. 218-228.

16. Chessa, S., Self-Diagnosis of Grid Interconnected Systems, with Application to Self-Test of VLSI Wafers, PhD Thesis, Dipartimento di Informatica, Università di Pisa, January 1999.

17. Peterson, W. W. and Weldon, E. J., Error Correcting Codes, Boston, MIT Press, 1972.

18. Siewiorek, D. P. and Swarz, R. S., The Theory and Practice of Reliable System Design, Bedford, MS, Digital Press, 1982.

Session 8

Built-In Self-Test

Chair: Bernd Straube, Fraunhofer Gesellschaft, Institute for Integrated Circuits, Germany

Pseudorandom, Weighted Random and Pseudoexhaustive Test Patterns Generated in Universal Cellular Automata

Ondřej Novák

Technical University Liberec, Hálkova 6, 461 17 Liberec I,
Czech Republic
tel.: + 420 48 53553460,   fax: + 420 48 5353112 e-mail: ondrej.novak@vslib.cz

Abstract. The paper presents a design method for Built-In Self Test (BIST) that uses a cellular automaton (CA) for test pattern generation. We have extensively studied the quality of generated patterns and we have found several interesting properties of them. The first possibility how to use the CA is to generate pseudoexhaustive test sets as the CA can generate code words of codes with higher minimal code distance of the dual code. There is no need of reseeding the CA in order to generate all the code words. This type of test set can be advantageously used for testing with low number of inputs and low size of cones in the circuits under test (CUT). The proposed CA can also generate weighted random patterns with different global weights which can be used instead of linear feedback shift register (LFSR) pseudorandom sequences, the fault coverage is higher. It can also be used as deterministic pattern compactor in mixed mode testing. The generated sequence can be also easily used for testing CUTs with input-oriented weighted random patterns. The CA is formed by T flip-flops and does not contain any additional logic in the feedback. We proposed a new scheme of BIST where the CA is a part of a modified scan chain. Several experiments were done with ISCAS 85 and 89 benchmark circuits. We compared the quality of the generated test patterns with the quality of the patterns generated in an LFSR .

Key words: Cellular automata, BIST, linear cyclic codes, linear feedback shift registers, hardware test pattern generators, weighted random testing, pseudoexhaustive testing

1 Introduction

Built-in self-test (BIST) is a concept useful for testing the VLSI circuits, where it solves the problem of limited access to the circuit-under-test (CUT), offers on-line and in-line applicability of the test sets and very radically reduces the amount of output information - see e.g. [16]. To implement BIST, we must embed both the test pattern generator (TPG) and output data compactor into the structure of the CUT which naturally imposes limits on their size, complexity and level of control which may lead to a loss of fault coverage. Our task was to find BIST structures and their function algorithms, which will guarantee the required level of fault coverage when observing the simplicity requirements.

The techniques for hardware test pattern generation can be classified in the following groups: pseudoexhaustive testing [22], pseudorandom testing [1], weighted random testing [22], deterministic tests [5] and mixed mode pattern generation [13], [12].

A pseudoexhaustive or (n,w)-exhaustive test set is a sequence of n-bit input vectors which exercises every w-bit subset of CUT inputs feeding one output with 2^w different binary patterns. It can be generated e.g. by a built-in test pattern generator using a linear feedback shift register (LFSR) [22] or cellular automaton (CA) [18]. It was proved by simulation of the ISCAS benchmark circuits, that the effectiveness of the pseudoexhaustive testing is limited on the cases of CUT with small number of inputs and small values of w.

The mixed mode pattern generation consists in generation of a given number of pseudorandom patterns and after it in exercising the CUT with deterministic test vectors. The deterministic vectors have to detect random resistant faults.

It was shown that for a substantial part of designed circuits it is practically impossible to detect all faults by a pseudorandom test set. One way how to improve the fault coverage and or to reduce the number of generated test patterns is to generate weighted random patterns. There exist a relatively large number of proposals [2, 17, 23, ...] how an optimized set of weights can be determined such that the required number of random patterns is minimized. Usually the input-oriented weight computation is used, the resulting test set has different probabilities of zeros and ones for each CUT input. This approach is very efficient but in the case of hardware test pattern generation it demands quite a lot of additional hardware .

In [15] it was shown that it could be very efficient to calculate and apply global weights for weighted random testing (pattern oriented WRT). By the term global weight we mean the ratio between ones and zeros in a test pattern. This kind of testing means that the weights are not input-oriented but they are common for CUT inputs. During testing there are generated several pattern subsets with different weights. This approach provides lower hardware overhead and shorter computational time which is necessary for estimating the optimal weights. The method uses single LFSR for generation of patterns with the probability of ones equal to 0.5, weight computational block for deriving patterns with modified weights and a multiplexer which switches between patterns with different weights. The multiplexer is controlled by a counter which enables us to generate in one test set patterns with different weights. The output of the multiplexer feeds the scan chain of a CUT.

Cellular automata (CA) can be seen as a tool for decomposing a system into very simple elementary units (cells) which are very well suited for implementation in VLSI circuits, above all due to the uniformity of the cells and due to the locality of connections [3]. Among the recently identified fields of their application, the test pattern generation plays an important role.

In [24] the CA formed by T flip-flops was designed. It generates primitive polynomial code sequences for the polynomials which have the form $p(x) = 1 + x^{n-1} + x^n$. In [8], there is introduced a method how to transform the primitive polynomial LFSR sequences into sequences with the same period which can be generated with the help of cyclic CA which can be formed by D and T flip-flops without any combination logic between the flip-flops. These CA could be used as pseudo random test pattern generators.

The cellular automata were proposed to be used in BIST in [11]. It is shown there, that the random properties of the CA outputs are better than those of LFSRs. CA were used in [6] for testing circuits with boundary scan and in [7] for testing the sequential circuits. Several experiments with the benchmark circuits were done, the fault coverage was higher for the case of CA, the testability of delay faults was higher than in the case of using LFSRs.

In this paper we introduce a new universal scheme which can be used both for pseudoexhaustive, weighted random pattern generation and compressing the deterministic patterns. Instead of using an external LFSR for pattern generation we modify the scan chain in such a way that it forms a CA. The CA can be used for generating code words of chosen code with greater minimal code distance of its dual code or for generating non code words. The CA can generate all code words after seeding with one seed only, usually it can generate the same number of non code words after seeding with one non code seed, too. We have verified that the quality of generated test patterns is better than the quality of the patterns generated in the LFSR with primitive polynomial.

In the following section the design of the CA will be introduced. An analysis of the CA parallel output sequences can be found in section 3. In section 4, the proposed arrangement of BIST using the CA is presented. In section 5, experimental data underline the efficiency of the proposed method. In section 6 we compare hardware overhead for LFSR and CA test pattern generation. In section 7 we summarize the results.

2 Linear Code Based Test Pattern Generation

In the following we will be referring alternatively to a vector or code word or polynomial, taking into account that every vector $r = (r_0, r_1, ..., r_n)$ can be associated with a polynomial $r(x) = r_0 + r_1 x + ... + r_n x^n$.

An m-bit LFSR serially generates code words of a cyclic code $N=(n,k)$, $k=n-m$. If the minimal code distance of the dual code is d_{min}, then the code words of the code N form an (n,w)-exhaustive test set, where $w = d_{min}-1$, the LFSR has to be seeded with several seeds, see [20]. The problem of great number of seeds for $d_{min}>3$ is solved by using an n-stage LFSR in [22]. This method is based on the use of an n-bit LFSR which has a feedback connected in accordance with a polynomial $g(x) = p(x)c(x)$, where $p(x)$ is a primitive polynomial of degree m and $c(x)$ is a generator polynomial of an (n,k) code. When an (n,k) code word is used as a seed, all code words are generated during one LFSR period. Another solution of this problem was shown in [9], using only an m-stage LFSR with additional non-linear feedback. The LFSR has a linear feedback connected according to a non-primitive irreducible polynomial with roots of nth order. The non-linear feedback enables after finishing an LFSR cycle to add two code words of just generated code cycle. The modified LFSR can in some cases generate after being initiated with a nonzero seed all 2^m-1 different nonzero code words.

Further we develop another method of linear code generation. This method does not use any XOR in feedback and all the code words of a code with non primitive but irreducible polynomial can be generated in a CA after seeding with one vector only.

2.1 Properties of code sequences generated in LFSRs

As a first step, let us consider an m-bit serial LFSR with the XOR gates in the feedback which performs division by an irreducible polynomial $g(x)$ of the degree m (An example for $m=8$ is given in Fig.1).

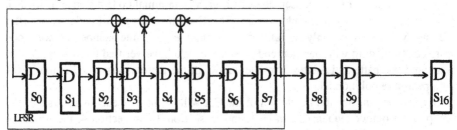

Fig. 1. An 8-bit LFSR created by D flip-flops with XOR gates in the feedback which performs division by the non-primitive irreducible polynomial $g(x) = x^8+x^5+x^4+x^3+1$. The LFSR generates code words of the (17,8) code. The first 8 bits of the code words are generated in the LFSR latches (denoted as S_0-S_7) the next 9 bits can be obtained by shifting into the adjacent shift register (denoted as S_8-S_{16}). The LFSR can generate 15 disjoint code word cycles, each having the period of 17.

The feedback is connected according to reciprocal polynomial $g^*(x)=x^m g(1/x)$, m-n latches are added as shift register. The LFSR generates code words of a code N=(n,k), $k=n$-m. The same code words can also be generated by an n-bit LFSR which performs cyclic shifting of one code word (Fig.2). However, to generate the whole code, we must use $c=(2^m-1)/n$ different initial states (seeds), because the LFSR states are distributed within c disjoint n-state nonzero cycles and one all-zero cycle of the length one. In the case of a primitive polynomial $c=1$.

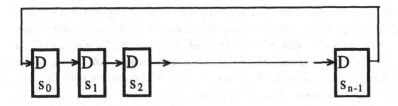

Fig. 2. A n-bit LFSR without XOR gates which after loading with a code word as a seed can be used for generation of a code word cycle of the length n.

The code words can be considered as multiples of the parity-check polynomial $h(x)$ = $(x^n-1)/g(x)$. Let us suppose that the initial state of the LFSR is $a(x) h(x)$ where $a(x)$ is an arbitrary polynomial. Then the ith state can be obtained as $x^i a(x)h(x)$.

Define T as a matrix that contains as rows all the nonzero code words of the code N. The rows of this matrix correspond to parallel outputs of the LFSR (Fig. 2). If we generate the code words with an LFSR with a non-primitive polynomial, we have to seed the register c times. This means that every n^{th} row will correspond to a new seed, whereas the following $n-1$ rows correspond to LFSR shifts.

$$T = \begin{bmatrix} a_0(x)h(x) \\ xa_0(x)h(x) \\ \dots \\ x^{n-1}a_0(x)h(x) \\ a_1(x)h(x) \\ \dots \\ x^{n-1}a_1(x)h(x) \\ \dots \\ a_{c-1}(x)h(x) \\ \dots \\ x^{n-1}a_{c-1}(x)h(x) \end{bmatrix}$$

The total number of rows is equal to $cn = 2^m-1$. The polynomials $a_i(x)$ are chosen in such a way that the seeds $a_i(x)h(x)$ initiate disjoint LFSR cycles.

2.2 Finding a primitive element of a field

We know from the theory of the fields, that all codes generated by irreducible polynomials form a field and that every field has at least one primitive element. In case of a primitive polynomial $g(x)$, the primitive element is x. For other cases we can find some other primitive elements. The second polynomial of degree 1 is $x+1$. It is the simplest polynomial worth testing whether it is a primitive element or not. In the following we will work with codes with non primitive polynomials for which $x+1$ is a primitive element. Define T' as a matrix that contains as rows all nonzero code words with a code word $a_0(x)h(x)$ as a seed. All code words can be obtained by multiplication of any of the rows by the powers of primitive element $x+1$.

$$T' = \begin{bmatrix} a_0(x)h(x) \\ (x+1)a_0(x)h(x) \\ ... \\ (x+1)^{cn} a_0(x)h(x) \end{bmatrix}$$

2.3   Design of a CA

The automaton performing the multiplication by $x+1$ is given in Fig. 3. If the automaton is seeded with a code word, the outputs of the D flip-flops correspond after every clock period to an (n,k) code word from the matrix T'. The automaton is an additive cellular automaton (CA) with the rule 60 for each cell [3], having a regular linear structure.

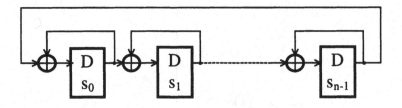

Fig. 3. Cellular automaton created from D flip-flops performing multiplication of the polynomials corresponding to code words by the polynomial x+1.

This CA can be further simplified. Instead of the D flip-flops and local feedback taps with XORs we can use T flip-flops because the T flip-flop performs a XOR function of its own state and the input signal in each clock period , the result is stored as a new internal state. Thus the CA given in Fig.4 has the same function as the CA in Fig. 3, but the hardware realization is simpler.

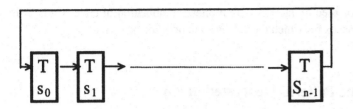

Fig. 4. Cellular automaton created from T flip-flops performing multiplication of the polynomials corresponding to code words by the polynomial x+1.

We have studied the state transition diagrams of the proposed CA. If we consider a CA with the length equal to a such code length that the corresponding polynomial can be irreducible, we obtain the state transition diagram with $2^{n-k}-1$ periodic states, 2^{n-k} "garden of Eden" states and one "graveyard" state. An example is given in Fig. 5.

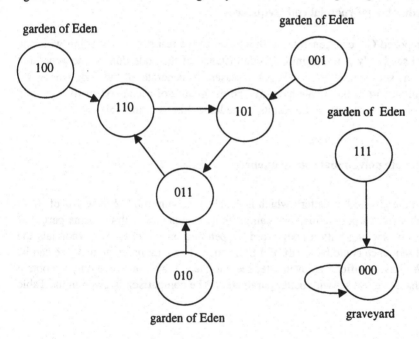

Fig. 5. State transition diagram of the 3 bit CA. The states with even number of ones are the code words of the (3,1) code

As far as we know, the proposed CA is the simplest possible automaton which can generate all code words of codes with non primitive polynomials with one seed only. It is universal in the sense that it can generate all possible code sequences of the given length without any hardware modification, we can also generate non code patterns which correspond to XOR of two or more code words of different codes. There is also possible to generate cyclic sequences of non code words, the period is usually the same as in the case of seeding the CA with a linear combination of code words. It is also possible to find seeds for which the CA has non periodic behavior.

3 Analysis of the Patterns Generated in CA

We have studied the properties of patterns generated in the proposed CA. There are substantial differences between the properties of the patterns generated in a LFSR and a CA. We have studied the possibility of generating code sequences, parts of code sequences with reducible characteristic polynomials, non-code sequences and possibility of test pattern compression.

3.1 Irreducible polynomial code sequences

The proposed CA can generate an (n,w) exhaustive test set after seeding with one code word seed only , w < minimal code distance of the code dual to the generated code. It was shown in [4] that it is not necessary to generate all the code words, we can use only a part of them. We have studied the quality of pseudoexhaustive test sets in [10]. Here we demonstrate the results in the left columns of the Table 1.

3.2 Reducible polynomial code sequences

If we seed the CA with a pattern which is equal to the sum mod. 2 of words of (n,k) codes with different polynomials we can generate a sequence with the same period as in the case of seeding with a code word. Depending on the chosen polynomials the generated sequence could be a part of a BCH code. The minimal code distance can be greater. We have verified that even after seeding the CA with one seed only we obtain pseudoexhaustive test set with better parameters. The comparison is given in the Table 1.

3.3 Test sequences with different weights

Let us suppose that we feed the serial output of an m bit LFSR to the s bit scan chain, $s>m$. The weights of the patterns from a LFSR with arbitrary primitive characteristic polynomial are very closed to the value $s/2$, where s is equal to the scan chain length. An example is given in Fig. 6. The weights are not distributed symmetrically around $s/2$. This is caused by seeding (resetting) the scan chain flip flops before testing to the zero states. .We can see that that the initial reset of the scan chain flip-flops has only a negligible influence on the weight rate.

CA generating code words			CA generating mod 2 sums of code words		
(n,w)-exhaustive test set	Generator polynomial (octal form)	No. of test patterns	type of (n,w)exhaustive test set	used poly-nomials (octal form)	number of test patterns
8 (17,4)	471	255	(17,5)	727, 471	255
11 (23,6)w	5343	2047	(23,7)	5343, 6135	2 047
12 (65,5)	10761	4095	(65,7)	10761, 13535, 111763	3 542
20 (41,8)	6647133	1048575	(41,9)	6647133, 5327265	41 943

Table 1. Comparison of pseudoexhaustive test set parameters for CA generating all code words of a code with $d_{min}>3$ and the same CA with modified seed. The CA were seeded only once with a mod. 2 sum of selected code words of the given codes. The last column shows the lowest sufficient number of test patterns which create a pseudoexhaustive test set.

	Number of test patterns		
(n,w)-ex-haustive test set	Use of incomplete LFSR period [4]	method of const-ant weights [21]	proposed CA
(31,3)	42	62	31
(63,3)	64	126	58
(127,3)	93	254	67
(17,5)	382	272	255
(23,7)	3 302	3 542	2 047
(65,7)	2 579130	87 360	3 588
(41,9)	695 860	202 540	41 943

Table 2. Comparison of test lengths for different test methods and given test parameters

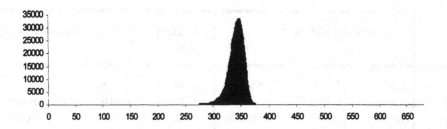

Fig. 6. The rate of global test pattern weights. The patterns were generated in a 23 bit LFSR with a primitive characteristic polynomial. The LFSR output was serially fed to the scan chain of the length 683 bits. X axis - pattern weights, Y axis - the number of test patterns which have the given weight . The number of generated test patterns:1 000 000. The scan chain flip-flops were set to log 0 before testing.

We have compared the weights of the LFSR patterns with the weights of CA patterns. The generated code was chosen in such a way that the number of information bits was the same as in the case of LFSR. In the Fig. 7 we can see the weight rates of code words generated in the CA. The polynomial of the code was non primitive and irreducible. In the Figures 8 and 9 we can see weight rates with different non code seeds. We can conclude that depending on the seed we can generate patterns with different weight rates.

Let us define a weight of one output sequence to be a ratio between the number of ones and zeros on the output within the test period. The weight during the test sequence is approximately the same for each of the CA parallel output. We have experimentally verified this fact for each of the 683 bit CA outputs. The weight depends on the CA seed properties only. This is demonstrated in Fig. 10. The different seeds caused that the weights were on all the different outputs equal to 0,5 for the first seed ; 0,4 for the second seed and 0,1 for the third seed.

3.4 Deterministic test pattern compaction

The CA can be used for compaction of deterministic test patterns which will test random, pseudoexhaustive and weighted-random resistant faults in mixed mode testing similarly to [12]. In this scheme we suppose to store seeds for the CA in a memory. After a given number of clock periods we get the demanded test cubes on CUT inputs. It is possible to store only the first k bits of the CA the rested bits are set to one or to zero. We have done several experiments which show that the CA is an efficient tool for decompressing such stored seeds of the deterministic test patterns, the efficiency is similar or better than it is for an LFSR.

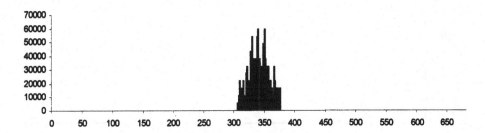

Fig.7 The rate of global test pattern weights. The 683 bit CA generated code patterns. X axis - pattern weights, Y axis - the number of test patterns which have the given weight. The number of generated test patterns:1 000 000

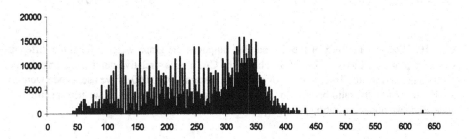

Fig. 8. The rate of global test pattern weights. The 683 bit CA generated non code patterns. X axis - pattern weights, Y axis - the number of test patterns which have the given weight . The number of generated test patterns:1 000 000.

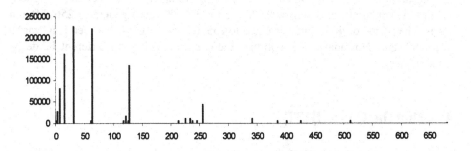

Fig 9. The rate of global test pattern weights. The 683 bit CA generated non code patterns. The seed was different from that one in Fig. 5. X axis - pattern weights, Y axis - the number of test patterns which have given weight. The number of generated test patterns:1 000 000.

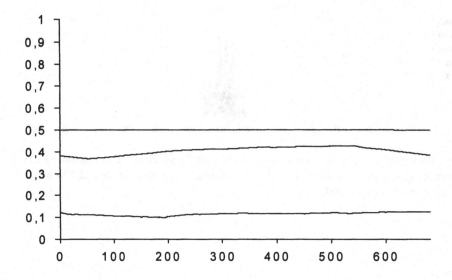

Fig. 10. Weights for each of the CA parallel output in the graph weights for three different seeds are plotted . X axis - position of a bit in the CA, Y axis - relative number of ones in the set of generated words. Total number of generated patterns 1 000 000. If we use a code word as a seed we obtain the ratio between ones and zeros approx. equal to 0.5, if we use specific non code seeds we obtain the ratio approx. equal to 0,4 and 0.1 respectively.

3.5 CA as a fast counter

The CA can be used as a fast synchronous counter. There is no additional delay of signal propagation between the flip-flops. The delay caused by the global feedback can be eliminated by arranging the CA into a ring similarly to [8]. We have designed a 17 bit CA, which after seeding with the vector 300000 (oct.) generates 256 different states. The period of the counter is equal to 255, the vector used as a seed is a "garden of Eden" state. Nowadays, we optimize the counter topology in different IC design technologies.

4 Using the CA in BIST

We can use the CA in BIST in several different ways: We can generate an (n,w) exhaustive test set according to Tab. 1. We can choose such a seed of the CA that we can consider the sequence to be pseudorandom (the test patterns weight rates similar to those shown in Fig. 7, the probability of ones on each CA output approximately equal to 0.5 during the test as it is shown in Fig. 10). We can choose such a seed of the CA that the patterns generated on the parallel CA outputs have different global weights (Fig. 8 or 9). If we modify the CA according to Fig. 12 we can use the inverted outputs for stimulating the CUT inputs with complement weights.

Example: For a specific seeds of the 683 bit CA we obtained the global weights 0.5, 0,4 and 0.1. If we use the inverted outputs, we can simultaneously stimulate arbitrary selected CUT inputs with the weights 0.6 and 0.9.

In order to use the CA in BIST we have to do several practical steps:

1.Choose an (n,k) code, $n \geq$ number of CUT inputs, $2^{n-k} -1 \geq$ considered test sequence length. In order to keep the period of CA maximal it is necessary to choose n equal to the length of some code with irreducible polynomial. For our experiments we have chosen the codes with lengths 17, 23, 25, 41, 47, 55, 69, 267, 765, 1687, ... [19].

2.Verify whether the polynomial $x+1$ is either a primitive element of the corresponding field or it guarantees the period et least equal to the test sequence length . Otherwise we have to chose another characteristic polynomial of the (n,k) code .

3.Verify whether the selected code or non code sequence is suitable for testing the CUT. We have either to simulate fault coverage of the test sets for the seeds with different properties or we have to estimate the optimal weights of test patterns [15, 23] .

One possibility of using the CA in BIST is shown in Fig. 11. Let us suppose that the CUT is designed in accordance with Scan Design methodology with modified Boundary Scan cells in such a way that the D flip-flops in the input part of scan chain are replaced by T flip/flops . We can also determine whether we will stimulate any of the CUT inputs with inverted CA output or with the non inverted one. We separate the input and output part of the chain and we complete the CA with the feedback. We suppose to use the CA with the number of flip-flops equal to or greater then the number of CUT inputs. If there are internal flip-flops in the CUT we have to include them into the scan chain and we have to avoid influencing the CUT inputs by the CUT outputs in the testing mode.

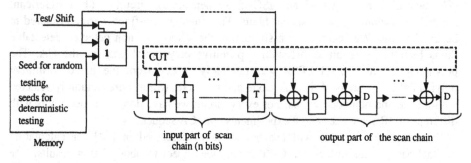

Fig. 11. BIST scheme

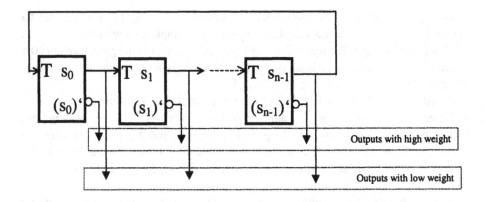

Fig. 12. Modified CA created from T flip-flops with non inverted and inverted outputs.

This can be done by any known technique similar to BILBO [14]. The testing starts after resetting of all flip flops and seeding the CA from the memory. At each clock cycle the CA generates a new pattern, and the CUT responds are compacted in the output part of the chain. After performing a given number of test steps the deterministic test patterns are shifted into the chain and the CUT responses are compacted in the output part of the chain.

We have to keep in mind that the seeds which are stored in the memory have to be modified for both parts of testing in such a way that after shifting into the scan chain the desired test cube would be present at the CUT inputs.

5 Results Obtained

We have chosen ISCAS 85 and ISCAS 89 benchmark circuits with a significant number of random pattern resistant faults. The internal flip-flops were considered to be CUT inputs. We checked by a simulation the number of non detected detectable faults both for a 32 bit LFSR with a primitive polynomial and for the CA. The polynomial of the 32 bit LFSR was randomly chosen from the list of primitive polynomials. The seeds of the CA code and non code words were randomly selected within code and non code words. For every circuit we have done 8 experiments with different LFSR sequences and 8 experiments with CA sequences.

In further research we will use the method described in [23] for calculating optimal pattern weights for the CUT inputs, we expect to obtain better results. The simulated results are given in Tab. 3.

circuit	length of test cubes	32 bit LFSR : No. of undetected faults after 10 000 generated patterns	CA: No. of undetected faults after 10 000 generated patterns
s 641	54	12	7
s 713	54	11	7
s 820	23	9	6
s 832	23	17	5
s 953	45	10	3
s 1238	32	10	11
s 5378	214	38	27
s1196	32	17	11
s 13207	700	624	472
s 9234	247	648	602
s 9234.1	247	681	642
s 15850	611	605	565
s 953	45	10	5
c 2670	157	304	292
c 7552	206	324	130

Table 3. Comparison of the numbers of faults which remain undetected after 10 000 test patterns. In the case of the LFSR we have chosen 32 bit LFSRs with primitive polynomial. The length of CA is equal or higher than the number of transformed circuit inputs.

6 Hardware Overhead

We have designed the CA in MIETEC 2.4 mm CMOS technology. In this technology we have the following sizes of the flip-flops:
D flip-flop with set or reset – 180mm x 106 mm
T flip-flop with set – 170mm x 106 mm
T flip-flop with reset – 190mm x 106 mm
XOR gate – 80mm x 106 mm.

If we compare the solution of T flip-flop CA with asynchronous set from Fig. 2 with the simple chain formed by D flip-flops with set or reset we can see that the used chip area will be similar. If we compare the solution of T flip-flop CA with the D flip flop CA we can see that we use only about 65 % of silicon for the flip-flops and gates, we also spare some area because of simpler routing.

7 Conclusion

A linear cellular automaton which can be used as a TPG for BIST was designed. Its main features are its simple structure and high fault coverage. The simplicity of the structure is due to the existence of only one feedback with no XOR. The cyclic CA can be implemented in the CUT by replacing the D flip flops in the scan chain with the T flip/flops and by adding a feedback from the last to the first flip-flop. There is no hardware overhead necessary for this replacing. The properties of the generated patterns depend on the seed of the CA. No additional hardware changes have to be done when we want to change the rate of global weights in generated patterns.

We compared the properties of the CA with the properties of a LFSR with a primitive characteristic polynomial which is usually used for pseudorandom test pattern generation. The CA has the following advantages:
- no hardware overhead, the whole TPG can be built by converting the existing scan chain
- depending on the seed the CA can generate weighted pseudorandom test sets with different rates of weights, we can individually modify weights for any of the CUT inputs by using inverted or non inverted CA outputs
- the fault coverage for ISCAS benchmark circuits is better than it is for an external LFSR.

Disadvantages:
- all flip-flops have to be reset-able, a seed for the CA has to be calculated in more complex manner than for an LFSR
- the patterns are generated in the scan chain and thus the CUT responses must not influence the flip/flops in the input part of the chain during the test.

The TPG can be advantageously used in mixed mode testing where we generate a given number of patterns and after it we exercise the circuit with deterministic test patterns which are stored in a memory. It is useful to test circuits in the following way: at first pseudoexhaustive test set is generated, after it weighted random test set is generated with the help of the same CA and after if we can test the resistant faults with the help of compressed patterns stored in the memory. which are decompressed in the CA.

The first experiments we have done with ISCAS benchmark circuits showed that by selecting an appropriate seed we can improve the fault coverage. Because of these promising results we continue in arranging new experiments. We want to arrange experiments with CUT input oriented WRT, the properties of the CA as we have demonstrated are useful for this kind of testing.

Acknowledgment

The author wishes to thank H.-J. Wunderlich and S. Hellebrand for their help with the simulation of fault coverage of the benchmark circuits. The research was in part supported by the research grants of the Czech Grant Agency GACR 102/98/1003 and of the Ministry of Education, Youth and Sport VS 96006.

References

1.   Bardell, P. – McAnney, W. H.- Savir, J.: Built-In Test for VLSI. New York: Wiley-Interscience, 1987

2.   Bershteyn, M.: Calculation of Multiple Sets of Weights for Weighted Random Testing. Proc. ITC, 1993, pp. 1031-1040

3.   Chaudhuri, P.P. et al.: Additive Cellular Automata Theory and Applications Volume I. IEEE Computer Society Press, 1997, 340 pp.

4.   Chen, C.L.: Exhaustive Test Pattern Generation Using Cyclic Codes. IEEE Trans. on Comp., Vol. 37, No. 2, February 1988, pp. 225-228

5.   Daehn, W., Mucha, J.: Hardware test pattern generators for built-in test. Proc. of IEEE ITC,1981, pp. 110-113

6.   Gloster,C., Brglez. F.: Cellular Scan Test Generation for Sequential Circuits. In European Design Automation Conference (EURO-DAC '92), pages 530-536, September 1992.

7.   Gloster,C., Brglez, F.: Boundary Scan with Cellular-Based Built-In Self-Test. In Proc. IEEE International Test Conference, pages 138-145, September 1988.

8.   Garbolino, T., Hlawiczka, A. : A new LFSR with D and T flip-flops as an effective test pattern generator for VLSI circuits. To appear in these proceedings.

9.   Golan, P.: Pseudoexhaustive Test Pattern Generation for Structured Digital Circuits. Proc.   FTSD9, Brno, Czechoslovakia, 1986, pp. 214-220

10.   Hlavicka, J, Novak, O.: Methods of Pseudoexhaustive Test Pattern Generation. Research Report DC-98-08, Dept. of Computer Science, Czech Technical University Prague, 27 pages

11.   Hortensius et al. Cellular automata circuits for BIST, IBM J. R&Dev, vol 34, no 2/3, pp. 389-405, 1990.

12.   Hellebrand, S., Rajski, J., Tarnick, S., Venkataraman, S., Courtois, B.: Built-In Test for Circuits with Scan Based on Reseeding of Multiple-Polynomial Linear Feedback Shift Registers. IEEE Trans. on Comp.,   vol. 44, No. 2, February 1995, pp. 223-233

13.   Koenemann, B.: LFSR – coded test patterns for scan designs. Proc. Europ. Test Conf., Munich , Germany, 1991, pp. 237-242

14.   Koenemann, B., Mucha, J., Zwiehoff, G.: Built-in Logic Block Observation Techniques. Proc. IEEE Test Conf., Cherry Hill, 1979, pp. 37-41

15.   Kunzmann, A. : Efficient Random Testing with Global Weights. Proc. of IEEE EURO-DAC `96

16.   McCluskey, E.J.: Built-in self-test techniques. IEEE Design & Test of Comput., Vol. 2., April 1985, pp. 21-28

17.   Miranda,M.A., Lopez-Bario, C. A.: Generation of Optimized Single Distributions of Weights for Random Built-In Self Test. Proc. ITC conf., 1993, pp. 1023- 1030

18. Novak, O., Hlavicka, J.: Design of a Cellular Automaton for Efficient Test Pattern Generation. Proc. IEEE ETW 1998, pp. 30-31

19. Peterson, W. W. - Weldon, E. J.: Error-Correcting Codes. Cambridge, Massachusetts, MIT Press, 1972

20. Tang, D.T., Chen, Ch.L.: Logic Test Pattern Generation Using Linear Codes. IEEE Trans. on Comp., Vol. C-33, No. 9, 1984, pp. 845-850

21. Tang, D. T., Woo, L. S.: Exhaustive Test Pattern Generation with Constant Weight Vectors. IEEE Trans. on Comp. , C-32, No.12, 1983, pp. 1145-1150

22. Wang, L.T., McCluskey, E.J.: Condensed linear feedback shift register (LFSR) testing - A pseudoexhaustive test technique. IEEE Trans. on Comp. Vol. C-35, Apr. 1986, pp. 367-370

23. Wunderlich, H. J.: Self Test Using Unequiprobable Random Patterns. Proc. IEEE 17 FTCS, Pittsburgh 1987, pp.236-244

24. Yarmolik, V. N., Muraskho, I. A.: A new tests pattern generator design approach for VLSI built-in self-testing. Automatic Control & Computer Sciences, 1995, No. 6, pp. 25-35

A New LFSR with D and T Flip-Flops as an Effective Test Pattern Generator for VLSI Circuits

Tomasz Garbolino, Andrzej Hławiczka

Institute of Electronics, Silesian Technical University of Gliwice
ul. Akademicka 16, 44-101 Gliwice, POLAND
e-mails: {garbol, hlawicz}@boss.iele.polsl.gliwice.pl

Abstract. *In the paper authors analyse properties of the various structures of linear registers (LFSRs) that are used as the test pattern generators in VLSI circuits. It is shown that the majority of them have one or more of the following drawbacks:*

- *large area overhead that is caused by the large number of XOR gates,*
- *reduced operational frequency due to presence of the long connection in the main feed-back loop and the high fan-out on the outputs of the flip-flops,*
- *inflexible structure that cannot be easily redesigned and adjusted to the needs of the digital circuit efficient testing.*

In the paper we present a new type of LFSR that is free from all mentioned above disadvantages. We also develop the algebraic description of its operation and the methods of its designing. Finally we give numerous examples of its structures for different lengths of the register.

1   Introduction

Nowadays linear registers are very often used in built-in self-test logic for VLSI circuits. Mainly, they act as the pseudorandom or deterministic test pattern generators (LFSR) and test response compactors (MISR) [3]. These register are composed of only two kinds of elements - D-type flip-flops and XOR gates, which are the part of the internal (Internal Exclusive OR LFSR - IED-LFSR) or external (External Exclusive OR LFSR - EED-LFSR) linear feedback path [3].

The important drawback of such classic linear registers is the strong cross-correlation between the majority of the binary sequences that appear at the outputs of the adjacent stages of the register. It results from the fact that the value of the phase shift between these binary sequences equals to 1. The strong cross-correlation between the above binary sequences leads to the strong correlation between consecutive test patterns that are produced at the outputs of the linear register. Therefore the conventional linear registers can not be considered to be a high quality pseudorandom test pattern generators. There was shown in [12] that the test patterns produced by the classic EED-LFSR do not detect considerable amount of stuck-at faults in the digital circuit with registered inputs.

There is an example of the fifteen input circuit under test (CUT) shown in Fig.1a. It contains four bit register on the inputs 4-7, which is composed of D-type flip-flops. The EED-LFSR implementing primitive polynomial $p(x)=1+x^{14}+x^{15}$ acts as the test pattern generator for this circuit. The flip-flops in the CUT as well as the test pattern generator are clocked by the same signal.

a)

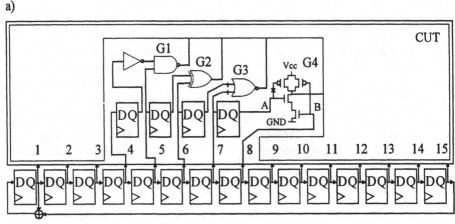

test pattern generator

b)

Fig. 1. Testing scheme for the exemplar CUT.
(a) Example of the CUT which inputs 4-7 are registered; The EED-LFSR acts as the test pattern generator for the CUT; (b) State-time diagram for the EED-LFSR (*length 480, initial state with a single non-zero site*)

In the above example the following faults: stuck-at-1 at the output of the NAND gate (G1), stuck-at-0 at the output of the XOR gate (G2), bridging fault at the inputs of the NOR gate (G4) and stuck-open fault at the p-type transistor input in the NAND gate (G4) are not detected by the test patterns produced by the EED-LFSR. In order to detect these faults the value of the phase shift between binary sequences which are applied to the inputs 4-8 of the CUT needs to be larger than 1. The value of the phase shift between binary sequences produced at every pair of the adjacent outputs of the EED-LFSR is 1. It results in the strong cross-correlation between these sequences and the correlation between consecutive pattern appearing at the outputs of the EED-LFSR. They both can be observed in the state-time diagram for this register presented in Fig. 1b. This state-time diagram is a result of simulating the EED-LFSR

a)

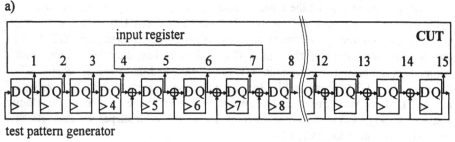

test pattern generator

b)

Fig. 2. Testing scheme for the exemplar CUT: (a) The use of the IED-LFSR as the test pattern generator for the CUT; (b) State-time diagram for the EED-LFSR (*length 480, initial state with a single non-zero site*)

operation using the techniques developed in [9]. Its very regular shape testifies to the poor randomness of the EED-LFSR output patterns.

There are several solutions to the above issue but all of them possess essential drawbacks. One of these solutions is the use of the IED-LFSR as the test pattern generator for the exemplar CUT. The example of the IED-LFSR that implements polynomial $p(x)=1+x^4+x^5+x^6+x^7+x^{12}+x^{13}+x^{14}+x^{15}$ and the way it is connected to the exemplar CUT is shown in Fig. 2a. Because there are XOR gates of the main feedback loop path at the inputs of D flip-flops 5-8 in the IED-LFSR the value of the phase shift between the binary sequences produced at the outputs 4-8 of this register is much larger than 1. It reduces the cross-correlation between these sequences. The state-time diagram of the IED-LFSR displays larger irregularity than one presented in Fig. 2b. This irregularity is particularly visible in the areas of the diagram corresponding to the stages of the IED-LFSR including the XOR gates of the main feedback loop of the register. Unfortunately this type of the linear register has several substantial drawbacks. Due to the large number of the XOR gates in the main feedback loop path of the IED-LFSR the cost of such a solution is high. It also leads to high fan-out at the output of the last stage of the register, which is 8 in the case of the IED-LFSR shown in a. In general, the fan-out at the output of the last stage in the IED-LFSR equals to K+1, where K is the number of the XOR gates in the main feedback loop of the register. Moreover the main feedback loop contains the long connection between the last and the first stage of the IED-LFSR that reduces the maximal operational frequency of the register. Other disadvantages of the IED-LFSR is the inflexibility of its structure, which can not be easily redesigned without changing the characteristic polynomial of the register. There exists only one structure of the IED-LFSR for a given primitive polynomial. The number and the arrangement of the XOR gates in this structure is determined by the form of the polynomial. If we change the arrangement of the registered inputs in the CUT in Fig. 1a we usually need to find a new IED-LFSR that implements different primitive polynomial.

It was proven in [9] that the cross-correlation between binary sequences produced at the outputs of the linear CA composed of the rule 90 and 150 cells is very small. Thus the CA is a very good quality test pattern generator for exemplar CUT. One of the possible structures of the linear CA with null boundary conditions, which implements the primitive polynomial $p(x)=1+x^{14}+x^{15}$, and the way it is connected to the exemplar CUT is shown in Fig. 3a. The state-time diagram of this CA is presented in Fig. 3b. It is very irregular. Notice the triangular shapes which are randomly scattered throughout the state-time diagram. These triangular shapes are characteristic for many one dimensional CA's [9].

a)

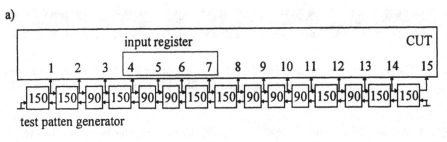

test patten generator

b)

Fig. 3. Testing scheme for the exemplar CUT.
(a) CA acts as the test pattern generator for the CUT; (b) State-time diagram for the CA (*length 480, initial state with a single non-zero site*)

The advantage of the CA is the small length and the local nature of the connections between its adjacent stages. On the other hand the essential drawback of this register is its extremely large cost. It contains 23 XOR gates. In general, to build an n-bit CA the n+k-1 XOR gates are necessary. The n-1 XOR gates are needed in local feedback and feedforward loops between the adjacent stages of CA. In addition there is the k XOR gates necessary to construct the k rule 150 cells, where 0<k<n.

In [12] authors proposed to use External Exclusive OR type LFSR that includes T-type flip-flop instead of D-type flip-flop in every stage to solve the problem mentioned above. The structure of the register of such a type, which implements polynomial $p(x)=1+x+x^3+x^5+x^7+x^9+x^{11}+x^{13}+x^{15}=1+(1+x)^{14}+(1+x)^{15}$, and the way it is connected to the exemplar CUT is shown in Fig. 4a. It was proven in [12] that the value of the phase shift between binary sequences produced at the outputs of the register under consideration is always larger than 1. The state-time diagram of this register is shown in Fig. 4b. It is irregular to the same degree as the state-time diagram of the CA. Notice the triangular shapes which are randomly scattered throughout the state-time diagram. These triangular shapes seem to be characteristic for LFSRs including T flip-flops.

a)

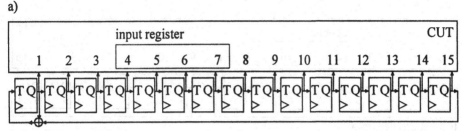

test pattern generator

b)

Fig. 4. Testing scheme for the exemplar CUT.
(a) The use of the External Exclusive OR type LFSR containing T flip-flop in every stage as the test pattern generator for the CUT; (b) State-time diagram for this type of the linear register (*length 480, initial state with a single non-zero site*)

The synthesis method of the LFSR with T flip-flops and external feedback loop was also presented in [12]. This method is based on substitution of the variable x with expression (1+x) in the primitive polynomial $p(x)=1+x^{n-1}+x^n$ that results in polynomial $p'(x)=p(1+x)=1+(1+x)^{n-1}+(1+x)^n$. Unfortunately the primitive polynomials of the form $1+x^{n-1}+x^n$ exist only for n=2, 3, 4, 6, 7, 15, 22, 60, 127, 153, ... [12]. Moreover, the transformation of the polynomial p(x) for n=4, 15, 22, for example, results in the polynomial p'(x) which is prime but not primitive.

The proposed solution is also expensive. The 15 T flip-flops and 1 XOR gate, which gives 16 XOR gates in total, are necessary to built the LFSR shown in Fig. 4a. In general, at least n+1 XOR gates are needed to construct the LFSR of the type proposed in [12]. Moreover there is a long connection in the main feedback loop that reduces maximal operational frequency of this LFSR.

None of the above presented implementations of the test pattern generator is the optimal solution to the problem pointed out previously because each of them has one or more of the following drawbacks:

- the value of the phase shift between the binary sequences produced at the outputs of the adjacent stages of the linear register is 1, what results in strong cross-correlation between these sequences,
- inflexible structure, which cannot be redesigned without changing the characteristic polynomial of the register,
- reduced operational frequency due to presence of the long connection in the main feedback loop and the high fan-out at the outputs of the flip-flops,
- large area overhead.

The optimal solution to the problem under consideration, which is free from the above disadvantages, is linear register DT-LFRS introduced in [7]. The large flexibility of its structure allows for the unrestricted arrangement of the D and T

a)

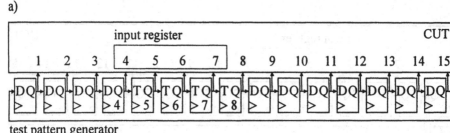

test pattern generator

b)

Fig. 5. Testing scheme for the exemplar CUT.
(a) The use of DT-LFSR as the test pattern generator for the CUT; (b) State-time diagram for the DT-LFSR *(length 480, initial state with a single non-zero site)*

flip-flops in the register. The long connection in the main feedback loop of the DT-LFSR can by radically shortened using interlacing technique [2]. The fan-out in this register is less or equal to 2. Owing to the last two features, the DT-LFSR can operate with its maximal frequency, which is higher than in the case of the IED-LFSR and LFSR developed in [12] and similar to the maximal operational frequency of CA. Furthermore, there exist the n-bit DT-LFSRs for many values of n.

The example of the DT-LFSR register, which implements the primitive polynomial $p(x)=1+x^{11}+x^{15}$, and the way it is connected to the exemplar CUT is shown in Fig. 5a. It includes 4 T flip-flops - so there are 4 XOR gates needed to construct this register. These T flip-flops cause the value of the phase shift between the binary sequences at the outputs of the DT-LFSR that feed inputs 4-8 of the CUT to be larger than 1. Thus the value of this phase shift is larger than 1 only at these inputs of the CUT where it is necessary. The state-time diagram for the DT-LFSR, which is shown in Fig. 5b, displays irregularity in the area corresponding to the outputs of the T-type flip-flops in the DT-LFSR.

So, in summary, the advantages of the DT-LFSR are as follows:

- the value of the phase shift between the binary sequences produced at some pairs of the adjacent outputs of the register is larger than 1,
- low area overhead,
- flexibility of the structure, which can be easily redesigned and adjusted to the needs of the efficient testing of the digital circuit without changing the characteristic polynomial of the register,
- high operational frequency due to the low fan-out and the radical length reduction of the long connection in the main feedback loop path of the register.

The above mentioned advantages of the DT-LFSRs led the authors to do research work on the properties of these registers. In particular, they analysed the phase shifts of the binary sequences produced at the outputs of the DT-LFSRs. Moreover, the authors also adopted the methods given in [7] to synthesis of the LFSRs with D and T flip-flops.

The remaining part of the paper is organised as follows. In section 2 we present an algebraic description of the operation of the new type registers. We also show examples of the structures of the IEDT-ILFSR and EEDT-LFSR and introduce the abbreviated notation of their structures there. The synthesis methods of the registers with D and T flip-flops are proposed in section 3. Section 4 is devoted to analysis of the phase shifts between the binary sequences produced at the outputs of these registers. In section 5 the properties of the new type registers are presented. We conclude in section 6.

2 Algebraic Description of the Operation of the New Type Linear Registers

General models of a structure of the IEDT-LFSR and EEDT-LFSR registers are presented in Fig. 6 and Fig. 7, respectively.

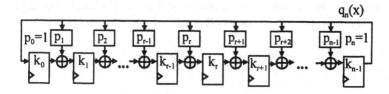

Fig. 6. General model of the IEDT-LFSR structure

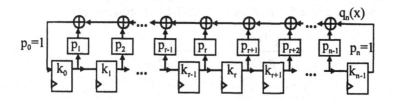

Fig. 7. General model of the EEDT-LFSR structure

The models of a single stage of the both of these registers are shown in Fig. 8.
The meaning of the symbols used in Fig. 6, Fig. 7 and Fig. 8 is as follows:

$q_{r+1}(x)$ - represents the polynomial over $GF(2)$ of the binary stream occurring at the output of the r-th flip-flop,

$q_n(x)$ - represents the polynomial over $GF(2)$ of the binary stream occurring at the feedback line,

$$p_r = \begin{cases} 0 \text{ - there is no connection} \\ 1 \text{ - there is a wire connection}, \end{cases} \qquad k_r = \begin{cases} 0 \text{ - D - type flip - flop} \\ 1 \text{ - T - type flip - flop}. \end{cases}$$

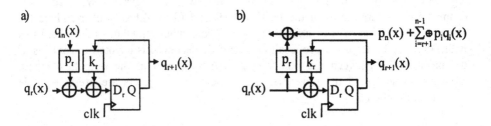

a)

b)

Fig. 8. Single stage models for the two LFSRs: (a) IEDT-LFSR, (b) EEDT-LFSR

The algebraic description of the operation of the all stages of the IEDT-LFSR during m clock cycles, using the polynomial ring over GF(2), is illustrated by the set of equations (1):

$$\{q_{r+1}(x) = [s_r + h_r x^m + p_r q_n(x) + q_r(x)] / (k_r + x)\}_{\; r \in \{0, 1, ..., n-1\}}. \tag{1}$$

The algebraic description of the operation of 0-th and the remaining stages of the EEDT-LFSR is presented by equation (2) and the set of equations (3):

$$q_0(x) = \sum_{r=1}^{n} p_r q_r(x), \tag{2}$$

$$\{q_{r+1}(x) = [s_r + h_r x^m + q_r(x)] / (k_r + x)\}_{\; r \in \{0, 1, ..., n-1\}}. \tag{3}$$

On the basis of the set of equations (1) and the set of equations (2) and (3) we obtain the equation which describes, in the form of the polynomial division over GF(2), operation of the IEDT-LFSR and EEDT-LFSR, respectively:

$$\frac{x^m h(x)}{p_C(x)} = q(x) + \frac{r(x)}{p_C(x)}, \tag{4}$$

where:

$c \in \{\text{IEDT, EEDT}\}$ - is the index pointing out the type of the register - IEDT-LFSR and EEDT-LFSR, respectively,

$$p_{IEDT}(x) = p_0 + \sum_{r=1}^{n} \oplus p_r \prod_{j=0}^{r-1} (k_j + x)$$

is the characteristic polynomial of the IEDT-LFSR; deg $p_{IEDT}(x) = n$,

$$p_{IEDTr}(x) = \prod_{j=0}^{r-1} (k_j + x)$$

is the polynomial representing the influence the r-th stage of the IEDT-LFSR has on division (4); deg $p_{IEDTr}(x) = r$,

$$p_{EEDT}(x) = p_0 + \sum_{r=0}^{n-1} \oplus p_r \prod_{j=r}^{n-1}(k_j + x) + p_n$$

is the characteristic polynomial of the EEDT-LFSR; deg $p_{IEDT}(x)$=n,

$$p_{EEDTr}(x) = \sum_{i=0}^{r-1} \oplus p_i \prod_{j=1}^{r-1}(k_j + x) + p_r$$

is the polynomial representing the influence the r-th stage of the EEDT-LFSR has on division (4); deg $p_{EEDTr}(x)$=r,

$$h(x) = \sum_{r=0}^{n-1} \oplus h_r\, p_{cr}(x)$$

is the polynomial including the bits h_r of the c-LFSR initial state; deg $h(x)$=n-1,

$$r(x) = \sum_{r=0}^{n-1} \oplus s_r\, p_{cr}(x)$$

is the polynomial representing the reminder of division (4) that contains the bits s_r of the c-LFSR signature (the final state); deg $r(x)$=n-1,

$q(x)$

represents the quotient of division (4) that in the form of the binary stream appears at the output of the last (n-1) stage of the c-LFSR; deg q(x)=m-1.

The exemplar structure of the IEDT-LFSR that implements primitive polynomial $p(x)=1+x^4+x^5+x^8+x^9$ is shown in Fig. 9. The example of the structure of the EEDT-LFSR that implements the same polynomial is presented in Fig. 10.

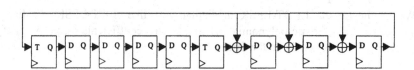

Fig. 9. Example of the structure of IEDT-LFSR

The structures of the registers in Fig. 9 and Fig. 10 can be denoted in symbolic way as TDDDDT$_\oplus$D$_\oplus$D$_\oplus$D and D$^\oplus$D$^\oplus$D$^\oplus$TDDDDT, respectively. Symbols D and T denote D-type and T-type flip-flops, respectively, and symbols $_\oplus$ and $^\oplus$ denotes the XOR gates in the internal and external feedback loop, respectively.

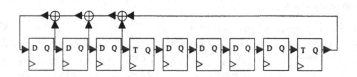

Fig. 10. Example of the structure of EEDT-LFSR

Moreover, the set of the i consecutive D or T flip-flops will be denoted as D^i and T^i, respectively. The every stage of the IEDT-LFSR takes one of the four possible forms: D, T, $_\oplus$D, $_\oplus$T. Similarly, the every stage of the EEDT-LFSR also takes one of the four possible forms: D, T, $^\oplus$D, $^\oplus$T.

3 Synthesis of the LFSRs with D and T Flip-Flops

The method of the synthesis of the IEDT-LFSR and EEDT-LFSR registers that implement given polynomial was developed in [7]. Let us assume that p_0, p_s, p_t and p_n, where $n>t>s>0$, are non-zero coefficients of the polynomial $p_{IEDT}(x)$ (see Fig. 6 in section 2). Let us further assume that $b1+c1=s$, $b2+c2=t-s$ and $b3+c3=n-t$ for some combination of 0s and 1s assigned to the coefficients k_j.

Then the polynomial $p_{IEDT}(x)$ can be written in the following form:

$$p_{IEDT}(x) = p_0 + x^{b1}(1+x)^{c1}[p_s + x^{b2}(1+x)^{c2}[p_t + x^{b3}(1+x)^{c3}]],$$ (5)

$$\text{where } \sum_{j=1}^{3}(b_j + c_j) = n.$$

The final form of the polynomial $p_{IEDT}(x)$, which is named the structural form $p_{IEDTw}(x)$ in this paper, we obtain by substituting coefficients p_0, p_s, p_t, p_n with 1s:

$$p_{IEDT}(x) = p_0 + x^{b1}(1+x)^{c1}[1 + x^{b2}(1+x)^{c2}[1 + x^{b3}(1+x)^{c3}]].$$ (6)

The structure of the IEDT-LFSR corresponding to the above polynomial $p_{IEDTw}(x)$ is $D^{b1}T^{c1}{}_\oplus D^{b2}T^{c2}{}_\oplus D^{b3}T^{c3}$.

We synthesise the EEDT-LFSR in similar way like IEDT-LFSR. At first we transform its characteristic polynomial $p_{EEDT}(x)$, which coefficients p_0, p_s, p_t, p_n equal to 1 (see Fig. 7 in section 2), to the form:

$$p_{EEDT}(x) = p_n + x^{b3}(1+x)^{c3}[p_t + x^{b2}(1+x)^{c2}[p_s + x^{b1}(1+x)^{c1}]],$$ (7)

$$\text{where } \sum_{j=1}^{3}(b_j + c_j) = n.$$

Then we transform it to the structural form $p_{EEDTw}(x)$:

$$p_{EEDTw}(x) = 1 + x^{b3}(1+x)^{c3}[1 + x^{b2}(1+x)^{c2}[1 + x^{b1}(1+x)^{c1}]].$$ (8)

The structure of the EEDT-LFSR corresponding to the polynomial $p_{EEDTw}(x)$ is $D^{b1}T^{c1\oplus}D^{b2}T^{c2\oplus}D^{b3}T^{c3}$.

Notice that if $p_{IEDTw}(x)= p_{EEDTw}(x)= 1+x^{b1}(1+x)^{c1}[1+x^{b2}(1+x^{c2})[1+x^{b3}(1+x)^{c3}]]$, then knowing the structure $D^{b1}T^{c1}{}_\oplus D^{b2}T^{c2}{}_\oplus D^{b3}T^{c3}$ of the IEDT-LFSR we can easily find the structure $T^{c3}D^{b3\oplus}T^{c2}D^{b2\oplus}T^{c1}D^{b1}$ of the EEDT-LFSR. All we need to do is to write symbols in symbolic notation $D^{b1}T^{c1}{}_\oplus D^{b2}T^{c2}{}_\oplus D^{b3}T^{c3}$ of the IEDT-LFSR structure in the reverse order and substitute symbols $_\oplus$ with symbols $^\oplus$.

If a given polynomial p(x) can be expressed in the structural form:

$$p_{DTw}(x) = 1 + x^b(1+x)^c,$$ (9)

then the corresponding to this polynomial structure of the DT-LFSR is composed of b D-type flip-flops c T-type flip-flops.

Example 1.

We are looking for the structures of the IEDT-LFSR, EEDT-LFSR and DT-LFSR that implement primitive polynomial $p(x)=1+x^4+x^5+x^8+x^9$.

IEDT-LFSR:

  We transform polynomial $p(x)$ to the structural form $p_{IEDTw}(x)$:

  a) $p_{IEDT}(x)=1+x^4(1+x+x^4+x^5)$; $p_{IEDTw}(x)=1+x^4[1+x[1+x^3(1+x)]]$; the structure of the IEDT-LFSR corresponding to polynomial $p_{IEDTw}(x)$ is DDDD$_\oplus$D$_\oplus$DDDT; Some other transformations of polynomial $p(x)$ result in:

  b) $p_{IEDT}(x)=1+x^4(1+x)(1+x^4)$; $p_{IEDTw}(x)=1+x^4(1+x)[1+x^4]$; DTDDD$_\oplus$DDDD;

  c) $p_{IEDT}(x)=1+x^4(1+x)^2(1+x+x^2+x^3)$; $p_{IEDTw}(x)=1+x^4(1+x)^2[1+x[1+x[1+x]]]$; TDDDDT$_\oplus$D$_\oplus$D$_\oplus$D;

EEDT-LFSR:

  Some of the EEDT-LFSR structures that implement polynomial $p(x)$ can be obtained by arranging the stages of the IEDT-LFSRs that have been developed above (see points a-c) in reverse order and substituting the internal feedback loop with the external feedback loop: TDDD$^\oplus$D$^\oplus$DDDD, DDDD$^\oplus$DDDTD, D$^\oplus$D$^\oplus$D$^\oplus$TDDDDT.

DT-LFSR:

  We transform polynomial $p(x)$ to the structural form $p_{DTw}(x)=1+x^4(1+x)^5$; some structures that correspond to the polynomial $p_{DTw}(x)$ are: DDDDTTTT, TTTTTDDDD, TTDDTTDDT.

4 Analysis of Phase Shifts of Binary Sequences Produced at the Outputs of the LFSRs with D and T Flip-Flops

The value of the phase shift between the binary sequences produced at the outputs of the test pattern generator is one of the parameters influencing the quality of this generator. Let us consider the phase shifts in the D^kT^f register. Its corresponding structural polynomial is $p_{DTw}(x)=1+x^k(1+x)^f$, where $k+f=n$. The $q_i(t)$ denotes the value of the i-th output of the register in t-th clock cycle and $q_i(t+1)$ denotes the value of this output in the clock cycle $t+1$. The operation of the DT-LFSR register can be described in the form of the following set of equations:

$$q_1(t+1) = q_n(t), \tag{10}$$
$$q_i(t+1) = q_{i-1}(t), \text{ for } i \in [2,k],$$
$$q_i(t+1) = q_{i-1}(t) + q_i(t), \text{ for } i \in [k+1,n].$$

Let us introduce the shift operator s that expresses the dependency between the previous and the next state of the i-th stage of the register:

$$q_i(t+1) = sq_i(t), \text{ for } i \in [1, n]. \tag{11}$$

Thus, the set of equations (10) can be written in the form:

$$sq_1(t) = q_n(t), \tag{12}$$
$$sq_i(t) = q_{i-1}(t), \text{ for } i \in [2, k],$$
$$sq_i(t) = q_{i-1}(t) + q_i(t), \text{ for } i \in [k+1, n].$$

Now we compute the discrete logarithms for the left-hand side as well as the right-hand side of the equations in the set of equations (12). This results in the set of the following congruencies (13):

$$\log(q_n(t)) - \log(q_1(t)) = \log(s) \bmod 2^n - 1, \tag{13}$$
$$\log(q_{i-1}(t)) - \log(q_i(t)) = \log(s) \bmod 2^n - 1, \text{ for } i \in [2, k],$$
$$\log(q_{i-1}(t)) - \log(q_i(t)) = \log(s+1) \bmod 2^n - 1, \text{ for } i \in [k+1, n],$$

where $\log(x)=1$ and the value of the expression $\log(q_{i-1}(t))$ - $\log(q_i(t))$ is the value of the phase shift between binary sequences appearing at the outputs i-1 and i of the DT-LFSR and i=2, 3, ..., n.

On the basis of the set of equations (12) we can obtain the following equation:

$$q_n(t) = s^k (s+1)^{n-k} q_n(t). \tag{14}$$

Computing the discrete logarithms of the both left-hand side and right-hand side of the equation (14) results in congruence:

$$(n-k)\log(s+1) + k\log(s) = 0 \bmod 2^n - 1. \tag{15}$$

Substituting 1 for log(s) in (15) we obtain the congruence:

$$(n-k)\log(s+1) + k = 0 \bmod 2^n - 1. \tag{16}$$

The last congruence allows us to compute the value of log(s+1). It also indicates that $\log(s+1) \neq 1$ for all n>1. Moreover, on the basis of the set of congruencies (13) we can draw the conclusion that in the case of every D-type flip-flop in the DT-LFSR the value of the phase shift between binary sequence at the input of the flip-flop and the binary sequence at its output equals to $\log(s)=1$. In the case of every T-type flip-flop in the DT-LFSR the value of the phase shift equals to the value of $\log(s+1)$, which satisfies congruence (16).

In order to compute the values of the phase shift between the binary sequences produced at the outputs of the IEDT-LFSR or EEDT-LFSR we need to use sophisticated techniques of computing discrete logarithms, which can be found in [11]. Discussing these techniques is out of scope of the paper. What is important, the T-type flip-flops present in the both types of the linear registers introduce the phase shift which value is larger than 1.

5   Properties of the Structure of the DT-LFSR

Flexibility of the structure of the DT-LFSR

Freedom in arrangement of the D and T flip-flops in the structure of the DT-LFSR

The structure of the DT-LFSR is very flexible due to the lack of the XOR gates in its main feedback loop. We are able to arrange the D and T flip-flops in the structure of the DT-LFSR in many different ways. Thus, the structure of the DT-LFSR can be easily redesigned and adjusted to the needs of the efficient test pattern generation.

Example 2.

One of possible structures of the DT-LFSR that implements primitive polynomial $p(x)=1+x^4+x^5+x^8+x^9$ is DDDDTTTTT. Changing the arrangement of the D and T flip-flops in this structure results in many others structures of this register, e.g.: TDTDTDTDT, TTTTTDDDD, TTTDDDDTT, TDTTDDTTD.

Possibility of changing the number of T flip-flops

We can change the number of the T-type flip-flops in the structure of the DT-LFSR by converting it to the IEDT-LFSR or EEDT-LFSR structure, which has only one XOR gate in the main feedback loop.

Example 3.

Let us consider the DT-LFSR that implements primitive polynomial $p(x)=1+x^7+x^8+x^9+x^{10}+x^{15}+x^{16}+x^{17}+x^{18}$. The structural form of this polynomial is $p_{DTw}(x)=1+x^7(1+x)^{11}$ and its corresponding structure is D^7T^{11}. Some transformed forms $p_w(x)$ of $p_{DTw}(x)$ and their corresponding structures of the IEDT-LFSR and EEDT-LFSR are shown below.

1. Increasing the number of T flip-flops:
   a) $p_w(x)=1+x^6(1+x)^{11}[1+(1+x)]$; $D^6T^{11}{}_{\oplus}T$; $T^{\oplus}T^{11}D^6$;
   b) $p_w(x)=1+x^5(1+x)^{11}[1+(1+x)^2]$; $D^5T^{11}{}_{\oplus}T^2$; $T^{2\oplus}T^{11}D^5$;
   c) $p_w(x)=1+x^3(1+x)^{11}[1+(1+x)^4]$; $D^3T^{11}{}_{\oplus}T^4$; $T^{4\oplus}T^{11}D^3$;

2. Decreasing the number of T flip-flops:
   a) $p_w(x)=1+x^7(1+x)^{10}[1+x]$; $D^7T^{10}{}_{\oplus}D$; $D^{\oplus}T^{10}D^7$;
   b) $p_w(x)=1+x^7(1+x)^9[1+x^2]$; $D^7T^9{}_{\oplus}D^2$; $D^{2\oplus}T^9D^7$;
   c) $p_w(x)=1+x^7(1+x)^7[1+x^4]$; $D^7T^7{}_{\oplus}D^4$; $D^{4\oplus}T^7D^7$;
   d) $p_w(x)=1+x^7(1+x)^3[1+x^8]$; $D^7T^3{}_{\oplus}D^8$; $D^{8\oplus}T^3D^7$;

Good timing parameters

Low fan-out

The very important advantage of the DT-LFSRs is their low fan-out, which is less than or equal to 2. The fan-out in the IEDT-LFSRs and EEDT-LFSRs which include only one XOR gate in the main feedback loop is less than or equal to 3.

Shortening of the long connection in the main feedback loop

The form of the structure of the DT-LFSR as well as IEDT-LFSR and EEDT-LFSR that include only one XOR gate in the main feedback loop facilitates such a design of their topology in the integrated circuit (IC) that does not contain long connections.

The typical topology of the $D^bT^f{}_\oplus D^cT^g$ structure of the IEDT-LFSR, which implements polynomial $1+x^b(1+x)^f[1+x^c(1+x)^g]$, where $b+f=i$, $b+f+c+g=n$, $b\neq0$ and $c\neq0$, is shown in Fig. 11a. This register is composed of n standard cells containing D or T flip-flops and one standard cell including XOR gate of the main feedback loop. These cells are arranged in the form of a single well-ordered row in the way that provides minimal length of connections between i-th and i+1 stage of the register, where i=1, 2, ..., n-1. The feedback loop of this register includes one long connection between the output of the stage n and the input of the stage 1 of the register. The propagation delay through this long line impose the limit to the maximal operational frequency of the IEDT-LFSR, particularly in the case of submicron technologies.

One way to shorten this long connection is to design the topology of the IEDT-LFSR in the form of a ring. The implementation of such a ring for the IEDT-LFSR corresponding to the above-mentioned $p_{IEDTw}(x)$ is presented in Fig. 11b. The ring comprises two rows of flip-flops. The connection between the n-th and the 1st stage in the upper row is short. The connection between the output of the n-th stage and the XOR gate at the input of the i+1 stage is short as well. Interlacing the flip-flops from the upper row with the flip-flops in the lower row we obtain the topology of the IEDT-LFSR shown in Fig. 11c (A type interlace).

Table 1.

No.	i+1	n	Left part		Right part	
			k	type	r	type
1	even	even	(i+1)/2	A	(n+i+1)/2	A
2	even	odd	(i+1)/2	A	(n+i+2)/2	B
3	odd	even	(i+2)/2	B	(n+i+2)/2	B
4	odd	odd	(i+2)/2	B	(n+i+1)/2	A

Another way of interlacing the upper and the lower rows of the flip-flops is illustrated in Fig. 11d (B type interlace). There are two more types of flip-flops interlacing possible, in which the left part is the A (B) type interlace and the right part is the B (A) type interlace.

The idea of flip-flops interlacing in the one row was first time developed in [2]. However, there was no rules provided indicating how to arrange the flip-flops of the IEDT-LFSR into two groups which, after interlacing one to another, result in the topology of the IEDT-LFSR that is free from the long connections. The solution to this problem is proposed in this paper. The expressions in Table 1 allow for choosing the k-th stage of the linear register for the left part and the r-th stage of this register for the right part of the interlace structure when the values of the coefficients n and i are given.

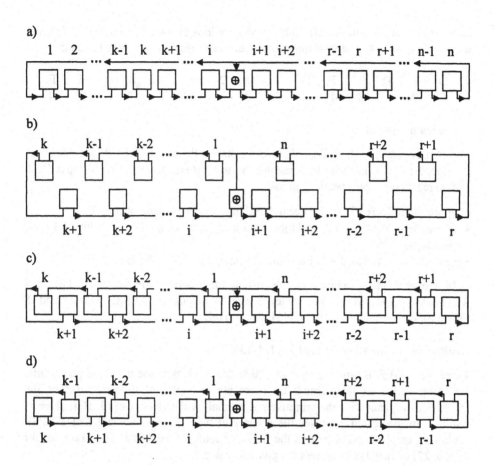

Fig. 11. Distribution of the linear register flip-flops: (a) well-ordered row, (b) ring, (c) A type interlace, (d) B type interlace

The technique shown above can also be used in the case of the EEDT-LFSR and DT-LFSR registers which implement the following polynomials, respectively:

- $p_{EEDTw}(x) = 1+x^b(1+x)^f[1+x^c(1+x)^g]$, where $b+f=i$, $b+f+c+g=n$, $b\neq0$ and $c\neq0$,
- $p_{DTw}(x) = 1+x^b(1+x)^f$.

Example 4.

There is given primitive polynomial $p(x)=1+x^{11}+x^{15}$. Its structural form corresponding to the IEDT-LFSR type register is $p_{IEDTw}(x)=1+x^7(1+x)^4[1+(1+x)^4]$. The well-ordered row of the flip-flops designed on the basis of the $p_{IEDTw}(x)$ is shown bellow, where $n=15$ (odd number) and $i+1=12$ (even number):

D	D	T	T	D	D	T	T	D	D	D	$_\oplus$T	T	T	T
1	2	3	4	5	6	7	8	9	10	11	12	13	14	15

In order to determine the coefficients k and r, we look into the second row of Table 1, where k=6 and r=14. The final interlaced structure of IEDT-LFSR is as follows:

D	T	D	T	T	D	T	D	D	D	D	$\oplus$T	T	T	T
6	7	5	8	4	9	3	10	2	11	1	12	15	13	14

Low area overhead

The area overhead of the DT-LFSR is lower than in the case of the CA and the LFSR developed in [12]. In order to construct the test pattern generator for n-input CUT with m registered inputs we need to use:

- approximately $n+n/2$ XOR gates to build the TPG in the form of n-bit CA,
- at least $n+1$ XOR gates to build the TPG in the form of n-bit LFSR with all T-type flip-flops,
- only about m XOR gates to build the TPG in the form of n-bit DT-LFSR.

Moreover, some examples of the testing logic area reduction in ACTEL and ALTERA FPGAs, which was achieved due to the use of LFSRs with D and T flip-flops, can be found in [10] and [8], respectively.

Availability of the structures of the DT-LFSR

There are DT-LFSR type registers available that implement the primitive polynomial for many values of their length n. There are examples of the structures of the DT-LFSRs implementing the primitive polynomial for the values $n \in [15, 100]$ given in Table 2. In the remaining cases the register of type IEDT-LFSR and EEDT-LFSR containing only one XOR gate in the feedback loop can be found. The examples for $n \in [16, 27]$ of such type registers are given in Table 3.

Table 2.

n	DT-LFSR with structure $D^k T^r$							
15	$D^{14}T$,	$D^{11}T^4$,	D^7T^8,	D^4T^{11}				
17	$D^{14}T^3$,	$D^{12}T^5$,	$D^{11}T^6$,	D^6T^{11},	D^5T^{12},	D^3T^{14}		
18	D^7T^{11}							
20	D^3T^{17}							
21	$D^{19}T^2$,	D^2T^{19}						
22	$D^{21}T$							
23	$D^{18}T^5$,	$D^{14}T^9$,	D^9T^{14},	D^5T^{18}				
25	$D^{22}T^3$,	$D^{18}T^7$,	D^7T^{18},	D^3T^{22}				
28	$D^{15}T^{13}$,	D^9T^{19}						
29	D^2T^{27},	$D^{27}T^2$						
31	$D^{28}T^3$,	$D^{25}T^6$,	$D^{24}T^7$,	$D^{18}T^{13}$,	$D^{13}T^{18}$,	D^7T^{24},	D^6T^{25},	D^3T^{28}
33	$D^{20}T^{13}$,	$D^{13}T^{20}$						
35	$D^{33}T^2$,	D^2T^{33}						
36	$D^{25}T^{11}$							

n	DT-LFSR with structure D^kT^f						
39	$D^{35}T^4$,	$D^{31}T^8$,	$D^{14}T^{25}$,	D^8T^{31}			
41	$D^{38}T^3$,	$D^{21}T^{20}$,	$D^{20}T^{21}$,	D^3T^{28}			
47	$D^{42}T^5$,	$D^{33}T^{14}$,	$D^{27}T^{20}$,	$D^{26}T^{21}$,	$D^{21}T^{26}$,	$D^{20}T^{27}$,	$D^{14}T^{33}$, D^5T^{42}
49	$D^{40}T^9$,	$D^{37}T^{12}$,	$D^{34}T^{15}$,	$D^{27}T^{22}$,	$D^{22}T^{27}$,	$D^{15}T^{34}$,	$D^{12}T^{37}$, D^9T^{40}
52	$D^{33}T^{19}$,	$D^{21}T^{31}$,	D^3T^{49}				
56	$D^{32}T^{24}$						
57	$D^{35}T^{22}$,	D^7T^{50}					
58	$D^{39}T^{19}$						
60	$D^{59}T$,	DT^{59}					
63	$D^{62}T$,	$D^{58}T^5$,	$D^{32}T^{31}$,	$D^{31}T^{32}$,	D^5T^{58},	DT^{62}	
65	$D^{47}T^{18}$,	$D^{33}T^{32}$,	$D^{32}T^{33}$,	$D^{18}T^{47}$			
68	D^9T^{59}						
71	$D^{65}T^6$,	$D^{62}T^9$,	$D^{53}T^{18}$,	$D^{51}T^{20}$,	$D^{36}T^{35}$,	$D^{35}T^{36}$,	$D^{20}T^{51}$, $D^{18}T^{53}$,
	D^9T^{62},	D^6T^{65}					
73	$D^{48}T^{25}$,	$D^{45}T^{28}$,	$D^{42}T^{31}$,	$D^{31}T^{42}$,	$D^{28}T^{45}$,	$D^{25}T^{48}$	
79	$D^{70}T^9$,	$D^{60}T^{19}$,	$D^{19}T^{60}$,	D^9T^{70}			
81	$D^{77}T^4$,	$D^{65}T^{16}$,	$D^{35}T^{46}$,	$D^{16}T^{65}$			
84	$D^{13}T^{71}$						
87	$D^{74}T^{13}$,	$D^{13}T^{74}$					
89	$D^{51}T^{38}$,	$D^{38}T^{51}$					
93	$D^{91}T^2$						
94	$D^{21}T^{73}$						
95	$D^{84}T^{11}$,	$D^{78}T^{17}$,	$D^{17}T^{78}$,	$D^{11}T^{84}$			
97	$D^{91}T^6$,	$D^{85}T^{12}$,	$D^{64}T^{33}$,	$D^{63}T^{34}$,	$D^{34}T^{63}$,	$D^{33}T^{64}$,	$D^{12}T^{85}$, D^6T^{91}
98	$D^{87}T^{11}$,	$D^{27}T^{71}$					
100	$D^{63}T^{37}$						

Table 3.

n	IEDT-LFSR with structure $D^bT^f \oplus D^cT^g$	EEDT-LFSR with structure $D^cT^g \oplus D^bT^f$
16	$D^7T^8 \oplus T^2D^5$	$D^5T^2 \oplus T^8D^7$
19	$D^5T^8 \oplus T^6$	$T^6 \oplus T^8D^5$
24	$D^{19}T^2 \oplus T^3$	$T^3 \oplus T^2D^{19}$
26	$D^{15}T^8 \oplus T^3$	$T^3 \oplus T^8D^{15}$
27	$D^{10}T^8 \oplus T^9$	$T^9 \oplus T^8D^{10}$

6 Conclusions

The use of the DT-LFSRs, IEDT-LFSRs and EEDT-LFSRs as the cheap, efficient and operating with high frequency test pattern generators is proposed in this paper. The overall model and the algebraic description of the operation of these registers have been introduced. The methods of the new type registers synthesis have also been developed. Moreover, the formula that allows to compute the values of the phase shift in the DT-LFSR have been derived. The DT-LFSR structure and topology modification techniques, which allow for changing the number and the arrangement of the T flip-flops in the register as well as the improvement of the DT-LFSR timing parameters, have been developed, too. The list of the available structures of the n-bit DT-LFSR for $n \in [15, 100]$ is included in the paper.

DT-LFSR is the type of dedicated solution for the test pattern generator. Its structure depends on the structure of the CUT. In particular, the number and the arrangement of the T flip-flops in the DT-LFSR have to be adjusted to the needs of CUT efficient testing. However, due to the large flexibility of the structure of the DT-LFSR this task can be easily accomplished using one of the methods which has been presented in the paper.

References

1. Bardell P.H.: Discrete logarithms in a parallel pseudorandom pattern generator analysis method. J. Elect. Testing: Theory and Appl., Vol. 3. (1992) 17-31
2. Bhavsar D.K., Edmondson J.H.: Alpha 21164 Testability Strategy. IEEE Design and Test of Computers, vol. 14, No 1 (January-March 1997) 25-33.
3. David R.: Random Testing of Digital Circuits. Theory and Applications, Marcel Dekker, Inc., New York (1998)
4. Garbolino T., Hławiczka A.: Test Pattern Generator for Delay Faults Based on LFSR with D, T Flip-Flops and Internal Inverters. Proc. of Design and Diagnostics of Electronic Circuits and Systems Workshop, Szczyrk, Poland (2-4 September 1998) 153-160
5. Garbolino T., Hławiczka A.: Synthesis and Analysis of New LFSRs with D- and T-Flip-Flops, Inverters, XOR- and IOR-Gates. Proc. of 11th Workshop on Test Technology and Reliability of Circuits and Systems (TWS'99), Potsdam, Germany, (28th February-2nd March 1999) 34-37
6. Hławiczka A.: Built-in Self-test Using Time Linear Compression. Journal on New Generation of Computer Systems. Akademie-Verlag, Berlin, (1990) 337-352
7. Hławiczka A.: D or T Flip-Flop Based Linear Registers. Archives of Control Sciences, vol. 1, (XXXVII), No 3-4 (1992) 249-268
8. Hławiczka A., Binda J.: The Optimized Synthesis of Self-Testable Finite State Machines Using BIST-PST Structures in ALTERA Structures. Proc. of 4th International Workshop on Field Programmable Logic and Applications, September 7-9, 1994, Prague. Lecture Notes in Computer Science No 849. Springer Verlag Press (1994) 120-122
9. Hortensius P.D., McLeod R.D., Pries W., Miller D.M., Card H.C.: Cellular Automata-Based Pseudorandom Number Generators for Built-In Self-Test. IEEE Transactions on Computer-Aided Design, Vol. 8, No. 8 (August 1989) 842-858
10. Muszyński J., Hławiczka A.: Design of Fast LFSR and MISR Linear Registers Using Resources of OTP Type FPGA Circuits Produced by ACTEL and XILINX. Proc. of Design and Diagnostics of Electronic Circuits and Systems Workshop, Szczyrk, Poland (September 2-4 1998) 193-199
11. Odlyzko A.M., Discrete Logarithms in Finite Fields and Their Cryptographic Significance. Lecture Notes in Computer Science, Vol. 209 (1984) 224
12. Yarmolik V.N., Murashko I.A.: A new test pattern generator design approach for VLSI built-in self-testing. Automatic Control & Computer Sciences, No 6 (1995) 25-35

Transparent Word-Oriented Memory BIST Based on Symmetric March Algorithms

V.N. Yarmolik[1,2], I.V. Bykov[1] S. Hellebrand[3], H.-J. Wunderlich[3]

[1] Computer Systems Department, Belarussian State University of Informatics and Radioelectronics, P.Brovki 6, Minsk, 220027, Belarus
yarmolik@yvn_poit.minsk.by
[2] Bialystok University of Technology, Department of Computer Science, Poland
[3] Division of Computer Architecture, University of Stuttgart, Breitwiesenstr. 20/22, 70656 Stuttgart, Germany

Abstract. The paper presents a new approach to transparent BIST for word-oriented RAMs which is based on the transformation of March transparent test algorithms to the symmetric versions. This approach allows to skip the signature prediction phase inherent to conventional transparent memory testing and therefore to significantly reduce test time. The hardware overhead and fault coverage of the new BIST scheme are comparable to the conventional transparent BIST structures. Experimental results show that in many cases the proposed test techniques achieve a higher fault coverage in shorter test time.

1 Introduction

Today semiconductor memory testing becomes one of the strategic position in the area of computer systems design and diagnosis. It can be explained by the following two main reasons: memory devices are used in any computer and most other digital systems and play a key role in terms of correct functioning the complete system, and on the other hand, advances in memory technology make memory testing more and more complicated due to appearance of the new defect mechanisms in memory devices and constraints of fault coverage and the time spent on the test procedures.

In this paper we concentrate our attention on one of the most important group of test techniques used for solving the problem of memory testing: transparent Built-In Self-Test (BIST) for Random Access Memories. These techniques were introduced due to the problem of the limited accessibility of embedded memories which are widely used in many critical applications (medical electronics, railway control, avionics, telecommunications etc.) and allow to restore the initial contents of memories at the end of the test session.

A number of BIST approaches were developed in the past [1-10]. These approaches are devoted to many aspects of BIST for RAMs: test algorithms, test hardware implementation, efficient mechanisms for consistency checking etc.

Taking into account the results related to transparent memory testing [2, 4, 10, 11] it should be concluded that the most frequently used test algorithms for transparent RAM BIST are march tests [12-14] which combine a high fault coverage with an acceptable test time even for memories of the large sizes (1M and higher). Another advantage of these algorithms is that they can be easily extended to transparent versions [11]. However, the traditional approaches to transforming non-transparent march algorithms to transparent tests implies significant increasing test time needed for calculating the learnt signature. It can be illustrated by the following example. Let us consider four-bit memory and transparent version of the MATS+ algorithm [12] (see Fig 1.) which can be written as {⇔ (w0); ⇑ (r0, w1); ⇓ (r1, w1)}. Throughout the paper we will use the notations presented below:

1. a^c: complementary value of $a \in \{0, 1\}$;
2. ⇑: increasing addressing order;
3. ⇓: decreasing addressing order;
4. ⇔: arbitrary addressing order;
5. w0, w1: write 0, 1 into memory cell;
6. r0, r1: read memory cell, expected value is 0, 1;
7. wa, wa^c: write a, a^c into memory cell;
8. ra, ra^c: read memory cell and feed result into signature register, expected value is a, a^c;
9. (ra^c): read memory cell with expected value a and feed a^c into signature register.

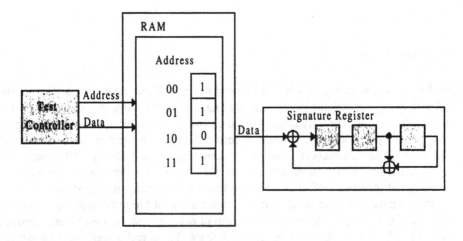

Fig. 1. BIST Scheme for RAMs

MATS+ algorithm can be transformed into a transparent test by removing the first march element (w0) which is used for RAMs initialization and replacing read and write operation with fixed values "0" and "1" with the appropriate values which depend on the sequence of Read and Write operations of the initial algorithm [11]. For MATS+ its transparent version consists of the following two phases:

1. {⇑ (ra); ⇓ (ra^c)};

2. $\{\Uparrow (ra, wa^\circ); \Downarrow (ra^c, wa)\}$.

The former phase called "signature prediction phase" is needed for calculating the learnt signature which depends on the memory contents, and the latter phase is used for RAM's testing. During the testing process after each Read operation the obtained data is fed into the signature register, and at the end of the test session the final signature S is compared with the learnt signature S^*.

In general, the signature prediction phase consists of all Read operations of the complete march algorithm. For the considered example it implies that one third of the test time is required for signature prediction. and this ratio is similar for any transparent march algorithm. To cope with this problem a new technique for transparent testing bit-oriented RAMs was proposed in [15]. In this paper we extend it to the case of word-oriented memories and show that this systematic approach allows to avoid spending extra time on performing signature prediction phase without any losses in fault coverage. The paper is organized as follows: The basic principles of the proposed BIST schemes are presented in Section 2. Section 3 demonstrates the general applicability of the new approach and Section 4 analyzes the experimental results and the fault coverage of the proposed technology for transparent RAMs testing.

2 March Algorithms Symmetry and Signature Prediction

It should be noticed that most of the march test algorithms used for transparent RAM BIST produce test data with a high degree of symmetry. To illustrate this statement, consider MATS+ algorithm again and the BISTed four-bit RAM shown in Figure 1. For the fault-free memory during the both phase the data sequence read from the memory can be represented the binary vector $(a_1, a_2, a_3, a_4, a_4^c, a_3^c, a_2^c, a_1^\circ) = (1, 1, 0, 1, 0, 1, 0, 0)$. The so-called property of symmetry of march algorithms is concluded in generation of bit sequence on the output of the RAM in reverse order and with complemented entries compared to the sequence produced by the previous march elements. Combining such a kind of symmetry with a certain type of signature register allows to completely omit the signature prediction phase of conventional transparent memory BIST techniques. The proposed transparent technique is based on the switching between the regular feedback polynomial and its reciprocal polynomial during signature analysis. To detail the new test methodology, consider the following formal definitions first introduced in [15].

Definition 1: The signature obtained for a test data string $d \in \{1, 0\}^n$ using single input signature register with feedback polynomial $h(X) \in GF(2)[X]$ and initial state $s \in \{1, 0\}^k$ is denoted by $sig(d, s, h)$.

Definition 2: Let $h(X) = h_k X^k + h_{k-1} X^{k-1} + \ldots + h_1 X + h_0$ be a polynomial of degree k. Then $h^*(X) = X^k h(X^{-1}) = h_k + h_{k-1} X + \ldots + h_1 X^{k-1} + h_0 X^k$ denotes the reciprocal polynomial (the general structures of signature registers corresponding to $h(X)$ and $h^*(X)$ are shown in Figure 2).

Definition 3: Let $d=(d_0, ..., d_{n-1}) \in \{1, 0\}^n$ be a data stream, then $d^*=(d_{n-1}, ..., d_0)$ $\in \{1, 0\}^n$ denotes the data stream with components in reverse order, and $d^c=(d_0^c, ..., d_{n-1}^c) \in \{1, 0\}^n$ denotes the data stream with inverted components.

Consider a single input signature register with initial state $s \in \{1, 0\}^k$ with structure defined by feedback polynomial $h(X) \in GF(2)[X]$. Let $d \in \{1, 0\}^n$ be a test data stream with corresponding signature $\sigma = sig(d, s, h)$. It was shown [15] that signature analysis using $h^*(X)$ as feedback polynomial and the reversed signature σ^* as an initial state provides the original state s as signature for the data stream d^*. In other words,

$$sig(d^*, sig(d, s, h)^*, h^*)=s.$$

Figure 3 illustrates the above proposition.

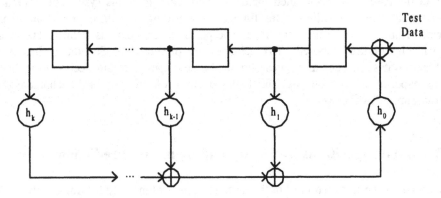

a) single-input signature register with feedback polynomial h(X)

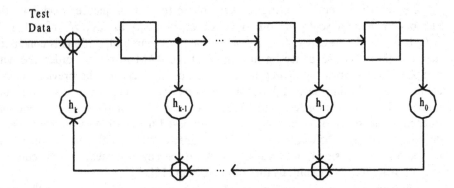

b) single-input signature register with feedback polynomial h*(X)

Fig. 2. Single-input signature registers with original and reciprocal feedback polynomial

The results obtained for single output signature analyzer can be extended to the case of multi-input signature register (MISR) and word-oriented RAM which is typical in practice. Let us consider BILBO-type MISR [16] presented in Figure 4.

This kind of signature analyzer (Type 1) is described by the original polynomial $h(X)=h_kX^k+ h_{k-1}X^{k-1}+...+ h_1X+h_0$, however a state of the register depends on a k-bit word $d_{k-1}...d_1d_0$ compacted instead just one bit d. The functioning of such an analyzer can be described by the following recursive expressions:

$$s_{k-1}(n)=d_{k-1}(n)+ \sum_{i=0}^{k-1}s_i(n-1)h_i \tag{1}$$

...

$$s_1(n)=d_1(n)+s_2(n-1) \tag{2}$$

$$s_0(n)=d_0(n)+s_1(n-1) \tag{3}$$

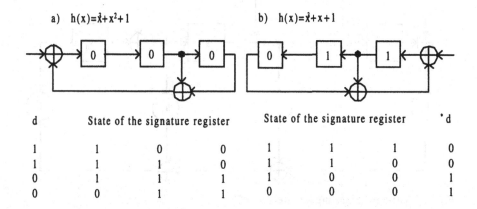

a) $h(x)=x^3+x^2+1$ b) $h(x)=x^3+x+1$

d	State of the signature register			State of the signature register			'd
1	1	0	0	1	1	1	0
1	1	1	0	1	1	0	0
0	1	1	1	1	0	0	1
0	0	1	1	0	0	0	1

Fig. 3. Signature analysis with the original and reciprocal feedback polynomial

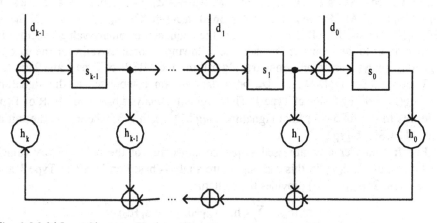

Fig. 4. Multi-Input Signature Register (Type1)

It is obvious, that the previous states of the register $s_{k-1}(n-1)$, ..., $s_1(n-1)$, $s_0(n-1)$ can be found from (1)-(3) as follows:

$$s_{k-1}(n-1)=s_{k-2}(n)+d_{k-2}(n) \qquad (4)$$

$$\cdots$$

$$s_1(n-1)=s_0(n)+d_0(n) \qquad (5)$$

$$s_0(n-1)=s_{k-1}(n)+d_{k-}$$

$$_1(n)+\sum_{i=0}^{k-2}(s_i(n)+d_i(n))h_{i+1} \qquad (6)$$

The expressions (4)-(6) define the structure of the MISR (Type 2) corresponding to the reciprocal polynomial $h^*(X) = h_k + h_{k-1}X + ... + h_1 X^{k-1} + h_0 X^k$ (see Figure 5).

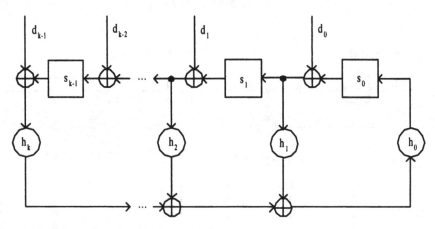

Fig. 5. Multi-Input Signature Register (Type2)

Let $msig(D, S, h)$ be a signature obtained using MISR of Type 1 for a sequence of binary-valued vectors $D=D_0 D_1, ..., D_m$, where $D_i=(d_0, d_1, ..., d_{k-1})$, $S \in \{0, k\}^k$ is initial state of MISR, and h is polynomial $h(X)=h_k X^k + h_{k-1}X^{k-1}+...+ h_1 X + h_0 \in$ GF(2)[X]. Denote $D^* = D_m, D_{m-1}, ..., D_0$ the sequence of binary-valued vectors in reverse order to the sequence D. Then the following theorem is valid for the case of signature analysis based on symmetric algorithms and MISRs of Type 1 and Type2.

Theorem: Let $D=D_0 D_1, ..., D_m$ be a data stream compressed to the signature $\sigma=msig(D, S, h)$ by MISR of Type 1. Then signature analysis based on MISR of Type 2 results in the following final signature $msig^{-1}(D^*, \sigma, h^*)=S$, where σ is the initial state of MISR of Type 2.

Proof: Consider a compressed sequence consisting of the only binary-valued vector $(d_0, d_1, ..., d_{k-1})$. In this case signature analysis based on MISR of Type 1 and initial state $S=(s_{k-1}, ..., s_0)$ provides the signature

$$\sigma=(d_{k-1}+\sum_{i=0}^{k-1} s_i h_i, s_{k-1}+d_{k-2}, ..., s_1+d_0).$$

Signature analysis based on MISR of Type 2 results in

$$(s_{k-1}+d_{k-2}+d_{k-2}, ..., s_1+d_0+d_0, d_{k-1}+(d_{k-1}+\sum_{i=0}^{k-1}s_i h_i)h_k+$$

$$\sum_{i=1}^{k-1}(s_i+d_{i-1})h_i+\sum_{i=1}^{k-1}d_{i-1}h_i)=(s_{k-1}, ..., s_0)=S.$$

The proof for a sequence of binary-valued vectors with an arbitrary length m follows by induction.

q.e.d.

An example of signature analysis with MISRs is presented in Figure 6.

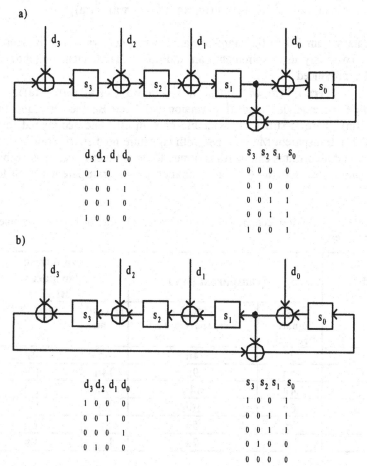

Fig. 6. Signature analysis with multi-input registers

3 Symmetric March Algorithms Construction

The proposed BIST schemes for bit- and word-oriented RAMs can be used with any transparent march test which is symmetric in the following sense.

Definition 4: Let $D \in \{0, 1\}^{2n}$ be a data string. D is called symmetric, if there exists a data string $d \in \{0, 1\}^n$ with $D=(d, d^*)$ or $D=(d, d^{*c})$. A transparent march test is called symmetric, if it produces a symmetric data string D.

In general, it cannot be expected, that an arbitrary transparent march test is symmetric. However, any march test can be easily extended to fully symmetric version. Consider the March C- algorithm as an example [14]. The initial algorithm version is defined as

$$\{\Leftrightarrow(w0);\ \Uparrow(r0, w1);\ \Uparrow(r1, w0);\ \Downarrow(r0, w1);\ \Downarrow(r1, w0);\ \Leftrightarrow(r0)\}$$

and its transparent version is

$$\{\Uparrow(ra, wa^c);\ \Uparrow(ra^c, wa);\ \Downarrow(ra, wa^c);\ \Downarrow(ra^c, wa);\ \Downarrow(ra)\}.$$

The test data stream fed to the signature analyzer is not symmetric in sense of Definition 4. To satisfy its requirements an additional march element (shown in bold) has to be introduced:

$$\{\Uparrow(\mathbf{ra^c});\ \Uparrow(ra, wa^c);\ \Uparrow(ra^c, wa);\ \Downarrow(ra, wa^c);\ \Downarrow(ra^c, wa);\ \Downarrow(ra)\}.$$

Despite the extended algorithm version will increase the test time from $O(9n)$ to $O(10n)$, there is still a considerable gain in efficiency compared to the conventional 14n transparent Marc C- test with signature prediction. Similarly, any known transparent algorithms can be transformed to its symmetric versions. Table 1 shows the resulting test lengths for some commonly used transparent march tests [12].

Table 1. Comparison of test complexities for conventional transparent and symmetric transparent march tests

Algorithm	Transparent BIST		Symmetric Transparent BIST	
	Time for Signature Prediction	Time for Transparent Test	Overall Time	Overall Time
MATS+	2n	4n	6n	4n
March C-	5n	9n	14n	10n
March A	4n	14n	18n	16n
March B	6n	16n	22n	18n
March X	3n	5n	8n	6n
March Y	5n	7n	12n	8n

4 Fault Coverage Issues

For investigation the ability of the proposed approach to transparent BIST for word-oriented memories 16K RAM of organization 8x2K was simulated (discussion of the investigated fault models (SAF: stuck-at faults, TF: transition faults, CFid:

idempotent coupling faults, CFin: inversion coupling faults can be found in [12, 13]). As can be observed (see Table 2), the new BIST scheme provides fault coverage comparable with conventional BIST technique.

5 Conclusions

A new approach to transparent BIST for word-oriented RAMs has been proposed which exploits symmetries in march algorithms. Compared to traditional transparent BIST schemes this new approach provides significant reduction in test time while preserving the benefits of conventional approaches with respect to hardware overhead and fault coverage.

Table 2. Simulation results (fault coverage in % for single faults) for 8x2K RAM

Algorithm	March C		March C-		March X	
Fault Model	Conventional	Symmetric	Conventional	Symmetric	Conventional	Symmetric
SAF	100	100	99.59	100	100	100
TF	100	100	99.69	100	99.70	99.95
Cfid	99.98	100	99.91	100	49.98	49.98
Cfin	99.94	100	99.78	100	99.87	99.89

References

1. V.C. Alves, M. Nicolaidis, P.Lestrat, and B.Courtois: Built-In Self-Test for Multi-Port RAMs; Proceedings IEEE International Conference on Computer-Aided Design, ICCAD-91, November 1991, pp. 248-251.
2. S. Barbagallo, F. Corno, P.Prinetto, M.Sonza Reorda: Testing a Switching Memory in Telecommunication System; Proceedings IEEE International Test Conference, Washington, DC, Oct. 1995, pp. 947-953.
3. H. Cheung, S. K. Gupta: A BIST Methodology for Comprehensive Testing of RAM with Reduced Heat Dissipation; Proceedings IEEE International Test Conference, Washington, DC, Oct. 1996, pp. 386-395.
4. B. Cockburn, Y.-F. Sat: Synthesized Transparent BIST for Detecting Scrambled Pattern-Sensitive Faults in RAMs; Proceedings IEEE International Test Conference, Washington, DC, Oct. 1995, pp. 23-32.
5. R. Dekker, F. Beenker, and L. Thijssen: Realistic Built-In Self-Test for Static RAMs; IEEE Desing & Test of Computers, Vol. 6, No. 1, Feb. 1989, pp. 26-34.
6. K. Kinoshita, K. K. Saluja: Built-In Testing of Memory Using an On-Chip Compact Testing Scheme; IEEE Transactions on Computers, Vol. C-35, No. 10, October 1986, pp. 862-870.
7. K.T. Le, K.K. Saluja: A Novel Approach for Testing Memories Using a Built-In Self-Testing Technique; Proceedings IEEE International Test Conference, Washington, DC, Oct. 1986, pp. 830-839.

8. P. Olivo, M. Dalpasso: Self-Learning Signature Analysis for Non-Volatile Memory Testing; Proceedings IEEE International Test Conference, Washington, DC, Oct. 1996, pp. 303-308.

9. N. Sakashita et al.: A Built-in Self-Test Circuit with Timing Margin Test Function in a 1 Gbit Synchronous DRAM; Proceedings IEEE International Test Conference, Washington, DC, Oct. 1996, pp. 319-324.

10. V. N. Yarmolik, S. Hellebrand, H.-J. Wunderlich; Self-Adjusting Output Data Compression: An Efficient BIST Technique for RAMs; Proceedings Design and Test in Europe (DATE'98), Paris, February 1998, pp. 173-179.

11. M. Nicolaidis: Transparent BIST for RAMs; Proceedings IEEE International Test Conference, Baltimore, MD, Oct. 1992, pp. 598-607.

12. A. J. Van de Goor: Testing Semiconductor Memories, Theory and Practice; Chichester: John Wiley & Sons, 1991.

13. A. J. Van de Goor: Using March Tests to Test SRAMs; IEEE Desing & Test of Computers, Vol. 10, No. 1, March 1993, pp. 8-14.

14. M. Marinescu: Simple and Efficient Algorithms for Functional RAM Testing; Proceedings IEEE International Test Conference, 1982, pp. 236-239.

15. V.N.Yarmolik, S.Hellebrand, H.-J.Wunderlich: Symmetric Transparent BIST for RAMs, DATE-99, Munich, March 9-12, 1999, pp. 702-707.

16. B. Koenemann, J. Mucha, G. Zwihoff: Built-In Logic Block Observation Technique; Proceedings IEEE International Test Conference, 1979, pp. 37-41.

Session 9

Networks and Distributed Systems

Chair: Gilles Muller, INRIA/IRISA, Rennes, France

Achieving Fault-Tolerant Ordered Broadcasts in CAN

Jörg Kaiser, Mohammad Ali Livani
University of Ulm, Department of Computer Structures, 89069 Ulm, Germany
{kaiser, mohammad}@informatik.uni-ulm.de

Abstract. The paper focuses on the problem to guarantee reliable and ordered message delivery to the operational sites of a CAN-Bus network. The contributions of the paper are firstly a hardware mechanism to handle rare failure situations and secondly, a protocol to guarantee the same order of messages on all nodes. After analyzing the error handling mechanism, we suggest a hardware extension to capture situations, which may lead to inconsistent views about the status of a message between the nodes. Based on this mechanism, which enhances the guarantees of the CAN-Bus with respect to reliable message transmission, we develop a deadline-based total ordering scheme. By carefully exploiting the properties of CAN, this can be achieved with very low additional message overhead.

Keywords. Real-time communication, fault-tolerance, reliable broadcast, CAN.

1 Introduction

Dependability is one of the most important design dimensions for many applications in the area of real-time control systems. A distributed real-time architecture supports in many ways the aspect of dependability as well as other related demands of process control like modularity and improved extensibility. Therefore, distributed systems, composed from a network of micro-controllers connected via a field-bus network become increasingly popular in process control and automotive applications. In these cooperative distributed systems, reliable coordination of distributed actions becomes a critical issue. Atomic broadcast protocols represent a mature technology to support this coordination of distributed actions in the presence of network and node failures. In contrast to general-purpose applications, real-time control systems put some additional challenging requirements to these protocols. Firstly, they have to meet temporal constraints dictated by the controlled external environment, usually given in terms of deadlines. This means that the communication has to be predictable and bounded in the temporal domain. Secondly, the nodes in these systems consisting of micro-controllers typically offer limited processing and memory capacity. Additionally, field-bus networks connecting these nodes generally exhibit a lower bandwidth compared to general purpose LANs. These constraints demand for efficient mechanisms, which carefully exploit the capability and functionality of the underlying hardware basis.

Reliable atomic broadcast protocols are widely used in dependable distributed computing. There is, however, a wide class of protocols, which are not designed for real-time systems and therefore completely lack respective properties [3, 4, 5]. Even those protocols which are explicitly designed for dependable real-time systems, like [6,7] cannot be used in a fieldbus environment straightforwardly. The reasons are mainly the constraints, set by low performance micro-controllers and low network bandwidth. In a control system composed from micro-controllers it is vital to free the host processor as much as possible from executing complex protocol algorithms. Equally important, these systems demand for minimizing the communication overhead usually necessary to achieve a consensus about the message status and order in a reliable broadcast protocol. Therefore, it is important to carefully analyze the properties of the network to exploit the functionality that is already available on the controller level.

The paper focuses on mechanisms to support reliable atomic broadcast on the CAN-bus. Among the established field bus networks, CAN constitutes an emerging standard and particularly supports a decentralized control architecture. Developed by BOSCH [1], CAN is primarily aimed at automotive applications which omit a single point of control or a master-slave communication relation often found in industrial automation. Because CAN was designed for reliable operation in a control environment, it has a number of comprehensive mechanisms to detect and handle communication faults. Particularly, CAN has a built-in mechanism which aims at achieving consensus about the success of a message transfer for all participants immediately, i.e. before the message is delivered to the host processor by the CAN communication controller. Thus, in most situations, the sender handles the fault transparently on the controller level by automatically discarding the faulty message and initiating retransmission. However, a careful analysis of the CAN-bus mechanisms with respect to atomic broadcast protocols in [2] reveals that in specific situations inconsistencies may arise which cannot be handled by the standard CAN protocol.

An atomic broadcast protocol provides reliable message transmission to all operational nodes under anticipated fault assumptions and guarantees that all nodes received the messages in the same order. The paper presents solutions to these two requirements. To provide reliable message transfer under omission and crash failures we describe a new hardware mechanism SHARE (SHadow REtransmitter), which guarantees an all-or-nothing property of message delivery. This means that a message is eventually correctly delivered or discarded at all operational nodes. Based on this atomicity property, we develop an ordering scheme based on deadlines. The specific feature of our scheme compared to other approaches [6, 19] is that it considers the coexistence of hard and soft real-time messages. While hard real-time messages are critical and must be delivered at some specified deadline, soft real-time messages may miss their deadlines under transient overload.

The achievement of the paper is to provide the atomic broadcast protocol for CAN with very low overhead for the host processors and the communication network. By using SHARE, error detection and retransmissions of messages is completely handled at the network controller level. Order is established by exploiting the CAN properties without additional communication overhead. Another important benefit of the protocol is that the temporal behaviour of the system is highly predictable and does not change with the number of nodes in the system.

The paper sets out with the problem analysis. It comprises a brief description of the basic CAN mechanisms, which are a prerequisite to understand the critical faults which lead to inconsistencies. These inconsistencies are analyzed in the subsequent section. Chapter 3 describes the SHARE hardware component to achieve consistent delivery of messages in spite of sender crashes. Based on these results, chapter 4 presents our mechanism to establish order between the messages based on their deadlines. Chapter 5 summarizes related work and a conclusion is presented in Chapter 6.

2 Problem Analysis

CAN handles arbitration and performs message validation and error signaling in a very specific way. Because this is exploited by our mechanisms, we will briefly introduce the basic CAN properties. CAN (ISO 11898 an 11519-1) is a broadcast CSMA-network targeted to operate in an automotive or industrial automation environment with speeds of up to 1 Mbit/sec, exchanging small real-time control messages. The CAN-specification [1] developed by BOSCH covers the functionality of layers 1 (physical layer) and 2 (data link layer) of the ISO/OSI protocol stack. CAN is a variant of a polled bus [8], which relies on three properties.

1. Every bit of a message will propagate to all connected nodes before the next bit will be sent, thus enabling all nodes to see the same bit value during a certain time window.
2. The sender monitors the bus at the same time it transmits. For every bit, a sender can check if the bus carries the signal level which was transmitted.
3. There are dominant and recessive signal levels. A single dominant signal level overrides any number of recessive signal levels.

If two stations start transmission at the same time, a collision will occur. Different from other CSMA-networks, however, collisions always lead to a well-defined signal level on the bus because of the property 1 and 3. In most implementations, the CAN-bus behaves like a wired AND circuit for all bit values sent at the same time, i.e. a "0" denotes a dominant and a "1" denotes a recessive value. This basic feature of the CAN-bus is exploited for:

- Efficient use of available network bandwidth by providing a non-destructive arbitration of the bus based on the priority of messages.
- Immediate error detection, signaling and automatic retransmission of messages.

2.1 CAN arbitration

The priority-based non-destructive arbitration scheme assures that a collision does not destroy the messages on the bus, but the message with the highest priority will be transferred without further delay. Collisions are resolved during the arbitration process, i.e. when sending the arbitration field, which contains a unique ID for each message. If a node during the arbitration process sends out a recessive level but monitors a dominant level on the bus, it stops transmission because it knows that a message with higher priority is competing for the bus. The CAN arbitration mechanism thus acts as a global priority-based non-preemptive message dispatcher, guaranteeing that the message with the highest priority always is sent without delay. Additionally, the non-destructive arbitration scheme overcomes the drawback of general CSMA networks of low predictability and lost bandwidth because of collisions under high load conditions.

2.2 CAN error detection and fault handling

The second important feature of CAN is that it provides a validation mechanisms to achieve a consistent view about the status of a message at the end of every individual message transfer. Every message will be accepted or rejected by all participants. CAN has a comprehensive set of error detection mechanisms, which comprise bit monitoring, bit stuffing, cyclic redundancy checking and frame consistency checks [1]. Here, only the error signaling mechanism will be examined in more detail because it takes part in providing consensus about the message status in CAN. The error signaling mechanism is realized by exploiting bit monitoring and the CAN bit-stuffing mechanism. The CAN bit-stuffing mechanism always inserts an additional complementary bit in the bit-stream of a message when a string of 5 consecutive bits with the same value are detected. When a CAN controller (sender or receiver) detects an error locally it will invalidate the ongoing message transfer by sending out an error frame consisting of a string of 6 dominant bits. This violates the CAN bit-stuffing rule and consequently, will be detected by all other nodes, including the sender. As a result, the receivers will discard the current message from their local in-queues and start error signaling themselves. After error signaling is terminated, the sender will automatically retransmit the message. Thus, relating a corrupted message to its source and retransmitting it will be done at the controller level. For the host processor the automatic retransmission procedure is transparent.

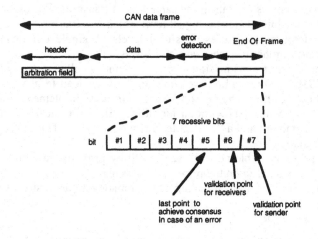

Fig. 1. Schematic outline of a CAN data frame

To allow last moment frame error detection for nodes which are completely out of synchronization, CAN provides an end-of-frame field (EOF) consisting of 7 recessive bits (see Fig. 1). Nodes which are aware of receiving the EOF will disable the mechanism detecting a bit-stuffing violation. Only nodes which are not aware of receiving an EOF will detect a bit-stuffing error when sampling bit #6. They will start error signaling in bit #7 of the EOF.

If the receivers did not observe the start of an error frame until the bit #6 of the EOF, they assume that the message is transmitted correctly and deliver it to their respective host processors. Let us term the point when the receiver locally samples bit #6 the validation point for receivers. The error frame can be viewed as a variant of a negative acknowledge (NAK). If no NAK occurs, the message is assumed to be transmitted correctly.

2.3 Sources of inconsistencies

Now consider that some receivers detect an error just in the bit #6 of the EOF. These receivers will discard the message and start an error frame. Obviously the error frame can only start in the subsequent bit, i.e. the bit #7 of EOF. At that time all receivers which did not detect or were not affected by the error have already accepted and delivered the message. They basically ignore the error frame. To cope with this situation and to prevent that some receivers have obtained the message and some others have not, the sender of the message waits until the bit #7 of the EOF before it assumes a correct message transmission. In the situation sketched above, the sender would recognize the error frame and initiate retransmission. This leads to "inconsistent message duplicates" [2] of the message at those nodes, which previously accepted the message. If the message is retransmitted immediately, these inconsistent duplicates can easily be detected by a sequence number which consists of a single toggle bit [9] in its simplest form.

However, there may be situations in which a higher priority message "b" becomes ready to transmit on some node which now competes with the message "a" to be retransmitted. Because of the global CAN priority scheme, the message "b" (or any number of higher priority messages) will be sent before the retransmission of message "a". In this situation, we encounter a problem affecting the order of messages. The nodes which have already received message "a" will see it before message "b" while the other nodes observe "a" after "b". This is not solved by the raw CAN protocol nor by the mechanisms provided by popular CAN application level protocols [9, 10, 11].

The CAN protocol guarantees that if the sender remains operational, it will retransmit the message until it is eventually received by all nodes. In case of a sender crash, however, there will be nodes, which have received the message while others never will receive the message. This constitutes an "inconsistent message omission" [2]. In the following two chapters, we introduce the concepts to deal with sender crashes and inconsistent order of messages. We start with describing SHARE, a hardware component to handle inconsistent omissions transparently, i.e. without any additional load for the nodes in the system. Built on this, we sketch the protocol that provides a deadline-based ordering scheme.

3 Using Shadow Retransmitters to Mask Sender Crashes

As discussed previously, CAN provides reliable message transmission (sometimes with duplicates) unless a sender crashes after a frame was received only by a subset of the receivers. In this case the sender cannot retransmit the frame which results in a permanent frame-level inconsistency.

This problem is solved by adding dedicated nodes to the system, which act as 'Shadow Retransmitters' (SHARE). A SHARE, schematically sketched in Fig. 2, captures frames, which are transmitted over CAN and detect the situation when an inconsistent omission is possible. In these situations they behave just like the sender and transmit the frame *simultaneously* with the original sender. This is feasible because of the physical properties of CAN; i.e. multiple senders may transmit *identical* frames. Hence, if the original sender crashes, the SHARE will mask the fault and retransmit the message. The SHARE mechanism is transparent and can be used in a system to cope with inconsistent omissions without changing the existing system components or affecting the temporal properties of the system. Currently, a SHARE consists of a dedicated micro-controller with CAN interface and a simple additional state machine to detect a unique bit pattern on the bus. This bit pattern only is generated when a situation occurs which may lead to inconsistent omissions.

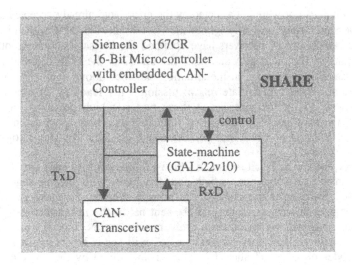

Fig. 2. Components of a SHARE

The detection of a possible inconsistent omission is based on a simple fact: a frame-level inconsistency is only possible if at least one non-faulty node observes an error, i.e. a dominant level in bit #6 in the EOF pattern. In this case, the sender is expected to retransmit the frame, thus a SHARE should also retransmit the frame.

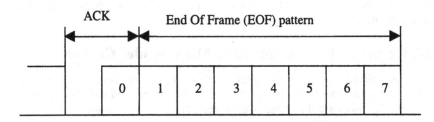

Fig. 3. Bit pattern terminating a CAN message frame

The terminating bit sequence of a CAN message frame comprises a total number of 8 recessive bits, one bit from the acknowledge field and seven bits of the EOF. It is shown in Fig. 3. As we stated before, retransmission by a SHARE is not allowed if an error occurs before bit #6 of the EOF. These situations are handled consistently by the standard CAN protocol.

The situation, in which a SHARE is expected to retransmit a frame, occurs if set of nodes E (with at least one element) detects an error during the bit #6 of EOF. These nodes will start an error frame at bit #7, which is observed by all nodes including the SHARE. The sender is now obliged to retransmit. To prevent an inconsistent message omission in case of a sender crash, the SHARE is expected to transmit the message simultaneously.

We observe, that the bit pattern, which is generated by this error is unique, i.e. it cannot be generated by some single error at some other section of the message frame. If some node detects an error in bit #6 the error is flagged in bit#7 of the EOF by sending a dominant bit value. Thus, the characteristic sequence is 7 recessive bits followed by a dominant bit. This sequence cannot occur during normal message transfer or error processing because of the bit stuffing rule and subsequent error signaling. Thus, a SHARE can easily be implemented by a state machine, which detects this particular sequence. Note, that at this time, the CAN-Controller of the SHARE has a valid message frame in his receive buffer.

Finally, the situation may occur that a node detects an error during bit #7. This node will be the sender or a SHARE because all receivers already have accepted the message. If any SHARE detects the message during bit #7, then it will retransmit. In this situation, a SHARE exactly behaves like any sender which detects an error in bit #7. Hence, a sender crash is always masked by a SHARE.

The actions of a SHARE are time critical. In order to start the frame retransmission simultaneously with the sender; a SHARE must be ready to retransmit a frame immediately after receiving it. To be more precise, after detecting an error at the last bit of a frame, a SHARE must start its retransmission within 3 bit-times. At the maximum bit-rate of 1Mbit/s, a SHARE has no more than 3 μ-seconds to start the retransmission of the last received frame. Currently, SHARE components are realized by dedicated hardware. The main component of a SHARE is a 16-bit Siemens microcontroller C167 [12], which has an embedded CAN controller and a special fast interrupt handling unit. This unit, called PEC (Peripheral Event Controller) enables the transfer of a word or byte from a source address to a destination address with minimal CPU interaction. SHARE uses 3 PEC transfer channels to:

1) convert the CAN receive buffer of the last received frame to a transmit buffer,
2) initiate its transmission, and
3) prepare the next free buffer for receiving another frame.

A PEC transfer only takes 2 processor clock cycles. Because the processor interrupt response delay (due to the pipeline) takes no more than 7 processor bus access cycles [12], the necessary steps (1-3) for retransmission are completed in less than 2 μs at a processor clock rate of 20MHz. Hence, a SHARE is fast enough for operating at the highest bit-rate of 1Mbit/s.

The error detection including the special treatment of bit #6 is realized by a relatively simple 22v10 Gate-Array Logic (GAL) which is directly connected to the CAN transceivers. The logic detects a characteristic sequence on the bus indicating that a dominant level occurred in bit #7 of the EOF. The error detector immediately raises an interrupt, which activates the PEC transfer channels. A listing of the GAL map can be found in [13].

The main advantage of dedicated SHARE components is their transparency. Existing CAN networks may add a SHARE to the bus in order to guarantee consistent frame delivery in the case of an inconsistent omission failure caused by a sender crash. No additional protocol overhead is necessary in fault-free situations. Even when an omission occurs, there is no additional effort to detect and handle the situation. A SHARE realizes a fault-tolerant sender, which retransmit a message with very high reliability. This is important when considering the overall bus scheduling which needs not to distinguish between consistent and inconsistent omission failures.

4 Achieving Order

With the introduction of SHARE components we solved the problem of inconsistent omission failures. We now can safely assume that each message which is received by a node will eventually be received by all operational nodes in the system even if the sender crashes and fails to retransmit. This is summarized in assumption (A1): If one non-faulty node receives a message, then all non-faulty nodes eventually receive this message.

Our scheme to establish order between messages assumes that in a real-time control system, a message has to be delivered at its deadline. We further assume the coexistence of critical hard real-time messages and less critical soft real-time messages. The former have to meet their deadlines otherwise the system fails unpredictably. Soft real-time messages may miss their deadlines under transient overload. Temporal constraints like deadlines or laxities can be converted into a priority scheme [8, 14, 22], which is used by the CAN priority-based message dispatching mechanism to globally schedule the messages. We use the eight most significant bits of the CAN-ID as an explicit priority field. In [14, 15] we develop a scheme which is a combination of a reservation-based, time triggered message scheduling for hard real-time communication requirements and least laxity first (LLF) for soft real-time messages. Because the detailed description of the mechanism is beyond the scope of this paper, we will only roughly sketch the basic ideas of the scheme. Let us start with the assumption for hard real-time messages (A2): Hard real-time messages are received before their deadlines by all operational nodes under an omission fault assumption.

For hard real-time messages fixed time slots are reserved like in a TDMA [16] or TTP [17] approach. Conflicting resource requirements between hard real-time messages are resolved off-line, i.e. at run-time two hard real-time messages never will compete for the CAN-bus. If a time slot for a specific hard real-time message arrives, the dynamic priority mechanism assures that the message has the highest priority of all messages currently competing for the bus. To cope with communication failures, our scheme provides time redundancy and multiple transmissions of the same message. If k omissions must be tolerated for a message needing the time Δt to be transmitted, the respective reserved time slot must be of length: $k * (\Delta t + \Delta r) + \Delta t$ where Δr is the recovery time (a more detailed discussion can be found in [15]). Because a SHARE handles inconsistent omissions (assumption A1) we can assume that A2 holds.

Soft real-time messages are scheduled according to the LLF (Least Laxity First) algorithm [8]. This means that in overload situations deadlines may be missed (assumption A3). Finally, we assume that the communication system can rely on the fact that the local real-time operating system will provide a message timely, i.e. before the transmission deadline is expired (assumption A4).

Based on these assumptions, we now can develop an ordering scheme. The algorithm relies on the reliable message transfer and on the knowledge about the message transmission deadlines. The *transmission deadline (TD)* of a message denotes the point of time, at which the message must be successfully transmitted to all non-faulty destination nodes. The transmission deadline is tightly related to the point in time, where the message delivery to all receiving application objects is expected. Therefore, the ordering mechanism reflects an application specific order related to temporal requirements. We maintain the order for hard real-time messages and soft real-time messages in two totally ordered sets separately. This is because consensus about the order of soft real-time messages cannot be derived under hard real-time constraints. This property has formally been proved in [20].

Let m and m' be two real-time messages with deadlines d_m and $d_{m'}$. Then the deadline-based ordering algorithm implements the following rule:

$$(O1): \quad dm < dm' \Rightarrow delj(m) \rightarrow delj(m')$$

This means that if the deadline of the message m is before the deadline of the message m', then m must be delivered to destination objects before m'. For hard real-time messages this is easy to show. Because hard real-time messages are scheduled off-line according to a time-triggered scheme and are transmitted in reserved time slots, the above rule follows immediately. The order between hard real-time messages can straightforwardly be formulated by the following delivery rule: Every hard real-time message is delivered at its deadline. Total order of hard real-time messages is guaranteed according to their deadlines.

To establish a total order between soft real-time messages is more complicated. Firstly, soft real-time messages may have identical transmission deadlines. This results in the same laxity that is mapped on the same priority. Secondly, under transient overload, multiple messages that already have missed their deadlines end up with the same laxity. In both cases we cannot use the priority field (8 most significant bits) in the CAN message ID alone to establish the order. However, because CAN IDs all must be different (to enable an unambiguous arbitration decision), some (arbitrary) order in which the messages are scheduled on the bus is determined by the unique less significant bits of the CAN-ID. Note, that in case of equal deadlines and in the situation that all laxities are "0", no relationship between the messages can exist because none of the messages has yet been sent. The following rule is used to ensure a global decision on the delivery order of messages m and m'.

$$(O2): \quad dm = dm' \Rightarrow (delj(m) \rightarrow delj(m')) \Leftrightarrow message\text{-}IDm < message\text{-}IDm')$$

In $O2$, $message\text{-}ID_m$ consists of a tuple $(d_m, sender\text{-}ID_m, r_m)$ with $sender\text{-}ID_m$ is some unique number for the sender and "r_m" are the remaining bits of the arbitration field. The $sender\text{-}ID_m$ makes sure that messages from different nodes competing for the bus have different CAN-IDs.

Soft real-time messages can become ready for transmission at any point in time. No a priori reservation or conflict resolution is performed. We may have messages with different and equal priorities. The ordering is based on the following properties:

P1: If a node has received a message m, and then another message with lower priority is observed on the CAN bus, or the bus is idle, then the sender of m will not retransmit it in future.

Assume that a message m is transmitted at least once on the CAN bus. Further, assume that the sending CAN controller still attempts to retransmit due to the inconsistent transmission. According to the CAN specification [1] the sender will try to retransmit m immediately, thus no bus idle period will be observed before the retransmission of m. Furthermore, no lower-priority message will be transmitted before the retransmission of m, because m will win the arbitration process against any lower-priority message. Because we assume reliable retransmission through a SHARE even in the case of sender crashes, we can enforce this property:

P2: Any receiver of a soft real-time message m can assume that the message has been received by all nodes when the receiver observes an idle bus or a message with a lower priority on the bus after receiving m.

P2 states the condition under which a receiver can detect that all nodes received a particular message. Now, to deliver this message, the receiver must be sure that it is delivered in the same order in all nodes. This order should be based on the transmission deadline. Therefore, we now must first clarify the question whether a message with an earlier deadline still can arrive. Based on our previous considerations we can conclude:

P3: A soft real-time message with a higher priority has an earlier deadline than a soft real-time message with a lower priority. If after the transmission deadline of a soft real-time message m another message with lower priority is transmitted on the CAN bus, or the bus is idle, then there is no other soft real-time message m' with an earlier or equal deadline, which is pending for transmission.

P3 is proved by the following considerations: Assume that a message m' with the deadline $d_{m'} < d_m$ is pending for transmission at the time $t > d_m$. Because of the deadline-based priority assignment the priority of m' is not lower than the priority of m. Due to assumption A4, m' has been pending for transmission at least since $d_{m'}$, hence at least since d_m. Hence the sender of m' must have been trying to transmit m' at the beginning of every bus-idle period since d_m. Therefore no idle bus can be observed before the successful transmission of m'. Also, no lower-priority message transmission can be observed on the bus before the successful transmission of m', because m' would win the arbitration process against any lower-priority message. Thus, if after d_m a message with a lower priority is transmitted on the CAN bus, or the bus is unused for some period of time, then m' has been already transmitted successfully before and hence has been received before m.

We now can derive the property which enables a total order between soft real-time messages:

P4: For any soft real-time message m, no preceding soft real-time message will arrive later, if after the transmission deadline d_m a lower-priority message is observed on the bus.

Therefore, the delivery rule which maintains total order of soft real-time messages can finally be established as follows:

SRTD: *(Soft Real-Time message Delivery)* Every received soft real-time message can be delivered in total order as soon as either another message with later deadline, or a bus idle time is observed after its transmission deadline.

In situations which are not affected by overload, soft real-time messages are transmitted and delivered in strict deadline order. If there is no idle bus detected (in this case an immediate delivery is performed) the message has at most to wait for one message transmission time to be delivered. In overload situations, no temporal guarantees can be granted. The deadlines cannot be used for ordering the messages. However, total order between soft real-time messages is still preserved. Duplication of messages is handled by a sequence number.

5 Discussion and Related Work

We presented a scheme to provide reliable atomic broadcast for CAN. Considering the broadcast mechanisms specifically developed for CAN, we examined some of the popular application level protocols available for industrial automation [9, 10, 11]. These protocols provide reliable message delivery for situations, which are covered by the standard CAN error detection and fault handling mechanisms. Thus, they fail to provide measures for inconsistent omissions. Additionally, they cannot guarantee the same order of messages in all nodes even under moderate fault assumptions. This is because message duplicates cannot be safely distinguished from new messages.

Reliable message transmission to all operational receivers can be achieved by appropriate retransmission mechanisms [2, 6, 18, 21]. A problem occurs when a sender crashes before it performs the retransmission. All approaches to handle this situation are based on the assumption that the sender has correctly transmitted the message at least once and at least one receiver has correctly received it. This receiver then can retransmit the message. In an eager approach, the receivers try to retransmit the message until they have observed a certain number of retransmissions [2, 6]. In the lazy approach the message is retransmitted only if a sender crash has been detected. It is obvious that the first approach incurs additional message overhead while the second approach relies on the detection of a sender crash that requires a time-out mechanism. What distinguishes our approach is the use of masking redundancy. With the introduction of SHARE components, the retransmission in case of a sender crash becomes completely transparent. No additional overhead is added to the protocol that would increase network load or affect the basic timing properties.

Concerning the mechanism to establish order, our scheme accommodates hard and soft real-time messages. We maintain order separately for the two classes of real-time messages. This is because the delivery of a hard real-time message should not rely on the successfully established order between soft real-time messages, which in overload situations is not time-bounded. To our knowledge, the only work specifically addressing ordering schemes for CAN is described in [2] and [19]. In [19] a CAD-tool is used to determine off-line, which messages in an application may be causally related. The deadlines of related messages are adjusted according to this analysis. Then, their dynamic priority scheme [22] is used to schedule the messages on the CAN-bus according to their fixed deadlines. The approach is only valid in systems in which all causal relationships can be determined off-line. Secondly, the approach treats all messages as hard real-time messages.

In [2] a protocol suite is presented which provides fault-tolerant broadcast in CAN under varying system assumptions. The protocols are referred as EDCAN (CAN Eager-Diffusion), RELCAN (Lazy Diffusion-based Protocol), and TOTCAN (Totally Ordered CAN-protocol). The EDCAN (CAN Eager-Diffusion) protocol is based on a multiple transmission policy similar to [6]. The problem with EDCAN is the high communication overhead of about 200% under normal operation. To overcome this efficiency problem, the authors propose a more efficient protocol called RELCAN. In this protocol, efficiency in the fault-free case is traded against a certain waiting time in case of a sender crash. Although this delay is predictable, it has to be considered in the worst case estimation of every message transfer. Finally the TOTCAN protocol is proposed which provides total order of messages. TOTCAN uses a two-phase scheme. Sender crashes are not tolerated by TOTCAN, although consistency of messages is maintained b y discarding a message for which it cannot be guaranteed that it has been received by all nodes. In contrast to our hardware-based solution to reliable message transfer, the software-oriented protocols require a substantial overhead. This overhead involves not only the communication system, which has to carry a higher load, but also the processing nodes, which explicitly have to perform retransmissions.

6 Conclusion

The paper presented mechanisms to achieve fault-tolerant broadcasts in CAN. The mechanisms for error detection and fault handling in CAN already cover a considerable fault class. However, there still exist situations in which CAN alone is not able to guarantee the all-or-nothing property of message reception and the consistent order of messages. We first introduced a hardware extension SHARE to provide atomicity of message reception. A SHARE component detects the specific situation where some nodes may have accepted a message while others have not. In this situation a retransmission is necessary. In combination with the mechanisms provided by CAN, SHARE components mask sender crashes. The hardware of a SHARE is simple and can be added to any existing CAN-bus network. Multiple SHARE components can be added to increase reliability. Based on the atomicity property, we develop a deadline-based consistent ordering mechanism. We treat hard real-time messages and soft real-time messages separately. Hard real-time messages are strictly ordered according to their deadlines: This is possible because all deadlines of hard real-time messages are different and conflicts are resolved off-line. In contrast, soft real-time messages, which are created dynamically, may have identical deadlines. Moreover, soft real-time messages may miss their deadlines under transient overload. By carefully exploiting the properties of CAN, we provide total order for hard real-time and soft real-time messages, respectively, without additional message overhead. By treating hard and soft real-time messages separately, we make sure that a hard real-time message never is delayed because it has to wait on the decision about the order of a soft real-time message.

Currently the protocol is implemented and we investigate the integration with an application level protocol using the publisher/subscriber communication model [23]. For the publisher/subscriber model which is based on anonymous communication, it is highly beneficial that the protocols devised in this paper can achieve atomicity and order without explicit knowledge of the sender and receivers of messages.

7 References

[1] ROBERT BOSCH GmbH: „CAN Specification Version 2.0", Sep. 1991.
[2] J. Rufino, P. Veríssimo, C. Almeida , L. Rodrigues: „Fault-Tolerant Broadcasts in CAN", Proc. FTCS-28, Munich, Germany, June 1998.
[3] K.P. Birman and T.A. Joseph: "Reliable Communication in the Presence of Failures", ACM Tr. Computer Systems, 5(1):47-76, Feb. 1987.
[4] J.M. Chang and N.F. Maxemchuk: „Reliable broadcast protocols", ACM Trans. on Computer Systems, 2(3), Aug. 1984, pp. 251-273.
[5] Weijia Jia, J. Kaiser, E. Nett:RMP: "Fault-Tolerant Group Communication", IEEE Micro, IEEE Computer Society Press, Los Alamitos, USAS. 59-67, April 1996
[6] F. Cristian: „Synchronous Atomic Broadcast for Redundant Broadcast Channels", The Journal of Real-Time Systems, Vol. 2, pp. 195-212, 1990.
[7] L. Rodrigues and P. Veríssimo: „xAMP: a Multi-primitive Group Communication Service", IEEE Proc. 11th Symposium on Reliable Distributed Systems, Houston TX, Oct. 1992.
[8] C.M. Krishna, K.G. Shin: „Real-Time Systems", McGraw-Hill, 1997
[9] CiA Draft Standards 201..207: „CAN Application Layer (CAL) for Industrial Applications", may 1993.
[10] DeviceNet Specification 2.0 Vol. 1, Published by ODVA, 8222 Wiles Road - Suite 287 - Coral Springs, FL 33067 USA.
[11] Smart Distributed Systems, Application Layer Protocol Version 2, Honeywell Inc, Micro Switch Specification GS 052 103 Issue 3, USA, 1996

[12] Siemens AG: „C167 User's Manual 03.96", Published by Siemens AG, Bereich Halbleiter, Marketing-Kommunikation, 1996.

[13] M.A. Livani:"SHARE: A Transparent Mechanism for Reliable Broadcast Delivery in CAN", Informatik Bericht 98-14, University of Ulm, 1998

[14] M.A. Livani, J. Kaiser, W. Jia: „Scheduling Hard and Soft Real-Time Communication in the Controller Area Network (CAN)", 23rd IFAC/IFIP Workshop on Real Time Programming, Shantou, China, June 1998.

[15] M.A. Livani and J. Kaiser: „Evaluation of a Hybrid Real-time Bus Scheduling Mechanism for CAN", 7th Int'l Workshop on Parallel and Distributed Real-Time Systems (WPDRTS'99), San Juan, Puerto Rico, Apr. 1999.

[16] Maruti 3, Design Overview 1st Edition, System Design and Analysis Group, Dept. of Comp. Science, Univ. of Maryland, 1995.

[17] H. Kopetz and G. Grünsteidl: „TTP - A Time-Triggered Protocol for Fault-Tolerant Real-Time Systems", Res. Report 12/92, Inst. f. Techn. Informatik, Tech. Univ. of Vienna, 1992.

[18] F. Cristian et. al.: „Atomic Broadcast: From Simple Message Diffusion to Byzantine Agreement", IEEE 15th Int'l Symposium on Fault-Tolerant Computing Systems, Ann Arbor, Michigan, 1985.

[19] K. M. Zuberi and K. G. Shin: „A Causal Message Ordering Scheme for Distributed Embedded Real-Time Systems", Proc. Symp. on Reliable and Distributed Systems, Oct 1996.

[20] M.A. Livani, J. Kaiser:"A Total Ordering Scheme for Real-Time Multicasts in CAN", The Proc. Third International Workshop on Active and Real-Time Database Systems, Schloß Dagstuhl, Mai 1999

[21] P. Ramanathan and K.G. Shin: "Delivery of Time-Critical Messages Using a Multiple Copy Approach", ACM Tr. Computer Systems, 10(2):144-166, May 1992.

[22] K. M. Zuberi and K. G. Shin, „Non-Preemptive Scheduling of messages on Controller Area Network for Real-Time Control Applications", Technical Report, University of Michigan, 1995.

[23] J. Kaiser, M. Mock : "Implementing the Real-Time Publisher/Subscriber Model on the Controller Area Network (CAN)", 2nd Int'l Symposium on Object-Oriented Distributed Real-Time Computing Systems, San Malo, May 1999.

Directional Gossip: Gossip in a Wide Area Network *

Meng-Jang Lin[1] and Keith Marzullo[2]

[1] University of Texas at Austin
Department of Electrical and Computer Engineering
Austin, TX
`mj@ece.utexas.edu`
[2] University of California, San Diego
Department of Computer Science and Engineering
La Jolla, CA
`marzullo@cs.ucsd.edu`

1 Introduction

A *reliable multicast* protocol ensures that all of the intended recipients of a message m that do not fail eventually deliver m. For example, consider the reliable multicast protocol of [11], and consider a message m, sent by process p_1, that is intended to be delivered by p_1, p_2, and p_3. We impose a directed spanning tree on these processes that is rooted at the message source. For example, for m we could have the directed spanning tree $p_1 \to p_2 \to p_3$. The message m propagates down this spanning tree and acknowledgments of the receipt of m propagate back up the tree. A leaf process in this tree delivers m when it receives m, and a non-leaf process delivers m when it gets the acknowledgment for m from all of its children. If a non-leaf process (say, p_1) does not get an acknowledgment for m from one of its children (here, p_2), then it removes the child from the tree and "adopts" that child's children (here, p_3). The process sends m to the newly-adopted children and continues the broadcast. A similar monitoring and adoption approach is used to recover from the failure of the root of the tree.

Reliable multicast protocols are intended for local area networks. Unfortunately, most implementations of reliable multicast do not scale well to large numbers of processes even when all are in the same local area network [2]. For example, with the protocol given above, the sender cannot deliver its own message m until it knows that all non-failed processes have already delivered m. The latency can be reduced by using a bushy directed spanning tree, but doing so increases the overhead of some processes, where by overhead we mean the number of messages a process sends and receives in the reliable multicast of a single m. As the number of processes increases, either the latency or the overhead at some processes increases. Hence, when a multicast is to be sent to a large

---

* Supported by DOD-ARPA under contract number F30602-96-1-0313. The views and conclusions contained in this document are those of the authors and should not be interpreted as necessarily representing the official policies or endorsements, either expressed or implied, of the Air Force or the U.S. Government.

number of processes or processes located on a wide area network, a protocol like IP Multicast [3] that has been specifically designed for these cases is preferable even though it is not as reliable as reliable multicast.

More recently, *gossip-based protocols* have been developed to address scalability while still providing high reliability of message delivery. These protocols, which were first developed for replicated database consistency management in the Xerox Corporate Internet [4], have been built to implement not only reliable multicast [2,7] but also failure detection [12] and garbage collection [8]. Gossip protocols are scalable because they do not require as much synchronization as traditional reliable multicast protocols. A generic gossip protocol running at process p has a structure something like the following:

```
when (p receives a new message m)
while (p believes that not enough of its neighbors have received m) {
    q = a neighbor process of p;
    send m to q;
}
```

Since a recipient may receive a message more than once, gossip protocols can have a higher reliability than IP Multicast. Indeed, the natural resiliency and graceful degradation of gossip protocols is one of their attractions. However, there are techniques one can use with gossip protocols to improve its reliability even more (e.g., see [4,2]). For example, a process can periodically exchange information with another randomly selected process in the background and resolve any difference. This technique, called *anti-entropy*, implements a much simpler mechanism for loss recovery than those used in reliable multicast protocols such as SRM [5].

Since they lack the amount of synchronization that traditional multicast protocols have, the reliability of gossip-based protocols is determined using different analytical tools. The mathematics of *epidemiology* are often applied, since the spread of a message with a gossip protocol is much like the spread of a disease in a susceptible population. When the mathematics become intractable, simulation is often used.

If one wished to implement gossip-based reliable multicast with as high reliability as possible, then one would use a *flooding protocol* [1] like the following

```
when (p receives a new message m from neighbor q)
for each (r : r neighbor of p)
    if (r != q) send m to r;
```

Flooding can be thought of as a degenerate gossip protocol in which a process chooses all the neighbors that it does not know already have the message. Flooding, however, can have a high overhead. Consider the undirected graph $G = (V, E)$ in which the nodes V are processes and edges E connect processes that are neighbors. The total number of messages sent in flooding a single message in G is between $|E|$ and $2|E|$. If the processes are all on a single local area network, then one can consider G to be a clique (that is, all processes can directly communicate with each other), and so the number of messages is quadratic in $|V|$. Gossip protocols are attractive when G is a clique because they provide negligibly less reliability than flooding with a much lower overhead.

If G is not a clique, then the reliability of gossip protocols is less. This is not hard to see, and has already been observed in the context of the spreading of computer viruses [9, 10]. Consider a process p_1 that is in a clique of n processes $p_1, p_2, ...p_n$ and that has a pendant neighbor q: that is, the only neighbor of q is p_1. Suppose that these processes are running a gossip protocol in which p_1 continues to forward a new message m to B of its neighbors that p_1 believes may not yet have m. If p_1 receives a new message m from p_2 and p_1 selects its neighbors uniformly, then the probability that q will receive m is $1 - \binom{n-2}{B}/\binom{n-1}{B} = B/(n-1)$. Thus, B must be close to $n-1$ (and the corresponding overhead high) for the reliability of this protocol to be high. A more intelligent protocol would have p_1 always forward new messages to q and use gossip to communicate with the rest of its neighbors.

We present a protocol that behaves like this more intelligent protocol. Each process determines a *weight* for each of its neighbors. This weight is measured dynamically and is the minimum number of edges that must be removed for the process to become disconnected from its neighbor. For example, assuming no links are down, p_1 would assign a weight of 1 to q and weights of $n-1$ to each of its remaining $n-1$ neighbors. A process floods to neighbors that have small weights and gossips to neighbors that have large weights.

The protocol we present is a broadcast protocol rather than a multicast protocol. That is, the set of processes G that comprise the intended recipients of the message is assumed to be static and well-known. A multicast protocol would allow G to change. We believe that in the context of gossip in a wide-area network, the problem of a dynamic G is separable from the delivery of messages to G.

2 Architecture

It has already been observed [12] that the overhead of gossip protocols in a wide area network can be reduced by taking the network topology into account. For example, consider two local area networks, each with the same number of processors and that are connected by a single router. If one ignores the network topology, then on average a processor will have half of its neighbors in one local area network and half of its neighbors in the other. Hence, on average half of the gossip messages will traverse the router, which is an unnecessarily high load. The work in [12] addresses this problem by having each processor aware of which local area network each of its neighbors is in. A processor then only rarely decides to send a gossip message to a processor in another local area network. This approach is attractive because it attenuates the traffic across a router without adding any additional changes to the gossip protocol. Its drawback is that it does not differentiate between wide area traffic and local area traffic. The performance characteristics and the link failure probabilities are different for wide area networks and local area networks. Hence, we adopt a two-level gossip hierarchy: one level for gossip within a local area network and another level for gossip among local area networks (that is, within a wide area network).

Each local area network runs a *gossip server* that directs gossip to the local area networks that are one hop away. Two gossip servers are neighbors if the local area networks with which they are associated are connected by an internetwork router. For example, Figure 1 shows three local area networks connected by routers A, B and C. Each gossip server is labeled with the routers that are connected to its local area network. Two gossip servers are neighbors if they both have the same internetwork router listed in their label. Hence, the neighbors relation of these three gossip servers in this figure is a three-clique. As will be discussed in the next section, the state that a gossip server maintains is small, and so a gossip server could easily be replicated if the reliability of a single server is not adequately high.

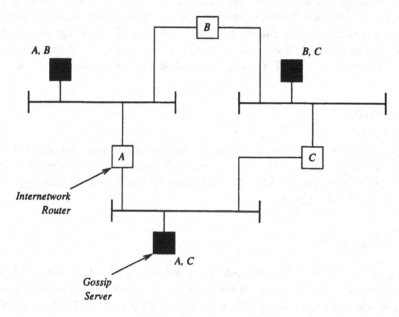

Fig. 1. Gossip Server Architecture

Messages are disseminated to the processes in a local area network, including the gossip servers, using a traditional gossip protocol. When a gossip server receives a message m for the first time via the local area network gossip protocol, it initiates a *wide area network* gossip protocol with message m. When a gossip server receives for the first time a message m via the wide area network gossip protocol, it injects m into its local area network using the local area network gossip protocol.

The protocol that we develop in this paper is the wide area network gossip protocol; we do not address local area network issues further. In Section 1 we argued that to have a high reliability of message delivery, a wide area network gossip protocol needs to have some information about the network topology. Wide area networks can be large and their topology may change frequently, and so we decided not to require each gossip server to have *a priori* knowledge about the entire network topology. Instead, all a gossip server needs to know is its neighbors, which is equivalent to knowing the identity of all local area networks that are one hop away. This is the kind of information that a network administrator will know about a local area network, and so a gossip server can obtain this information from an administrator-generated configuration file.

We believe that the wide area gossip protocol should run on top of IP. Since the gossip protocol determines information about the internetwork connectivity on the fly, it needs to circumvent to some degree the internet routing protocol. As will be described in the next section, a gossip server records the trajectory a gossip message follows to determine the number of link-disjoint paths between itself and a neighbor. Internet routing, on the other hand, abstracts away the notion of a path; routing can change the trajectory of a message as routers fail or become overloaded. Hence, wide area network gossip must thwart routing, which can be done with IP by using either hop counts or source routing.

3 Protocol

In this section we develop a wide area gossip protocol that we call *directional gossip*. We first review some ideas from graph theory and then describe how we use them to measure weights. We then describe the directional gossip protocol in terms of these weights.

3.1 Weights

A *link cut set* of a connected graph G is a set of edges that, if removed from G, will disconnect G. A link cut set with respect to a pair of nodes p and q is a set of edges that, if removed from G, will disconnect p and q. Clearly, the link cut set with respect to a pair of nodes is also a link cut set of the graph.

A gossip server p assigns as a weight to a neighbor gossip server q the size of the smallest link cut set with respect to p and q. If this weight is low, then p will always send new messages to q; else it will send them to q only if p selects q as a neighbor with whom to gossip. The intuition behind this strategy is similar to what was illustrated in Section 1. For example, if this weight is 2, then there are two links, at least one of which must be up and selected when gossiping, for a message to propagate from p to q. As the weight of a neighbor increases, the likelihood of at least one link in the link cut set being up and selected becomes sufficiently large that p and q can exchange information using gossip. Otherwise, p always forwards each new message to q.

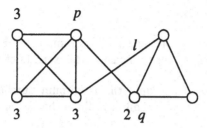

Fig. 2. Weights

Figure 2 gives an example of the weights of a gossip server p. All of the neighbors of p in the four-clique have a weight three, since three edges must be deleted to isolate p from any of these neighbors. The neighbor of p in the three-clique, however, has a weight of two since only the two links connecting the four-clique and the three-clique need be deleted to isolate q from p.

One can imagine other weights that might be interesting. For example, consider the graph in Figure 3 that consists of many long cycles, each distinct except for the (p, q) edge. The weight that p would assign to q is large (in this graph, seven) since there are many link-disjoint paths that connect p and q. Thus, our strategy would most likely have p only probabilistically choose q. If links fail frequently enough, however, then the probability that a message will make it along one of the long cycles from p to q may be low. Hence, under these conditions p should always forward to q. The benefit of the strategy that we have is that the weights are easy to compute dynamically and the strategy works well for common internetwork interconnection topologies. In addition, our protocol measures the dynamic connectivity between two neighboring nodes. Under the assumptions that the long links are often broken, the weight that p would assign q would in fact be low.

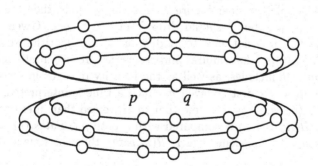

Fig. 3. Pathological Graph

3.2 Measuring Weights

We use the following version of Menger's Theorem, due to Ford and Fulkerson [6], in a method for a gossip server to measure the weights of its neighbors.

For any two nodes of a graph, the maximum number of link-disjoint paths equals the minimum number of links that separate them.

Thus, a gossip server can maintain for each of its neighbors a list of link-disjoint paths between itself and that neighbor. The size of this set is the weight of the neighbor. A gossip server collects these paths by observing the trajectories that gossip messages traverse, and it ensures through randomization that all such paths are found.

Each message m carries $m.path$ which is the trajectory that m has traversed. Each element in this trajectory identifies an internetwork router that has forwarded m. The internetwork router is implicitly identified by the pair of gossip servers that communicate via that router. Before a gossip server s forwards m to another gossip server r, s adds an identifier for r to the end of $m.path$ if $m.path$ is not empty; otherwise, it sets $m.path$ to the list $\langle s; r \rangle$. Thus, given a trajectory $m.path$ of $g > 1$ gossip servers, we can construct a path of $g - 1$ internetwork routers, which we denote by $INR(m.path)$. Note that the length of $m.path$ is bounded by the diameter D of the wide area network.

Let $Neighbors_s$ be the set of neighbors of a gossip server s. For each neighbor $r \in Neighbors_s$, each gossip server s maintains a list $Paths_s(r)$ of link-disjoint paths that connect s and r. This list contains no more than $|Neighbors_s|$ paths. When a gossip server s receives a gossip message m, for every $r \in Neighbors_s$ such that r is in $m.path$, if for every path $p \in Paths_s(r)$, p and $INR(m.path)$ do not have any common elements, then $INR(m.path)$ is added to $Paths_s(r)$. A simple implementation of this algorithm has $O(D(\log(D) + |Neighbors_s|^2))$ running time for each gossip message that a gossip server receives. The weight a gossip server s computes for its neighbor r is then simply $|Paths_s(r)|$.

The weights that a gossip server computes for its neighbors should be dynamic. For example, consider Figure 2. If the link ℓ fails, then the weight that p assigns to its neighbor q should drop from two to one. Given loosely synchronized clocks[1], it is not hard to modify the above algorithm to dynamically maintain $Paths_s(r)$ so that failures and recoveries are taken into account. Each element in $m.path$ includes, as well as the identity of a gossip server, the time that the gossip server first received m. Such a time is interpreted, for each element in $INR(m.path)$, as the time that m traversed that internetwork router. Then, when $INR(m.path)$ is compared with a path $p \in Paths_s(r)$, when an element of p is equal to an element of $INR(m.path)$, then the time associated with

---

[1] Clocks are used to measure how long has elapsed since a link has been traversed. The required degree of synchronization depends on the mean time to failure of links and the impact on reliability of having too high a weight for a node. We have not determined this exact relationship, but we believe that clock synchronized within tens of seconds should be sufficient.

the link in p is set to the maximum of its current time and the time associated with the same link in $INR(m.path)$. We can then associate a time $Time(p)$ with each element $p \in Paths_s(r)$ as the oldest time of any link in p. If $Time(p)$ is too far in the past, then s can remove p from $Paths_s(r)$.

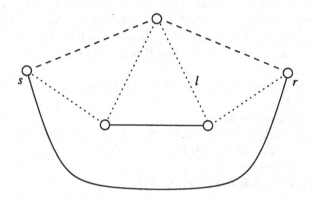

Fig. 4. Dynamic Weight Computation

This simple method of aging link-disjoint paths can result in a temporarily low weight. For example, consider the two gossip servers s and r in Figure 4. Assume that $Paths_s(r)$ contains three paths: the direct path connecting s and r, the path indicated by dashed lines, and the path indicated by dotted lines. Hence, s computes a weight of three for r. Now assume that the link ℓ fails. Eventually, the time associated with the dotted path will become old enough that this path is removed from $Paths_s(r)$, at which point s computes a weight of two for r. This weight is too low: three links must be removed for these two nodes to become disconnected. Eventually, though, s will receive a message following the remaining link-disjoint path, and thus will again compute a weight of three for r. And, as discussed in the next section, computing a too-low weight does not hurt the reliability of the gossip protocol, but only increases the overhead.

3.3 Directional Gossip

The protocol that a gossip server s executes is the following. We first give the initialization. A gossip server only knows about the direct path connecting itself to a neighbor. Thus, s will assign an initial weight of one to each of its neighbors. This weight may be low, and will have s forward new messages to all of its neighbors. As s learns of more paths, it will compute more accurate weights for its neighbors, and the overhead will correspondingly reduce.

init

    for each $r \in Neighbors_s : Paths_s(r) = \{INR(\langle s,r \rangle)\};$

Note that, in order to simplify the exposition, we have not given a time for the last traversal of this initial path. We assume that whenever a gossip server is added to a trajectory, the current time is also added to the trajectory.

A node starts the sending of a new gossip message by sending it to all of its neighbors. The following code block is executed when s receives a new gossip message m. It first updates $Paths_s(r)$ for each neighbor r that is in $m.path$. It then sends m to all neighbors that s believes may not have m and that have a weight less than K. Gossip server s then chooses enough of the remaining neighbors that may not have m so that B neighbors are sent m.

```
when s receives gossip message m for the first time: {
    int sent = 0;
    for each r ∈ Neighbors_s
        if (r ∈ m.path) UpdatePaths(Paths_s(r), INR(Trim(m.path, r)));
    for each r ∈ Neighbors_s AgePaths(Paths_s(r));
    for each r ∈ Neighbors_s
        if (r ∉ m.path &&|Paths_s(r)| < K){
            m' = m;
            append r to m'.path;
            send m' to r;
            sent = sent + 1;
        }
    for each r ∈ Choose(B − sent of Neighbors_s − {q : q ∈ m.path}){
        m' = m;
        append r to m'.path;
        send m' to r;
    }
}
```

The following procedure updates the set of link-disjoint paths between itself and a neighbor based on the trajectory that m has followed. It also updates the times that the links were last traversed. The test for common links can be efficiently implemented by having each path be a sorted list of links, and sorting the trajectory T.

```
void UpdatePaths(ref set of paths P, trajectory T) {
    if (all elements of P have no links in common with T) add T to P;
    else for each p in P:
        for each link ℓ_1 ∈ p and link ℓ_2 ∈ T:
            if (ℓ_1 and ℓ_2 name the same internetwork router)
                set the time ℓ_1 was last traversed to
                    max(time ℓ_1 was last traversed, time ℓ_2 was last traversed);
}
```

The following procedure determines if a path is to be removed because too much time has passed since a link in the path has been traversed.

```
void Age(ref set of paths P) {
    for each p in P:
        if (there is a link ℓ in p: Now() − the last time ℓ was traversed > Timeout)
            remove p from P;
}
```

Finally, the following function removes a prefix from the sequence of gossip servers a message has traversed.

```
server sequence Trim(server sequence S, gossip server s) {
    return (the sequence S with all servers visited before s removed)
}
```

4 Simulation

We built a simple discrete event simulator to measure the performance of directional gossip. The simulator takes as input a graph with nodes representing gossip servers and links representing internetwork routers. Messages are reliably sent between gossip servers and are delivered with a time chosen from a uniform distribution. We do not model link failures or gossip server failures, and hence do not implement the aging of links.

We simulated three protocols: flooding, gossip with a fanout B, and directional gossip with a fanout B and a critical weight K. We compared the message overheads of these three different protocols, and when interesting compared their reliability. We also measured the ability of directional gossip to accurately measure weights.

We considered four different network topologies: a ring of 16 gossip servers, a clique of 16 gossip servers, two cliques of eight gossip servers, connected by a single link, and a topology meant to resemble a wide area network.

We show two different kinds of graphs: overhead graphs and and weight graphs. An overhead graph plots for the initialization of each gossip message m the total number of messages that were sent. The curves plot the average value computed over 100 runs. A weight graph gives the maximum and the minimum of the weights a node computes for its neighbors against time. We calculate reliability as the percentage of 10,000 runs (done as 100 runs each sending 100 gossip messages) in which all nodes receive all gossip messages.

Ring When the fanout B is at least two, all three protocols should behave the same in a ring. A node that initiates a gossip message sends the gossip message to its two neighbors, and each neighbor forwards it to its next neighbor. This continues until the last two nodes send the gossip message to each other. Hence, the last two nodes receive the gossip message twice and the remaining nodes once.

Therefore, 18 messages are sent for a single initiation of a gossip message. The simulator shows this to be the case. The reliability is 1.0 for all three protocols.

Clique For a clique of size n, a node will eventually learn that there are $n-1$ link-disjoint paths to each of its neighbors. However, learning this will take time. Figure 5 shows how these estimates evolve in a clique of 16 nodes. This graph reflects a run in which 100 gossip messages were initiated and in which $B = 1$ and $K = 2$. A node was chosen at random. The x-axis measures the total number of messages the randomly-chosen node has received, and so is a measure of time. The upper curve shows the highest weight the node has assigned to a neighbor, and the lower curve shows the lowest weight it has assigned to a neighbor. Note that by the end of this run, this node still has not learned that it is in a clique.

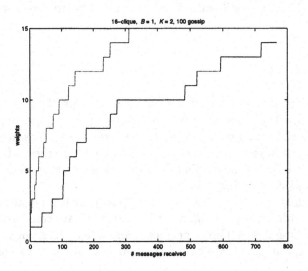

Fig. 5. Weight Graph (16-clique, B=1, K=2)

However, as soon as the minimum weight a node assigns to a neighbor reaches K, the node will simply use a gossip protocol to disseminate messages. Thus, the overhead reduces to that of gossip. This behavior is shown in Figure 6. In this figure, the top curve is the overhead of flooding, the middle curve that of directional gossip, and the bottom curve that of simple gossip. The overhead of flooding is expected to be the worst: $(n-1)^2$ messages sent for each initiation of a gossip message, and gossip uses the least number of messages. Directional gossip converges from initially having an overhead less than that of flooding to an overhead of gossip. All three protocols have a reliability of 1.0.

Two Cliques For two cliques that have only one link between them, the reliability of gossip protocols can suffer because a node incident on the cross-clique link must always forward across that link. Directional gossip overcomes this by identifying this critical link. For example, for two cliques of eight nodes connected by a single link, flooding provides a reliability of 1.0 and directional gossip with

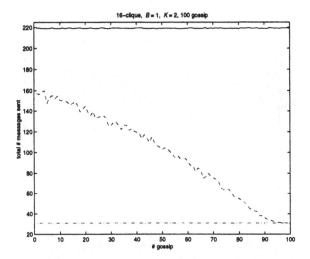

Fig. 6. Overhead Graph (16-clique, B=1, K=2)

$B = 4, K = 2$ a reliability of 0.9963. Gossip with $B = 4$ has a reliability of 0.6329.

Figure 7 shows the corresponding message overheads of the three protocols. As can be seen, initially directional gossip incurs a little more overhead than gossip and gradually decreases.

We have experimented with other values for B and K. The reliability of directional gossip is always significantly higher than that of gossip. Also, the larger the value of B, the better the reliability for both protocols. Increasing K, in general, improves the reliability of directional gossip. However, in the case of two cliques where there is only one critical link, the effect is not as pronounced.

Wide Area Networks We constructed a transit-stub graph to model a wide area network using the technique presented in [13]. We constructed two topologies:

1. A network of 66 nodes. This network consists of two transit domains each having on average three transit nodes. Each transit node connects to, on average, two stub domains. Each stub domain contains an average of five stub nodes. The average node degree within domains is two and is one between domains.
2. A network of 102 nodes. This has the same properties as the previous topology except that stub domains have, on average, eight nodes and each such node has, on average, a degree of five.

Since the flooding protocol always deliver messages to all nodes, it has a reliability of 1.0. Directional gossip in the 66-node WAN with $B = 2$ and $K = 4$ has a reliability of 0.9492, and in the 102-node WAN with $B = 4$ and $K = 4$ has

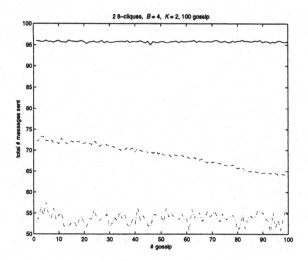

Fig. 7. Overhead Graph (2 8-cliques, B=4, K=2)

reliability of 0.8994. In contrast, gossip with $B = 2$ in the 66-node WAN has a reliability of 0 and with $B = 4$ in the 102-node WAN has a reliability of 0.0597.

Figures 8 and 9 compare the overheads of the three protocols in the two networks. It demonstrates that the high reliability of directional gossip comes at the expense of overhead: the overhead of directional gossip is not far from that of flooding. For the 66-node WAN the overhead of directional gossip is very close to that of flooding. This is not surprising. The average degree of each node is small, and so directional gossip will tend to behave more like flooding. The relatively lower overhead of directional gossip in the 102-node WAN is because the average degree of a node is higher. As we note in Section 5, we believe that the relatively lower reliability in the more richly-connected WAN can be increased.

We have looked at the reliability of directional gossip for different values of B and K. For the 66-node WAN, reliability is increased much more by increasing K than by increasing B. For the 102-node WAN and the two-clique examples we have looked at, however, reliability is increased more by increasing B rather than increasing K.

The reason why increasing K can increase the reliability in the 66-node WAN more is because the average node degree is small. For the 102-node WAN and the two-clique example, however, there are more nodes in a domain and so with a larger B, a gossip message spreads to mode nodes once it is forwarded across the cross-domain link.

5 Conclusions

Gossip protocols are becoming an attractive choice to disseminate information in a wide area network. They are appealing because they are relatively simple yet

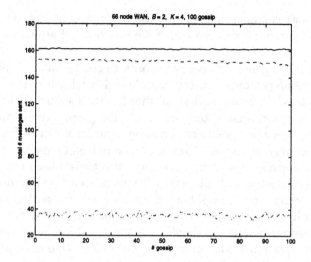

Fig. 8. Overhead Graph (66 node WAN, B=2, K=4)

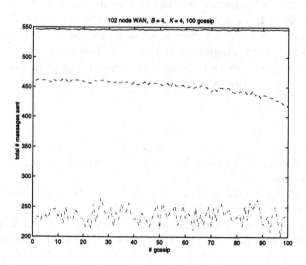

Fig. 9. Overhead Graph (102 node WAN, B=4, K=4)

are robust against common failures such as link failures and processor crashes. They also scale very well with the size of the network and are relatively easy to implement.

However, aimless gossiping does not guarantee good reliability. We have presented a new gossip protocol that can provide higher reliability than traditional gossip protocols while incurring less overhead than flooding. This protocol is part of an architecture that allows one to employ gossip servers and internetwork routers to propagate gossip on a wide area network more efficiently.

Our directional gossip protocol achieves good reliability and low to moderate overhead by having a node identify the critical directions it has to forward gossip messages. A node continuously observes the number of active link-disjoint paths there exist between it and its neighbors. If there are only few paths to a particular neighbor, then it will always pass new messages to that neighbor.

Reliable gossip is based on a simple heuristic: flood messages over links that are critical, and gossip over the other links. The two parameters that are important in these heuristics are K which defines what denotes a link to be critical, and B which defines how broadly the gossip should be. In general, when there are many nodes in a domain, B has to increase correspondingly for the reliability to be high. Generally the reliability can be improved with a large K. However, given the node degrees, increasing K beyond a certain value will not have much effect.

There are ways to push the reliability higher. Besides continuously running anti-entropy in the background, one can, for example, have a process forward a messages received from a neighbor with a weight less than K to all other neighbors. In other words, not only a message should be forwarded across a critical link, but also a message that arrives on a critical link should be flooded. However, this will incur more overhead. In general, the reliability achieved is proportional to the number of messages sent.

References

1. G. R. Andrews. *Concurrent programming: principles and practice*, Benjamin/Cummings, 1991.
2. K. Birman, *et al.* Bimodal multicast. Cornell University, Department of Computer Science Technical Report TR-98-1665, May 1998.
3. S. E. Deering. Multicast routing in internetworks and extended LANs. In *Proceedings of ACM SIGCOMM '88*, Stanford, California, USA, 16–19 August 1988, pp. 55–64.
4. A. Demers, *et al.* Epidemic algorithms for replicated database maintenance. In *Proceedings of 6th ACM Symposium on Principles of Distributed Computing*, Vancouver, British Columbia, Canada, 10–12 August 1987, pp. 1–12.
5. S. Floyd, *et al.* A Reliable Multicast Framework for Light-weight Sessions and Application Level Framing. *IEEE/ACM Transactions on Networking* 5(6):784–803, December 1997.
6. L. R. Ford and D. R. Fulkerson. Maximum flow through a network. *Canadian Journal of Mathematics* 8(1956):399–404.

7. R. A. Golding and D. E. Long. The performance of weak-consistency replication protocols. University of California at Santa Cruz, Computer Research Laboratory Technical Report UCSC-CRL-92-30, July 1992.

8. K. Guo, *et al.* GSGC: An Efficient Gossip-Style Garbage Collection Scheme for Scalable Reliable Multicast, Cornell University, Department of Computer Science Technical Report TR-97-1656, December 1997.

9. J. Kephart and S. White. Directed-graph epidemiological models of computer viruses. In *Proceedings of IEEE Computer Society Symposium on Research in Security and Privacy*, Oakland, California, USA, 20–22 May 1991, pp. 345–359.

10. M.-J. Lin, A. Ricciardi, and K. Marzullo. A new model for availability in the face of self-propagating attacks. In *Proceedings of New Security Paradigm Workshop*, Charlottesville, Virginia, USA, 22–25 September 1998.

11. F. B. Schneider, D. Gries, and R. D. Schlichting. Fault-tolerant broadcasts. *Science of Computer Programming* 4(1):1–15, April 1984.

12. R. van Renesse, Y. Minsky, and M. Hayden. A gossip-style failure detection service. In *Proceedings of the IFIP International Conference on Distributed Systems Platforms and Open Distributed Processing (Middleware '98)*, The Lake District, England, September 1998, pp. 55–70.

13. E. W. Zegura, K. L. Calvert, and S. Bhattacharjee. How to model an internetwork. In *Proceedings of IEEE Infocom '96*, San Francisco, California, USA, 24–28 March 1996, pp. 594–602, Volume 2.

Efficient Reliable Real-Time Group Communication
for
Wireless Local Area Networks

Michael Mock[1], Edgar Nett[2], and Stefan Schemmer[1]

[1]GMD – German Research Center for Information Technology
D-53754 St. Augustin
e-mail: {mock,schemmer}@gmd.de
Phone: +49 2241 142576
Fax: +49 2241 142324

[2]University of Magdeburg
Institute for Distributed Systems
Universitaetsplatz 2
D-39106 Magdeburg
email: nett@ivs.cs.uni-magdeburg.de
Phone: +49 391 67 18346

Abstract. We consider teams of mobile autonomous robot systems that coordinate their work via communication over a wireless local area network. In such a scenario, timely delivery and group support are the predominant requirements on the communication protocol. As the mobile robot systems are communicating via standard hardware, we base our work on the IEEE 802.11 standard for wireless local area networks. In this paper, we present a reliable real-time group communication protocol that enhances the IEEE 802.11 standard. The reliability and real-time properties of the protocol are based on time-bounded dynamic time redundancy. By this, network bandwidth is used much more efficiently than in a message diffusion approach based on static redundancy. The fault detection mechanism needed to implement the time-bounded dynamic redundancy concept is achieved by an implicit acknowledgement scheme that consumes no additional bandwidth for acknowledgement messages.

1 Introduction

We consider teams of mobile autonomous robot systems that cooperate to achieve a common goal (for instance, playing soccer in the RoboCup benchmark [16], or working in a flexible manufacturing system). A basic means for supporting cooperation of such mobile systems is their ability to communicate via wireless links.

Due to locomotion of the mobile systems, the communication is subject to strong real-time constraints when the execution of closely coupled cooperative actions is considered (e.g., cooperative object manipulation). Since the application consists of groups of robot systems, the reliable group communication paradigm is best adequate to support the coordination of the group. As the mobile robot systems are communicating via standard hardware, e.g. PCMCIA Cards, we must base our work on the IEEE 802.11 standard for wireless local area networks [8]. Hence, we are looking for a reliable real-time group communication protocol that can be used efficiently in wireless local area networks that conform to the IEEE 802.11 standard.

So far, there is no protocol providing reliable real-time group communication for wireless local area networks based on the IEEE 802.11 standard. There is, however, a number of proposals for achieving reliable real-time group communication on wired local area networks [20, 18, 11]. None of these protocols is directly suited for our target environment because, firstly, the protocols do not conform to the communication structure imposed by the IEEE 802.11 standard, and secondly, they are not designed to be efficient in the presence of a high degree of message losses. In [11], a static redundancy approach is used to tolerate message losses and meeting real-time requirements by sending every message a fixed number of times, independent of a successful transmittal in the meanwhile. This is the so-called message diffusion approach that consumes a considerable amount of bandwidth, especially when a high degree of message losses has to be tolerated. Hardware redundancy techniques making the message diffusion approach more efficiently can not be applied in the wireless environment. As argued in [20], time-bounded dynamic time redundancy can be used to retransmit a message only if necessary, while still meeting real-time requirements. This approach consumes less bandwidth in the average case than the static redundancy approach. However, it requires a mechanism to detect a message loss. In the context of communication protocols, this is achieved by the means of acknowledgements. The positive acknowledgement scheme as proposed in [20, 18] consumes a large amount of bandwidth. Therefore, it is not adequate for the wireless environment where network bandwidth is low.

In this paper, we present the design of a reliable real-time group communication protocol for wireless local area networks that implements time-bounded dynamic time redundancy but consumes no additional bandwidth for acknowledgement messages. The acknowledgement scheme implemented to achieve the detection of message omission faults exploits the protocol structure imposed by the IEEE 802.11 standard. Furthermore, the protocol allows to save network bandwidth by relaxing the reliability of message transfer. Due to the relaxed reliability, a message might not be transmitted reliably to all group members. However, the protocol still guarantees a time-bounded agreement among all group members on whether or not the message has been transmitted, so that the atomicity of message transfer is assured and group consistency is not violated.

The remainder of the paper is organized as follows: Chapter 2 describes the IEEE 802.11 standard and the fault assumptions on which our protocol is based. Chapter 3 presents our reliable real-time group communication protocol. Chapter 4 refers to related work and chapter 5 presents some concluding remarks and further work.

2 The IEEE 802.11 Standard and Fault Assumptions

The IEEE 802.11 standard is commonly accepted for wireless local area networks. In order to cope with the relatively high message loss rates encountered in a wireless environment compared to wired local area networks, the IEEE 802.11 standard provides the means to realize contention free and contention based medium access over a single physical channel. In particular, it specifies two alternating phases of medium access control: the "Contention Period (CP)" with distributed medium arbitration, and the "Contention Free Period (CFP)" with centralized medium arbitration.

The basic arbitration scheme used in the CP is carrier sense multiple access with collision avoidance (CSMA/CA). Furthermore, acknowledgments and retransmissions are used in order to cope with the (frequent) message losses. The CP is the adequate scheme for transmitting non real-time messages efficiently. But, as the CP is subject to contention, timing guarantees cannot be given. In contrast, the CFP is the adequate scheme on which a time-bounded message delivery can be built. As discussed in [14], the alternating phases of CP and CFP support the integration of real-time with non real-time communication. During the CP, the access to the medium for a group of stations is coordinated by a central station that is denoted as "access point" (see figure 1).

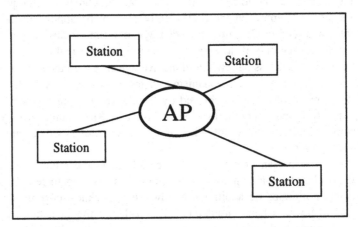

Fig. 1. Group definition according to the IEEE 802.11 standard.

The access point is a special fixed node that coordinates the medium access for all stations that are reachable over the wireless medium. Hence, a group consists of all stations that are within the reach of the access point which normally has a central location. Medium arbitration in the CFP works by imposing the following communication structure: the access point grants exclusive access to the medium by transmitting a polling message to some station in the group. Every station remains silent until it is polled by the access point. When being polled, it may transmit a message. This way, contention free access is accomplished. The access point is free to implement any strategy for polling stations during the CFP.

Contention periods and contention free periods alternate under the control of the access point. Since the CFP and the CP are both of variable length, the whole time that is scheduled but not needed for real-time communication during the CFP, can be used for the transmission of non real-time messages during the CP.

Although there are no contentions during the CFP, the problem of message losses still has to be tackled. The number of message losses is considerable higher than for wired local area networks, because the wireless medium is unshielded and thus exposed to external interference. In particular, broadcast messages are just unreliable datagrams sent on a best effort basis, neither order nor atomic delivery of broadcast messages is considered.

We base our protocol design on the following fault assumptions:

- Messages sent during the CFP are either lost (omission fault), or are delivered correctly within a fixed time-bound (t_m). Message losses may be asymmetric, i.e., some stations may receive a broadcast message and some may not. We assume that there is a so-called omission degree OD (as defined in [20, 6]) that denotes an upper bound on the number of omission faults that may affect a single message. For a broadcast message, this means that after $OD+1$ transmissions, every receiver has received at least one of these transmissions. It does not imply the existence of a single transmission that is received by all receivers. We furthermore assume that in any sequence of $OD+1$ broadcast messages issued by the same sender, each receiver has received at least on of these messages. With respect to point-to-point communication, we assume the bounded omission degree to hold for request/response type of communication, i.e., when considering $OD+1$ subsequent pairs of polling messages and reply messages exchanged between the access point and a particular station, at least one these pairs is transmitted successfully.

- Although the medium is a broadcast medium, messages have a limited reach: even if a station A may communicate with station B, and station B may communicate with station C, C may not be directly reachable from A because it is too far away. Since C is hidden from A, this situation is denoted as "hidden station problem", that, for instance, may cause asymmetric message losses.

- Stations may suffer crash failures. In addition, due to mobility, stations may leave the reach of the access point at arbitrary points in time, without crashing. This resembles a (permanent) crash of the link between the access point and the leaving station. This station is said to be no longer connected to the group. A station is said to be correct, if it does not crash and if it is connected to the group.

- The access point is stable, i.e., it is not subject to any kind of error. Note that our protocol only requires a limited amount of stable storage (see the description in section 3.2). The assumption of stability is already implied in the IEEE 802.11 standard that uses the access point as central coordinator during the CFP. However, the IEEE 802.11 standard does not indicate how the stability is achieved. From our point of view, standard techniques of fault tolerance (such as hot-standby) should be used to implement this assumption.

The assumption of having a worst case bounded omission degree is critical for the reliable operation of the protocol. In fact, every protocol that intends to guarantee real-time properties on an unreliable medium must base on such an assumption. The distinguishing aspect is how to deal with the inherent tradeoff: on one side, the *OD* should be determined large enough to ensure that the worst case assumption holds. On the other side, an *OD* that turns out to be beyond any realistic worst case situation will unnecessarily affect the performance of the protocol. We are able to cope with this tradeoff in a twofold manner. Firstly, our protocol introduces an additional protocol parameter *res(c)* that allows specifying the reliability of message transfer (without sacrificing consistency) independent of *OD*. The performance overhead devoted to achieving reliability is mainly determined by *res(c)* such that we can afford to choose a generous worst case value for *OD* without jeopardizing the performance of the protocol. Secondly, determining realistic values for *OD* and *res(c)* is supported by measuring the length of bursts of message losses under different physical conditions and workloads. First results indicate that a large value for the omission degree (about 20 in our office environment) must be taken while setting *res(c)* to 2 has turned out to be a reasonable choice.

3 Reliable Real-Time Group Communication

In this chapter, we present the design of our protocol. Section 3.1 defines the properties achieved by the protocol. Section 3.2 presents the basic operation of our protocol, followed by a timing analysis given in section 3.3. An extension of the basic operation of the protocol, that allows trading reliability for bandwidth, is presented in section 3.4, the respective timing analysis can be found in section 3.5. A more formal description of the protocol based on finite state automatons can be found in [19].

3.1 Properties of the Protocol

Our protocol implements atomic, time-bounded broadcast. According to [7], atomic broadcast is defined in terms of broadcasting and delivering messages. Here, the term "broadcast" refers to the sending of a message and the term "deliver" refers to forwarding the message to the application process on the receiving site. In particular, a message can be received by a certain site but not yet be delivered. Our protocol satisfies the following properties:

validity: A message broadcasted by a correct station is eventually delivered by every correct station, as long as less than a specified number of message losses occur.

agreement: A message delivered by a station is eventually delivered by every correct station. This implies that either all or none of the correct stations deliver a given message.

integrity: For any message *m*, every correct station delivers *m* at most once and only if *m* has been broadcasted.

total order: If the messages m_1 and m_2 are delivered by stations s_1 and s_2, then station s_1 delivers message m_1 before message m_2 if and only if station s_2 delivers message m_1 before m_2.

timeliness: A message broadcasted by a correct station at real time *t* either is delivered to all stations before real-time $t+\Delta t$, or not at all, for some known constant Δt.

We say, a protocol is reliable if it satisfies the properties of validity, agreement and integrity.

3.2 Basic Operation of the Protocol

We base our protocol on the CFP because this offers us the possibility to assume bounded message delays and a bounded omission degree. As the CFP already makes use of the access point as central coordinator, we use the centralized approach as described in [5, 13] to achieve the total ordering of broadcast messages. In our approach, the access point is used as so called token site or sequencer, that has the right to order messages, i.e., to assign a sequence number to a broadcast. After being polled, a station sends a broadcast request message (or a null message) to the access point, which assigns a sequence number to that message and broadcasts it. Obviously, with the access point assigning a global unique sequence number to each broadcast, and with every station delivering messages according to their sequence number, total order is achieved.

Let us now consider how reliability and timeliness are achieved. Relying on a negative acknowledgment scheme between the access point and the receivers for detecting omission faults of the broadcast, such as done in [5, 13, 10], is not feasible for time-bounded message transfer. Relying on a static time redundancy scheme would require the access point to broadcast every message *OD+1* times. By this, the number of message retransmissions would be far beyond the average number of message omission faults and thus, this would waste expensive bandwidth. Hence, we are using a dynamic redundancy scheme, where time redundancy becomes effective only upon detection of message losses (fault detection/recovery). On the planning level, message retransmissions are still scheduled with worst case assumptions on the number of message omission faults that have to be tolerated, but in the actual execution of the protocol, messages are only retransmitted (and thus network bandwidth is only used) upon the occurrence of message losses. Due to the variable length of the communication phases CP and CFP, all the time scheduled but not needed for message retransmission in the CFP can be utilized for message transmission in the CP. The main problem of this approach is that sending lots of acknowledgements (*groupSize* acknowledgements per broadcast, where *groupSize* is the number of group members) to detect message losses may consume a not negligible amount of bandwidth, which would make dynamic redundancy as inefficient as diffusion.

In order to implement an efficient acknowledgement scheme, we structure the communication of the group into rounds. We assume that there is a maximum number n_{max} of stations in a group. During each round, the access point polls each station of the group exactly once. We use the broadcast request message to acknowledge each of the *groupSize* preceding broadcasts by piggy-backing a bit field of n_{max}-bits on the header of the request message. Each bit is used to acknowledge one of the *groupSize* preceding broadcasts. By this, one round after sending a broadcast message, the access point is able to decide whether each group member has received the message or not. In the latter case, the access point will retransmit the affected message. In particular, this acknowledgement scheme does not need any extra message for error detection at all, because the acknowledgements are piggy-backed on the broadcast request messages that have to be sent anyway. Piggy-backing the acknowledgements on the request message instead of sending them on extra messages contributes to performance improvement in two ways: Firstly, additional headers of lower level protocols needed for extra messages are avoided. Secondly, as we are working in the CFP, any extra acknowledgment message would have to be polled for, resulting in at least two extra messages.

In more detail, after being polled, a station (denoted as originator in the following) sends a broadcast request message *bc_rqu(acks[], sl, m)* to the access point. This message is composed of the acknowledgement field *acks[i]*, the local sequence number *sl*, and the message data *m*. In the acknowledgement field, *acks[i]* is set to *true*, if and only if the *i*th broadcast of the *groupSize* preceding broadcasts has been received correctly. The local sequence number is increased for every new request message and, together with the network address of the originator, yields a unique identification of *m*. There are three possibilities for the originator to choose *m*. First, if no message has to be broadcasted, *m* is empty, i.e., only the acknowledgement field is sent. Second, if the originator has not received the broadcast of its last request, it supposes that its last request message might have been lost and retransmits it. This implements an implicit positive acknowledgement scheme for the broadcast request messages between the originator and the access point. This is executed in at most *OD + 1* rounds. Third, otherwise, the next broadcast request message is transmitted.

Upon reception of the broadcast request message, two cases have to be distinguished: Either, there is still a not yet acknowledged broadcast message from the same originator to be retransmitted by the access point. In this case, the access point stores the new broadcast request message for later transmission (when the previous broadcast message of the originator has been processed). Otherwise, it assigns a global sequence number *sg* to the message *m*, broadcasts it (*bc(m, orig, sl, sg)*) and increments *sg* for the next broadcast. Besides *sg*, also the local sequence number *sl* and the address *orig* of the originator are included. This enables the originator *orig* to recognize a broadcast *bc(m, orig, sl, sg)* as an implicit acknowledgement for its broadcast request *bc_rqu(m,sl)*.

If the access point does not receive the request message within a certain period of time after polling the station, it considers the request message (or polling message) to be lost. In this case, as described above, the access point transmits the last broadcast message of the originator if it has not yet been acknowledged by all stations.

Subsequently, the access point polls the next station. If the access point has not received the request message for more than *OD* times, it considers the originator to have left the group and broadcasts a message indicating the change in the group membership. This message is then processed in the same way as a regular broadcast message.

Each station maintains its local view of the global sequence number *sta.sg* denoting the next global sequence number that station *sta* expects to receive. Upon reception of a broadcast *bc(m, orig, sl, sg)*, the station first checks whether the message is totally ordered (*sg == sta.sg*). If this is the case, the message is delivered to the user, otherwise it is put to a pending queue until the missing messages are received. Each station that has received a broadcast will set the corresponding bit in the header of its next broadcast request message.

The access point keeps a bit field for every pending message in its storage: in this field, *global_ack[sender.id, receiver.id] == true* if and only if the last broadcast of station *sender* has been acknowledged by station *receiver* (*.id* denotes the position of the station in the group list). Upon reception of a broadcast request *bc_rqu(acks[], sl, m)*, the access point uses the acknowledgement field to update *global_ack[* , originator.id]*. As *acks[i]* is the acknowledgement of station *originator* for the broadcast of station with id *(originator.id + i) mod groupSize*, the bit field *global_ack[]* is updated as follows:

$$global\_ack[(originator.id + i) \bmod groupSize, originator.id] = \qquad (1)$$
$$global\_ack[(originator.id + i) \bmod groupSize, originator.id] \text{ or } acks[i].$$

Obviously, *global_ack[sta$_1$, sta$_2$] == true* $\forall sta_2$ indicates that the last broadcast message of *sta$_1$* has been received by all stations. Accordingly, the next broadcast of *sta$_1$* can take place. Otherwise, the access point retransmits the last broadcast message of the station *sta$_1$* in the next round.

By choosing the access point as the sequencer, we force every message to be routed through the access point. As, by definition, the access point reaches every station of the group, a broadcast that is done by the access point is received by every station as long as no message omission faults occur. Thus, the hidden station problem is solved without the need to deploy sophisticated routing protocols. In addition, we can best profit from the fact that we assume the access point to be stable. Every broadcast request message that is sent to the access point is stored in the access point and can be considered to be stable. Since the access point must store at most two broadcast messages for each station (one currently being processed and one being the next broadcast request), at most 2 × *groupSize* messages have to be stored at the access point.

Furthermore, with the access point being responsible (as defined in the IEEE 802.11 standard) for coordinating the group reformation, the membership algorithm becomes simple. When a certain threshold of succeeding failed polling-request message pairs is exceeded and no broadcast request message has been received by the access point, the station is considered to have crashed or left the group and is eliminated from the group membership. Instead of broadcasting a message of that (now eliminated) station, the access point broadcasts this membership change to the remaining group members, thus achieving a consistent view of the group among all the group members. Reintegrations and the associations of new members are handled in the non real-time phase (contention period) of the IEEE 802.11 standard using the ordinary procedure of the standard. By this, integration of arbitrary stations becomes possible without sacrificing the predictability of the real-time traffic.

3.3 Timing Analysis

Let us now consider the message delays achieved by this approach. Recall that the delay of a single message is bounded by t_m. We first consider the transmission of a single message in the fault-free case. This requires three messages: the access point polling the originator, the broadcast request message sent by the originator to the access point, and the broadcast issued by the access point. Consequently, the time needed for a broadcast in the best case is:

$$\Delta bc_{min} = 3 \times t_m. \tag{2}$$

Now, message losses are taken into account. Since the number of group members is limited by n_{max}, the upper bound for a round of communication can be calculated as:

$$\Delta round = n_{max} \times 3 \times t_m. \tag{3}$$

The process of broadcasting message m of station sta_i is depicted in figure 2 (for $OD = 2$).

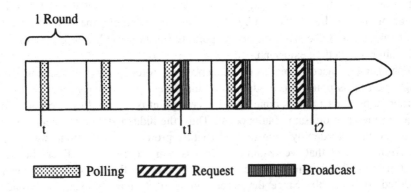

Fig. 2. Broadcast of a single message (worst case).

In the worst case, OD pairs of polling-request messages fail, so that the broadcast request message will be received by the access point in round $OD+1$ (t_1). After the reception of the request message (still in round $OD+1$), m is broadcasted. Broadcasting the message may also fail for OD times, yielding that the message will be delivered in round $OD+1+OD$ (t_2) in the worst case.

This shows that Δt – the upper bound of the timeliness definition – can be calculated as:

$$\Delta t = \Delta bc_{max} = 2 \times OD \times \Delta round + 3 \times t_m. \tag{4}$$

Next, $\Delta t(k)$ – the worst case time in the case of each station transmitting k messages – is considered (depicted in figure 3).

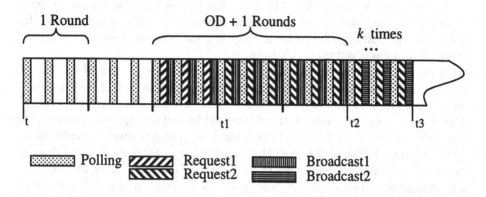

Fig. 3. Broadcast of k messages by each station (worst case).

Again, after $OD+1$ rounds (t_1), all requests are received by the access point and they are all broadcasted for the first time (in the worst case). Another OD rounds later (t_2), each broadcast is received by every station and OD tries for transmitting the next request message have taken place. Hence, a single round later (t_3), all the next broadcast request messages are received by the access point and are broadcasted the first time. Yet another OD rounds later, this broadcast will be received by all stations and so forth until all the broadcasts are received and delivered.

This yields that $\Delta t(k)$ can be calculated as follows:

$$\Delta t(k) = [(OD+1) \times k + OD] \times \Delta round, \tag{5}$$

because after $(OD+1) \times k$ rounds the last request message is received by the access point and broadcasted the first time. OD rounds after this, the broadcast is received be all stations and all messages are transmitted.

3.4 Relaxing Reliability

Up to now, it was shown that by using dynamic time redundancy, we are able to improve the utilization of the medium in favor of the CP. The number of real-time messages, however, that can be accepted for transmission during the CFP (real-time throughput), can not be increased as long as guaranteeing reliable transfer of every message requires to schedule up to $OD+1$ retries for each accepted message. Increasing the throughput of real-time messages can be achieved by reducing the scheduled number of message retransmissions from OD to a user specified number $res(c)$ of messages for all messages of class c. Surely, neither the dynamic nor the static redundancy approach can keep the full reliability guarantee as long as *res(c)* < *OD*. As a consequence, a message that is broadcasted may not be received by all stations in the group but only by some of them (asymmetric message loss). But, as long as all stations agree in time not to deliver that message, this situation is acceptable for many applications [1]. Thus, our goal is to allow the user to trade reliability for real-time throughput, while guaranteed timely agreement enables consistent error handling. Furthermore, consistent and timely delivery of membership change indications is still to be guaranteed.

To prevent the system from reaching an inconsistent state in case of asymmetric message losses, the stations are allowed to deliver a message only if the message is safe (received by all stations). The access point decides that a message can be delivered if it has got a positive acknowledgement for that message from every station (see the description in section 3.2 of acknowledgments piggy-backed on the broadcast request messages). Else, if after *res(c)* broadcasts the message is not acknowledged by all stations, the access point decides that the message is to be rejected. Note that the acknowledgement based scheme here again is superior to the diffusion based approach. If not all stations receive the message in the diffusion based approach, in spite of *res(c)* tries have taken place, no station will recognize this and the system may remain in an inconsistent state (some stations have delivered the message and some have not).

As we want to reach time bounded agreement among the stations, distribution of the access point's decision has to be reliable and timely. So, what we need is a small bandwidth synchronous channel that the access point can use to transmit its decision. Again, this information can be piggy-backed on messages that have to be sent anyway. In order to implement this channel, we use the diffusion based approach and the known upper bound *OD* on message losses. In particular, we extend the header of a broadcast message with a field of *OD+1* bit tuples, and provide by this "accept field" the access point with the means for broadcasting its decision *OD+1* times to the stations in an effective manner. The resulting message structure is shown in figure 4.

The access point uses the bit tuples that are provided in the new header to transmit its decision about delivering/rejecting messages to the stations. The two bits in a tuple have the following meaning: If the first bit b_1 of a tuple (b_1, b_2) is *true*, this tuple represents a decision of the access point regarding a broadcast message. In that case, the second bit b_2 denotes whether to deliver (b_2 is *true*) or reject the message (b_2 is *false*). If b_1 is *false*, this tuple either indicates that the corresponding message is retransmitted and the decision is still to come (b_2 is *false*), or that the station corresponding to the tuple is to be removed from the group membership (b_2 is *true*). The access point comes to a decision on removing a station when a certain threshold of lost polling/request messages is exceeded (as described in 3.2)

Each tuple is included in exactly *OD+1* broadcasts. The first time a tuple is transmitted, it is put to position 0 of the *accept* field, next time to position 1 and so forth until it finally rotates out of the field. By this we have assured the following properties for the synchronous channel:

1. Each tuple is received by every correct station, because we transmit each tuple *OD+1* times.
2. Each tuple is received at most $t_m + OD \times 3 \times t_m$ time units after it has been broadcasted
3. All stations receive the tuples in the same sequence.

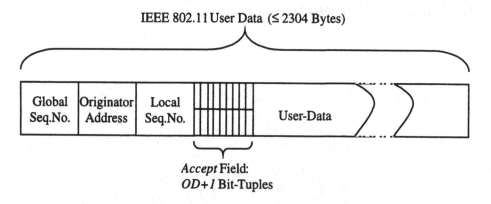

Fig. 4. A broadcast sent by the access point.

4. Every station can calculate the sequence number of the broadcast to which a tuple (i.e., decision of the access point) corresponds, no matter which of the *OD+1* broadcasts including the tuple it receives. If a tuple (b_1, b_2) occupies position i in the *accept* field of a broadcast with global sequence number *sg*, it represents the access points decision with regard to broadcast *sg – groupSize - i* (see figure 5).[1]

Figure 5 gives an example for the above mentioned unique assignment of bit tuples to broadcasts. The upper part of figure 5 depicts the *accept* field of a broadcast message with sequence number *90* (denoted as broadcast *90*), whereas the lower part depicts the overall sequence of communication rounds (*groupSize = 4, OD = 5*). If a station receives the broadcast *90*, it knows that the tuple *0* refers to the broadcast *90 - 4- 0 = 86*. Similarily, tuple *1* refers to broadcast *85*, and tuples *2* to *5* refer to the broadcasts *84, 83, 82,* and *81*, respectively. An accept decision for the broadcasts *86* and *85* has not yet taken place, these broadcast are retransmitted (as broadcast *90* and *89*). Broadcasts *84, 83,* and *81* are accepted and thus can be delivered to the application process. However, broadcast *82* is rejected.

In the normal case, when no message losses occur, a station *sta$_i$* that intends to transmit a broadcast message, after being polled, sends this message to the access point using a request message *bc_rqu(acks[], sl, m)*. Upon reception of the request message, the access point assigns a new sequence number to the message and

---

[1] The assignment of the global sequence number has changed to allow for this easy computation. A new sequence number is assigned to every broadcast the access point issues, no matter whether it is a new broadcast or a retransmission. The global message order then is determined by the sequence in which messages are accepted.

broadcasts it (as already described in section 3.2). As before, the access point evaluates the *acks* fields of the request messages of the succeeding round, and, after one round of communication, concludes that the broadcast has been received by all stations. Therefore, the access point now sets *accept[0]* to *(true,true)*, indicating that the preceding message of *sta$_i$* can be delivered by all stations. This pair of bits will be transmitted in *accept[1]* of the next broadcast, in *accept[2]* in the next but one broadcast, and so forth for *OD+1* broadcasts.

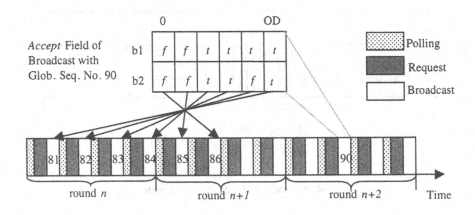

Fig. 5. Assigning Bit Tuples to Broadcasts.

In the event of message losses disturbing the polling-request communication between a *sta$_i$* and the access point, *sta$_i$* is polled again in the next round. The originator retransmits the request message in at most *res(c) + 1* rounds.

Now, we consider the case in which message losses disturb the broadcast of a message, i.e., the broadcast is not received by all stations, or acknowledgements are lost. Let the access point broadcast message *m* with global sequence number *s* in round *r*. In round *r+1* the access point decides, due to missing acknowledgements, that *m* has to be retransmitted. So, the broadcast with sequence number *s + groupSize* that takes place in round *r+1*, will be a retransmission of broadcast *s*. The access point sets *accept[0]* of that broadcast to *(false,false)*, indicating that it has not yet decided whether to accept or reject the message and that a retransmission is taking place. Similar to the polling and broadcast request messages, the broadcast is at most repeated *res(c)+1* times. If, even after the $(res(c)+1)^{st}$ broadcast (in round *r + res(c)*), positive acknowledgements for *m* have not be received from all stations, the access point decides that *m* should be rejected and diffuses its decision via the synchronous channel.

This way a message of class *c* will reach every station, and will be delivered also, as long as less than *res(c)+1* polling-request messages are lost and less than *res(c)+1* messages are lost during the broadcast of the message. If more than *res(c)* errors occur in one of the two phases, in the worst case the message will not reach all intended stations. The access point, however, will decide *reject* and, by using the synchronous channel for transmission of his decision, ensure that all stations will timely agree upon the rejection of the message.

3.5 Timing Analysis for Relaxed Reliability

As in the former timing analyses in section 3.3, we first consider the transmission of a single broadcast in the normal case, where no message losses occur. In this scenario, station sta_i is polled, transmits the request for m, m is broadcasted and received by all stations, but not yet delivered. One round of communication later, the access point has positive acknowledgements for the broadcast of m from all station and piggy-backs the accept decision on the next broadcast of sta_i. By this, m will be delivered $\Delta bc_{min} = 3 \times t_m + \Delta round$ time units after transmission of the polling message started.

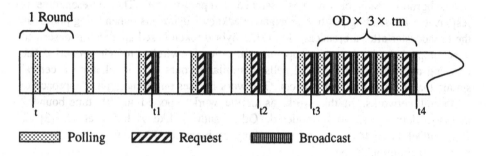

Fig. 6. Broadcast of a single message (worst case)

Now, we consider the worst-case scenario, where the maximum value for Δbc is needed. This is the case, if sta_i has to be polled $res(c)+1$ times until the request message of m is received at the access point, m has to be broadcasted $res(c)+1$ times until the access point has got positive acknowledgements from all stations, and the last station receives the decision in the last broadcast that includes the corresponding bit tuple. This scenario is depicted in figure 6, with $res(c)=2$.

According to figure 6, the access point polls sta_i for m at time t. By time $t_1 = t + res(c) \times \Delta round + 2 \times t_m$, m is finally received at the access point (otherwise m is not broadcasted at all). By time $t_2 = t_1 + res(c) \times \Delta round$, the access point broadcasts m for the last time, and at time $t_3 = t_2 + \Delta round$, comes to the decision about m. Thus, at time $t_4 = t_3 + t_m + OD \times 3 \times t_m$ the last station will have received that decision. Altogether, this yields:

$$\Delta t = t_4 - t = (2 \times res(c) + 1) \times \Delta round + (OD+1) \times 3 \times t_m \qquad (6)$$

as worst-case upper bound for the message delay.

4 Related Work

Relying on a rotating token based approach for achieving reliable group communication as described in [10, 15] makes the provision of real-time guarantees difficult because the handling of the token loss must be predictable. Also, in the mobile wireless environment, network topology is unknown and very dynamic implying an unacceptable high frequency of losses of the token. Therefore, these types of protocols are beyond the scope of what is considered in this paper.

There is no other protocol providing reliable real-time group communication for wireless local area networks based on the IEEE 802.11 standard. Inoue et al. [9] have tackled the reliability problem for wireless group communication. They enhanced reliability of multicast using a representative acknowledgement scheme that tries to reduce the number of acknowledgements. They subdivide the communication group into subgroups, each of which is assigned a representative. The representative is responsible for sending positive or negative acknowledgements, when being polled by the broadcaster after a broadcast. In [17], a hybrid token based approach is described to accomplish totally ordered group communication for wireless mobile networks. The ordering approach used for local cells is similar to ours, i.e., it relies on a central station that is responsible for that cell. The work focuses on extending that approach to multi-cell networks. In this work, as in the work reported in [9], time-bounded message delivery is not considered. Other authors like Acharya et al. [3] or Bruschi/Del Pinto [4] focus on the routing problem for IP multicasts that require multi-hop communication.

A number of protocols have been published on real-time group communication for wired networks. Kopetz et al. [6, 12] use message diffusion on physically redundant channels. This approach cannot be transferred to the wireless environment, where all communication shares the same medium. Using the static message diffusion approach for transmitting real-time messages during the CFP would always consume the worst case bandwidth whereas our approach does not. Kopetz et al. [11] structure the communication in rounds and use bit fields to acknowledge the broadcast of the previous round as we do. However, the information is not used to detect the need for the retransmission of lost messages (message transmission is reliable by the means of hardware redundancy), but for maintaining a consistent view of the group membership.

Veríssimo et al. [20, 18] consider real-time communication in local area networks that have no hardware redundancy. They argue that the retransmission/acknowledgment based communication scheme can be used for achieving reliable and time-bounded message transfer and that this dynamic approach in the average uses less bandwidth than the static message diffusion approach. We adopt this argument. However, their protocol is not suitable for the wireless environment as defined by the IEEE 802.11 standard. Firstly, the protocol does not consider the hidden station problem, which is solved in our approach by routing all broadcast messages through the access point. Secondly, their basic broadcast procedure is based on receiving individual positive acknowledgement messages from each receiver. However, collecting n explicit acknowledges for each broadcast reduces the effective utilization of the small network bandwidth encountered in the wireless environment. In addition, as time bounded message transfer is only possible during the CFP, receiver stations cannot send acknowledgements immediately upon reception of a broadcast message. According to the communication structure defined for the CFP, they would have to wait until being polled by the access point. Therefore, after each broadcast, the access point would have to poll each station for the transmission of its acknowledgement message. Thus, in the best (fault-free) case, at least 2n+2 messages are needed for a single broadcast (the first polling message, the broadcast message itself, n polling messages for the acknowledgements, and the acknowledgements). In contrast, our protocol piggy-backs acknowledgements to broadcast request messages of the next communication round and thus only requires 3 messages in the best case (see the timing analysis in section 3.3).

Moreover, Veríssimo et al. [2] describe how a small synchronous channel can be used to achieve a timely agreement on message delivery for messages that are scheduled with expected transmission times. They use the small synchronous channel to prevent contamination of the system (for example reach timely agreement for broadcasts). Our argumentation is analogous for the user definable resiliency degree and the synchronous channel used to achieve timely agreement. Again, our protocol implements this channel without extra messages by piggy-backing the necessary information on other broadcast messages.

5 Conclusions

Providing a reliable real-time group communication protocol is essential for applications that consist of teams of mobile robotic systems. Since the protocol should run on standard hardware, it must base on the IEEE 802.11 standard for wireless local area networks. Existing protocols do not conform to the communication structure imposed by that standard and are not designed to work efficiently in the presence of high message loss rates combined with a low transmission bandwidth (as encountered in the wireless environment). Two basic approaches can be distinguished when message losses must be dealt with: message diffusion representing a static redundancy approach and the retransmission/acknowledgement based approach representing dynamic redundancy. The message diffusion approach consumes too much bandwidth, whereas the retransmission/acknowledgement requires the implementation of an acknowledgement scheme. Especially when considering group communication, the acknowledgement scheme must be carefully designed in order not to counteract the goals of small bandwidth consumption and timeliness. Our protocol includes a sophisticated time-bounded acknowledgement scheme that explicitly makes use of the communication structure imposed by the IEEE 802.11 standard. Since all acknowledgements are piggy-backed on messages sent anyway, we do not need extra messages for sending acknowledgements, and we can transmit group messages with lower bandwidth consumption than the diffusion based approach needs. In addition, our protocol offers the option to trade reliability for bandwidth consumption. Relaxing reliability implies that group messages may not be transmitted reliably, but we still guarantee ordered delivery and consistent and timely decision on whether a message has been received by all group members or not.

The protocol is currently being implemented on Lucent WaveLan PCMCIA cards that support a bandwidth of 2 Mbits/sec. Since the currently available access points do not include the CFP functionality defined in the IEEE 802.11 standard, we are emulating this functionality on a normal, but dedicated station.

Acknowledgement

We would like to thank the anonymous referees for their constructive and valuable comments on this paper. They have helped us a lot to improve the quality of the paper.

References

1. C. Almeida and P. Veríssimo. An Adaptive Real-Time Group Communication Protocol. In *Proceedings of the 1ˢᵗ IEEE Workshop on Factory Communication Systems*, Lausanne, Switzerland, Oct. 1995.
2. C. Almeida and P. Veríssimo. Timing Failure Detection and Real-Time Group Communication in Quasi-Synchronous Systems. In *Proceedings of the 8ᵗʰ Euromicro Workshop on Real-Time Systems*, L'Aquila, Italy, 1996
3. A. Acharya, A. Bakre, and B. R. Badrinath. Delivering Multicast Message in Networks with Mobile Hosts. In *Proceedings of the 13ᵗʰ IEEE Distributed Computing Systems*, pp. 292-299, Pittsburgh, Pennsylvania, U.S.A., 1993.
4. D. Brushi and M. Del Pinto. Lower bounds for the broadcast problem in mobile radio networks. In *Distributed Computing* 10:129-135, 1997. Springer Verlag.
5. J.-M. Chang and N. F. Maxemchuck. Reliable Broadcast Protocols. *ACM Transactions on Computing Systems*, 2(3):251-273, Aug. 1984.
6. G. Grünsteidl and H. Kopetz. A Reliable Multicast Protocol for Distributed Real-Time Systems. In *Proceedings of the 8ᵗʰ IEEE Workshop on Real-Time Operating Systems and Software*, Atlanta, U.S.A., 1991.
7. V. Hadzilacos and S. Toueg. Fault-Tolerant Broadcast and Related Problems. In: S. Mullender (Ed.). *Distributed Systems*, 1993. Addison-Wesley.
8. IEEE 802.11: Wireless LAN Medium Access Control (MAC) and Physical Layer (PHY) secifications, IEEE 1997.
9. Y. Inoue, M. Iizuka, H. Takanashi, and M. Morikura. A Reliable Multicast Protocol for Wireless Systems with Representative Acknowledgement Scheme. In *Proceedings. of the 5ᵗʰ International Workshop on Mobile Multimedia Communication*, Berlin, Germany, 1998.
10. W. Jia, J. Kaiser, and E. Nett. RMP: Fault-Tolerant Group Communication. *IEEE Micro*, 16(2):59-67, April 1996.
11. H. Kopetz and G. Grünsteidl. TTP – A Time Triggered Protocol For Fault-Tolerant Real-Time Systems. In *Proceedings of the 23ʳᵈ International Symposium on Fault-Tolerant Computing*, pp. 524-532, Toulouse, France, 1993.
12. H. Kopetz, Real-Time Systems, Kluwer Academic Press, Boston, 1997.

13. M. F. Kaashoek and A. S. Tanenbaum: Group Communication in the Amoeba Distributed Operating Systems. In *Proceedings of the 11ᵗʰ International Conference on Distributed Computing Systems*, pp. 222-230, Arlington, Texas, U.S.A., 1991.

14. M. Mock and E. Nett. Real-Time Communication in Autonomous Robot Systems. In *Proceedings of the 4ᵗʰ International Symposium on Autonomous Decentralized Systems*, Tokyo, Japan, 1999.

15. L. E. Moser, P. M. Melliar-Smith, D. A. Agarwal, R. K. Budhia, and C. A. Lingley-Papadopoulos. Totem: A Fault-Tolerant Multicast Group Communication System. *Communications of the ACM*, 39(4):54-63, Apr. 1996.

16. The Robot Worldcup Initiative, http://www.robocup.org.

17. L. Rodrigues, H. Fonseca, and P. Veríssimo. Reliable Computing over Mobile Networks. In *Proceedings of the 5ᵗʰ Workshop on Future Trends of Distributed Computing Systems*, Cheju Island, Korea, Aug. 1995.

18. L. Rodrigues and P. Veríssimo. xAMP: a Multi-Primitive Group Communication Service. In *Proceedings of the 11ᵗʰ Symposium On Reliable Distributed Systems*, Houston, Texas, U.S.A., 1992.

19. S. Schemmer. Zuverlässige Gruppenkommunikation über einem lokalen Funknetz. Diplomarbeit an der Universität Bonn. To appear 1999.

20. P. Veríssimo, J. Rufino, and L. Rodrigues. Enforcing Real-Time Behavior on LAN-Based Protocols. In *Proceedings of the 10ᵗʰ IFAC Workshop on Distributed Computer Control Systems*, Semmering, Austria, September 1991. IFAC.

Session 10

Software Testing and Self-Checking

Chair: Luca Simoncini, CNUCE/CNR, Pisa, Italy

A Case Study in Statistical Testing of Reusable Concurrent Objects

Hélène Waeselynck and Pascale Thévenod-Fosse

LAAS - CNRS, 7 Avenue du Colonel Roche, 31077 Toulouse Cedex 4 - FRANCE
{waeselyn, thevenod}@laas.fr

Abstract. A test strategy is presented which makes use of the information got from OO analysis and design documents to determine the testing levels (unit, integration) and the associated test objectives. It defines solutions for some of the OO testing issues: here, emphasis is put on applications which consist of concurrent objects linked by client-server relationships. Two major concerns have guided the choice of the proposed techniques: component reusability, and nondeterminism induced by asynchronous communication between objects. The strategy is illustrated on a control program for an existing production cell taken from a metal-processing plant in Karlsruhe. The program was developed using the Fusion method and implemented in Ada 95. We used a probabilistic method for generating test inputs, called statistical testing. Test experiments were conducted from the unit to the system levels, and a few errors were detected.

1 Introduction

A large number of testing techniques have already been defined for programs developed according to hierarchical approaches and written in procedural languages (see e.g., [3]). But object-oriented (OO) development process corresponds to a different approach to software construction. The design of a program is organized around the data it manipulates and their relationships, which leads to highly decentralized architecture. OO languages provide powerful mechanisms like entity instantiation, genericity, inheritance, that have no equivalent in procedural languages. Hence, testing approaches must be revisited to take into account the characteristics of OO technology (see e.g., [5, 12]). Yet, few complete experiments that follow design and testing in a systematic way have been reported. The paper focuses on such an experiment.

We present a test strategy based on the information got from analysis and design documents produced during an OO development process. This strategy defines proper solutions for some of the OO testing issues: here, emphasis is put on applications which consist of *concurrent objects* linked by *client-server relationships*. The case study used as an experimental support to our investigation is adapted from an existing industrial production cell [13]. Its aim is to forge metal blanks got from a feed belt. An OO version of the control program [1] provides us with an example of a complete OO development: Fusion analysis and design [6], Ada 95 implementation.

Some OO specific difficulties are raised by the case study: How to determine the unit and integration testing levels (decentralized architecture of objects)? At each testing level, how to define the test objectives from the analysis and design documents? How to determine conformance of the test results to the expected ones (oracle checks)? How to solve the controllability and observability problems that are drastically increased by object encapsulation? The choice of the proposed solutions is guided by the consideration of two major concerns:

- *Component reusability*. OO design is intended to favor reusability: components are defined by interface models, and their internal behavior is hidden (encapsulation). In order to define a cost-effective strategy, testing of reusable components has to be performed without making any assumption on the operational context.
- *Nondeterminism* involved by concurrency between objects communicating by asynchronous events. It means that there are many possible interleavings of event reception and event treatment, depending on the reaction time of the environment. This issue has already been identified in work on protocol testing [14]; unlike in protocol testing where the hypothesis of a slow environment may sometimes be acceptable, no timing assumption may be done for concurrent objects.

Main related work is briefly reviewed in Section 2. Section 3 introduces the probabilistic method for generating test inputs we use to automatically generate test input sequences in accordance with given test objectives [15]. Section 4 describes the case study. An overview of the global strategy is presented in Section 5. Then, emphasis is put on unit testing (Section 6). Section 7 summarizes the results of the experiments conducted from the unit to the system levels; and finally, we highlight the main lessons learnt from this theoretical and experimental investigation.

2   Related Work

There is now a general agreement among the testing community that OO concepts raise a number of problems from the perspective of testing (see e.g., [5, 12]). The case study presented in this paper does not exhibit all of these problems. For example, its design is more object-based than object-oriented: there are few inheritance relations, and only between very basic classes. Hence this paper does not address the problem of how to test new and inherited features (see e.g., [8]). The focus is on decentralized architecture of communicating concurrent objects, which raises the following issues:

- *Determination of testing levels*. The traditional unit and integration levels of testing do not fit well in the case of OO programs. Their decentralized architecture makes it difficult to determine where to start testing, and there is no obvious order for an integration strategy. Related work defines the testing levels by considering the number of stubs to be produced [10], or the most significant paths and interactions in the application [9].
- *Selection and control of test sequences*. State-based testing techniques are usual for small OO subsystems [11, 16]. But concurrency introduces nondeterminism, which

has to be taken into account. The problem is well-known in the field of protocol testing. For example, it is shown in [14] that a simple system of two communicating deterministic automata yields nondeterministic behavior that cannot be modeled by a finite number of states. Transferring classical state-based criteria – such as the Wp method chosen by these authors – to communicating systems requires assumptions to be made (bounded queues and communication channels, system run in a "slow" environment).

- *Observability and oracle checks.* Observability is impeded by the principle of encapsulation and information hiding: as shown in [17], this is detrimental to state error propagation, and hence to the revealing of faults during testing. The systematic introduction of built-in test capabilities in the design of classes (set/reset capabilities, executable assertions, operations reporting the internal state) is studied in [4]. In our case, the issue is further compounded by concurrency which raises the problems of (i) choosing an appropriate conformance relation as the basis of the oracle checks and, (ii) synchronizing the control and observation with the activities of the objects.

Reusability is also one of our concerns: we are interested in assessing the behavior of software components that may be reused in the framework of different applications. This problem shares similarities with other work concerned with the interface robustness of commercial off-the-shelf software components [7, 18]; however, unlike them, we do not consider fault injection and fault containment techniques. Our aim is not to assess the ability of the component to handle faults in its environment, but to increase confidence in its ability to react according to its interface model for a large population of possible users. Hence we have to consider a larger range of solicitation profiles (e.g., frequency and sequencing of calls to the operations of the objects) than the ones that are possible in the original application.

Central to the case study is the problem of the interactions of objects with their environment. The interaction schemes may be very complex depending on the many possible interleavings of concurrent events. Since it is not tractable to test for all possible interleavings in a given operational context, and since reusable objects should be tested for several operational contexts, sampling approaches have to be defined. The approach that we propose is based on statistical testing designed according to functional criteria.

3 Statistical Testing Designed According to a Test Criterion

Test criteria are related to the coverage of either a white box or a black box model of the software (see e.g., [3]). For example, the program control flow graph is a well-known white box model; automata are black box models that may be used to describe some software functions. Given a criterion (e.g., branch or transition coverage), the conventional method for generating test inputs proceeds according to the *deterministic principle*: it consists in selecting a priori a set of test inputs such that each element defined by the criterion is exercised (at least) once. But a major limitation is due to the imperfect connection of the criteria with the real faults: exercising once, or very few times, each element defined by such criteria cannot ensure a high fault exposure power. Yet, the criteria provide us with relevant information about the target piece of software.

A practical way to compensate for criteria weakness is to require that each element be exercised several times. This involves larger sets of test inputs that have to be automatically generated: it is the motivation of *statistical testing* designed according to a test criterion [15]. In this approach, the information provided by criteria is combined with an automatic way of producing input patterns, that is, a random generation.

The statistical test sets are defined by two parameters, which have to be determined according to the test criterion: (i) the input distribution, from which the inputs are randomly drawn and, (ii) the test size, or equivalently the number of inputs that are generated. As in the case of deterministic testing, test criteria may be related to a model of either the program structure, which defines *statistical structural testing*, or of its functionality, which defines *statistical functional testing*.

The *determination of the input distribution* is the corner stone of the method. The aim is to search for a probability distribution that is proper to rapidly exercise each element defined by the criterion. Given a criterion C – say, transition coverage – let S be the corresponding set of elements – the set of transitions. Let P be the occurrence probability per execution of the least likely element of S. Then, the distribution must accommodate the highest possible P value. Depending on the complexity of this optimization problem, the determination of the distribution may proceed either in an analytical or in an empirical way (see [15] for detailed examples). The latter way is used in the case study presented in this paper (Section 6.3).

The *test size* N must be large enough to ensure that each element is exercised several times under the input distribution defined. The assessment of a minimum test size N is based on the notion of test quality with respect to the retained criterion. This quality, denoted q_N, is the probability of exercising at least once the least likely element of S. Relation (1) gives the value of N under the assumption of statistical independence (see [15] for examples where the assumption does not hold). It can be explained as follows: $(1-P)^N$ is an upper bound of the probability of never exercising some element during N executions with random inputs. Then, for a required upper bound of $1-q_N$, where the target test quality q_N will be typically taken close to 1.0, a minimum test size is derived.

$$N = \ln(1-q_N) / \ln(1-P) \tag{1}$$

Returning to the motivation of statistical testing – exercising several times each element defined by the criterion, it is worth noting that Relation (1) establishes a link between q_N and the expected number of times, denoted n, the least likely element is exercised: $n \cong - \ln(1-q_N)$. For example, $n \cong 7$ for $q_N = 0.999$. This relation is used to tune the test size N when the input distribution is empirically determined.

The main conclusions arising from previous work conducted on procedural programs were that: (i) statistical testing is a suitable means to compensate for the tricky link between test criteria and software design faults, (ii) the most efficient approach should be to retain weak criteria (e.g., transition coverage) facilitating the search for an input distribution, and to require a high test quality with respect to them (e.g., $q_N = 0.999$).

We are now studying the use of statistical testing for OO software. In the work presented in Sections 5 and 6, we adopt a functional approach consisting in basing the probabilistic generation of test patterns on the information got from the OO analysis and design documents. The production cell case study allows us to investigate this issue taking the example of the Fusion method [6].

4   Presentation of the Case Study

The case study is adapted from an industrial production cell. It was launched by the FZI (Forschungszentrum Informatik) inside the framework of the German Korso Project [13]. In addition to the informal specification, a Tcl/Tk simulator was made available by the FZI: it mimics the movements of the physical devices of the cell (Fig. 1).

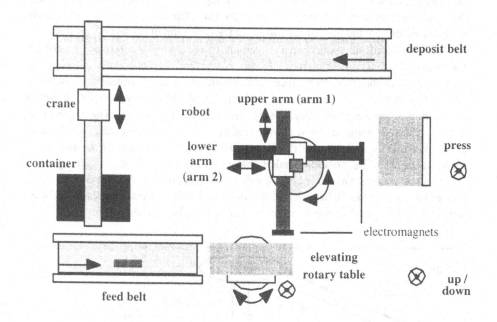

Fig. 1. Top view of the production cell

The aim of the production cell is the transformation of metal blanks into forged plates and their transportation from the feed belt into a container. The production cycle of each blank is the following: the blank is put on the feed belt by an operator; the feed belt conveys the blank to the table which rotates and lifts to put the blank in the position where the first robot arm is able to magnetize it; this arm places the blank into the press where it is forged; the second robot arm places the resulting plate on the deposit belt; then the crane magnetizes the plate and brings it from the deposit belt into a container. At a given time, several blanks may be in transit within the cell.

The cell is an industry-oriented problem where safety requirements play a significant role: 21 safety requirements and 1 liveness requirement (« every blank introduced in the cell will be forged and eventually dropped into the container ») are listed in the informal specification. Two examples of safety requirements are given below.

Requirement 18. A new plate may only be put on the deposit belt if the photoelectric cell, installed at the end of the belt, has detected the previous plate.

Requirement 21. If there is a blank on the table, the robot arm 1 may not be moved above the table if it also conveys a blank (otherwise the two blanks collide).

A control program for the production cell has been developed using the Fusion method [1]. This provides us with an example of a complete OO development process: Fusion analysis, Fusion design, and Ada 95 implementation. Fusion [6] is presented by its authors as a synthesis of prominent OO methods (OMT/Rumbaugh, Booch, Objectory, CRC). It includes some aspects coming from formal specification methods (pre- and postconditions). In this section, only few elements of the Fusion analysis phase are described: the ones that are used for the definition of the test experiments.

The Fusion analysis starts with the creation of the *system context diagram* of the controller (Fig. 2): it consists of six concurrent agents communicating by asynchronous events. Note that, since the controller is an active concurrent system, it has been separated – as proposed in Section 3.5 of [6] – to view it as a set of cooperating agents, each of which being developed using Fusion. The meaning of arrows is the following: an event may be sent at any time; the receiving agent queues the event until it is able to treat it; the sending agent is blocked until the end of the event treatment. The principle underlying event emission is that each agent is autonomous: it will do as many actions as it can independently. And for this, an agent may reorder the events it has queued: the order of event treatments does not always correspond to the order of event receptions into the waiting queues.

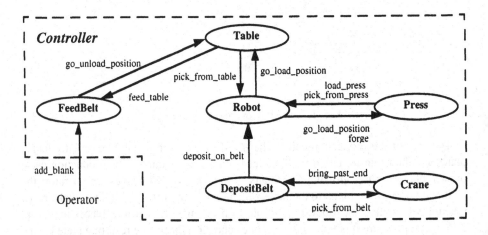

Fig. 2. System context diagram (inside view)

The expected behavior of an agent is described by its *interface model* which consists of a lifecycle and an operation model. The *lifecycle* specifies the order of event treatments and emissions by the agent. It is defined in terms of regular expressions. For example, the Table lifecycle is shown below:

initialize.#feed_table.(go_unload_position.#pick_from_table.go_load_position.#feed_table)*

It means that the first event to be treated is initialize which leads to the emission of feed_table (prefix # denotes emission); then any number of cycles of go_unload_position and go_load_position (with event emissions) may be treated by the Table agent.

The treatment of each event by the receiving agent is specified in the operation model which includes pre- and postconditions. For example, the treatment of go_load_position by Table corresponds to the following conditions:

Precondition: No blank on the table.
Postcondition: The table is in load position.
                          An event feed_table has been sent to FeedBelt.

In this example, the precondition of go_load_position is implied by the postcondition of pick_from_table treated by the Robot agent. But the order specified in the lifecycle does not always guarantee that the preconditions hold. In such cases, the receiving agent has to queue the event until the precondition becomes true: other events can be treated in the meantime. Thus, the interface model implies the reordering of events by the receiving agent: the order of event treatments must comply with both the agent lifecycle and the operation preconditions.

5   Overview of the Test Strategy

The test strategy is based on two kinds of information: the list of 21 safety requirements, and the models got from the Fusion analysis phase. A first problem is the determination of testing levels. To tackle this problem, we consider the possibility of associating a functional description with a (set of) class(es):

- The *unit level* corresponds to small subsystems that are meaningful enough to have interface models in Fusion. From Section 4, there are 6 such subsystems: FeedBelt, Table, Robot, Press, DepositBelt and Crane. Each of them is already an aggregation of classes. It means that basic classes (e.g., the Electro_Magnet class) are not tested in isolation: they are tested through their embodying subsystems (e.g., Robot).
- The *integration process* is guided by the consideration of the safety and liveness requirements. For example, requirement 21 leads to the definition of an integration test for the subsystem Robot+Table. Thus, four integration tests (FeedBelt+Table, Robot+Table, Robot+Press, Robot+DepositBelt) and one system test are defined.

The respective focus of each testing level (unit, integration) is determined in order to define a cost-effective test strategy for *reusable* components. The concern is to identify what can be tested once for all at the unit level and what has to be tested during the integration process specific to each application.

Unit testing is focused on verifying conformance to interface models. For reusability purposes, unit testing is designed without making any assumption on the operational context: it is well-recognized that a component that has been adequately tested in a given environment is not always adequately tested for another environment. Hence the test sequences are not restricted to the ones that are possible in the production cell context. Roughly speaking, the units are placed in an "hostile" environment: there is no timing or sequence assumption related to the events sent to them. This allows us to verify the correct reordering of events, and the correct treatment of the reordered events, in response to arbitrary solicitations. If the unit is not robust enough to pass the test, its design can be improved. Or, at least, the test results allow the identification of usage assumptions that must be added to its interface model.

Whether or not these assumptions hold in a given context (e.g., the production cell) has to be verified during the *integration process*. Also, integration testing allows the verification of safety requirements involving several units of the production cell. The liveness requirement is verified by the final system test. Contrary to the design of unit testing, the design of integration testing takes into account some characteristics of the cell. This leads to a more constrained version of the environment. For example, when testing Robot+Table, it is not possible to sent a load_press event to Robot while the previous one had not yet been treated. This is so because the robot is connected to a single press, and this press is blocked until the previous load_press is treated.

An overview of all experimental results is shown at the end of this paper. Section 6 focuses on the design of unit testing only (see [2] for the complete case study).

6   Unit Testing of Reusable Components

The unit testing process can be decomposed into phases that accompany the Fusion phases. The main objective – verify the conformance of the units to their interface models – has first to be refined in terms of workable test criteria and conformance relations. Fusion analysis models are examined with a view to testing: this leads to their reformulation in a compact and non ambiguous form (Section 6.1) from which test criteria are derived (Section 6.2). Statistical test sets are designed in accordance with the criteria (Section 6.3) and an oracle procedure is specified (Section 6.4). Then the development of a test environment supporting the refined objective requires a number of controllability and observability problems to be handled (Section 6.5): solutions to these problems must be determined in relation to the choices taken in the late phases of the production cell development (Fusion design and Ada implementation). Experiments are performed using the resulting test environments (Section 6.6).

6.1   Reformulation of the Fusion Interface Model

The lifecycle model specifies the order in which each unit should process input events and send output events. The processing of input events is made more precise in the operation model, where in particular pre- and postconditions are stated. The textual lifecycle expression can be put into an equivalent form: a finite state automaton recognizing the regular expression. However, this automaton is not sufficient to describe the allowed sequences of processed events because no operation should be triggered outside its precondition: the set of allowed sequences should be further constrained by considering whether the postcondition of one operation implies the precondition of the next one. This leads us to reformulate the Fusion interface model.

First, a *completed version of the operation model* is required for testing purposes. According to the Fusion method, a condition that has to be true both before and after the operation is not listed, neither as a precondition nor as a postcondition; and the granularity of the operation model does not distinguish between the case where the condition remains true throughout the operation execution, and the case where it turns to false and then returns to true before the end of the operation. In both cases, it is important to check the validity of the condition after the operation. Hence, pre- and postconditions are expanded in the completed operation model. For example, in the model of the Table operation go_load_position (Section 4), pre- and postconditions are added, including the following ones: the rotation and elevation motors are off.

Then, combining the lifecycle expression and the completed operation model, the allowed sequences of event treatment for each unit are reformulated as *finite state automata*. Figure 3 shows the reformulation of the lifecycle of Robot which is the most complex unit (for the other units, we get 2-states automata). The textual lifecycle expression would have given us a 4-states automaton, depending on which arm is carrying a plate. The examination of the operation model shows that presence or absence of a plate in the press should also be taken into account: Robot is not allowed to process pick_from_press if it did not previously load the press.

The lifecycle automata describe the allowed sequences of event treatments, but they say nothing about the event reordering functionality to be supplied by the units. Input events are supposed to be stored in a waiting queue if the unit is not ready to process them. When no timing and sequence assumption related to the events sent to the unit is made, the size of the waiting queue may be infinite: the reordering mechanisms of event processing cannot be modeled by an automaton with a finite number of states.

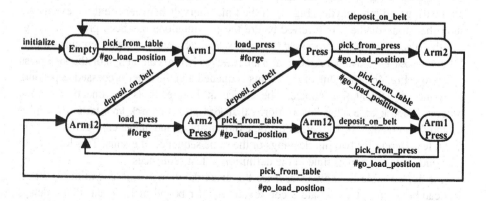

Fig. 3. Robot lifecycle automaton

In order to represent both the reordering mechanisms and the allowed sequences of event treatments, we need a formalism that is more powerful than finite state automata. The solution retained is to attach an *input event queue* to each state of the lifecycle automaton: this queue is characterized by the number of events of each category (for Robot, pick_from_table, pick_from_press, load_press, deposit_on_belt) that are waiting to be processed. It is worth noting that the reformulated model (automaton + queues) may involve nondeterminism, for example (Fig. 3) when state Arm12 is reached while both deposit_on_belt and load_press events are queued.

6.2 Test Criteria

Two different test criteria are needed, based on the reformulated models. As regards the *correct treatment of reordered events*, the criterion retained is the coverage of the *transitions of the lifecycle automata* with a high test quality of $q_N = 0.999$. This test quality implies that the least likely transition should be exercised 7 times on average by a given test set (Section 3).

As regards the *correct reordering of events*, the retained criterion is the coverage of *four classes of queue configurations* for each category of event: the number of queued events of that category is 0, 1, 2 or ≥3. We require the same test quality as previously. Note that queue configurations with more than one event are not possible in the production cell context. Yet, they are forced during testing for reusability purposes.

6.3 Design of Statistical Test Sets

Controlling coverage of transitions and queue configurations is not trivial. Due to concurrency, the internal behavior of one unit depends not only on the order in which events are received, but also on the interleavings of event reception and event treatment.

To illustrate the problem, let us assume that a test sequence first takes the robot to the Arm12 state (Fig. 3) with no queued event, and then is continued by subsequence load_press.deposit_on_belt.pick_from_table. The robot behavior may be different depending on the triggered interleaving (Fig. 4). If the time intervals between the three events are such that none of them is received before the previous one has been processed (Fig. 4a), then deposit_on_belt is processed before pick_from_table and the queue remains empty. If both deposit_on_belt and pick_from_table are received before completion of the load_press operation (Fig. 4b), then one of the events is queued and the other processed depending on some implementation choice. The choice in Figure 4b is the one of the Ada program: deposit_on_belt has lower priority than load_press and pick_from_table. Examples 4a and 4b show that the triggered coverage of transitions and queue configurations may be quite different for two interleavings of the same sequence of events. This leads us to introduce some notion of time in the definition of test sequences.

It is not possible to know in advance the exact duration of one operation: the best that can be done is to estimate a conservative upper bound of it. Then, if the delays between input events are long enough compared to the reaction time of the units (slow environment), specific interleavings such as the one of Figure 4a are forced, making it possible to assess the coverage supplied by a given sequence of events. Such an a priori assessment is impossible when the units are not run in a slow environment, because the occurrence of a specific interleaving depends on uncontrollable factors: the behavior may be non reproducible from one run to the other. Yet, interleavings such as the one of Figure 4b should not be excluded from the test input domain if they may occur in operational contexts. For example, if the treatment of events is not atomic, it must be possible to trigger the reception of events during an on-going treatment. And irrespective of the atomicity hypothesis, it must be possible to trigger schemes where several concurrent events are received in the meantime between two treatments. To account for all these schemes, the proposed sampling approach is to consider several load profiles, i.e. profiles of time intervals between two successive events. Then a test sequence is defined as a sequence of input events with time intervals between events.

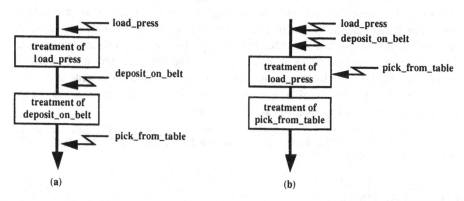

Fig. 4. Different possible interleavings for a same sequence of events

Event sequences are first designed. Assuming a slow environment, it is possible to search for a probability distribution of input events that is proper to ensure rapid coverage of the criteria. The analysis proceeds empirically: coverage measures are collected from programs simulating the reformulated model of each unit (automaton + queues). Then, input distributions are determined by successive trials with random sets of events. Robot is the unit for which the empirical process required the largest number of trials: in the retained distribution, the probability of events is tuned according to the current state and queue configuration. For the other units, making all events equally likely (uniform stimulation) turns out to provide a balanced coverage of transitions and queue configurations. Sets of event sequences are randomly generated according to the retained distributions. Each set provides the required test quality of $q_N = 0.999$ with respect to the criteria: every transition and queue configuration is exercised more than 7 times. Note that since the initialization is one of the transitions to be exercised, each set contains at least 7 test sequences beginning with initialize. For example, the Robot test set contains 12 test sequences involving a total number of $N = 306$ events. An example of sequence included in this set is provided below. It is one of the shortest sequences (the size varying over the range [5..40]):

initialize . pick_from_table . load_press . deposit_on_belt . pick_from_table . pick_from_press . load_press . pick_from_press . load_press . pick_from_table . deposit_on_belt

The *time intervals* between successive events are generated according to 3 load profiles:

- A low load profile: the time intervals are large compared to the reaction time of the unit (long delays).
- A high load profile: the time intervals are shorter than, or the same order of magnitude as, the reaction time of the unit (short delays).
- An intermediate load profile (mix of short, long and middle delays).

Hence, each set of events will be executed three times, once under each load profile. In this way, different interleavings are triggered for a same sequence of events. One of these interleavings, the one forced by the low load profile, ensures coverage of the criteria with the test quality previously assessed. The other two profiles induce interleavings like the one of Figure 4b, possibly in a nondeterministic way.

The values associated to the three profiles take into account the average response time of the FZI simulator, but could be calibrated for other environments in a similar way. With the simulator, the reaction time of each unit to process one event is of the order of magnitude of a few seconds. Accordingly, the time intervals are generated as follows: 1) uniform generation over [15s..20s] for the low load profile; 2) uniform generation over [1s..15s] for the intermediate load profile; 3) uniform generation over [0s..5s] for the high load profile. For the previous Robot test sequence, the values generated under the low load profile are shown below:

initialize . (16s) pick_from_table . (15s) load_press . (18s) deposit_on_belt . (15s) pick_from_table . (15s) pick_from_press . (17s) load_press . (15s) pick_from_press . (18s) load_press . (20s) pick_from_table . (18s) deposit_on_belt

6.4 Oracle Checks

The role of the oracle is to determine conformance of the test results to the expected ones. Most of the corresponding checks are based on our reformulation of the interface models. They take advantage of the fact that the lifecycle automata turn out to possess a remarkable property: for any test sequence, the final state and the number of processed events at the end of the sequence do not depend on the nondeterministic choices made during the execution. For example, the interleavings of Figure 4 both take the robot to the Arm1/Press state with an empty queue, irrespective of the intermediate behavior. Accordingly, the oracle conformance checks are specified as follows:

- The observed sequences of input events processed and output events sent must be recognized by the lifecycle automaton.
- The number of events that are processed by the unit is the same as the number of events that would be processed by the lifecycle automaton exercised with the same test sequence. Due to the property mentioned above, adding this check to the previous one ensures that the implementation has the same deadlocks as the specification.
- After each treatment of event, the associated postconditions got from the completed operation model must hold.

In addition to the previous checks, our oracle procedures include the verification of 15 safety requirements that can be related to one unit taken in isolation. For example, requirement 18 (see Section 4) is included in the DepositBelt oracle. Although verifying safety requirements is not the main objective of unit testing, it is interesting to consider them at the unit level: if they are shown to hold when testing in a "hostile" environment, then *a fortiori* they should hold in the production cell context. Indeed, the experimental results will provide examples of requirements that are violated at the unit level when no assumption is made on the operational context; yet, integration tests show that they hold when the unit is placed in the production cell.

6.5 Unit Test Environments

Having defined the test sets and test oracles, we have now to develop the test environments allowing us to perform the experiments. As expected, this raises a number of controllability and observability issues.

Let us recall that the test environment must be able to *control any arbitrary input sequence*: there is no ordering assumption related to the events sent to the units. Since the sending of events is blocking, we must be careful not to introduce deadlocks when the event order departs from the one specified in the lifecycle. Let us take the example of a unit having a lifecycle defined as (E1.#e1.E2#e2)*, and exercised with an input sequence having order E2.E1. The expected behavior of the unit is to treat both events in the lifecycle order: the treatment of E2 is delayed until E1 has been processed and e1 has been sent. If the test driver is implemented by a single Ada task sequentially sending E2 and E1, then the driver will be blocked on E2: E1 will never be sent. This is not acceptable since the test environment should always be able to send the next event, as defined in the sequence. To handle this controllability problem, the adopted solution is to have the input events sent by several concurrent drivers.

Observability is prerequisite to the feasibility of oracle checks: appropriate information is to be monitored by the test environment. Checking conformance to the lifecycle automata relates to the observation of the treatment of input events and emission of output events. However, the reordering of input events according to the lifecycle is encapsulated in the units: once the input events have been received by a unit, the test environment may be unable to know the order of their internal treatment. This problem is solved by inserting a print statement at the start point of the treatment in the Ada code, thus making observable the beginning of each operation. Postconditions and safety requirements relate to the state of the physical devices controlled by the software units (e.g., position of the robot arms). In our test environment, their verification is implemented by instrumenting the FZI simulator used to mimic the reaction of the physical devices. All the observations must be synchronized with the behavior of the units, and some ordering relations must be preserved by the results of (possibly concurrent) observers: for example, for a given unit, observation of the beginning of one operation is always reported before the end of this operation; postconditions checks are always performed and reported before the beginning of the next operation of this unit.

A generic view of the resulting test environments is provided in Figure 5. The corresponding design choices are justified in [2], and we do not further detail them in this paper. Let us just mention two important remarks. First, it can be seen that a number of test components had to be developed in order to control and observe the unit under test. Second, it is worth noting that a few postconditions were not implemented in the oracle procedures: due to synchronization constraints, making them observable would have required an important instrumentation of the corresponding units and this was considered as too intrusive.

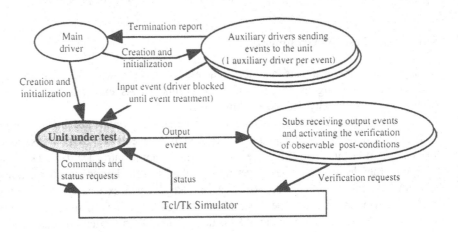

Fig. 5. Generic view of unit test environments

With these test environments, each test experiment generates a trace file recording:

- The sequence of every event treated or sent by the unit under test.
- The number and category of input events not treated at the end of the test experiment.
- The results of the checks for the status of the devices at the end of the operations.
- The error messages of the FZI simulator. The FZI simulator has built-in mechanisms to issue an error message in case of abnormal situations like collision of devices, or falling of metal plates.

Then the trace file is analyzed off-line by an oracle program in order to issue an acceptance or rejection report.

6.6 Experimental Results

The test experiments first revealed a *synchronization problem* that was observed whatever the unit under test (violation of postconditions and safety requirements). It concerns communication with the FZI simulator: the synchronization mechanisms do not ensure that requests to stop the physical devices are received in time by the simulator. For example, when the Robot operation load_press is executed, the extension of the upper arm (arm 1) over the press may be actually stopped too late so that the blank falls beside the press. Failures are all the more frequent as the load profile is high, but their occurrences are not repetitive from one run to the other: executing several times a same test set systematically produces failures, but possibly at different times during the experiment. These intermittent faulty behaviors are closely related to the real-time behavior of the program which is not adequately addressed by the Fusion method. Nevertheless, the fault is repeatedly exposed by the statistical test sets. It is fixed by modifying the Ada code of two basic classes (Sensor_Server, Actuator_Server) in charge of the communication with the physical devices. With this fix, four agents (FeedBelt, Table, Press, Crane) pass their test. For the other two agents (Robot, DepositBelt) errors are detected.

As regards *Robot*, the number of deposit_on_belt treated by the Ada program is lower than the expected one: when several deposit_on_belt are queued, only one of them is treated and the others are ignored. Failures are observed whatever the load profile, but their rate is raised under the high load profile since the waiting queues are larger. These test results show that the Robot agent is not robust enough to be used in any context of applications: its correct behavior assumes that no new deposit_on_belt event is sent to Robot before the previous one has been processed. The fault is fixed by a simple modification of the deposit_on_belt operation (replacement of a Boolean flag by a counter), and the fixed Robot passes its unit test.

As regards *DepositBelt*, it is first observed that two events sent during the treatment of the initialize operation occur in the reverse order compared to the one defined in the Fusion lifecycle. After analysis, our diagnosis is that both orders are consistent with the initial (informal) specification of the application, and none of them may lead to the violation of safety requirements. Our oracle procedure is modified in accordance with this diagnosis and it is requested that this modification is integrated in the Fusion analysis document. A second and more significant problem is related to the dropping of plates on the belt. It is observed that plates may be dropped too close to each other, so that they collide or fall at the end of the belt; two safety requirements are violated (e.g., requirement 18 in Section 4). The problem is due to the fact that the dropping of plates is not encapsulated into an operation of DepositBelt. Then the DepositBelt agent is not robust enough to be used in any context of applications: its correct behavior assumes that plates are dropped only when expected by the belt, that is, when the previous plate has already reached the end of the belt.

Fixing this fault requires the modification of the DepositBelt interface, and thus of the interface of the Robot agent which interacts with DepositBelt. The modifications would have repercussions at every level from the Fusion analysis document to the Ada code. In the context of the production cell, such substantial modifications are not needed if it can be shown that the correct usage assumption holds. Indeed, one of the preconditions of the Robot operation deposit_on_belt should ensure that the robot cannot drop a plate while there is another one at the beginning of the belt. Hence, the decision to perform the modifications is delayed: the correct behavior of the subsystem Robot+DepositBelt has to be verified by integration testing (Section 7).

Besides the exposure of faults, the test experiments give us feedback on the internal behavior of the Ada program under the various load profiles. We have instrumented the oracle procedures checking conformance to the lifecycle automata, in order to collect statistics on the number of times each transition is actually executed. The statistics confirm that transition coverage heavily depends on the load profile. For instance, some transitions of the Robot automaton are never or seldom executed under the high load profile, and others are much more exercised. This is due to the fact that when numerous events are available in the waiting queues, their order of treatment is enforced by the priority choices taken in the Ada implementation. For example (Fig. 3), the robot transition from Arm2 to Arm12 state (triggered by pick_from_table) is never exercised under the high load profile: lower load profiles are required to reveal faults related to this transition. Conversely, our test results show that the high load profile may be more effective in some cases. This corroborates our expectation that the use of different load levels should strengthen the fault revealing power of test sets.

7 Summary and Conclusion

Table 1 displays the results of the whole set of test experiments. A complete description of the integration testing process is available in [2]. Let us note that the integration test experiments do not reveal any fault related to the joint behavior of the units under test: in particular, the two safety requirements violated during unit testing of DepositBelt are satisfied by the subsystem Robot+DepositBelt: as expected from the Robot interface model (Section 6.6), the assumption governing the correct behavior of DepositBelt does hold. At the system level, only one input can be controlled: the introduction of blanks in the production cell; it is worth noting that the experiments confirm that the interleaving of the internal events is quite different depending on the time intervals between the successive blanks.

This theoretical and experimental investigation allows us to draw more general conclusions on testing of reusable concurrent objects. The main lessons learnt are summarized below. They are classified according to three issues: object-oriented technology, concurrency and reusability.

Table 1. Overview of the test results

Unit Tests	FeedBelt, Table, Press, Crane	Robusts, 8 safety requirements satisfied
	Robot	Made robust ➡ 5 safety requirements satisfied
	DepositBelt	Assumption on the usage context, 2 safety requirements violated
Integration Tests	Robot+DepositBelt	Assumption holds in the production cell context ➡ the 2 safety requirements are satisfied
	FeedBelt+Table Robot+Table Robot+Press	2 safety requirements satisfied 1 safety requirement satisfied 2 safety requirements satisfied
System Test	1 liveness requirement satisfied	

As regards *object-oriented* technology, the information got from OO development methods should allow us to design efficient statistical functional test sets: this has been exemplified using Fusion analysis document; but, the information used is quite similar to the one provided by other OO methods. However, whatever the chosen testing approach, the requirements of the test environments must be identified early in the development process, in accordance with the pursued test objectives. Especially, it must be identified what is to be controlled and what is to be observed. Then, how to handle the resulting controllability and observability issues is necessarily constrained by the design and the implementation choices taken for the application. This leads us to recommend that the development of the test environments accompany the corresponding development phases of the application. This is not new, since recommended for a long while in the well-known "V development process". But, it is still more crucial in cases of OO software because of the testability problems increased by encapsulation mechanisms. Returning to the Fusion example, the determination of the testing levels, test criteria and oracle checks must accompany the analysis phase; as for the design and implementation of the test environments, they must be conducted during the Fusion design and implementation phases.

As regards *concurrency*, the concern is not to exclude any event interleaving that may occur in operational contexts, that is, to account for nondeterminism induced by asynchronous communication. To tackle this problem, it is necessary to introduce some notion of time in the definition of the test sequences: for each sequence of events to be sent during testing, time intervals between successive events must be generated according to several load profiles that mimic different types of operational contexts. We propose to use a sampling technique based on three typical load profiles: long delays compared to the reaction time of the subsystem under test; short delays; and a mix of short, long and middle delays. Another notable impact of concurrency is related to the design of test environments which may become complex compared to the subsystem under test: the environments must consist of concurrent drivers and stubs in order to handle the controllability and observability problems added by concurrency.

Finally, the *reusability* concern influences the choice of the test criteria that guide the selection of test inputs: the test sequences must not be restricted to the ones that are possible in the context of the application under test. The test input domain is enlarged. Yet, the benefit of testing for reusability – when it remains feasible – is significant: either the unit under test is robust enough to pass the test, or it is not. If it is, it may be used in any context without requiring further testing. If it is not, its design can be made robust, or at least the test results allow the identification of usage assumptions that are required for the unit to conform to its interface model.

Acknowledgments. This work was partially supported by the European Community (ESPRIT Project n° 20072: DeVa). It has benefited from many fruitful discussions with our DeVa partners, in particular: Stéphane Barbey, Didier Buchs, Marie-Claude Gaudel, Bruno Marre and Cécile Péraire. We also wish to thank Damien Guibouret and Olfa Kaddour very much for their useful contribution to the case study, within the framework of student projects.

References

1. Barbey, S., Buchs, D., Péraire, C.: Modelling the Production Cell Case Study Using the Fusion Method. Technical Report 98/298, EPFL-DI, 1998
2. Barbey, S., Buchs, D., Gaudel, M-C., Marre, B., Péraire, C., Thévenod-Fosse, P., Waeselynck, H.: From Requirements to Tests via Object-Oriented Design. DeVa Year 3 Deliverables (1998) 331-383. Also available as LAAS Report no 98476
3. Beizer, B.: Software Testing Techniques. 2nd edn. Van Nostrand Reinhold, New York (1990)
4. Binder, R.: Design for Testability in Object-Oriented Systems. Communications of the ACM 37 (1994) 87-101. Also available in [12]
5. Binder, R.: Testing Object-Oriented Software – A Survey. Software Testing, Verification & Reliability 6 (1996) 125-252
6. Coleman, D., Arnold, P., Bodoff, S., Dollin, C., Gilchrist, H., Hayes, F., Jeremaes, P.: Object-Oriented Development – The Fusion Method. Object-Oriented Series, Prentice Hall (1994)
7. Fabre, J-C., Salles, F., Rodriguez Moreno, M., Arlat, J.: Assessment of COTS Microkernels by Fault Injection. In Proc. 7th IFIP International Working Conference on Dependable Computing for Critical Applications (DCCA-7), San Jose (1999) 19-38
8. Harrold, M-J., McGregor, J., Fitzpatrick, K.: Incremental Testing of Object-Oriented Class Structures. In Proc. 14th IEEE Int. Conf. on Software Engineering (ICSE-14), Melbourne (1992) 68-80. Also available in [12]
9. Jorgensen, P., Erickson, C.: Object-Oriented Integration Testing. Communications of the ACM 37 (1994) 30-38. Also available in [12]
10. Kung, D., Gao, J., Hsia, P., Toyoshima, Y., Chen, C., Kim, Y-S., Song, Y-K.: Developping an Object-Oriented Software Testing and Maintenance Environment. Communications of the ACM 38 (1995) 75-87. Also available in [12]
11. Kung, D., Lu, Y., Venugopala, N., Hsia, P., Toyoshima, Y., Chen, C., Gao, J.: Object State Testing and Fault Analysis for Reliable Software Systems. In Proc. 7th IEEE International Symposium on Software Reliability Engineering (ISSRE'96), White Plains (1996) 76-85. Also available in [12]
12. Kung, D., Hsia, P., Gao, J. (eds): Testing Object-Oriented Software. IEEE Computer Society (1998)
13. Lewerens, C., Linder, T. (eds): Formal Development of Reactive Systems – Case Study Production Cell. Lecture Notes in Computer Science, Vol. 891, Springer-Verlag (1995)
14. Luo, G., Bochman, G. v., Petrenko, A.: Test Selection Based on Communicating Nondeterministic Finite-State Machines Using a Generalized Wp-Method. IEEE Trans. on Software Engineering 20 (1994) 149-162
15. Thévenod-Fosse, P., Waeselynck, H., Crouzet, Y.: Software Statistical Testing. In: Randell, B., Laprie, J-C., Kopetz, H., Littlewood, B. (eds): Predictably Dependable Computing Systems. Springer-Verlag (1995) 253-272
16. Turner, C., Robson, D.: The State-Based Testing of Object-Oriented Programs. In Proc. IEEE Conference on Software Maintenance (1993) 302-310. Also available in [12]
17. Voas, J.: Object-Oriented Software Testability. In Proc. 3rd International Conference on Achieving Quality in Software , Chapman & Hall (1996) 279-290
18. Voas, J.: Certifying Off-the-Shelf Software Components. IEEE Computer 31 (June 1998) 53-59.

Fault-Detection by Result-Checking for the Eigenproblem[1]

Paula Prata[&], João Gabriel Silva[*]

[&] Universidade da Beira Interior – Dep. Matemática/Informática
Rua Marquês d'Ávila e Bolama
P- 6200 Covilhã, Portugal
[*]Universidade de Coimbra - Dep. Eng. Informática/CISUC
Pinhal de Marrocos
P-3030 Coimbra - Portugal
{pprata, jgabriel }@dei.uc.pt

Abstract. This paper proposes a new fault detection mechanism for the computation of eigenvalues and eigenvectors, the so called eigenproblem, for which no such scheme existed before, to the best of our knowledge. It consists of a number of assertions that can be executed on the results of the computation to determine their correctness. The proposed scheme follows the Result Checking principle, since it does not depend on the particular numerical algorithm used. It can handle both real and complex matrices, symmetric or not. Many practical issues are handled, like rounding errors and eigenvalue ordering, and a practical implementation was built on top of unmodified routines of the well-known LAPACK library. The proposed scheme is simultaneously very efficient, with less than 2% performance overhead for medium to large matrices, very effective, since it exhibited a fault coverage greater than 99.7% with a confidence level of 99%, when subjected to extensive fault-injection experiments, and very easy to adapt to other libraries of mathematical routines besides LAPACK.

1   Introduction

When solving systems of differential equations, the calculation of eigenvalues and eigenvectors, collectively called the Eigenproblem, is almost always required. Differential equations turn up in such different areas as stability theory, quantum mechanics, statistical analysis, and control systems. Many of these applications process large amounts of data, taking hours of computer time to execute. Since the probability of some perturbation occurring that affects the computation cannot be neglected, it is important to use fault tolerant techniques to assert the correctness of the results.

---

[1] This work was partially supported by the Portuguese Ministério da Ciência e Tecnologia, the European Union through the R&D Unit 326/94 (CISUC) and the project PRAXIS XXI 2/2.1/TIT/1625/95 (PARQUANTUM).

For computations that mainly do linear transformations of matrices, Algorithm Based Fault Tolerance (ABFT) [1] is such a technique, providing very high fault coverage with low performance overhead, [2][3]. ABFT exploits algorithm properties in order to introduce in the program some extra calculations that check its correctness. The basic approach is to apply some encoding to the input data of the calculation, execute the algorithm on the encoded data, and check that the encoding is preserved at the end. Moreover, it was shown that ABFT is particularly effective at detecting faults that just affect data, which is exactly the type of errors that other error detection methods like memory protection or control flow checking [4][5] have greater difficulty in detecting. For the eigenvalues computation there are also some ABFT schemes described in the literature [6] [7].

An alternative to ABFT that has been the subject of some theoretic work being done by the Computer Science community is Result-Checking (RC), where the results of a computation are verified in a way independent of the used algorithm. Formally presented in [8], it is based on the fact that checking the solution is usually easier than computing it. Recently we have shown that ABFT and RC are equivalent in terms of error detection coverage for some matrix operations like matrix multiplication and QR factorization [9]. Chen [6] proposed a RC scheme for the calculation of eigenvalues, using some of its properties. For the calculation of eigenvectors, no RC technique has been proposed in the literature, to the best of our knowledge.

This paper proposes a new fault detection mechanism based on RC for the eigenvalue and eigenvector computation. Computing the eigenvalues remains an open problem and new algorithms have been studied in recent years, for parallel and distributed architectures [10]. Until now, there hasn't been a total convergence proof for the most used algorithm, the QR iteration with implicit shifts, although this algorithm is considered quite reliable [11].

We claim that for the purpose of error detection for the Eigenproblem, RC has some advantages over ABFT:

- ABFT techniques are only known for some steps of the QR algorithm. Although they are the most important, we need to protect all the remaining calculations. For instance, the ABFT proposed for the QR iteration doesn't consider the use of shifts, a practical technique used to speedup the convergence of the algorithm.

- RC is problem-based, so that it doesn't depend on the algorithm used. Thus our checker can be applied to the QR algorithm or to any other algorithm for eigenvalue calculation (sequential or parallel), as for instance the recently proposed Divide-and-Conquer algorithm, [11], for which there isn't until now any ABFT known to us.

- RC can be easily applied to off-the-shelf routines, like those from highly optimized mathematical libraries. Introducing ABFT code in any such existing routine can be very hard.

We have implemented our Result-Checker on top of routines from the well known LAPACK library [12], which calculate the eigenvalues and optionally the eigenvectors. While the most obvious way of checking those computations would be the direct use of the definition of eigenvalues/eigenvectors, this possibility is not interesting because it would be almost as expensive as initial calculation itself.

Instead we proposed a simplified checker whose overhead is smaller than 2% for large matrices. The experimental evaluation of our proposed scheme with random matrices has shown a fault coverage greater than 99.7% with a confidence level of 99%.

The structure of this paper is as follows: in section 2 the concept of Result-Checking is reviewed, in section 3, after a short description of the eigenproblem, subsection 3.1 reviews the scheme proposed by Chen for the eigenvalues [6] and subsection 3.2 presents the new RC for the eigenproblem. Section 4 presents the experimental evaluation, briefly describes the fault injection tool (subsection 4.1), and shows the fault coverage results and performance overheads for the symmetric case (subsection 4.2), for the general real case (subsection 4.3) and the general complex case (subsection 4.4). Finally section 5 presents the conclusions and future work directions.

2 Result-Checking

Checking the result of a mathematical function is often easier than computing it. Starting from this idea, some theoretical work has been done in the Result-Checking field [8]. The concept of a simple checker for a function f [13], is presented as: "*a program which, given inputs x and y, returns the correct answer to the question, does $f(x) = y$?; [...] Moreover, the checker must take asymptotically less time than any possible program for computing f*". The initial motivation of this work was to assure software-fault tolerance by checking the result, instead of testing the program with a set of random inputs or by a formal proof of correctness. There are checkers proposed for very different areas such as sorting, [8], linear transformations ([14], [13], [15]) and algebraic expressions of trigonometric functions [16].

Proposed RC schemes do not consider faults that affect the execution of the checker itself. Some authors of RC schemes [15] claim that there is no need to do it, because it is very unlikely that the result and the checker are simultaneously affected in such a way that the checker incorrectly accepts a wrong result. In [17] we have shown that this may not always be the case. Another problem that RC algorithms face is the possible corruption of the data outside the part of the program covered by the checker, the so-called *protection window* of the checker. For instance, data errors can happen before the calculation, so that the results are computed and checked with wrong inputs, or the results can be corrupted after having been verified. In this work we have handled these problems by protecting all the application code, including the RC execution, using the method of Robust Assertions [17], which has been proposed to complement the fault tolerant capabilities of any kind of assertion (like e.g. a result-checker or ABFT).

Robust Assertions (see Fig. 1), to solve the problem of data corruption outside the "protection window" of the checker, use some error detection code to protect the data, since data is not transformed there, just moved around. For instance, whoever generates the input matrix should also generate a CRC of all their elements. The program should then proceed in the following sequence: read the data, compute all the values needed to check the result (we call this "encode data") and verify the input

CRC (verifies data integrity). A similar procedure occurs at the end: the program calculates a CRC over the results (protects the results), executes the checker and, if the results are correct, writes them to the output file together with the CRC. If the results are somehow corrupted in the process, whoever reads it from the output file will be able to detect the corruption by verifying the CRC.

To prevent the problem of a possible incorrect execution of the checker (e.g. a control-flow error can jump over the whole checking code), a very simple software-based control flow checking technique is used (*Gold Code* in Fig.1): a double execution of the checker and the use of a "magic" number, written together with the results to the output file, that is e.g. the sum of two unrelated numbers. At the start of the test, that number is set to zero; if the first execution of the checker is successful the first number is added to it; if the second execution of the checker is also successful, the second number is also added to form the magic number. The resulting number is then written to the disk together with the results, using the same "write" statement. We call "gold code" to this carefully protected piece of code. When the program using the output file reads it, it just has to verify that the magic number is there (it is independent of the contents of the matrix) to have the guaranty of that the results were indeed checked.

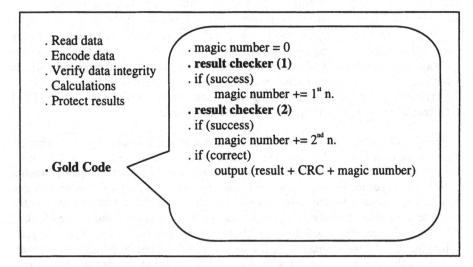

Fig. 1. Robust Result-Checking

We have shown in [17] that with a very high probability the results produced under such a scheme are indeed filtered by a correctly executed test. We say that the system follows a Fail-Bounded failure model: if we have results, they are as correct as the assertion over the data transformations can guarantee.

423

3 The Eigenproblem

The eigenproblem includes a variety of problems, such as finding all the eigenvalues and eigenvectors, finding the eigenvalues only, and for some applications, finding only a subset of the eigenvalues (and possibly the eigenvectors). The following two definitions are from [18]:

Definition 1 - "The **eigenvalues** of a matrix $A \in \forall^{n \times n}$ are the n roots of its characteristic polynomial $p(z) = det\ (zI-A)$. The set of these roots is called the spectrum and is denoted by $\lambda(A) = \{\lambda_1, \ldots, \lambda_n\}$". (Where I represents the n-by-n identity matrix and $det(M)$ represents the determinant of matrix M).

Definition 2 - "If $\lambda \in \lambda(A)$ then the nonzero vectors $x \in \forall^{n \times n}$ that satisfy $Ax = \lambda x$ are referred to as **eigenvectors**". We say that x is a right eigenvector for the eigenvalue λ. (If $y^H A = y^H \lambda$, then y is a left eigenvector for λ, where $-^H$ is the notation for conjugate transposition.)

Finding the eigenvalues of a n-by-n matrix is mathematically equivalent to calculating the roots of a polynomial of degree n. That means there is no general formula to find the eigenvalues of an n-by-n matrix if $n > 4$ [19]. The most widely used method to compute all eigenvalues and eigenvectors on dense matrices is the QR algorithm [11]. On each step of the algorithm, the matrix is transformed into a similar one, which has the same eigenvalues. This sequence of similar matrices converges to an upper-triangular matrix whose main diagonal elements are the eigenvalues. Each QR iteration consists of a QR decomposition and a matrix multiplication. Thus we can apply the known ABFT.s for these operations ([1], [20], [21], [7], [6]). But in practice this method is too expensive, and certain techniques are needed to accelerate the convergence:

Usually the matrix is first reduced to an upper Hessenberg form (this means that the matrix is zero below the first sub-diagonal). After that is applied a strategy of shifting and matrix deflation to increase the convergence rate of eigenvalues. Regarding the eigenvectors, although the QR procedure could also be used to compute them, inverse iteration is a cheaper method, and that means doing LU decompositions, solving systems of equations and doing rescaling operations [19].

Introducing the ABFT scheme in a complex algorithm like this is not a trivial problem. The algorithm includes several linear transformations that can be protected by partial ABFT.s, but also includes non-linear operations such as computing shifts, deflation, or testing the convergence in each iteration.

Our main purpose is building a low-overhead checker that verifies whether the eigenvalues and eigenvectors are correct and then evaluating it by fault injection. The algorithm used to compute the result doesn't matter, we only need to take into account that known algorithms are all approximately $O(n^3)$.

Next section reviews the scheme proposed in [6], which uses some properties of eigenvalues and similarity transformations to check the calculated eigenvalues without data codification. Next we describe the checker we propose for each pair eigenvalue/eigenvector.

3.1   Checking the Eigenvalues

Defining the trace of an n-by-n matrix A by $trace(A) = \sum_{i=1}^{n} a_{ii}$, it can be shown that

$trace(A) = \lambda_1 + \cdots + \lambda_n$ [18]. That is, the sum of the main diagonal matrix elements is equal to the sum of all eigenvalues. It's a very simple O(n) assertion, proposed in [6], although quite weak because it is an invariant based on a small set of A entries. Our study has shown that errors in the calculation of non-diagonal matrix elements may not be detected.

To improve the fault coverage a second assertion based on norm preservation was proposed [6]. Since similarity transformations are generated using orthogonal matrices, the norm of the successive similar matrices is also an invariant [18]. Then we can test if the norm of the initial matrix A is equal to the norm of the final updated matrix. This assertion works very well for symmetric matrices because in the symmetric case we reach a diagonal matrix whose entries are the eigenvalues, and we

only need to verify the expression $\|A\|_2 = \sqrt{\sum_{i=1}^{n} \lambda_i^2}$, where $\|A\|_2$ denotes the 2-norm

of matrix A ($\sqrt{\sum_{i=1}^{n}\sum_{j=1}^{n} a_{ij}^2}$). Moreover we can say that this checker is independent of

the algorithm because the assertion is also true even if we don't use orthogonal transformations to find the eigenvalues. (The spectral theorem [19], guarantees that if A is symmetric then there exists an orthogonal matrix that transforms A into a similar diagonal matrix that has the eigenvalues of A in the main-diagonal entries). Our experimental evaluation has shown that this second assertion greatly improves the fault-coverage obtained with the trace assertion. That $O(n^2)$ checker (trace plus norm preservation assertions) for the symmetric eigenvalue calculation can have a fault-coverage greater than 99.7%.

For general matrices, we must have the final upper-triangular matrix in order to compare both norms. Since that depends on the algorithm used we didn't apply the norm assertion in the non-symmetric case.

3.2   A Result-Checker for the Eigenproblem

When the eigenvectors are also calculated, it's possible to verify the result using the definition, that is: given one eigenvalue λ and the associated eigenvector v, we can verify if $Av=\lambda v$. This verification is an $O(n^2)$ assertion. When all the eigenvalues/eigenvectors are required we have n x $O(n^2)$ verifications, resulting in an $O(n^3)$ checker with a high overhead. To lower it, we propose a novel scheme where a column checksum vector (CCS_A) is built, with each element being the sum of the elements from the corresponding column of A. Then $CCS_A \times v$ should be equal to $\lambda \times$ ccs_v, where ccs_v is the sum of the eigenvector elements. That is, instead of testing the initial definition $\begin{bmatrix} & & \\ & A & \\ & & \end{bmatrix} \times \begin{bmatrix} v \\ \end{bmatrix} = \lambda \begin{bmatrix} v \\ \end{bmatrix}$, we will check a slightly weaker

condition $\begin{bmatrix} & CCS_A & \end{bmatrix} \times \begin{bmatrix} v \\ \end{bmatrix} = \lambda \times ccsv$. This is an O(n) assertion, and even if

we compute it for the n eigenvectors we have an O(n^2) checker. We will call it the (λ, v)-checker.

All the (λ, v) pairs that verify the definition will also verify this checker. The probability of a wrong random (λ, v) pair satisfying the checker, is similar to the probability that a random n-vector verifies one equation in n unknowns. Let us consider, as an example, an equation in one unknown: the probability that a random double precision value verifies the equation is one over the number of double values that can be represented on 64 bits (2^{-64}); such a probability is essentially zero. When $n>1$, the solution belongs to 3^n, and the probability that a random error won't be detected is even smaller. Correlated errors, such as having two components of CCS_A with the same value and the corresponding entries of v being interchanged are very unlikely.

In this problem there is an obvious situation that can originate undetected wrong results. The first one is that, if v is an eigenvector associated with λ, then every nonzero multiple of v is also an eigenvector associated with λ. Usually an eigenvector with unit norm is calculated, but even so the solution is not unique. Then the checker won't detect a fault that produces a multiple of v. This is not strictly a failure, since a multiple of v is also an eigenvector of the original matrix, but is a failure from the point of view of the user since she/he expected a vector with unit norm.

Another special situation arises from the order in which the eigenvalues are generated. A fault can lead to the correct eigenvalues, but generate them in a different order of a fault-less execution. This cannot be considered a failure, but can lead to a false alarm of our *wrong result detector* routine. This is the routine we use to compare the results of a run without errors injected with the results of the runs were errors were injected. In order to have a deterministic result we added to the program an additional requirement about the expected solution. The results must be sorted in ascending order of the real part of the eigenvalues and conjugate pairs appear consecutively with the eigenvalue having the positive imaginary part first. To have unique eigenvectors they must be normalized to have Euclidean norm equal to 1 and the largest component real and positive.

Some of these specifications were already implemented by LAPACK routines. For each case studied we implemented the missing code after calling the LAPACK routine. We needed to convert each computed eigenvector into the one that has the largest component positive. In the general real and complex cases we also needed to sort the results as described above.

Finally, as in any numerical algorithm, we have the problem of finite precision inherent to floating point arithmetic. To apply the result-checker, we need to calculate a tolerance interval that bounds the rounding error of the performed computations. This error bound will also be used to interpret the results. Errors, whose magnitude is comparable to the rounding error that is expected for the algorithm used, are not significant errors. That is, we try to build a Fail-Bounded system [17]: *if it produces a wrong output, the error it exhibits has an upper error bound defined by the assertions used.*

In summary, we consider that the fault-detection mechanism proposed fails when it doesn't detect errors greater than the rounding error considered. The rounding errors applied in this work were calculated from the reciprocal condition numbers computed by the LAPACK routines for each case studied.

4 Experimental Evaluation

To study the fault/error coverage of the result-checker proposed we have considered real and complex double precision matrices with random entries from the range (-1,+1). The real symmetric case was implemented with the LAPACK routine DSYEVX using 200-by-200 matrices. In the case of general real and complex matrices we worked with 100-by-100 matrices to save time in the injection process. LAPACK routines DGEEVX and ZGEEVX were used to compute the eigenvalues and right eigenvectors of real and complex matrices respectively.

As stated before, we need to determine a rounding error bound for the expected results. Let $A \in \forall^{nm}$ have n distinct eigenvalues. The eigenvalue λ with associated right and left unit eigenvectors x and y, respectively, has an approximate error bound given by $k\varepsilon$, where $k(=1/|y^H x|)$ is the condition number of λ and ε the perturbation of the initial matrix. A similar result holds for eigenvectors replacing k by the eigenvector condition number [19]. For a stable algorithm, such as QR iteration, the perturbation of matrix A is given by $\varepsilon \approx cu\|A\|_2$, where c is a modest constant depending on the dimension of A and u the machine precision [22].

Since the condition number of an eigenvalue depends on the associated right and left eigenvectors, we can have very different rounding errors for the eigenvalues of a matrix. Moreover for each eigenvector we have an error bound that is affected by the distance of the associated λ from the other eigenvalues and by the condition number of the eigenvalues other than λ. That is, a matrix can have a mixture of well-conditioned and ill-conditioned eigenvalues, and close eigenvalues can have ill-conditioned associated eigenvectors. In such case we must check each (λ, v) pair with the adequate tolerance.

We worked with random matrices whose expected error bounds, for the eigenvalues and eigenvectors, have a maximum difference of two significant digits. We did the simplification of using the maximum error bound as the tolerance for the

(λ,v)-checker. The condition numbers and the machine precision were computed using LAPACK routines and constant c was considered equal to the matrix dimension, n.

In the symmetric case the error bound expressions become simplified because the left and right eigenvectors associated to an eigenvalue are equal, thus $y^H x=1$. Then in the symmetric case we can compute the tolerance at run-time. To calculate the error bounds for the general case, we need to compute also the left eigenvectors. So in that case we used a tolerance previously computed. It should be noted that the left eigenvectors could be verified exactly in the same way. The only difference is using a row checksum vector instead of the CCS of A.

The structure of each program follows the Robust Assertions technique [17] described in section 2: All the matrices were generated with a checksum. The program reads the matrix and the respective checksum, codifies the data, that is, computes the trace, the column checksum vector and, in the symmetric case, computes the norm. Then it verifies the integrity of the data and performs the main computation. At the end, the program again protects the results with a checksum, and executes the assertions following the gold code structure. If the results pass all the tests then they are outputted.

To classify the outputs we started by verifying if the results were indeed checked and if they were not corrupted. That is, we test if the magic number is the right number and we check the result checksum. After that we performed a component-wise comparison between the computed eigenvalues and eigenvectors and a reference solution obtained in a run with no injected fault. We call "eigenvalue error" to the maximum absolute difference between two corresponding eigenvalues and "eigenvector error" to the maximum absolute difference between two corresponding elements of the eigenvectors. The possible outcomes are:
- Correct output;
- No output because of a crash;
- No output because an error was detected by an assertion;
- Detected wrong output (if either the checksum or the magic number is not correct)
- Wrong output but within tolerance;
- Wrong output outside tolerance.

To classify the wrong outputs we used the maximum eigenvalue error bound for comparing the eigenvalues and used the maximum eigenvector error bound for the eigenvector entries.

Finally for each case studied is calculated an upper 99% confidence limit estimate for the fault/error non-coverage of the overall scheme implemented. We assume that the injected faults are representative faults, that is, the selection probability of each injected fault is equal to its occurrence probability. Then f/n is an unbiased estimator for the non-coverage of the mechanism (n is the number of injected faults and f the number of undetected faults). An upper $100\gamma\%$ confidence limit estimator

for the non-coverage is given by $\dfrac{(f+1)\,F_{2(f+1),2(n-f),\gamma}}{(n+f)+(f+1)\,F_{2(f+1),2(n-f),\gamma}}$ [23], where

$F_{v1,v2,\gamma}$ is the $100\gamma\%$ percentile point of the F distribution with $v1, v2$ degrees of freedom.

After describing the fault injection process we present the results for the eigenvalue calculation of symmetric matrices, and then the results obtained with the checker proposed in this work considering the symmetric case and the general cases: real and complex non-symmetric matrices.

4.1 Fault Injection

The fault-detection mechanism was evaluated with a fault injection tool, called Xception [24], which emulates hardware faults at a very low level. Xception is a software fault injection and environment monitoring that can inject transient faults in specific microprocessor functional units such as Floating-point ALU, Integer ALU, Data Bus, Address Bus, General Purpose Registers, Condition Code Register(s), Memory Management Unit and Memory. Each fault affects only one machine instruction and one functional unit at a time. It provides means to automatically define and execute fault injection experiments, to monitor the fault impact on the application and to collect statistic results. The system used is a Parsytec PowerXplorer with 4 PowerPCs 601, each with 8 Mbytes of memory, running Parix, a parallel OS similar to UNIX, with a Sun SparcStation as the host.

The faults injected were transient bit flips of one bit, randomly chosen, applied to a randomly selected functional unit, time triggered (i.e. randomly distributed during the program execution time).

4.2 Symmetric Case

4.2.1 Eigenvalues. We started by evaluating the assertions proposed in [6] and described in section 3.1, for the eigenvalues of a real symmetric matrix: trace assertion and norm preservation assertion. In order to identify all the possible sources of undetected wrong results we added two more tests. Checking the eigenvalues order and verifying if some result is a NaN. (Not a Numbers (NaNs) are special codes used in the IEEE floating point format, that when compared with anything, including itself, always returns false). Besides, the LAPACK routine can itself detect some errors. For instance, it can detect if an argument received an illegal value or verify that the algorithm failed to converge.

The results of the fault injection experiments are shown in table 1. As can be seen only 0.2% of the outcomes are wrong results out of the tolerance. Moreover most of those errors (33) are smaller than *tolerance* $\times$ 10^3 (the tolerance value was approx. 10^{-12}). Then we can conclude that they are not arbitrary errors but probably weren't detected because of an effect of cancellation when calculating the sum of the eigenvalues or the sum of the eigenvector elements. The other 6 faults were injected in the routine that performs the matrix-vector product (dsymv). The injection of faults directly on that routine lead to some clearly wrong results (the cases studied have a maximum error of 0.2 and we are working with a set of eigenvalues whose minimum difference between two elements is app. 0.01). But those 6 cases represent only 0.03% of the injected faults.

Table 1. Results of fault injection for the eigenvalue computation of a symmetric matrix

Symmetric matrix: eigenvalues computation	N. of faults	% of total
Correct output	10839	57.1%
No Output (crash)	4188	22.1%
No output (error detected)	3435	18.1%
Detected wrong output	0	0.0%
Wrong output within tolerance	466	2.5%
Wrong output out of tolerance	39	0.2%
TOTAL	18967	100.0%

The distribution of detected faults by assertion type is shown in table 2. Besides the assertions described above, we have also the faults detected when the program checks the input data integrity and when it checks the computed tolerance. In the symmetric case the eigenvalue tolerance is computed twice before the data be codified, and both values are compared before executing the assertions. The order by which the assertions were executed is the same as presented in the table.

Table 2. Distribution of detected faults by assertion for the eigenvalue computation of a symmetric matrix

Faults detected by assertion:	N. of faults	% of total
Checking data integrity	303	1.6%
Lapack error flag	82	0.4%
Comparing eigenvalue tolerance	572	3.0%
$trace(A) = \lambda_1 + \cdots + \lambda_n$	962	5.1%
$\|A\|_2 = \sqrt{\lambda_1^2 + \cdots + \lambda_n^2}$	1516	8.0%
$\lambda_1 \geq \lambda_2 \cdots \geq \lambda_n$	0	0.0%
NaNs	0	0.0%
TOTAL	3435	18.1%

As can be seen only 5.1% of the errors were detected by the trace assertion. Without the norm-preservation assertion 8% of the outcomes will be undetected wrong results. Thus if we are not able to use the norm assertion (as can be the case with general matrices) the trace is a weak checker for the eigenvalues.

Finally table 3 shows the execution times for some matrix dimensions. As expected the overheads are very small. We have $O(n^2)$ checkers for $O(n^3)$ computations.

In summary the scheme implemented has a non-coverage of 0.2%, with an upper 99% confidence limit estimate of 0.30%. That is a fault detection mechanism for the symmetric eigenvalue computation with very low execution overhead that, for the data set studied, has a fault/error coverage greater than 99.7% with a confidence level of 99%.

Table 3. Execution time of computing the eigenvalues of a symmetric matrix

Execution time of eigenvalues of symmetric:	Total time (second)	Input / Output		Calculations		Checking	
		sec.	% of total	sec.	% total	sec.	% of total
100-by-100 matrices	1.39	0.55	39.6%	0.79	56.8%	0.05	3.6%
200-by-200 matrices	5.71	1.74	30.4%	3.88	67.9%	0.09	1.7%
300-by-300 matrices	14.30	3.68	25.7%	10.46	73.2%	0.16	1.1%

4.2.2. Eigenvalues and eigenvectors. Next we have computed the eigenvalues and also the eigenvectors. If the eigenvalues pass the assertions described above, each pair eigenvalue/eigenvector will be verified using the (λ, v)-checker proposed. Two more assertions were added: checking the norm of each eigenvector, it must be a unit vector, and checking if the largest component of the eigenvector is positive. The outcomes of the fault injection experiments are shown in table 4.

Table 4. Results of fault injection for the eigenproblem using a symmetric matrix

Symmetric matrix: eigenvalues and eigenvectors	Number of faults	% of total
Correct output	9226	49.64%
No Output (crash)	4298	23.13%
No output (error detected)	4338	23.34%
Detected wrong output	6	0.03%
Wrong output within tolerance	695	3.74%
Wrong output out of tolerance	22	0.12%
TOTAL	18585	100.0%

As can be seen only 0.12% of the faults (22) lead to wrong results out of the tolerance. From those, 19 are eigenvalue and eigenvector errors smaller than *tolerance* $\times 10^{3}$. The other 3 have an eigenvalue error smaller than *tolerance* $\times 10^{3}$ but the eigenvector error is greater than that. It seems that the clearly wrong eigenvalues are detected with the additional (λ, v)-checker.

Table 5 shows the distribution of detected faults by assertion type. As can be seen the errors are mainly detected by the (λ, v) assertion. Indeed we have done some preliminary experiments without the eigenvalue assertions and we have got an equivalent coverage.

We decided to keep the norm and trace assertions because there is a trivial situation not detected by the (λ, v)-checker that can be easily detected by them. If a wrong eigenvalue becomes equal to one other correctly computed λ, and the eigenvector is computed accordingly, both pairs pass the checker. But probably the trace or the norm assertion will detect the error.

Table 5. Distribution of detected faults by assertion for the eigenvalue and eigenvector computation of a symmetric matrix

Faults detected by assertion:	N. of faults	% of total
Checking data integrity	138	0.74%
Lapack error flag	0	0.0%
Comparing eigenvalue tolerance	300	1.61%
$trace(A) = \lambda_1 + \cdots + \lambda_n$	432	2.33%
$\|A\|_2 = \sqrt{\lambda_1^2 + \cdots + \lambda_n^2}$	634	3.41%
$\lambda_1 \geq \lambda_2 \cdots \geq \lambda_n$	1	0.01%
(λ, v)-checker	2779	14.95%
$\|v\|_2 = 1$	22	0.12%
Largest component of v positive	0	0.0%
NaNs	32	0.17%
TOTAL	4338	23.34%

Finally table 6 shows the execution times for the same matrix dimensions as in the previous case.

Table 6. Execution time of computing the eigenvalues and eigenvectors of a symmetric matrix

Execution time for symmetric matrices:	Total time (second)	Input / Output		Calculations		Checking	
		sec.	% of total	sec.	% of total	sec.	% of total
100-by-100	2.61	0.77	29.5%	1.73	66.3%	0.11	4.2%
200-by-200	13.08	2.51	19.2%	10.23	78.2%	0.34	2.6%
300-by-300	36.91	5.47	14.8%	30.73	83.3%	0.71	1.9%

In conclusion the overall scheme implemented has a non-coverage of 0.12%, with an upper 99% confidence limit estimate of 0.19%. That is a fault detection mechanism for the symmetric eigenproblem computation with a execution overhead smaller than 5% that, for the data set studied, has a fault/error coverage greater than 99.81% with a confidence level of 99%.

4.3 General Real Case

When we move to the general real case the eigenvalues can be real or complex, in which case they appear in conjugate pairs. Associated with a complex conjugate pair there is a pair of conjugate eigenvectors. To classify the outputs we used the maximum absolute difference between two elements, which is the maximum difference obtained comparing the real parts and the imaginary parts.

The norm-preservation assertion is removed and the order of the results is now tested at the end.

The outcomes of the experiments for the general real case are shown in table 7. Table 8 shows the distribution of detected faults by assertion type.

Table 7. Results of fault injection for the eigenproblem using a general real matrix

General real matrix: eigenvalues and eigenvectors	Number of faults	% of total
Correct output	4133	44.27%
No Output (crash)	2233	23.92%
No output (error detected)	2662	28.51%
Detected wrong output	5	0.05%
Wrong output within tolerance	294	3.15%
Wrong output out of tolerance	9	0.10%
TOTAL	9336	100.0%

Table 8. Distribution of detected faults by assertion for the eigenvalue and eigenvector computation of a general real matrix

Faults detected by assertion:	N. of faults	% of total
Checking data integrity	94	1.01%
Lapack error flag	45	0.48%
$trace(A) = \lambda_1 + \cdots + \lambda_n$	610	6.53%
(λ, v)-checker	1874	20.07%
$\|v\|_2 = 1$	21	0.23%
Checking eigenvalues order and Largest component of v real and positive	1	0.01%
NaNs	17	0.18%
TOTAL	2662	28.51%

As can be seen from the table the wrong results out of the tolerance are only 0.1% of the injected faults. All these 9 faults lead to eigenvalue and eigenvector errors smaller than $tolerance \times 10^3$.

The scheme has a non-coverage of 0.1% with an upper 99% confidence limit estimate of 0.20%. Thus, for the data set studied, we have a fault detection mechanism for the general real eigenproblem with a fault/error coverage greater than 99.80% (at a confidence level of 99%).

The execution overhead is lower than in the symmetric case because the complexity of the calculations increases while the checkers are almost the same. The execution times are shown in table 9.

Table 9. Execution time of computing the eigenvalues and eigenvectors of a real matrix

Execution time for real matrices:	Total time (second)	Input / Output		Calculations		Checking	
		sec.	% of total	sec.	% of total	sec.	% of total
100-by-100	4.18	0.79	18.9%	3.31	79.2%	0.08	1.9%
200-by-200	32.07	2.41	7.5%	29.40	91.7%	0.26	0.8%
300-by-300	105.08	5.19	4.9%	99.34	94.5%	0.55	0.5%

4.4 General Complex Case

We have also studied the complex case. The assertions were the same as in the previous case and the results are not very different. All the undetected wrong outputs out of tolerance correspond to eigenvalue and eigenvector errors smaller than *tolerance* $\times 10^3$.

Table 10 shows the outcomes of the experiments, table 11 presents the distribution of detected faults by assertion type and table 12 shows the execution times.

One curiosity is that the LAPACK routine doesn't detect any fault in this case. With real matrices it has detected 0.5% of the errors.

Table 10. Results of fault injection for the eigenproblem using a general complex matrix

General complex matrix: eigenvalues and eigenvectors	Number of faults	% of total
Correct output	3410	42.07%
No Output (crash)	1770	21.84%
No output (error detected)	2550	31.46%
Detected wrong output	5	0.06%
Wrong output within tolerance	362	4.46%
Wrong output out of tolerance	9	0.11%
TOTAL	8106	100.0%

Finally, for the complex cases we have an upper 99% confidence limit estimate for the non-coverage of 0.23%. The proposed fault-detection scheme has a fault/error coverage greater than 99.77% with a confidence level of 99% for the complex data set studied. Comparing with previous cases again we can see that the overhead decreases when the calculation complexity grows.

Table 11. Distribution of detected faults by assertion for eigenvalue and eigenvector
computation of a general complex matrix

Faults detected by assertion	N. of faults	% of total
Checking data integrity	41	0.51%
Lapack error flag	0	0.0%
$trace(A) = \lambda_1 + \cdots + \lambda_n$	476	5.87%
(λ, v)-checker	1960	24.18%
$\|v\|_2 = 1$	19	0.23%
Checking eigenvalues order and Largest component of v real and positive	0	0.0%
NaNs	54	0.67%
TOTAL	2550	31.46%

Table 12. Execution time of computing the eigenvalues and eigenvectors of a complex matrix

Execution time for complex matrices:	Total time (second)	Input / Output		Calculations		Checking	
		sec.	%of total	sec.	% of total	sec.	% of total
100-by-100	9.92	1.45	14.6%	8.36	84.3%	0.11	1.1%
200-by-200	76.99	4.81	6.2%	71.81	93.3%	0.37	0.5%
300-by-300	244.92	10.82	4.4%	233.18	95.2%	0.92	0.4%

5. Conclusions

In this work we proposed a new fault-detection mechanism based on result checking for the computation of eigenvalues and eigenvectors. In the described implementation we checked the results computed by well-known LAPACK routines for the eigenproblem, using a set of low-overhead assertions. This checker is weaker than a direct application of the definition, which would have a very high overhead, but even so, when subjected to fault injection, it exhibits an error detection coverage greater than 99.7% with a confidence level of 99%. For medium and large matrices the execution overhead of the mechanism is lower than 2%. The data set used includes random symmetric matrices and general real and complex matrices. The new RC was implemented using the ideas of Robust Assertions, following a Fail-Bounded failure model.

Devising faster and numerically stable algorithms for the eigenproblem is an open area of research. Thus we think that RC is a very appropriate scheme for checking it. Fault detection mechanisms based on result checking have the advantage of being applicable to any algorithm without change.

We left for future work the study of matrices with very different rounding error bounds for their eigenvalues/eigenvectors. If a matrix has some ill-conditioned eigenvalues we will need a rounding error analysis for each eigenvalue/eigenvector pair but the checker remains the same.

References

1. Huang, K.-H. and J. A. Abraham, Algorithm-Based Fault Tolerance for Matrix Operations, in IEEE Transactions on Computers, 1984, p. 518-528.
2. Banerjee, P., et al., Algorithm-Based Fault Tolerance on a Hypercube Multiprocessor, in IEEE Transactions on Computers, 1990, p. 1132-1144.
3. Chowdhury, A. R. and P. Banerjee. Algorithm-Based Fault Location and Recovery for Matrix Computations in 24th International Symposium on Fault-Tolerant Computing, 1994. Austin, Texas, p. 38-47.
4. Rela, M. Z., H. Madeira, and J. G. Silva. Experimental Evaluation of the Fail-Silent Behavior of Programs with Consistency Checks in 26th International Symposium on Fault-Tolerant Computing, 1996. Sendai-Japan, p. 394-403.
5. Silva, J. G., J. Carreira, H. Madeira, D. Costa, and F. Moreira. *Experimental Assessment of Parallel Systems* in *26th International Symposium on Fault-Tolerant Computing*, 1996. Sendai, Japan, p. 415-424.
6. Chen, C.-Y. and A. Abraham. Fault-tolerant Systems for the computation of Eigenvalues and Singular Values in Proc. SPIE, Advanced Algorithms Architectures Signal Processing, 1986, p. 228-237.
7. Balasubramanian, V. and P. Banerjee, Algorithm-Based Error Detection for Signal Processing Applications on a Hypercube Multiprocessor, in Real-Time Systems Symposium, 1989, p. 134-143.
8. Blum, M. and S. Kannan, *Designing Programs that Check Their Work.* Journal of the Association for Computing Machinery, 1995. 42(1): p. 269-291.
9. Prata, P. and J. G. Silva. Algorithm Based Fault Tolerance Versus Result-Checking for Matrix Computations. To appear in 29th International Symposium on Fault-Tolerant Computing, 1999. Madison, Wisconsin, USA.
10. Velde, E. F. V. d., *Concurrent Scientific Computing.* 1994: Springer-Verlag.
11. Demmel, J. W., *Applied Numerical Linear Algebra.* 1997: SIAM.
12. Anderson, E., Z. Bai, C. Bischof, and e. al., *LAPACK Users' Guide.* 1995: SIAM.
13. Blum, M. and H. Wasserman, Reflections on The Pentium Division Bug, in IEEE Transactions on Computers, 1996, p. 385-393.
14. Rubinfeld, R., *A Mathematical Theory of Self-Checking, Self-Testing and Self-Correcting Programs*, PhD Thesis. University of California at Berkeley, 1990. 103 pages.
15. Wasserman, H. and M. Blum, *Software Reliability via Run-Time Result-Checking.* Journal of the ACM, 1997. 44(6): p. 826-849.
16. Rubinfeld, R. Robust functional equations with applications to self-testing / correcting in 35th IEEE Conference on Foundations of Computer Science, 1994, p. 288-299.
17. Silva, J. G., P. Prata, M. Rela, and H. Madeira. Practical Issues in the Use of ABFT and a New Failure Model in 28th International Symposium on Fault-Tolerant Computing, 1998. Munich, Germany, p. 26-35.
18. Golub, G. H. and C. F. V. Loan, *Matrix Computations.* Second edition ed. 1989: Johns Hopkins University Press.
19. Watkins, D. S., *Fundamentals of Matrix Computations.* 1991: John Wiley & Sons.
20. Reddy, A. L. N. and P. Banerjee, Algorithm-Based Fault Detection for Signal Processing Applications, in IEEE Transactions on Computers, 1990, p. 1304-1308.

21. Jou, J.-Y. and J. A. Abraham, Fault-Tolerant Matrix Arithmetic and Signal Processing on Highly Concurrent Computing Structures, in Proceedings of the IEEE, 1986, p. 732-741.
22. Higham, N., Accuracy and Stability of Numerical Algorithms. 1996: SIAM.
23. Powell, D., M. Cukier, and J. Arlat. On Stratified Sampling for High Coverage Estimations in 2nd European Dependable Computing Conference, 1996. Taormina, Italy, p. 37-54.
24. Carreira, J., H. Madeira, and J. G. Silva, Xception: A Technique for the Experimental Evaluation of Dependability in Modern Computers, in IEEE Transactions on Software Engineering, 1998, p. 125-135.

Concurrent Detection of Processor Control Errors by Hybrid Signature Monitoring

Yung-Yuan Chen

Department of Computer Science, Chung-Hua University
Hsin-Chu, Taiwan, R.O.C.
chenyy@chu.edu.tw

Abstract. In this study, we present a new concurrent error-detection scheme by hybrid signature to the on-line detection of control flow errors caused by transient and intermittent faults. The proposed hybrid signature monitoring technique combines the vertical signature scheme with the horizontal signature scheme. We first develop a new vertical signature scheme. The length of vertical signature is adjustable. The attribute of adjustable length can be employed to reduce the length of vertical signature, but at meantime it also decreases the coverage. The rest of signature word can be utilized for the horizontal signature and recording the block length. The horizontal signature can offset the coverage degradation due to the reduction of vertical signature length, and decrease the latency significantly. The simulation is conducted to justify the effectiveness of the proposed technique and compared with the previous schemes.

The main contribution of this research is to integrate the vertical signature, horizontal signature and watchdog timer techniques into a single signature word, and without the using of the memory system equipped with the SEC-DED code. Therefore, with no increase or even lower of memory space overhead and watchdog processor complexity, our scheme has higher error-detection coverage and much shorter error-detection latency compared with the previous representative techniques.

1 Introduction

Basically, a fault-tolerant computer system consists of the following three steps: error detection, rollback recovery and reconfiguration. Before performing the rollback recovery or reconfiguration process, we need to detect the faults/errors. Therefore, error detection plays an important role in fault-tolerant computer systems. Concurrent error detection provides especially the ability of detection the errors caused by transient and intermittent faults. The concurrent error-detection by watchdog processor can be used to monitor the behavior of program execution, such as the attributes of memory access, control flow, control signal and the execution results. The experimental results of Schmid [1] showed that the 80% faults would result in the control flow errors, and Gunneflo [2] also indicated that the control flow error detection is an effective approach to find out the existence of faults at system level. Therefore, watchdog processor is a sound approach for concurrent error detection at system level [3,4,5] from the consideration of hardware complexity. The experimental studies of a 32-bit RISC with an on-chip watchdog processor were performed by Ohlsson et. al [6,7]. K. Wilken and T. Kong [8] have extended the existing signature monitoring approach to detect software and hardware data-access faults. I. Majzik et.

al [9] have demonstrated a low-cost control flow checking scheme, which is suitable for a multitasking, multiprocessor environment.

The implementation of watchdog processor is generally by the scheme of signature monitoring and it is mainly used to detect two types of program errors known as bit errors and sequencing errors [10]. The effectiveness of signature monitoring can be measured by: (1) error-detection coverage, (2) error-detection latency, (3) memory space overhead, (4) watchdog processor complexity and (5) main processor performance loss. Error-detection coverage, henceforth referred to as coverage, is the ratio of the number of errors detectable to the total number of errors possible. Error-detection latency is the average time taken to detect an error after it has occurred. This is commonly measured in terms of the number of instructions. In order to lower the latency, we need to increase the number of signatures and the frequency of signature checking and it will increase the overhead of signature memory space and lower the run-time performance.

The Embedded Signature Monitoring (ESM) is the scheme of embedding the signatures into the instruction stream [3,11,12]. The ESM approach requires the use of tag bits for instructions to distinguish the signatures from regular instructions. The use of tag bits has several drawbacks: First of all, it increases the memory space overhead. Secondly, a couple of errors may not be detected or cause the longer latency, such as the program counter stuck-at faults, faults resulting in the false loop and no reference signature inside the false loop, tag bit errors and branching to data segment. The tag bits can be eliminated by branch address hashing [13] or by using software delimiters and a monitor [11]. This may, however, affect the run-time performance or increase the hardware complexity.

Most of the previous signature monitoring technologies is devoted to the vertical signature scheme only. The main drawback of vertical signature scheme is its lengthy error-detection latency. The horizontal signature concept combined with the vertical signature scheme is first presented in the Wilken and Shen paper [14] in order to shorten the error-detection latency. The horizontal signature method proposed in [14] needs to employ the memory system equipped with a parity code or single-error-correcting, double-error-detecting (SEC-DED) code. Consequently, the memory space overhead for Wilken and Shen approach should include both the vertical signature and the horizontal signature. Another conspicuous problem for this horizontal signature scheme is the information overload on the parity bit as indicated by Upadhyaya and Ramamurthy [15]. In [15], the authors mentioned that to extract the useful information from the parity bit, hashing and rehashing is required, which results in increased latency and run-time performance degradation.

To solve the above problems, with no increase or even lower of the signature memory space overhead and watchdog processor complexity, we propose a new hybrid signature monitoring scheme which combines the vertical signature, the horizontal signature and watchdog timer techniques into a single signature word.

The paper is organized as follows. In Section 2, the vertical signature scheme and its property analysis are presented. In Section 3, hybrid signature monitoring techniques and algorithms are proposed. In Section 4, the simulation is conducted to validate the effectiveness of the proposed scheme and the comparison results are given. The implementation consideration is addressed in Section 5. Conclusions appear in Section 6.

2 The New Vertical Signature Scheme

The length of the proposed vertical signature is adjustable, and it is unlike the most commonly used modulo-2 sum signature generating function, which requires the whole instruction word for storing the vertical signature of a block. The attribute of adjustable length can be employed to reduce the length of vertical signature, but at meantime it also decreases the coverage. The rest of signature word can be utilized for the horizontal signature and recording the block length. The horizontal signature can offset the coverage degradation due to the reduction of vertical signature length, and decrease the latency significantly.

2.1 Vertical Signature Scheme

The following notations are developed:

BL : Number of instructions in a block;

W : Number of bits for an instruction word;

I_i : The ith instruction in block, $1 \le i \le BL$;

$I_{i,j}$: The jth bit (from left to right) of ith instruction in block, $1 \le j \le W$.

Definition 1: Let state set $S = (s_1, s_2, s_3, s_4) = \left(\binom{0}{0}, \binom{0}{1}, \binom{1}{0}, \binom{1}{1} \right)$. We define the vertical signature generating function $V(I_i, I_{i+1})$ as $V(I_i, I_{i+1}) =$

$$V \begin{pmatrix} I_{i,1} & I_{i,2} & \cdot & I_{i,j} & \cdot & I_{i,w} \\ I_{i+1,1} & I_{i+1,2} & \cdot & I_{i+1,j} & \cdot & I_{i+1,w} \end{pmatrix} = \left(V_{i+1,1}, \cdots, V_{i+1,j}, \cdots V_{i+1,w} \right),$$

where $\left(V_{i+1,1}, \cdots, V_{i+1,j}, \cdots V_{i+1,w} \right)$ is called a state vector, and $V_{i+1,j} \in S$, $1 \le i \le BL-1, 1 \le j \le W$. □

In the two-dimensional coordinate (X, Y), we assume that the current coordinate is in (x, y). If next state $V_{i+1,j}$ is

$s_1 : \binom{0}{0}$, then coordinate moves to (x+1, y); $s_2 : \binom{0}{1}$, then coordinate moves to (x-1, y);

$s_3 : \binom{1}{0}$, then coordinate moves to (x , y-1); $s_4 : \binom{1}{1}$, then coordinate moves to (x, y+1).

The vertical signature scheme is presented as follows:

Algorithm 1:

Let (x_{vs}, y_{vs}) be the block vertical signature; (x_{vs}, y_{vs}) ← (0, 0);

Step 1: Initial signature generation

$$V(I_1 , I_1) = V \begin{pmatrix} I_{1,1} \cdots I_{1,j} \cdots I_{1,w} \\ I_{1,1} \cdots I_{1,j} \cdots I_{1,w} \end{pmatrix} = \left(V_{1,1}, \cdots, V_{1,j}, \cdots V_{1,w} \right)$$

for ($j = 1, W$)

switch ($V_{1,j}$)

{case s_1: (x_{vs}, y_{vs}) ← (x_{vs}+1, y_{vs}); case s_2: (x_{vs}, y_{vs}) ← (x_{vs}-1, y_{vs});

case s_3: (x_{vs}, y_{vs}) ← (x_{vs}, y_{vs}-1); case s_4: (x_{vs}, y_{vs}) ← (x_{vs}, y_{vs}+1);}

Step 2: for ($i = 1, BL - 1$)

    for ($j = 1, W$)

    switch ($V_{i+1,j}$)

    {case s_1: (x_{vs}, y_{vs}) $\leftarrow$ ($x_{vs}+1, y_{vs}$); case s_2: (x_{vs}, y_{vs}) $\leftarrow$ ($x_{vs}-1, y_{vs}$);

    case s_3: (x_{vs}, y_{vs}) $\leftarrow$ ($x_{vs}, y_{vs}-1$); case s_4: (x_{vs}, y_{vs}) $\leftarrow$ ($x_{vs}, y_{vs}+1$);}

Step 3: End $\Box$

2.1.1 Effect of state assignment on fault coverage

In Algorithm 1, we assign state set $S = (s_1, s_2, s_3, s_4)$ as ($\rightarrow, \leftarrow, \downarrow, \uparrow$). This is we call the state assignment in two-dimensional coordinate. As we know, two-bit has four combinations or states $(s_1, s_2, s_3, s_4) = \left(\binom{0}{0}, \binom{0}{1}, \binom{1}{0}, \binom{1}{1} \right)$. Each state can be assigned by any one of the set element ($\rightarrow, \leftarrow, \downarrow, \uparrow$) under the constraint of each set element occurring only once in the state assignment. The state assignment has an effect on fault coverage as discussed below. Two bits have four states $\left(\binom{0}{0}, \binom{0}{1}, \binom{1}{0}, \binom{1}{1} \right)$, and each state can be assigned one element from the set of ($\rightarrow, \leftarrow, \downarrow, \uparrow$). Therefore, twenty-four possible state assignments can be derived, and how to choose one assignment from these possible state assignments is discussed below. The main concern in selection of state assignment is the issue of fault coverage. We can classify these twenty-four state assignments into two groups A and B:

A. $\binom{0}{1}$ and $\binom{1}{0}$ assignments are at the same axis, but in opposite direction. There are eight state assignments that belong to this class. We observed that when a single column in block has n number of $\binom{0}{1}$ states, where $n \geq 1$, then this column must also have at least $(n-1)$ number of $\binom{1}{0}$ states, and at most $(n+1)$ number of $\binom{1}{0}$ states. But $\binom{0}{1}$ and $\binom{1}{0}$ assignments are at the same axis, and in opposite direction, the movement in two-dimensional coordinate will be offset each other. Consequently, this column will be left either one $\binom{0}{1}$ state or one $\binom{1}{0}$ state or $\binom{0}{1}, \binom{1}{0}$ offset each other completely. For instance, if $\binom{0}{1}$ and $\binom{1}{0}$ assignment is $\left(\binom{0}{1}, \binom{1}{0} \right) = (\rightarrow, \leftarrow)$, then the signature of x-axis for this single column is confined within (-1,1). Due to this limitation, we can not guarantee to obtain a good balance of signature distribution in two-dimensional coordinate. The imbalance of signature distribution will raise the probability of fault-masking errors. Therefore, the probability of error escaping from detection for vertical signature checking increases, and decreases the fault coverage.

B. $\binom{0}{1}$ and $\binom{1}{0}$ assignments are not at the same axis. The rest of sixteen assignments are for this group. For each state assignment, we were based on the simulation to investigate the distribution of block signature. Several block length BL and instruction width W was selected, and all possible program code patterns for each selected BL and W were generated. For each program code pattern, we evaluated its corresponding signature coordinate, so we can obtain the signature distribution for each state assignment. The number of bits of x-axis and y-axis used to represent the signature coordinate restricts the signature space. We observed that the signature distribution is not uniform. If the number of various code patterns which are mapped to the same signature increase then the probability of error escaping from detection for these patterns increases too. From the simulation results, we found that the signature distributions of these sixteen assignments are quite similar and are more balance than class A is. Therefore, class B has lower probability of error escaping from detection than class A. There is no obvious effect on fault coverage among state assignments of this class. From the above discussion, we decide to use state assignment from this group to gain a better fault coverage.

2.1.2 Signature space analysis

The numbers of bits of x-axis and y-axis represent the signature space. The size of signature space will affect the fault coverage. The larger signature space can reduce the probability of error escaping from detection but needs more memory space to store the vertical signatures.

Given block length BL and instruction width W, an upper bound of signature space can be derived such that the fault coverage reaches the maximum. Therefore, within the upper bound of signature space, the fault coverage increases as the signature space increases. The block signature generated can not fall over the area beyond the space bound, so the signature space exceeding the upper bound, it is no use to raise the fault coverage any more. The derivation of the upper bound of signature space is depicted below:

A. A single column analysis: The range of the signature value for x-axis and y-axis is calculated as follows.

1. The maximal value of x is BL and it occurs when all values of the column are zero.
2. The minimal value of x occurs when zero and one alternate with each other in the column, because this situation produces the largest number of $\binom{0}{1}=(\leftarrow)$ state. When the first bit of column is zero, based on Algorithm 1, Step 1, this zero bit will generate a state of $\binom{0}{0}=(\rightarrow)$. From above discussion, the minimal value of x is $-\lfloor \frac{BL-1}{2} \rfloor$.
3. The maximal value of y is BL when the values of the column are all one.
4. The minimal value of y is $-\lfloor \frac{BL-1}{2} \rfloor$. The analysis is similar to the minimal value of x.

Based on above explanation, the range of x, y is $-\lfloor \frac{BL-1}{2} \rfloor \leq x, y \leq BL$. It should be noted that the positive side of x, y and negative side of x, y are not length balance. This phenomenon will raise the implementation complexity. From the aspects of representation of x, y values, efficient usage of signature space and easy hardware implementation, only the positive signature space is considered here. Therefore, we should add value of $\left\lfloor \frac{BL-1}{2} \right\rfloor$ to both sides of x, y inequality equation, and it becomes of $0 \leq x, y \leq BL + \left\lfloor \frac{BL-1}{2} \right\rfloor$. So the number of bits needed to express the x and y signature is $\left\lceil \log_2 \left(BL + \left\lfloor \frac{BL-1}{2} \right\rfloor + 1 \right) \right\rceil$.

B. General case analysis: For various block length BL and instruction width W, the upper bound of number of x bits and y bits can be derived from the result of single column block analysis. The columns in a block are independent each other, so it is clear to see that the range of x and y is $-W \times \left\lfloor \frac{BL-1}{2} \right\rfloor \leq x, y \leq W \times BL$. For positive signature space consideration, both sides of x, y inequality equation are added the term of $W \times \left\lfloor \frac{BL-1}{2} \right\rfloor$. Consequently, the number of bits needed to represent the x and y signature is $\left\lceil \log_2 \left[W \times \left(BL + \left\lfloor \frac{BL-1}{2} \right\rfloor \right) + 1 \right] \right\rceil$.

In practical applications, if the numbers of x bits and y bits are less than the upper bound of x and y, when the signature exceeds the signature space currently used, the overflow values of signature are modulated by the function of modulo arithmetic. So, the probability of errors escaping from detection for vertical signature decreases when the signature moves away from the central coordinate $(0,0)$. Reduction of signature space can save the memory space, but it also lowers the fault coverage.

2.2 Property Analysis

Due to space limitation, we omit the proofs of the following theorems.

Theorem 1: The signature distribution of the proposed vertical scheme is not uniform.

Theorem 2: All unidirectional errors can be detected by our vertical signature technique.

Theorem 3: All the odd number of errors can be detected completely by our vertical mechanism.

Theorem 4: When width of instruction word is even, the x coordinate plus the y coordinate of any signature can not be odd.

Theorem 4 means that the values of x and y are either all even or all odd. This feature can be used to save one bit space in either x or y signature field.

3 Hybrid Signature Scheme

The hybrid signature monitoring technique combines the vertical signature scheme with the horizontal signature scheme. The bit length of our vertical signature is adjustable as presented in last section, and therefore, we can combine the vertical signature, the horizontal signature and watchdog timer technique into a single signature word. Our horizontal signature does not need the parity code or SEC/DED memory mechanism and no extra memory space overhead compared with the CSM scheme [14]. We now present the hybrid signature scheme as follows.

3.1 Signature Word Structure

A signature word is partitioned into three fields: Block Length, Horizontal Signature and Vertical Signature as shown in Fig. 1. Let BL_B, HS_B and VS_B be the numbers of bits for Block Length field, Horizontal Signature and Vertical Signature fields, respectively. So, $BL_B + HS_B + VS_B = W$. Every block is associated with a signature word, which is added to the beginning of the block.

Block Length (BL_B)	Horizontal Signature (HS_B)	Vertical Signature (VS_B)

Fig. 1. Signature word structure

Block Length field stores the value of, the number of instructions in the block. Its function is similar to the watchdog timer. Block length subtracts one when each instruction is executed. When block length reaches to zero, it indicates that the end of block is encountered, and the checking of vertical signature is performed. Thus, the use of block length field in signature word allows us to remove the tag bits from the instruction words, and saves a lot of memory space and the memory system and data bus do not require to be modified.

Our signature scheme is especially suitable for the instruction width greater than or equal to thirty-two bits, which is the current and future trend of CPU processors. The selection of the values of BL_B, HS_B and VS_B has the effect on coverage, latency and signature memory space overhead. The choice of values depends on the design specification and application requirements. How to decide the BL_B, HS_B and VS_B to obtain the better results under some constraints is difficult to be analyzed theoretically, but by using the simulation approach. The distribution of block length for thirty-two-bit wide instruction word is given in [16]. From the data of [16] described, we choose $BL_B = \log_2 W$ for the reasons explained below. The choice of BL_B is mainly based on the compromise among the memory space overhead, coverage and latency.

Given $W = 32$, if we select $BL_B = \log_2 W - 1$, the maximal block length BL_B is sixteen and the probability of block length less than or equal to sixteen instructions is around 0.7 based on the distribution data of block length given in [16]. If we choose $BL_B = \log_2 W$, the block length field of a signature word can handle the maximal length of thirty-two instructions for a block, and the probability of block length less than or equal to thirty-two instructions is around 0.85. If $BL_B = \log_2 W + 1$ is selected, the probability of block length less than or equal to sixty-four is around 0.98. It should be noted that when the number of instructions of a branch-free block is greater than 2^{BL_B}, we have to partition this block to several smaller blocks. This effect will increase the memory space overhead. The increasing rate of memory space overhead depends on the value of BL_B. For $BL_B = \log_2 W - 1$, the rate is about 30% more compared with no restriction of block length approaches. The raised rate of $BL_B = \log_2 W$ is about 15% more, and $BL_B = \log_2 W + 1$ is about 2% more. Among these three choices, $BL_B = \log_2 W - 1$ has the highest coverage and the lowest latency, and $BL_B = \log_2 W + 1$ has the lowest coverage and the highest latency. Based on above discussion, we choose $BL_B = \log_2 W$ as the compromise between space, coverage and latency to demonstrate our approach.

The technique of horizontal signature for each instruction word in a block is depicted next. The concept of parity is used to generate the horizontal signature and a simple parity scheme is adopted here to lower the hardware complexity. If the horizontal signature is derived only from the information of current instruction word, it will suffer from the lower error-detection coverage and higher latency because the effect of errors can not be accumulated. If an instruction error occurs in a block and the horizontal signature scheme fails to detect this instruction error, then it is clear to see that this instruction error has no chance to be detected again until the vertical signature checking. To overcome this drawback, the intermediate vertical signature is joined with the current instruction word to compute the horizontal signature. The horizontal signature of each instruction word is derived basically from the information of current instruction word and the portion of intermediate vertical signature obtained from the beginning of block through current instruction word. The merit of this approach is to improve the coverage and latency significantly because the errors still have extremely high opportunity to be detected between the erroneous instruction and end of block.

We now continue to consider how to utilize the information of immediate vertical signature to raise the coverage and lower the latency. Obviously, an instruction error has much higher opportunity to affect the portion of lower bits of intermediate vertical signature. In other words, the bit difference of correct and incorrect intermediate vertical signatures is mainly located at lower bit portion. From the analysis of simulation, the lower three bits from least significant bit are adopted in the generation of horizontal signature for each instruction word. This mechanism enhances the coverage and lowers the latency effectively and increases the hardware cost slightly.

We know that the length of block is restricted within 2^{BL_B}. To simplify the hardware design and effectively utilize the power of horizontal signature, we choose $HS_B = 2^{BL_B - 1}$ and the following space assignment of horizontal signature for each instruction word is adopted. This assignment is based on the value of block length.

$$BL \le 2^{BL_B - 4} \Rightarrow \quad 8 \text{ bit/per instruction}$$

$$2^{BL_B - 4} < BL \le 2^{BL_B - 3} \Rightarrow \quad 4 \text{ bit/per instruction}$$

$$2^{BL_B - 3} < BL \le 2^{BL_B - 2} \Rightarrow \quad 2 \text{ bit/per instruction}$$

$$2^{BL_B - 2} < BL \le 2^{BL_B - 1} \Rightarrow \quad 1 \text{ bit/per instruction}$$

$$2^{BL_B - 1} < BL \le 2^{BL_B} \Rightarrow \quad \text{for } I_i, \ 1 \le i \le 2^{BL_B - 1}, \ 1 \text{ bit/per instruction}$$

$$\text{for } I_i, \ 2^{BL_B - 1} < i \le 2^{BL_B}, \ 0 \text{ bit/per instruction}$$

The details of horizontal signature scheme are described in Algorithm 2 as shown in the following.

Finally, $VS_B = W - BL_B - HS_B$. The VS_B can be even or odd. If VS_B is odd, the number of bits for x coordinate of vertical signature is $\left\lceil \frac{VS_B}{2} \right\rceil$, and the number of bits for y coordinate is $\left\lfloor \frac{VS_B}{2} \right\rfloor$. From Theorem 4 in Section 2.2, we know that when width of instruction word is even, the x coordinate plus the y coordinate of any signature can not be odd. Consequently, it is obvious to see that the x coordinate and the y coordinate of any signature are either all even or all odd. Based on this feature, we don't need to store the least significant bit of y coordinate because the least significant bit of x coordinate and y coordinate is the same. Thus, one bit space can be saved by this property of our vertical signature scheme. Consequently, this property can be used further to save the memory space of signatures. The proposed signature-monitoring algorithms of compilation phase and execution phase are presented next.

Algorithm 2: compilation phase

The following notations are defined:

I_o : signature word of block;

I_{ij} : the jth bit (from left to right) of ith instruction in block, $1 \le i \le BL$, $1 \le j \le W$;

X_{ivs} , Y_{ivs} : x coordinate and y coordinate of intermediate vertical signature;

$X_{ivs}(1)$, $X_{ivs}(2)$, $X_{ivs}(3)$: the lower three bits of X_{ivs} ;

$y_{ivs}(1)$, $y_{ivs}(2)$, $y_{ivs}(3)$: the lower three bits of y_{ivs} ;

X_{vs} , Y_{vs} : x coordinate and y coordinate of vertical reference signature;

If VS_B is even, then X_{vs} and y_{vs} have $\frac{VS_B}{2}$ number of bits each, else X_{vs} has $\left\lceil \frac{VS_B}{2} \right\rceil$ number of bits, and y_{vs} has $\left\lfloor \frac{VS_B}{2} \right\rfloor$ number of bits;

HS : horizontal reference signature of block;

HS_k : the kth bit of HS, $1 \le k \le 2^{BL_B-1}$;

BLOCK BEGIN

1) $i \leftarrow 1$;   /* initialize i to first instruction */

2) a. While I_i is not a branch and $i < 2^{BL_B}$
   $i \leftarrow i+1$;
   end while   /* calculate the length of the block */
   b. $BL \leftarrow i$;

3) $i \leftarrow 1$; $(X_{ivs}, y_{ivs}) \leftarrow (0,0)$;
   $cs_1 \leftarrow cs_2 \leftarrow cs_3 \leftarrow cs_4 \leftarrow 0$; /*These are the counters of (s_1, s_2, s_3,
   $$s_4) = \left(\begin{pmatrix} 0 \\ 0 \end{pmatrix}, \begin{pmatrix} 0 \\ 1 \end{pmatrix}, \begin{pmatrix} 1 \\ 0 \end{pmatrix}, \begin{pmatrix} 1 \\ 1 \end{pmatrix} \right) */$$

4)   /* initial vertical signature */
   $$V(I_i, I_i) = V \begin{pmatrix} I_{i,1} \cdots I_{i,j} \cdots I_{i,w} \\ I_{i,1} \cdots I_{i,j} \cdots I_{i,w} \end{pmatrix} = \left(V_{i,1}, \cdots, V_{i,j}, \cdots V_{i,w} \right)$$
   for ($j = 1, W$)

{ switch (η, j)

  {case s_1: $CS_1 \leftarrow CS_1 +1$; case s_2: $CS_2 \leftarrow CS_2 +1$;

   case s_3: $CS_3 \leftarrow CS_3 +1$; case s_4: $CS_4 \leftarrow CS_4 +1$;}}

$X_{ivs} \leftarrow X_{ivs} + CS_1 - CS_2$; $y_{ivs} \leftarrow y_{ivs} + CS_4 - CS_3$;

$X_{ivs} \leftarrow X_{ivs} \bmod 2^{\left\lfloor \frac{VS_a}{2} \right\rfloor}$; /* bound the size of 2-D coordinate

$y_{ivs} \leftarrow y_{ivs} \bmod 2^{\left\lfloor \frac{VS_a}{2} \right\rfloor}$; for vertical signature */

5) generate horizontal signature for each instruction word and intermediate vertical signature

    While $BL \geq i$ do

      a. generate 8 bits of interlaced parity; We use the bit-interlaced approach for coverage consideration.

$$H_1 \leftarrow I_A \oplus I_B \oplus ... \oplus I_{i(w-7)} \oplus x_{ivs}(1) \oplus x_{ivs}(2) \oplus x_{ivs}(3);$$

$$H_2 \leftarrow I_2 \oplus I_{A0} \oplus ... \oplus I_{i(w-6)} \oplus y_{ivs}(1) \oplus y_{ivs}(2) \oplus y_{ivs}(3);$$

$$H_3 \leftarrow I_B \oplus I_{A1} \oplus ... \oplus I_{i(w-5)};$$

$$H_8 \leftarrow I_B \oplus I_{A6} \oplus ... \oplus I_{iw};$$

/* $H_1 ... H_8$ store the results of interlaced parity */

      b. according to the size of BL ,put horizontal signature for each instruction word to HS

        case A : $BL \leq 2^{BL_B-4}$

          $b \leftarrow 1$;

          while $b \leq 8$ do

              $HS_{i+(b-1)*2^{BL_B-4}} \leftarrow H_b$; $b \leftarrow b+1$;

          end while

        case B : $2^{BL_B-4} < BL \leq 2^{BL_B-3}$

          $H_1 \leftarrow H_1 \oplus H_5$; $H_2 \leftarrow H_2 \oplus H_6$;

          $H_3 \leftarrow H_3 \oplus H_7$; $H_4 \leftarrow H_4 \oplus H_8$;

          $b \leftarrow 1$;

          while $b \leq 4$ do

              $HS_{i+(b-1)*2^{BL_B-3}} \leftarrow H_b$; $b \leftarrow b+1$;

          end while

        case C : $2^{BL_B-3} < BL \leq 2^{BL_B-2}$

          $H_1 \leftarrow H_1 \oplus H_3 \oplus H_5 \oplus H_7$; $H_2 \leftarrow H_2 \oplus H_4 \oplus H_6 \oplus H_8$;

          $b \leftarrow 1$;

          while $b \leq 2$ do

              $HS_{i+(b-1)*2^{BL_B-2}} \leftarrow H_b$;

              $b \leftarrow b+1$;

          end while

        case D : $2^{BL_B-2} < BL$

$$H_1 \leftarrow H_1 \oplus H_2 \oplus H_3 \oplus H_4 \oplus H_5 \oplus H_6 \oplus H_7 \oplus H_8;$$

if $i \leq 2^{BLB-1}$

$$HS_i \leftarrow H_i$$

end if

c. generate the intermediate vertical signature

if $BL \neq i$

$CS_1 \leftarrow CS_2 \leftarrow CS_3 \leftarrow CS_4 \leftarrow 0$; /* These are counters of $s_1 s_2 s_3 s_4$ */

for ($j = 1, W$)

{ switch ($V_{i+1,j}$)   /* Please refer to Algorithm 1 */

{case s_1: $CS_1 \leftarrow CS_1$ +1; case s_2: $CS_2 \leftarrow CS_2$ +1;

case s_3: $CS_3 \leftarrow CS_3$ +1; case s_4: $CS_4 \leftarrow CS_4$ +1; }}

$x_{ivs} \leftarrow x_{ivs} + CS_1 - CS_2$; $y_{ivs} \leftarrow y_{ivs} + CS_4 - CS_3$;

$$x_{ivs} \leftarrow x_{ivs} \bmod 2^{\left\lceil \frac{VS_B}{2} \right\rceil} ; \quad y_{ivs} \leftarrow y_{ivs} \bmod 2^{\left\lceil \frac{VS_B}{2} \right\rceil} ;$$

end if

$i \leftarrow i + 1$;

end while

6) $x_{ivs} \leftarrow x_{ivs} + W \times \left\lfloor \dfrac{BL-1}{2} \right\rfloor$; $y_{ivs} \leftarrow y_{ivs} + W \times \left\lfloor \dfrac{BL-1}{2} \right\rfloor$; /* To shift the signature

space to positive coordinate, the term of $W \times \left\lfloor \dfrac{BL-1}{2} \right\rfloor$ is added to

the x coordinate and y coordinate. The details can be found in Section 2.1.2 */

$$x_{vs} \leftarrow x_{ivs} \bmod 2^{\left\lceil \frac{VS_B}{2} \right\rceil} ; \quad y_{vs} \leftarrow y_{ivs} \bmod 2^{\left\lceil \frac{VS_B}{2} \right\rceil} ;$$

7) $I_0 \leftarrow (BL, HS, x_{vs}, y_{vs})$; /* put reference signature to the beginning of the block */

BLOCK END

Algorithm 3: execution phase

Watchdog processor checks the run-time horizontal signature with horizontal reference signature for each instruction. The comparison of run-time vertical signature with vertical reference signature is performed when the end of block is encountered. If some of the comparisons do not match, then the errors occur. The concept of this algorithm is the same as the algorithm of compilation phase. Thus, we omit the details of this algorithm.

3.2 Error-Detection Capability

Two types of program errors known as bit errors and sequencing errors can be detected mostly. We summarize several specific control flow errors that can be detected by our scheme as follows.

● Stuck-at PC/ False loops

● Program–bound violations: The control flow errors cause the instruction execution from data space. The horizontal signature is used first to detect the errors then the vertical signature follows if needed.

- Branch address errors: This kind of error can be detected by our technique except that the branch address is the beginning of the wrong block. The probability of this type of errors should be quite low.
- Data-bit errors in stack pointer (SP) register/ PC: One situation of data-bit errors in SP register can not be detected in that the SP points to a wrong entry of the stack whose content is the beginning address of the other block. One case of data-bit errors in PC can not be detected as described below. The data-bit errors happen in PC when PC represents the starting address of a block. If the erroneous address of PC coincidentally points to the beginning address of the other block, then this error can not be detected.

4 Simulation and Comparisons

Based on [16], the control flow errors can be modeled as bit errors for the analysis of coverage and latency. Thus we use the bit errors in the simulation to calculate the coverage and latency. In this demonstration, we use the width of instruction word $W = 32$. Therefore, the signature word structure is $BL_B = 5$ bits, $HS_B = 16$ bits and $VS_B = 11$ bits. Clearly, the length of branch-free block can not be larger than thirty-two instructions. In this instance, we let x coordinate be six-bit and y coordinate be five-bit to represent a 64×64 signature space. Here, the least significant bit of y coordinate doesn't need to be stored as we mentioned before.

For a specific BL and W, the following notations are developed:

- $P_{error-rate}$: the probability of a bit error;
- $P_{i-bit-error}$: the probability of i-bit errors occurring in the block, where $0 \le i \le BL \times W$;
- $C_{i-bit-error}$: the coverage of i-bit errors happening in the block, where $0 \le i \le BL \times W$;
- $L_{i-bit-error}$: the latency of i-bit errors happening in the block, where $0 \le i \le BL \times W$;
- $C_{BL\ error-rate}$: the expected coverage of the block for a specific BL and $P_{error-rate}$;
- $L_{BL\ error-rate}$: the expected latency of the block for a specific block length and $P_{error-rate}$;
- P_{BL} : the probability of a block whose length is BL ;
- $C_{mean}(W)$: the expected coverage for a specific instruction width W ;
- $L_{mean}(W)$: the expected latency for a specific instruction width W ;

The terms of $C_{BL\ error-rate}$ and $L_{BL\ error-rate}$ can be expressed as

$$C_{BL\ error-rate} = \sum_{i=0}^{BL*W} C_{i-bit-error} * P_{i-bit-error} \tag{1}$$

$$L_{BL\ error-rate} = \sum_{i=0}^{BL*W} L_{i-bit-error} * P_{i-bit-error} \tag{2}$$

$$P_{i-bit-error} = \binom{BL*W}{i} \left(P_{error-rate}\right)^i \left(1 - P_{error-rate}\right)^{BL*W-i} \tag{3}$$

To compute $C_{BL\ error-rate}$ and $L_{BL\ error-rate}$, we employ the simulation approach to obtain the values of $C_{i-bit-error}$ and $L_{i-bit-error}$, where i from zero to $BL \times W$. For a specific block length BL, we randomly generate two thousand different code patterns for the block; for each block code pattern, we inject the bit errors into it: one thousand i-bit error's patterns are generated for $1 \le i \le BL \times W$. In other words, two million simulations are performed for each number of bit errors. The terms of $C_{i-bit-error}$ and $L_{i-bit-error}$ can be derived from this simulation approach. A point should be pointed out that to calculate the equations (1) and (2), we need to obtain the values of $C_{i-bit-error}$ and $L_{i-bit-error}$, for $0 \le i \le BL \times W$. This may require enormous simulation time. Fortunately, from the analysis of $P_{i-bit-error}$ expression, we found that we are not necessary to evaluate the terms of $C_{i-bit-error}$ and $L_{i-bit-error}$ when the $P_{i-bit-error}$ approaches to zero. Therefore, the data derived from this approximation methodology seems to be a little bit pessimistic.

4.1 Coverage and Latency

We observe that for even bit errors, two-bit errors have the worst coverage, and the coverage increases when the number of bit errors increases too. This is because that the effect on vertical signature of a bit error may be offset by the other bit error. Thus, for even bit errors, the effect of error bits on vertical signature may be canceled each other, and it may result in the errors going undetected. Among even bit errors, two-bit errors have the highest probability to make the effect of error bits on vertical signature canceled each other, and then four-bit errors, and so on.

Fig. 2 shows the block coverage $C_{BL\ error-rate}$ for vertical signature scheme and hybrid signature scheme, respectively. Fig. 3 illustrates the block latency $L_{BL\ error-rate}$ of hybrid scheme for various $P_{error-rate}$. The average latency of vertical signature for $BL=4$ and $BL=10$ is two and five instructions, respectively. From Figures 2 and 3, it is obvious to see that the hybrid signature scheme has much better coverage and latency than vertical signature scheme. Fig. 3 illustrates the significant effect of horizontal signature on latency. If the block has more horizontal signature bits for each instruction, then clearly it has higher coverage for horizontal signature part and lower latency as shown in Fig. 3.

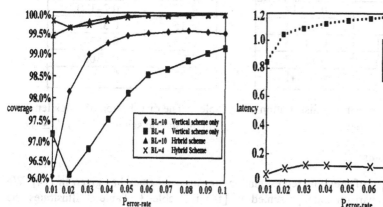

Fig. 2. The comparison of block coverage for   Fig. 3. The block latency of hybrid scheme
vertical scheme and hybrid scheme   for various bit-error rate

Next, we are going to calculate the $C_{mean}(W)$ and $L_{mean}(W)$, and they can be written as

$$C_{mean}(W) = \sum_{BL=1}^{W} P_{BL} * C_{BL\ error-rate} \qquad (4)$$

$$L_{mean}(W) = \sum_{BL=1}^{W} P_{BL} * L_{BL\ error-rate} \qquad (5)$$

Previously, we have demonstrated how to derive $C_{BL\ error-rate}$ and $L_{BL\ error-rate}$. To evaluate equation (4) and (5), we need to resolve the term of P_{BL}, the probability of a block whose length being BL. Table 1 from [16] presents the probability distribution of block length P_{BL}. We can not directly utilize this table to compute the equation (4) and (5) because of the reason described below. For our scheme, the maximal allowable block length is thirty-two in this example, when the block length is larger than thirty-two, then it needs to be partitioned into several blocks. Therefore, the block length distribution is not the same as Table 1. We use the following approach to derive the P_{BL}, where $1 \le BL \le 32$. As can be seen from Table 1, the probability of block length larger than or equal to sixty-four is quite small, so we ignore this part in this demonstration. Consequently, the only part of blocks, which should be partitioned in Table 1, is block length from thirty-three to sixty-three, and they are partitioned into two smaller blocks. The first block is from the beginning to the thirty-second instruction, and the rest of the instructions is assigned to the second block. From Table 1, we only have the total probability of block length 32-63. For demonstration only, we here assume that the probability of each block length in the range of 32-63 is all the same. Based on this assumption, the P_{BL}, $1 \le BL \le 32$, is illustrated in Table 2.

Fig. 4 shows the $C_{mean}(W)$ for vertical scheme and hybrid scheme, where $W = 32$. Fig. 5 shows the $L_{mean}(W)$ for hybrid scheme, where $W = 32$. Figures 4 and 5 demonstrate the significance of our hybrid scheme.

BL	P_{BL}
1	0.01921
2-3	0.08645
4-7	0.23812
8-15	0.35224
16-31	0.14996
32-63	0.13757
≥ 64	0.01641

Table 1: The probability distribution of block length

BL	P_{BL}
1	0.02339
2-3	0.09029
4-7	0.24120
8-15	0.35475
16-31	0.15348
32	0.13688
> 32	0

Table 2: The distribution of block length in our hybrid scheme, $1 \le BL \le 32$.

4.2 Comparisons

The comparison of previous representative signature schemes has given in [14]. We adopt the comparison data presented in [14] in Table 3. Table 3 illustrates the comparison results of our hybrid scheme with several previous techniques.

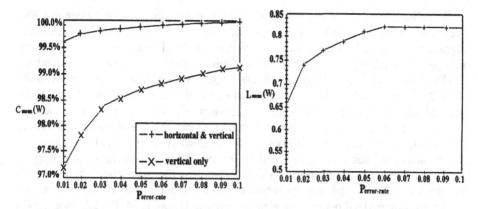

Fig. 4. The comparison of the expected coverage for vertical and hybrid schemes, W=32

Fig. 5. The expected latency for hybrid scheme, where W=32

	Basic	PSA[3]	SIS[11]	CSM[14]	Our scheme (W=32)	Our scheme (W=64)
Control-Bit Coverage	99.9999%	100%	85-93%	99.9999%	**99.66-99.99%**	**99.99-99.9999%**
Control-Flow Coverage	96-99%	99.5-99.9%	85-93%	99.9999%	**99.66-99.99%**	**99.99-99.9999%**
Error-Detection Latency	2-5	7-17	7-17	0.016-1.0	**0.65- 0.8**	**0.07- 0.42**
Total Memory Overhead	10-25%*	12-21%	6-15%	4-11%#	**10-25%**	**10-25%**

*Not include the overhead of tag bit part.
#Not include the overhead of horizontal signature space.

Table 3: The comparison results.

In Table 3, one thing should be pointed out that the total memory overhead for basic technique and CSM [14] does not include the part of tag bits and horizontal signature part, respectively. Even though our scheme needs to add extra signature words when the length of branch-free block exceeds the instruction width W, the tag bits are eliminated in our scheme. Normally, two tag bits are inserted into each instruction for basic technique. For block length less than or equal to W, our scheme needs one signature word, W number of bits. The tag bit approach requires one signature word plus two tag bits multiplying the block length. Therefore, our scheme can save up to $2W$ bits, i.e., two instruction words. If $W < BL \leq 2W$, our technique needs two signature words. The tag bit approach requires one signature word plus two tag bits multiplying the block length. The size of tag bit part is $2W$ bits < tag bit part $\leq 4W$ bits. So, $3W <$ signature part + tag bit part $\leq 5W$ Thus, the saving of memory bits for our scheme is larger than W and less than or equal to $3W$. The analysis is similar for block length larger than $2W$. So, it is obvious to see that the memory space overhead of our approach is far less than the basic technique.

As indicated in [15], if multiple bits are used for the horizontal signature in CSM, the entire memory has to be padded with as many bits as required for the horizontal signature. It results in a large memory overhead in CSM, and we should not ignore this part of overhead. For instance, if combining CSM with single-error-correcting, double-error-detecting code for horizontal signature, when instruction word width $W = 32$, the memory overhead of horizontal signature part is 21.875%. Clearly, when we add up this memory overhead of horizontal signature part to total memory overhead of CSM in Table 3, our hybrid scheme has much less memory overhead than CSM, and our scheme is still competitive to CSM in coverage and latency.

The above measurements are based on the synthesized benchmarks consisting of randomly generated instructions. We now perform the simulation on three real benchmark programs and they are factorial, quick sort and matrix multiplication. The results are summarized below. The memory space overhead is 34.8%, 22.5% and 14% respectively. The factorial program code is optimized such that the block length is small. Consequently, its overhead is higher than 25%. Theoretically, the performance degradation of our technique is the same as the signature overhead of memory space that is 10-25% for basic block sizes of 4 to 10. The fault coverage is 99.2-99.48% and the latency is 0.07-0.13.

5 Implementation Consideration

In this section, we briefly describe the implementation issues of our signature scheme. A five-stage pipeline DSP processor developed by our team is used as a target to be monitored. First of all, the compiler needs to be modified based on the Algorithm 2. One signature instruction, "Initsig", is provided to initialize the signature monitoring and is put in the beginning of each program. We know that the instruction next to the "Initsig" is the signature word for the first block. The DSP won't execute the signature word when it is fetched, so it needs to insert a NOP for signature word. When the instruction "Initsig" is executed, the DSP will insert a NOP for signature word fetched in next clock cycle and send an initial_setup signal to watchdog processor. Once the signature word is fetched in, the DSP saves the block length into a counter. Meanwhile, the watchdog processor resets and loads in the reference signature and starts performing the signature monitoring when it receives the initial_setup signal from DSP. The DSP and watchdog processors are synchronized each other. The counter decrements when DSP fetches an instruction. Once the counter reaches to zero, it means that the next fetch is the signature word for next block. Therefore, DSP knows when to insert a NOP to pipeline. Meantime, the watchdog processor uses the block length as timer and controls when to end of the current block checking, to clear of the registers of the vertical signature and counter and when to load in the next signature word.

Exception handling: Our DSP processor adopts the concept of precise exception to handle the interrupt. An interrupt controller is also on-chip. When interrupt happens, DSP sends interrupt signal to watchdog processor immediately, then the watchdog processor pushes the signature word, intermediate vertical signature and instruction counter into stack. Thereafter, watchdog processor enters to the idle state until DSP saves the status and return address from interrupt. When DSP is ready to execute the interrupt service routine, it will inform the watchdog processor. Once the watchdog processor receives the signals from DSP, it resumes its state and begins the signature monitoring. The first instruction of interrupt service routine is always the signature word. The processing of return from interrupt is quite the same as mentioned before. When DSP executes the return from interrupt instruction, it will send the signals to watchdog processor immediately, then watchdog processor restores the signature word, intermediate vertical signature and instruction counter from stack for previous interrupted block. The watchdog processor then waits for the starting signals from DSP to perform the signature monitoring for previous interrupted block.

To process the exception handling, the watchdog processor uses three signal pins to distinguish the various situations. Table 4 lists the functions of these signal pins.

Enable	Sig1	Sig2	Function
0	X	X	Regular signature monitoring
1	0	0	Save signature word, intermediate vertical signature & counter; enter to idle state
1	0	1	Start signature monitoring for interrupt service routine
1	1	0	Restore the signature word, intermediate vertical signature & counter; enter to idle state
1	1	1	Start signature monitoring for previous interrupted block

Table 4: Signal pins of watchdog processor

We now briefly explain a couple of circuit blocks whose errors can be detected through our on-chip watchdog processor. The address decoder errors of memory system can be detected because these errors can be modeled as control flow errors. The errors located in program sequencer (PSQ) can be detected. The purpose of PSQ is to generate the address of next instruction, and the PSQ errors can be modeled as control flow errors. Two cases should be considered. First case is that the errors cause the sequential address changing to branching address. In this case, our technique can detect the errors except that the sequential address is the address of the beginning of next executed block and the wrong branching address points to also the beginning of the other block. Under the circumstances, our scheme can not distinguish the block executed next being the wrong flow. The other case is the branching address changing to sequential address due to errors. Our approach can not detect this kind of error because sequential address is also the starting address of the other block.

6 Conclusions

We have presented a new concurrent error-detection scheme by hybrid signature to the on-line detection of control flow errors caused by transient and intermittent faults. The main contribution of this research is to reduce the overhead of memory space significantly, and meanwhile the quality of coverage and latency is still achieved. The much lower latency of our scheme is a very important feature when watchdog processor is used as an error-detection tool for rollback recovery in real-time fault tolerant computer systems.

The usage of block length information in our scheme has several merits. First, only one signature instruction should be offered and one clock cycle performance loss for each program due to the signature instruction. Secondly, the DSP complexity won't increase much owing to the insertion of watchdog processor for error detection. We found that the overall design can be simplified much by our approach. Finally, the memory system and data bus does not require to be modified, because the information of block length is stored in the signature word. The drawback of this approach is that it can not utilize the delayed slot in the approach of delayed branch. The proposed watchdog processor will be integrated into our DSP processor and the fault injection and experimental study will be conducted next.

Our scheme is applicable to single RISC pipeline processor and it requires monitoring the instruction bus of the processors. The program control-flow graph is not necessary in our scheme. Based on the above points, our approach and target are different from Majzik et. al technique [9] that addressed the hierarchical control flow checking for a multitasking, multiprocessor environment.

Acknowledgments

The research was supported by the National Science Council, R.O.C., under Grant NSC 87-2213-E-216-001. The author would like to thank Professor I. Majzik and the referees for constructive comments that led to improvements of the paper.

References:

[1] M. Schmid, R. Trapp, A. Davidoff, and G. Masson, " Upset exposure by means of abstraction verification, " in Proc. 12th IEEE FTCS, 1982, pp. 237-244.

[2] U. Gunneflo, J. Karlsson, and J. Torin, " Evaluation of error detection schemes using fault injection by heavy-ion radiation," in Proc. 19th IEEE FTCS, 1989, pp. 340-347.

[3] M. Namjoo, " Techniques for concurrent testing of VLSI processor operation, " in Proc. 12th IEEE ITC, November 1982, pp. 461-468.

[4] A. Mahmood, D. J. Lu, and E. J. McCluskey, " Concurrent Fault Detection using a Watchdog Processor and Assertions, " in Proc. 13th IEEE ITC, 1983, pp. 622-628.

[5] A. Mahmood and E. J. McCluskey, " Concurrent error detection using watchdog processor - A survey, " IEEE Trans. on Computers, Vol. 37, No. 2, pp. 160-174, Feb. 1988.

[6] J. Ohlsson, M. Rimen, and U.Gunneflo, "A Study of the Effects of Transient Fault Injection into a 32-bit RISC with Built-in Watchdog", FTCS-22, 1992, pp. 316-325.

[7] J. Ohlsson and M. Rimen, "Implicit Signature Checking", FTCS-25, 1995, pp. 218-227.

[8] K. Wilken and T. Kong, "Concurrent Detection of Software and Hardware Data-Access Faults", IEEE Trans. on Computers, vol. 46, No. 4, pp. 412-424, April 1997.

[9] I. Majzik, A. Pataricza et. al, "Hierarchical Checking of Multiprocessors Using Watchdog Processors", EDCC-1, 1994, pp. 386-403.

[10] T. Sridhar and S. M. Thatte, " Concurrent Checking of Program Flow in VLSI processors, " in Proc. 12th IEEE ITC, 1982, pp. 191-199.

[11] M. Schuette and J. Shen, " Processor Control Flow Monitoring Using Signatured Instruction Streams, " IEEE Trans. on Computers, Vol. C-36, No.3, pp.264-276, March 1987.

[12] K. Wilken and J. Shen, " Embedded Signature Monitoring: Analysis and Technique, " in Proc. 17th IEEE ITC, 1987, pp. 324-333.

[13] K. Wilken and J. Shen, "Continuous signature monitoring: Efficient concurrent detection of processor control errors, " in Proc. 18th Int. Test Conf., 1988, pp. 914-925.

[14] K. Wilken, J. Shen, " Continuous Signature Monitoring: Low-Cost Concurrent Detection of Processor Control Errors, " IEEE Trans. Computer-Aided Design, Vol. 9, No. 6, June 1990, pp. 629-641.

[15] S. J. Upadhyaya, B. Ramamurthy, " Concurrent Process Monitoring with No Reference Signatures, " IEEE Trans. on Computers, Vol. 43, No. 4, pp. 475-480, April 1994.

[16] A. Mahmood and E. J. McCluskey, " Watchdog Processors: Error Coverage and Overhead, " in Proc. 15th IEEE FTCS, 1985, pp. 214-219.

Author Index

Apfeld, R.   231
Arlat, J.   145

Baraza, J.C.   193
Belli, F.   63
Bellos, M.   269
Bondavalli, A.   7
Busquets, J.V.   193
Bykov, I.V.   341

Chen, Y.-Y.   439
Chessa, S.   285
Constantinescu, C.   163
Cunha, J.C.   211

Doudou, A.   71

Echtle, K.   106

Fabre, J.-C.   145
Folkesson, P.   173
Futsuhara, K.   241

Garbinato, B.   71
Garbolino, T.   323
Gil, D.   193
Gil, P.J.   193
Greblicki, J.W.   253
Guerraoui, R.   71

Heidtmann, K.   24
Hellebrand, S.   341
Henn, H.H.   3
Hławiczka, A.   323

Kaiser, J.   353
Kanoun, K.   42
Karlsson, J.   173

Lin, M.-J.   366
Livani, M.A.   353

Lonn, H.   88

Maestrini, P.   285
Martínez, R.   193
Marzullo, K.   366
Mock, M.   382
Mukaidono, M.   241
Mura, I.   7

Nett, E.   382
Nikolos, D.   269
Novák, O.   305

Piestrak, S.J.   253
Prata, P.   421

Rabah, M.   42
Rela, M.Z.   211
Rodríguez, M.   145

Sakai, M.   241
Sallay, B.   285
Salles, F.   145
Schemmer, S.   382
Schiper, A.   71
Shirai, T.   241
Silva, J.G.   124, 211, 421
Silva, L.M.   124

Thévenod-Fosse, P.   403
Trivedi, K.S.   7

Umbreit, M.   231

Vergos, H.T.   269

Waeselynck, H.   403
Wunderlich, H.-J.   341

Yarmolik, V.N.   341

Lecture Notes in Computer Science

For information about Vols. 1–1606
please contact your bookseller or Springer-Verlag

Vol. 1607: J. Mira, J.V. Sánchez-Andrés (Eds.), Engineering Applications of Bio-Inspired Artificial Neural Networks. Proceedings, Vol. II, 1999. XXIII, 907 pages. 1999.

Vol. 1608: S. Doaitse Swierstra, P.R. Henriques, J.N. Oliveira (Eds.), Advanced Functional Programming. Proceedings, 1998. XII, 289 pages. 1999.

Vol. 1609: Z. W. Raś, A. Skowron (Eds.), Foundations of Intelligent Systems. Proceedings, 1999. XII, 676 pages. 1999. (Subseries LNAI).

Vol. 1610: G. Cornuéjols, R.E. Burkard, G.J. Woeginger (Eds.), Integer Programming and Combinatorial Optimization. Proceedings, 1999. IX, 453 pages. 1999.

Vol. 1611: I. Imam, Y. Kodratoff, A. El-Dessouki, M. Ali (Eds.), Multiple Approaches to Intelligent Systems. Proceedings, 1999. XIX, 899 pages. 1999. (Subseries LNAI).

Vol. 1612: R. Bergmann, S. Breen, M. Göker, M. Manago, S. Wess, Developing Industrial Case-Based Reasoning Applications. XX, 188 pages. 1999. (Subseries LNAI).

Vol. 1613: A. Kuba, M. Šámal, A. Todd-Pokropek (Eds.), Information Processing in Medical Imaging. Proceedings, 1999. XVII, 508 pages. 1999.

Vol. 1614: D.P. Huijsmans, A.W.M. Smeulders (Eds.), Visual Information and Information Systems. Proceedings, 1999. XVII, 827 pages. 1999.

Vol. 1615: C. Polychronopoulos, K. Joe, A. Fukuda, S. Tomita (Eds.), High Performance Computing. Proceedings, 1999. XIV, 408 pages. 1999.

Vol. 1616: P. Cointe (Ed.), Meta-Level Architectures and Reflection. Proceedings, 1999. XI, 273 pages. 1999.

Vol. 1617: N.V. Murray (Ed.), Automated Reasoning with Analytic Tableaux and Related Methods. Proceedings, 1999. X, 325 pages. 1999. (Subseries LNAI).

Vol. 1618: J. Bézivin, P.-A. Muller (Eds.), The Unified Modeling Language. Proceedings, 1998. IX, 443 pages. 1999.

Vol. 1619: M.T. Goodrich, C.C. McGeoch (Eds.), Algorithm Engineering and Experimentation. Proceedings, 1999. VIII, 349 pages. 1999.

Vol. 1620: W. Horn, Y. Shahar, G. Lindberg, S. Andreassen, J. Wyatt (Eds.), Artificial Intelligence in Medicine. Proceedings, 1999. XIII, 454 pages. 1999. (Subseries LNAI).

Vol. 1621: D. Fensel, R. Studer (Eds.), Knowledge Acquisition Modeling and Management. Proceedings, 1999. XI, 404 pages. 1999. (Subseries LNAI).

Vol. 1622: M. González Harbour, J.A. de la Puente (Eds.), Reliable Software Technologies – Ada-Europe'99. Proceedings, 1999. XIII, 451 pages. 1999.

Vol. 1623: T. Reinartz, Focusing Solutions for Data Mining. XV, 309 pages. 1999. (Subseries LNAI).

Vol. 1625: B. Reusch (Ed.), Computational Intelligence. Proceedings, 1999. XIV, 710 pages. 1999.

Vol. 1626: M. Jarke, A. Oberweis (Eds.), Advanced Information Systems Engineering. Proceedings, 1999. XIV, 478 pages. 1999.

Vol. 1627: T. Asano, H. Imai, D.T. Lee, S.-i. Nakano, T. Tokuyama (Eds.), Computing and Combinatorics. Proceedings, 1999. XIV, 494 pages. 1999.

Col. 1628: R. Guerraoui (Ed.), ECOOP'99 - Object-Oriented Programming. Proceedings, 1999. XIII, 529 pages. 1999.

Vol. 1629: H. Leopold, N. García (Eds.), Multimedia Applications, Services and Techniques - ECMAST'99. Proceedings, 1999. XV, 574 pages. 1999.

Vol. 1631: P. Narendran, M. Rusinowitch (Eds.), Rewriting Techniques and Applications. Proceedings, 1999. XI, 397 pages. 1999.

Vol. 1632: H. Ganzinger (Ed.), Automated Deduction – Cade-16. Proceedings, 1999. XIV, 429 pages. 1999. (Subseries LNAI).

Vol. 1633: N. Halbwachs, D. Peled (Eds.), Computer Aided Verification. Proceedings, 1999. XII, 506 pages. 1999.

Vol. 1634: S. Džeroski, P. Flach (Eds.), Inductive Logic Programming. Proceedings, 1999. VIII, 303 pages. 1999. (Subseries LNAI).

Vol. 1636: L. Knudsen (Ed.), Fast Software Encryption. Proceedings, 1999. VIII, 317 pages. 1999.

Vol. 1637: J.P. Walser, Integer Optimization by Local Search. XIX, 137 pages. 1999. (Subseries LNAI).

Vol. 1638: A. Hunter, S. Parsons (Eds.), Symbolic and Quantitative Approaches to Reasoning and Uncertainty. Proceedings, 1999. IX, 397 pages. 1999. (Subseries LNAI).

Vol. 1639: S. Donatelli, J. Kleijn (Eds.), Application and Theory of Petri Nets 1999. Proceedings, 1999. VIII, 425 pages. 1999.

Vol. 1640: W. Tepfenhart, W. Cyre (Eds.), Conceptual Structures: Standards and Practices. Proceedings, 1999. XII, 515 pages. 1999. (Subseries LNAI).

Vol. 1641: D. Hutter, W. Stephan, P. Traverso, M. Ullmann (Eds.), Applied Formal Methods – FM-Trends 98. Proceedings, 1998. XI, 377 pages. 1999.

Vol. 1642: D.J. Hand, J.N. Kok, M.R. Berthold (Eds.), Advances in Intelligent Data Analysis. Proceedings, 1999. XII, 538 pages. 1999.

Vol. 1643: J. Nešetřil (Ed.), Algorithms – ESA '99. Proceedings, 1999. XII, 552 pages. 1999.

Vol. 1644: J. Wiedermann, P. van Emde Boas, M. Nielsen (Eds.), Automata, Languages, and Programming. Proceedings, 1999. XIV, 720 pages. 1999.

Vol. 1645: M. Crochemore, M. Paterson (Eds.), Combinatorial Pattern Matching. Proceedings, 1999. VIII, 295 pages. 1999.

Vol. 1647: F.J. Garijo, M. Boman (Eds.), Multi-Agent System Engineering. Proceedings, 1999. X, 233 pages. 1999. (Subseries LNAI).

Vol. 1648: M. Franklin (Ed.), Financial Cryptography. Proceedings, 1999. VIII, 269 pages. 1999.

Vol. 1649: R.Y. Pinter, S. Tsur (Eds.), Next Generation Information Technologies and Systems. Proceedings, 1999. IX, 327 pages. 1999.

Vol. 1650: K.-D. Althoff, R. Bergmann, L.K. Branting (Eds.), Case-Based Reasoning Research and Development. Proceedings, 1999. XII, 598 pages. 1999. (Subseries LNAI).

Vol. 1651: R.H. Güting, D. Papadias, F. Lochovsky (Eds.), Advances in Spatial Databases. Proceedings, 1999. XI, 371 pages. 1999.

Vol. 1652: M. Klusch, O.M. Shehory, G. Weiss (Eds.), Cooperative Information Agents III. Proceedings, 1999. XI, 404 pages. 1999. (Subseries LNAI).

Vol. 1653: S. Covaci (Ed.), Active Networks. Proceedings, 1999. XIII, 346 pages. 1999.

Vol. 1654: E.R. Hancock, M. Pelillo (Eds.), Energy Minimization Methods in Computer Vision and Pattern Recognition. Proceedings, 1999. IX, 331 pages. 1999.

Vol. 1655: S.-W. Lee, Y. Nakano (Eds.), Document Analysis Systems: Theory and Practice. Proceedings, 1998. XI, 377 pages. 1999.

Vol. 1656: S. Chatterjee, J.F. Prins, L. Carter, J. Ferrante, Z. Li, D. Sehr, P.-C. Yew (Eds.), Languages and Compilers for Parallel Computing. Proceedings, 1998. XI, 384 pages. 1999.

Vol. 1661: C. Freksa, D.M. Mark (Eds.), Spatial Information Theory. Proceedings, 1999. XIII, 477 pages. 1999.

Vol. 1662: V. Malyshkin (Ed.), Parallel Computing Technologies. Proceedings, 1999. XIX, 510 pages. 1999.

Vol. 1663: F. Dehne, A. Gupta. J.-R. Sack, R. Tamassia (Eds.), Algorithms and Data Structures. Proceedings, 1999. IX, 366 pages. 1999.

Vol. 1664: J.C.M. Baeten, S. Mauw (Eds.), CONCUR'99. Concurrency Theory. Proceedings, 1999. XI, 573 pages. 1999.

Vol. 1666: M. Wiener (Ed.), Advances in Cryptology – CRYPTO '99. Proceedings, 1999. XII, 639 pages. 1999.

Vol. 1667: J. Hlavička, E. Maehle, A. Pataricza (Eds.), Dependable Computing – EDCC-3. Proceedings, 1999. XVIII, 455 pages. 1999.

Vol. 1668: J.S. Vitter, C.D. Zaroliagis (Eds.), Algorithm Engineering. Proceedings, 1999. VIII, 361 pages. 1999.

Vol. 1671: D. Hochbaum, K. Jansen, J.D.P. Rolim, A. Sinclair (Eds.), Randomization, Approximation, and Combinatorial Optimization. Proceedings, 1999. IX, 289 pages. 1999.

Vol. 1672: M. Kutylowski, L. Pacholski, T. Wierzbicki (Eds.), Mathematical Foundations of Computer Science 1999. Proceedings, 1999. XII, 455 pages. 1999.

Vol. 1673: P. Lysaght, J. Irvine, R. Hartenstein (Eds.), Field Programmable Logic and Applications. Proceedings, 1999. XI, 541 pages. 1999.

Vol. 1674: D. Floreano, J.-D. Nicoud, F. Mondada (Eds.), Advances in Artificial Life. Proceedings, 1999. XVI, 737 pages. 1999. (Subseries LNAI).

Vol. 1675: J. Estublier (Ed.), System Configuration Management. Proceedings, 1999. VIII, 255 pages. 1999.

Vol. 1976: M. Mohania, A M. Tjoa (Eds.), Data Warehousing and Knowledge Discovery. Proceedings, 1999. XII, 400 pages. 1999.

Vol. 1677: T. Bench-Capon, G. Soda, A M. Tjoa (Eds.), Database and Expert Systems Applications. Proceedings, 1999. XVIII, 1105 pages. 1999.

Vol. 1678: M.H. Böhlen, C.S. Jensen, M.O. Scholl (Eds.), Spatio-Temporal Database Management. Proceedings, 1999. X, 243 pages. 1999.

Vol. 1679: C. Taylor, A. Colchester (Eds.), Medical Image Computing and Computer-Assisted Intervention – MICCAI'99. Proceedings, 1999. XXI, 1240 pages. 1999.

Vol. 1680: D. Dams, R. Gerth, S. Leue, M. Massink (Eds.), Practical Aspects of SPIN Model-Checking. Proceedings, 1999. X, 277 pages. 1999.

Vol. 1682: M. Nielsen, P. Johansen, O.F. Olsen, J. Weickert (Eds.), Scale-Space Theories in Computer Vision. Proceedings, 1999. XI, 532 pages. 1999.

Vol. 1684: G. Ciobanu, G. Păun (Eds.), Fundamentals of Computation Theory. Proceedings, 1999. XI, 570 pages. 1999.

Vol. 1685: P. Amestoy, P. Berger, M. Daydé, I. Duff, V. Frayssé, L. Giraud, D. Ruiz (Eds.), Euro-Par'99. Parallel Processing. Proceedings, 1999. XXXII, 1503 pages. 1999.

Vol. 1688: P. Bouquet, L. Serafini, P. Brézillon, M. Benerecetti, F. Castellani (Eds.), Modeling and Using Context. Proceedings, 1999. XII, 528 pages. 1999. (Subseries LNAI).

Vol. 1689: F. Solina, A. Leonardis (Eds.), Computer Analysis of Images and Patterns. Proceedings, 1999. XIV, 650 pages. 1999.

Vol. 1690: Y. Bertot, G. Dowek, A. Hirschowitz, C. Paulin, L. Théry (Eds.), Theorem Proving in Higher Order Logics. Proceedings, 1999. VIII, 359 pages. 1999.

Vol. 1691: J. Eder, I. Rozman, T. Welzer (Eds.), Advances in Databases and Information Systems. Proceedings, 1999. XIII, 383 pages. 1999.

Vol. 1692: V. Matoušek, P. Mautner, J. Ocelíková, P. Sojka (Eds.), Text, Speech, and Dialogue. Proceedings, 1999. XI, 396 pages. 1999. (Subseries LNAI).

Vol. 1694: A. Cortesi, G. Filé (Eds.), Static Analysis. Proceedings, 1999. VIII, 357 pages. 1999.

Vol. 1701: W. Burgard, T. Christaller, A.B. Cremers (Eds.), KI-99: Advances in Artificial Intelligence. Proceedings, 1999. XI, 311 pages. 1999. (Subseries LNAI).

Vol. 1704: Jan M. Żytkow, J. Rauch (Eds.), Principles of Data Mining and Knowledge Discovery. Proceedings, 1999. XIV, 593 pages. 1999. (Subseries LNAI).

Vol. 1705: H. Ganzinger, D. McAllester, A. Voronkov (Eds.), Logic for Programming and Automated Reasoning. Proceedings, 1999. XII, 397 pages. 1999. (Subseries LNAI).